T0258714

Performance, Reliability, and Availability Evaluation of Computational Systems, Volume 2

This textbook intends to be a comprehensive and substantially self-contained two-volume book covering performance, reliability, and availability evaluation subjects. The volumes focus on computing systems, although the methods may also be applied to other systems. The first volume covers Chapter 1 to Chapter 14, whose subtitle is "Performance Modeling and Background". The second volume encompasses Chapter 15 to Chapter 25 and has the subtitle "Reliability and Availability Modeling, Measuring and Workload, and Lifetime Data Analysis".

This text is helpful for computer performance professionals for supporting planning, design, configuring, and tuning the performance, reliability, and availability of computing systems. Such professionals may use these volumes to get acquainted with specific subjects by looking at the particular chapters. Many examples in the textbook on computing systems will help them understand the concepts covered in each chapter. The text may also be helpful for the instructor who teaches performance, reliability, and availability evaluation subjects. Many possible threads could be configured according to the interest of the audience and the duration of the course. Chapter 1 presents a good number of possible courses programs that could be organized using this text.

Volume 2 is composed of the last two parts. Part III examines reliability and availability modeling by covering a set of fundamental notions, definitions, redundancy procedures, and modeling methods such as Reliability Block Diagrams (RBD) and Fault Trees (FT) with the respective evaluation methods, adopts Markov chains, Stochastic Petri nets and even hierarchical and heterogeneous modeling to represent more complex systems. Part IV discusses performance measurements and reliability data analysis. It first depicts some basic measuring mechanisms applied in computer systems, then discusses workload generation. After, we examine failure monitoring and fault injection, and finally, we discuss a set of techniques for reliability and maintainability data analysis.

Performance, Reliability, and Availability Evaluation of Computational Systems, Volume 2

Reliability, Availability Modeling, Measuring, and Data Analysis

Paulo Romero
Martins Maciel

CRC Press
Taylor & Francis Group
Boca Raton London New York

CRC Press is an imprint of the
Taylor & Francis Group, an **informa** business

A CHAPMAN & HALL BOOK

First edition published 2023
by CRC Press
6000 Broken Sound Parkway NW, Suite 300, Boca Raton, FL 33487-2742

and by CRC Press
4 Park Square, Milton Park, Abingdon, Oxon, OX14 4RN

CRC Press is an imprint of Taylor & Francis Group, LLC

ISBN: 978-1-032-30640-7 (hbk)
ISBN: 978-1-032-30642-1 (pbk)
ISBN: 978-1-003-30603-0 (ebk)

DOI: 10.1201/9781003306030

Typeset in Nimbus Roman
by KnowledgeWorks Global Ltd.

Publisher's note: This book has been prepared from camera-ready copy provided by the authors.

Dedication

To the One and Triune God, the Holy Mystery that is Wholly Love.

Contents

PART III   *Reliability and Availability Modeling*

PART IV   Measuring and Data Analysis

Contents of Volume 1

Preface

This text intends to be a comprehensive and substantially self-contained two-volume book covering performance, reliability, and availability evaluation subjects. The volumes focus on computing systems, although the methods may also be applied to other systems. Like many other parallel or concurrent systems, computing systems often lead to conflicts because processes attempt to access resources simultaneously or with time overlapping. Such conflict may cause errors, processes congestion, and system deadlocks. Moreover, when planning a cost-effective system, the policies, mechanisms, systems' structures, and the respective phenomena are usually hard to represent by deterministic models. On the other hand, such systems commonly have statistical regularities that make them suitable for dealing with stochastic processes and statistics that quantify the collected data's central tendencies, variability, and shapes. Due to its size, the document was divided into two volumes. The first volume covers from Chapter 1 to Chapter 14, whose subtitle is "Performance Modeling and Background". The second volume encompasses from Chapter 16 to Chapter 26 and has the subtitle "Reliability and Availability Modeling, Measuring and Workload, and Lifetime Data Analysis".

This text is helpful for computer performance professionals for supporting planning, design, configuring, and tuning the performance, reliability, and availability of computing systems. Such professionals may use these volumes to get acquainted with specific subjects by looking at the particular chapters. Many examples in the textbook on computing systems will help them understand the concepts covered in each chapter. The text may also be helpful for the instructor who teaches performance, reliability, and availability evaluation subjects. Many possible threads could be configured according to the interest of the audience and the duration of the course. Chapter 1 presents a good number of possible courses programs that could be organized using this text. Students following a course organized by an instructor should observe the sequence proposed by the instructor. If the students need extra assistance on some particular background topic, they may go to the specific material shown in the text to fill the specific gaps. The performance analyst may also self-teach topics of interest. In such a case, the guidelines for students and instructors may serve them well. Each chapter has a good number of unsolved exercises to assist the students in consolidating the covered materials. In the case of self-teaching a particular topic of interest, a plausible direction is to adopt one of the threads suggested for students and instructors on Chapter 1.

The first chapter of Volume 1 introduces the text and provides a glimpse of performance evaluation planning, describes the intended public, suggests several threads for getting acquainted with the subjects covered in these volumes. This document comprises two volumes, each of which has two parts, totaling twenty-five chapters. Volume 1 is composed of the first two parts, besides Chapter 1. Part I gives the knowledge required for the subsequent parts of the text. This part includes six chapters. It covers an introduction to probability, descriptive statistics and exploratory data analysis, random variables, moments, covariance, some helpful discrete and continuous random variables, Taylor series, inference methods, distribution fitting, regression, interpolation, data scaling, distance measures, and some clustering methods. Part II presents methods for performance evaluation modeling, such as operational analysis, Discrete-Time Markov Chains (DTMC), and Continuous Time Markov Chains (CTMC), Markovian queues, Stochastic Petri nets (SPN), and discrete event simulation. Volume 2 is composed of the last two parts. Part III examines reliability and availability modeling by covering a set of fundamental notions, definitions, redundancy procedures, and modeling methods such as Reliability Block Diagrams (RBD) and Fault Trees (FT) with the respective evaluation methods, adopts Markov chains, Stochastic Petri nets and even hierarchical and heterogeneous modeling to represent more complex systems. Part IV discusses performance measurements and reliability data analysis. It first depicts some basic measuring mechanisms applied in computer systems, then discusses workload generation. After, we examine failure monitoring and fault injection, and finally, we discuss a set of techniques for reliability and maintainability data analysis. Several parts of the text have been used for performance, reliability, and availability evaluation courses for graduate and undergraduate students at Centro de Informática at Universidade Federal de Pernambuco, and as short courses and seminaries for students and companies.

The Mercury tool[1], which one that is adopted to model and evaluate many of the proposed examples and problems, can be obtained by contacting the author.

---

[1] https://www.modcs.org/

Acknowledgement

First and before all, I would like to thank the One and Triune God who gave strength and perseverance to his humblest slave to accomplish this task.

I thank my late father, Abelardo, who passed away in December, the 9th, 2016. His example as a self-made man, whose limitless capacity of work and discipline taught me persistence under all circumstances. I thank my mother, Aliete, for her love, care, immeasurable and unconditional support, and for what she went through with my father to bring me up to the man I am together with my brother Abelardo Jr., and my sisters Roberta and Fernanda.

I also thank my students, as I see them as a figure of other students who may benefit from this textbook. This document was carefully planned, conceived, and written thinking of you. My aim was to provide a comprehensive book and reasonably self-contained to support educating, teaching, training, and instructing students and professionals on performance, reliability, and availability evaluation.

When I was finishing writing the one before the last chapter, I got COVID-19. My case was critical. I was intubated, but the oxygen saturation level kept declining to the level that medical staff was setting up to use extracorporeal membrane oxygenation (ECMO). Dozen of prayer groups, hundreds of people prayed to the Lord. At that critical moment, my organism started to react, and in five more days, I was at home. I firmly believe that they were heard, and God gave me more time to be a better person and carry out tasks that I consigned to last priority.

Renata and my son Rodrigo, the greatest gifts in my life; thank you for your love and support. It is for you my struggle in this land. I try, fall, stand up, fall and stand again, and keep striving to follow the path to Life by the grace of God. I hope you follow the trail that leads to the Truth. To my wife, Teresa, I am in debt of having our most precious gifts, our son and daughter, by the grace of God. Teresa has supported me in the most painful and challenging moments of my life. Thank you for your love and care. Finally, I would like to thanks my in-laws Gilberto and Laélia for their love.

15 Introduction

This text aims to be self-contained to support one's instruction without requiring extra material, at least to some extent. Due to its size, the manuscript was divided into two volumes. The first volume covers Chapter 1 to Chapter 14, whose subtitle is "Performance Modeling and Background". This volume (**Volume 2**) encloses Chapter 15 to Chapter 25 and has the subtitle "Reliability and Availability Modeling, Measuring and Workload, and Lifetime Data Analysis". This chapter introduces the book by first providing an overview of how the text is divided and how the interested reader may use the document, and also offers courses' configurations with the respective sequences of chapters, besides a list of possible short courses on specific subjects for instructors and students.

Performance evaluation refers to a set of methods for investigating the temporal behavior of systems. It has a long tradition in studying and designing communication and manufacturing systems, operational research, and computer systems. Reliability and availability evaluation refers to studying system behavior in the presence of failure and repair events of the system components. This book focuses on the performance, reliability, and availability evaluation of computational systems.

The computer systems may be broadly classified into two categories: real-time and resource-sharing systems. A real-time system is a system that provides its services subject to time constraints. Such systems may even be classified as soft real-time and hard real-time systems depending on if the constraints violation degrades the system performance or if the result is considered useless. On the other hand, many computational systems are resource-sharing systems due to cost-effectiveness and technological motivations. Some examples are online delivery services, streaming services, online reservation services, online content sharing, online ticket booking, communication networks, computer servers, manufacturing production systems, etc.

Sharing of system resources often leads to conflicts because processes attempt to access them simultaneously or with some time overlap what should be avoided to lead to reliable results. This, however, causes processes congestion and may even cause the system deadlock. Moreover, varying service times, error situations, arrival events, burst events, faults, and so forth make it extremely hard (if not impossible) to represent such phenomena by deterministic models. However, such systems and phenomena usually have statistical regularities that make them suitable to be defined by stochastic processes. Nevertheless, it is worth noting that depending on the abstraction level, a system may be viewed as a real-time system and in another as a resource-sharing system [177]. This book focuses on resource-sharing computational systems.

This text is divided into two volumes, and each volume is divided into two parts. The Volume 1 is composed of Part I and Part II. This volume (**Volume 2**) is divided into

Part III and **Part IV**. Part I is composed of six chapters, Part II has seven chapters, Part III is divided into seven chapters, and Part IV has four chapters. Each chapter has many solved examples and questions for students to consolidate their knowledge on the topics covered in each chapter. This particular volume covers the last two parts.

Part I offers the background needed for the following parts of the document. This part contains six chapters. Chapter 2 presents an introduction to probability by encompassing algebra of sets, probability space, conditional probability, the law of total probability and independence, Bayes' Rule, and counting methods. Chapter 3 offers an extensive summary of descriptive statistics analysis by presenting statistics for measuring central tendency, variability, shape, and graphical description of data for exploratory data analysis. Chapter 4 gives the notion of random variables, discrete random variables and continuous random moments, joint random variables distribution, covariance, and other related measures. Chapter 5 presents some valuable discrete and continuous random variable distributions as well as describes the concepts of functions of random variables and Taylor series. Chapter 6 introduces a set of inference techniques for assessing system parameters with confidence, distribution fitting strategies, and methods for data fitting such as regression and interpolation. Finally, Chapter 7 presents the ideas of data scaling, distance measures, and some classical data clustering methods.

The system performance can be assessed via different methods and strategies depending on the context, criticality, and costs affected. In a general context, the performance evaluation may be conducted through Measuring, Analysis, and Simulation. Part II covers methods for performance evaluation modeling. Part II of the book is organized into seven chapters. Chapter 8 presents the operational analysis. Chapter 9 and Chapter 10 introduce Discrete-Time Markov Chains (DTMC) and Continuous Time Markov Chains (CTMC). Chapter 11 depicts basic Markovian queue models. Chapters 12 and Chapter 13 details Stochastic Petri nets (SPN), and Chapter 14 introduces discrete event simulation. Measuring methods are discussed in Part IV.

The dependability of a system can be understood as the capability of carrying out a stipulated functionality that can be trustworthy. Due to the widespread provision of online services, dependability has become a requirement of primary concern. Providing fault-tolerant services is intrinsically attached to the adoption of redundancy. Replication of services is often supplied through distributed hosts across the world so that whenever the service, the underlying host, or network fails, an alternative service is eager to take over. Among the dependability attributes, some critical are reliability and availability-related measures. A reliability or availability problem may be evaluated through combinatorial or state-space models, simulation, or lifetime data analysis.

Part III studies reliability and availability-related measures via combinatorial and state-space models. Simulation, which is introduced in Part II (Chapter 14), may also be adopted to evaluate the models presented in this part of the book. Lifetime data analysis is covered in Part IV. Part III is divided into seven chapters. Chapter 16 describes some early and pivotal works on reliability, availability, and dependability evaluation, a set of fundamental notions and definitions, the essential redundancy procedures, and the modeling methods are classified. Chapter 18 and Chapter 19 introduce the Reliability Block Diagrams (RBD) and Fault Trees (FT) and their applications. Their evaluation methods are discussed in Chapter 20. Chapter 21 studies more complex systems than those studied in the previous chapter. Markov chains are applied to model such systems, which are not well characterized by combinatorial models. Chapter 22 adopts SPN to model systems that are not precisely described by combinatorial methods and whose state spaces are large what turns out to be challenging to represent directly via Markov chains. In these two last chapters, multiple formalisms (RBD + CTMC, RBD + SPN, FT + CTMC + FT + SPN, for instance) are also employed to model even more convoluted systems through hierarchy and refinement.

Computer system performance measurements are founded on monitoring the system while being exposed to a workload. Such a workload could be observed during the system's typical operation or a workload test. Therefore, for obtaining meaningful measurements, the workload should be carefully characterized. The analyst may also ponder different workloads, how the system is monitored, and how the measured data are summarized and presented.

Contrasting performance, reliability, and availability-related measures are tougher to assess since system behavior depends on failure incidents. Nevertheless, as the mean time between failures (MTBF) in a dependable system is typically in the order of years, the fault occurrences have to be synthetically speeded up and injected into the system under test to analyze faults effects on the system behavior. Reliability data analysis concerns the analysis of observed product lifetimes. Such lifetime data can be of products in the market or associated with the system in operation. The data analysis and prediction are described as lifetime data analysis or reliability data analysis.

Part IV is divided into four chapters. Chapter 23 presents the basic performance measuring mechanism applied in computer systems. Chapter 24 discusses workload generation methods. Chapter 26 examines failure monitoring and fault injection procedures. Finally, Chapter 25 presents a set of methods for reliability and maintainability data analysis.

For Instructors

Here, we present some possible course configurations to support the instructor to define courses according to their aims, syllabus, and students' background. The suggestions are just alternatives that may serve as a road map to guide the interested instructor. Instructors may also choose alternative paths that better suit their courses' requirements.

Performance Measurement

This course plan aims at studying computer systems performance through measurements. This study supports comparing systems, upgrading, or tuning the system's performance or components by either replacing them with new devices with better capabilities or the whole system. More detailed descriptions of cases are briefly mentioned below.

An possible objective may be selecting systems from competing systems where some performance features are essential as decision criteria for the decision process.

Poor system performance could be either inadequate hardware devices or system management. Hence the performance study objective may be to identify and locate bottleneck devices or the cause of sluggish behavior. If an insufficient hardware device causes the problem, the system has to be upgraded, and if it is caused by poor management, the system has to be tuned up.

Assume the analyst team is confronted with several different computer system alternatives to choose. Furthermore, the analyst team may have several choices within each system that may affect economic value and performance, such as the dimension, main capacity, the number of processor units, network interface, the size and number of storage devices, etc. In such cases, the performance study goal might be to provide quantitative information about which configurations are best under specific conditions.

Consider two or more computer system alternatives should be compared in terms of its performance. Therefore, the decision-maker is confronted with different systems from which one should be chosen. Furthermore, each system may have several other configuration options that impact both cost and performance, such as the size of the main memory, the number of processors, the type of network interface, the size and number of disk drives, the kind of system software, etc. The goal of the performance analysis, in this case, would be to provide quantitative information about which configurations are best under specific conditions.

Debugging a program for correct execution is a fundamental prerequisite for any application program. Once the program is functionally correct, the performance analysis may be required to find performance issues. For instance, consider that a program produces the right results, but such results are produced after a stipulated deadline. The goal of the performance analyst would be to apply the appropriate tools and analysis methods to find out why the program is not meeting performance requirements. All these cases are possible studies that could be tackled through the content covered in this course plan.

Content sequence

Chapter 1 → Chapter 23 (up to the first to two paragraphs of Section 23.6) → Chapter 3 → Chapter 2 → Chapter 4 → Chapter 5 → Chapter 6 → Chapter 8 → Chapter 23 (from Section 23.6 onwards) → Chapter 24.

Some sections of Chapter 4 may be omitted according to the depth of knowledge intended to approach. In Chapter 5, the essential distributions are Bernoulli, Geometric, Binomial, Poisson, uniform, triangular, Student's t, and chi-square for this course. It is important to note that each specific content of Chapter 5 may be studied when needed.

Performance Evaluation: Measuring and Modeling

This course plan aims at studying computer systems' performance through modeling and measurements. Such a study supports modeling computational systems through stochastic models to tackle complexities related to conflicts, resource sharing, uncertainties, failures, discard, etc. Performance evaluation through models can be applied during the initial design stages of the system development activities to safeguard the product meets the performance needs. Even when systems are already available and in operation, it may be too costly or unfeasible to stop the system to evaluate specific scenarios. The modeling portion covers operational analysis, Markov chains, Markovian queues, stochastic Petri nets, and simulation. In such cases, the system performance may be assessed through measuring, but it represents the operational conditions of the system. It is impossible to create specific scenarios and test the system performance in such new scenarios. Having an accurate system model allows the analyst to evaluate such performance cases, better tuning system parameters, and planning system capacity. Besides, this course also covers the measuring process. This part covers the topics already seen in the previous plan.

Content sequence

Chapter 1 → Chapter 23 (up to the first to two paragraphs of Section 23.6) → Chapter 3 → Chapter 2 → Chapter 4 → Chapter 5 → Chapter 6 → Chapter 8 → Chapter 23 (from Section 23.6 onwards) → Chapter 24 → Chapter 5 → Chapter 9 → Chapter 10 → Chapter 11 → Chapter 12 → Chapter 13 → Chapter 14. Optional chapter: Chapter 7.

In the first passage of Chapter 5, the essential distributions to look at are Bernoulli, Geometric, Binomial, Poisson, uniform, triangular, Student's t, and chi-square. In the second passage of Chapter 5, the essential distributions to look at are the exponential, Erlang, hypoexponential, hyperexponential, and Cox distributions. Other distributions may be needed according to specific interests and studies. Chapter 23 and Chapter 24 may be summarized to cover only particular topics according to the course requirements and duration. However, it is worth mentioning that the specific contents of Chapter 5 may be covered when needed.

Performance Evaluation: Modeling

This course is the content of the course Performance Evaluation: Measuring and Modeling removing the content of course Performance Measurement. It focuses specifically on performance modeling by covering Operational Laws, Markov Chains, Markovian Queues, Stochastic Petri Nets, and Simulation.

Content sequence

Chapter 1 → Chapter 2 → Chapter 3 → Chapter 4 → Chapter 5 → Chapter 6 →
Chapter 7 → Chapter 8 → Chapter 9 → Chapter 10 → Chapter 11 → Chapter 12 →
Chapter 13 → Chapter 14.

It is worth mentioning that some parts of this chapter may be omitted according to
the instructor's aim and the course duration. Each specific content of Chapter 5 may
be studied when required.

Reliability and Availability Evaluation

Due to the widespread availability of services on the Internet, dependability has become a need of significant interest in system design and operation. Among the fundamental attributes of dependability, we have reliability and availability. The reliability
of a system at a time instant t is the probability of that system performing its function accordingly without failure in the interval $t - t_0$, assuming t_0 is the instant the
system begins to function. The most straightforward system availability in period T
if the ratio between the period of which the system is operational, T_o, by the observation period T.

This course covers the topics on reliability and availability evaluation of systems.
First, the necessary background is introduced (in case the students need an update on
statistics and probability basis); otherwise, these chapters may be skipped. After that,
the basic definitions of the subject are introduced. Then, a model classification is introduced, and later on, the combinatorial model is presented, that is, RBD and FT.
This is followed by a description of several methods for evaluating non-state-based
models. Markov chains are, then, adopted to represent reliability and availability
problems that combinatorial models fail to describe accurately. Then, SPN is also
assumed to model systems' reliability and availability features. Simulation may also
be adopted as an alternative method of evaluation. Then, system reliability, availability, and maintainability are studied through parametric and nonparametric lifetime
data analysis. Finally, an introduction to fault injection is presented.

Content sequence

Chapter 1 → Chapter 2 → Chapter 3 → Chapter 4 → Chapter 5 → Chapter 6 →
Chapter 16 → Chapter 17 → Chapter 18 → Chapter 19 → Chapter 20 → Chapter
21 → Chapter 22 → Chapter 25 → Chapter 26.

If the students already know statistics and basic probability subjects, the respective
chapters or part of them may be skipped. If the class has no knowledge of Markov
chain and stochastic Petri nets, an overview of chapters 9, 10, 12, and 13 is required.
Optional chapters: Chapters 7 and Chapters 14. The examples for Chapters 14 may
be taken from Chapter 22.

Reliability and Availability Evaluation: Modeling

This course covers the background, fundamentals on dependability, reliability, availability and related metrics, and the modeling subjects of the previous course.

Content sequence

Chapter 1 → Chapter 2 → Chapter 3 → Chapter 4 → Chapter 5 → Chapter 6 → Chapter 16 → Chapter 17 → Chapter 18 → Chapter 19 → Chapter 20 → Chapter 21 → Chapter 22.

If the students are already versed in introductory statistics and probability subjects, the respective chapters or part of them may be skipped. If the class has no knowledge of Markov chain and stochastic Petri nets, an overview of chapters 9, 10, 12, and 13 is required. Optional chapter: Chapters 14. The examples for Chapters 14 may be taken from Chapter 22.

Lifetime Data Analysis or Reliability and Availability Data Analysis

covers the background, fundamentals on dependability, reliability, availability and related metrics, and lifetime data analysis and fault injection subjects. In a general sense, there are two broad approaches for dealing with failure and repairing data: the parametric and nonparametric approaches. This curse covers many methods of both general approaches.

Content sequence

Chapter 1 → Chapter 2 → Chapter 3 → Chapter 4 → Chapter 5 → Chapter 6 → Chapter 16 → Chapter 17 → Chapter 25 → Chapter 26.

Besides the long courses, a short course could be conceived from this document. This course is much more straightforward than the previous one. The background topics may be significantly reduced, or if the audience is already acquainted with the background, it could be skipped entirely, and the courses may start directly on the core subject. For instance, the list below summarizes a short course that the instructor may compose from the text.

- **Introduction to Statistics and Probability.**
  This course may be composed of Chapter 1, Chapter 2, Chapter 3, Chapter 4, Chapter 5 and Chapter 7 or specific part of them.

- **Operational Analysis: Bottleneck Analysis and Bounds.**
  Sequence of chapters: Chapter 1, Chapter 3 and Chapter 8.

- **Introduction to Markov Chain.**
  Sequence of chapters: Chapter 2, Chapter 5, Chapter 9, Chapter 10, Chapter 11.

- **Performance Modeling with Markov Chain.**
  Sequence of chapters: Chapter 1, Chapter 2, Chapter 3, Section 4.1, Section 4.2, Chapter 6, Chapter 9, Chapter 10, Chapter 11.

- **Performance Modeling with Stochastic Petri Nets.**
  Sequence of chapters: Chapter 1, Chapter 12, Chapter 13, Chapter 14 Optional chapter: Chapter 14 and Chapter 22. Requirement: Course Performance Modeling with Markov Chain or Introduction to Markov Chain.

- **Performance Simulation.**
  Sequence of chapters: Chapter 1, Chapter 14 and examples from Chapter 13 and Chapter 22. Requirement: Course Performance Modeling with Stochastic Petri Nets.

- **Reliability, Availability and Related Metrics Evaluation via RBD and FT.**
  This course may be formed of Chapter 1, Chapter 2, Chapter 5, Chapter 16, Chapter 17, Chapter 18, Chapter 19 and Chapter 20.

- **Reliability, Availability and Related Metrics Evaluation with Markov Chain**
  This course may be composed of Chapter 1, Chapter 2, Chapter 5, Chapter 16, Chapter 17, Chapter 9, Chapter 10 and Chapter 21.

- **Reliability, Availability and Related Metrics Evaluation with Stochastic Petri Nets.**
  This course may composed of Chapter 12, Chapter 13 and Chapter 22. Requirement: Course Performance Modeling with Markov Chain or Introduction to Markov Chain.

- **Lifetime Data Analysis and Fault Injection.**
  This course may be defined of parts of Chapter 1, Chapter 2, Chapter 3, Chapter 4, Chapter 5 (Choose the distributions according your need), Chapter 26 and Chapter 25.

- **Introduction to to Workload Generation.**
  This course may be composed of parts of Chapter 1, Chapter 2, Chapter 3, Chapter 4, Chapter 5, Chapter 7 and Chapter 24.

For Students

Students following a course organized by an instructor should follow the sequence suggested by the instructor. For instance, if the instructor adopts the plan proposed for the course Reliability and Availability Evaluation: Modeling, the students should follow the steps depicted in the course plan. If the students need extra support on some specific background topic, they may go to the particular topic shown on the book (or on the references quoted) to fill the specific gaps. Each chapter has a good number of unsolved exercises to help the students to consolidate the covered subjects.

For self-studying, the interested person should first define the topic of interest. Such a topic of interest could be confined to a specific subject or broad as one other as one of the long courses proposed. In the latter case, we also suggest following the plans already defined. Next, the student should look at the core chapter of the topic of interest in specific subjects and check the necessary background. This book aims to be self-contained to support one's instruction without requiring extra material, at least to some extent.

For Analyst

Analysts may use this book to get acquainted with specific subjects by looking at the particular chapters. A large number of examples will help them to understand the concepts covered in each chapter. The analyst may also self-teach topics of interest. In such a case, the guidelines for students and instructors may serve them well.

Part III

Reliability and Availability Modeling

Due to the pervasive provision of services on the Internet, dependability has become a requirement of prime concern in hardware/software design, development, deployment, and operation. Providing fault-tolerant services is inherently related to the use of redundancy. Redundancy can be exploited either in time or space. Replication of services is usually provided through distributed hosts across the world, so that whenever the service, the underlying host, or network fails, another service is ready to take over [161]. Dependability of a system can be understood as the ability to deliver a specified functionality that can be justifiably trusted [227, 228]. Functionality is a set of roles or services (functions) observed by an outside agent (a human being, another system) interacting with a system at its interfaces. The defined functionality of a system is what the system is intended to do.

Figure 15.1 shows a guideline for reliability and availability modeling. This guideline helps the analyst decide the evaluation approach to follow by considering the probability distributions, the state-space size, and the access to the analytic solution. In addition, this recommendation considers the representation capacity and the time to get a solution inherent to the models.

Once one has a reliability or availability problem to be evaluated through a model, a first question to be answered is if the system is complex enough to be subdivided into subsystems. Then, we may have a monolithic system or a system represented by subsystems. Afterward, for each subsystem (in case the system is represented by subsystems) or in case of a monolithic system, the analyst may ask if phase-type distributions are suitable to represent the system or the respective subsystem. If they are not suitable, simulation is the alternative. If phase-type distributions are appropriate,

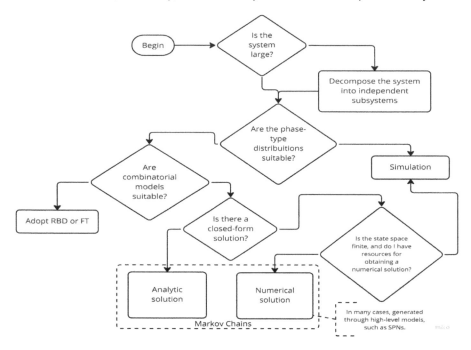

Figure 15.1   Reliability and Availability Modeling Guideline.

one may ask if combinatorial models are suitable to represent the system[1]. If the answer is affirmative, adopt a Reliability Block Diagram (RBD) or Fault Tree as the modeling formalism. If combinatorial models are inadequate, the analyst may ask if a known analytic model represents the system (closed-form algebraic expressions). If no analytic model is known, the analyst should ask if the state space size is finite and if the evaluation platform (computers) has enough memory to represent the state space. If these last two questions are positively answered, numerical solutions are likely to be the best choice; otherwise, the analyst should employ simulation.

This part is divided into seven chapters. Chapter 16 describes some early and seminal works on reliability, availability, and dependability evaluation and a set of fundamental concepts and definitions. Subsequently, the essential redundancy mechanisms are introduced, and finally, the modeling techniques are classified. Chapter 18 and Chapter 19 introduce the two most relevant combinatorial model types for reliability and availability evaluation, namely, Reliability Block Diagrams (RBD) and Fault Trees (FT) and applications. Their evaluation methods are presented in Chapter 20. Chapter 21 studies more complex systems than those studied in the previous chapter, where Markov chains are applied to model systems that combinatorial models do not represent well. Chapter 22 adopts SPN to model systems that are not accurately

---

[1]Details about the modeling capacity and constraints of combinatorial models are discussed in Chapter 18.

described by combinatorial methods and whose state space is large, making them hard to represent using Markov chains. In these two last chapters, multiple formalisms (RBD + CTMC, RBD + SPN, FT + CTMC + FT + SPN, for instance) are also applied to model an even more complex system through hierarchy and refinement.

16 Fundamentals of Dependability

This chapter describes early and seminal works on reliability, availability, and dependability evaluation. Afterward, we introduce a set of fundamental concepts and definitions. Subsequently, some important lifetime probability distribution is introduced.

16.1 A BRIEF HISTORY

This section provides a summary of early work related to dependability and briefly describes some seminal efforts and the respective relations with current prevalent methods. This effort is undoubtedly incomplete; nonetheless, we hope it provides fundamental events, people, and important research related to what is now called dependability modeling.

Dependability is related to disciplines such as fault tolerance and reliability. The concept of dependable computing first appeared in the 1820s when Charles Babbage carried out the initiative to conceive and build a mechanical calculating engine to get rid of the risk of human errors [227] [371]. In his book, "On the Economy of Machinery and Manufacture," he remarks " 'The first objective of every person who attempts to make any article of consumption is, or ought to be, to produce it in perfect form" [49]. In the nineteenth century, reliability theory advanced from probability and statistics to support estimating maritime and life insurance rates. In the early twentieth century, methods had been proposed to estimate survivorship of railroad equipment [416] [418].

The first IEEE (formerly AIEE and IRE) public document to mention reliability is "Answers to Questions Relative to High Tension Transmission," that digests the meeting of the Board of Directors of the American Institute of Electrical Engineers, held on September 26, 1902 [39]. In 1905, H. G. Stott and H. R. Stuart discussed "Time-Limit Relays and Duplication of Electrical Apparatus to Secure Reliability of Services at New York [416] and at Pittsburg", [418]. In these works, the concept of reliability was chiefly qualitative. In 1907, A. A. Markov began the study of a notable sort of chance process. In this process, the outcome of a given experiment can modify the outcome of the next experiment. This sort of process is now called a Markov chain [445]. Markov's classic textbook, "Calculus of Probabilities," was published four times in Russian and was translated into German [38]. In 1926, twenty years after Markov's initial discoveries, a paper by Russian mathematician S. N. Bernstein used the term "Markov chain" [43]. In the 1910s, A. K. Erlang studied telephone traffic planning for reliable service provisioning [131]. Later in the 1930s, the theory of extreme value was adopted to the model fatigue life of materials by W. Weibull, and Gumbel [220]. In 1931, Kolmogorov, in his famous paper "Über die analytischen Methoden in der Wahrscheinlichkeitsrechnung" (Analytic Methods in Probability Theory) set the foundations for the modern theory of Markov processes[216] [38]. Finally, in the 1940s quantitative analysis of reliability was adopted for many operational and strategic problems in World War II [49] [83].

The first generation of electronic computers was entirely undependable; thence, many techniques were investigated for improving their reliability. Among such techniques, many researchers investigated design strategies and evaluation methods. Many methods were then proposed for improving system dependability, such as error control codes, replication of components, comparison monitoring, and diagnostic routines. The leading researchers during that period were Shannon [379], Von Neumann [304], and Moore [289], who proposed and developed theories for building reliable systems by using redundant and less reliable components [290]. These were the forerunners of the statistical and probabilistic techniques that form the groundwork of modern dependability theory [11, 29].

In the 1950s, reliability turned out to be a subject of great interest as a consequence of the cold war efforts, failures of American and Soviet rockets, and failures of the first commercial jet, the British de Havilland comet [344] [37]. Epstein and Sobel's 1953 paper on exponential distribution was a landmark contribution [128]. In 1954, the first Symposium on Reliability and Quality Control (it is now the IEEE Transactions on Reliability) was held in the United States, and in 1958 the First All-Union Conference on Reliability was held in Moscow [159] [446]. In 1957 S. J. Einhorn and F. B. Thiess applied Markov chains for modeling system intermittence [427], and in 1960, P. M. Anselone employed Markov chains for evaluating the availability of radar systems [16]. In 1961 Birnbaum, Esary, and Saunders published a pioneering paper introducing coherent structures [46].

The reliability models might be classified as combinatorial (non-state space model) and state-space models. Reliability Block Diagrams (RBD) and Fault Trees (FT) are combinatorial models and the most widely adopted models in reliability evaluation. RBD is probably the oldest combinatorial technique for reliability analysis [290]. Fault Tree Analysis (FTA) was initially developed in 1962 at Bell Laboratories by H. A. Watson to analyze the Minuteman I Intercontinental Ballistic Missile Launch Control System. Afterward, in 1962, Boeing and AVCO expanded the use of FTA to the entire Minuteman II [129]. In 1965, W. H. Pierce unified Shannon, Von Neumann, and Moore's theories of masking and redundancy as the concept of failure tolerance [339]. In 1967, A. Avizienis combined masking methods with error detection, fault diagnosis, and recovery into the concept of fault-tolerant systems [30].

The formation of the IEEE Computer Society Technical Committee on Fault-Tolerant Computing (now Dependable Computing and Fault Tolerance TC) in 1970 and of IFIP Working Group 10.4 on Dependable Computing and Fault Tolerance in 1980 were essential means for defining a consistent set of concepts and terminology. In the early 1980s, Laprie coined the term dependability for covering concepts such as reliability, availability, safety, confidentiality, maintainability, security, and integrity [227] [228].

In late 1970s some works were proposed for mapping Petri nets to Markov chains [286] [302] [421]. These models have been extensively adopted as high-level Markov chain automatic generation models and for discrete event simulation. Natkin was the first to apply what is now generally called stochastic Petri nets to dependability evaluation of systems [8].

16.2 FUNDAMENTAL CONCEPTS

This section presents several fundamental concepts, taxonomy, and quantitative measures for dependability [246].

As mentioned, the dependability of a system is the capability to deliver a set of reliable services observed by outside agents. A service is trustworthy when it implements the system's specified functionality. On the other hand, a system failure occurs when the system fails to provide its specified functionality. A computer system failure can be either hardware defects or software bugs. In everyday language, the words fault, failure, and error are reciprocally used. However, in fault-tolerant computing system jargon, they have different meanings. Therefore, distinguishing faults, errors, and failures is fundamental for understanding fault tolerance concepts.

A system **failure** is an event that occurs when the delivered service deviates from correct service. Therefore, a failure is a transition from right service to incorrect service. Consider a Bernoulli random variable $X(t)$ that represents the system (S) state at time t. $X(t) = 1$ represents the system operational state and $X(t) = 0$ denotes the faulty state (see Figure 16.1). More formally,

$$X(t) = \begin{cases} 0 & \text{with probability } 1\text{-p, if } S \text{ has failed} \\ 1 & \text{with probability } p, \text{ if } S \text{ is operational.} \end{cases}$$

A transition from incorrect service to correct service is service restoration.

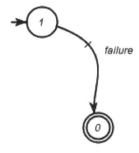

Figure 16.1 States of $X(t)$ and Failure Event.

An **error** is a state of a component of a system (a system substate) that may cause a subsequent failure (Figure 16.2). A failure occurs when an error is not contained, reaches the system interface, and alters the system service. A **fault** is an event that causes an erroneous substate [31]. A system with faults that delivers its specified functionality is fault-tolerant; that is, the system does not fail even when there are faulty components.

Summarizing, a fault causes an erroneous substate. The error can spread through the system because the output of one component may be an input of other components. If the erroneous substate is not contained, it propagates to the system interface and causes a failure.

$$\ldots \longrightarrow \text{fault} \longrightarrow \text{error} \longrightarrow \text{failure} \longrightarrow \text{fault} \longrightarrow \ldots$$

Figure 16.2   Fault, Error, and Failure Sequence.

For instance, consider an air conditioner switch contact that is stuck open; that is, it is always open independently on the switch position. Thus, we already fault the beginning of operations (switch position in open) but there is not yet an error. However, if we change the switch position to closed, the fault causes an error (that if not contained), which, in turn, causes a malfunctioning (failure) since the switch contact does not close, and the air conditioner does not start.

Hardware faults can be classified based on several aspects. A fault may be *active* or *dormant*. It is active when it produces an error; otherwise, it is dormant. Concerning durations, faults can be *permanent, transient*, or *intermittent*. A permanent fault is a component that is permanently out of service. One example is a burned-out incandescent lamp. A transient fault causes a component to malfunction for some time, but the component is fully restored after that time. Intermittent faults, on the other hand, never go away completely. They oscillate between being dormant and active. A loose electrical connection is an example of an intermittent fault. Faults can also be classified as *benign* and *malicious*. A fault that only causes a component to go out of service is called benign. Malicious faults produce plausible but incorrect output. As an example, assume an altitude sensor in an airplane that reports 2000 m altitude to one component and a 1200 m altitude to another component [218].

A programming bug (fault) causes erroneous states. For instance, assume a function is presumed to calculate the volume of three-dimensional space, but it calculates two-thirds of the respective space due to a programming bug. This bug (fault) will results in an erroneous state (error) only when the particular function is executed, and if the erroneous state is not contained, it will propagate to generate a failure. It is worth mentioning that software bugs may be malicious or non-malicious, whereas non-malicious bugs could be caused by accident, inexperience, or inability. The standard approach for removing software faults involves finding and removing software bugs in the operational period (debugging). Such an approach is considerably more costly than avoiding or removing faults during the developing or testing phase. However, diagnosing and confining the underlying fault accountable for an observed failure becomes uncertain if the failure cannot be reproduced. Software testing is suitable for dealing with faults that consistently results in failure under particular circumstances. Testers sometimes call such faults Bohrbugs, a reference to Niels Bohr's atomic model [164, 439]. However, when testers fail to reproduce the failure under apparently similar conditions, the debugging can sometimes lead to the failure but may also not reach the failure. For instance, inadequate synchronization in multi-threaded programs can yield race conditions depending on the threads' timing and operating system schedules. As a failure exclusively occurs if the operating system schedules the threads, using the debugging process is uncertain about reproducing failures and confining the underlying faults. A fault can prompt the software systems to manifest an uncontrolled and even seemingly non-deterministic behavior. Software developers sometimes name such faults Mandelbugs (a reference to the preeminent researcher in fractal analysis). The literature also designates such software faults as Heisenbugs as an allusion to Heisenberg's uncertainty principle [439].

As Heisenbugs resemble non-deterministic behaviors, a new execution of the failed operation usually leads to success. Nevertheless, when the specific unknown internal conditions are met, the failure may be exposed again. Therefore, in many cases, simply restarting a program or rebooting a computer after experiencing a failure can be valuable for preventing future failure incidents. Nevertheless, such proactive actions (software rejuvenation) are only effective if the failure rate increases with the runtime. Indeed, many software systems running continuously for long periods tend to manifest degraded performance and reliability decay due to the increased failure rate. Such a phenomenon is called software aging [439].

As described earlier, service failure is defined as an event that occurs when the delivered service deviates from correct service. An *operational mode* is a system behavior that delivers a service according to a specification. On the other hand, the different ways in which the services deviation are manifested are a system's service failure modes [352]. The failure modes may be characterized by the *domain*, *perception*, and *consequence* (see Figure 16.3). The failure domain distinguishes between *content failures* and *timing failures*. A content failure occurs when the information delivered at the service interface departs from what is defined in the specification. A timing failure occurs when the timing at which the information is delivered diverges from the timing specification. The user perception of failures leads us to distinguish them as *consistent* and *inconsistent*. A consistent failure occurs when the incorrect service is identically perceived by system users, whereas the system users perceive an inconsistent failure differently.

The consequence of a failure may be ordered into severity levels. The severity levels are usually related to the acceptable probabilities of occurrence. The definition of the severity levels and the acceptable probabilities of occurrence are application-specific

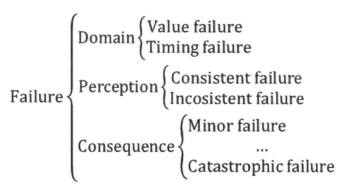

$$\text{Failure} \begin{cases} \text{Domain} \begin{cases} \text{Value failure} \\ \text{Timing failure} \end{cases} \\ \text{Perception} \begin{cases} \text{Consistent failure} \\ \text{Incosistent failure} \end{cases} \\ \text{Consequence} \begin{cases} \text{Minor failure} \\ \quad \dots \\ \text{Catastrophic failure} \end{cases} \end{cases}$$

Figure 16.3   Failure Classification.

and involve dependability and security attributes like reliability, availability, safety, confidentiality, and integrity. Generally speaking, two limiting levels can be defined: *minor failures* and *catastrophic failures*. The consequence of a minor failure is similar to the benefits provided by the correct service. On the other hand, the consequence of a catastrophic failure is orders of magnitude higher than the benefit provided by correct service delivery or is even inadmissible. A comprehensive taxonomy of faults and failures is presented in [30].

Now, consider a random variable T as the time to reach the state $X(t) = 0$, given that the system started in state $X(t) = 1$ at time $t = 0$. Therefore, the random variable T represents the time to failure of the system S, $F_T(t)$ its cumulative distribution function (CDF), and $f_T(t)$ the respective density function (DF). Figure 16.4) shows these functions. Therefore

$$F_T(0) = 0 \text{ and } \lim_{t \to \infty} F_T(t) = 1,$$

$$f_T(t) = \frac{dF_T(t)}{dt}, \tag{16.2.1}$$

where $f_T(t) \geq 0$ and $\int_0^\infty f_T(t)\,dt = 1$.

The probability that the system S does not fail up to time t is the system **reliability** ($R(t)$). Hence, reliability (also called survivability) is complementary with the cumulative distribution function (see Figure 16.5). In other words, $F_T(t)$ is the **unreliability** function ($UR(t)$). The reliability is formally defined by

$$P(T > t) = R(t) = 1 - F_T(t), \tag{16.2.2}$$

$$R(0) = 1 \text{ and } \lim_{t \to \infty} R(t) = 0.$$

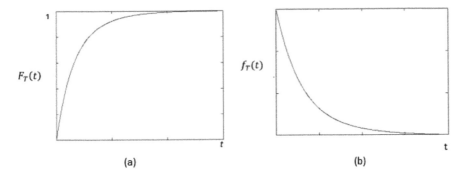

(a)   (b)

Figure 16.4 (a): Cumulative Distribution Function and (b): Density Function.

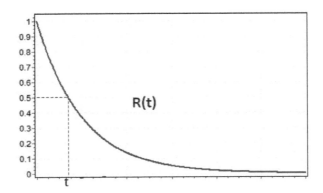

Figure 16.5 Reliability Function – $R(t) \times t$.

Now assume n similar devices have been placed under a test. If after a testing period of Δt, n_i devices survived, the reliability may be estimated by

$$\widehat{R}(t) = \frac{n_i}{n}.$$

Therefore, the unreliability may also be estimated by

$$\widehat{UR}(t) = \widehat{F_T}(t) = 1 - \widehat{F_T}(t) = 1 - \frac{n_i}{n} = \frac{n - n_i}{n},$$

where $D = n - n_i$ is the number of failures (defects - D) in the test period. Therefore

$$D = \widehat{UR}(t) \times n.$$

If $n = 10^6$ (one million), then the defects per million is estimated by

$$DPM = \widehat{UR}(t) \times 10^6.$$

Therefore

$$DPM = UR(t) \times 10^6,$$ (16.2.3)

$$DPM = (1 - R(t)) \times 10^6$$ (16.2.4)

and

$$R(t) = 1 - DPM \times 10^{-6}.$$ (16.2.5)

The probability of that the system S fails within the interval $[t, t + \Delta t]$ may be calculated by:

$$P(t \leq T \leq t + \Delta t) = F_T(t + \Delta t) - F_T(t) =$$

$$R(t) - R(t + \Delta t) =$$

$$\int_0^\infty f_T(t)\,dt.$$

The probability of that the system S fails during the interval $[t, t + \Delta t]$ if it has survived to the time t (conditional probability of failure) is

$$P(t \leq T \leq t + \Delta t \,|\, T > t) = \frac{R(t) - R(t + \Delta t)}{R(t)}.$$

$P(t \leq T \leq t + \Delta t \,|\, T > t)/\Delta t$ is the conditional probability of failure per time unit. When $\Delta t \to 0$, then

$$\lim_{\Delta t \to 0} \frac{R(t) - R(t + \Delta t)}{R(t) \times \Delta t} = \lim_{\Delta t \to 0} \frac{-[R(t + \Delta t) - R(t)]}{\Delta t} \times \frac{1}{R(t)} =$$

$$-\frac{dR(t)}{dt} \times \frac{1}{R(t)} = \frac{dF_T(t)}{dt} \times \frac{1}{R(t)} = \frac{f_T(t)}{R(t)} = \lambda(t),$$ (16.2.6)

where $\lambda(t)$ is named the **hazard function (failure rate** function). Hazard rates may be characterized as decreasing failure rate (DFR), constant failure rate (CFR), or increasing failure rate (IFR).

Since,

$$\lambda(t) = -\frac{dR(t)}{dt} \times \frac{1}{R(t)},$$ (16.2.7)

$$\lambda(t) \times dt = -\frac{dR(t)}{R(t)}.$$

Thus

$$\int_0^t \lambda(t) \times dt = -\int_0^t \frac{dR(t)}{R(t)} =$$

$$-\int_0^t \lambda(t) \times dt = \ln R(t).$$

Therefore,

$$R(t) = e^{-\int_0^t \lambda(t) \times dt} = e^{-H(t)}, \qquad (16.2.8)$$

where

$$H(t) = -\ln R(t)\, dt = \int_0^t \lambda(t) \times dt \qquad (16.2.9)$$

is the cumulative hazard rate function (cumulative failure rate function).

Consider a hazard rate of an entire population of products over time ($\lambda(t)$), where some products will fail in early life ("infant mortality"), others will last until wear-out ("end of life"), and others will fail during their useful life period ("normal life"). Infant mortality failures are usually caused by material, design, and manufacturing problems, whereas wear-out failures are related to fatigue or exhaustion [377]. Regular life failures are considered to be random.

Infant mortality is commonly represented by decreasing hazard rate (see Figure 16.6.a), wear-out failures are typically represented by increasing hazard rate (Figure 16.6.c), and regular life failures are usually depicted by constant hazard rate (see Figure 16.6.b). The overlapping of these three separate hazard rate functions forms the so-called bathtub curve (Figure 16.6.d).

The **mean time to fail** ($MTTF$) is defined by

$$MTTF = \int_0^\infty t\, f_T(t)\, dt. \qquad (16.2.10)$$

As

$$f_T(t) = \frac{dF_T(t)}{dt} = -\frac{dR(t)}{dt},$$

thus,

$$MTTF = -\int_0^\infty \frac{dR(t)}{dt} \times t\, dt.$$

Let $u = t$ and $dv = \frac{dR(t)}{dt} \times t\, dt$; then $du = dt$ and $dv = R(t)$. Then, integrate by parts[1]

$$MTTF = -\int_0^\infty \frac{dR(t)}{dt} \times t\, dt = -\left[t R(t) \Big|_0^\infty - \int_0^\infty R(t)\, dt \right]$$

$$= -\left[0 - \int_0^\infty R(t)\, dt \right].$$

---

[1] $\int u\, dv = uv - \int v\, du.$

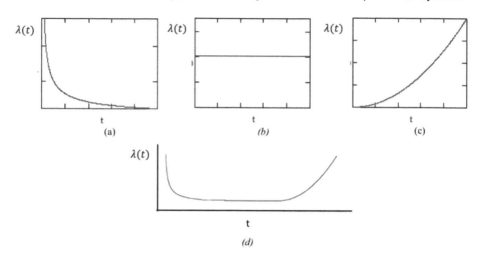

Figure 16.6   Hazard Rate: **(a)** Decreasing, **(b)** Constant, **(c)** Increasing, **(d)** Bathtub curve.

Thus

$$MTTF = \int_0^\infty R(t)\,dt, \qquad\qquad (16.2.11)$$

and

$$MTTF = \int_0^\infty (1 - F_T(t))\,dt, \qquad\qquad (16.2.12)$$

which is often easier to compute than using 16.2.10.

Another central tendency reliability measure is the **median time to failure** (*MedTTF*), defined by the time instant, t, when $R(t) = 0.5$. The *MedTTF* divides the time to fail distribution into two halves, where 50% of failures occur before MedTTF and the other 50% after (see Figure 16.5).

Example 16.2.1. Assume the CDF of the time to failure of the computational system is represented by

$$F_T(t) = 1 - \frac{1}{30 \times 10^{-6}t^2 + 1},$$

where t is the time in hours. Compute **(a)** $F_T(720\,h)$, **(b)** the reliability at $t = 720\,h$, **(c)** $\lambda(t)$ at $720\,h$, and **(d)** $MTTF$.

$$F_T(720\,h) = 1 - \frac{1}{30 \times 10^{-6} \times 720^2 + 1} = 0.9396.$$

As $R(t) = 1 - F_T(t)$, then $R(t) = \frac{1}{30 \times 10^{-6} t^2 + 1}$, so

$$R(720h) = \frac{1}{30 \times 10^{-6} \times 720^2 + 1} = 0.0604.$$

Using 16.2.7 (or $F_T(t)$ in 16.2.6), we get

$$\lambda(t) = 0.006 - \frac{400}{33333.3333 + t^2}.$$

So, $\lambda(720h) = 5.2750 \times 10^{-3}$.

Taking 16.2.11, we have

$$MTTF = \int_0^\infty \frac{1}{30 \times 10^{-6} t^2 + 1} dt = 286.787\,h.$$

The median time to failure can be obtained by solving

$$R(t) = 0.5 = \frac{1}{30 \times 10^{-6} t^2 + 1}$$

for t. Hence $MedTTF = 182.574\,h$.

□

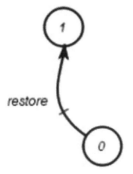

Figure 16.7 States of $X(t)$ and Restore Event.

Now consider that the system is out of service at time instant $t = 0$, that is $X(0) = 0$ (see Figure 16.7). When the system is restored, it reaches the state $X(t) = 1$. Assume a random variable D that represents the time to reach the state $X(t) = 1$, given the system started in state $X(t) = 0$ at time $t = 0$. Therefore, the random variable D represents the system time to restore (recover), $F_D(t)$ its cumulative distribution function, and $f_D(t)$ the respective density function, where:

$$F_D(0) = 0 \text{ and } \lim_{t \to \infty} F_D(t) = 1,$$

$$f_D(t) = \frac{dF_D(t)}{dt}, \tag{16.2.13}$$

where $f_D(t) \geq 0$ and $\int_0^\infty f_D(t)\,dt = 1$.

The probability that the system S will be repaired by t is defined as **maintainability**, $M(t)$. Thus

$$P(D \leq t) = F_D(t) = M(t) = \int_0^t f_D(t)\,dt. \tag{16.2.14}$$

The **mean time to restore** $(MTTR)$ is defined by

$$MTTR = \int_0^\infty t\, f_D(t)\,dt. \tag{16.2.15}$$

Let us define $UM(t) = 1 - M(t)$ (as $M(t) = F_D(t)$, $UM(t) = 1 - F_D(t)$ – complementary cumulative distribution function – $CCDF$). Hence

$$f_D(t) = -\frac{dUM(t)}{dt}.$$

Thus,

$$MTTR = -\int_0^\infty \frac{dUM(t)}{dt} \times t\,dt.$$

Let $u = t$ and $dv = \frac{dUM(t)}{dt}$, then $du = dt$ and $V = UM(t)$. Then, integrating by parts we have

$$MTTR = -\left[t\,UM(t) \Big|_0^\infty - \int_0^\infty UM(t)dt \right].$$

$$MTTR = \int_0^\infty UM(t)dt,$$

since at $t = 0$, $UM(0) = 1$ and $\lim_{t \to \infty} UM(t) = 0$. Therefore

$$MTTR = \int_0^\infty (1 - M(t))dt, \tag{16.2.16}$$

which is often easier to compute than 16.2.15.

Consider a repairable system S that is either operational (Up) or faulty $(Down)$. Figure 16.8 shows the system state transition model, $X(t) = 1$ when S is Up and $X(t) = 0$ when S is $Down$. Whenever the system fails, a set of activities is conducted to restore (recover) the system. These activities comprehend administrative, transportation, and logistic times, for instance. When the maintenance team arrives at the system site, the actual repairing process may start. Further, this time may also be divided into diagnosis time and actual repair time, checking time. However, for the sake of simplicity, we group these times such that the downtime equals the time to restore – TR, which is composed of non-repair time $--$ NRT – (that groups transportation time, order times, delivery times.) and time to repair – TTR (see Figure 16.9). Thus, $Downtime = TR = NRT + TTR$.

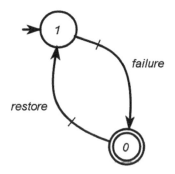

Figure 16.8   States of a Repairable System.

The simplest definition of **availability** is expressed as the ratio of the expected system uptime to the expected system up and downtimes:

$$A = \frac{E(Uptime)}{E(Uptime) + E(Downtime)}. \qquad (16.2.17)$$

Consider the system started operating at time $t = t'$ and fails at $t = t''$; thus $\Delta t = t'' - t' = Uptime$ (see Figure 16.9). Therefore, the system availability may also be expressed by

$$A = \frac{MTTF}{MTTF + MTR},$$

where MTR is the mean time to restore, which in turn is defined by $MTR = MNRT + MTTR$. Therefore

$$A = \frac{MTTF}{MTTF + MNRT + MTTR},$$

where $MTTR$ is the mean time to repair, and $MNRT$ is the mean non-repair time, that is the portion of the MTR that is not related to the actual repair of the system [401].

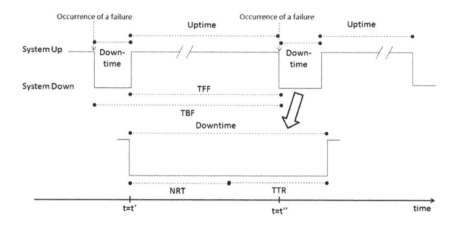

Figure 16.9 Downtime and Uptime.

If $MNRT \simeq 0$ or if the analyst is not interested in detailing the $MNRT$, and this delay is added to the respective $MTTR$, we have

$$A = \frac{MTTF}{MTTF + MTTR}. \tag{16.2.18}$$

As mean time between failures is $MTBF = MTTF + MTR = MTTF + MNRT + MTTR$ (see Figure 16.9), and if $MNRT \simeq 0$, then $MTBF = MTTF + MTTR$. Since $MTTF \gg MTTR$; thus $MTBF \simeq MTTF$, so

$$A \simeq \frac{MTBF}{MTBF + MTTR}. \tag{16.2.19}$$

The instantaneous availability is the probability that the system is operational at t ($X(t) = 1$ in Figure 16.8), that is

$$A(t) = P(X(t) = 1) = E(X(t)), \quad t \geq 0. \tag{16.2.20}$$

If repairing is not possible, the instantaneous availability, $A(t)$, is equivalent to the reliability, $R(t)$.

If the system approaches stationary states as the time increases, it is possible to quantify the steady-state availability, such that it is possible to estimate the long-term fraction of time the system is available.

$$A = \lim_{t \to \infty} A(t), \quad t \geq 0. \tag{16.2.21}$$

Occasionally, we are required to estimate the system availability in a time interval $(0,t]$. The interval availability $(A_I(t'))$ is estimated by

$$A_I(t') = \frac{1}{t'} \int_0^{t'} A(t)dt. \tag{16.2.22}$$

Assume we are required to estimate if the system S is operational and if it can deliver a specified service capacity. Assuming the system has n operational, functional unities able to provide the specified service, the system may deliver the service in a full operational capacity, that is, when n functional unities are operational, or may still provide the service with smaller processing capacity when some functional unities are out of service. Even when only one functional unity is available, the system delivers the specified service but with the smallest operational capacity possible. The system availability considering the processing capacity, defined as the **capacity-oriented availability**(*COA*), is estimated by

$$COA = \frac{\sum_{i=1}^n i \times \pi_i}{n}, \tag{16.2.23}$$

where π_i is the probability of i functional unities being operational.

The system **downtime** (DT) in a given time period T may is defined by

$$DT = UA \times T, \tag{16.2.24}$$

$UA = 1 - A$ is the system **unavailability**. The system **uptime** (UT) in the time period T is defined by

$$UT = A \times T. \tag{16.2.25}$$

Availability may also be commonly expressed as the number of nines:

$$\#9s = -\log UA. \tag{16.2.26}$$

Table 16.1 presents the steady-state availability, the respective number of nines, and the system downtime for a year of 365 days.

Sometimes the $MTTF$ (and $MTBF$) are confused with the **expected life time**. Let us discuss one example to highlight the differences. Assume 1000 brand new mechanical devices. We monitored these devices for one year. During this period, we observed ten failures. Hence the failure rate calculated was $10/1000 = 0.01$ a year. We were considering the time to failure exponentially distributed, the $MTTF = 100\,years$. Now, consider that we monitored 1000 devices of the same model for one year, but only those that survived four years of use. We observed 230 failures.

Table 16.1

Availability, Number of Nines, and Downtime

A	$\#9s$	DT
0.99999	5	$5.256\,min$
0.9999	4	$52.56\,min$
0.999	3	$8.76\,h$
0.99	2	$87.6\,h$
0.9	1	$36.5\,days$

Thus the failures estimated are $230/1000 = 0.23$ failures a year. This example shows that the $MTTF$ is different from the expected lifetime since failures occur more often as the devices become older. Thus, the best way to estimate the $MTTF$ would be to watch each sample device until each fails. Afterward, the mean of the time to failure would be computed.

Let us consider a second example in which 100,000 twenty-year-old people are watched for one year. In this period, 100 people died. Hence, the failure rate (deaths per year - dpy) is estimated by $100/100,000 = 0.001\,dpy$. Assume the time to failure is exponentially distributed; the $MTTF$ is obtained, $MTTF = 1,000$ years. Therefore, it is clear that the $MTTF$ is different from the expected lifetime since people get old. Hence, the death rate increases so that the expected lifetime reaches values much more realistic, around 80 years.

Example 16.2.2. Considering the results obtained in Example 16.2.1, now assume the $MTTR = 24\,h$ and calculate the steady-state availability. Taking 16.2.18, we obtain

$$A = \frac{MTTF}{MTTF + MTTR} = \frac{28.6787}{28.6787 + 24} = 0.9228.$$

The monthly downtime (in hours) is

$$DT = (1 - A) \times T = (1 - 0.9228) \times 720 = 55.584\,h.$$

□

16.3   SOME IMPORTANT PROBABILITY DISTRIBUTIONS

This section discusses the concepts introduced in the previous section considering some important specific probability distributions for reliability and availability studies. However, the distributions themselves have already been introduced in Chapter 2.

Exponential Distribution

The reliability is specified by 16.2.8. If the failure rate function is constant, $\lambda(t) = \lambda$, then the reliability is

$$R(t) = e^{-\int_0^\infty \lambda \times dt} = e^{-\lambda t}, \quad t \geq 0. \tag{16.3.1}$$

The constant failure rate implies no aging or wear-out effects. The probability that a running system that will operate for the next period T is equal to that of a brand new system will operate for the same period T, since

$$R(t|T) = \frac{R(t+T)}{R(T)} = \frac{e^{-\lambda(t+T)}}{e^{-\lambda T}},$$

which results in

$$R(t|T) = \frac{e^{-\lambda t} \times e^{-\lambda T}}{e^{-\lambda T}} = e^{-\lambda t} = R(t). \tag{16.3.2}$$

The result presented above shows that the only continuous random variable with the memoryless property is the random variable exponentially distributed. The *CDF* is

$$F_T(t) = 1 - e^{-\lambda t}, \quad t \geq 0, \tag{16.3.3}$$

the density function is

$$f_T(t) = \lambda e^{-\lambda t}, \quad t \geq 0, \tag{16.3.4}$$

and the cumulative failure rate function is

$$H(t) = \lambda \times t, \quad t \geq 0. \tag{16.3.5}$$

As $MTTF = \int_0^\infty R(t)\,dt$, then the mean time to fail is

$$MTTF = \int_0^\infty e^{-\lambda t}\,dt = \frac{1}{\lambda}. \tag{16.3.6}$$

If the failure rate is constant, but a failure will never occur before a specified period, t_0, the exponential distribution with threshold should be adopted [115]. Now, t_0 is the location parameter that shifts the distribution to the right. Therefore,

$$R(t) = e^{-\lambda(t-t_0)}, \quad t \geq 0, \tag{16.3.7}$$

$$F_T(t) = 1 - e^{-\lambda(t-t_0)}, \quad t \geq 0, \tag{16.3.8}$$

the density function is

$$f_T(t) = \lambda e^{-\lambda (t-t_0)}, \quad t \geq 0, \tag{16.3.9}$$

and

$$MTTF = t_0 + \frac{1}{\lambda}. \tag{16.3.10}$$

Considering a repairable system (see 16.8), if the time to restore (D) is also exponentially distributed, $M(t) = 1 - e^{\mu t}$, where μ is the restore rate. Hence, using 16.2.16, the mean time to restore is

$$MTTR = \int_0^\infty (1 - M(t))dt = \int_0^\infty e^{\mu t} dt = \frac{1}{\mu}. \tag{16.3.11}$$

Using 16.2.18, we get the steady-state availability.

$$A = \frac{MTTF}{MTTF + MTTR} = \frac{1/\lambda}{1/\lambda + 1/\mu} = \frac{\mu}{\lambda + \mu}. \tag{16.3.12}$$

Using 10.5.8 (or 10.5.13), we obtain the instantaneous availability.

$$A(t) = \frac{\mu}{\lambda + \mu} + \frac{\lambda}{\lambda + \mu} e^{-(\lambda + \mu)t}. \tag{16.3.13}$$

Example 16.3.1. Assume the cumulative failure rate of the server is equal to $H(t) = 2.5 \times 10^{-4}t$, where t is hours. Compute **(a)** the failure rate, **(b)** $MTTF$, **(c)** the reliability at $t = 720h$, and **(d)** $F_T(720h)$. The failure rate can be obtained by deriving $H(t)$, so $\lambda = 2.5 \times 10^{-4}fph$. As the failure rate is constant, the time to failure is exponentially distributed; hence $MTTF = 1/\lambda = 4000h$. The reliability at $720h$ is $R(720h) = e^{-2.5 \times 10^{-4} \times 720} = 0.83527$, and $F_T(720h) = 1 - R(720h) = 0.16473$.

Consider the TTR is exponentially distributed with rate $\mu = 25 \times 10^{-3}rph^2$. Calculate **(e)** $M(t)$ at $t = 20h$, **(f)** MTTR, and **(g)** the steady-state availability. As $M(t) = 1 - e^{-\mu t}$, then $M(20h) = 1 - e^{-25 \times 10^{-3} \times 20} = 0.3935$, and $MTTR = 1/\mu = 1/(25 \times 10^{-3}) = 40h$. Since $A = \mu/(\lambda + \mu) = 25 \times 10^{-3}/(2.5 \times 10^{-4} + 25 \times 10^{-3}) = 0.9901$. ☐

Assume a set of n devices was simultaneously observed for a period of days T. In this period, nf devices failed. The so-called "annualized failure rate" (AFR) is a failure rate, $nf/(n \times T)$, prorated in a one year period, that is $(nf/(n \times T)) \times 365$ days. It is indeed a ratio that vendors have used to estimate the failure probability of

---

[2]Repair per hour - rph

the device's models in a year of use. Assuming $MTBF$ is exponentially distributed, the following relations (see Equation 16.3.8) may be applied to estimate the $MTBF$ from the AFR and vice versa:

$$AFR = 1 - e^{\frac{-8760h}{MTBF}} \tag{16.3.14}$$

and from this we get

$$MTBF = \frac{8760\,h}{-ln(1-AFR)}. \tag{16.3.15}$$

Example 16.3.2. A company tested a set of disks of a specific model for in a period. After this period, the company determined the annualized failure rate as $AFR = 3.626117 \times 10^{-3}$. Assuming the time to failure is exponentially distributed, an estimated mean time between failures is $MTBF = \frac{8760\,h}{-ln(1-AFR)} = 2414150.7\,h$.

$\square$

Hyperexponential Distribution

Let us assume a device of the specified type is produced in n different plants. These devices have constant failure rates; however, their failure rates are different as the production processes are slightly different. Consider that the produced devices are mixed up before being delivered to retailers. Now, assume we pick up one item at random; the reliability of this item is

$$R(t) = \sum_{i=1}^{n} p_i R_i(t),$$

where $R_i(t) = e^{-\lambda_i t}$ is the reliability of an item produced in plant i, $-\lambda_i$ is the constant failure rate, p_i is the fraction of items coming from plant i, and $\sum_{i=1}^{n} p_i = 1$. Thus,

$$R(t) = \sum_{i=1}^{n} p_i e^{-\lambda_i t} \quad t \geq 0. \tag{16.3.16}$$

Hence

$$F(t) = \sum_{i=1}^{n} p_i(1 - e^{-\lambda_i t}) \quad t \geq 0, \tag{16.3.17}$$

which is the hyperexponential distribution (see Chapter 2, Section 14.3.4 and Section 13.3.8.3). The density function is

$$f(t) = \sum_{i=1}^{n} p_i \lambda_i e^{-\lambda_i t} \quad t \geq 0. \tag{16.3.18}$$

The $MTTF = \int_0^\infty R(t)\,dt = \int_0^\infty \sum_{i=1}^n p_i e^{-\lambda_i t}\,dt$, so

$$MTTF = \sum_{i=1}^n \frac{p_i}{\lambda_i}, \qquad \text{where } \sum_{i=1}^n p_i = 1. \qquad (16.3.19)$$

Applying 16.2.7, we get the hazard rate function

$$\lambda(t) = -\frac{dR(t)}{dt} \times \frac{1}{R(t)}.$$

$$\lambda(t) = \frac{d\sum_{i=1}^n p_i e^{-\lambda_i t} / dt}{\sum_{i=1}^n p_i e^{-\lambda_i t}}.$$

$$\lambda(t) = \frac{\sum_{i=1}^n p_i \lambda_i e^{-\lambda_i t}}{\sum_{i=1}^n p_i e^{-\lambda_i t}}, \qquad \text{where } \sum_{i=1}^n p_i = 1 \ \text{ and } \ t \geq 0. \qquad (16.3.20)$$

Erlang Distribution

Consider a device is subjected to hits that occur as a Poisson process with rate λ_i. Assume this device fails after k hits (increasing failure rate). This model leads to a reliability function that belongs to the gamma distribution family with a k integer. If the rate is the same for every hit, this gamma distribution is an Erlang distribution; otherwise, it is a hypoexponential distribution (see Chapter 2 and Section 13.3.8.3). The Erlang CDF is

$$F(t) = 1 - \sum_{i=1}^k \frac{e^{-\lambda t}(\lambda t)^i}{i!}, \quad t \geq 0. \qquad (16.3.21)$$

The reliability is defined by

$$R(t) = \sum_{i=1}^k \frac{e^{-\lambda t}(\lambda t)^i}{i!}, \quad t \geq 0. \qquad (16.3.22)$$

The density function is specified by

$$f(t) = \frac{\lambda^k x^{k-1} e^{-\lambda(t)}}{(k-1)!}, \quad t \geq 0. \qquad (16.3.23)$$

The hazard function is

$$\lambda(t) = \frac{\lambda^k t^{k-1} e^{-\lambda t}}{(k-1)!}, \quad t \geq 0. \qquad (16.3.24)$$

The mean time to failure is

$$MTTF = \frac{k}{\lambda}.$$

(16.3.25)

The variance of the time to failure is

$$Var(TTF)\frac{k}{\lambda^2}.$$

(16.3.26)

Cox Distributions

As mentioned in Chapter 5 and Section 13.3.8, the advantage of using phase-type distributions is the fact that they can approximate any non-negative distribution arbitrarily closely. Cox distributions can be adopted to match the first central moment about the origin (mean) and the second central moment (variance) of empirical devices' lifetime. For details about this process, please refer to Section 13.3.8.

Weibull Distribution is widely used in reliability and life data analysis due to its versatility. Depending on the parameter values, the reliability and the hazard function are affected. In general, it is defined by three parameters, $\alpha \in \mathbb{R}$ ("shape parameter"), $\beta \in \mathbb{R}^+$ ("scale parameter"), and $\mu \in \mathbb{R}^+$ ("location parameter"). In addition, the distribution has support on the interval $[\mu, \infty)$.

The value of α modifies the shape of the failure rate (see Figure 16.10). Values below one ($\alpha < 1$) specify a failure rate that decreases with time. If $\alpha = 1$, the failure rate is constant (it is an exponential distribution). Failure rates increasing with time are obtained when $\alpha > 1$.

$$\lambda(t) = \frac{\alpha\left(\frac{t-\mu}{\beta}\right)^{\alpha-1}}{\beta}, \quad t \geq \mu.$$

(16.3.27)

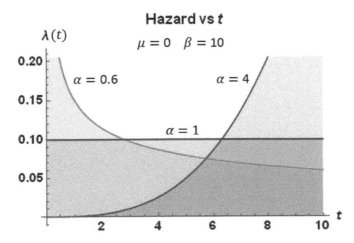

Figure 16.10   Hazard Function - $\alpha = 0.6$, $\alpha = 1$, and $\alpha = 4$ - $\mu = 0$ and $\beta = 10$.

CDF:

$$F(t) = 1 - e^{-\left(\frac{t-\mu}{\beta}\right)^{\alpha}}, \quad t \geq \mu. \tag{16.3.28}$$

Reliability:

$$R(t) = e^{-\left(\frac{t-\mu}{\beta}\right)^{\alpha}}, \quad t \geq \mu. \tag{16.3.29}$$

PDF:

$$f(t) = \frac{\alpha e^{-\left(\frac{t-\mu}{\beta}\right)^{\alpha}}\left(\frac{t-\mu}{\beta}\right)^{\alpha-1}}{\beta}, \quad t \geq \mu. \tag{16.3.30}$$

Mean time to failure:

$$MTTF = \beta\Gamma\left(1 + \frac{1}{\alpha}\right) + \mu. \tag{16.3.31}$$

Example 16.3.3. Consider a system with a hazard rate function equal to $\lambda(t) = bt^{a}$, $a > 0$, $b > 0$ (a monotonically increasing function). As the cumulative hazard function is $H(t) = \int_0^t \lambda(t)\,dt$, then

$$H(t) = \frac{b}{a+1}t^{a+1}.$$

If $a = \alpha - 1$, then

$$H(t) = \frac{bt^{\alpha}}{\alpha}.$$

If $b = \frac{\alpha}{\beta^{\alpha}}$, then

$$H(t) = \left(\frac{t}{\beta}\right)^{\alpha}.$$

Therefore,

$$R(t) = e^{-\left(\frac{t}{\beta}\right)^{\alpha}},$$

and

$$F(t) = 1 - e^{-\left(\frac{t}{\beta}\right)^{\alpha}},$$

which is a Weibull distribution with parameters α, β and $\mu = 0$.

$\square$

Normal Distribution (also known as the Gaussian distribution) is defined over the real numbers. The distribution is parametrized by a real number μ, and a positive real number σ, where μ is the mean of the distribution, σ is the standard deviation, and σ^2 is the variance. The normal distribution is certainly the most widely adopted general-purpose distribution. This is the reason for including it among the lifetime distributions. Some authors argue that the normal distribution is not suitable for modeling lifetime data since its domain encompasses negative numbers, resulting in modeling negative times to failure. However, if the distribution has a relatively high mean and a small standard deviation, negative failure times should not present a problem.

PDF:

$$f(t) = \frac{e^{-\frac{(t-\mu)^2}{2\sigma^2}}}{\sqrt{2\pi}\sigma}. \tag{16.3.32}$$

$$F(t) = \int_{-\infty}^{t} \frac{e^{-\frac{(x-\mu)^2}{2\sigma^2}}}{\sqrt{2\pi}\sigma}\, dx. \tag{16.3.33}$$

$$R(t) = \int_{t}^{\infty} \frac{e^{-\frac{(x-\mu)^2}{2\sigma^2}}}{\sqrt{2\pi}\sigma}\, dx. \tag{16.3.34}$$

Mean time to failure:

$$MTTF = \mu. \tag{16.3.35}$$

Standard deviation of time to failure:

$$SD(TTF) = \sigma. \tag{16.3.36}$$

Log-Normal Distribution is supported over the interval $[0,\infty)$, parametrized by a real number μ and by a positive real number σ. The lognormal distribution is usually adopted as a model of the lifetime of components whose failures due to fatigue-stress. A random variable is lognormally distributed if the logarithm of the random variable is normally distributed.

PDF:

$$f(t) = \frac{e^{-\frac{(\log(t)-\mu)^2}{2\sigma^2}}}{\sqrt{2\pi}\sigma t}, \quad t \geq 0. \tag{16.3.37}$$

$$F(t) = \int_{0}^{t} \frac{e^{-\frac{(\log(x)-\mu)^2}{2\sigma^2}}}{\sqrt{2\pi}\sigma x}\, dx, \quad t \geq 0. \tag{16.3.38}$$

$$R(t) = \int_t^\infty \frac{e^{-\frac{(\log(x)-\mu)^2}{2\sigma^2}}}{\sqrt{2\pi}\sigma x}\, dx, \ t \geq 0. \tag{16.3.39}$$

Mean time to failure:

$$MTTF = e^{\mu + \frac{\sigma^2}{2}}. \tag{16.3.40}$$

Standard deviation of time to failure:

$$SD(TTF) = \sqrt{\left(e^{\sigma^2} - 1\right) e^{2\mu + \sigma^2}}. \tag{16.3.41}$$

The Logistic Distribution has a shape very similar to the normal distribution, however with heavier tails. Since the logistic distribution has closed-form solutions for the $R(t)$, CDF, and $\lambda(t)$, it is sometimes favored over the normal distribution when modeling systems whose failure rates increase over time. The logistic distribution is supported over the set of real numbers and parametrized by μ, the "mean" of the distribution, and a positive real number β, called the "scale parameter".

PDF:

$$f(t) = \frac{e^{-\frac{t-\mu}{\beta}}}{\beta \left(e^{-\frac{t-\mu}{\beta}} + 1\right)^2}. \tag{16.3.42}$$

CDF:

$$F(t) = \frac{1}{e^{-\frac{t-\mu}{\beta}} + 1}. \tag{16.3.43}$$

Reliability:

$$R(t) = 1 - \frac{1}{e^{\frac{\mu-t}{\beta}} + 1}. \tag{16.3.44}$$

Hazard function:

$$\lambda(t) = \frac{1}{\beta \left(e^{\frac{\mu-t}{\beta}} + 1\right)}. \tag{16.3.45}$$

Mean time to failure:

$$MTTF = \mu. \tag{16.3.46}$$

Standard deviation:

$$SD(TTF) = \frac{\pi \beta}{\sqrt{3}}. \tag{16.3.47}$$

The Loglogistic Distribution is similar to the logistic distribution. Lifetime data follows a loglogistic distribution if the natural logarithms to failure obey a logistic distribution. The relation between the loglogistic and logistic distribution is similar to the relation between normal and lognormal distributions. Accordingly, the loglogistic and lognormal distributions share many similarities. This distribution is continuous, supported over the interval $[0, \infty)$, and is parametrized by two positive real numbers γ ("shape parameter") and σ ("scale parameter").

PDF:

$$f(t) = \frac{\gamma \sigma^{-\gamma} t^{\gamma - 1}}{\left(\left(\frac{t}{\sigma} \right)^{\gamma} + 1 \right)^2}. \tag{16.3.48}$$

CDF:

$$F(t) = \frac{1}{\left(\frac{t}{\sigma} \right)^{-\gamma} + 1}. \tag{16.3.49}$$

Reliability:

$$R(t) = \frac{1}{\left(\frac{t}{\sigma} \right)^{\gamma} + 1}. \tag{16.3.50}$$

Hazard function:

$$\lambda(t) = \frac{\gamma}{t \left(\left(\frac{t}{\sigma} \right)^{-\gamma} + 1 \right)}. \tag{16.3.51}$$

Mean time to failure:

$$MTTF = \frac{\pi \sigma \csc \left(\frac{\pi}{\gamma} \right)}{\gamma} \quad \gamma > 1. \tag{16.3.52}$$

Standard deviation:

$$SD(TTF) = \frac{\sqrt{\pi} \sigma \sqrt{2\gamma \csc \left(\frac{2\pi}{\gamma} \right) - \pi \csc^2 \left(\frac{\pi}{\gamma} \right)}}{\gamma} \quad \gamma > 2. \tag{16.3.53}$$

The **Dagun Distribution** represents a continuous distribution defined over the interval $(0, \infty)$ with three positive parameters p, a, and b. The parameters $p > 0$ and $a > 0$ are "shape parameters," and the parameter $b > 0$ is a "scale parameter". This distribution is also referred to as a Burr III distribution. The main motivation is that the hazard rate of this model is very flexible, according to the values of the parameters. For instance, considering $p = 0.5$ and $b = 2$, taking $a = \{1, 2, 4\}$, we have the following hazard plots shown in Figure 16.11.

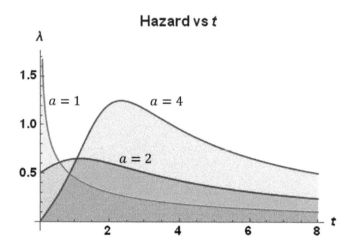

Figure 16.11   Hazard Function - $p = 0.5$ and $b = 2$ - $a = 1$, $a = 2$, and $a = 4$.

$$\lambda(t) = \frac{ap}{t\left(\left(\frac{t}{b}\right)^a + 1\right)\left(\left(\left(\frac{b}{t}\right)^a + 1\right)^p - 1\right)}, \quad t \geq 0. \tag{16.3.54}$$

CDF:

$$F(t) = \left(\left(\frac{t}{b}\right)^{-a} + 1\right)^{-p}, \quad t \geq 0. \tag{16.3.55}$$

Reliability:

$$R(t) = 1 - \left(\left(\frac{t}{b}\right)^{-a} + 1\right)^{-p}, \quad t \geq 0. \tag{16.3.56}$$

PDF:

$$f(t) = apb^{-ap}t^{ap-1}\left(\left(\frac{t}{b}\right)^a + 1\right)^{-p-1}, \quad t \geq 0. \tag{16.3.57}$$

Mean time to failure:

$$MTTF = \frac{b\Gamma\left(\frac{a-1}{a}\right)\Gamma\left(p+\frac{1}{a}\right)}{\Gamma(p)}, \quad a > 1. \qquad (16.3.58)$$

Gumbel Distribution (Extreme Value Type I Distribution) has the PDF skewed to the left. The Gumbel distribution is suitable for modeling the life of products that experience quick wear-out after reaching a certain age. The Gumbel distribution has two parameters, where $\mu \in \mathbb{R}$ is the location parameter and $\sigma \in \mathbb{R}^+$ is the scale parameter.

PDF:

$$f(t) = \frac{e^{\frac{t-\mu}{\sigma} - e^{\frac{t-\mu}{\sigma}}}}{\sigma} \qquad (16.3.59)$$

CDF:

$$F(x) = 1 - e^{-e^{\frac{x-\mu}{\sigma}}}. \qquad (16.3.60)$$

Reliability:

$$R(t) = e^{-e^{\frac{t-\mu}{\sigma}}}. \qquad (16.3.61)$$

Hazard function:

$$\lambda(t) = \frac{e^{\frac{t-\mu}{\sigma}}}{\sigma} \qquad (16.3.62)$$

Mean time to failure:

$$MTTF = \mu - \gamma\sigma \qquad (16.3.63)$$

where $\gamma \approx 0.5772$ is the Euler–Mascheroni constant.

EXERCISES

Exercise 1. Explain the concepts of fault, error, and failure.

Exercise 2. Describe the meanings of permanent, transient, or intermittent faults.

Exercise 3. If the cumulative hazard function is a line with a positive slope, what can you say about the distribution of the failure time associated with that function?

Exercise 4. Consider a database system with time to failure distribution represented by the CDF $F(t) = 1 + e^{-0.0005t} - 2e^{-0.00025t}$. Calculate the reliability at $t = 5,500 h$ and compute the $MTTF$.

Exercise 5. Assume the system reliability in $t = 720 h$ is $7,500 DPM$. Calculate the probability of failure by $t = 720 h$.

Exercise 6. Use the CDF of the Exercise 4, and obtain the system hazard function, $\lambda(t)$. Afterward, calculate $\lambda(t)$ at $t = 5,500 h$.

Exercise 7. Assume the reliability of a system that is represented by

$$R(t) = \begin{cases} \frac{1 - 0.0004t}{0.96} & 100 \leq t \leq 2500 \\ 0 & t > 2500. \end{cases}$$

Obtain the density function of the time to failure and calculate the $MTTF$ and $MedTTF$.

Exercise 8. The time to failure of a web server is exponentially distributed with rate $5 \times 10^{-4} fph$. **(a)** What is the probability that the system does not fail in the first two months? Assume the time to repair rate is constant and equal to 5×10^{-2}. **(b)** Estimate the probability of being operational at $720 h$. **(c)** Compute the steady-state availability.

Exercise 9. The time to failure of a system is distributed according to a Weibull distribution with shape parameter equal to $\alpha = 2$, scale parameter equal to $\beta = 1000 h$, and location parameter equal to zero. **(a)** What is the reliability at $720 h$? **(b)** Calculate the $MTTF$.

Exercise 10. Now, consider that the distribution of the previous example has a shape parameter is equal to $\alpha = 0.8$. **(a)** What is the reliability at $720 h$? **(b)** Calculate the $MTTF$.

Exercise 11. Assume the hazard function of a system is $t/250000$. **(a)** Calculate the reliability of the system at $t = 720 h$, and **(b)** the $MTTF$.

Exercise 12. If the cumulative rate function of a system is $7.5 \times 10^{-7} \times t^3$, **(a)** compute the reliability at $720 h$, **(b)** the failure rate at $500 h$, and **(c)** the MTTF.

Exercise 13. Let us assume the failure and the repair rates are equal to $\lambda = 1.2 \times 10^{-6}$ and $\mu = 1,2 \times 10^{-3}$, respectively. **(a)** Calculate the $MTTF$ and $MTBF$, and **(b)** the reliability at $t = 8760 h$. **(c)** If the annual downtime is $15 h$, what is the steady-state availability? **(d)** What is the effect on the availability if we triple the $MTTR$?

Exercise 14. Consider that the distribution of the time to failure of a data base system is represented by a logistic distribution with parameters $\mu = 600 h$ and $\beta = 25 h$. **(a)** What is the probability of survival at $t = 500 h$? **(b)** Calculate $MedTTF$.

Exercise 15. The time to failure of system is distributed according to a Dagun distribution with shape parameters $p = 0.5$, $a = 2$, and the scale parameter equal to $b = 2000 h$. **(a)** What is the reliability at $720 h$? **(b)** Calculate the $MTTF$. Change $a = 4$ and calculate **(c)** the reliability at $720 h$, and **(d)** calculate the $MTTF$.

17 Redundancy

System dependability can be attained by fault prevention, fault removal, fault tolerance, and fault forecasting [29–31, 151, 227, 228]. **Fault prevention** concerns the development and use of methodologies for system (hardware and software) designing aiming at reducing the number of faults introduced in the implemented systems. **Fault removal** can be accomplished during the system development cycle or throughout its use. During the development phases, fault removal is carried out in three steps: validation and verification, diagnosis, and correction. In this context, the validation process consists of finding evidence for rejecting a model as a representation of a system or another model at a different level of abstraction. The model is never entirely validated. We may only say that for a model tested considering a given set of constraints and parameters' values, and for such and such conditions, we found no evidence to reject the claim that the model indeed represents the system (or the other model) given the specified constraints and conditions.

In verification, the system is checked to determine whether it adheres to given properties. If the system does not observe the specified behavior nor holds the required properties, the causes should be found (diagnosis) and removed (correction). Corrective maintenance concerns removing faults once errors are reported, whereas preventive maintenance aims at uncovering and removing faults before system failures. **Fault forecasting** is conducted by evaluating the system behavior concerning fault occurrence. The two main approaches are accomplished by modeling (see Chapters 18 and 21) and testing (see Chapter 26). These approaches are complementary since modeling needs data that may be obtained either by testing or by the processing of failure data (see Chapter 25), and models can support testing. **Fault tolerance** is intended to preserve the delivery of correct service in the presence of faults. It is generally implemented either by (**I**) error detection and subsequent system recovery (dynamic) or by (**II**) fault-masking (static). Fault masking uses sufficient redundancy to support recovery without error detection. This chapter introduces some important mechanisms for enhancing system reliability through fault tolerance.

Redundancy is the replication of components or functions of a system aiming at increasing its dependability. Redundancy implies adding resources or time beyond what is required for the system to deliver its specified service.

Redundancy can be divided into resource and time redundancies [198]. **Resource redundancy** requires additional resources whereas **time redundancy** demands extra time to perform tasks for fault tolerance. Redundancy may also be divided into hardware and software redundancy mechanisms. **Hardware redundancy** is applied by incorporating extra hardware into the system to either detect or mask the effects of a failed component. Hardware redundancy can be static, dynamic, or hybrid. **Static hardware redundancy** aims at masking faults in order to avoid failure. **Dynamic**

redundancy activates spare components upon a failure. Hybrid hardware redundancy adopts a combination of static and dynamic redundancy.

Software redundancy is mainly applied against software failures. One way to implement it is by independently coding two or more versions of that software, assuming the different versions will not fail on the same input. **Multiple versions** of the program can be executed either concurrently (requiring redundant hardware) or sequentially (requiring extra time, that is, time redundancy) upon failure detection.

Failures can be handled by error detection and correction coding (in hardware or software), where extra bits (called check bits) are added to the original data so that an error can be detected or even corrected.

This chapter aims to introduce some important mechanisms and strategies for implementing redundancy in computing systems.

17.1   HARDWARE REDUNDANCY

As already mentioned, hardware redundancy may be classified as static, dynamic, or hybrid, where static redundancy masks faults to avoid failure, dynamic redundancy triggers spare units upon a failure, hybrid redundancy combines static and dynamic redundancy.

Assumed a very small lighting system composed only of two lamps (L_1 and L_2) each able to deliver 4,000 lumens (see Figure 17.1). This system sheds light on a specific location. Both lamps are usually kept switched on.

The system correctly works as long as it provides at least 1,800 lumens. Thus, if both lamps are operational, the system is appropriately delivering its service. On the other hand, if one of the lamps fails, the system is still functional since the required lumens are still delivered. Therefore, the system is only considered in failure when both lamps fail.

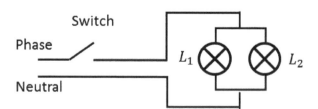

Figure 17.1   Two-Lamps System.

This simple **parallel redundancy** mechanism refers to an approach of having multiple units in execution in parallel. Thus, all units are highly synchronized and receive the same input information at the same time. However, because all the units are powered up and actively engaged, the system is at risk of encountering failures in many units.

Now assume a computing system with one web-server that receives requests sent by clients. This web-server operates in a simplex mode since if it fails, web-services requests cannot be handled. If the system is updated with a second equivalent web-server (the duplex mode - see Figure 17.2), the client's requests may be handled by a load balancer (*LB*) that directs the requests to each web-server according to their actual load (100% duplex mode - Figure 17.3.a).

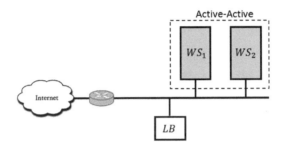

Figure 17.2   Active-Active Redundancy.

When one of the web-servers fails, the other assumes the total workload. This sort of redundant system is called **active-active redundancy**. Hence, a sub-system with two components sharing the load is usually denoted as an active-active redundant mechanism since both components are actively serving.

Let us describe this general process in more detail. When one server fails, the erroneous state may be detected or not. Detecting the erroneous state takes a time length (detection latency). During such a period, the load balance is still not aware of the faulty server. Hence, it keeps distributing requests to both web-servers. Therefore, part of such requests is lost. The request sent to the operational server, on the other hand, is adequately served. Therefore, 50% of transaction requests are lost, assuming both servers receive the same number of requests (50% simplex mode - Figure 17.3.b). After the latency period, the load balancer is finally aware of the faulty server. From then on, all transaction requests are directed to an operational web-server, which will process the total workload (100% simplex mode - Figure 17.3.c); thus affecting its utilization. If the erroneous state is not detected, the load balancer will keep sending part of the requests to the faulty server (50% simplex mode); thus causing a significant impact on the system service.

Let us consider two synchronized graphics processing units (GPU_1 and GPU_2) that simultaneously receive input data, through the input data bus, compute the same function, and each delivers the particular result through the specific output data bus (see Figure 17.4), then if one *GPU* fails to provide a correct result, decide which

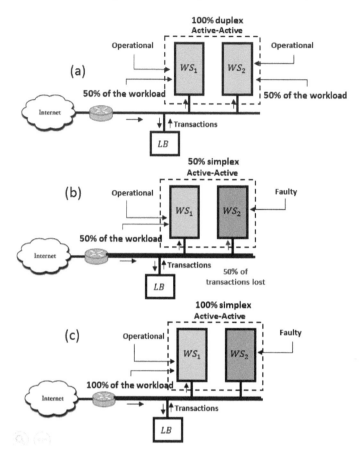

Figure 17.3   100% Duplex Mode (a), 50% Simplex Mode (b), and 100% Simplex Mode (c).

GPU is appropriately functioning. Consider, for instance, three units; the problem can be solved by adopting majority voting.

Most **static hardware redundancy** is based on majority voting mechanisms to mask faults. Static approaches accomplish fault tolerance without requiring fault detection and reconfiguration. An *NMR* (**N modular redundancy**) structure is a system with *N* components which need the majority of them to deliver the specified service correctly. The best-known example of this type of system is the *TMR* (**triple modular redundancy**) mechanism. The *TMR* mechanism consists of triplicating a component and performing a **majority vote** (which could be implemented in hardware or software) to decide the output of the system. If one of the modules fails, the two remaining components mask the wrong result delivered by the faulty device when the majority vote is performed. Figure 17.5 illustrates the basic *TMR* mechanism.

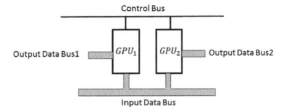

Figure 17.4   Two-GPUs System.

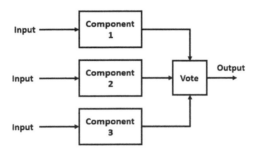

Figure 17.5 TMR Mechanism.

A $5MR$ system is composed of five replicated components and a voter. The majority voting allows the system to deliver correct results if at least three components work correctly. Thus, the fundamental tradeoff in NMR mechanisms is the fault tolerance achieved versus the hardware required, in which a trade-off between costs, size, performance, availability, and reliability defines the number of components.

Dynamic hardware redundancies attempt to achieve fault tolerance by fault detection and recovery. Such strategies are usually adopted when temporary erroneous results or longer delays in producing results are acceptable as long as the system regains its operational status in an acceptable length of time. The fundamental operation of a dynamic redundant mechanism is the following. When during a routine operation a fault happens, after a latency period, the fault produces an error. The erroneous state may be detected or not. If the error is undetected, the system will fail. If the error is detected, the faulty component is detached from the operation, and a spare component is enabled so that the system is brought back to an operational state [198]. The dynamic hardware redundancies are classified as hot-standby, warm-standby, and cold-standby spare, besides the active-active mechanism already shown.

Assume the web-server system introduced earlier in this section. Now, consider the second server (WS_2) does not receive a request as soon as WS_1 is active (see Figure

17.6.a). Nevertheless, WS_2 is operational and can assume the transaction processing as soon as transactions are delivered to it; that is, WS_2 is turned on and available.

This redundant strategy is usually called **hot-standby** sparing. The difference between hot-standby and active-active is that in the former, the second server (WS_2) does not process transactions while the primary server (WS_1) is active, whereas, in the latter, requests are sent to both servers. In the hot-standby strategy, when the active server (WS_1) fails, the erroneous state may be detected or not. If the erroneous state is detected, the spare server (WS_2)immediately assumes the total workload (see Figure 17.6.c).

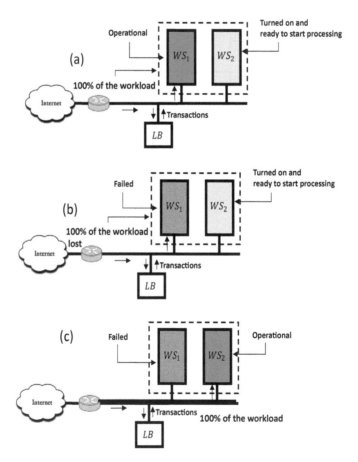

Figure 17.6   Hot-Standby.

However, if the erroneous state is not detected, the load balancer keeps sending the requests to the faulty server (Figure 17.6.b); thus causing a significant impact on the system service. The error detection is usually implemented through heartbeat messages that are periodically sent between the servers. Upon the main component's failure, the system instantaneously switches over to the spare server if the switching mechanism is considered fault-free. This is usually called perfect switching or perfect switch-over. Manual failover may also be adopted if the requirements are not too strict. It is important to stress that the error detection mechanism may also be implemented directly by the servers (without the interference of a manager). In such a case, the heartbeat messages are sent directly from each server to each server.

Now, consider that WS_1 processes all requests and that, during normal operation, WS_2 is switched off (Figure 17.7.a). Hence, when WS_1 fails (Figure 17.7.b), after the manager (LB) detects the erroneous state, it switches on the spare server (WS_2), which sets up the whole software stack and begins processing the transaction requests (Figure 17.7.c). This strategy is named **cold-standby** sparing. The switching delay is much longer than the one considered in the hot-standby mechanism.

Assume a computational system composed of two servers. One of the servers is operationally active (S_1) and processes all transaction requests. The software stack running on S_1 is composed of a host operational system (OS_1), a hypervisor (HV_1), and two virtual machines (VM_1 and VM_2), each running two applications, respectively. The applications running on VM_1 are A_1 and A_2, whereas the applications running on VM_2 are A_3, and A_4. S_1 is operational as long as it provides the services executed by A_1, A_2, A_3 and A_4. The second server (S_2) is in standby mode (see Figure 17.8.a). However, differently from the standby server of the hot-standby and cold-standby mechanisms, S_2 is neither completely ready to process transactions when a failure occurs in the active server (S_1), nor is it turned off. The software stack executing on S_2 when it is the standby mode is composed of the host operating system (OS_2) and the hypervisor (HV_2). Assume a failure occurs in the S_1 hardware; thus taking the active server to a failed state. The standby server is not yet ready to process transactions (see Figure 17.8.b), but as it already has a significant part of the software stack in an operational state, what is required is to mount the virtual machines (VM_1 and VM_2) and to start the respective application on each VM. This process is much shorter than it was required if S_2 started from an off state. After mounting the virtual machines and starting the applications, S_2 begins processing the transactions (see Figure 17.8.c). This mechanism is usually called **warm-standby** sparing.

Data errors may occur when the data are transferred or stored. Information redundancy is a mechanism that aims at tolerating such errors. Many information redundancy strategies are based on coding. Codes allow verifying data correctness, and even data correction [218]. The most common codes adopted in data storage are parity codes, Hamming codes, checksum, and cyclic codes. Coding is a well-established research area, and many textbooks on this topic are available.

An interesting case of applying for information redundancy through coding is the Redundant Arrays of Independent Disks (**RAID**). The generic term for such storage system was redundant disk arrays [155], but it was soon modified to a redundant

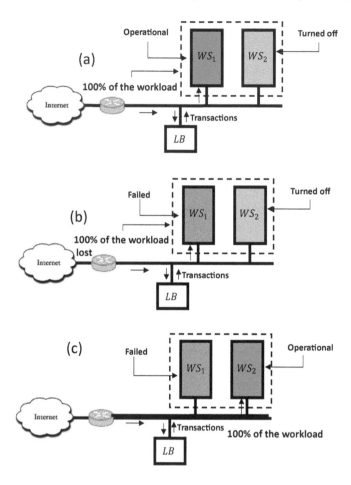

Figure 17.7   Cold-Standby.

array of inexpensive disks (RAID). However, as technology advanced, the term "inexpensive" was replaced by the term "independent." In this context, "array" means a set of disks organized in a particular fashion to improve the performance and reliability of data storage. A RAID system consists of two or more disks working in parallel. This technology is driven by many methods available for connecting disks, coding techniques, and read-and-write strategies. Many types of RAID have been developed, and more will probably come out in the future. Here we introduce some important RAID architectures.

Let us first consider a storage system composed of only one disk as depicted in Figure 17.9.a. The data to be stored are divided into chunks (blocks) of bytes. When writing the data in the disk, each block is stored at a time. Similarly, when a set of blocks is

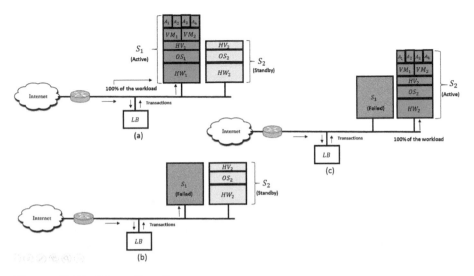

Figure 17.8   Warm-Standby.

required to be read, each block is read at a time, since the disk is a shared resource and the system has only one disk controller [372] [125].

RAID 0 stripes data evenly across two or more disks, without parity information or redundancy. Here, when one disk fails, the system fails since RAID 0 is non-fault-tolerant. RAID 0 is normally used to increase performance. Increasing the number of disks supports superior I/O performance since more data can be transferred simultaneously. Figure 17.9.b shows a RAID 0 structure composed of two disks (Disk 0 and Disk 1), each with its specific controller. The set of data blocks (chunks) is distributed to the disks, where the blocks A_1, A_3, A_5, and A_7 are stored in Disk 0, and the blocks A_2, A_4, A_6, and A_8 are stored in Disk 1. Each data set, that is A_1 and A_2, A_3 and A_4, and A_5, A_6, A_7, and A_8, are called stripes. As the structure is composed of two disks, it is possible to read or write blocks in one disk while performing read-write operations in the other disk. Hence, an n-disk RAID 0 array appears as a single large disk with a data rate n times higher than the single-disk rate. The reliability, however, may decrease in comparison to a single disk since more than one single disk is required to store the same set of data.

RAID 1 mirrors the set of data in two or more disks (at least two disks are required). For instance, when the disk array is composed of two disks, data are stored twice by writing them to both the data disk (or set of data disks) and a mirror disk (or set of mirror disks). Figure 17.10 shows a RAID 1 structure implemented with two disks (data disk + mirror disk).

Observe that the stored dataset is replicated in both disks. If one disk fails, the other continues to serve requests. If both disks are working, this mechanism can speed up

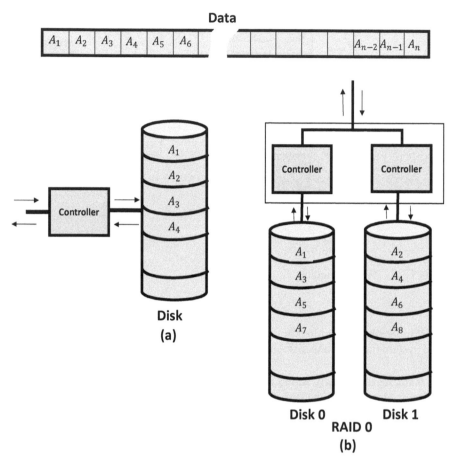

Figure 17.9   Single Disk Storage and RAID 0.

read accesses by dividing them among the two disks. However, write accesses are slowed down because both disks must finish the update before completing the operation. Hence, RAID 1 offers read and write throughput comparable to that of a single drive. In case of a drive failure, data must be copied to a replacement drive to achieve fault tolerance again. The downside is the storage capacity efficiency (SCE) because effective storage capacity (ESC) is half of the total disk capacity (TDC) since all data is written twice. Thus considering n disks with capacity DC, the efficiency is defined by

$$SCE = \frac{ESC}{TDC} = \frac{TDC/2}{TDC} = 0.5, \qquad (17.1.1)$$

where $TDC = n \times DC$, and $ESC = TDC/2$.

Another possible drawback is when some RAID 1 solutions do not accept the failed disk hot-swapping. In such a case, the disk can only be replaced after powering down the system, which may not be acceptable in many circumstances. However, this difficulty can be overcome by the use of hardware controllers that support hot-swapping.

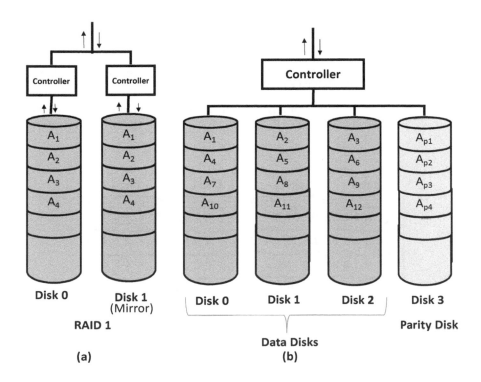

Figure 17.10   RAID 1 and RAID 4.

RAID 2 is seldom used; data are organized at the bit level rather than in block, and it uses a Hamming code for error correction. RAID 3 is also rarely used. It is a modification of RAID 2 with a dedicated parity disk. RAID 3 consists of a bank of data disks with one parity disk. Neither RAID 2 nor RAID 3 is discussed here.

RAID 4 stripes data across two or more disks and adds a dedicated parity disk. **RAID 4** tolerates one disk failure in an array of n disks. Hence, RAID 4 requires at least three disks to be implemented. Figure 17.10.b shows a RAID 4 system with four data disks and a parity disk. For instance, if the parity disk fails, the remaining data disks are not affected, but redundancy is lost. If a data disk fails, the RAID controller uses the remaining data disks and the parity disk to recover the missing data on the fly. The system performance degrades until the failed disk is replaced, but no data is lost. Besides, as a read request for block A_1 would be serviced by Disk 0, a simultaneous read request for block A_2 is possible since it is in Disk 1. Nevertheless, a concurrent reading for A_2 would have to wait since A_1 and A_4 share the same disk (Disk 0).

Consider a block has a size equal to 4 bits. Figure 17.11 depicts the set of blocks stored in the data disk and the respective parity block. The parity block is obtained by just performing the exclusive or (XOR) operation of the i bits of respective blocks $A_j = a_3^j a_2^j a_1^j$, $A_{j+1} = a_3^{j+1} a_2^{j+1} a_1^{j+1}$, and $A_{j+2} = a_3^{j+2} a_2^{j+2} a_1^{j+2}$; that is the parity block $A_{p_j} = pb_3^j pb_2^j pb_1^j$ is obtained by computing each of its parity bits using

$$pb_i^j = a_i^j \oplus a_i^{j+1} \oplus a_i^{j+2}, \tag{17.1.2}$$

where $j = \{1, 4, 7, 10, ...\}$ and $i = \{1, 2, 3, 4\}$.

Hence, considering the values of A_1, A_2, and A_3 shown in Figure 17.11, we have $A_{p1} = pb_1^1 \ pb_2^1 \ pb_3^1 \ pb_4^1 = 0 \oplus 1 \oplus 0, 0 \oplus 1 \oplus 1, 1 \oplus 0 \oplus 0, 0 \oplus 1 \oplus 1 = 1010$.

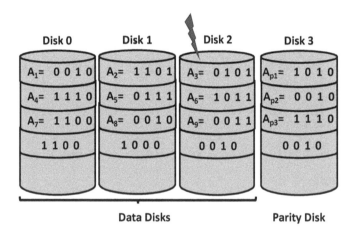

Figure 17.11   RAID 4 - Parity Bits.

If Disk 0, 1, or 2 breaks, the parity disk (Disk 3) is used to regenerate the missing data. Let us look at how this works. Assume Disk 2 failed, so we have lost all read and write access to this disk. Nevertheless, the parity disk is used to calculate the missing data. The parity data is calculated by performing the same XOR operation over the remaining data disks and the parity information on the parity disk. Thus, assuming a failure in Disk 2, the words A_3, A_6, A_9 are lost. However, the word A_3 (see Figure 17.11) can be regenerated by executing

$$a_i^3 = a_i^1 \oplus a_i^2 \oplus pb_i^1, \quad i = \{1, 2, 3, 4\},$$

thus $A_3 = 0 \oplus 1 \oplus 1, 0 \oplus 1 \oplus 0, 1 \oplus 0 \oplus 1, 0 \oplus 1 \oplus 0 = 0101$. Therefore, RAID 4 structure allows the storage system to tolerate and recover from one disk failure. Considering the infrastructure shown in Figure 17.10, which is composed of three data disks and one parity disk, as long as three out of four disks are functioning the storage system will properly work. The storage capacity efficiency is specified by

$$SCE = \frac{ESC}{TDC},$$

where $ESC = (n-1) \times DC$, and $TDC = n \times DC$. Hence

$$SCE = \frac{n-1}{n}. \qquad (17.1.3)$$

For an infrastructure with eight disks, $SCE = 0.875$, which is much better than the storage capacity efficiency of RAID 1.

It is worth mentioning that if only two disks are used to implement RAID 4, the structure is equivalent to RAID 1 since the exclusive-or operations would result in parity blocks with identical content to the data blocks.

RAID 5 is similar to RAID 4 except that the parity data blocks are striped across all disks, instead of being written on a dedicated disk (see Figure 17.12). In RAID 4 structure, each write operation generates a write operation on the parity disk, leading to bottlenecks. In RAID 5, as the block of parity bits is distributed across the disks, it avoids the single disk bottleneck. As in RAID 4, it requires at least three disks. **RAID 6** extends RAID 5 by adopting two parity blocks and storing them, as in RAID 5, in different disks. There are several possibilities for implementing two independent parity checks. One of such approaches is a horizontal-vertical parity strategy. However, this is only one of many approaches to Level 6. Indeed, any method that independently calculates two parity bits is classified as RAID 6. The storage capacity efficiency is specified by

$$SCE = \frac{ESC}{TDC} = \frac{(n-2) \times DC}{n \times DC} = \frac{n-2}{n}, \qquad (17.1.4)$$

where $ESC = (n-2) \times DC$.

The RAID architectures can be nested to generate hybrid RAIDs (nested RAIDs). Hybrid RAID combines two or more of the standard RAID levels to improve performance, reliability, or both. Nested RAIDs are named using numbers that denote the standard RAID levels adopted to implement the hybrid RAID. In the numeric designation, the left numbers denote the lower RAID level, whereas the numbers to the right denote the highest layered RAID level. The most common nested RAIDs are a combination of two standards; hence the names are represented by two numbers only, where the first digit denotes the lowest RAID level and the second digit denotes the highest RAID level. RAID 10 combines RAID 1 (mirroring) and RAID 0 (striping) in one single system (see Figure 17.13.a). RAID 01 combines striping (RAID 0) and mirroring (RAID 1) (see Figure 17.13.b). Both require at least four disks. Their

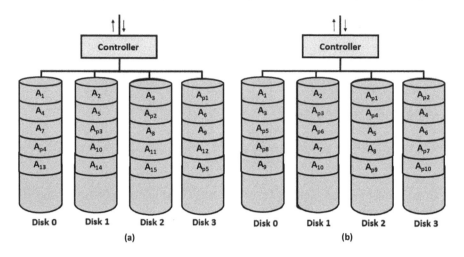

Figure 17.12   RAID 5 (a) and RAID 6 (b).

storage capacity efficiency is 0.5. However, the fault tolerance is different. Consider, for instance, a RAID 10 with four disks. This system is composed of two groups of disks, G_1 and G_2. G_1 is composed of Disk 1 and Disk 2, whereas G_2 is composed of Disk 3 and Disk 4. Two blocks of data, A_1 and A_2, are stored in this system. In RAID 10, when writing these blocks of data, first A_1 is written in Disk 1; then it is mirrored in Disk 2. After, the other block (A_2) is written (striping) in Disk 3 and then mirrored in Disk 4. Hence, A_1 is stored in Disk 1 *AND* Disk 2, and A_2 is stored in Disk 3 *AND* Disk 4. If, for instance, Disk 2 fails, the system still survives a failure either in Disk 3 or Disk 4, since A_1 is in Disk 1. However, the system fails if Disk 1 fails. Now, let us assume a RAID 01 system composed of two groups of disks also named as G_1 and G_2. When the data, A_1 and A_2, are stored in this system, we have the following: first, A_1 and A_2 are written to Disk 1 *AND* Disk 2 (striping), respectively; then A_1 and A_2 are mirrored in Disk 3 *AND* Disk 4. If Disk 2 fails, then the system neither tolerates a failure in Disk 3 nor in Disk 4. Chapter 18 discusses these aspects in detail.

RAID 50 is implemented by striping data (RAID 0) across two RAID 5 arrays (see Figure 17.14.b). RAID 50 requires at least 6 disks, and tolerates up to one disk failure in each sub-array (for more details see Chapter 18). The storage capacity efficiency is specified by

$$SCE = \frac{ESC}{TDC} = \frac{n-2}{n},$$ (17.1.5)

where $ESC = (n-2) \times DC$.

RAID 51 is implemented by mirroring (RAID 1) in an entire RAID 5 array (see Figure 17.14.a). RAID 51 also requires at least six disks and tolerates up to four disk failures. The storage capacity efficiency is specified by

$$SCE = \frac{ESC}{TDC} = \frac{((n-2)/2)}{n}, \tag{17.1.6}$$

where $ESC = ((n-2)/2) \times DC$.

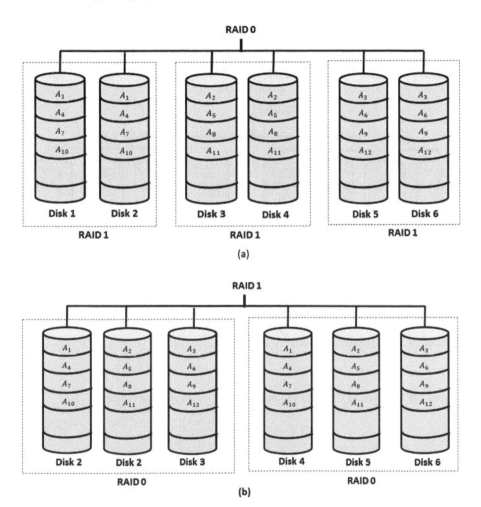

Figure 17.13   RAID 10 (a) and RAID 01 (b)

RAID 60 adopts striping data (RAID 0) across two RAID 6 arrays, and requires at least 8 disks. RAID 60 tolerates up to two disk failures in each sub-array (for more

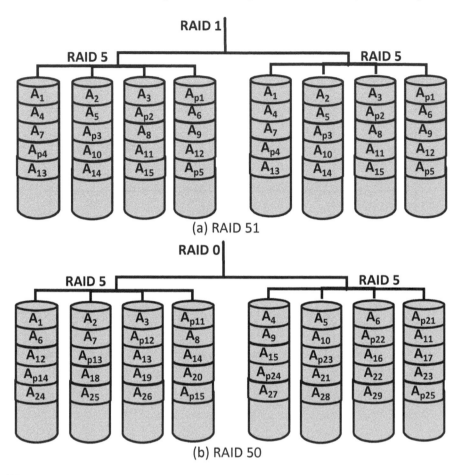

Figure 17.14   RAID 51 (a) and RAID 50 (b)

details, see Chapter 18). The storage capacity efficiency is specified by

$$SCE = \frac{ESC}{TDC} = \frac{(n-4)}{n},\tag{17.1.7}$$

where $ESC = (n-4) \times DC$.

RAID 61 is implemented by mirroring (RAID 1) in an entire RAID 6 array. RAID 61 requires at least eight disks and tolerates up to four disk failures (see Figure 17.14.b). The storage capacity efficiency is specified by

$$SCE = \frac{ESC}{TDC} = \frac{(n-4)/2}{n},\tag{17.1.8}$$

where $ESC = ((n-4)/2) \times DC$.

In both mirrored and parity RAIDs, every write operation causes input-output (I/O) operation overhead. This overhead is usually called a write penalty. In RAID 1, the write penalty is two because each block is written twice due to the mirror disk. RAID 5 has a significant write penalty. For each change to the disk, the RAID controller should read the data (first I/O operation) and the respective parity (second I/O operation), the new parity should be calculated, the data should be written (third I/O operation), and the new parity should also be written (fourth I/O operation) before the operation is complete. RAID 6 works similarly to RAID 5, apart from the fact that the parity reading and writing take two I/O operations, each due to the two parity blocks for each stripe. To summarize, the writing penalty is expressed in the number of I/O operations for each write operation. For instance, the number of I/O operations for one write operation in RAID 0 is also one. However, the number of I/O operations for one write operation in RAID 5 is four because four I/O operations are required.

Table 17.1 summarizes some essential features of the RAID architectures presented in this section. The features considered are the minimal number of disks required to implement the architecture (MND), the storage capacity efficiency (SCE), the number of disk failures tolerated (NDF), I/O performance ($Perf$), and writing penalty (WP).

Table 17.1

RAID Architecture Features – n is the Number of Disks and DC is the Disk Capacity

Architecture	MND	SCE	NDF	$Perf$	WP
RAID 0	2	1	0	High	No
RAID 1	2	0.5	1	High	Moderate
RAID 4	3	$\frac{n-1}{n}$	1	Low	High
RAID 5	3	$\frac{n-1}{n}$	1	Moderate	High
RAID 6	4	$\frac{n-2}{n}$	2	Moderate	High
RAID 10	4	0.5	Up to one disk failure in each sub-array	High	Moderate
RAID 50	6	$\frac{n-2}{n}$	Up to one disk failure in each sub-array	Moderate	High
RAID 51	6	$\frac{(n-2)/2}{n}$	4	High	Very High
RAID 60	8	$\frac{(n-4)}{n}$	Up to two disk failures in each sub-array	Moderate	High
RAID 61	8	$\frac{(n-4)/2}{n}$	4	Moderate	Very High

17.2 SOFTWARE REDUNDANCY

Software failure is an out-of-specification result produced by the software system for the respective specified input value. This definition is consistent with the system failure definition. Hence, the reader might ask: why should we pay particular attention to software dependability issues? However, the reader should bear in mind that the scientific software communities involved in subjects have specific backgrounds, many of which are not rooted in system reliability. These communities have developed a specific vocabulary that does not necessarily match the common system dependability terminology [247].

Software research communities have long pursued dependable software systems. Correction of codification problems and software testing begins with the very origin of software development itself. Since then, the term software bug has been broadly applied to refer to mistakes, failures, and faults in a software system, whereas debugging is referred to the methodical process of finding bugs.

The formal methods community has produced significant contributions on models, methods, and strategies for checking software correctness and validity. In addition, these researchers and dependability communities have proposed and applied failure avoidance techniques and redundancy mechanisms to achieve highly dependable software systems.

In 1985 Jim Gray classified software failures (bugs) as **Bohrsbugs** and **Heisenbugs** [164]. This terminology was extended in [439]. The word Bohrbug comes from the deterministic representation of an atom proposed by Niels Bohr in 1913. If a Bohrbug is present in the software, there would always be a failure in retrying the operation, which caused the failure. Bohrbugs are detectable by standard debugging methods. Heisenbugs, on the other hand, are transient or intermittent failures [380], since restarting the program, the functionality will usually not fail again. Heisenbug is derived from Heisenberg's Uncertainty Principle, which states that it is impossible to predict a particle's location and time simultaneously.

Many researchers have proposed methods to reduce the failure rate of software systems. These methods rely on software testing, debugging, verification techniques, formal specification, and fault tolerance. Fault tolerance aims at mitigating the impact of software failures (bugs). In the single version software environments, software fault-tolerant mechanisms involve first fault detection and recovery features. In addition, these underlying mechanisms comprehend modularity, monitoring, decision verification, and exception handling.

When a process in the presence of a transient fault is reset to some previous consistent state, and re-executed, it may not fail again. This is a simple fault-tolerant method that can be applied to solve Heisenbugs. For example, consider a software system that interacts with the physical device, a printer, for instance. If the device happens to be offline, the software can reach an error state. However, if the device is switched on and the software process is re-executed, there is a reasonable probability that the erroneous state is no longer reached. The fundamental assumption here is that the problem is not a hard error (a Bohrbug) but a transient error (a Heisenbug).

Advanced architectures may adopt independently developed software versions to support fault tolerance. The two basic most essential techniques of multiple version software are **recovery blocks** and **N-version programming** [244]. When considering Bohrbugs, the software does not break as hardware does since these faults result from incorrect software design or coding mistakes. Therefore, a simple duplication and comparison procedure will not detect such faults if the duplicated software modules are identical. The fundamental concept of N-version programming is the design and coding of the software module N times and voting on the N results produced by these modules. Each N module should be designed and coded by a separate group of programmers but considering the same specification. The recovery block strategy to software fault tolerance is analogous to the active approaches to hardware fault tolerance, specifically the cold-standby sparing approach.

The common property of both strategies is that two or more diverse software units (variants) are employed to form fault-tolerant software. The most fundamental difference is how the decision is made that determines the outputs to be produced by fault-tolerant software. Besides at least two system variants, tolerance of design faults necessitates a decider to provide an error-free result. In the recovery block strategy, the decider is an acceptance test, which is applied sequentially to the results provided by the variants, in which if the results provided by the first variant do not satisfy the acceptance test, the second variant is executed, and so on. In the N-version programming approach, the variants (versions) and the decider look for a consensus of two or more outputs by voting on all variants' results.

The recovery blocks strategy is usually classified as forwarding or backward recovery methods. In forward recovery, the systems continue processing in the presence of an erroneous state in computation for correcting the detected error a little later. In backward recovery, the system rolls back the computation process before the error and restarts the computation.

The hardware-fault tolerant architectures equivalent to recovery block strategy and N-version programming are standby sparing (also termed as passive dynamic redundancy) and N modular redundancy (also termed as static redundancy), respectively. For more details on software redundancy methods, the reader is referred to [244] and [112].

EXERCISES

Exercise 1. What do you understand of passive and active redundancy mechanisms?

Exercise 2. Explain the following redundant mechanisms, and describe their pros and cons: **a)** active-active redundancy, **b)** hot-standby redundancy, **c)** warm-standby redundancy, **d)** cold-standby redundancy.

Exercise 3. How many faults, does the 5MR system tolerates? Explain.

Exercise 4. Explain the circumstances in which a system manager should favor using a cold-standby spare instead of an active-active redundancy.

Exercise 5. Explain the pros and cons of the following RAID architecture: **a)** RAID 0, **b)** RAID 1, **c)** RAID 5, and **d)** RAID 6.

Exercise 6. Considering a RAID 50 with ten disks, each with two TB, provide: **a)** the storage capacity efficiency, **b)** the effective storage capacity, **c)** the number of disk faults the system tolerates.

Exercise 7. Assuming a RAID 60 with twelve disks, each with two TB, provide: **a)** the storage capacity efficiency, **b)** the effective storage capacity, **c)** the number of disk faults the system tolerates.

Exercise 8. Considering a RAID 10 with eight disks, each with three TB, provide: **a)** the storage capacity efficiency, **b)** the effective storage capacity, **c)** the number of disk faults the system tolerates.

Exercise 9. Assuming a RAID 51 with ten disks, each with three TB, provide: **a)** the storage capacity efficiency, **b)** the effective storage capacity, **c)** the number of disk faults the system tolerates.

Exercise 10. How is a software fault different from a hardware fault?

Exercise 11. The stochastic independence of n-version programming can be compromised by a number of factors. Depict them and comment how they can compromise the solution.

18 Reliability Block Diagram

The two most widely used combinatorial models for reliability and availability evaluation are the Reliability Block Diagram (RBD) and the Fault Tree (FT). This chapter presents the RBDs. First, however, reliability and availability modeling methods are classified. This classification supports choosing the suitable method of evaluation for each specific problem by taking into account the modeling capacity and the evaluation complexity. Afterward, the RBD compositions are described. These compositions are illustrated with many examples. Measures of importance are also introduced.

18.1 MODELS CLASSIFICATION

This section presents a classification of models used for availability and reliability evaluation. These models may be broadly classified into combinatorial and state-space models. State-space models may also be referred to as non-combinatorial, and combinatorial can be identified as non-state space models.

Combinatorial models capture conditions that make a system fail (or to be working) regarding structural relationships between the system components. These relations observe the set of components (and sub-systems) of the system that should be either properly working or faulty for the system as a whole to be working correctly.

State-space models represent the system behavior (failures and repair activities) by its states and event occurrence expressed as labeled state transitions. These models allow representing more complex relations between components of the system, such as dependencies involving sub-systems and resource constraints, and complex maintenance policies. Some state-space models may also be evaluated by discrete event simulation in the case of intractable large state spaces or when a combination of non-exponential distributions prohibits an analytic (closed-form) or numerical solution.

The most prominent combinatorial model types are Reliability Block Diagrams (**RBD**) and Fault Trees (**FT**) [290] [224] [438] [247]. Markov chains, stochastic Petri nets, and stochastic process algebras are most widely used state-space models [413] [437] [256] [153]. Next, we introduce the combinatorial models and their respective evaluation methods.

18.2 BASIC COMPONENTS

This section presents the reliability block diagram. An RBD is a success-oriented model that links functional blocks to the effect of components' failures on the system reliability. RBDs are composed of two special nodes, named **source** vertex and **target** vertex, **blocks** (usually rectangles), and **arcs** connecting the blocks and the vertices. The source node is usually placed at the left-hand side of the diagram whereas the target vertex is positioned at the right. Figure 18.1 shows one RBD with three blocks, $BS = \{b_1, b_2, b_3\}$.

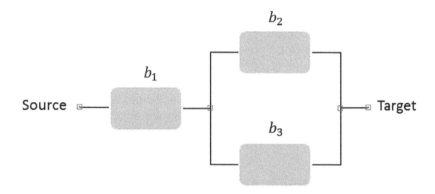

Figure 18.1   Reliability Block Diagram - an Example.

The system functions are represented by a set of blocks ($BS = \{b_i\}$), where each block, b_i, represents a specific function state. A Bernoulli random variable specifies each function state i

$$x_i(t) = \begin{cases} 0 & \text{if } b_i \text{ has failed at } t. \\ 1 & \text{if } b_i \text{ is operational at } t. \end{cases} \qquad (18.2.1)$$

The probability function, PDF, of $x_i(t)$ is defined by

$$P(x_i(t)) = \begin{cases} 1 - p_i & \text{if } x_i(t) = 0 \text{ at } t \\ p_i & \text{if } x_i(t) = 1 \text{ at } t. \end{cases}$$

The expected value of $x_i(t)$ is $E(x_i(t)) = p_i$.

The reader can think of a block as a switch that is open when the respective function failed and closed when the function is correctly operating (see Figure 18.2). Failures of individual functions (blocks) are also assumed to be independent.

RBDs are not a block schematic diagrams systems, although they might be isomorphic in some particular cases. RBDs only indicate how the functioning of the system's components affects the functioning of the system. Although RBD was initially proposed as a model for calculating reliability, it can be used for computing other dependability metrics, such as availability and maintainability.

Assume a component i is correctly operating at $t = 0$ ($x_i(0) = 1$); the time to reach the state $x_i(t) = 0$ is the time to failure (see Section 16.2). Therefore, the probability

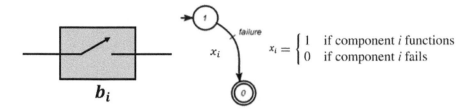

Figure 18.2 Functional Block and Block States.

of staying in $x_i(t) = 1$ by t, $P(x_i(t) = 1)$, is the component i reliability, that is $R_i(t) = E(x_i(t)) = p_i$.

If the component is repairable such as the one shown in Figure 18.3, $P(x_i(t) = 1)$ represents the instantaneous availability; hence $A_i(t) = E(x_i(t)) = p_i$. Likewise, when $lim_{t \to \infty}$, $A_i = E(x_i(t)) = p_i$ represents the steady-state availability.

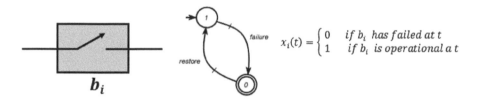

Figure 18.3 Repairable Block and Its States.

18.3 LOGICAL AND STRUCTURE FUNCTIONS

This section presents the logical and the structure functions.

Logical Function

Assume a system S represented by an RBD with set of n components (blocks) $CS = \{b_i\}$, $|CS| = n$. The system state is described through a **logical function** of its components. The logical function is evaluated as true whenever at least a minimal number of components is operationally enabled to perform the indented functionality. More formally, let us define n Boolean variables $BS = \{s_i\}$, $i = 1, ...n$, each representing the state of each component. Each variable is defined by

$$s_i = \begin{cases} F & \text{if } b_i \text{ has failed.} \\ T & \text{if } b_i \text{ is operational.} \end{cases}$$

Now, consider $\mathbf{B} = (s_i)$ is a vector of the Boolean variables of the set BS, and its cardinality is $|BS| = n$. The logical function that represents the operational mode depicted by the RBD is defined by

$$\Psi(\mathbf{B}) = \begin{cases} F & \text{if } S \text{ has failed.} \\ T & \text{if } S \text{ is operational.} \end{cases} \qquad (18.3.1)$$

If the system performs more than one functionality (operation), logical functions should be defined for representing each functionality (**operational mode**). The meaning of an intended functionality must be specified and depends on the objective of the study. Hence, the system being operational for a particular functionality does not mean it also is operational for another functionality.

Let us illustrate the concept described. Assume a system depicted by the RBD shown in Figure 18.1. This system is operational as long as there is a path that connects the source node to the target node. Hence, if b_1, and b_2 or b_3 are in operational states, the system is operational. The set of Boolean variables that describes the states of the blocks of this RBD is $BS = \{s_1, s_2, s_3\}$, and the vector $\mathbf{B} = (s_3, s_2, s_1)$, $|BS| = 3$. Table 18.1 shows the enumeration of the whole set of vector, and evaluates the respective logical function.

Table 18.1
State Enumeration - Logical Function

s_3	s_2	s_1	$\Psi(\mathbf{B})$
F	F	F	F
F	F	T	F
F	T	F	F
F	T	T	T
T	F	F	F
T	F	T	T
T	T	F	F
T	T	T	T

All we have to do is examine the Column $\Psi(\mathbf{B})$ of the enumeration in Table 18.1 for any rows where the output is "T", and write the conjunction that would equal a value of "T" given those input conditions. The obtained function is

$$\Psi(\mathbf{B}) = (\overline{s_3} \wedge s_2 \wedge s_1) \vee (s_3 \wedge \overline{s_2} \wedge s_1) \vee (s_3 \wedge s_2 \wedge s_1).$$

Minimizing the expression above, we get

$$\Psi(\mathbf{B}) = s_1 \wedge (s_2 \vee s_3).$$ (18.3.2)

The logical function shows that the system is operational as long as the component b_1, and b_2 or b_3 (or both) are operational.

Structure Function

The system state may also be described by the respective structure function of its components. The structure function of the system S is evaluated to one whenever at least the minimal number of components is operational. More formally, let us define a set of n Bernoulli random variables $XS = \{x_i\}$, $i = 1,...n$, where each variable represents the state of each component i. Each variable is defined as in 18.2.1. Consider $\mathbf{X} = (x_i)$ is a vector of the random variables of the set XS, and its cardinality is $|XS| = n$. The structure function that represents the operational mode depicted by the RBD is defined by

$$\Phi(\mathbf{X}) = \begin{cases} 0 & \text{if } S \text{ has failed.} \\ 1 & \text{if } S \text{ is operational.} \end{cases}$$ (18.3.3)

If the system has more than one operational mode, structure functions should be specified for representing each operational mode. Thus, if that system is operational for a particular mode does not mean it also is operational for another operational mode.

Now, assume the RBD depicted in Figure 18.1. This system is operational if b_1, and b_2 or b_3 are in operational states. The set of random variables that describes the states of the blocks of this RBD is $XS = \{x_1, x_2, x_3\}$, and the vector $\mathbf{X} = (x_3, x_2, x_1)$, $|XS| = 3$. Table 18.2 shows the enumeration of the whole set of vectors and the respective structure function.

All we have to do is examine the Column $\Phi(\mathbf{X})$ of the enumeration Table 18.2 for any rows where the output is "1", and write the products that would equal a value of "1" given those input conditions. The obtained function is

$$\Phi(\mathbf{X}) = ((1 - x_3) \times x_2 \times x_1) + (x_3 \times (1 - x_2) \times x_1) + (x_3 \times x_2 \times x_1).$$

Doing some algebra, we get

$$\Phi(\mathbf{X}) = x_1 \times (1 - (1 - x_2) \times (1 - x_3)).$$

The structure function may also be obtained from the logical function by converting Boolean variables to random variables, and logical operators to arithmetic operators as depicted in Table 18.3.

Table 18.2

State Enumeration - Structure Function

x_3	x_2	x_1	$\Phi(\mathbf{X})$
0	0	0	0
0	0	1	0
0	1	0	0
0	1	1	1
1	0	0	0
1	0	1	1
1	1	0	0
1	1	1	1

Table 18.3

Transformation

Logical Function	Structure Function
s_i	x_i
$\overline{s_i}$	$1 - x_i$
$\wedge$	$\times$
$\vee$	$+$
$\Psi(\mathbf{B})$	$\Phi(\mathbf{X}) = 1$
$\overline{\Psi(\mathbf{B})}$	$\Phi(\mathbf{X}) = 0$

The conversion process begins by (1) transforming the logical function to a normal form in which only $\wedge$ and negation operators are present. Then (2) the conversion from the logical domain to the arithmetic domain is performed. Considering the logical function 18.3.2 and transforming it to the normal form, we get

$$\Psi(\mathbf{B}) = \overline{\overline{s_1 \wedge (s_2 \vee s_3)}}.$$

$$\Psi(\mathbf{B}) = \overline{\overline{s_1} \vee \overline{s_2 \vee s_3}}.$$

$$\Psi(\mathbf{B}) = \overline{\overline{\overline{s_1}} \wedge \overline{s_2} \wedge \overline{s_3}}.$$

$$\Psi(\mathbf{B}) = \overline{s_1 \wedge \overline{s_2} \wedge \overline{s_3}}. \tag{18.3.4}$$

Now, applying the transformation rules depicted in Table 18.3, we get

$$\Phi(\mathbf{X}) = x_1 \times (1 - (1 - x_2) \times (1 - x_3)). \tag{18.3.5}$$

The structure function may also be obtained by conditioning the RBD in terms of its components. **Conditioning** is also called **factoring, pivoting,** or **expansion** [54] (see Chapter 20). The structure function $\Phi(\mathbf{X})$ may be re-written by

$$\Phi(\mathbf{X}) = x_i \times \Phi(1_i, \mathbf{X}) + (1 - x_i) \times \Phi(0_i, \mathbf{X}), \tag{18.3.6}$$

where $\Phi(1_i, \mathbf{X})$ represents a state in which the component c_i is operational and the states of the other components are random variables ($\Phi(x_1, x_2, ..., 1_i, ..., x_n)$). Likewise, $\Phi(0_i, \mathbf{X})$ denotes a state in which the component c_i has failed and the states of the other components are random variables ($\Phi(x_1, x_2, ..., 0_i, ..., x_n)$). Factoring the structure function is a very useful strategy when modeling complex systems, since with its repeated application one can eventually reach a subsystem whose structure function is simpler to deal with.

Now, let us apply such a strategy to the RBD depicted in Figure 18.1. First, let us conditioning on the component b_1. Hence, we get

$$\Phi(x_1, x_2, x_3) = x_1 \Phi(1, x_2, x_3)) + (1 - x_1) \Phi(0, x_2, x_3).$$

As $\Phi(0, x_2, x_3) = 0$, we have

$$\Phi(x_1, x_2, x_3) = x_1 \Phi(1, x_2, x_3)).$$

Now, conditioning $\Phi(1, x_2, x_3))$ on component b_2, we obtain

$$\Phi(1, x_2, x_3)) = x_2 \Phi(1, 1, x_3) + (1 - x_2) \Phi(1, 0, x_3).$$

As $\Phi(1, 1, x_3) = 1$, then

$$\Phi(1, x_2, x_3)) = x_2 + (1 - x_2) \Phi(1, 0, x_3).$$

Therefore

$$\Phi(x_1, x_2, x_3) = x_1 (x_2 + (1 - x_2) \Phi(1, 0, x_3)).$$

Now, let us conditioning $\Phi(1, 0, x_3)$ on component b_3. Hence

$$\Phi(1, 0, x_3)) = x_3 \Phi(1, 0, 1) + (1 - x_3) \Phi(1, 0, 0).$$

As $\Phi(1,0,1) = 1$ and $\Phi(1,0,0) = 0$, we get

$$\Phi(1,0,x_3)) = x_3.$$

Hence,

$$\Phi(x_1,x_2,x_3) = x_1\,(x_2 + (1-x_2)x_3).$$

Doing some algebra, we obtain

$$\Phi(x_1,x_2,x_3) = x_1 \times (1 - (1-x_2) \times (1-x_3)).$$

18.4 COHERENT SYSTEM

A component i is irrelevant to the system, if $\Phi(\mathbf{X})$ is not affected by the state of the component, x_i. More formally, $\Phi(1_i,\mathbf{X}) = \Phi(0_i,\mathbf{X})$, $\forall i$. If a component i is not irrelevant, it is relevant to the system.

Irrelevant components cannot directly modify the state of the system. A system is **co-herent** if (1) its structure function, $\Phi(\mathbf{X})$, is nondecreasing and (2) each component is relevant. Here, all systems are coherent [346] [224].

Condition (1) implies $\Phi(\mathbf{X}) \leq \Phi(\mathbf{Y})$, for any $\mathbf{X}$ and $\mathbf{Y}$ such that $\mathbf{X} \leq \mathbf{Y}$. In other words, replacing a failed component in a functioning system does not make the system fail. It is worth noting that for two vectors with n elements, $\mathbf{X}$ and $\mathbf{Y}$, $\mathbf{X} < \mathbf{Y}$, if $x_i \leq y_i$, $\forall i$, and $\exists i$ such that $x_i < y_i$.

Therefore, in a coherent system, $\Phi(\mathbf{0}) = 0$ and $\Phi(\mathbf{1}) = 1 = 1^1$. In other words, the system fails when all components fail, and the system functions when all components function.

18.5 COMPOSITIONS

This section presents the blocks composition.

Series Composition

Let us consider a system S composed of n components (see Figure 18.4). If the system is only operational if every component b_i is operational, the structure function is

$$\Phi(\mathbf{X}) = \prod_{i=1}^{n} x_i.$$

---

[1]Bold 0, **0**, and bold 1, **1**, denote vectors of zeros and ones.

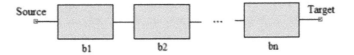

Figure 18.4   Series Composition.

As $\Phi(\mathbf{X})$ is a Bernoulli random variable, we have

$$E(\Phi(\mathbf{X})) = P(\Phi(\mathbf{X}) = 1).$$

Thus,

$$P(\Phi(\mathbf{X}) = 1) = E\left(\prod_{i=1}^{n} x_i\right).$$

Considering the components are independent, we have

$$P(\Phi(\mathbf{X}) = 1) = \prod_{i=1}^{n} E(x_i). \qquad (18.5.1)$$

If $E(x_i) = R_i(t)$ (component's b_i reliability), then

$$R_S(t) = P(\Phi(\mathbf{X}) = 1).$$

Therefore, the system reliability is

$$R_S(t) = \prod_{i=1}^{n} R_i(t). \qquad (18.5.2)$$

If $E(x_i) = A_i(t)$ (component's b_i instantaneous availability), then the system instantaneous availability is

$$A_S(t) = \prod_{i=1}^{n} A_i(t). \qquad (18.5.3)$$

Similarly, if $E(x_i) = A_i$ (component's b_i steady-state availability), then the system steady-state availability is

$$A_S = \prod_{i=1}^{n} A_i. \qquad (18.5.4)$$

If the TTFs and the TTRs of all components are identically distributed, then $A_i = MTTF/(MTTF + MTTR)$ for every component b_i. Hence, the system steady-state availability is

$$A_S = \left(\frac{MTTF}{MTTF + MTTR} \right)^n.$$ (18.5.5)

If the time to failure of every component is identically distributed according to an exponential distribution with rate λ, and if the time to repair of every component is also identically distributed and follows an exponential distribution with rate μ, the system's steady-state availability is

$$A_S = \left(\frac{\mu}{\lambda + \mu} \right)^n.$$ (18.5.6)

Suppose each component b_i time to failure, TTF_i, is exponentially distributed with rate λ_i. Hence the component b_i reliability is

$$R_i(t) = e^{-\lambda_i t}.$$

Thus, the system S reliability is

$$R_S(t) = \prod_{i=1}^{n} e^{-\lambda_i t}.$$ (18.5.7)

Hence

$$R_S(t) = e^{-\sum_{i=1}^{n} \lambda_i t},$$ (18.5.8)

where $\lambda_{eq} = \sum_{i=1}^{n} \lambda_i$ is the equivalent failure rate, and as

$$MTTF = \int_0^\infty R(t)\, dt,$$

$$MTTF = \int_0^\infty e^{-\sum_{i=1}^{n} \lambda_i t}\, dt.$$

Therefore

$$MTTF = \frac{1}{\sum_{i=1}^{n} \lambda_i}.$$ (18.5.9)

Example 18.5.1. Assume a computer system is composed of a physical server (hardware - HW) with an operating system (OS), and two application programs A_1 and A_2 (see Figure 18.5.a). These components are assumed to be independent. Consider the time to failure of each component (HW, OS, A_1, and A_2) is exponentially distributed with the respective rates: $\lambda_{HW} = 6.25 \times 10^{-5}$, $\lambda_{OS} = 3.3333 \times 10^{-4}$, $\lambda_{A_1} = 5.00 \times 10^{-4}$, and $\lambda_{A_2} = 6.6667 \times 10^{-4}$. The system is assumed to be operational only if the physical server, the operating system, and both application programs are operational. Thus, the logical function depicting the operational mode is

$$\Psi(\mathbf{B}) = s_{hw} \wedge s_{os} \wedge s_{a_1} \wedge s_{a_2},$$

where s_{hw}, s_{os}, s_{a_1}, and s_{a_2} are the logical variables that describe the components'state. Therefore, the RBD that represents this operational mode composes the components in series as depicted in Figure 18.5.b.

The structure function is

$$\Phi(\mathbf{X}) = x_{hw} \times x_{os} \times x_{a_1} \times x_{a_2},$$

where x_{hw}, x_{os}, x_{a_1}, and x_{a_2} are the structure variables that describe the components'state.

As the system reliability of series system is $R(t) = E(\Phi(\mathbf{X}))$, then

$$R(t) = E(x_{hw} \times x_{os} \times x_{a_1} \times x_{a_2}).$$

$$R(t) = E(x_{hw}) \times E(x_{os}) \times E(x_{a_1}) \times E(x_{a_2}).$$

$$R(t) = R_{hw}(t) \times R_{os}(t) \times R_{a_1}(t) \times R_{a_2}(t).$$

$$R(t) = e^{-\lambda_{hw}t} \times e^{-\lambda_{os}t} \times e^{-\lambda_{a_1}t} \times e^{-\lambda_{a_2}t}.$$

$$R(t) = e^{-(\lambda_{hw}+\lambda_{os}+\lambda_{a_1}+\lambda_{a_2})t}.$$

$$R(720h) = 0.3247.$$

As when $R(t) = e^{-\lambda_{eq}t}$, the $MTTF = 1/\lambda_{eq}$, and as $\lambda_{eq} = (\lambda_{hw} + \lambda_{os} + \lambda_{a_1} + \lambda_{a_2})$, then the system time to failure is $MTTF = 640h$.

Figure 18.6 shows the system reliability in the interval $(0, 720h)$.

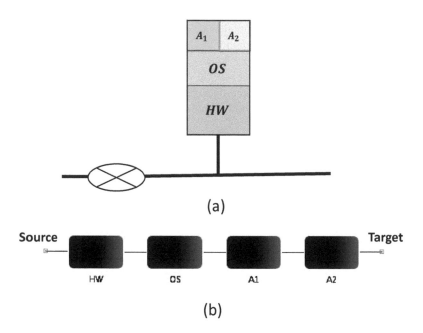

(a)

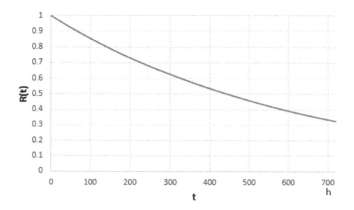

(b)

Figure 18.5 Four-Component Computational System (a) – Four-Component Series RBD (b).

Figure 18.6 Four-Component Computational System – Reliability.

Now, consider that the time to repair each component is also exponentially distributed. If the mean time to repair the hardware is $24h$, the mean time to repair the operating system is $8h$, and the respective times to repair the programs are $4h$, the steady-state availability can be estimated by

$$A = \prod_{i \in \{hw, os, a_1, a_2\}} A_i,$$

where $A_i = \mu_i/(\lambda_i + \mu_i) = MTTF_i/(MTTF_i + MTTR_i)$.

The system steady-state availability is $A = 0.99122$. The annual downtime in hours is $DTyh = (1 - A) \times 8760h = 76.9128h$. The system mean time to restore may be estimated from $A = MTTF/(MTTF + MTTR)$, because

$$A \times (MTTF + MTTR) = MTTF.$$

$$A \times MTTR = MTTF - A \times MTTF.$$

$$MTTR = \frac{MTTF \times (1 - A)}{A}.$$

$$MTTR = \frac{MTTF \times UA}{A}, \qquad (18.5.10)$$

where UA is the steady-state unavailability.

Taking the steady-state availability, we have $UA = 1 - 0.99122 = 0.00878$. As $MTTF = 640h$, then $MTTR = (640 \times 0.00878)/(0.99122) = 5.67h$.

Assume the mean time to failure of the program A_2 may lay in the interval $(1000h, 2000h)$. The steady-state system availability and yearly downtime in hours are depicted in Figure 18.7.

□

Example 18.5.2. A system S of 8 functions serially composed was conceived aiming at reliability not smaller than 0.9 ($R(t) \geq 0.9$) for mission time of $t = 400h$. If the functions' time to failure are independent and identically distributed (i.i.d.) according to an exponential distribution, what is the maximal failure rate allowed for each function?

The system reliability for an eight-component i.i.d. serial system is $R(t) = e^{-8\lambda t}$. Then,

$$\lambda = \frac{-lnR(t)}{8 \times t}.$$

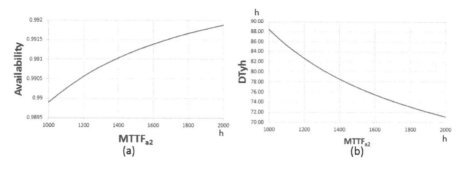

Figure 18.7 Steady-State Availability (a) and Downtime (b) as Function of $MTTF_{a_2}$.

As $R(t) \geq 0.9$, then

$$\lambda < \frac{-lnR(t)}{8 \times t}.$$

Hence

$$\lambda < \frac{-ln0.9}{8 \times 400} = 3.2925 \, 10^{-5} \, f/h.$$

The required system mean time to failure is

$$MTTF = \frac{1}{8 \times \lambda} = \frac{1}{2.63401 \, 10^{-4}} = 3796.49 \, h.$$

□

Parallel Composition

Let us consider a system S composed of n components (see Figure 18.8). If the system is operational if at least one component b_i is operational, the structure function is

$$\Phi(\mathbf{X}) = 1 - \prod_{i=1}^{n}(1 - x_i).$$

Since $\Phi(\mathbf{X})$ is a Bernoulli random variable, we have

$$E(\Phi(\mathbf{X})) = P(\Phi(\mathbf{X}) = 1).$$

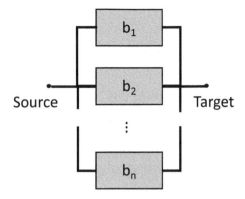

Figure 18.8 Parallel Composition.

Hence,

$$P(\Phi(\mathbf{X}) = 1) = E(1 - \prod_{i=1}^{n}(1 - x_i)).$$

Assuming the components are independent, we have

$$P(\Phi(\mathbf{X}) = 1) = 1 - E(\prod_{i=1}^{n}(1 - x_i)).$$

$$P(\Phi(\mathbf{X}) = 1) = 1 - \prod_{i=1}^{n} E((1 - x_i)).$$

$$P(\Phi(\mathbf{X}) = 1) = 1 - \prod_{i=1}^{n}(1 - E(x_i)).$$

If $E(x_i) = R_i(t)$ (component's b_i reliability), then

$$R_P(t) = P(\Phi(\mathbf{X}) = 1).$$

Thus, the system reliability is

$$R_P(t) = 1 - \prod_{i=1}^{n}(1 - R_i(t)), \tag{18.5.11}$$

and the system unreliability is

$$UR_P(t) = \prod_{i=1}^{n} UR_i(t) = \prod_{i=1}^{n} (1 - R_i(t)), \qquad (18.5.12)$$

where $UR_i(t)$ is the component b_i unreliability.

Another way of thinking of the system reliability is through its unreliability. The system composed of n components in parallel fails if every component fails. Hence, the system unrelaibility, $UR(t)$, is the product of the components' unreliability, $\prod_{i=1}^{n} UR(t)_i$. Therefore, as system reliability is $R(t) = 1 - UR(t)$, $R(t) = 1 - \prod_{i=1}^{n} UR(t)_i$.

If $E(x_i) = A_i(t)$ (component's b_i instantaneous availability), then the system instantaneous availability is

$$A_P(t) = 1 - \prod_{i=1}^{n} (1 - A_i(t)), \qquad (18.5.13)$$

and the instantaneous system unavailability is

$$UA_P(t) = \prod_{i=1}^{n} UA_i(t) = \prod_{i=1}^{n} (1 - A_i(t)). \qquad (18.5.14)$$

Likewise, if $E(x_i) = A_i$ (component's b_i steady-state availability), then the system steady-state availability is

$$A_P = 1 - \prod_{i=1}^{n} (1 - A_i), \qquad (18.5.15)$$

and the steady-state system unavailability is

$$UA_P = \prod_{i=1}^{n} UA_i = \prod_{i=1}^{n} (1 - A_i). \qquad (18.5.16)$$

If the n components are identically distributed, then $A_i = MTTF/(MTTF + MTTR)$ for every component b_i, and the system steady-state availability is

$$A_P = 1 - \prod_{i=1}^{n} (1 - \frac{MTTF}{MTTF + MTTR}).$$

Hence,

$$A_P = 1 - \left(1 - \frac{MTTF}{MTTF + MTTR}\right)^n. \qquad (18.5.17)$$

Thus,

$$A_P = 1 - \left(\frac{MTTR}{MTTF + MTTR} \right)^n. \qquad (18.5.18)$$

If the time to failure of every component is identically distributed according to an exponential distribution with rate λ, and if the time to repair of every component is also identically distributed and follows an exponential distribution with rate μ, the components' steady-state availability is

$$A_i = \frac{\mu}{\lambda + \mu}.$$

Therefore, the system S steady-state availability is

$$A = 1 - \left(1 - \frac{\mu}{\lambda + \mu} \right)^n. \qquad (18.5.19)$$

Hence

$$A = 1 - \left(\frac{\lambda}{\lambda + \mu} \right)^n, \qquad (18.5.20)$$

and the system unavailability is

$$UA = \left(\frac{\lambda}{\lambda + \mu} \right)^n. \qquad (18.5.21)$$

Consider a system composed of two parallel components with time to failure exponentially distributed with rates λ_1 and λ_2. The system reliability is

$$R(t) = 1 - (1 - e^{-\lambda_1 t})(1 - e^{-\lambda_2 t}).$$

The $MTTF$ of this system is obtained from

$$MTTF = \int_0^\infty R(t)\, dt = \int_0^\infty (1 - (1 - e^{-\lambda_1 t})(1 - e^{-\lambda_2 t}))\, dt.$$

$$MTTF = \int_0^\infty (e^{-\lambda_1 t} + e^{-\lambda_2 t} - e^{-(\lambda_1 + \lambda_2)t})\, dt.$$

$$MTTF = \int_0^\infty e^{-\lambda_1 t}\, dt + \int_0^\infty e^{-\lambda_2 t}\, dt - \int_0^\infty e^{-(\lambda_1 + \lambda_2)t}\, dt.$$

$$MTTF = \frac{1}{\lambda_1} + \frac{1}{\lambda_2} - \frac{1}{\lambda_1 + \lambda_2}. \qquad (18.5.22)$$

Assume a system composed of three parallel components with time to failure exponentially distributed with rates λ_1, λ_2, and λ_3. The system reliability is

$$R(t) = 1 - (1 - e^{-\lambda_1 t})(1 - e^{-\lambda_2 t})(1 - e^{-\lambda_3 t}).$$

Thus, the system mean time to failure is

$$MTTF = \int_0^\infty R(t)\, dt.$$

$$MTTF = \int_0^\infty (1 - (1 - e^{-\lambda_1 t})(1 - e^{-\lambda_2 t})(1 - e^{-\lambda_3 t}))\, dt.$$

$$MTTF = \int_0^\infty (e^{-\lambda_1 t} + e^{-\lambda_2 t} + e^{-\lambda_3 t} - e^{-(\lambda_1 + \lambda_2)t} -$$
$$e^{-(\lambda_1 + \lambda_3)t} - e^{-(\lambda_2 + \lambda_3)t} + e^{-(\lambda_1 + \lambda_2 + \lambda_3)t})\, dt.$$

$$MTTF = \frac{1}{\lambda_1} + \frac{1}{\lambda_2} + \frac{1}{\lambda_3} - \frac{1}{\lambda_1 + \lambda_2} - \frac{1}{\lambda_1 + \lambda_3} - \frac{1}{\lambda_2 + \lambda_3} + \frac{1}{\lambda_1 + \lambda_2 + \lambda_3}. \quad (18.5.23)$$

Likewise, the $MTTF$ of systems with a large number of components should be obtained. If, however, the components are identically distributed, a closed-form expression is available. Consider a system S composed of n blocks with TTF_i identically distributed according to an exponential distribution with rate λ. The system reliability is

$$R(t) = 1 - \prod_{i=1}^n (1 - e^{-\lambda t}).$$

$$R(t) = 1 - (1 - e^{-\lambda t})^n. \quad (18.5.24)$$

Therefore the mean time to failure is

$$MTTF = \int_0^\infty R(t)\, dt = \int_0^\infty (1 - (1 - e^{-\lambda t})^n)\, dt.$$

Let $x = 1 - e^{-\lambda t}$. Hence, when $t = 0$, $x = 0$, and when $t \to \infty$, $x = 1$. Differentiating x, we get $dx = \lambda e^{-\lambda t} dt$. Therefore, since

$$\int_0^\infty R(t)\, dt = \int_0^\infty (1 - (1 - e^{-\lambda t})^n)\, dt = \frac{1}{\lambda} \int_0^\infty \frac{(1 - (1 - e^{-\lambda t})^n)}{e^{-\lambda t}} \times e^{-\lambda t} \times \lambda\, dt,$$

we have

$$MTTF = \frac{1}{\lambda} \int_0^\infty \frac{(1 - x^n)}{(1 - x)} dx,$$

since $e^{-\lambda t} = 1 - x$.

As

$$\sum_{i=0}^n x^i = \frac{1 - x^n}{1 - x},$$

then

$$MTTF = \frac{1}{\lambda} \int_0^1 \sum_{i=0}^n x^i dx.$$

Thus,

$$MTTF = \frac{1}{\lambda} \int_0^1 (1 + x + x^2 + \ldots + x^{n-1}) dx.$$

$$MTTF = \frac{1}{\lambda} \left(\int_0^1 dx + \int_0^1 x \, dx + \int_0^1 x^2 \, dx + \ldots + \int_0^1 x^{n-1} \, dx \right).$$

$$MTTF = \frac{1}{\lambda} \left(1 + \frac{1}{2} + \frac{1}{3} + \ldots + \frac{1}{n} \right).$$

Hence

$$MTTF \frac{1}{\lambda} \sum_{i=1}^n \frac{1}{i}. \tag{18.5.25}$$

The system density function may be obtained from system reliability by $f(t) = -\frac{dR(t)}{dt}$ (see 16.2.1 and 16.2.2). Hence,

$$f(t) = n\lambda e^{-\lambda t}(1 - e^{-\lambda t})^{n-1}. \tag{18.5.26}$$

Figure 18.9 shows the failure density function of a parallel system composed by $n = \{1, 2, 3, 4\}$ i.i.d. blocks, where each has a constant failure rate equal to $\lambda = 10^{-4} f/h$. The **mode time to failure**, which is the time that maximized the density function, the MedTTF, and MTTF are depicted in Table 18.4.

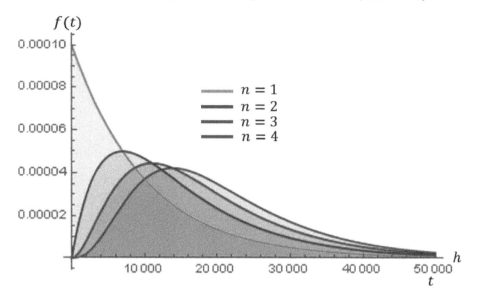

Figure 18.9 Failure Density Function – Parallel Composition with n Blocks.

Table 18.4

$ModeTTF, MedTTF, MTTF$ **- Parallel Composition with n Blocks**

n	$ModeTTF$ (h)	$MedTTF$ (h)	$MTTF$ (h)
1	0	6931.47	10000.00
2	6931.47	12279.50	15000.00
3	10986.10	15784.30	18333.33
4	13862.90	18382.00	20833.33

Since the failure rate (hazard rate - $h(t)$, $\lambda(t)$) function is $\lambda(t) = -\frac{dR(t)}{dt} \times \frac{1}{R(t)}$ (see 16.2.7), and using 18.5.24, we have

$$\lambda(t) = -\frac{d(1-(1-e^{-\lambda t})^n)}{dt} \times \frac{1}{R(t)}.$$

$$\lambda(t) = \frac{n\lambda e^{-\lambda t}\left(1-e^{-\lambda t}\right)^{n-1}}{1-\left(1-e^{-\lambda t}\right)^n}. \tag{18.5.27}$$

Figure 18.10 shows the failure rates of a parallel system composed by $n = \{1,2,3,4\}$ i.i.d. blocks, where each has a constant failure rate equal to $\lambda = 10^{-4} f/h$. It is important to highlight that for $n = 1$ the system failure rate is constant, whereas, for $n > 1$, the failure rate is no longer steady. In such cases, the failure rates increase over time. However, they are smaller than the single component failure rate ($n = 1$) and approach the single component failure rate as the time increases.

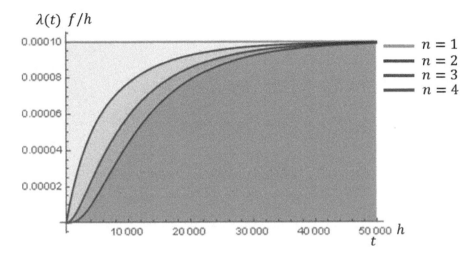

Figure 18.10   Failure Rate Function – Parallel Composition with n Blocks.

Now consider four systems, named S_1, S_2, S_3, and S_4, where S_1 is composed of a single block, and S_2, S_3, and S_4 are composed of two, three, and four i.d.d blocks in parallel, respectively. Assume the failure rate of the single block of S_1 is $\lambda_1 = 10^{-4} f/h$. Also consider the failure rate of each block of the system S_2, S_3, and S_4 is $\lambda_2 = 3/2\,10^{-4} f/h$, $\lambda_3 = 11/6\,10^{-4} f/h$, and $\lambda_4 = 25/12\,10^{-4} f/h$, respectively. The mean time to failure of each of these systems are equal to $MTTF_{S_i} = 10000h$, $i = \{1,2,3,4\}$. The reliability of each system is depicted in Figure 18.11.

It is important to stress that although the four systems have the same $MTTF$, the reliability curves are distinct. The parallel systems have higher reliability for a mission period shorten than t, whereas the simplex system has higher reliability for t. One should also observe that the reliability improvements reduces at each new component addition. Inversely, the reliability decrease reduces at each new component inclusion when considering mission periods higher than t. The time t in which the system S_i and S_j ($i = \{1,2,3\}$, $j = \{2,3,4\}$) reliabilities are equal is depicted in Table 18.5. These time instants are also graphically shown in Figure 18.11.

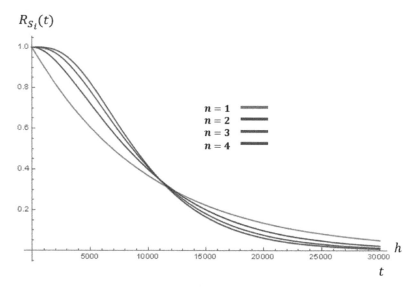

Figure 18.11   Reliability - Parallel Composition with n Blocks - $MTTF_{S_i} = 10000\,h$.

Table 18.5
Time Instants t (h) at Which $R_{S_i}(t) = R_{S_j}(t)$

Systems	S_2	S_3	S_4
S_1	12187.6	11769.7	11536.2
S_2		11154.9	10991.7
S_3			10777.3

Example 18.5.3. Assume a computational system composed of one application server (S_1 - main server) and a hot-standby server (S_2). S_1 is operational if its hardware infrastructure (HW), operating system (OS), and applications (A_1, ..., A_n) are operational. Assume the time to failure (TTF_{S_1}) of S_1 is exponentially distributed with failure rate equal to $\lambda = 4 \times 10^{-4}\,f/h$. S_2 has an identical configuration and TTF. Figure 18.12.a shows the system. S_1 delivers the services required to the system. When S_1 fails, S_2 assumes the transaction processing. Hence, the system is operational as long as at least one of the servers is operational.

Considering the logical variable as homonyms of the servers identification, the logical function is $\Psi(\mathbf{S}) = S_1 \vee S_2$. The RBD that represents this system is shown in Figure 18.12.b. The respective structure function is $\Phi(\mathbf{X}) = 1 - (1 - x_1)(1 - x_2)$, where x_1 and x_2 are the state random variables that represent the servers. As the com-

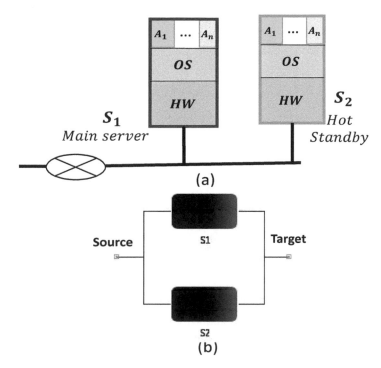

Figure 18.12   Hot-Standby Configuration (a) - RBD Parallel Composition (b).

ponents x_1 and x_2 are i.i.d, then the structure function reduces to $\Phi(\mathbf{X}) = 1 - (1-x)^2$. The system reliability is calculated by

$$R(t) = 1 - (1 - e^{-\lambda t})^2. \tag{18.5.28}$$

Figure 18.13 shows the reliability function curve of the system. The system reliability at $t = 2500h$ is $R(t) = 0.6$, and its $MTTF = 3750h$. This reliability expressed in DPM is $DPM = (1 - R(t)) \times 10^6 = 4 \times 10^5$. The system steady-state availability is estimated by

$$A = 1 - (\lambda/(\lambda + \mu))^2, \tag{18.5.29}$$

and the respective yearly downtime in minutes is computed by $DT = (1 - A) \times 525,600\,min$. If the time to repair a server is exponentially distributed with mean $MTTR = 20h$, the steady-state availability is $A = 0.999937$, the availability expressed in number of nines is $\#9s = 4.2$, and annual downtime in minutes is $DT = 33.1285\,min.$.

□

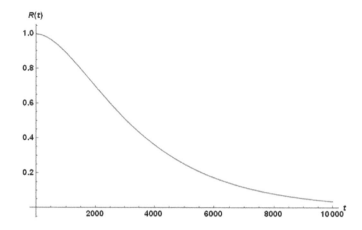

Figure 18.13   Hot-Standby Configuration – Reliability Function.

Composing Parallel and Series Structures

Series and parallel structures can be combined to form more complex system configurations. In practice, a system may be decomposed into subsystems, and each subsystem may also be decomposed into smaller subsystems or components. Decomposition is very convenient when defining the structure, reliability, and availability
functions of systems.

As one example, consider a computational system composed of a computer (HW),
an operating system (OS), and three application (A_1, A_2 and A_3) programs (Figure
18.14.a). The application program A_2 is composed of two modules named A_{21} and
A_{22}, respectively. The computer is composed of a mother board (MB), a video controller (VC), a network controller (NC), a disk controller DC, a disk, and a power-
source subsystem (PSS), which is composed of two power sources (S_1 and S_2) configured in hot-standby (Figure 18.14.b).

The power-source subsystem is configured in hot-standby; thus it is operational as
long as one of the power sources correctly works. Thus

$$\Psi(\mathbf{S_{pss}}) = S_1 \lor S_2,$$

where $\mathbf{S_{pss}} = (S_1, S_2)$. Figure 18.15.a shows the RBD describing the power-source
subsystem.

The hardware is operational if

$$\Psi_{hw}(\mathbf{S_{hw}}) = MB \land VC \land NC \land DC \land D \land \Psi(\mathbf{S_{pss}}),$$

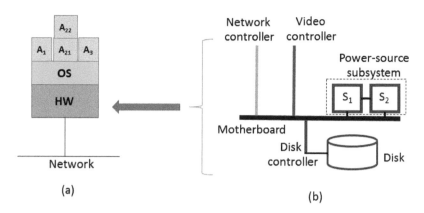

Figure 18.14 Computer System.

where $\mathbf{S_{hw}} = (MB, VC, NC, DC, D, \mathbf{S_{pss}}) = (MB, VC, NC, DC, D, S_1, S_2)$. Figure 18.15.b shows the RBD describing the hardware subsystem. Therefore,

$$\Psi(\mathbf{S_{hw}}) = MB \wedge VC \wedge NC \wedge DC \wedge D \wedge (S_1 \vee S_2).$$

The computational system is operational as long as the hardware subsystem $(\Psi_{hw}(\mathbf{S_{hw}}))$, the operating system ($OS$), and the application program A_1 are operational as well as at least one of A_2 and $A3$ are operational. Hence

$$\Psi(\mathbf{S_{cs}}) = \Psi(\mathbf{S_{hw}}) \wedge OS \wedge A_1 \wedge ((A_{21} \wedge A_{22}) \vee A_3),$$

$$\Psi(\mathbf{S_{cs}}) = MB \wedge VC \wedge NC \wedge DC \wedge D \wedge (S_1 \vee S_2) \wedge OS \wedge A_1 \wedge ((A_{21} \wedge A_{22}) \vee A_3),$$

where $\mathbf{S_{cs}} = (MB, VC, NC, DC, D, S_1, S_2, \mathbf{S_{cs}}) = (MB, VC, NC, DC, D, S_1, S_2, OS, A_1, A_2, A_3)$. It is worth stressing the application A_2 is composed of modules A_{21} and A_{22}, and it properly works if both modules are operational. Figure 18.15.c shows the RBD describing the computational system.

If the time to failure of each hardware device is exponentially distributed with rate λ_i, then the hardware reliability is

$$R(t)_{hw} = (1 - (1 - R(t)_{S1})(1 - R(t)_{S1})) \times \prod_{i \in \{MB, NC, VC, DC, D\}} R(t)_i.$$

$$R(t)_{hw} = (1 - (1 - e^{-\lambda_{s1} t})(1 - e^{-\lambda_{s1} t})) \times \prod_{i \in \{MB, NC, VC, DC, D\}} e^{-\lambda_i t}.$$

If $\lambda_{s1} = \lambda_{s1} = \lambda_s$, then

$$R(t)_{hw} = (1 - (1 - e^{-\lambda_s t})^2) \times \prod_{i \in \{MB, NC, VC, DC, D\}} e^{-\lambda_i t}.$$

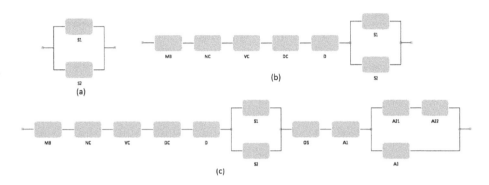

Figure 18.15   Computer System –] RBD.

Assuming the failure rates shown in Table 18.6, the hardware mean time to failure can be computed by $MTTF_{hw} = \int_0^\infty R(t)_{hw}\, dt$. Hence

$$MTTF_{hw} = \frac{2}{\lambda_d + \lambda_{dc} + \lambda_{mb} + \lambda_{nc} + \lambda_s + \lambda_{vc}} - \frac{1}{\lambda_d + \lambda_{dc} + \lambda_{mb} + \lambda_{nc} + 2\lambda_s + \lambda_{vc}}.$$

The hardware mean time to failure is $MTTF_{hw} = 27122.934\, h$. The hardware reliability is depicted in Figure 18.16.a.

The system steady-state availability is computed by

$$A_{CS} = A_{hw} \times A_{os} \times A_{a_1} \times (1 - ((1 - A_{a_3}) \times (1 - A_{a_{21}} \times A_{a_{22}}))),$$

where $A_i = MTTF_i / (MTTF_i + MTTR_i)$.

Now assume the time to repair the hardware, and the software components are exponentially distributed with the parameters presented in Table 18.7. The steady-state system availability is $A = 0.99694$, the system mean time to failure is $MTTF = 638.74\, h$, the system mean time to restore is $MTTR = 1.963\, h$, and the yearly downtime in hours is $DT = 26.85724\, h$.

Assuming the mean time to repair each program application (MTT_a) module is equal, Figure 18.16.b shows the system availability (in number of nines) for $MTT_a = \{0.1, 0.2, 0.3, 0.4, 0.5\}$.

Table 18.6
MTTFs and Failure Rates

Component	$MTTF\,(h)$	$\lambda\,(f/h)$
MB	430000	2.32558×10^{-6}
NC	220000	4.54545×10^{-6}
VC	185000	5.40541×10^{-6}
DC	140000	7.14286×10^{-6}
D	120000	8.33333×10^{-6}
S	50000	2.00×10^{-5}
OS	2000	5×10^{-4}
A_1	1500	6.67×10^{-4}
A_{21}	1800	5.56×10^{-4}
A_{22}	1800	5.56×10^{-4}
A_3	1600	6.25×10^{-4}

Table 18.7
Time to Repair - Parameters

Component	$MTTR\,(h)$	$\mu\,(r/h)$
Hw	20	5×10^{-2}
OS	4	2.5×10^{-1}
A_1	0.5	2
A_{21}	0.5	2
A_{22}	0.5	2
A_3	0.50	2

KooN

A system that is operational if at least K out of N components are operational is called a *KooN* structure. A series system is, therefore, a *NooN* structure, whereas parallel composition is a *1ooN* structure. *NMR* redundancies are represented by *KooN* structures. Structures like K out of N, bridges, delta and star arrangements [224] have been customarily represented by RBD; nevertheless such structures can only be represented if the components are replicated in the model [246].

Consider a data center with an ordered set of N similar servers, where $\mathbf{X_N} = (x_1, x_2, x_n)$ denotes the data center state, and x_i represents the state of the server i. These servers are observed during a period. At the end of the period, each server can be in one of these two states, operational ($x_i = 1$) or failed ($x_i = 0$). Assume the data center is considered operational if K out of the N servers are operational. If

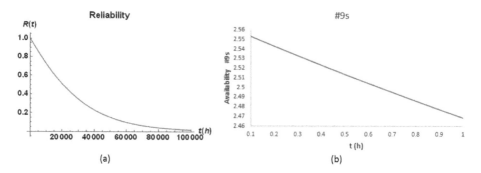

Figure 18.16   Reliability (a) - Availability in #9s (b).

exactly K out of the N servers are operational, the data center is considered operational. One possible outcome ($\mathbf{x_N}$) of the observation is when servers 1, 2, ..., k are operational, and servers $k+1$, $k+2$, ..., n have failed. This outcome is depicted by

$$\mathbf{X_{N1}} = (x_1, x_2, \dots, x_{k-1}, x_k, x_{k+1}, \dots, x_n).$$

$$\mathbf{X_{N1}} = (1, 1, \dots, 1, 1, 0, \dots, 0).$$

Let $Y_1 = \sum_{i=1}^{K} x_i$ be the total number of operational servers observed in the outcome $\mathbf{x_1}$.

Therefore, if $P(x_i = 1)$ is the probability of server i being operational, the probability of having exactly K out of the N servers operational is

$$P(Y_1 = K) = \prod_{i=1}^{K} P(x_i = 1) \times \prod_{i=K+1}^{n} P(x_i = 0).$$

If the mean time to failure of the system's components is i.i.d., then

$$P(Y_1 = K) = P(x = 1)^K \times P(x = 0)^{N-K}.$$

If $P(x = 1)$ is the component's reliability ($R_c(t)$), and $P(x = 0)$ is the component's unreliability ($UR_c(t)$), then

$$P(Y_1 = K) = R_c(t)^K \times UR_c(t)^{N-K}.$$

Thus,

$$P(Y_1 = K) = R_c(t)^K \times (1 - R_c(t))^{N-K}.$$

The outcome observed is one of many possible outcomes ($\mathbf{x_N}$) that represent precisely K out of N servers in an operational state ($Y = K$). The total number of outcomes with exactly K out of N is $\binom{N}{K}$. Therefore

$$P(Y = K) = \binom{N}{K} R_c(t)^K \times (1 - R_c(t))^{N-K}.$$

As the system is operational if K or more servers are operational, the system reliability is obtained by

$$R(t) = \sum_{i=k}^{N} \binom{N}{i} R_c(t)^i \times (1 - R_c(t))^{N-i}. \tag{18.5.30}$$

Likewise, the steady-state and the instantaneous availabilities are calculated.

$$A = \sum_{i=k}^{N} \binom{N}{i} A_c^i \times (1 - A_c)^{N-i}, \tag{18.5.31}$$

$$A(t) = \sum_{i=k}^{N} \binom{N}{i} A_c(t)^i \times (1 - A_c(t))^{N-i}, \tag{18.5.32}$$

where A_c and $A_c(t)$ are the steady-state and the instantaneous components' availability.

Example 18.5.4. Consider a system composed of 3 identical and independent components (b_1, b_2, b_3) that is operational if at least 2 out of its 3 components are working properly. The success probability of each of those blocks is p (reliability, availability or maintainability). This system can be considered as a single block (see Figure 18.17.a) where its success probability (P_S) is depicted by

$$P_S = \sum_{i=2}^{3} \binom{3}{i} p^i \times (1 - p)^{3-i} = 3p^2 - 2p^3. \tag{18.5.33}$$

Figure 18.17 shows three representations of the K out of N structure, in this particular case, a 2oo3 structure. The notation adopted in Figure 18.17.a uses a single block and allows representing $KooN$ with identical components, whereas the notation depicted in Figure 18.17.b allows representing blocks with distinct parameters. Figure 18.17.c represents the 2oo3 structure using replicated components.

The structure function of the $KooN$ system can be expressed by

$$\Phi(\mathbf{X}) = \begin{cases} 0 & \text{if } \sum_{i=1}^{N} x_i < K. \\ 1 & \text{if } \sum_{i=1}^{N} x_i \geq K. \end{cases} \tag{18.5.34}$$

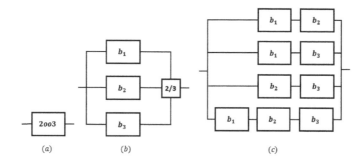

Figure 18.17 $2oo3$ Block - $KooN$ $K = 2, N = 3$.

Considering the $2oo3$ system represented by the RBD shown in Figure 18.17.c, the structure function is

$$\Phi(\mathbf{X}) = 1 - (1 - x_1 x_2)(1 - x_1 x_3)(1 - x_2 x_3)(1 - x_1 x_2 x_3).$$

$$\Phi(\mathbf{X}) = -x_2^3 x_3^3 x_1^3 + x_2^2 x_3^2 x_1^3 + x_2^2 x_3^3 x_1^2 + x_2^3 x_3^2 x_1^2$$
$$+x_2^2 x_3^2 x_1^2 - x_2 x_3^2 x_1^2 - x_2^2 x_3 x_1^2 - x_2 x_3 x_1^2 - x_2^2 x_3^2 x_1 - x_2 x_3^2 x_1$$
$$+x_2 x_1 - x_2^2 x_3 x_1 + x_2 x_3 x_1 + x_3 x_1 + x_2 x_3.$$

As $x_i^k = x_i$, we get

$$\Phi(\mathbf{X}) = x_1 x_2 + x_1 x_3 + x_2 x_3 - 2x_1 x_2 x_3.$$

As the system success probability (P_S - availability, reliability) is $P_S = E(\Phi(\mathbf{X}))$, then

$$P_S = E(x_1 x_2 + x_1 x_3 + x_2 x_3 - 2x_1 x_2 x_3).$$

$$P_S = E(x_1 x_2) + E(x_1 x_3) + E(x_2 x_3) - E(2x_1 x_2 x_3).$$

If x_1, x_2, and x_3 are independent, then

$$P_S = E(x_1)E(x_2) + E(x_1)E(x_3) + E(x_2)E(x_3) - 2E(x_1)E(x_2)E(x_3).$$

$$P_S = p(x_1)p(x_2) + p(x_1)p(x_3) + p(x_2)p(x_3) - 2p(x_1)p(x_2)p(x_3).$$

If x_1, x_2, and x_3 are identically distributed, then x may represent them. Hence

$$P_S = 3p(x)^2 - 2p(x)^3.$$

If $p(x) = p$, then we have

$$P_S = 3p^2 - 2p^3, \tag{18.5.35}$$

which is equal to expression 18.5.33.

If the component's time to failure is exponentially distributed with rate λ, the system reliability is

$$R(t) = 3e^{-2\lambda t} - 2e^{-3\lambda t}. \tag{18.5.36}$$

As $MTTF = \int_0^\infty R(t)\,dt$, then

$$MTTF = \int_0^\infty (3e^{-2\lambda t} - 2e^{-3\lambda t})\,dt = \frac{5}{6\lambda} = \frac{1}{\lambda}\sum_{i=2}^3 \frac{1}{i}. \tag{18.5.37}$$

Since

$$f(t) = \frac{-dR(t)}{dt},$$

then the density functions is

$$f(t) = 6\lambda e^{-2\lambda t} - 6\lambda e^{-3\lambda t}. \tag{18.5.38}$$

As the hazard function is

$$h(t) = -\frac{dR(t)}{dt} \times \frac{1}{R(t)},$$

then

$$h(t) = \frac{6\lambda}{3 - 2e^{\lambda(-t)}} - \frac{6\lambda e^{\lambda(-t)}}{3 - 2e^{\lambda(-t)}}. \tag{18.5.39}$$

□

Now, let us assume a non-repairable *KooN* system with i.i.d. components' time to failure that are exponentially distributed with rate λ. The system reliability is then calculated by

$$R(t) = \sum_{i=K}^{N} \binom{N}{i} e^{-i\lambda t} (1 - e^{-\lambda t})^{N-i}. \tag{18.5.40}$$

The system mean time to failure is

$$MTTF = \int_{0}^{\infty} R(t)\,dt.$$

$$MTTF = \int_{0}^{\infty} \sum_{i=K}^{N} \binom{N}{i} e^{-i\lambda t} (1 - e^{-\lambda t})^{N-i}\,dt.$$

$$MTTF = \sum_{i=K}^{N} \binom{N}{i} \int_{0}^{\infty} e^{-i\lambda t} (1 - e^{-\lambda t})^{N-i}\,dt.$$

Let $u = 1 - e^{-\lambda t}$, then $e^{-\lambda t} = 1 - u$, $e^{-(i-1)\lambda t} = (1-u)^{i-1}$, and $du = \lambda e^{-\lambda t}\,dt$. Therefore

$$MTTF = \frac{1}{\lambda} \sum_{i=K}^{N} \binom{N}{i} \int_{0}^{\infty} e^{-(i-1)\lambda t} (1 - e^{-\lambda t})^{N-i} \lambda e^{-\lambda t}\,dt.$$

As when $t = 0$, $u = 0$, and $t \to \infty$, $u = 1$, then

$$MTTF = \frac{1}{\lambda} \sum_{i=K}^{N} \binom{N}{i} \int_{0}^{1} (1-u)^{i-1} u^{N-i}\,du,$$

which leads to[2]

$$MTTF = \frac{1}{\lambda} \sum_{i=K}^{N} \frac{1}{i}. \tag{18.5.41}$$

Example 18.5.5. Consider a system represented by a $2oo5$ structure, such that its components are i.i.d. with constant rates equal to λ. The system reliability is represented by

$$R(t) = \sum_{i=2}^{5} \binom{5}{i} e^{-i\lambda t} (1 - e^{-\lambda t})^{5-i}.$$

---

[2](see Appendix A).

Hence

$$R(t) = \binom{5}{2} e^{-2\lambda t}(1 - e^{-\lambda t})^{5-2} + \binom{5}{3} e^{-3\lambda t}(1 - e^{-\lambda t})^{5-3} +$$

$$\binom{5}{4} e^{-4\lambda t}(1 - e^{-\lambda t})^{5-4} + \binom{5}{5} e^{-5\lambda t}(1 - e^{-\lambda t})^{5-5}.$$

$$R(t) = 10e^{-2\lambda t}(1 - e^{-\lambda t})^3 + 10e^{-3\lambda t}(1 - e^{-\lambda t})^2 +$$

$$5e^{-4\lambda t}(1 - e^{-\lambda t}) + e^{-5\lambda t}.$$

Then, the mean time to failure can be obtained directly from

$$MTTF = \int_0^\infty R(t)\,dt = \int_0^\infty (10e^{-2\lambda t}(1 - e^{-\lambda t})^3 + 10e^{-3\lambda t}(1 - e^{-\lambda t})^2 +$$

$$5e^{-4\lambda t}(1 - e^{-\lambda t}) + e^{-5\lambda t})\,dt.$$

$$MTTF = \int_0^\infty 10e^{-2\lambda t}(1 - e^{-\lambda t})^3\,dt + \int_0^\infty 10e^{-3\lambda t}(1 - e^{-\lambda t})^2\,dt +$$

$$\int_0^\infty 5e^{-4\lambda t}(1 - e^{-\lambda t})\,dt + \int_0^\infty e^{-5\lambda t}\,dt.$$

For sake of clarity, consider each term of the summation above as A, B, C, and H; hence

$$MTTF = A + B + C + D.$$

Now, first consider A:

$$A = \int_0^\infty 10e^{-2\lambda t}(1 - e^{-\lambda t})^3\,dt.$$

Let $u = 1 - e^{-\lambda t}$, then $e^{-\lambda t} = 1 - u$, and $du = \lambda e^{-\lambda t}\,dt$. Hence

$$A = \frac{10}{\lambda} \int_0^\infty e^{-\lambda t}(1 - e^{-\lambda t})^3 \lambda e^{-\lambda t}\,dt.$$

As when $t = 0$, $u = 0$, and $t \to \infty$, $u = 1$, then

$$A = \frac{10}{\lambda} \int_0^1 (1 - u) u^3 \, du.$$

$$A = \frac{10}{\lambda} \left(\int_0^1 u^3 \, du + \int_0^1 u^4 \, du \right)$$

$$A = \frac{10}{\lambda} \left(\frac{u^4}{4} \Big|_0^1 + \frac{u^5}{5} \Big|_0^1 \right)$$

$$A = \frac{1}{2\lambda}.$$

Now considering B, we get

$$B = \int_0^\infty 10 e^{-3\lambda t} (1 - e^{-\lambda t})^2 \, dt.$$

Let $u = 1 - e^{-\lambda t}$, then $e^{-\lambda t} = 1 - u$, $e^{-2\lambda t} = (1 - u)^2$, and $du = \lambda e^{-\lambda t} \, dt$. Thus

$$B = \frac{10}{\lambda} \int_0^\infty e^{-2\lambda t} (1 - e^{-\lambda t})^2 \lambda e^{-\lambda t} \, dt.$$

Likewise, as when $t = 0$, $u = 0$, and $t \to \infty$, $u = 1$, then

$$B = \frac{10}{\lambda} \int_0^1 (1 - u)^2 u^2 \, du = \frac{1}{3\lambda}.$$

Now take C:

$$C = \int_0^\infty 5 e^{-4\lambda t} (1 - e^{-\lambda t}) \, dt.$$

Let $u = 1 - e^{-\lambda t}$, then $e^{-\lambda t} = 1 - u$, $e^{-3\lambda t} = (1 - u)^3$, and $du = \lambda e^{-\lambda t} \, dt$. Hence

$$C = \frac{5}{\lambda} \int_0^\infty e^{-3\lambda t} (1 - e^{-\lambda t}) \lambda e^{-\lambda t} \, dt.$$

As when $t = 0$, $u = 0$, and $t \to \infty$, $u = 1$, then

$$C = \frac{5}{\lambda} \int_0^1 (1 - u)^3 u \, du = \frac{1}{4\lambda}.$$

Finally, take D:

$$D = \int_0^\infty e^{-5\lambda t}\, dt = \frac{1}{5\lambda}.$$

Therefore

$$MTTF = \frac{1}{2\lambda} + \frac{1}{3\lambda} + \frac{1}{4\lambda} + \frac{1}{5\lambda} = \frac{77}{60\lambda} =$$

$$\frac{1}{\lambda} \sum_{i=2}^{5} \frac{1}{i}.$$

□

Example 18.5.6. Assume a system represented by a *KooN* system composed of identical components. Also consider the time to failure of each component to be exponentially distributed with rate $\lambda = 10^{-4} f/h$. Figure 18.18.a shows the system reliability for the *Koo5* structure considering $K = \{1,2,3,4,5\}$. Figure 18.18.b depicts the *2ooN* reliability taking into account $N = \{1,2,3,4,5\}$.

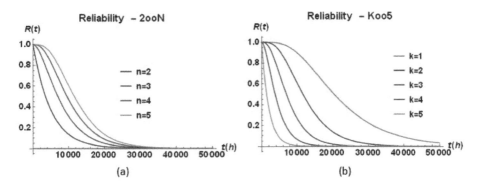

Figure 18.18 *KooN* Structure – Reliability.

Figure 18.19.a and Figure 18.19.b presents the density and the hazard functions for the *Koo5* system. It is important to stress the failure rate function (hazard function) of the *5oo5* configuration. It is constant since it represents a series structure. The *1oo5* configuration denotes the parallel configuration; hence the hazard function representing this structure shows the failure rate curve of the parallel structure.

For the *2oo3* structure, the $MTTF = 8333.33\,h$, the $MedTTF = 6931.47\,h$ ($t \leftarrow F(t) = 0.5$), and the $ModeTTF = 4054.65\,h$ (the time that maximizes the density

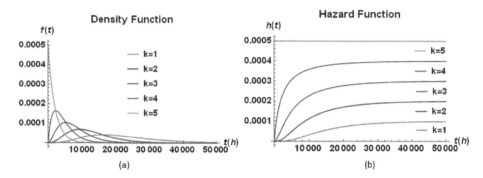

Figure 18.19   *KooN* Structure - Density and Hazard Functions.

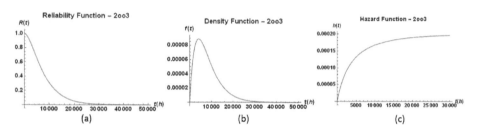

Figure 18.20   2*oo*3 Structure - Reliability (a), Density (b) and Hazard (c) Functions.

function $f(t)$.). The reliability, the density, and the hazard rate curves for the 2*oo*3 structure are shown in Figure 18.20.

□

Bridge

A bridge structure is a non-series-parallel configuration of blocks. In standard RBD, blocks are unidirectional, where the block's left-hand side is its input and the block's right-hand side is its output. The bridge structure, however, has a bidirectional block. Figure 18.21 shows a bridge configuration, represented by source and target nodes (S and T), and the set of blocks $CS = \{b_1, b_2, b_3, b_4, b_5\}$. The blocks b_1, b_2, b_4, and b_5 are unidirectional, but b_3 is bidirectional. The system represented by this bridge is operational if at least the following sets of components are operational: $\{b_1, b_2\}$, $\{b_4, b_5\}$, $\{b_1, b_3, b_5\}$, and $\{b_3, b_4, b_5\}$.

The bridge structure can be decomposed into two standard RBDs by conditioning on block b_3. Therefore, applying 18.3.6, we have

$$\Phi(\mathbf{X}) = x_3 \times \Phi(1_3, \mathbf{X}) + (1 - x_3) \times \Phi(0_3, \mathbf{X}).$$

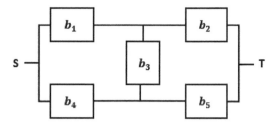

Figure 18.21 Bridge.

$\Phi(1_3, \mathbf{X})$ denotes the system structure function conditioned to when b_3 is operational, whereas $\Phi(0_3, \mathbf{X})$ represents the structure function conditioned to when b_3 has failed. Both cases are represented by the RBDs shown in Figure 18.22.a and Figure 18.22.b, respectively.

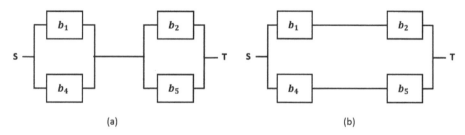

Figure 18.22 Block b_3 Operational (a) - Block b_3 Failed (b).

As $P(\Phi(\mathbf{X}) = 1) = E(\Phi(\mathbf{X}))$, then

$$P(\Phi(\mathbf{X}) = 1) = E(x_3 \times \Phi(1_3, \mathbf{X}) + (1 - x_3) \times \Phi(0_3, \mathbf{X})).$$

As the blocks are independents, we get

$$P(\Phi(\mathbf{X}) = 1) = E(x_3) \times E(\Phi(1_3, \mathbf{X})) + E((1 - x_3)) \times E(\Phi(0_3, \mathbf{X}))).$$

If $E(x_3) = p_3$ and $E(1 - x_3) = 1 - p_3$, then

$$P(\Phi(\mathbf{X}) = 1) = p_3 \times E(\Phi(1_3, \mathbf{X})) + (1 - p_3) \times E(\Phi(0_3, \mathbf{X}))).$$

As $E(\Phi(1_3,\mathbf{X})) = P(\Phi(1_3,\mathbf{X}) = 1)$ and $E(\Phi(0_3,\mathbf{X}))) = P(\Phi(0_3,\mathbf{X}) = 0)$, then

$$P(\Phi(\mathbf{X}) = 1) = p_3 \times P(\Phi(1_3,\mathbf{X}) = 1) + (1-p_3) \times P(\Phi(0_3,\mathbf{X}) = 0). \quad (18.5.42)$$

As

$$P(\Phi(1_3,\mathbf{X}) = 1) = 1 - ((1-p_1) \times (1-p_4))) \times (1 - ((1-p_2) \times (1-p_5))$$

and

$$P(\Phi(1_3,\mathbf{X}) = 0) = 1 - ((1-(p_1\,p_2))\,(1-(p_4\,p_5))),$$

then

$$P(\Phi(\mathbf{X}) = 1) = p_3 \times ((1-(1-p_1) \times (1-p_4)) \times (1-(1-p_2) \times (1-p_5))) \quad (18.5.43)$$

$$+ (1-p_3) \times (1-(1-p_1p_2)(1-p_4\,p_5)).$$

Assuming $p_i = p$ ($i \in \{1,2,3,4,5\}$), we get

$$P(\Phi(\mathbf{X}) = 1) = p^2(p(p-2)(2p-1)+2). \quad (18.5.44)$$

Considering $p = 0.9$, we obtain $P(\Phi(\mathbf{X}) = 1) = 0.97848^3$.

If the time to failure of each block is exponentially distributed with rate λ_i ($i \in \{1,2,3,4,5\}$), the reliability of each block is $R_i(t) = e^{-\lambda_i t}$. Hence, using the Expression 18.5.43, the system reliability is

$$R(t) = -e^{-(\lambda_1+\lambda_2+\lambda_3+\lambda_4+\lambda_5)t}(e^{\lambda_1 t} + e^{\lambda_2 t} + e^{\lambda_3 t} \quad (18.5.45)$$

$$-e^{(\lambda_1+\lambda_2+\lambda_3)t} + e^{\lambda_4 t} - e^{(\lambda_2+\lambda_4)t}+$$

$$e^{\lambda_5 t} - e^{(\lambda_1+\lambda_5)t} - e^{(\lambda_3+\lambda_4+\lambda_5)t} - 2).$$

---

[3] Also see the results obtained in Section 20.4 and in Section 20.5.

The system mean time to failure is

$$MTTF = \frac{1}{\lambda_2 + \lambda_3 + \lambda_4} - \frac{1}{\lambda_1 + \lambda_2 + \lambda_3 + \lambda_4} + \frac{1}{\lambda_1 + \lambda_3 + \lambda_5} \qquad (18.5.46)$$

$$-\frac{1}{\lambda_1 + \lambda_2 + \lambda_3 + \lambda_5} + \frac{1}{\lambda_4 + \lambda_5} - \frac{1}{\lambda_1 + \lambda_2 + \lambda_4 + \lambda_5}$$

$$-\frac{1}{\lambda_1 + \lambda_3 + \lambda_4 + \lambda_5} - \frac{1}{\lambda_2 + \lambda_3 + \lambda_4 + \lambda_5} +$$

$$\frac{2}{\lambda_1 + \lambda_2 + \lambda_3 + \lambda_4 + \lambda_5} + \frac{1}{\lambda_1 + \lambda_2}.$$

If $\lambda_i = \lambda$ ($i \in \{1,2,3,4,5\}$), then

$$R(t) = e^{-\lambda t}\left(1 - \left(1 - e^{-\lambda t}\right)^2\right)^2 + \left(1 - e^{-\lambda t}\right)\left(1 - \left(1 - e^{-2\lambda t}\right)^2\right), \quad (18.5.47)$$

which leads to

$$R(t) = e^{-5\lambda t}\left(e^{\lambda t}\left(2e^{\lambda t}\left(e^{\lambda t} + 1\right) - 5\right) + 2\right). \qquad (18.5.48)$$

$$MTTF = \frac{49}{60\lambda}. \qquad (18.5.49)$$

As $f(t) = -dR(t)/dt$ and $\lambda(t) = f(t)/R(t)$, we get

$$f(t) = 2\lambda e^{-5\lambda t}\left(e^{\lambda t} - 1\right)\left(5e^{\lambda t} + 2e^{2\lambda t} - 5\right). \qquad (18.5.50)$$

and

$$\lambda(t) = 2\lambda\left(\frac{1}{\frac{49e^{\lambda t} - 34}{e^{2\lambda t} - 5e^{\lambda t} + 3} + 2e^{\lambda t} + 12} + 1\right). \qquad (18.5.51)$$

Example 18.5.7. Figure 18.23 shows the reliability, the density, and the hazard function in the interval $[0, 30000\,h]$, when considering the failure rate of each component as $\lambda = 10^{-4}\,f/h$.

The mean time to failure is

$$MTTF = \frac{49}{60\lambda} = 8166.67\,h.$$

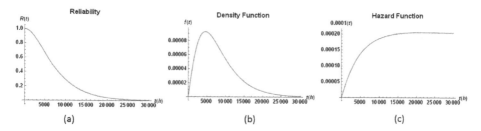

Figure 18.23   Reliability (a) - Density Function (b) - Hazard Function (c) - Bridge Structure.

The median time to failure can be obtained by finding t such that $R(t) = 0.5$. The median time to failure is $MedTTF = 6931.47\,h$, as mode time to failure is the time that maximizes the density function. In this example, $ModeTTF = 4558.75\,h$.

□

If p_i in Expression 18.5.43 is the component $i's$ availability, then the system availability is

$$A = A_3 \times ((1 - ((1 - A_1) \times (1 - A_4))) \times (1 - ((1 - A_2) \times (1 - A_5)))) \quad (18.5.52)$$
$$+ (1 - A_3) \times (1 - ((1 - (A_1 A_2))(1 - (A_4 A_5))))),$$

where $A_i = MTTF_i/(MTTF_i + MTTR_i)$.

If the time to repair and the time to failure of each block are exponentially distributed with rates μ and λ, respectively; then the availability of each block is $A_i = \mu/(\lambda + \mu)$. Hence, system availability is

$$A = \frac{\mu}{\lambda + \mu} \times (1 - (1 - \frac{\mu}{\lambda + \mu})^2)^2 + (1 - \frac{\mu}{\lambda + \mu}) \times (1 - (1 - (\frac{\mu}{\lambda + \mu})^2)^2),$$
$$(18.5.53)$$

which leads to

$$A = \frac{\mu^2 (2\lambda^3 + 8\lambda^2\mu + 5\lambda\mu^2 + \mu^3)}{(\lambda + \mu)^5}. \quad (18.5.54)$$

Example 18.5.8.   Figure 18.24 shows the availability represented in number of nines of the bridge structure with five similar blocks. The time to failure and the time to repair of each block are exponentially distributed with parameters $\lambda = 10^{-4} f/h$ and $\mu \in \{5 \times 10^{-2} r/h, 7.5 \times 10^{-2} r/h, 10^{-1} r/h\}$, respectively.

□

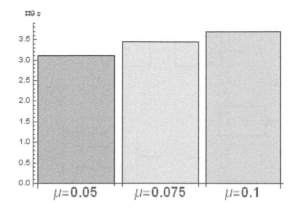

Figure 18.24 Number of Nines.

18.6 SYSTEM REDUNDANCY AND COMPONENT REDUNDANCY

Consider a system S formed by two components, a and b, composed in series (see Figure 18.25.a). Assume the reliability of each component is $R_a(t)$ and $R_b(t)$, respectively. Therefore, the system reliability is $R_S(t) = R_a(t) \times R_b(t)$. We are interested in increasing the system reliability by adopting redundancy. Two alternative solutions are devised, named $S1$ and $S2$. Solution $S1$ (system redundancy) consists of replicating the original system. In this solution a subsystem, S', equivalent to the original one (S), is composed in parallel with S. The system S' is composed of blocks a' and b', which are equivalent to a and b, respectively. Figure 18.25.b shows this composition. The system $S1$ reliability is

$$R_{S1}(t) = 1 - (1 - R_a(t)R_b(t))^2,$$

which leads to

$$R_{S1}(t) = R_a(t)R_b(t)(2 - R_a(t)R_b(t)).$$

Solution $S2$ consists of replicating the component a with a', and the component b with b'. It is worth mentioning that a is equivalent to a', and b is equivalent to b'. Therefore, each component of the original system S is configured in parallel with an equivalent component (component redundancy). Figure 18.25.c shows this composition. The system $S2$ reliability is

$$R_{S2}(t) = \left(1 - (1 - R_a(t))^2\right)\left(1 - (1 - R_b(t))^2\right),$$

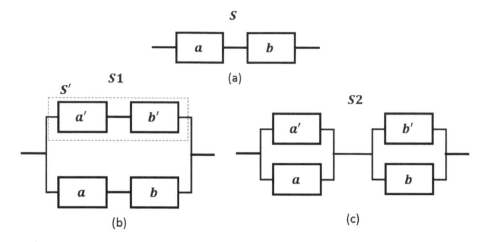

Figure 18.25   System Redundancy and Component Redundancy

which is simplified to

$$R_{S2}(t) = (R_a(t) - 2)R_a(t)(R_b(t) - 2)R_b(t).$$

Let us consider the relation

$$\frac{R_{S2}(t)}{R_{S1}(t)} = \frac{(R_a(t) - 2)R_a(t)(R_b(t) - 2)R_b(t)}{R_a(t)R_b(t)(2 - R_a(t)R_b(t))}.$$

Applying some algebra yields

$$\frac{(R_a(t) - 2)(R_b(t) - 2)}{2 - R_a(t)R_b(t)} = \tag{18.6.1}$$

$$\frac{R_a(t)R_b(t) - 2R_a(t) - 2R_b(t) + 4}{2 - R_a(t)R_b(t)} =$$

$$\frac{R_a(t)R_b(t) - 2(R_a(t) + R_b(t)) + 4}{2 - R_a(t)R_b(t)} =$$

$$\frac{R_a(t) \times R_b(t) - 2 \times (R_a(t) + R_b(t)) + 4 - 2 \times (R_a(t) \times R_b(t)) - 2 + 2 \times R_a(t) \times R_b(t) + 2}{2 - R_a(t) \times R_b(t)} =$$

$$\frac{R_a(t) \times R_b(t) - 2 \times (R_a(t) + R_b(t)) + 4 - 2 \times R_a(t) \times R_b(t) - 2}{2 - R_a(t) \times R_b(t)} + \frac{2 \times R_a(t) \times R_b(t) + 2}{2 - R_a(t) \times R_b(t)} =$$

$$\frac{2 - R_a(t) \times R_b(t) - 2 \times (R_a(t) + R_b(t))}{2 - R_a(t) \times R_b(t)} + \frac{2 \times R_a(t) \times R_b(t) + 2}{2 - R_a(t) \times R_b(t)} =$$

$$\frac{2 - R_a(t) \times R_b(t)}{2 - R_a(t) \times R_b(t)} + \frac{2 \times R_a(t) \times R_b(t) - 2 \times (R_a(t) + R_b(t)) + 2}{2 - R_a(t) \times R_b(t)} =$$

which finally leads to

$$1 + 2 \times \frac{1 - (R_a(t) + R_b(t)) + R_a(t) \times R_a(t)}{2 - R_b(t) \times R_b(t)}.$$

As $R_a(t) \in [0,1]$ and $R_b(t) \in [0,1]$, $\frac{R_{S2}(t)}{R_{S1}(t)} \geq 1$.

Therefore, component redundancy (Figure 18.25.c) is more reliable than system redundancy (Figure 18.25.b) [381].

Example 18.6.1. Assume the times to failure of the components of the systems shown in Figure 18.25 are exponentially distributed with rate $\lambda_1 = \lambda_2 = 10^{-4} f/h$, respectively. The reliability of system S and the respective redundant systems S_1 (system redundancy) and S_2 (component redundancy) are depicted in Figure 18.26. It is worth observing the higher reliability of the component redundant system ($R_{S2}(t)$).

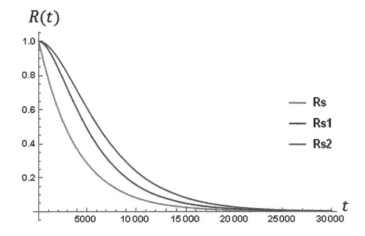

Figure 18.26   System Redundancy and Component Redundancy Reliabilities.

If $R_a(t) = R_b(t)$, Equation 18.6.1 becomes

$$\frac{(R(t) - 2)^2}{2 - R^2(t)}. \tag{18.6.2}$$

If the structures depicted in Figure 18.25.a, Figure 18.25.b, and Figure 18.25.c are respectively extended into an n-component series, a parallel configuration of n-components system-redundant, and a series of n structures of two parallel components, Equation 18.6.2 [381] becomes

$$\frac{(R(t) - 2)^n}{2 - R^n(t)}. \tag{18.6.3}$$

We have seen that component redundancy provides higher reliability than system redundancy. In many practical cases, however, it could be far from simple to implement component redundancy. For instance, consider a computer composed of a motherboard, video controller, network controller, disk controller, disk, and power source. Implementing component redundancy in this system is far from simple. Nevertheless, system-redundancy is straightforwardly implemented by using a second computer.

18.7   COMMON CAUSE FAILURE

A common cause failure (CCF) is the result of events, concurrent with system events and local states, which lead to system failure. A common cause failure can be internal or external to the system and can act simultaneously on significant (if not all) components of a system. Therefore, a common cause fault is a major concern in many critical systems. Some typical common causes failures are external events such as power outages, storms, earthquakes, tsunamis, flooding, hurricanes, and lightning. For example, if a lightning strike hits a server rack, it can destroy all levels of redundancy at once.

The term common mode failure (CMF) is also frequent. CMF refers to coincident failures of the same mode; that is, failures that have an identical effect. On the other hand, CCF implies the failures have the same underlying cause. It is possible for two CMFs not to have a common cause and vice-versa. Since the models studied in this section assess the cause of coincident failure, CCF will be used throughout [401].

Consider a redundant system composed of two subsystems represented by two blocks in parallel (b_1 and b_2) (see Figure 18.27.a). Assume the failure rates of both components are equal and constant, λ. However, if a percentage (p) of failures ($\lambda_{ccf} = p \times \lambda$) affect both subsystems (CCF) and thus defeat the redundancy, it is necessary to add a block (b_3) in series to represent the CCF (see Figure 18.27.b).

Assume $\lambda = 10^{-4} h^1$. The MTTF of the system depicted in Figure 18.27.a is $1500h$ and the system reliability at $t = 10000h$ is $R(10000h) = 0.6004$. If CCF is considered and its rate is equal to $\lambda_{ccf} = 10^{-5} h^1$, the system's MTTF is $13419.91 h$ and $R(10000h) = 0.5433$.

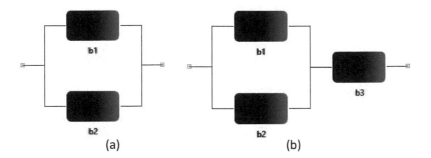

Figure 18.27 Common Cause Failure.

18.8 PATHS AND CUTS

Consider a coherent system represented by an RBD, and its set of components $CS = \{b_i\}$. A **path** P is a set of components (blocks), $P \subseteq CS$, that if operational connects the source node (S) to the target node (T). Otherwise stated, a path set P is a set of components which by functioning ensures the system is functioning.

The vector state $\mathbf{X_P}$ that represents the path P is denoted a path vector. In other words, $\mathbf{X_P}$ is called a path vector if $\Phi(\mathbf{X_P}) = 1$. A path vector is called minimal if $\Phi(\mathbf{Y}) = 0$ for every $\mathbf{Y} < \mathbf{X_P}$. The corresponding set of components P is called a **minimal path** (minpath). In a series system of n components, there is only one minimal path set, and it is composed of every component of the system. On the other hand, in a parallel system with n components, there are n minimal paths, each set formed by only one component.

Assume the RBD depicted in Figure 18.22.a. The set of blocks $B = \{b_1, b_2\}$, represented by its respective vector $\mathbf{X_B} = (1, 1, x_3, x_4, x_5)$, is a path, since if $x_1 = 1$ and $x_2 = 1$, $\Phi(\mathbf{X_B}) = x_1 \, x_2 = 1$.

The set $B' = \{b_1, b_2, b_4\}$, and respective state vector $\mathbf{X_B} = (1, 1, x_3, 1, x_5)$, also leads to $\Phi(\mathbf{X_{B'}}) = 1$; thus B' is also a path. However, B is minimal, whereas B' is not. Observe that $\mathbf{X_B} < \mathbf{X_{B'}}$ and $\Phi(\mathbf{X_B}) = 1$; hence B' is not minimal. However, for every $\mathbf{Y} < \mathbf{X_B}$, $\Phi(\mathbf{Y}) = 0$; thus B is minimal.

The complementary notion of a path is termed a **cut**. A **cut** C is a set of components, $C \subseteq CS$, that if failed does not connect the source node (S) to the target node (T). In other words, a cut C is a set of components of a system which by failing causes the system to fail.

A cut vector X_C is a vector that represents a cut set C; thus $\Phi(\mathbf{X_C}) = 0$. A cut vector is called minimal if $\Phi(\mathbf{Y}) = 1$ for every $\mathbf{Y} > \mathbf{X_C}$. The corresponding set of components C is called a **minimal cut** (mincut). In the series system, there are n minimal cuts, each formed by only one component. The minimal cut set of the parallel system is composed of all the components of the system.

Consider the RBD depicted in Figure 18.22.a. The set of blocks $B = \{b_1, b_4\}$, represented by its respective vector $\mathbf{X_B} = (0, x_2, x_3, 0, x_5)$, is a cut, since $x_1 = 0$, and $x_4 = 0$, $\Phi(\mathbf{X_B}) = 1 - ((1 - x_1)(1 - x_2)) = 0$.

The set $B' = \{b_1, b_2, b_4\}$, represented by the state vector $\mathbf{X_{B'}} = (0, 0, x_3, 0, x_5)$, is also a cut, since $x_1 = 0$, $x_2 = 0$, and $x_4 = 0$ leads to $\Phi(\mathbf{X_{B'}}) = 0$. However, B is minimal, whereas B' is not. Observe that for any $\mathbf{Y} > \mathbf{X_B}$, it does not ensure $\Phi(\mathbf{Y}) = 0$. However, for $\mathbf{Y} = (0, 0, x_3, 1, x_5)$, which is $\mathbf{Y} > \mathbf{X_{B'}}$, $\Phi(\mathbf{Y}) = 0$.

Example 18.8.1. The RBD depicted in Figure 18.1 has three pathes and three cuts. The paths are $P_1 = \{b_1, b_2, b_3\}$, $P_2 = \{b_1, b_2\}$, and $P_3 = \{b_1, b_3\}$. The paths $P_2 = \{b_1, b_2\}$ and $P_3 = \{b_1, b_3\}$ are minimal paths. The cuts are $C_1 = \{b_1, b_2, b_3\}$, $C_1 = \{b_1\}$, and $C_3 = \{b_2, b_3\}$. The cuts $C_1 = \{b_1\}$ and $C_3 = \{b_2, b_3\}$ are minimal cuts.

□

Example 18.8.2. The model shown in Figure 18.17.c is an RBD with replicated components that represents the $2oo3$ structure. The minimal paths are $P_1 = \{b_1, b_2\}$, $P_2 = \{b_1, b_3\}$, and $P_3 = \{b_2, b_3\}$. These sets are also the minimal cuts.

□

Example 18.8.3. The bridge structure depicted in Figure 18.21 has four minimal paths and four minimal cuts. The minimal paths are $P_1 = \{b_1, b_2\}$, $P_2 = \{b_4, b_5\}$, $P_3 = \{b_1, b_3, b_4\}$, and $P_4 = \{b_2, b_3, b_4\}$. The minimal cuts are $C_1 = \{b_1, b_4\}$, $C_2 = \{b_2, b_5\}$, $C_3 = \{b_1, b_3, b_5\}$, and $C_4 = \{b_2, b_3, b_4\}$.

□

Some components in a system may be more critical than others when defining whether the system is in an operational or failed state. For instance, a component in a series system is at least as necessary as any other component. Hence, importance measures of components in the system are useful tools for planning and improving systems dependability.

A **critical path** vector for component i is a state vector $(1_i, \mathbf{X})$ that $\Phi(1_i\mathbf{X}) = 1$ and $\Phi(0_i\mathbf{X}) = 0$. It is worth stressing that the state above is equivalent to $\Phi(1_i\mathbf{X}) - \Phi(0_i\mathbf{X}) = 1$. In other words, given the states of the other components, the system is operational if and only if component i is operational [352]. A critical path set is the set of components that are operational in a critical path vector.

18.9 IMPORTANCE INDICES

Assume a system consists of multiple components. Such a system is often designed, enhanced, or maintained. The system's components are usually not equally important to the system performance[4] (reliability importance, criticality importance, availability importance.). For complex systems, it may be too time-consuming or not

---

[4]The term performance here is considered in its broad sense.

even possible to find an optimal configuration. Measures of importance are valuable means to support resource allocation according to how important each system is to the performance [265, 270, 390]. This section briefly presents the following measures of importance: structural measure, the Birnbaum (reliability) measure (and some variants), risk achievement worth, risk reduction worth, and the criticality importance. These measures are mainly dependent on two factors: the location of the component in the system, and the probability of the component being operational [103, 140, 224, 225].

In the system design, the importance measure may be adopted to identify critical components that should be analyzed to improve the system reliability. The reliability of a component may be enhanced by considering higher quality modules, by adopting redundancy, by reducing the workloads, or by adjusting the maintainability. The component importance measure aims to support designers to spot components that should be enhanced and grade these components in order of their importance. In the operational phase, the component importance may be adopted to support allocating maintenance teams to the most critical subsystems or components. These measures may also be considered to identify parts that should be improved or replaced with higher quality components.

First let introduce the concept of **structural importance** [47, 48]. The structural importance of component i in a system measures the importance of the respective *position* of component i in the system. This importance measure is useful in early design stages, mainly when data on reliability of components are still unavailable.

Consider a system specified by an RBD with a set of n components and the set of all possible states SS ($SS = \{\mathbf{X} | \mathbf{X} = (x_i)_{|n|}\}$). The function $1_i(\mathbf{X})$ is an indicator function that is evaluated as one if the structure function is evaluated as one for a specific state $\mathbf{X}$ and the component i is operational. The function $0_i(\mathbf{X})$ is also an indicator function that is evaluated as one if the structure function is evaluated as one for a specific state $\mathbf{X}$ and the component i failed.

$$1_i : SS \rightarrow \begin{cases} 1 & \text{if} \quad \Phi(x_1, ..., x_{i-1}, 1, x_{i+1}, ..., x_n) = 1, \\ 0 & \text{otherwise;} \end{cases}$$

and

$$0_i : SS \rightarrow \begin{cases} 1 & \text{if} \quad \Phi(x_1, ..., x_{i-1}, 0, x_{i+1}, ..., x_n) = 1, \\ 0 & \text{otherwise.} \end{cases}$$

The vector $(x_1, ..., x_{i-1}, 1, x_{i+1}, ..., x_n)$ is also represented by $(1_i, \mathbf{X})$. Likewise, the vector $(x_1, ..., x_{i-1}, 0, x_{i+1}, ..., x_n)$ is also denoted by $(0_i, \mathbf{X})$ (see the structure function 18.3.6).

The structural importance of a component i is defined by

$$I_i^S = \frac{1}{2^{n-1}} \sum_{\forall j \in SS} (1_i(j) - 0_i(j)), \tag{18.9.1}$$

where $\sum_{\forall j \in SS} 1_i(j)$ is the total number of states that yields the system to operational state $(Phi(x_1, ..., x_{i-1}, 1, x_{i+1}, ..., x_n) = 1)$ given the component i is operational; and $\sum_{\forall j \in SS} 0_i(j)$ is the total number of states that yields the system to an operational state $(\Phi(x_1, ..., x_{i-1}, 0, x_{i+1}, ..., x_n) = 1)$ given the component i failed.

Example 18.9.1. Assume a system represented by the RBD shown in Figure 18.1. Table 18.8 depicts the values of the structure function and of the indicator functions (1_i and 0_i) for each state, and Table 18.9 presents the structural importance for each component. Component b_1 is the most important component, since $I_1^S = 0.75$, and $I_2^S = I_3^S = 0.25$. Figure 18.28 also shows the structural importance of each component.

Table 18.8

Structure Function

j	x_3	x_2	x_1	$\Phi(x_3, x_2, x_1)$	1_1	0_1	1_2	0_2	1_3	0_3
0	0	0	0	0	0	0	0	0	0	0
1	0	0	1	0	0	0	0	0	0	0
2	0	1	0	0	0	0	0	0	0	0
3	0	1	1	1	1	0	1	0	0	1
4	1	0	0	0	0	0	0	0	0	0
5	1	0	1	1	1	0	0	1	1	0
6	1	1	0	0	0	0	0	0	0	0
7	1	1	1	1	1	0	1	0	1	0

Table 18.9

Structural Importance - $n = 3$

Metrics	b_1	b_2	b_3
$\sum 1_i = \sum_{j=0}^{7} 1_i(j)$	3	2	2
$\sum 0_i = \sum_{j=0}^{7} 0_i(j)$	0	1	1
$\sum 1_i - \sum 0_i$	3	1	1
I_i^B	0.75	0.25	0.25

□

The **reliability importance**, also called **Birnbaum importance** (B-Importance) of a component i at time t is defined by the partial derivative of the system reliability

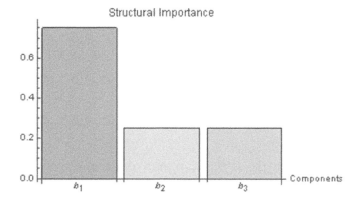

Figure 18.28   Structural Importance.

concerning the component i's reliability.

$$I_i^B(t) = \frac{\partial R_s(t)}{\partial R_i(t)}. \tag{18.9.2}$$

We may omit t whenever the context is clear; that is we may write I_i^B.

Consider the structure function represented by 18.3.6; that is

$$\Phi(\mathbf{X}(t)) = x_i(t) \times \Phi(1_i, \mathbf{X}(t)) + (1 - x_i(t)) \times \Phi(0_i, \mathbf{X}(t)).$$

As

$$R_s(t) = P(\Phi(\mathbf{X}(t)) = 1) = E(\Phi(\mathbf{X}(t))),$$

then

$$R_s(t) = E(x_i(t) \times \Phi(1_i, \mathbf{X}(t)) + (1 - x_i(t)) \times \Phi(0_i, \mathbf{X}(t))).$$

$$R_s(t) = E(x_i(t) \times \Phi(1_i, \mathbf{X}(t))) + E((1 - x_i(t)) \times \Phi(0_i, \mathbf{X}(t))).$$

Assuming the components are independents, we get

$$R_s(t) = E(x_i(t)) \times E(\Phi(1_i, \mathbf{X}(t))) + E((1 - x_i(t))) \times E(\Phi(0_i, \mathbf{X}(t))).$$

$$R_s(t) = R_i(t) \times E(\Phi(1_i, \mathbf{X}(t))) + (1 - R_i(t)) \times E(\Phi(0_i, \mathbf{X}(t))).$$

Let $E(\Phi(1_i, \mathbf{X(t)})) = R_s(1_i, \mathbf{X(t)})$, and $E(\Phi(0_i, \mathbf{X(t)})) = R_s(0_i, \mathbf{X(t)})$, then

$$R_s(t) = R_i(t) \times R_s(1_i, \mathbf{X(t)}) + (1 - R_i(t)) \times R_s(0_i, \mathbf{X(t)}).$$

Therefore

$$R_s(t) = R_i(t) \times R_s(1_i, \mathbf{X(t)}) + R_s(0_i, \mathbf{X(t)}) - R_i(t)) R_s(0_i, \mathbf{X(t)}).$$

$$R_s(t) = R_i(t) (R_s(1_i, \mathbf{X(t)}) - R_s(0_i, \mathbf{X(t)})) + R_s(0_i, \mathbf{X(t)}).$$

As $I_i^B = \partial R_s(t)/\partial R_i(t)$ (see 18.9.2), we have

$$I_i^B = \frac{\partial R_s(t)}{\partial R_i(t)} = R_s(1_i, \mathbf{X(t)}) - R_s(0_i, \mathbf{X(t)}). \qquad (18.9.3)$$

Example 18.9.2. Let us consider a system represented by the RBD depicted in Figure 18.29.a. As these blocks are configured in series, the system reliability is $R_s(t) = R_1(t) \times R_2(t) \times R_3(t)$.

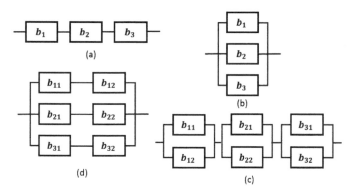

(a) Series Composition, (b) Parallel Composition

(c) Series of Parallel Composition, and (d) Parallel Composition of Series Blocks.

Figure 18.29   Compositions.

The reliability importance of each component is

$$I_1^B = \frac{\partial R_s(t)}{\partial R_1(t)} = \frac{\partial (R_1(t) \times R_2(t) \times R_3(t))}{\partial R_1(t)} = R_2(t) \times R_3(t).$$

$$I_2^B = \frac{\partial R_s(t)}{\partial R_2(t)} = \frac{\partial \left(R_1(t) \times R_2(t) \times R_3(t) \right)}{\partial R_2(t)} = R_1(t) \times R_3(t).$$

$$I_3^B = \frac{\partial R_s(t)}{\partial R_3(t)} = \frac{\partial \left(R_1(t) \times R_2(t) \times R_3(t) \right)}{\partial R_3(t)} = R_1(t) \times R_2(t).$$

The maximal importance (*MBI*) is obtained by

$$MBI = \max_{i \in \{1,2,3\}} \{I_i^B\}.$$

Assume the reliability of blocks b_1, b_2 and b_3 at a specific time t is $R_1(t) = 0.95$, $R_2(t) = 0.93$, and $R_3(t) = 0.9$, respectively. Therefore, the reliability importance of each component is $I_1^B = 0.837$, $I_2^B = 0.855$, and $I_3^B = 0.8835$ (see Figure 18.30). Therefore, in series configurations, the less reliable component is the one that is most important with respect to the reliability importance. This finding confirms the intuition, since in series structures, the system is likely to fail when one component (probably the least reliable component) fails. A series system is as strong as its weakest component.

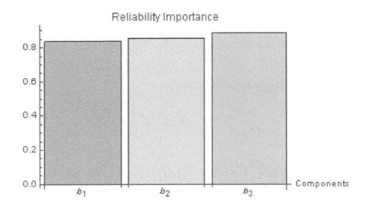

Figure 18.30 Reliability Importance - Series Structure.

The reliability importance may also be presented in relation to the most reliable component (**normalized reliability importance**) [260, 263, 264, 390]. This measure is obtained by normalizing the components' importance with the maximal importance, that is

$$NI_i^B = \frac{I_i^B}{MBI}, \tag{18.9.4}$$

where $MBI = \max_{\forall i} \{I_i^B\}$.

Considering the series composition of this example, the normalized Birnbaum importance of each component is $NI_1^B = 0.947368$, $NI_2^B = 0.967742$, and $NI_3^B = 1$ (see Figure 18.31), respectively.

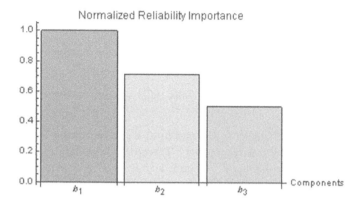

Figure 18.31   Normalized Reliability Importance - Parallel Structure.

□

Example 18.9.3. The RBD depicted in Figure 18.29.b is composed of three blocks in parallel. The system reliability is $R_s(t) = 1 - ((1 - R_1(t)) \times (1 - R_2(t)) \times (1 - R_3(t)))$.

The reliability importance of each component is

$$I_1^B = \frac{\partial R_s(t)}{\partial R_1(t)} = (1 - R_2(t))(1 - R_3(t)).$$

$$I_2^B = \frac{\partial R_s(t)}{\partial R_2(t)} = (1 - R_1(t))(1 - R_3(t)).$$

$$I_3^B = \frac{\partial R_s(t)}{\partial R_3(t)} = (1 - R_1(t))(1 - R_3(t)).$$

Considering the reliability of blocks b_1, b_2 and b_3 at t is $R_1(t) = 0.95$, $R_2(t) = 0.93$, and $R_3(t) = 0.9$, respectively, the reliability importance of each component is $I_1^B = 0.007$, $I_2^B = 0.005$, and $I_3^B = 0.0035$. Hence, in parallel structures, the most reliable component is the one that is most important with respect to the reliability importance. This result confirms the intuition, since in parallel structures, the system will only fail when all components fail, that is when even the most reliable component fails. A parallel system is as weak as its strongest component.

Considering the series composition of this example, the normalized Birnbaum importance of each component is $NI_1^B = 1$, $NI_2^B = 0.714286$, and $NI_3^B = 0.5$, respectively.

$\square$

Example 18.9.4. The RBD depicted in Figure 18.29.c is a series composition of two-blocks parallel structures. The system is composed of six blocks, $\{b_{11}, b_{12}, b_{21}, b_{22}, b_{31}, b_{32}\}$. The system reliability is

$$R_s(t) = \prod_{j=1}^{3}(1 - ((1 - R_{j1}(t)) \times (1 - R_{j2}(t)))).$$

The reliability importance of each component is

$$I_{11}^B = \frac{\partial R_s(t)}{\partial R_{11}(t)} = (1 - R_{12}(t))(1 - (1 - R_{21}(t))(1 - R_{22}(t)))(1 - (1 - R_{31}(t))(1 - R_{32}(t))).$$

$$I_{12}^B = \frac{\partial R_s(t)}{\partial R_{12}(t)} = 1 - R_{11}(t))(1 - (1 - R_{21}(t))(1 - R_{22}(t)))(1 - (1 - R_{31}(t))(1 - R_{32}(t))).$$

$$I_{21}^B = \frac{\partial R_s(t)}{\partial R_{22}(t)} = (1 - (1 - R_{11}(t))(1 - R_{12}(t)))(1 - R_{22}(t))(1 - (1 - R_{31}(t))(1 - R_{32}(t))).$$

$$I_{22}^B = \frac{\partial R_s(t)}{\partial R_{22}(t)} = (1 - (1 - R_{11}(t))(1 - R_{12}(t)))(1 - R_{21}(t))(1 - (1 - R_{31}(t))(1 - R_{32}(t))).$$

$$I_{31}^B = \frac{\partial R_s(t)}{\partial R_{31}(t)} = (1 - (1 - R_{11}(t))(1 - R_{12}(t)))(1 - (1 - R_{21}(t))(1 - R_{22}(t)))(1 - R_{32}(t)).$$

$$I_{32}^B = \frac{\partial R_s(t)}{\partial R_{32}(t)} = (1 - (1 - R_{11}(t))(1 - R_{12}(t)))(1 - (1 - R_{21}(t))(1 - R_{22}(t)))(1 - R_{31}(t)).$$

Considering the reliability of blocks at a specific time t is $R_{11}(t) = 0.95$, $R_{12}(t) = 0.94$, $R_{21}(t) = 0.93$, $R_{22}(t) = 0.92$, $R_{31}(t) = 0.9$, and $R_{32}(t) = 0.89$, respectively; therefore, the reliability importance of each component is $I_{11}^B = 0.0590077$, $I_{12}^B = $

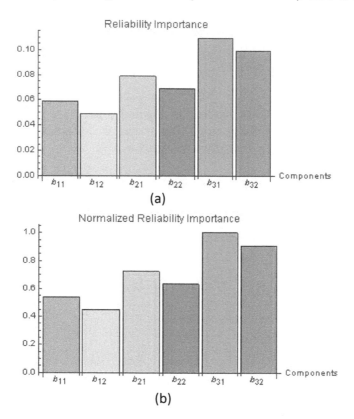

(a)

(b)

Figure 18.32 Reliability Importance - Series Composition of Parallel Structures.

0.0491731, $I_{21}^B = 0.0788826$, $I_{22}^B = 0.0690223$, $I_{31}^B = 0.109056$, and $I_{32}^B = 0.0991417$ (see Figure 18.32.a). The maximal reliability importance $MBI = 0.109056$.

The normalized reliability measures are $NI_{11}^B = 0.541078$, $NI_{12}^B = 0.450898$, $NI_{21}^B = 0.723323$, $NI_{22}^B = 0.632908$, $NI_{31}^B = 1$, and $NI_{32}^B = 0.909091$ (see Figure 18.32.b). These results shows that the most important block is the one with highest reliability that belongs to the parallel structure that has the smallest reliability, since it is a series composition of two-blocks-parallel structures.

□

Example 18.9.5. The RBD depicted in Figure 18.29.c is a parallel composition of two-blocks series structures. The system is composed of six blocks, $\{b_{11}, b_{12}, b_{21}, b_{22}, b_{31}, b_{32}\}$. The system reliability is

$$R_s(t) = 1 - ((1 - R_{11}(t)R_{12}(t)) \times (1 - R_{21}(t)R_{22}(t)) \times (1 - R_{31}(t)R_{32}(t))).$$

The reliability importance of each component is

$$I_{11}^B = \frac{\partial R_s(t)}{\partial R_{11}(t)} = R_{12}(t)(1 - R_{21}(t)R_{22}(t))(1 - R_{31}(t)R_{32}(t)).$$

$$I_{12}^B = \frac{\partial R_s(t)}{\partial R_{12}(t)} = R_{11}(t)(1 - R_{21}(t)R_{22}(t))(1 - R_{31}(t)R_{32}(t)).$$

$$I_{21}^B = \frac{\partial R_s(t)}{\partial R_{22}(t)} = R_{22}(t)(1 - R_{11}(t)R_{12}(t))(1 - R_{31}(t)R_{32}(t)).$$

$$I_{22}^B = \frac{\partial R_s(t)}{\partial R_{22}(t)} = R_{21}(t)(1 - R_{11}(t)R_{12}(t))(1 - R_{31}(t)R_{32}(t)).$$

$$I_{31}^B = \frac{\partial R_s(t)}{\partial R_{31}(t)} = R_{32}(t)(1 - R_{11}(t)R_{12}(t))(1 - R_{21}(t)R_{22}(t)).$$

$$I_{32}^B = \frac{\partial R_s(t)}{\partial R_{32}(t)} = R_{31}(t)(1 - R_{11}(t)R_{12}(t))(1 - R_{21}(t)R_{22}(t)).$$

Considering the reliability of blocks at a specific time t is $R_{11}(t) = 0.95$, $R_{12}(t) = 0.94$, $R_{21}(t) = 0.93$, $R_{22}(t) = 0.92$, $R_{31}(t) = 0.9$, and $R_{32}(t) = 0.89$, respectively; therefore, the reliability importance of each component is $I_{11}^B = 0.0270115$, $I_{12}^B = 0.0272988$, $I_{21}^B = 0.0195896$, $I_{22}^B = 0.0198025$, $I_{31}^B = 0.0137512$, and $I_{32}^B = 0.0139057$ (see Figure 18.33.a). The maximal reliability importance $MBI = 0.0272988$.

The normalized reliability measures are $NI_{11}^B = 0.989474$, $NI_{12}^B = 1$, $NI_{21}^B = 0.717597$, $NI_{22}^B = 0.725397$, $NI_{31}^B = 0.503729$, and $NI_{32}^B = 0.509389$ (see Figure 18.33.b). These results shows that the most important block is the one with smallest reliability that belongs to the series structure that has the highest reliability, since it is a parallel composition of two-block series structures.

□

The Birnbaum importance may also represent the **availability importance** of components in a system [36, 71, 140, 163]. In such cases, we have a partial derivative of the system availability concerning the component i's availability. Transient and steady-state availability may be considered.

$$I_i^A = \frac{\partial A_s}{\partial A_i}. \tag{18.9.5}$$

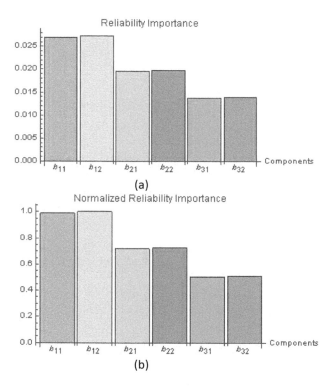

Figure 18.33 Reliability Importance - Parallel Composition of Series Structures.

The maximal availability importance (MAI) is obtained by

$$MAI = \max_{i \in \{1,2,3\}} \{I_i^A\}.$$

The availability importance may also be presented in relation to the most available component (**normalized availability importance**). This measure is obtained by normalizing the components' importance with the maximal availability importance, that is

$$NI_i^A = \frac{I_i^A}{MAI}, \qquad (18.9.6)$$

Example 18.9.6. Assume a computational system composed of a hardware server (hw), an operational system (os), and three application programs (a_1, a_2, and a_3).

The application program a_2 is composed of two modules, a_{21} and a_{22}. This system is operational if application programs a_1, and a_2 or a_3 are operational. The operational mode may be represented by the logical function

$$\Psi(hw, os, a_1, a_{21}, a_{22}, a_3) = hw \wedge os \wedge a_1 \wedge ((a_{21} \wedge a_{22}) \vee a_3).$$

The RBD shown in Figure 18.34 represents this system.

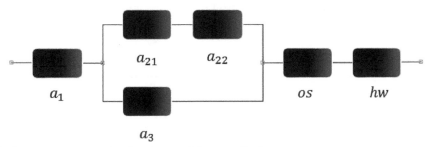

Hardware server, operational system, and three application programs.

Figure 18.34   Computational System.

Consider the time to failure of each component is exponentially distributed. The system reliability is

$$R_s(t) = e^{-(\lambda_{hw} + \lambda_{os} + \lambda_{a1})t} \left(1 - \left(1 - e^{-\lambda_{a3}t}\right)\left(1 - e^{-(\lambda_{a21} + \lambda_{a22})t}\right)\right).$$

The reliability importance of each component is

$$I_{hw}^{B} = \left(e^{t(\lambda_{a21} + \lambda_{a22})} + e^{t\lambda_{a3}} - 1\right)e^{-t(\lambda_{a1} + \lambda_{a21} + \lambda_{a22} + \lambda_{a3} + \lambda_{os})}.$$

$$I_{os}^{B} = \left(e^{t(\lambda_{a21} + \lambda_{a22})} + e^{t\lambda_{a3}} - 1\right)e^{-t(\lambda_{a1} + \lambda_{a21} + \lambda_{a22} + \lambda_{a3} + \lambda_{hw})}.$$

$$I_{a1}^{B} = \left(e^{t(\lambda_{a21} + \lambda_{a22})} + e^{t\lambda_{a3}} - 1\right)e^{-t(\lambda_{a21} + \lambda_{a22} + \lambda_{a3} + \lambda_{hw} + \lambda_{os})}.$$

$$I_{a21}^{B} = \left(e^{t\lambda_{a3}} - 1\right)e^{-t(\lambda_{a1} + \lambda_{a22} + \lambda_{a3} + \lambda_{hw} + \lambda_{os})}.$$

$$I^B_{a22} = \left(e^{t\lambda_{a3}} - 1 \right) e^{-t(\lambda_{a1}+\lambda_{a21}+\lambda_{a3}+\lambda_{hw}+\lambda_{os})}.$$

$$I^B_{a3} = \left(e^{t(\lambda_{a21}+\lambda_{a22})} - 1 \right) e^{-t(\lambda_{a1}+\lambda_{a21}+\lambda_{a22}+\lambda_{hw}+\lambda_{os})}.$$

Assuming the respective mean times are presented in Table 18.10, the reliability importance of each component can be calculated. Figure 18.35 shows the reliability importance of each component considering for $t \in (0\ 2500\,h)$. It is worth noting the reliability importance of component a_{21} and a_{22} are very close in the range $t \in (0\ 2500\,h)$.

Table 18.10
Mean Time to Failure and Mean Time to Repair

Component	$MTTF(h)$	$MTTR(h)$
hw	27000	24
os	2000	4
a_1	1500	0.5
a_{21}	1800	0.5
a_{22}	1400	0.5
a_3	1600	0.5

□

Example 18.9.7. Considering the system shown in the previous examples, and assuming the time to failure and the time to repair of each component are exponentially distributed, the system availability is

$$A_s = \frac{\mu_{a1}\mu_{hw}\mu_{os} \left(1 - \left(1 - \frac{\mu_{a3}}{\lambda_{a3}+\mu_{a3}} \right) \left(1 - \frac{\mu_{a21}\mu_{a22}}{(\lambda_{a21}+\mu_{a21})(\lambda_{a22}+\mu_{a22})} \right) \right)}{(\lambda_{a1}+\mu_{a1})(\lambda_{hw}+\mu_{hw})(\lambda_{os}+\mu_{os})}.$$

The availability importances of each component are

$$I^A_{hw} = \frac{\mu_{a1}\mu_{os} \left(\mu_{a21}\mu_{a22}\lambda_{a3} + \mu_{a3}(\lambda_{a21}+\mu_{a21})(\lambda_{a22}+\mu_{a22}) \right)}{(\lambda_{a1}+\mu_{a1})(\lambda_{a21}+\mu_{a21})(\lambda_{a22}+\mu_{a22})(\lambda_{a3}+\mu_{a3})(\lambda_{os}+\mu_{os})},$$

$$I^A_{os} = \frac{\mu_{a1}\mu_{hw} \left(\mu_{a21}\mu_{a22}\lambda_{a3} + \mu_{a3}(\lambda_{a21}+\mu_{a21})(\lambda_{a22}+\mu_{a22}) \right)}{(\lambda_{a1}+\mu_{a1})(\lambda_{a21}+\mu_{a21})(\lambda_{a22}+\mu_{a22})(\lambda_{a3}+\mu_{a3})(\lambda_{hw}+\mu_{hw})},$$

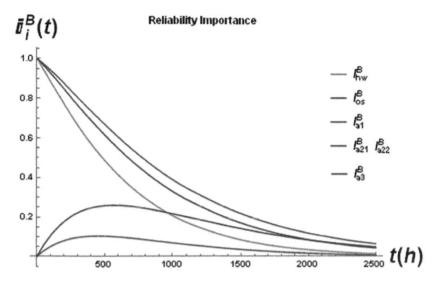

Figure 18.35 Reliability Importance for $t \in (0, 2500\,h)$.

$$I_{a1}^A = \frac{\mu_{hw}\mu_{os}\left(\mu_{a21}\mu_{a22}\lambda_{a3} + \mu_{a3}\left(\lambda_{a21} + \mu_{a21}\right)\left(\lambda_{a22} + \mu_{a22}\right)\right)}{\left(\lambda_{a21} + \mu_{a21}\right)\left(\lambda_{a22} + \mu_{a22}\right)\left(\lambda_{a3} + \mu_{a3}\right)\left(\lambda_{hw} + \mu_{hw}\right)\left(\lambda_{os} + \mu_{os}\right)},$$

$$I_{a21}^A = \frac{\mu_{a1}\mu_{a22}\lambda_{a3}\mu_{hw}\mu_{os}}{\left(\lambda_{a1} + \mu_{a1}\right)\left(\lambda_{a22} + \mu_{a22}\right)\left(\lambda_{a3} + \mu_{a3}\right)\left(\lambda_{hw} + \mu_{hw}\right)\left(\lambda_{os} + \mu_{os}\right)},$$

$$I_{a22}^A = \frac{\mu_{a1}\mu_{a21}\lambda_{a3}\mu_{hw}\mu_{os}}{\left(\lambda_{a1} + \mu_{a1}\right)\left(\lambda_{a21} + \mu_{a21}\right)\left(\lambda_{a3} + \mu_{a3}\right)\left(\lambda_{hw} + \mu_{hw}\right)\left(\lambda_{os} + \mu_{os}\right)},$$

and

$$I_{a3}^A = \frac{\mu_{a1}\mu_{hw}\mu_{os}\left(\mu_{a21}\lambda_{a22} + \lambda_{a21}\left(\lambda_{a22} + \mu_{a22}\right)\right)}{\left(\lambda_{a1} + \mu_{a1}\right)\left(\lambda_{a21} + \mu_{a21}\right)\left(\lambda_{a22} + \mu_{a22}\right)\left(\lambda_{hw} + \mu_{hw}\right)\left(\lambda_{os} + \mu_{os}\right)}.$$

Considering the respective mean times to failure and mean time to repair of each component are presented in Table 18.10, the availability importance of each component is shown in Figure 18.36.

$\square$

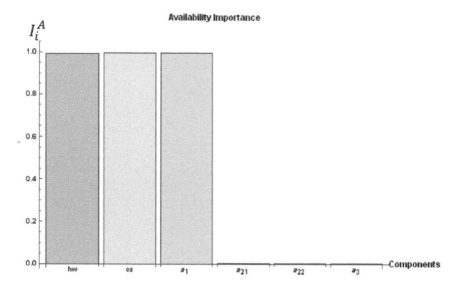

Figure 18.36 Availability Importance.

The normalized reliability importance of a component can be weighed by the relative cost of that component in a system - **Reliability-Cost Importance**. Such weights allow the analyst to ponder not only the reliability importance of a component to the system's reliability but also the financial aspect when designing a system [140]. This measure is obtained by

$$NI_i^{CB} = NI_i^B \times (1 - \frac{c_i}{c_{sys}}),$$ (18.9.7)

where c_i is the cost of component i and $c_{sys} = \sum_{\forall i} c_i$ is the system cost.

Similarly, the normalized availability importance of a component can be weighed by the relative cost of that component in a system - **Availability-Cost Importance**. This measure may be represented by

$$NI_i^{CA} = NI_i^A \times (1 - \frac{c_i}{c_{sys}}).$$ (18.9.8)

Example 18.9.8. Consider the acquisition cost of each component of the system shown in Figure 18.34 is presented in Table 18.11. The system total cost is $c_{sys} = \sum_{i=\{hw,os,a1,a21,a22,a3\}} c_i = \$ 3880.00$.

Table 18.11

Components' Costs

Component	Cost ($)
hw	2000.00
os	300.00
a_1	600.00
a_{21}	300.00
a_{22}	280.00
a_3	400.00

The reliability importance at $t = 800 h$ and the respective reliability importance weighed by the respective component's costs are shown in Figure 18.37.a and Figure 18.37.b, respectively. Observe that the reliability of importance of hw at $t = 800 h$ is higher than a_3's, but when the cost is considered, these components change their relative positions.

□

Assume a system composed of n components. In some cases, we may be interested in measuring how much the system reliability is affected by making changes in a parameter p_i. The system **reliability sensitivity** can measured by

$$S_{p_i}^R = \frac{\partial R(t)}{\partial p_i}. \tag{18.9.9}$$

Example 18.9.9. Considering the system depicted in Figure 18.34, the reliability sensitivity with respect to the parameters λ_{hw}, λ_{os}, λ_{a1}, λ_{a21}, λ_{a22}, and λ_{a3} are shown in the following.

$$S_{\lambda_{hw}}^R = \left(e^{t(\lambda_{a21}+\lambda_{a22})} + e^{t\lambda_{a3}} - 1 \right) e^{-t(\lambda_{a1}+\lambda_{a21}+\lambda_{a22}+\lambda_{a3}+\lambda_{os})},$$

$$S_{\lambda_{os}}^R = \left(e^{t(\lambda_{a21}+\lambda_{a22})} + e^{t\lambda_{a3}} - 1 \right) e^{-t(\lambda_{a1}+\lambda_{a21}+\lambda_{a22}+\lambda_{a3}+\lambda_{hw})},$$

$$S_{\lambda_{a1}}^R = \left(e^{t(\lambda_{a21}+\lambda_{a22})} + e^{t\lambda_{a3}} - 1 \right) e^{-t(\lambda_{a21}+\lambda_{a22}+\lambda_{a3}+\lambda_{hw}+\lambda_{os})},$$

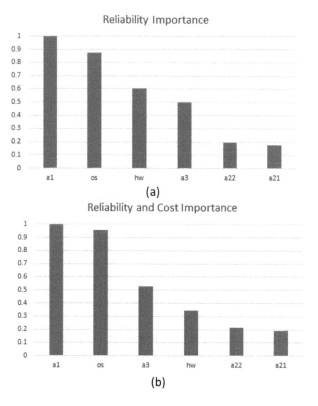

Figure 18.37 Reliability and Reliability-Cost Importances.

$$S^R_{\lambda_{a21}} = \left(e^{t\lambda_{a3}} - 1\right) e^{-t(\lambda_{a1}+\lambda_{a22}+\lambda_{a3}+\lambda_{hw}+\lambda_{os})},$$

$$S^R_{\lambda_{a22}} = \left(e^{t\lambda_{a3}} - 1\right) e^{-t(\lambda_{a1}+\lambda_{a21}+\lambda_{a3}+\lambda_{hw}+\lambda_{os})},$$

and

$$S^R_{\lambda_{a3}} = \left(e^{t(\lambda_{a21}+\lambda_{a22})} - 1\right) e^{-t(\lambda_{a1}+\lambda_{a21}+\lambda_{a22}+\lambda_{hw}+\lambda_{os})}.$$

Assuming the respective mean times are presented in Table 18.10, the reliability sensitivity of each parameter is shown in Figure 18.38, considering $t \in (0\ 2500\,h)$.

The reliability sensitivity of each parameter at $t = 600\,h$ is shown in Table 18.12.

□

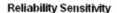

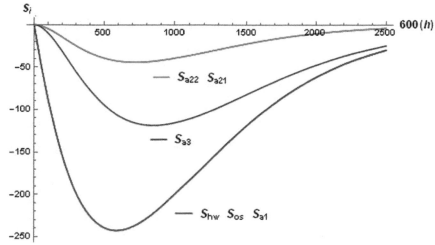

Parameters: λ_{hw}, λ_{os}, λ_{a1}, λ_{a21}, λ_{a22}, and λ_{a3} for $t \in (0, 2500\,h)$.

Figure 18.38 Reliability Sensitivity Analysis.

Table 18.12
Reliability Sensitivity at $t = 600\,h$

Parameter	$\partial R(t)/\partial \lambda_i$
λ_{hw}	-242.813
λ_{os}	-242.813
λ_{a1}	-242.813
λ_{a21}	-42.5349
λ_{a22}	-42.5349
λ_{a3}	-106.793

Now, lets us analyze how system availability is affected by changes in a parameter p_i. The system **availability sensitivity** can measured by

$$S_{p_i}^A = \frac{\partial A}{\partial p_i}. \tag{18.9.10}$$

Example 18.9.10. Considering the system depicted in Figure 18.34, the availability sensitivity with respect to the parameters λ_{hw}, μ_{hw}, λ_{os}, μ_{os}, λ_{a1}, μ_{a1}, λ_{a21}, μ_{a21}, λ_{a22}, μ_{a22}, λ_{a3}, and μ_{a3} are shown in the following.

$$\frac{\partial A}{\partial \lambda_{hw}} = -\frac{\mu_{a1}\mu_{hw}\mu_{os}\left(\mu_{a21}\mu_{a22}\lambda_{a3} + \mu_{a3}\left(\lambda_{a21} + \mu_{a21}\right)\left(\lambda_{a22} + \mu_{a22}\right)\right)}{\left(\lambda_{a1} + \mu_{a1}\right)\left(\lambda_{a21} + \mu_{a21}\right)\left(\lambda_{a22} + \mu_{a22}\right)\left(\lambda_{a3} + \mu_{a3}\right)\left(\lambda_{hw} + \mu_{hw}\right)^2\left(\lambda_{os} + \mu_{os}\right)},$$

$$\frac{\partial A}{\partial \mu_{hw}} = \frac{\mu_{a1}\lambda_{hw}\mu_{os}\left(\mu_{a21}\mu_{a22}\lambda_{a3} + \mu_{a3}\left(\lambda_{a21} + \mu_{a21}\right)\left(\lambda_{a22} + \mu_{a22}\right)\right)}{\left(\lambda_{a1} + \mu_{a1}\right)\left(\lambda_{a21} + \mu_{a21}\right)\left(\lambda_{a22} + \mu_{a22}\right)\left(\lambda_{a3} + \mu_{a3}\right)\left(\lambda_{hw} + \mu_{hw}\right)^2\left(\lambda_{os} + \mu_{os}\right)},$$

$$\frac{\partial A}{\partial \lambda_{os}} = -\frac{\mu_{a1}\mu_{hw}\mu_{os}\left(\mu_{a21}\mu_{a22}\lambda_{a3} + \mu_{a3}\left(\lambda_{a21} + \mu_{a21}\right)\left(\lambda_{a22} + \mu_{a22}\right)\right)}{\left(\lambda_{a1} + \mu_{a1}\right)\left(\lambda_{a21} + \mu_{a21}\right)\left(\lambda_{a22} + \mu_{a22}\right)\left(\lambda_{a3} + \mu_{a3}\right)\left(\lambda_{hw} + \mu_{hw}\right)\left(\lambda_{os} + \mu_{os}\right)^2},$$

$$\frac{\partial A}{\partial \mu_{os}} = \frac{\mu_{a1}\mu_{hw}\lambda_{os}\left(\mu_{a21}\mu_{a22}\lambda_{a3} + \mu_{a3}\left(\lambda_{a21} + \mu_{a21}\right)\left(\lambda_{a22} + \mu_{a22}\right)\right)}{\left(\lambda_{a1} + \mu_{a1}\right)\left(\lambda_{a21} + \mu_{a21}\right)\left(\lambda_{a22} + \mu_{a22}\right)\left(\lambda_{a3} + \mu_{a3}\right)\left(\lambda_{hw} + \mu_{hw}\right)\left(\lambda_{os} + \mu_{os}\right)^2},$$

$$\frac{\partial A}{\partial \lambda_{a1}} = -\frac{\mu_{a1}\mu_{hw}\mu_{os}\left(\mu_{a21}\mu_{a22}\lambda_{a3} + \mu_{a3}\left(\lambda_{a21} + \mu_{a21}\right)\left(\lambda_{a22} + \mu_{a22}\right)\right)}{\left(\lambda_{a1} + \mu_{a1}\right)^2\left(\lambda_{a21} + \mu_{a21}\right)\left(\lambda_{a22} + \mu_{a22}\right)\left(\lambda_{a3} + \mu_{a3}\right)\left(\lambda_{hw} + \mu_{hw}\right)\left(\lambda_{os} + \mu_{os}\right)},$$

$$\frac{\partial A}{\partial \mu_{a1}} = \frac{\lambda_{a1}\mu_{hw}\mu_{os}\left(\mu_{a21}\mu_{a22}\lambda_{a3} + \mu_{a3}\left(\lambda_{a21} + \mu_{a21}\right)\left(\lambda_{a22} + \mu_{a22}\right)\right)}{\left(\lambda_{a1} + \mu_{a1}\right)^2\left(\lambda_{a21} + \mu_{a21}\right)\left(\lambda_{a22} + \mu_{a22}\right)\left(\lambda_{a3} + \mu_{a3}\right)\left(\lambda_{hw} + \mu_{hw}\right)\left(\lambda_{os} + \mu_{os}\right)},$$

$$\frac{\partial A}{\partial \lambda_{a21}} = -\frac{\mu_{a1}\mu_{a21}\mu_{a22}\lambda_{a3}\mu_{hw}\mu_{os}}{\left(\lambda_{a1} + \mu_{a1}\right)\left(\lambda_{a21} + \mu_{a21}\right)^2\left(\lambda_{a22} + \mu_{a22}\right)\left(\lambda_{a3} + \mu_{a3}\right)\left(\lambda_{hw} + \mu_{hw}\right)\left(\lambda_{os} + \mu_{os}\right)},$$

$$\frac{\partial A}{\partial \mu_{a21}} = \frac{\mu_{a1}\lambda_{a21}\mu_{a22}\lambda_{a3}\mu_{hw}\mu_{os}}{\left(\lambda_{a1} + \mu_{a1}\right)\left(\lambda_{a21} + \mu_{a21}\right)^2\left(\lambda_{a22} + \mu_{a22}\right)\left(\lambda_{a3} + \mu_{a3}\right)\left(\lambda_{hw} + \mu_{hw}\right)\left(\lambda_{os} + \mu_{os}\right)},$$

$$\frac{\partial A}{\partial \lambda_{a22}} = -\frac{\mu_{a1}\mu_{a21}\mu_{a22}\lambda_{a3}\mu_{hw}\mu_{os}}{\left(\lambda_{a1} + \mu_{a1}\right)\left(\lambda_{a21} + \mu_{a21}\right)\left(\lambda_{a22} + \mu_{a22}\right)^2\left(\lambda_{a3} + \mu_{a3}\right)\left(\lambda_{hw} + \mu_{hw}\right)\left(\lambda_{os} + \mu_{os}\right)},$$

$$\frac{\partial A}{\partial \mu_{a22}} = \frac{\mu_{a1}\mu_{a21}\lambda_{a22}\lambda_{a3}\mu_{hw}\mu_{os}}{\left(\lambda_{a1} + \mu_{a1}\right)\left(\lambda_{a21} + \mu_{a21}\right)\left(\lambda_{a22} + \mu_{a22}\right)^2\left(\lambda_{a3} + \mu_{a3}\right)\left(\lambda_{hw} + \mu_{hw}\right)\left(\lambda_{os} + \mu_{os}\right)},$$

$$\frac{\partial A}{\partial \lambda_{a3}} = -\frac{\mu_{a1}\mu_{a3}\mu_{hw}\mu_{os}\left(\mu_{a21}\lambda_{a22} + \lambda_{a21}\left(\lambda_{a22} + \mu_{a22}\right)\right)}{\left(\lambda_{a1} + \mu_{a1}\right)\left(\lambda_{a21} + \mu_{a21}\right)\left(\lambda_{a22} + \mu_{a22}\right)\left(\lambda_{a3} + \mu_{a3}\right)^2\left(\lambda_{hw} + \mu_{hw}\right)\left(\lambda_{os} + \mu_{os}\right)},$$

and

$$\frac{\partial A}{\partial \mu_{a3}} = \frac{\mu_{a1} \lambda_{a3} \mu_{hw} \mu_{os} (\mu_{a21} \lambda_{a22} + \lambda_{a21} (\lambda_{a22} + \mu_{a22}))}{(\lambda_{a1} + \mu_{a1})(\lambda_{a21} + \mu_{a21})(\lambda_{a22} + \mu_{a22})(\lambda_{a3} + \mu_{a3})^2 (\lambda_{hw} + \mu_{hw})(\lambda_{os} + \mu_{os})},$$

Assuming the respective MTTFs and MTTRs are presented in Table 18.10, the availability sensitivity of each parameter is shown in Table 18.13. The parameters are presented in order of significance. It is worth mentioning that a positive number implies a positive impact on the availability. On the other hand, negative numbers depict the opposite relation.

Table 18.13
Availability Sensitivity

Parameter p_i	$\partial A / \partial p_i$	Component
λ_{hw}	-19.8378	hw
λ_{os}	-7.90935	os
λ_{a1}	-3.95993	a_1
μ_{os}	3.16374×10^{-2}	os
μ_{hw}	1.46947×10^{-2}	hw
λ_{a3}	-1.28233×10^{-2}	a_3
μ_{a1}	1.05598×10^{-2}	a_1
λ_{a22}	-7.38624×10^{-3}	a_{22}
λ_{a21}	-4.92924×10^{-3}	a_{21}
μ_{a3}	3.20581×10^{-5}	a_3
μ_{a22}	1.58277×10^{-5}	a_{22}
μ_{a21}	5.47693×10^{-6}	a_{21}

□

Consider a system composed of n components with reliability $R(t)$ at time t. We may be interested in quantifying the reliability improvement if a component i is replaced by a perfect component, that is $R_i(t) = 1$. The difference $R(1_i, \mathbf{X}(t)) - R(\mathbf{X}(t))$ is defined as the **Improvement Potential** (IP) with respect to component i, and it is denoted by IP_i [352].

$$IP_i = R(1_i, \mathbf{X}(t)) - R(\mathbf{X}(t)) \qquad (18.9.11)$$

As $I_i^B = \partial R_s(t) \, \partial R_i(t)$ (see Equation 18.9.2), it can also be represented by the slope of Figure 18.39, since

$$\frac{\partial R_s(t)}{\partial R_t} = \frac{R_s(1_i, \mathbf{X(t)}) - R_s(\mathbf{X(t)})}{1 - R_i(t)}.$$

Hence

$$I_i^B(t) = \frac{R_s(1_i, \mathbf{X(t)}) - R_s(\mathbf{X(t)})}{1 - R_i(t)}.$$

$$IP_i(t) = I_i^B(t) \times (1 - R_i(t)). \tag{18.9.12}$$

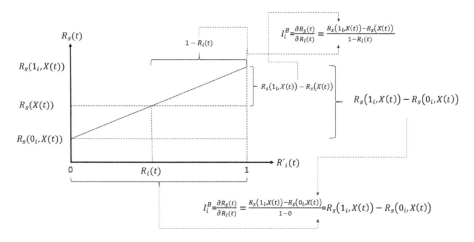

Figure 18.39   Reliability Importance - Slope.

In practice, it is not possible to improve the reliability of component i to 1. Therefore, let us consider it is possible to improve the component i's reliability from $R_i(t)$ to $R_i'(t)$. The **Credible Improvement Potential** (CIP) of component i at time t is defined by

$$CIP_i(t) = R(R_i'(t), \mathbf{X(t)}) - R(\mathbf{X(t)}), \tag{18.9.13}$$

where $R(R_i'(t), \mathbf{X(t)})$ denotes the system reliability if the component i's reliability at t is $R_i'(t)$. It is worth noting that these indexes may also be normalized.

Example 18.9.11. Let us consider the system depicted in Figure 18.34. The system reliability at $t = 800\,h$ is $R(800\,h) = 0.28594$. The improvement potential of each component at $t = 800\,h$ is shown in column IP_i of Table 18.15. Assuming the maximal reliability each component can achieve is shown in Table 18.14, the credible improvement potential of each component is presented in Column CIP_i of Table 18.15.

Table 18.14
Maximal Reliability

Component	$R'_i(800\,h)$
hw	0.99
os	0.9
a_1	0.9
a_{21}	0.9
a_{22}	0.9
a_3	0.9

Table 18.15
Reliability Improvements and Credible Reliability Improvements

Component	$R(1_i, \mathbf{X}(800\,h))$	$R(R'_i(800\,h), \mathbf{X}(800\,h))$	IP_i	CIP_i
hw	0.29454	0.29159	0.00860	0.00565
os	0.42657	0.38391	0.14063	0.09797
a_1	0.48741	0.43867	0.20147	0.15273
a_{21}	0.31638	0.30789	0.03044	0.02195
a_{22}	0.32786	0.31823	0.04192	0.03229
a_3	0.38176	0.35741	0.09582	0.07147

Figure 18.40 also presents the reliability improvements (a) and credible reliability improvements (b) of each component at $t = 800\,h$.

□

Risk Achievement Worth (RAW) is an importance measure that quantifies the ratio of the system unreliability given the component i has failed (or is not present) with

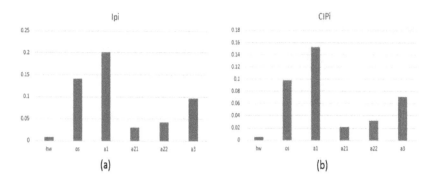

Figure 18.40   Reliability Improvements and Credible Reliability Improvements.

the actual system unreliability [352]. The RAW presents a measure that indicates the importance of maintaining the current level of reliability for the component.

$$I_i^{RAW}(t) = \frac{1 - R_s(0_i, \mathbf{X(t)})}{1 - R_s(t)},$$ (18.9.14)

where $R_s(t)$ is the system reliability at t, and $R_s(0_i, \mathbf{X(t)})$ is the system reliability given component i has failed (or is not present). It is worth mentioning that the RAW importance measure has also been adapted to consider steady-state availability [352].

Example 18.9.12.   Consider the system depicted in Figure 18.34. The system reliability at $t = 800h$ is $R(800h) = 0.28594$. The RAW importance measure of each component at $t = 800h$ is shown in column I_i^{RAW} of Table 18.16.

Table 18.16
Risk Achievement Worth - I_i^{RAW}

Component	$R(0_i, \mathbf{X}(800h))$	I_i^{RAW}
hw	0	1.40045
os	0	1.40045
a_1	0	1.40045
a_{21}	0.23155	1.07617
a_{22}	0.23155	1.07617
a_3	0.38176	0.86581

□

The **Risk Reduction Worth** (RRW) importance is the ratio of the actual system unreliability with the system unreliability given component i is replaced by a perfect component $(R_i(t) = 1)$ [352].

$$I_i^{RRW}(t) = \frac{1 - R_s(t)}{1 - R_s(1_i, \mathbf{X(t)})}, \qquad (18.9.15)$$

where $R_s(t)$ is the system reliability at t, and $R_s(1_i, \mathbf{X(t)})$ is the system reliability given component i is perfect.

Example 18.9.13. Consider the system depicted in Figure 18.34. The system reliability at $t = 800h$ is $R(800h) = 0.28594$. The RRW importance measure of each component at $t = 800h$ is shown in column I_i^{RRW} of Table 18.17.

Table 18.17
Risk Reduction Worth - I_i^{RRW}

Component	$R(1_i, \mathbf{X}(800h))$	I_i^{RRW}
hw	0.29453	1.01219
os	0.42657	1.24525
a_1	0.48741	1.39305
a_{21}	0.31638	1.04452
a_{22}	0.32786	1.06237
a_3	0.38176	1.15499

□

There are two definitions of **criticality importance** of components. One definition considers the system success and the second is specified in terms of the system failure. At this point it is worth reminding that a component is critical if a given state $\mathbf{X}$ is $\Phi(1_i \mathbf{X}) = 1$ and $\Phi(0_i \mathbf{X}) = 0$ (see Section 18.8), and that it is equivalent to

$$\Phi(1_i \mathbf{X}) - \Phi(0_i \mathbf{X}) = 1.$$

The criticality importance of a component i may be defined as the probability of that component being critical to the system operation (success) and the component i is operational, given the system is operational. Therefore, the criticality importance for success is

$$I_i^{CS} = \frac{R_s(1_i \mathbf{X(t)}) - R_s(0_i \mathbf{X(t)}) R_i(t)}{R_s(\mathbf{X(t)})}. \qquad (18.9.16)$$

Hence

$$I_i^{CS} = I_i^B \frac{R_i(t)}{R_s(\mathbf{X}(\mathbf{t}))}.$$
(18.9.17)

The criticality importance of component i in terms of success quantifies the probability that a component i is working and it is the one that supports the system operational state given the system is operational. Thus, the higher this index, the higher is the chance of the component i being the one the contributes to the system operational state [224].

The criticality importance may also be defined in terms of failure. This definition quantifies the probability that component i has failed and is the one that contributes to the system failure given the system has failed [224].

$$I_i^{CF} = \frac{UR_s(1_i\mathbf{X}(\mathbf{t})) - UR_s(0_i\mathbf{X}(\mathbf{t}))UR_i(t)}{UR_s(\mathbf{X}(\mathbf{t}))}.$$
(18.9.18)

Thus

$$I_i^{CF} = I_i^B \frac{UR_i(t)}{UR_s(\mathbf{X}(\mathbf{t}))}.$$
(18.9.19)

Example 18.9.14. Consider the system depicted in Figure 18.34. The system reliability at $t = 800\,h$ is $R(800\,h) = 0.28594$. The system reliabilities at $t = 800\,h$ when each component is operational are shown in column $R_s(1_i\mathbf{X}(\mathbf{t}))$ of Table 18.18. Likewise, the system reliability at $t = 800\,h$ when each component has failed are depicted in column $R_s(0_i\mathbf{X}(\mathbf{t}))$. The component reliabilities at $t = 800\,h$ are presented in column $R_i(t)$.

Table 18.18
Criticality Importance - I_i^{CS} and I_i^{CF}

Component	$R(1_i, \mathbf{X}(800\,h))$	$R(0_i, \mathbf{X}(800\,h))$	$Ri(800\,h)$	I_i^{CS}	I_i^{CF}
hw	0.29454	0	0.97081	1	0.01204
os	0.42657	0	0.67032	1	0.19695
a_1	0.48741	0	0.58665	1	0.28215
a_{21}	0.31638	0.23155	0.64118	0.19021	0.04263
a_{22}	0.32786	0.23155	0.56472	0.19021	0.05871
a_3	0.38176	0.38176	0.60653	0	0

The success and failure criticality importances of each component at $t = 800\,h$ are shown in column I_i^{CS} and column I_i^{CF}, respectively.

□

There are many other importance measures in the literature. For more detailed information on the subject, the reader is referred to [224, 225, 352].

EXERCISES

Exercise 1. What are the advantages and drawbacks of the state-based and combinatorial models?

Exercise 2. Why is it essential to define the operational mode when modeling a system?

Exercise 3. Given the logical function of a system $\Psi(s_1, s_2, s_3, s_4, s_5, s_6) = (s_1 \wedge s_2 \wedge s_3) \wedge ((s_4 \wedge s_5) \vee s_6)$, obtain the respective structure function.

Exercise 4. Describe the following concepts: (a) irrelevant component, and (b) coherent system.

Exercise 5. Considering a RAID 50 with ten disks, each with time to failure exponentially distributed with rate $\lambda = 5 \times 10^{-5}$, calculate (a) the reliability at $t = 8000\,h$ and (b) $MTTF$.

Exercise 6. Assuming a RAID 60 with twelve disks, each with time to failure exponentially distributed with rate $\lambda = 5 \times 10^{-5}$, obtain (a) the reliability at $t = 8000\,h$ and (b) $MTTF$.

Exercise 8. Considering a RAID 10 with eight disks, each with time to failure exponentially distributed with rate $\lambda = 5 \times 10^{-5}$, calculate (a) the reliability at $t = 8000\,h$ and (b) $MTTF$.

Exercise 9. Assuming a RAID 51 with ten disks, each with time to failure exponentially distributed with rate $\lambda = 5 \times 10^{-5}$, compute (a) the reliability at $t = 8000\,h$ and (b) $MTTF$.

Exercise 10. Consider a system in which software applications read, write, and modify the content of the storage device D_1(source). The system periodically replicates the production data (generated by the software application) of one storage device (D_1) in the storage system. The storage system is composed of three storage devices (D_2, D_3, D_4), arranged in a TMR configuration. Such a control is performed by the storage system controller (C) - see Figure 18.41.

The system is considered to have failed if the hardware infrastructure does not allow the software applications to read, write, or modify data on D_1, and if no safe data replica is available; that is two out of three data replicas are safely stored on the storage system. Consider that the constant failure rates are $\lambda_s = 2 \times 10^{-5}\,f/h$, $\lambda_C = 10^{-5}$, $\lambda_{D1} = 8 \times 10^{-5}$, and $\lambda_{D2} = \lambda_{D3} = \lambda_{D4} = 9 \times 10^{-5}$, respectively.

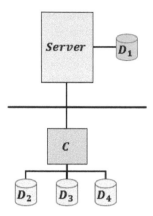

Figure 18.41 Data Consistent System.

a) Identify the operational mode and write down the logical function.

b) Write down the structure function.

c) Design the respective RBD.

d) Write down the expression for the $R(t)$.

e) Write down the expression for the MTTF.

f) Draw the reliability curve in the interval $(0, 1460h)$.

Exercise 11. Consider a two-component parallel-redundant system with distinct constant failure rates λ_1 and λ_2, respectively. Upon failure of a component, a repair process is invoked with the respective constant repair rates μ_1 and μ_2. Assume that a failure of a component, while another is being repaired, causes a system failure.

a) Derive the reliability and the MTTF of the system.

b) Derive the steady-state availability of the system and the downtime.

Exercise 12. For a database-server system composed of two servers (S1 and S2) operating in hot-standby sparing, a storage system (SS) and its controller (C), consider the system fails if SS or C or both servers fail. SS is RAID 5 storage composed of 6 disks (D) of 2 TB. Assume that the constant failure rates are $\lambda_{S1} = \lambda_{S2} = 0.00002\, f/h$, $\lambda_D = 0.00001\, f/h$, $\lambda_C = 0.00008\, f/h$.

a) Identify the failure mode and write down the respective logical function.

b) Write down the structure function.

c) Design the respective RBD.

d) Calculate the reliability at $1000\,h$.

e) What is the system MTTF?

f) Draw the reliability curve in the interval $(0, 2000h)$

Exercise 13. Consider a computer system composed of two servers (server sub-system: $S1$ and $S2$) operating in hot-standby sparing configuration, a storage sub-system (D1 and D2) configured in RAID 1, and controller (C) – see Figure 18.42. The system fails if the server sub-system or storage sub-system or C fails. Consider that the failure rates are $\lambda_{S1} = 1.14155 \times 10^{-4}h^{-1}$, $\lambda_{S2} = 7.61035 \times 10^{-5}h^{-1}$, $\lambda_c = 5.70776 \times 10^{-5}h^{-1}$, $\lambda_{D1} = \lambda_{D2} = 8 \times 10^{-5}h^{-1}$. The respective times to repair are exponentially distributed with rates $\mu_{S1} = \mu_{S2} = 20.833 \times 10^3\,h^{-1}$, $\mu_{D1} = \mu_{D2} = 10.417 \times 10^3\,h^{-1}$, and $\mu_{D2} = 41.667 \times 10^3\,h^{-1}$.

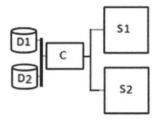

Figure 18.42   Data Consistent System.

a) Identify the operational mode and write down the respective logical function.

b) Propose an RBD model of the server sub-system and compute its availability.

c) Conceive an availability model of the whole system.

d) Compute the steady-state availability of the system.

e) Calculate the respective system's downtime in minutes per year.

f) Conceive a reliability model of the whole system.

g) Compute system's MTTF.

h) Draw the reliability curve in the interval $(0, 1460h)$.

Exercise 14. Considering a RAID 51 with ten disks, if the disk failure rate and disk controller failure rate are $\lambda_D = 8 \times 10^{-5}\,f/h$ and $\lambda_C = 5.70776 \times 10^{-5}\,f/h$, respectively, what is the system reliability at $2000h$?

Exercise 15. Consider a tiny-private cloud system (see Figure 18.43) composed of a cloud manager (*CM*), three servers (S_1, S_2, S_3), and a network attached storage (*NAS*), which is composed of an NAS controller (*NC*) and six disks configured in RAID 5. Each computer hardware is composed of a motherboard (*MB*), memory (*M*), a network controller (*NC*), a video controller (*VC*), an internal disk (*HD*), its disk controller (*HDC*), and the power source (*PS*). The cloud manager is operational if its hardware is operational as well as its operational system (*OS*) and the cloud manager software (*CMS*). Each server is operational if its hardware (*HW*) is operational, and its operational system (*OS*), the virtual machine manager (*HP* - hypervisor), and at least one virtual machine (*VM*) are functional. Each server provides four VMs. The tiny-private cloud system is operational if at least one virtual machine is operational. Assume the time-to-failures and the time-to-repairs are exponentially distributed. The MTTFs, the MTTRs, and the MTTS are depicted in Table 18.19. Calculate

a) the availability and the yearly downtime of the system,

b) the system reliability at $t = 720\,h$,

c) the system time to failure, and

d) the system time to recover.

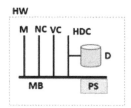

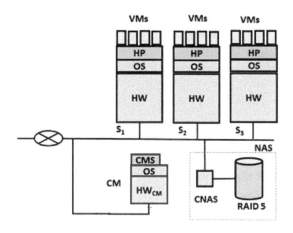

Figure 18.43 Tiny Cloud System.

Exercise 16. Assume the constant failure rates of the web-services 1, 2, 3, and 4 of a software system are $\lambda_1 = 10^{-5}\,f/h$, $\lambda_2 = 2 \times 10^{-5}\,f/h$, $\lambda_3 = 3 \times 10^{-5}\,f/h$, and $\lambda_4 = 4 \times 10^{-5}\,f/h$, respectively. The software system cannot work when any web service is down.

Table 18.19

Tiny Cloud System Parameters

/ Component	$MTTF(h)$	$MTTR(h)$
$Motherboard(MB)$	80000	
$Memory(M)$	40000	
$NetworkController(NC)$	60000	
$VideoController(VC)$	50000	
$HardDiskController(HDC)$	45000	
$HardDisk(HD)$	35000	
$PowerSource(PS)$	20000	
$OperationalSystem(OS)$	4000	1
$Hypervisor(HP)$	5000	1
$VirtualMachines(VMs)$	4000	0.1
$NASController(NASC)$	50000	4
$HardDisk(RAID)$	35000	4
$CloudManagerSoftware(CMS)$	3000	2
$HWServer(HW)$		24
$CloudManager(CM)$		8

a) Calculate the software system failure rate.

b) Compute the software system MTTF.

c) Obtain the reliability at $730\,h$.

Assuming the repair time of each web-service is exponentially distributed with $MTTR = 2\,h$

a) Calculate the steady-state web-service system downtime.

b) Obtain the yearly downtime in minutes.

Exercise 17. Consider the web-service system of Exercise 16. If this system provides a proper service, the web-service 1 or 3 are functional and the web-service 2 or 4 are operational.

a) Compute the web-service system MTTF.

b) Calculate the web-service system reliability at $730\,h$.

c) Obtain the steady-state availability.

d) Find the yearly downtime in minutes.

Exercise 18. Find the minimal cuts and paths of RBD of Exercise 17.

Exercise 19. Find the minimal cuts and paths of RBD of Exercise 15.

Exercise 20. Calculate the structural importance of the system represented by the RBD of the Figure 18.41.

Exercise 21. Obtain the reliability importance (Birnbaum importance) of the tiny cloud system shown in Exercise 15.

Exercise 22. Calculate (a) the reliability importance (Birnbaum importance) and (b) availability importance of the tiny cloud system shown in Exercise 15.

Exercise 23. Compute the reliability sensitivity with respect to the system parameters of the tiny cloud system shown in Exercise 15.

Exercise 24. Consider the system shown in Figure 18.43. Calculate the following importance measures for each component of the system: (a) IP, (b) CIP, (c) RAW, (d) RRC, (e) I^{CS}, and (f) I^{CF}. Compare them and comment.

19 Fault Tree

This chapter introduces the Fault Tree (FT) model. FT and RBD are the most widely used combinatorial models for reliability and availability evaluation. As mentioned in the previous chapter, combinatorial models suppose the system components are statistically independent and have a low modeling power concerning state-space models but with higher analytic tractability.

Fault Tree Analysis (FTA) was initially developed in 1962 at Bell Laboratories by H. A. Watson to evaluate the Minuteman I Intercontinental Ballistic Missile Launch Control System. Afterward, in 1962, Boeing and AVCO expanded the use of FTA to the entire Minuteman II [129]. The operation of a system can be considered from two distinct perspectives. We can specify the correct behavior, or we can enumerate the system failures [449]. Differently from RBDs, FT is a failure-oriented model, and as in RBDs, it was initially proposed for calculating reliability. Nevertheless, FT has also been extensively applied to evaluate other dependability metrics.

It is interesting to note that specific evident points in success-oriented models concur with certain analogous points in failure-oriented models. Thus, for instance, maximum success in RBDs can be thought of as the corresponding minimum failure in FTs. Although our first inclination might be to choose the optimistic view of our success-oriented model, this may not be the most advantageous one. Although hypothetically, the number of conditions in which a system can fail and the number of conditions a system can successfully operate are both unlimited, from a practical point of view, there are usually more ways to specify the system operation than the system failures. Thus, from a practical perspective, the set of events representing a system failure is usually smaller than the set of events representing the successful system operation.

The Fault Tree is a graphical model that depicts logical relations between components' faults that result in a system failure.

19.1 COMPONENTS OF A FAULT TREE

In FT, the system may be represented by a logical function that is evaluated as true whenever at least one minimal cut is evaluated as true. The system state may also be characterized by a structure-function, which is the opposite of the RBDs. If the system has more than system failure, a logical function (or a structure-function) should be specified for representing each failure mode. In other words, one function should be defined for representing the combination of events that cause each system failure.

The most common FT elements are the TOP event, AND, OR, and *KooN* gates, and basic events. Many extensions have been proposed; some of them adopt XOR, transfer, and priority gates (see Table 19.1). This chapter, however, does not cover these extensions.

Table 19.1

Fault Tree - Components

Description	Graphical Notation
TOP Event	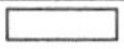
Basic events	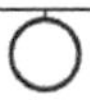
Repeated basic event.	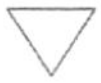
AND gate	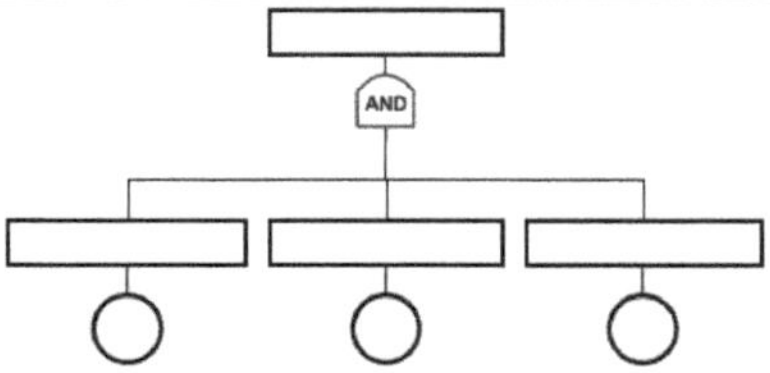
OR gate	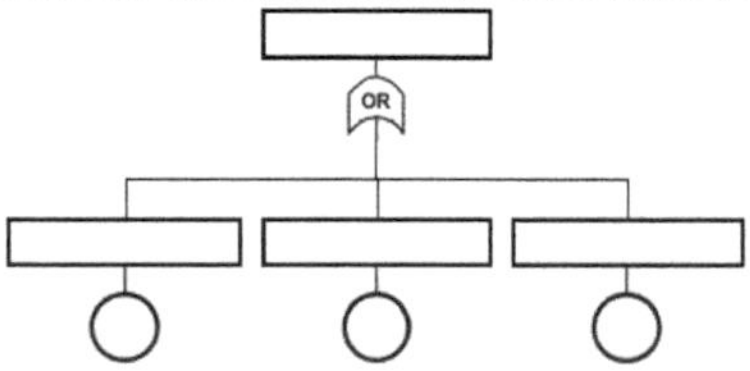
KooN gate	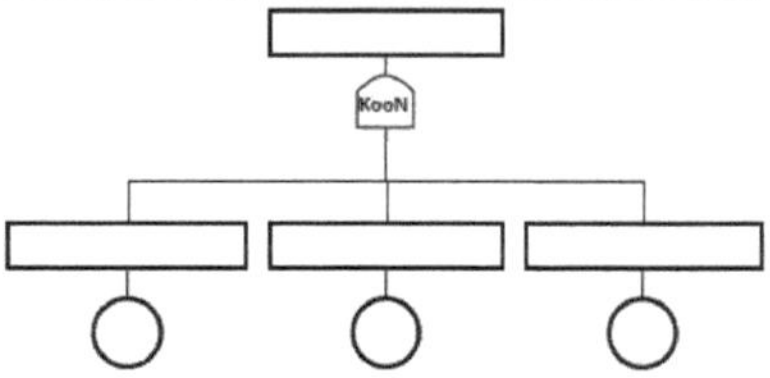
KooN gate (identical events)	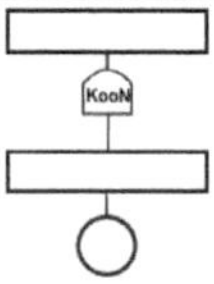
Comment rectangle	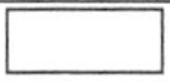

Assume a computational system S comprises two larger subsystems, a hardware subsystem (HS) and a software subsystem (SS). The hardware subsystem is composed of three subsystems: a motherboard component (MB), a power subsystem (PS), and a memory subsystem (MS). The power subsystem is composed of two hot-standby power sources (PS_1 and PS_2). The memory subsystem is composed of three memory banks (M_1, M_2, and M_3). The software subsystem has two components, the operating system (OS) and one application program (AP). The basic components are specified in the set $CS = \{PS_1, PS_2, M_1, M_2, M_3, MB, OS, AP\}$. This system is shown in Figure 19.1.

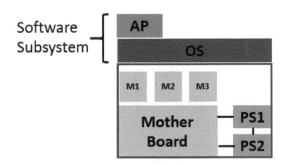

Figure 19.1   Computational System.

As in Section 18.3, the state of each basic component i may be represented by the logical variables s_i. The complement of s_i, that is $\overline{s_i}$, denotes the component i failure. Let us specify the state of the system basic components by logical variables denoted by the components' abbreviation PS_1, PS_1, M_1, M_2, M_3, MB, OS, and AP. Therefore, $\overline{PS_1}$, $\overline{PS_2}$, $\overline{M_1}$, $\overline{M_2}$, $\overline{M_3}$, $\overline{MB}$, $\overline{OS}$, and $\overline{AP}$ represent each component failure.

The TOP event of an FT is usually placed at the top of the diagram, whereas the gates, conditions, and basic event are introduced below. Figure 19.2 shows an FT that represents the system depicted in Figure 19.1. This FT has four gates and eight basic events. A system failure occurs if the power source system, the memory subsystem, the motherboard, or the software subsystem fails. The power system fails if both power sources fail, whereas the memory subsystem fails if the three memory banks fail. The software subsystem fails if the operating system fails, or the application program fails, or both.

The TOP event, that is, the system failure, is represented by the logical function

$$\overline{\Psi(\mathbf{B})} = (\overline{PS_1} \wedge \overline{PS_2}) \vee (\overline{M_1} \wedge \overline{M_2} \wedge \overline{M_3}) \vee \overline{MB} \vee (\overline{OS} \vee \overline{AP}),$$

where $\mathbf{B} = (PS_1, PS_2, M_1, M_2, M_3, MB, OS, AP)$ (see Equation 20.2.1).

If the system has more than one functionality (operation), logical functions should be specified for each functionality (**failure mode**). Hence, the failed system for a particular operation does not mean it also is failed for another functionality.

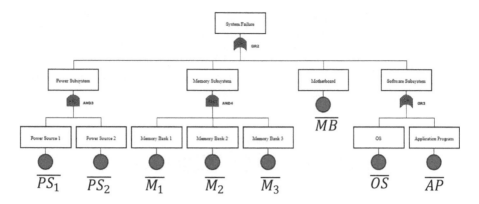

Figure 19.2 Fault Tree - Computational System.

The system state may also be specified by the structure function of its components. The structure function is evaluated to zero whenever at least a minimal number of components fails (see Definition 18.3.3). The structure function is specified in terms of structure variables. A structure variable i is evaluated to zero when a component i failed (see Definition 18.2.1). Let us define the structure variables x_{ps1}, x_{ps2}, x_{m1}, x_{m2}, x_{m3}, x_{mb}, x_{os}, and x_{ap} for representing the states of the components of the system shown in Figure 19.1. The structure function can be obtained from the logical function, since

$$\overline{\Psi(\mathbf{B})} = (\overline{PS_1} \wedge \overline{PS_2}) \vee (\overline{M_1} \wedge \overline{M_2} \wedge \overline{M_3}) \vee \overline{MB} \vee (\overline{OS} \wedge \overline{AP}).$$

$$\overline{\overline{\Psi(\mathbf{B})}} = \overline{(\overline{PS_1} \wedge \overline{PS_2}) \vee (\overline{M_1} \wedge \overline{M_2} \wedge \overline{M_3}) \vee \overline{MB} \vee (\overline{OS} \wedge \overline{AP})}$$

$$\Psi(\mathbf{B}) = \overline{(\overline{PS_1} \wedge \overline{PS_2})} \wedge \overline{(\overline{M_1} \wedge \overline{M_2} \wedge \overline{M_3})} \wedge \overline{MB} \wedge \overline{(\overline{OS} \wedge \overline{AP})}.$$

Applying the transformation rules depicted in Table 18.3, we obtain

$$\Phi(\mathbf{X}) = (1 - (1 - x_{ps1}) \times (1 - x_{ps2})) \times (1 - (1 - x_{m1}) \times (1 - x_{m2}) \times$$
$$(1 - x_{m3})) \times x_{mb} \times x_{os} \times x_{ap}.$$

If the expected value of x_i is the component i reliability, $E(x_i) = R_i(t)$, the system reliability is $R_S(t) = E(\Phi(\mathbf{X}))$; then

$$R_S(t) = E((1 - (1 - x_{ps1}) \times (1 - x_{ps2})) \times (1 - (1 - x_{m1}) \times$$
$$(1 - x_{m2}) \times (1 - x_{m3})) \times x_{mb} \times x_{os} \times x_{ap}).$$

Therefore

$$R_S(t) = (1 - (1 - E(x_{ps1})) \times (1 - E(x_{ps2}))) \times (1 - (1 - E(x_{m1})) \times (1 - E(x_{m2}))$$
$$\times (1 - E(x_{m3}))) \times E(x_{mb}) \times E(x_{os}) \times E(x_{ap}).$$

$$R(t) = (1 - (1 - R_{ps1}(t)) \times (1 - R_{ps2}(t))) \times (1 - (1 - R_{m1}(t)) \times (1 - R_{m2}(t))$$
$$\times (1 - R_{m3}(t))) \times R_{mb}(t) \times R_{os}(t) \times R_{ap}(t).$$

Example 19.1.1. Assume the time to failure of each basic component of the system depicted in Figure 19.1 is exponentially distributed with the respective rates $\lambda_{ps1} = \lambda_{ps2} = 6.67 \times 10^{-5} f/h$, $\lambda_{m1} = \lambda_{m2} = \lambda_{m3} = 3.33 \times 10^{-5} f/h$, $\lambda_{mb} = 2.5 \times 10^{-5} f/h$, $\lambda_{os} = 2.5 \times 10^{-4} f/h$, and $\lambda_{ap} = 5 \times 10^{-4} f/h$.

The system reliability is

$$R(t) = (1 - (1 - e^{-\lambda_{ps1} t}) \times (1 - e^{-\lambda_{ps2} t})) \times (1 - (1 - e^{-\lambda_{m1} t}) \times (1 - e^{-\lambda_{m2} t})$$
$$\times (1 - e^{-\lambda_{m3} t})) \times e^{-\lambda_{mb} t} \times e^{-\lambda_{os} t} \times e^{-\lambda_{ap} t}.$$

$MTTF = \int_0^\infty R(t)\, dt = 1274.88\, h$ and the reliability curve is shown in Figure 19.3.

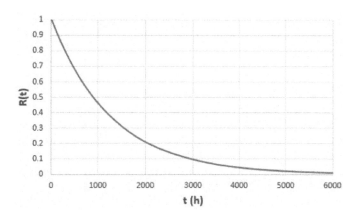

Figure 19.3 $R(t) \times t$.

Example 19.1.2. Let us consider the system studied in the previous example. Assume the components' times to repair are $MTTR_{ps1} = MTTR_{ps2} = 20\,h$, $MTTR_{m1} = MTTR_{m2} = MTTR_{m3} = 30\,h$, $MTTR_{mb} = 40\,h$, $MTTR_{os} = 4\,h$, and $MTTR_{ap} = 2\,h$; then the system availability may be estimated

$$A = (1 - (1 - A_{ps1}) \times (1 - A_{ps2})) \times (1 - (1 - A_{m1}) \times (1 - A_{m2})$$
$$\times (1 - A_{m3})) \times A_{mb} \times A_{os} \times A_{ap},$$

where $A_i = MTTF_i / (MTTF_i + MTTR_i)$, $i \in \{ps1, ps2, m1, m2m, m3, mb, os, ap\}$.

The steady-state system availability is $A = 0.997$, and the yearly downtime is $DT = 26.26\,h$.

$\square$

19.2   BASIC COMPOSITIONS

This section introduces the basic compositions used when representing a system through an FT. These basic compositions are referred to as the basic gates considered in the model, that is, *AND*, *OR*, and *KooN* gates.

OR Gate

Assume a system is composed of a hardware server, an operating system, and a program application (see Figure 19.4.a). If either component fails, the system fails. Hence, the system can be represented by the fault tree shown in Figure 19.4.c, since failure occurs if a basic event, that is $\overline{HW}$, $\overline{OS}$, or $\overline{AP}$, occurs. The RBD depicted in Figure 19.4.b also represents the system since the system is operational as long as the three components (*HW*, *OS*, and *AP*) are functional, and a series block diagram represents such a behavior.

Let us obtain the reliability from the logical function. Consider the name of each component is also adopted to represent the logical variables. Hence, let us define the Boolean vector as $B = (HW, OS, AP)$. Therefore,

$$\overline{\Psi(\mathbf{B})} = \overline{HW} \vee \overline{OS} \vee \overline{AP}.$$

If we negate both sides of the above expression, we get

$$\Psi(\mathbf{B}) = \overline{\overline{HW} \vee \overline{OS} \vee \overline{AP}};$$

then

$$\Psi(\mathbf{B}) = \overline{\overline{HW}} \wedge \overline{\overline{OS}} \wedge \overline{\overline{AP}}.$$
$$\Psi(\mathbf{B}) = HW \wedge OS \wedge AP.$$

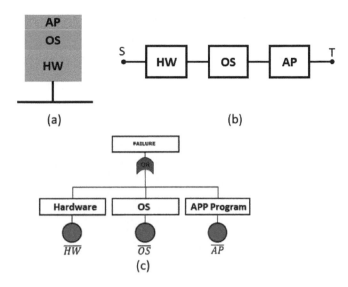

Figure 19.4 *OR* Gate.

The respective structure-function is obtained by applying the transformations rules shown in Table 18.3. Hence

$$\Phi(\mathbf{X}) = x_{hw} \times x_{os} \times x_{ap},$$

where $\mathbf{X} = (x_{hw}, x_{os}, x_{ap})$, and x_i is the respective structure variable.

As $R(t) = E(\Phi(\mathbf{X}))$, then

$$R(t) = R_{hw}(t) \times R_{os}(t) \times R_{ap}(t).$$

Therefore, the reliability for a system represented by an *OR* gate with i basic events is obtained by

$$R(t) = \prod_{i=1}^{n} R_i(t). \tag{19.2.1}$$

If $R_i(t) = R_c(t)$, then

$$R(t) = R_c(t)^n. \tag{19.2.2}$$

If the time to failure of each basic event is exponentially distributed with rate λ_i, the reliability is

$$R(t) = \prod_{i=1}^{n} e^{-\lambda_i t}, \tag{19.2.3}$$

and as $MTTF = \int_0^\infty R(t)\,dt$, we get

$$MTTF = \int_0^\infty \prod_{i=1}^n e^{-\lambda_i t}\,dt,$$

$$MTTF = \frac{1}{\sum_{i=1}^n \lambda_i}. \tag{19.2.4}$$

If $\lambda_i = \lambda$, then

$$R(t) = e^{-n\lambda t}, \tag{19.2.5}$$

and

$$MTTF = \frac{1}{n\lambda}. \tag{19.2.6}$$

Considering the system components can be repaired and that the component i's steady-state availability is A_i, the steady-state system availability is obtained by

$$A = \prod_{i=1}^n A_i. \tag{19.2.7}$$

If $A_i = A_c$, then

$$A = A_c^n. \tag{19.2.8}$$

If the component i's time to repair is exponentially distributed with rate μ_i, then $A_i = \mu_i/(\lambda_i + \mu_i)$. Hence

$$A = \prod_{i=1}^n \frac{\mu_i}{\lambda_i + \mu_i}. \tag{19.2.9}$$

The instantaneous availability is likewise obtained.

Example 19.2.1. Assume the time to failure of each component of the system shown in Figure 19.4.a is exponentially distributed with rate $\lambda_{hw} = 2.5 \times 10^{-5}\,f/h$, $\lambda_{os} = 5 \times 10^{-4}\,f/h$, and $\lambda_{ap} = 10^{-3}\,f/h$. The system reliability is

$$R(t) = \prod_{i \in \{hw, os, ap\}} R_i(t) = e^{-\lambda_{hw} t} \times e^{-\lambda_{os} t} \times e^{-\lambda_{ap} t},$$

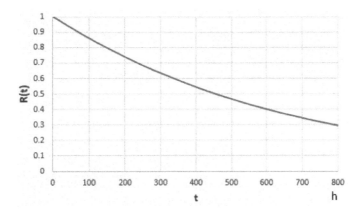

Figure 19.5 *OR* Gate - $R(t) \times t$.

since $R_i(t) = e^{-\lambda_i t}$, $i \in \{hw, os, ap\}$. Therefore,

$$R(t) = e^{-(\lambda_{hw} + \lambda_{os} + \lambda_{ap})t}.$$

The system reliability in the interval $(0, 800h)$ is shown in Figure 19.5.

The mean time to failure is

$$MTTF = \int_0^\infty R(t)\, dt = \int_0^\infty e^{-\lambda_{hw}t} \times e^{-\lambda_{os}t} \times e^{-\lambda_{ap}t}\, dt.$$

$$MTTF = \int_0^\infty e^{-(\lambda_{hw} + \lambda_{os} + \lambda_{ap})t}\, dt = \frac{1}{\lambda_{hw} + \lambda_{os} + \lambda_{ap}} = 655.7377\,h.$$

If the mean time to repair of each component is $MTTR_{hw} = 20h$ and $MTTR_{os} = MTTR_{ap} = 2h$, then the system availability is

$$A = \prod_{i \in \{hw, os, ap\}} A_i = \prod_{i \in \{hw, os, ap\}} \frac{MTTF_i}{MTTF_i + MTTR_i} = 0.9965.$$

$\square$

AND Gate

Assume a system is composed of three independent servers, S_1, S_2, and S_3 (see Figure 19.6.a). The system is faulty if all servers fail. Thus, the system can be represented by the fault tree shown in Figure 19.6.c, since failure occurs if the basic events $\overline{S_1}$, $\overline{S_2}$, and $\overline{S_3}$, occur. The RBD depicted in Figure 19.6.b also represents the system, since

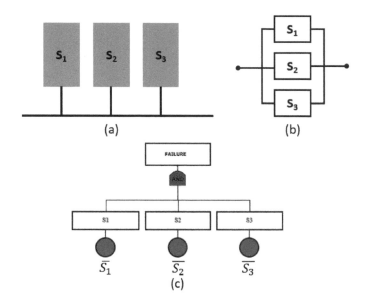

Figure 19.6 *AND* Gate.

the system is operational as long as at least one server (S_1, S_2, or S_3) is functional, and a parallel block diagram represents such a behavior.

Let us obtain the reliability from the logical function. Assume the name of each component is also adopted to represent the logical variables. Thus, let us define the Boolean vector as $B = (S_1, S_2, S_3)$. Therefore, the logical function that represents a failure is

$$\overline{\Psi(\mathbf{B})} = \overline{S_1} \wedge \overline{S_2} \wedge \overline{S_3}.$$

Hence, negating both sides of the expression above, we obtain

$$\overline{\overline{\Psi(\mathbf{B})}} = \overline{\overline{S_1} \wedge \overline{S_2} \wedge \overline{S_3}}.$$

Thus,

$$\Psi(\mathbf{B}) = \overline{\overline{S_1} \wedge \overline{S_2} \wedge \overline{S_3}}.$$

The respective structure-function is obtained by applying the transformations rules shown in Table 18.3. Hence

$$\Phi(\mathbf{X}) = 1 - ((1 - x_{S_1}) \times (1 - x_{S_2}) \times (1 - x_{S_3})).$$

If $R_i(t) = E(x_i(t))$, $i \in \{S_1, S_2, S_3\}$, then

$$R(t) = E(1 - ((1 - x_{S_1}(t)) \times (1 - x_{S_2}(t)) \times (1 - x_{S_3}(t)))),$$

which leads to

$$R(t) = 1 - ((1 - R_{S_1}(t)) \times (1 - R_{S_2}(t)) \times (1 - R_{S_3}(t))). \tag{19.2.10}$$

For a system with n parallel components, we have

$$R(t) = 1 - \prod_{i=1}^{n}(1 - R_i(t)). \tag{19.2.11}$$

If $R_i(t) = R_c(t)$, then

$$R(t) = 1 - (1 - R_c(t))^n. \tag{19.2.12}$$

As $MTTF = \int_0^\infty R(t)\, dt$, and if all components are identically distributed according to an exponential distribution with rate λ, then we obtain (see 18.5.25)

$$MTTF \frac{1}{\lambda} \sum_{i=1}^{n} \frac{1}{i}. \tag{19.2.13}$$

For components with different failure rates, see 18.5.23.

Assuming the system components can be repaired and that the steady-state availability of the component i is A_i, the steady-state system availability is calculated by

$$A = 1 - \prod_{i=1}^{n}(1 - A_i). \tag{19.2.14}$$

If $A_i = A_c$, then

$$A = 1 - (1 - A_c)^n. \tag{19.2.15}$$

As $A_i = MTTF_i/(MTTF_i + MTTR_i)$, then

$$A = 1 - \prod_{i=1}^{n}(1 - \frac{MTTF_i}{MTTF_i + MTTR_i}). \tag{19.2.16}$$

$$A = 1 - \prod_{i=1}^{n}(\frac{MTTR_i}{MTTF_i + MTTR_i}). \tag{19.2.17}$$

If $MTTF_i = MTTF$ and $MTTR_i = MTTR$, then

$$A = 1 - \left(\frac{MTTR_i}{MTTF_i + MTTR_i} \right)^n. \tag{19.2.18}$$

If the time to repair of component i is exponentially distributed with rate μ_i, then $A_i = \mu_i / (\lambda_i + \mu_i)$. Hence

$$A = 1 - \prod_{i=1}^{n} \frac{\mu_i}{\lambda_i + \mu_i}. \tag{19.2.19}$$

If $\lambda_i = \lambda$ and $\mu_i = \mu$, then

$$A = 1 - \left(\frac{\mu_i}{\lambda_i + \mu_i} \right)^n. \tag{19.2.20}$$

The instantaneous availability is similarly obtained.

Example 19.2.2. Let us assume the time to failure of each server S_i, $i \in \{1,2,3\}$, is exponentially distributed with rate $\lambda = 5 \times 10^{-5} f/h$. The system reliability in the interval $(0, 120000 h)$ is shown in Figure 19.7. The system mean time to failure is $MTTF = 36666.7 h$. Figure 19.8 shows the density function of the time to failure when the system is composed of one, two, and three servers. Assuming a server mean time to repair is $2.5 h$, the system steady-state availability expressed in number of nines ($\#9s = -\log_{10}(1 - A)$ - see 16.2.26) is $\#9s = 7.3668$.

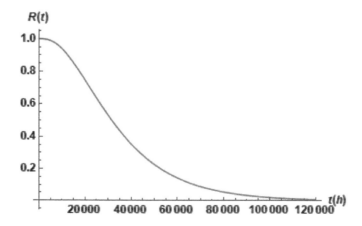

Figure 19.7   Three Servers System - Reliability $\times$ Time.

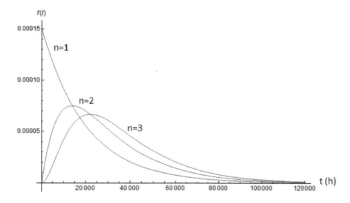

Figure 19.8 Three Servers System - Density × Time.

KooN Gate

Consider a system composed of n components. Suppose the system fails when at least k fails; such a system can be represented by composing *AND* and *OR* gates. This system has $\binom{n}{n-k+1}$ combinations of k basic events that lead to a failure. Assume, for instance, a system represented by three basic events, $\bar{a}$, $\bar{b}$, and $\bar{c}$. If this system fails when at least two out of three basic events occur, the FT can represent this system depicted in Figure 19.9. It is worth noting that the basic events appear more than once in the FT. Such an FT has repeated events. The gate shown in Figure 19.10.a is an implicit representation of the composition shown in Figure 19.9. The logical function that represents the system failure is

$$\overline{\Psi(a,b,c)} = (\bar{a}\wedge\bar{b}) \vee (\bar{a}\wedge\bar{c}) \vee (\bar{b}\wedge\bar{c}) \vee (\bar{a}\wedge\bar{b}\wedge\bar{c}).$$

Hence

$$\Psi(a,b,c) = \overline{(\bar{a}\wedge\bar{b}) \vee (\bar{a}\wedge\bar{c}) \vee (\bar{b}\wedge\bar{c}) \vee (\bar{a}\wedge\bar{b}\wedge\bar{c})}.$$

$$\Psi(a,b,c) = \overline{(\bar{a}\wedge\bar{b})} \wedge \overline{(\bar{a}\wedge\bar{c})} \wedge \overline{(\bar{b}\wedge\bar{c})} \wedge \overline{(\bar{a}\wedge\bar{b}\wedge\bar{c})}.$$

Applying the transformation rules presented in Table 18.3, we get

$$\Phi(x_a,x_b,x_c) = (1-(1-x_a)(1-x_b)) \times (1-(1-x_a)(1-x_c)) \times (1-(1-x_b)(1-x_c)) \times$$

$$(1-(1-x_a)(1-x_b)(1-x_c)).$$

As $x_i^n = x_i$, and doing some algebra, we get

$$\Phi(x_a, x_b, x_c) = x_b x_c + x_a x_b + x_a x_c - 2 x_a x_b x_c.$$

Considering x_a, x_b, and x_c are independent, $R_a(t) = E(x_a)$, $R_b(t) = E(x_b)$, $R_c(t) = E(x_c)$ and $E(\Phi(x_a, x_b, x_c)) = 1 = R(t)$, we have

$$R(t) = R_b(t)R_c(t) + R_a(t)R_b(t) + R_a(t)R_c(t) - 2R_a(t)R_b(t)R_c(t).$$

The system instantaneous and steady-state availability can be likewise obtained.

Example 19.2.3. Assume the FT depicted in Figure 19.9 represents a sensor system composed of three sensors, a, b, and c. If each sensor reliability at $t = 100h$ is $R_a(100h) = 0.81873$, $R_b(100h) = 0.84648$, and $R_c(100h) = 0.86688$, respectively, the system reliability at $t = 100h$ is $R(100h) = 0.93501$.

□

Example 19.2.4. If the basic events are identically distributed, and each sensor reliability at $t = 100h$ is $R_i(100h) = 0.81873$, $i \in \{a, b, c\}$, the system reliability at $t = 100h$ is $R(100h) = 0.91334$.

□

If the basic events are identically distributed, the system unreliability can be directly obtained by applying

$$UR(t) = \sum_{j=k}^{n} UR_e(t)^j (1 - UR_e(t))^{n-k},$$

where $UR_e(t)$ is the unreliability assigned to the basic event.

Therefore

$$UR(t) = \sum_{j=k}^{n} UR_e(t)^j R_e(t)^{n-k}. \tag{19.2.21}$$

Hence

$$R(t) = 1 - \sum_{j=k}^{n} UR_e(t)^j R_e(t)^{n-k}. \tag{19.2.22}$$

Similarly, the system steady-state and instantaneous availability is calculated by

$$A = 1 - \sum_{j=k}^{n} UA_e^j A_e^{n-k}, \tag{19.2.23}$$

and

$$A(t) = 1 - \sum_{j=k}^{n} UA_e(t)^j A_e(t)^{n-k}. \qquad (19.2.24)$$

If the basic events are independent and identically distributed, the gate notation depicted in Figure 19.10.b may be adopted.

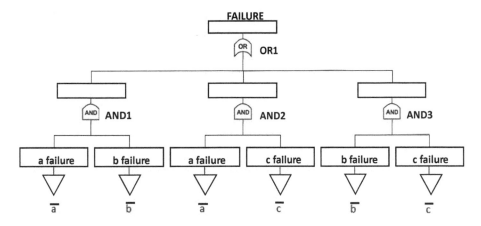

Figure 19.9 FT with *AND* and *OR* gates representing *KooN* configuration.

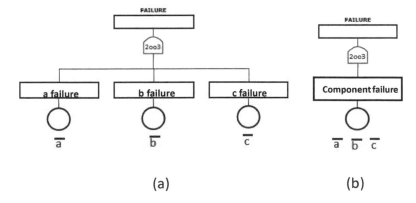

Figure 19.10 *KooN* gate (a) and its Simplified Representation (b)

Example 19.2.5. Consider the times to failure of each sensor are exponentially distributed with rate $\lambda = 2 \times 10^{-3} f/h$, and the times to repair of each sensor are also exponentially distributed with rate $\mu = 5 \times 10^{-2} r/h$. The system steady-state availability is 0.99568.

□

It is worth noting that the $K_f ooN$ gate is equivalent to the $K_r ooN$ block (of an RBD), where $K_r = N - K_f + 1$.

Example 19.2.6. If FT represents a system failure with only one $K_f ooN$ gate with $N = 7$ and $K_f = 3$, the respective RBD may also be represented by a single $K_r ooN$ block, where $K_r = 7 - 3 + 1 = 5$.

□

As the $K_f ooN$ gate is equivalent to the $K_r ooN$ block, and considering all basic events are identically distributed according to an exponential distribution with the rate λ, then the mean time to failure can be calculated using

$$MTTF = \frac{1}{\lambda} \sum_{i=N-K_f+1}^{n} \frac{1}{i}. \tag{19.2.25}$$

Example 19.2.7. Assume a system is represented by a $K_f ooN$ gate, where $N = 7$, $K_f = 3$, and the basic event times to failure are identically distributed according to an exponential distribution with rate $\lambda = 2 \times 10^{-3} f/h$. The mean time to failure is

$$MTTF = \frac{1}{2 \times 10^{-3}} \sum_{i=7-3+1}^{7} \frac{1}{i} = 254.7619\,h.$$

□

19.3 COMPOSITIONS

AND, *OR*, and *KooN* gates can be combined to form more complex system configurations. In practice, a system may be decomposed into smaller subsystems, and each subsystem may also be decomposed into other subsystems or components. As in RBDs, decomposition is convenient when defining a system's logic, structure, reliability, and availability functions.

Example 19.3.1. As one example, consider a computational system composed of two servers (Server 1 and Server 2) and a network. The servers have equal configuration (see Figure 19.11). The components that represent Server 1 are its hardware (hw_1), its operating system (os_1), and two program applications named a_1 and b_1. The components of the Server 2 are likewise named, that is hw_2, os_2, a_2, and b_2.

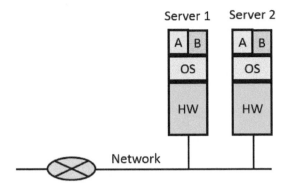

Figure 19.11   Server 1 and Server 2.

The system failure occurs when both servers fail or the network fails. For example, a server fails when its hardware fails, or its operating system or both application programs (*A* and *B*) fail. The fault tree shown in Figure 19.12 represents this system.

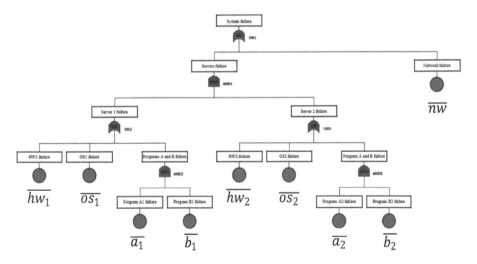

Figure 19.12   Server 1 and Server 2 – Fault Tree.

The logical function that represents the system failure is

$$\overline{\Psi(B)} = ((\overline{hw1} \vee \overline{os1} \vee (\overline{a1} \wedge \overline{b1})) \wedge (\overline{hw2} \vee \overline{os2} \vee (\overline{a2} \wedge \overline{b2}))) \vee \overline{nw},$$

where $B = (hw1, os1, a1, b1, hw2, os2, a2, b2, nw)$ is the Boolean vector.

Negating both sides, we get

$$\Psi(B) = \overline{((\overline{hw1} \vee \overline{os1} \vee (\overline{a1} \wedge \overline{b1})) \wedge (\overline{hw2} \vee \overline{os2} \vee (\overline{a2} \wedge \overline{b2})))} \vee \overline{nw}.$$

The structure-function can be obtained by applying the transformation rules depicted in Table 18.3.

$$\Phi(X) = (1 - (1 - x_{hw1} \times x_{os1} \times (1 - (1 - x_{a1}) \times (1 - x_{b1}))) \times$$

$$(1 - x_{hw2} \times x_{os2} \times (1 - (1 - x_{a2}) \times (1 - x_{b2}))))) \times x_{nw},$$

where x_i is the respective structure variable and $X = (x_{hw1}, x_{os1}, x_{a1}, x_{b1}, x_{hw2}, x_{os2}, x_{a2}, x_{b2}, x_{nw})$ is the structure vector.

Considering the structure variables are independent, $R_i(t) = E(x_i)$, the system reliability is

$$R(t) = (1 - (1 - R_{hw1}(t) \times R_{os1}(t) \times (1 - (1 - R_{a1}(t)) \times (1 - R_{b1}(t)))) \times$$

$$(1 - R_{hw2}(t) \times R_{os2}(t) \times (1 - (1 - R_{a2}(t)) \times (1 - R_{b2}(t)))))) \times R_{nw}(t).$$

Similarly, the steady-state availability is obtained.

$$A = (1 - (1 - A_{hw1} \times A_{os1} \times (1 - (1 - A_{a1}) \times (1 - A_{b1}))) \times$$

$$(1 - A_{hw2} \times A_{os2} \times (1 - (1 - A_{a2}(t \times (1 - A_{b2}))))) \times A_{nw}.$$

Consider the time to failure of each component i is exponentially distributed with the respective rate λ_i, and assume the rates are $\lambda_{hw1} = \lambda_{hw2} = 2.5 \times 10^{-5} f/h$, $\lambda_{os1} = \lambda_{os2} = 2.5 \times 10^{-4} f/h$, $\lambda_{a1} = \lambda_{a2} = 6.67 \times 10^{-4} f/h$, $\lambda_{b1} = \lambda_{b2} = 7.69 \times 10^{-4} f/h$, and $\lambda_{nw} = 2.22 \times 10^{-5} f/h$. The reliability in the interval $(0, 4000 h)$ is shown in Figure 19.13. The defects per million in $1000 h$ is $DPM = (1 - R(1000 h)) \times 10^6 = (1 - 0.21026) \times 10^6 = 789740.13$. Let us assume the time to repair of each component i is also exponentially distributed with the respective rate μ_i. If the rates are $\mu_{hw1} = \mu_{hw2} = 2.5 \times 10^{-2} r/h$, $\mu_{os1} = \mu_{os2} = 0.25 r/h$, $\mu_{a1} = \mu_{a2} = 1 r/h$, $\mu_{b1} = \mu_{b2} = 0.667 r/h$, and $\mu_{nw} = 0.25 r/h$, then the steady-state availability is $A = 0.999907$.

The reliability (Birnbaum) importance of each system component is obtained deriving the reliability function by the reliability of each component.

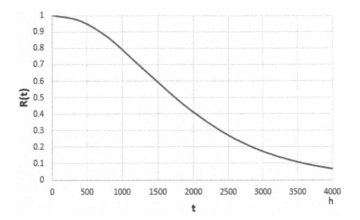

Figure 19.13 Server 1 and Server 2 - $R(t) \times t$.

$$\frac{\partial R(t)}{\partial R_{hw1}} = R_{nw}(t)R_{os1}(t)(1 - (1 - R_{a1}(t))(1 - R_{b1}(t)))$$
$$(1 - R_{hw2}(t)R_{os2}(t)(1 - (1 - R_{a2}(t))(1 - R_{b2}(t)))),$$

$$\frac{\partial R(t)}{\partial R_{hw2}} = R_{nw}(t)R_{os2}(t)(1 - (1 - R_{a2}(t))(1 - R_{b2}(t)))$$
$$(1 - R_{hw1}(t)R_{os1}(t)(1 - (1 - R_{a1}(t))(1 - R_{b1}(t)))),$$

$$\frac{\partial R(t)}{\partial R_{os1}} = R_{hw1}(t)R_{nw}(t)(1 - (1 - R_{a1}(t))(1 - R_{b1}(t)))$$
$$(1 - R_{hw2}(t)R_{os2}(t)(1 - (1 - R_{a2}(t))(1 - R_{b2}(t)))),$$

$$\frac{\partial R(t)}{\partial R_{os2}} = R_{hw2}(t)R_{nw}(t)(1 - (1 - R_{a2}(t))(1 - R_{b2}(t)))$$
$$(1 - R_{hw1}(t)R_{os1}(t)(1 - (1 - R_{a1}(t))(1 - R_{b1}(t)))),$$

$$\frac{\partial R(t)}{\partial R_{a1}} = (1 - R_{b1}(t))R_{hw1}(t)R_{nw}(t)R_{os1}(t)$$
$$(1 - R_{hw2}(t)R_{os2}(t)(1 - (1 - R_{a2}(t))(1 - R_{b2}(t)))),$$

$$\frac{\partial R(t)}{\partial R_{a2}} = (1 - R_{b2}(t))R_{hw2}(t)R_{nw}(t)R_{os2}(t)$$
$$(1 - R_{hw1}(t)R_{os1}(t)(1 - (1 - R_{a1}(t))(1 - R_{b1}(t)))),$$

$$\frac{\partial R(t)}{\partial R_{b1}} = (1 - R_{a1}(t))R_{hw1}(t)R_{nw}(t)R_{os1}(t)$$

$$(1 - R_{hw2}(t)R_{os2}(t)(1 - (1 - R_{a2}(t))(1 - R_{b2}(t)))),$$

$$\frac{\partial R(t)}{\partial R_{b2}} = (1 - R_{a2}(t))R_{hw2}(t)R_{nw}(t)R_{os2}(t)$$

$$(1 - R_{hw1}(t)R_{os1}(t)(1 - (1 - R_{a1}(t))(1 - R_{b1}(t)))),$$

and

$$\frac{\partial R(t)}{\partial R_{nw}} = 1 - (1 - R_{hw1}(t)R_{os1}(t)(1 - (1 - R_{a1}(t))(1 - R_{b1}(t))))(1 - R_{hw2}(t)R_{os2}(t) \times$$

$$(1 - (1 - R_{a2}(t))(1 - R_{b2}(t)))).$$

The reliability importance of each component in the interval $(0, 4000\,h)$ is shown in Figure 19.14. As the importance of each component changes over time, the mission time is essential when adopting these importance indices.

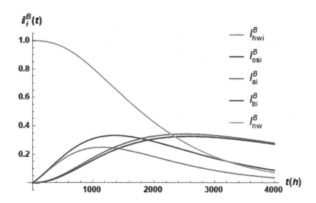

Figure 19.14   Reliability Importance - $\partial R(t)/\partial R_i(t) \times t$.

Example 19.3.2. Let us calculate the steady-state availability of a computational system composed of an application server (AS), one database-server (DBS), and network attached storage (NAS). Figure 19.15 shows this system. This system fails if the application server (AS) or database-server (DBS) or network attached storage (NAS)

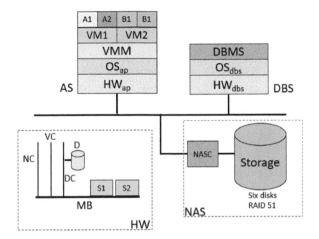

Figure 19.15   Application Server, Database server, and NAS.

(NAS) fails, that is $\overline{\Psi(AS, DBS, NAS)} = \overline{AS} \vee \overline{DBS} \vee \overline{NAS}$. The FT that represents computational system failure is shown in Figure 19.16.

The application server is composed of its hardware (HW_{as}), its operational system (OS_{as}), a virtual machine manager (VMM), and two virtual machines ($VM1$ and $VM2$). $VM1$ hostages two program applications, $A1$ and $A2$; and $VM2$ also hostages two two other program applications, $B1$ and $B2$. The application server fails if both virtual machine applications fail or the hardware server or the operating system or the virtual machine manager fails. This is specified by

$$\overline{\Psi(BS)_{as}} = \overline{HW_{as}} \vee \overline{OS_{as}} \vee \overline{VMM} \vee (\overline{VM1} \vee (\overline{A1} \wedge \overline{A2})) \vee (\overline{VM1} \vee (\overline{B1} \wedge \overline{B2})),$$

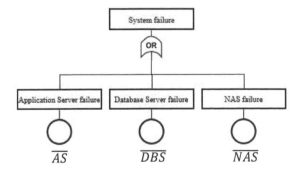

Figure 19.16   The Computational System Failure - $\overline{\Psi(AS, DBS, NAS)} = \overline{AS} \vee \overline{DBS}$ $\vee \overline{NAS}$.

$BS = (HW_{as}, OS_{as}, VMM, VM1, VM2, A1, A2, B1, B2)$. The FT in Figure 19.17 represents this failure mode.

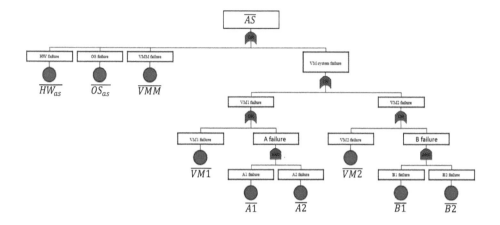

Figure 19.17 Application Server Failure.

The database-server is composed of its hardware (HW_{dbs}), its operational system (OS_{dbs}), and the database management system ($DBMS$). The database-server fails if its hardware or its operational system or database management system fail. More formally, $\Psi(HW_{dbs}, OS_{dbs}, DBMS) = \overline{HW_{dbs}} \vee \overline{OS_{dbs}} \vee \overline{DBMS}$. The FT the represents computational system failure is shown in Figure 19.18.

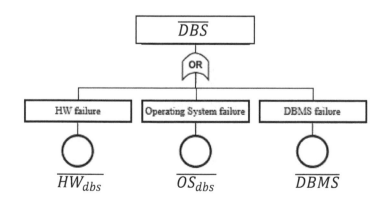

Figure 19.18 Database Server Failure.

The network-attached system is composed of a controller ($NASC$) and the storage, which is composed of six disks ($D1$, $D2$, $D3$, $D4$, $D5$, and $D6$) configured in RAID 51. The NAS fails if its controller or the storage fails. The storage (RAID51) fails if two disks out of $D1$, $D2$, and $D3$, and two disks out of $D4$, $D5$, and $D6$ fail. The network-attached system failure is represented by

$$\overline{\Psi(BS)_{nas}} = \overline{NASC} \vee (((\overline{D1} \wedge \overline{D2}) \vee (\overline{D1} \wedge \overline{D3}) \vee (\overline{D2} \wedge \overline{D3}) \vee (\overline{D1} \wedge \overline{D2} \wedge \overline{D3})) \wedge$$

$$((\overline{D4} \wedge \overline{D5}) \vee (\overline{D4} \wedge \overline{D6}) \vee (\overline{D5} \wedge \overline{D6}) \vee (\overline{D4} \wedge \overline{D5} \wedge \overline{D6}))),$$

$BS = (NASC, D1, D2, D3, D4, D5, D6)$. The FT of the NAS subsystem is depicted in Figure 19.19.

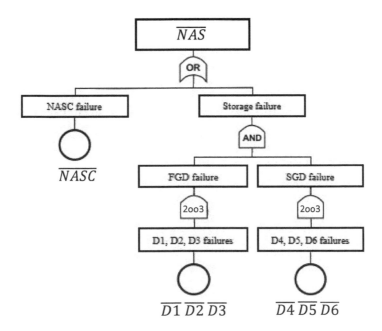

Figure 19.19   *NAS* Failure.

The hardware of each server (HW_{as} and HW_{dbs}) is composed of a motherboard (MB_i), a network controller (NC_i), a video controller (VC_i), a disk (D_i) and its controller (DC_i); and two power sources (S_1^i and S_2^i) configured in hot-standby ($i \in \{as, dbs\}$ - as denotes application server and dbs represents database server). The hardware server fails if its motherboard or any of its controllers or its respective disk or both power sources fail. More formally,

$$\overline{\Psi(BS)_{hw_i}} = \overline{MB_i} \vee \overline{NC_i} \vee \overline{VC_i} \vee \overline{HC_i} \vee \overline{D_i} \vee (\overline{S_1^i} \wedge \overline{S_2^i}),$$

$BS = (MB_i, NC_i, VC_i, DC_i, D_i, S_1^i, S_2^i)$, $i \in \{as, dbs\}$. The FT of the hardware server is depicted in Figure 19.20.

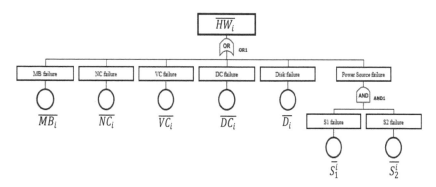

Figure 19.20   Hardware Failure.

The structure-function of each subsystem described above can be obtained by applying the transformation rules shown in Table 18.3. The reliability and the steady-state availability can, then, be obtained from the structure functions. Therefore, the hardware server reliability expression is

$$R_{HW_i}(t) = R_{MB}(t) \times R_{NC}(t) \times R_{VC}(t) \times R_{DC}(t) \times$$

$$R_D(t) \times (1 - (1 - R_{S1}(t)) \times (1 - R_{S2}(t))),$$

$i \in \{as, dbs\}$. Let us consider the time to failure of each hardware server component to be exponentially distributed with rate $\lambda_{MB} = 1.6667 \times 10^{-5} f/h$, $\lambda_{NC} = 2 \times 10^{-5} f/h$, $\lambda_{VC} = 2.2222 \times 10^{-5} f/h$, $\lambda_{DC} = 1.8181 \times 10^{-5} f/h$, $\lambda_D = 2.8571 \times 10^{-5} f/h$, and $\lambda_{S1} = \lambda_{S2} = 3.3333 \times 10^{-5} f/h$. Therefore, the reliability of the hardware is expressed by

$$R_{HW_i}(t) = e^{-\lambda_{MB} \times t} \times e^{-\lambda_{NC} \times t} \times e^{-\lambda_{VC} \times t} \times e^{-\lambda_{DC} \times t} \times e^{-\lambda_D \times t}$$

$$\times (1 - (1 - e^{-\lambda_{S1} \times t}) \times (1 - e^{-\lambda_{S2} \times t}))$$

Therefore,

$$MTTF_{HW_i} = \int_0^\infty R_{HW_i}(t)\, dt = 8587.49491\, h.$$

The application server availability is expressed by

$$A_{as} = A_{HW_{as}} \times A_{OS_{as}} \times A_{VMM} \times A_{VM1} \times (1 - (1 - A_{A1}) \times (1 - A_{A2})) \times$$

$$A_{VM2} \times (1 - (1 - A_{B1}) \times (1 - A_{B2})).$$

The hardware time to failure was already calculated. Let us assume the hardware time to repair is $24\,h$. The other components $MTTF$ and $MTTR$ are presented in Table 19.2.

Table 19.2
Mean Time to Failure and Mean Time to Repair

Component	MTTF (h)	MTTR (h)
OS	2000	4
VMM	3000	0.5
VM1	2000	0.1
VM2	2000	0.1
A1	1200	0.5
A2	1200	0.5
B1	1500	0.5
B2	1500	0.5

Using $A_i = MTTF_i/(MTTF_i + MTTR_i)$, $i \in \{HW, OS, VMM, VM1, VM2, A1, A2, B1, B2\}$, we get $A_{as} = 0.994956958$.

The steady-state availability of the database-server can be calculated similarly. The hardware $MTTF$ was already calculated. As in the application server, the hardware $MTTR$ is assumed as $24\,h$. The operational system and database management system time to failure are $MTTF_{OS} = 2000h$ and $MTTF_{DBMS} = 6000h$, respectively. Their mean time to repair are respectively $MTTR_{OS} = 4h$ and $MTTR_{DBMS} = 4h$. Hence

$$A_{dbs} = A_{HW_{dbs}} \times A_{OS_{dbs}} \times A_{DBMS} = 0.99455954,$$

where $A_i = MTTF_i/(MTTF_i + MTTR_i)$, $i \in \{HW_{dbs}, OS_{dbs}, DBMS\}$.

The NAS subsystem availability is expressed by

$$A_{NAS} = A_{NASC} \times A_{Storage} = A_{NASC} \times (3A_D^2 - 2A_D^3),$$

where $A_{Storage} = 3A_D^2 - 2A_D^3$ is the storage availability and A_D is the availability of a single disk. A_{NASC} is the availability of the NAS controller. As $A_i = MTTF_i/(MTTF_i + MTTR_i)$, $i \in \{NASC, D\}$, and $MTTF_{NASC} = 50000h$, $MTTF_D = 35000h$, and $MTTR_{NASC} = MTTR_D = 24h$, we obtain $A_{NAS} = 0.99952023$.

Thus, the system availability is $A = A_{as} \times A_{dbs} \times A_{NAS} = 0.9897596$. The yearly downtime in hours is $DT = (1 - A) \times 8760h = 89.7653\,h$.

□

Example 19.3.3. Consider a computer system composed of two processor units (P_1 and P_2), each with its local memory (M_1 and M_2, respectively), and a shared memory (M_3). Figure 19.21 depicts this system.

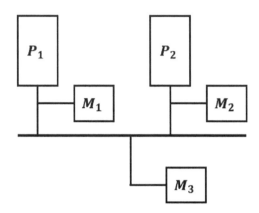

Figure 19.21 Computer System - Local and Shared Memories.

The system is considered failed if P_1 or M_1 and M_3 fail, and P_2 or M_2 and M_3 fail. More formally, a failure is defined by $\overline{\Psi(P_1,P_2,M_1,M_2,M_3)} = (P_1 \vee (M_1 \wedge M_3)) \wedge (P_2 \vee (M_2 \wedge M_3))$. The fault tree describing this failure mode is shown in Figure 19.22.

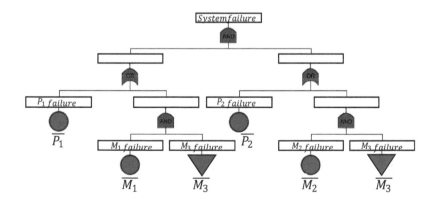

Figure 19.22 Fault Tree with Repeated Event.

It is worth noting that the basic event $\overline{M_3}$ appears twice in this model. Models such as this FT may be evaluated by factoring on the repeated events. In this example, we have one repeated event. Therefore, two conditions are possible, that is $\overline{M_3} = T$, representing a failure, or $\overline{M_3} = F$ that specifies the correct behavior of the memory module M_3. This strategy was already applied in the bridge structure in Section 18.5. Enumeration and summing of the disjoint product (see Chapter 20) may also be applied. The FT depicted in Figure 19.23.a is a model conditioned to $\overline{M_3} = T$ (failure) and Figure 19.23.b presents the FT conditioned to $\overline{M_3} = F$ (correct behavior).

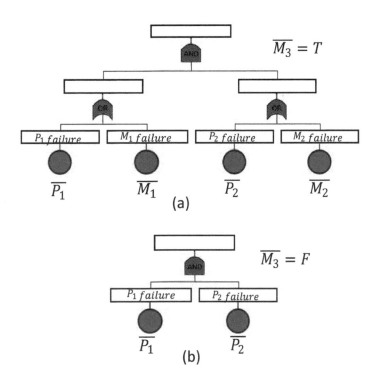

Figure 19.23   Factoring Repeated Event – Fault Trees.

The respective logical functions of each fault tree are

$$\Psi_{\overline{CM_3}}(P_1, P_2, M_1, M_2) = (\overline{P_1} \vee \overline{M_1}) \wedge (\overline{P_2} \vee \overline{M_2})$$

and

$$\overline{\Psi_{CM_3}}(P_1, P_2, M_1, M_2) = \overline{P_1} \wedge \overline{P_2}$$

The structure functions are obtained from the logical functions, and the respective reliability and availability expressions are derived. The reliability can be calculated from

$$R(t) = (1 - R_{M_3}(t)) \times R_{\overline{CM_3}}(t) + R_{M_3}(t) \times R_{CM_3}(t),$$

where $R_{M_3}(t)$ is the reliability of memory module M_3, $R_{\overline{CM_3}}(t)$ is the reliability computed from the FT shown in Figure 19.23.a, and $R_{CM_3}(t)$ is the reliability calculated from the model shown in Figure 19.23.b.

$$R_{\overline{CM_3}}(t) = 1 - ((1 - R_{P_1}(t) \times R_{M_1}(t)) \times (1 - R_{P_2}(t) \times R_{M_2}(t)))$$

and

$$R_{CM_3}(t) = 1 - (1 - R_{P_1}(t)) \times (1 - R_{P_2}(t)),$$

where $R_{P_1}(t)$, $R_{P_2}(t)$, $R_{M_1}(t)$, and $R_{M_2}(t)$ are the reliability of the processing unit P_1 and P_2, and of the memory module M_1 and M_2, respectively. The availability expression is obtained likewise.

$$A = (1 - A_{M_3}) \times A_{\overline{CM_3}} + A_{M_3} \times A_{CM_3},$$

where A_{M_3} is the availability of memory module M_3, $A_{\overline{CM_3}}$ is the availability calculated from the FT shown in Figure 19.23.a, and A_{CM_3} is the availability computed from the model shown in Figure 19.23.b.

$$A_{\overline{CM_3}} = 1 - ((1 - A_{P_1} \times A_{M_1}) \times (1 - A_{P_2} \times A_{M_2}))$$

and

$$A_{CM_3} = 1 - (1 - A_{P_1}) \times (1 - A_{P_2}),$$

where A_{P_1}, A_{P_2}, A_{M_1}, and A_{M_2} are the availability of the processing unit P_1 and P_2, and of the memory module M_1 and M_2, respectively.

The $MTTF$ and $MTTR$ of each system component are shown in Table 19.3. The component's steady-state availability is $A_i = MTTF_i/(MTTF_i + MTTR_i)$, $i \in \{P_1, P_2, M_1, M_2, M_3\}$, the system steady-state availability is $A = 0.999913$ and the yearly downtime is $(1 - A) \times 525600$ minutes $= 45.85$ minutes.

☐

Table 19.3
Computer System with Local and Shared Memories - $MTTFs$ **and** $MTTRs$

Component	MTTF (h)	MTTR (h)
P_1	4000	40
P_2	4500	40
M_1	30000	20
M_2	30000	20
M_3	35000	20

19.4 COMMON CAUSE FAILURE

This section shows how to model common cause failures using FT. The example adopted here is the same as depicted in Section 18.7. Hence, assume a redundant system specified by two subsystems (s_1 and s_2). These subsystems are represented by the events E_1 and E_2, respectively. The system is considered in failure if both subsystems fail; thus, a failure occurs when the expression $E_1 \wedge E_2$ is evaluated as true. (see Figure 19.24.a). Consider the failure rates of both subsystems are equal and constant, λ. Now, assume a percentage (p) of failures ($\lambda_{ccf} = p \times \lambda$) commonly affect both subsystems (CCF). This event is represented by including a two-input OR gate, in which the top event of the previous model (FT depicted in Figure 19.24.a) is one of its inputs, and the other event (E_3) represents the CCF. This model is shown in Figure 19.24.b. Therefore, a failure is represented when the expression $(E_1 \wedge E_2) \vee E_3$ is evaluated to true.

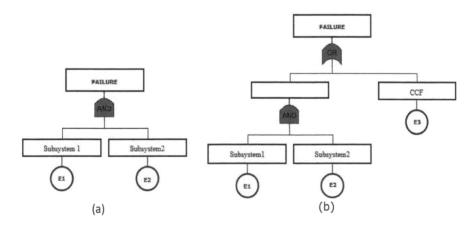

(a)   (b)

Figure 19.24   Common Cause Failure.

Let $\lambda = 10^{-4} h^1$. The MTTF of the system depicted in Figure 18.27.a is $1500 h$, and the system reliability at $t = 10000 h$ is $R(10000h) = 0.6004$. If the CCF rate is considered, and if it is equal to $\lambda_{ccf} = 10^{-5} h^1$, the system's MTTF is $13419.91 h$ and $R(10000h) = 0.5433$.

EXERCISES

Exercise 1. What are the reasons for choosing either RBD or FT as modeling notation?

Exercise 2. Why is it essential to define the failure mode when modeling a system using FT?

Exercise 3. Given the logical function of a system $\overline{\Psi(\bar{a},\bar{b},\bar{c},\bar{d})} = \bar{a} \vee \bar{d} \vee (\bar{b} \wedge \bar{c})$, obtain the respective structure function.

Exercise 4. Convert the RBD of Figure 18.34 into an FT, and find the logical and the respective structure function.

Exercise 5. Considering a RAID 50 with eight disks, each with time to failure exponentially distributed with rate $\lambda = 4.7 \times 10^{-5}$. Propose an FT and calculate (a) the reliability at $t = 7800 h$ and (b) $MTTF$.

Exercise 6. Assuming a RAID 61 with twelve disks, each with time to failure exponentially distributed with rate $\lambda = 5.5 \times 10^{-5}$. Propose an FT and obtain (a) the reliability at $t = 7000 h$ and (b) $MTTF$.

Exercise 7. Consider a system in which software applications read, write, and modify the content of the storage device D_1 (source). The system periodically replicates the production data (generated by the software application) of one storage device (D_1) in a storage system. The storage system comprises three storage devices (D_2, D_3, D_4) arranged in a TMR configuration. Such control is performed by the storage system controller (C) - see Figure 18.41.

The system is considered to have failed if the hardware infrastructure does not allow the software applications to read, write or modify data on D_1, and if no safe data replica is available, that is two out of three data replica are safely stored on the storage system. Consider that the constant failure rates are $\lambda_s = 2 \times 10^{-5} f/h$, $\lambda_C = 10^{-5}$, $\lambda_{D1} = 8 \times 10^{-5}$, and $\lambda_{D2} = \lambda_{D3} = \lambda_{D4} = 9 \times 10^{-5}$, respectively.

a) Identify the failure mode and write down the logical function.

b) Write down the structure function.

c) Design the respective FT.

d) Write down the expression for the $R(t)$.

e) Write down the expression for the MTTF.

f) Draw the reliability curve in the interval $(0, 1460 h)$.

Exercise 8. Consider a system represented by a two-inputs *AND* gate. Each basic event ($\overline{c_1}$ and $\overline{c_2}$) represents failures of two independent components (C_1 and C_2), which are specified by distinct constant failure rates λ_1 and λ_2, respectively. Upon failure of a component, a repair process is invoked with the respective constant repair rates μ_1 and μ_2. Assume that a failure of a component while another is being repaired causes a system failure.

a) Derive the reliability and MTTF of the system.

b) Derive the steady-state availability of the system and the downtime.

Exercise 9. Convert the RBD of Figure 18.22.a into an FT and find the reliability function, considering the failure rates of each component being constant and equal to λ_1, λ_2, λ_4, and λ_5, respectively. Assuming $\lambda_1 = 5.26 \times 10^{-4} f/h$, $\lambda_2 = 6.25 \times 10^{-4} f/h$, $\lambda_4 = 4 \times 10^{-4} f/h$, and $\lambda_5 = 7.14 \times 10^{-4} f/h$, plot the reliability function in the interval $(0, 720\,h)$. Calculate the system MTTF.

Exercise 10. Propose an FT for the system depicted in Figure 18.43, and calculate the steady-state availability and the yearly downtime assuming the parameter values shown in Table 19.4.

Table 19.4
System Parameters

Component	$MTTF\,(h)$	$MTTR\,(h)$
$Motherboard(MB)$	78000	
$Memory(M)$	36000	
$NetworkController(NC)$	56000	
$VideoController(VC)$	48000	
$HardDiskController(HDC)$	43000	
$HardDisk(HD)$	32000	
$PowerSource(PS)$	22000	
$OperationalSystem(OS)$	3800	1
$Hypervisor(HP)$	5000	1
$VirtualMachines(VMs)$	3800	0.1
$NASController(NASC)$	48000	4
$CloudManagerSoftware(CMS)$	3000	2
$HWServer(HW)$		24
$CloudManager(CM)$		8

Exercise 11. Consider the application server shown in Example 19.3.2. Assume the time to failure distribution of the program applications A_1 and A_2 are represented by

$F(t) = 1 - e^{-(\frac{t}{\beta})^{\alpha}}$, where $\alpha = 1.5$, and $\beta = 1500\,h$. Consider the other components' $TTFs$ and $TTRs$ are exponentially distributed, and their mean values are shown in Table 19.2. (a) Calculate the steady-state availability and (b) the yearly downtime.

Exercise 12. Obtain the reliability importance function (Birnbaum importance) of the system shown in Exercise 10, and calculate it for $t = 720\,h$.

Exercise 13. Compute the reliability sensitivity concerning the system parameters of the system shown in Exercise 10.

20 Combinatorial Model Analysis

This chapter presents some of the most important analytic methods for combinatorial models. These methods were divided into two groups: exact methods and methods for computing bounds. First, we introduce the exact methods; then the methods for calculating bounds are presented. The methods presented in this chapter are

- Exact Methods

  - Structure Function Method,

  - Enumeration Method,

  - Factoring Method (also called conditioning or pivoting method),

  - Reductions,

  - Inclusion-Exclusion Method,

  - Sum of Disjoint Product Method,

- Methods for Estimating Bounds

  - Method Based on Inclusion and Exclusion,

  - Method Based on the Sum of Disjoint Products,

  - Min-Max Bound Method,

  - Esary-Proschan Method, and

  - Decomposition.

20.1 STRUCTURE FUNCTION METHOD

The method based on structure-function has been the primary strategy adopted throughout the last two chapters. Hence, in this section, we only summarize the method already introduced.

This technique is based on the fact that $P(\Phi(X)) = E(\Phi(X))$, since $\Phi(X)$ is a Bernoulli random variable. Therefore, $P(\Phi(X))$ is the system reliability or availability, taking into account that the components are repairable or not. This method may be summarized in the following steps:

1. Obtain the structure function of the system.

2. Delete the powers of each variable x_i, $i \in \{1, 2, ..., n\}$, that is $x_i^n \to x_i$.

3. Replace x_i by p_i, where p_i is the component i's reliability or availability.

Most examples presented so far considered the structure-function strategy as the basic method for computing reliability and availability. However, it is worth looking at examples in which the state variables' power is higher than one. Examples 18.5.4 and 19.2 have state variables with power different from one. Therefore, it is worth having a look at the solutions presented for Examples 18.5.4 and 19.2.

20.2   ENUMERATION METHOD

The enumeration method is based on the explicit representation of all system states and on the respective structure-function that specifies the operational states. Thus, in theory, this method may be applied to all combinational models (RBD and FT) discussed.

As mentioned, the enumeration method is implemented by first determining the whole set of state vectors ($\{X_i\}$), and then applying each state to the structure function to check if the system is operational ($\Phi(X_i) = 1$) or not ($\Phi(X_i) = 0$). For a system with n components, the number of states is 2^n. Each state vector (X_i, $0 \leq i \leq 2^{n-1}$, $i \in \mathbb{N}^{*1}$) is considered an event (E_i), where $X_i = (x_j)_n$, x_j are the random variable that represents the state of the system component j (see Equation 18.2.1). The events E_i are all mutually exclusive (disjoints); hence the reliability (availability) can be computed by

$$P\left(\bigcup_{\forall E_i, \Phi(X_i)=1} E_i\right) = \sum_{\forall E_i, \Phi(X_i)=1} P(E_i), \qquad (20.2.1)$$

where $E_i \cap E_k$, $\forall i, k$, $i \neq k$. $P(E_i) = P(X_i) = \prod_{j=0}^{n-1} p_j$, $p_j = p(x_j = 1)$ – reliability or the availability of component j - or $p_j = p(x_j = 0)$ – unreliability or the unavailability of component z.

Consider the RBD shown in Figure 20.1. The model is composed of four ($n = 4$) components, represented by the set of Boolean variables $\{C_0, C_1, C_2, C_3\}$. As the RBD shows, the system is operational as long as the logical function $C_0 \wedge ((C_2 \wedge C_3) \wedge C_1)$ is evaluated as true. This logical function leads to the structure function

$$\Phi(X) = x_0 \times (1 - (1 - x_2 \times x_3) \times (1 - x_1)),$$

where $X = (x_0, x_1, x_2, x_3)$ is the vector of random variables (see Section 18.3). The variable x_j represents the state of the component j, $j = \{0, 1, 2, 3\}$.

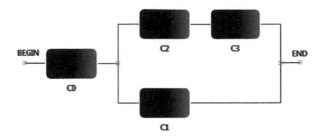

Figure 20.1 Enumeration – RBD.

Table 20.1 shows the enumeration of all system states (X_i, $i = \{0, 1, ..., 15\}$) and the respective evaluation of the structure function. The system probability (reliability and availability) computation takes into account the state $X = (x_3, x_2, x_1, x_0)$ that evaluates structure function to one. Therefore, in this specific example, the states of interest are only $(0, 0, 1, 1)$, $(0, 1, 1, 1)$, $(1, 0, 1, 1)$, $(1, 1, 0, 1)$, and $(1, 1, 1, 1)$.

Table 20.1
State Enumeration – RBD Shown in Figure 20.1

E_i	x_3	x_2	x_1	x_0	$\Phi(X)$
E_0	0	0	0	0	0
E_1	0	0	0	1	0
E_2	0	0	1	0	0
E_3	0	0	1	1	1
E_4	0	1	0	0	0
E_5	0	1	0	1	0
E_6	0	1	1	0	0
E_7	0	1	1	1	1
E_8	1	0	0	0	0
E_9	1	0	0	1	0
E_{10}	1	0	1	0	0
E_{11}	1	0	1	1	1
E_{12}	1	1	0	0	0
E_{13}	1	1	0	1	1
E_{14}	1	1	1	0	0
E_{15}	1	1	1	1	1

---

[1]$N^* = N \cup \{0\}$.

For each state that leads to $\Phi(X) = 1$, we multiply the probability – (un)reliability or the (un) availability – of each component. If the state of a component j is $x_j = 0$, we consider the unreliability or the unavailability $(p_j = P(x_j = 0) = 1 - E(x_{ij}))$. On the other hand, if the state of a component j is $x_j = 1$, we consider the reliability or the availability $(p_j = P(x_j = 1) = E(x_j))$.

Consider we are interested in the system reliability at t. If the components' reliabilities at t are $r_{c_3}(t) = 0.96$, $r_{c_2}(t) = 0.93$, $r_{c_1}(t) = 0.92$, and $r_{c_0}(t) = 0.95$, then when considering the state $(0,0,1,1)$, we have $ur_{c_3}(t) \times ur_{c_2}(t) \times r_{c_1}(t) \times r_{c_0}(t) = 0.04 \times 0.07 \times 0.92 \times 0.95 = 0.00245$ (see Table 20.2). Similarly, when considering the state $(0,1,1,1)$, we have $ur_{c_3}(t) \times r_{c_2}(t) \times r_{c_1}(t) \times r_{c_0}(t) = 0.04 \times 0.97 \times 0.92 \times 0.95 = 0.03251$. The probabilities related to the other states are shown in Table 20.2. Summing up the probabilities of the column $P(X)$, we have 0.94185.

Table 20.2

State Enumeration – Probabilities

E_i	x_3	x_2	x_1	x_0	p_3	p_2	p_1	p_0	$P(E_i) = \prod_{\forall j} p_j$
E_3	0	0	1	1	0.04	0.07	0.92	0.95	0.00245
E_7	0	1	1	1	0.04	0.93	0.92	0.95	0.03251
E_{11}	1	0	1	1	0.96	0.07	0.92	0.95	0.05873
E_{13}	1	1	0	1	0.96	0.93	0.08	0.95	0.06785
E_{15}	1	1	1	1	0.96	0.93	0.92	0.95	0.78031

Example 20.2.1. A system is composed of two servers (S_1 and S_2), each with its network-attached storage device (NAS_1 and NAS_2). Figure 20.2.a shows this system. A system failure occurs when both servers or their respective storage device fail. More formally, a failure is specified by

$$\overline{\Psi(B)} = (\overline{s_1} \vee \overline{nas_1}) \wedge (\overline{s_2} \vee \overline{nas_2}),$$

where $\overline{s_1}$, $\overline{s_2}$, $\overline{nas_1}$, and $\overline{nas_2}$ are Boolean variables, which if evaluated as true denote a component failure; otherwise the component is operational. $B = (\overline{s_1}, \overline{s_2}, \overline{nas_1}, \overline{nas_2})$ is Boolean vector.

Figure 20.2.b presents an FT that represents the system failure. Table 20.3 enumerates all states of the system and shows the respective evaluation of $\overline{\Psi}(B)$ and $1 - \Phi(X)$. In this table, F implies the system is operational and T represents a failure. Function $1 - \Phi(X)$ can be obtained from $\overline{\Psi}(B)$ by applying the rules shown in Table 18.3. It is worth noting that the basic events $\overline{s_1}$, $\overline{nas_1}$, s_2, and $\overline{nas_2}$ denote the respective component failure.

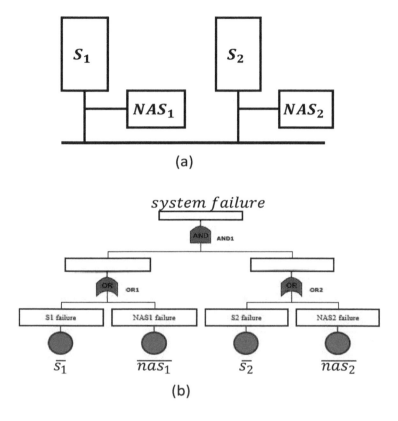

Figure 20.2   Two Servers and Two Storage Devices and FT.

Table 20.4 shows the respective structure variables and the structure function evaluation. Hence, it is important to stress that a Boolean variable $\overline{b_i}$ implies $x_i = 0$, and b_i corresponds to $x_i = 1$ (see rules presented in Table 18.3).

Assume the MTTFs and the MTTRs of each component are depicted in Table 20.5. The steady-state availability of each component is calculated by $A_i = MTTF_i/(MTTF_i + MTTR_i)$. Table 20.6 shows the events that evaluates the structure function ($\Phi(X)$) to one, and the respective availability or unavailability of each component in each specific event (state).

Consider we are interested in the system steady-state availability. For each state in which $\Phi(X) = 1$, we multiply the probability – (un)availability – of each component. If the state of a component $j \in \{S_1, S_2, NAS_1, NAS_2\}$ is $x_j = 0$, we consider the

Table 20.3

State Enumeration – Logical Function

Event	$\overline{s_1}$	$\overline{nas_1}$	$\overline{s_2}$	$\overline{nas_2}$	$\overline{\Psi}(B)$	$1 - \Phi(X)$
E_0	T	T	T	T	T	1
E_1	T	T	T	F	T	1
E_2	T	T	F	T	T	1
E_3	T	T	F	F	F	0
E_4	T	F	T	T	T	1
E_5	T	F	T	F	T	1
E_6	T	F	F	T	T	1
E_7	T	F	F	F	F	0
E_8	F	T	T	T	T	1
E_9	F	T	T	F	T	1
E_{10}	F	T	F	T	T	1
E_{11}	F	T	F	F	F	0
E_{12}	F	F	T	T	F	0
E_{13}	F	F	T	F	F	0
E_{14}	F	F	F	T	F	0
E_{15}	F	F	F	F	F	0

unavailability ($p_j = P(x_j = 0)$). On the other hand, if the state of a component $j \in \{s_1, s_2, nas_1, nas_2\}$ is $x_j = 1$, we consider the availability ($p_j = P(x_j = 1)$).

The components' availabilities are $A_{s_1} = 0.988142$, $A_{nas_1} = 0.99681$, $A_{s_2} = 0.989446$, and $A_{nas_2} = 0.99681$. For state $(0,0,1,1)$ – Event E_3, we have $UA_{s_1} \times UA_{nas_1} \times A_{s_2} \times A_{nas_2} = 0.011858 \times 0.00319 \times 0.989446 \times 0.99681 = 0.00004$ (see Table 20.6). The availabilities related to the other basic events (states) are shown in Table 20.6. Summing up the availabilities of the column $P(E_i)$, we obtain the steady-state availability 0.99979.

□

Example 20.2.2. Let us have a system composed of three identical components, C_1, C_2, and C_3. Each of these components may be operational ($x_i = 1$) or in failure ($x_i = 1$), $i \in \{1, 2, 3\}$. Table 20.7 shows all possible states of each component. If theses components are arranged in series, the respective structure function is only evaluated to 1 for the state $X = (1, 1, 1)$. This is shown in Column $\Phi_s(X)$. If theses components are arranged in parallel, the respective structure function is evaluated to 1 for all states except $X = (0, 0, 0)$. This is shown in Column $\Phi_p(X)$. For a 2oo3 structure, the respective structure function is evaluated to 1 for states $(0, 1, 1)$, $(1, 0, 1)$, $(1, 1, 0)$, and $(1, 1, 1)$. Column $\Phi_{2oo3}(X)$ of the Table 20.7 shows this function.

Table 20.4

State Enumeration – Structure Function

Event	x_{s_1}	x_{nas_1}	x_{s_2}	x_{nas_2}	$\Phi(X)$
E_0	0	0	0	0	0
E_1	0	0	0	1	0
E_2	0	0	1	0	0
E_3	0	0	1	1	1
E_4	0	1	0	0	0
E_5	0	1	0	1	0
E_6	0	1	1	0	0
E_7	0	1	1	1	1
E_8	1	0	0	0	0
E_9	1	0	0	1	0
E_{10}	1	0	1	0	0
E_{11}	1	0	1	1	1
E_{12}	1	1	0	0	1
E_{13}	1	1	0	1	1
E_{14}	1	1	1	0	1
E_{15}	1	1	1	1	1

Table 20.5

Two Servers and Two Storage Devices - $MTTF$s and $MTTR$s

Component	$MTTF$ (h)	$MTTR$ (h)
S_1	4000	48
S_2	4500	48
NAS_1	30000	96
NAS_2	30000	96

Consider the computation of the system reliability of the system. As the components are identical, $R_0(t) = R_1(t) = R_2(t) = R(t)$. Hence, in Table 20.8, the probabilities related to each component are $p_i = R(t)$ or $p_i = UR(t)$ depending on whether $x_i = 1$ or $x_i = 0$, $i \in \{0, 1, 2\}$. As the reliability is only calculated for states that $\Phi_s(X) = 1$; the system reliability is $R(t) \times R(t) \times R(t) = R^3(t)$.

The system reliability for the parallel system can be calculated by multiplying the probabilities (reliabilities or unreliabilities) of components of each line of the

Table 20.6

Probabilities of Events - Two Servers and Two Storage Devices

Event	p_{s_1}	p_{nas_1}	p_{s_2}	p_{nas_1}	$P(E_i) = \prod_{\forall j} p_j$
E_3	0.011858	0.00319	0.989446	0.99681	0.00004
E_7	0.011858	0.99681	0.989446	0.99681	0.01166
E_{11}	0.988142	0.00319	0.989446	0.99681	0.00311
E_{12}	0.988142	0.99681	0.010554	0.00319	0.00003
E_{13}	0.988142	0.99681	0.010554	0.99681	0.01036
E_{14}	0.988142	0.99681	0.989446	0.00319	0.00311
E_{15}	0.988142	0.99681	0.989446	0.99681	0.97149

Table 20.7

Three Components Systems - States Enumeration

Event	x_2	x_1	x_0	$\Phi_s(X)$	$\Phi_p(X)$	$\Phi_{2oo3}(X)$
E_0	0	0	0	0	0	0
E_1	0	0	1	0	1	0
E_2	0	1	0	0	1	0
E_3	0	1	1	0	1	1
E_4	1	0	0	0	1	0
E_5	1	0	1	0	1	1
E_6	1	1	0	0	1	1
E_7	1	1	1	1	1	1

Table 20.8

Three Components Systems - Series System

Event	x_2	x_1	x_0	$\Phi_s(X)$	p_2	p_1	p_0
E_0	0	0	0	0	$UR(t)$	$UR(t)$	$UR(t)$
E_1	0	0	1	0	$UR(t)$	$UR(t)$	$R(t)$
E_2	0	1	0	0	$UR(t)$	$R(t)$	$UR(t)$
E_3	0	1	1	0	$UR(t)$	$R(t)$	$R(t)$
E_4	1	0	0	0	$R(t)$	$UR(t)$	$UR(t)$
E_5	1	0	1	0	$R(t)$	$UR(t)$	$R(t)$
E_6	1	1	0	0	$R(t)$	$R(t)$	$UR(t)$
E_7	1	1	1	1	$R(t)$	$R(t)$	$R(t)$

Table 20.9 in which $\Phi(X) = 1$ and summing up the probabilities of the lines. An alternative is calculating the system unreliability by multiplying the unreliabilities of each component where $\Phi_p(X) = 0$ (Event $E0$) and subtracting from 1. Hence, the system unreliability is $UR(t) \times UR(t) \times UR(t) = UR^3(t) = (1 - R(t))^3$. Therefore, the system reliability is $1 - (1 - R(t))^3$.

Table 20.9

Three Components Systems - Parallel System

Event	x_2	x_1	x_0	$\Phi_p(X)$	p_2	p_1	p_0
E_0	0	0	0	0	$UR(t)$	$UR(t)$	$UR(t)$
E_1	0	0	1	1	$UR(t)$	$UR(t)$	$R(t)$
E_2	0	1	0	1	$UR(t)$	$R(t)$	$UR(t)$
E_3	0	1	1	1	$UR(t)$	$R(t)$	$R(t)$
E_4	1	0	0	1	$R(t)$	$UR(t)$	$UR(t)$
E_5	1	0	1	1	$R(t)$	$UR(t)$	$R(t)$
E_6	1	1	0	1	$R(t)$	$R(t)$	$UR(t)$
E_7	1	1	1	1	$R(t)$	$R(t)$	$R(t)$

The system reliability is computed from the line in which $\Phi_{2oo3}(X) = 1$ (see Table 20.10); thus

$$UR(t) \times R(t) \times R(t) + R(t) \times UR(t) \times R(t) + R(t) \times R(t) \times UR(t) + R(t) \times R(t) \times R(t) =$$

$$R^2(t) \times UR(t) + R^2(t) \times UR(t) + R^2(t) \times UR(t) + R^3(t) =$$

$$R^2(t) \times (1 - R(t)) + R^2(t) \times (1 - R(t)) + R^2(t) \times (1 - R(t)) + R^3(t) =$$

$$3R^2(t) \times (1 - R(t)) + R^3(t) =$$

$$3R^2(t) - 3R^3(t) + R^3(t) =$$

$$3R^2(t) - 2R^3(t).$$

□

Table 20.10

Three Components Systems - $2oo3$ System

Event	x_2	x_1	x_0	$\Phi_{2oo3}(X)$	p_2	p_1	p_0
E_0	0	0	0	0	$UR(t)$	$UR(t)$	$UR(t)$
E_1	0	0	1	0	$UR(t)$	$UR(t)$	$R(t)$
E_2	0	1	0	0	$UR(t)$	$R(t)$	$UR(t)$
E_3	0	1	1	1	$UR(t)$	$R(t)$	$R(t)$
E_4	1	0	0	0	$R(t)$	$UR(t)$	$UR(t)$
E_5	1	0	1	1	$R(t)$	$UR(t)$	$R(t)$
E_6	1	1	0	1	$R(t)$	$R(t)$	$UR(t)$
E_7	1	1	1	1	$R(t)$	$R(t)$	$R(t)$

20.3 FACTORING METHOD

In Chapters 18 and 19, we also applied the conditioning strategy for obtaining the structure-function of systems and the respective reliability or availability. Usually, this strategy is applied to decompose a system into simpler subsystems for which the solutions may be known. This method is particularly interesting for systems that parallel-series compositions can not represent due to more complex relations between the system components.

Consider a set of n independent components, $\{c_i\}$, whose states are represented by the respective variables x_i of the vector $X = (x_i)_{|n|}$. The structure function $\Phi(\mathbf{X})$ may be re-written by

$$\Phi(\mathbf{X}) = x_i \times \Phi(1_i, \mathbf{X}) + (1 - x_i) \times \Phi(0_i, \mathbf{X}), \qquad (20.3.1)$$

where $\Phi(1_i, \mathbf{X})$ represents the system state in which the component c_i is operational and the states of the other components are random variables ($\Phi(x_1, x_2, ..., 1_i, ..., x_n)$). Likewise, $\Phi(0_i, \mathbf{X})$ denotes the system state in which the component c_i has failed and the states of the other components are random variables ($\Phi(x_1, x_2, ..., 0_i, ..., x_n)$). Let us assume $p_i = P(x_i = 1)$ be the probability of the component i being operational (reliability or availability); hence the probability of the system being operational (reliability or availability) may be represented by

$$P(\Phi(\mathbf{X}) = 1) = P((x_i \times \Phi(1_i, \mathbf{X}) + (1 - x_i) \times \Phi(0_i, \mathbf{X})) = 1)$$

$$P(\Phi(\mathbf{X}) = 1) = P(x_i = 1) \times P(\Phi(1_i, \mathbf{X}) = 1) + P(1 - x_i = 1) \times P(\Phi(0_i, \mathbf{X}) = 1)$$

$$P(\Phi(\mathbf{X}) = 1) = P(x_i = 1) \times P(\Phi(1_i, \mathbf{X}) = 1) + P(x_i = 0) \times P(\Phi(0_i, \mathbf{X}) = 1)$$

$$P(\Phi(\mathbf{X}) = 1) = p_i \times P(\Phi(1_i, \mathbf{X}) = 1) + (1 - p_i) \times P(\Phi(0_i, \mathbf{X}) = 1).$$

Therefore, if the system is factored considering the state of the component i (x_i), the system probability can be computed based on the probability of component i

(p_i) and on the system's probabilities conditioned to $x_i = 1$ and to $x_i = 0$. If the system probabilities for these two conditions are known, the system reliability is straightforwardly calculated.

Some examples presented in previous chapters considered the pivoting strategy as an auxiliary method for computing reliability and availability. It is worth looking at the solutions presented for bridge structure in Section 18.5 and the Example 19.3.3.

Example 20.3.1. Let us study another system in which factoring helps find the system probability. Consider the RBD shown in Figure 20.3. This RBD is more complex than simple series-parallel structures. Particular attention should be paid to components C_2 and C_3. These two components are considered bidirectional (see the bridge structure in Section 18.5). Let us first define the structure variables of each component C_i by x_i, $i \in \{1,2,3,4,5,6,7\}$.

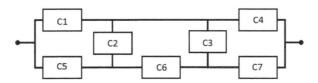

Figure 20.3 Non-Series-Parallel RBD.

The RBD shown in Figure 20.3 can be factored into two RBDs by, for instance, first conditioning on the states of C_2. If $x_2 = 1$, the RBD depicted in Figure 20.3 is transformed into the RBD shown in Figure 20.4.a. On the other hand, if $x_2 = 0$, the RBD presented in Figure 20.3 is represented by the RBD depicted in Figure 20.4.b. The system structure function can; thus, be represented by

$$\Phi(X) = x_2 \times \Phi(1_2, X) + (1 - x_2) \times \Phi(0_2, X).$$

Therefore

$$P(\Phi(X) = 1) = p_2 \times P(\Phi(1_2, X) = 1) + (1 - p_2) \times P(\Phi(0_2, X) = 1).$$

The RBD shown in Figure 20.4.a is a simple series-parallel structure. Hence

$$P(\Phi(1_2, X) = 1) = (1 - (1 - p_1)(1 - p_5)) \times (1 - (1 - p_4) \times$$
$$(1 - ((1 - (1 - p_3)(1 - p_6))p_7))).$$

In the RBD depicted in Figure 20.4.b, components C_5 and C_6 are in series; hence the probability of these two components is

$$P(\Phi(x_5, x_6) = 1) = p_5 \times p_6.$$

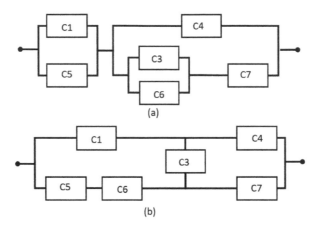

(a)

(b)

Figure 20.4   Factoring the RBD of Figure 20.3.

Consider C_5 and C_6 as one component (C_{56}) with probability $p_{56} = p_5 \times p_6$. Thus, the RBD depicted in Figure 20.4.b is represented by a bridge structure. Using the solution presented in Section 18.5 for the bridge structure, we obtain

$$P(\Phi(0_2, X) = 1) = p_3 \times P(\Phi(0_2, 1_3, X) = 1) + (1 - p_3) \times P(\Phi(0_2, 0_3, X) = 1).$$

$$P(\Phi(0_2, 1_3, X) = 1) = (1 - (1 - p_1) \times (1 - p_5 p_6)) \times (1 - (1 - p_4) \times (1 - p_7)).$$

$$P(\Phi(0_2, 0_3, X) = 1) = (1 - (1 - p_1 p_4) \times (1 - p_5 p_6 p_7)).$$

Therefore,

$$P(\Phi(X) = 1) = p_2 \times ((1 - (1 - p_1)(1 - p_5)) \times (1 - (1 - p_4) \times$$

$$(1 - ((1 - (1 - p_3)(1 - p_6))p_7)))) + (1 - p_2) \times (p_3 \times ((1 - (1 - p_1) \times (1 - p_5 p_6))$$

$$(1 - (1 - p_4) \times (1 - p_7))) + (1 - p_3) \times ((1 - (1 - p_1 p_4) \times (1 - p_5 p_6 p_7)))).$$

□

Example 20.3.2. Consider a sensor network, depicted in Figure 20.5.a, composed of 5 nodes, $\{n_a, n_b, n_c, n_d, n_e\}$, that are connected through the dedicated links $\{l_{ae}, l_{ad}, l_{bd}, l_{cd}, l_{de}\}$ [90]. The system is considered operational if n_a, n_b, or n_c can send data to node n_e through the respective links. Assume the functioning probability of the nodes are p_i, $i \in \{n_a, n_b, n_c, n_d, n_e\}$, and the respective links' functioning probabilities are p_j, $j \in \{l_{ae}, l_{ad}, l_{bd}, l_{cd}, l_{de}\}$. Figure 20.5.b shows the respective RBD. It is worth stressing that all blocks of the RBD are considered unidirectional.

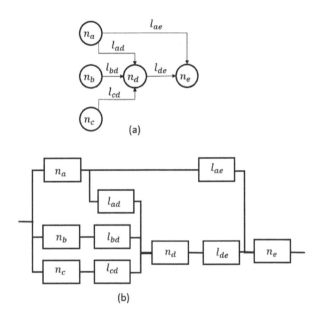

Figure 20.5   Sensor Network and Its RBD.

If the RBD is factored on node *na* ($x_a = 1$ and $x_a = 0$), then the RBD is represented by the two respective RBDs shown in Figure 20.6. Simple series-parallel structures represent these two RBDs.

Therefore,

$$P(\Phi(X) = 1) = p_{n_a} \times P(\Phi(1_{n_a}, X) = 1) + (1 - p_{n_a}) \times P(\Phi(0_{n_a}, X) = 1),$$

where

$$P(\Phi(1_{n_a}, X) = 1) = (1 - ((1 - (1 - p_{l_{ad}})(1 - p_{n_b} p_{l_{bd}})(1 - p_{n_c} p_{l_{cd}})) p_{n_d} p_{l_{de}})$$

$$(1 - p_{l_{ae}})) p_{n_e},$$

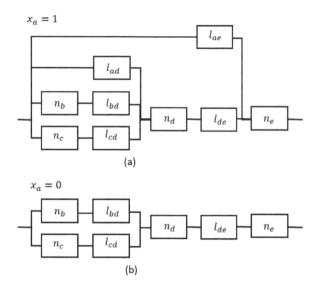

Figure 20.6 Factoring.

and

$$P(\Phi(0_{n_a}, X) = 1) = (1 - (1 - p_{n_b} p_{l_{lbd}})(1 - p_{n_c} p_{l_{lcd}})) p_{n_d} p_{l_{lde}} p_{n_e}.$$

☐

20.4 REDUCTIONS

This section presents a set of transformations that allows calculating the system probability (reliability or availability) by computing the respective probability of its subsystems and combining the individual results. The basic idea consists of calculating the probabilities of system components, then transforming the subsystems into single components of the system, and adopting such a procedure until the system is represented by one single component. Now, let us introduce a few reduction rules that support the evaluation process.

Series Reduction - Consider a series system is represented by an RBD with n components C_i, $i = \{1, 2, ..., n\}$. Assume each component C_i's functioning probability (reliability or availability) is p_i (see Figure 20.7.a); hence this system can be represented by a single component, and its respective probability is $P(\Phi(X) = 1) = \prod_{i=1}^{n} p_i$. Figure 20.7.b shows the single component that represents the system. Such a system may also be represented by the FT shown in Figure 20.7.c. As the failure probability of each basic event $(\overline{C_i})$ is $1 - p_i$, the system failure probability is

$P(\Phi(X) = 0) = \prod_{i=1}^{n}(1 - p_i)$ (see Section 19.2). After applying the reduction, the resulting FT consists of only one single basic event.

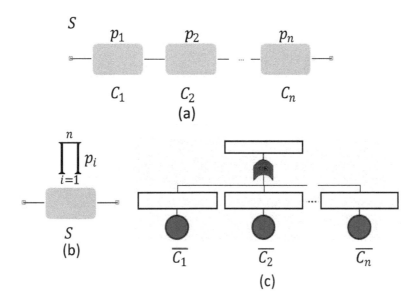

Figure 20.7 Series Reduction.

Parallel Reduction - Now assume a system is represented by an RBD with n components C_i, $i = \{1, 2, ..., n\}$. Consider each component C_i's success probability (reliability or availability) is p_i (see Figure 20.8.a); thus this system can be represented by a single component with success probability equal to $P(\Phi(X) = 1) = 1 - \prod_{i=1}^{n}(1 - p_i)$. Figure 20.8.b shows the single component that represents the system. This system may also be specified by the FT shown in Figure 20.8.c, and the resulting FT consists only of one single basic event.

Bridge Reduction - Consider a system is represented by a bridge structure with 5 components C_i, $i = \{1, 2, 3, 4, 5\}$. It is worth noting the component C_3 is bidirectional. Consider each component C_i's success probability (reliability or availability) is p_i (see Figure 20.9.a); thus this system can be represented by a single component with success probability equal to

$$P(\Phi(X = 1)) = p_3 \times ((1 - (1 - p_1) \times (1 - p_4)) \times (1 - (1 - p_2) \times (1 - p_5)))$$

$$+ (1 - p_3) \times (1 - (1 - p_1 p_2)(1 - p_4 p_5)).[2]$$

---

[2] See Equation 18.5.43.

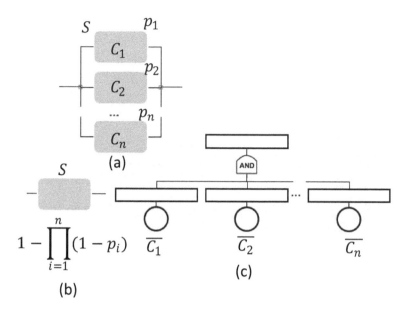

Figure 20.8   Parallel Blocks Reduction.

Assuming $p_1 = p_2 = p_3 = p_4 = p_5 = 0.9$, $P(\Phi(X = 1)) = 0.97848^3$. Figure 20.9.b shows the single component that represents the system.

Many strategies can be adopted to reduce the system model to calculate its probability. First, one possibility is decomposing the original system model into modules (subsystems) and then applying the reduction to each module. As one extreme case, the modules can be represented by individual components. In the other extreme case, one module defines the whole system. Usually, however, the system is decomposed into independent modules between these two extremes [352]. Another possibility is applying a possible reduction to a set of components, obtaining a resulting system model, and then continuing applying possible reductions until obtaining either a single component or a system specification to which a solution is already known.

Example 20.4.1.   A system is represented by an RBD shown in Figure 20.10. This model is specified by ten blocks. The blocks b_6, b_7, b_8, b_9, and b_{10} are a bridge, and the block b_4 represents a $2oo3$ configuration. Assume r_i is the block i reliability at specific time t.

---

[3]Also see the results obtained using Equation 18.5.44 and in Section 20.5.

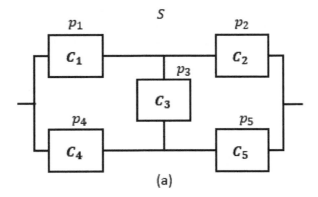

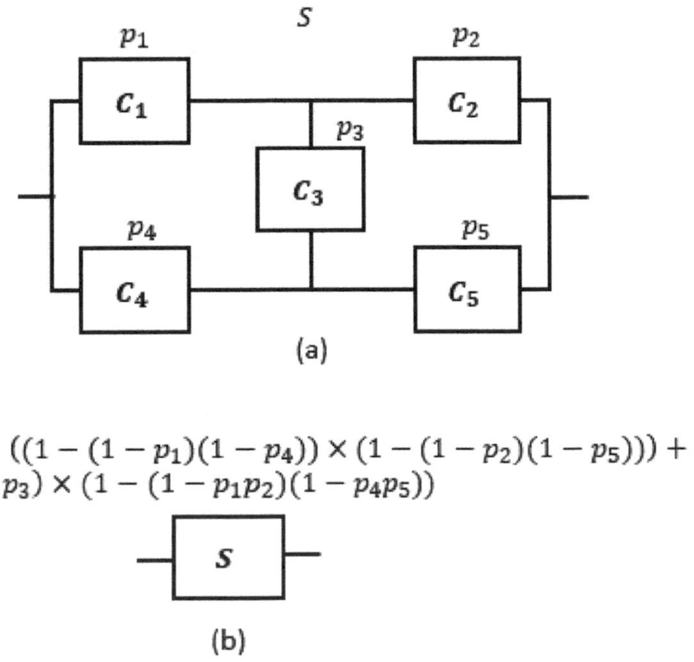

S
p1
p2
C1
C2
p3
C3
p4
p5
C4
C5
(a)
p3 × ((1 − (1 − p1)(1 − p4)) × (1 − (1 − p2)(1 − p5))) +
(1 − p3) × (1 − (1 − p1p2)(1 − p4p5))
S
(b)

Figure 20.9 Bridge Reduction.

The system reliability can be estimated by applying the reduction depicted in this section. A first possible reduction can be applied in the blocks that depict the bridge. These blocks can be reduced and represented by one block (b_{12} - see Figure 20.11). The reliability of b_{11} at t is

$$r_{11} = r_8 \times ((1-(1-r_6)\times(1-r_9))\times(1-(1-r_7)\times(1-r_{10})))$$

$$+(1-r_8)\times(1-(1-r_6r_7)(1-r_9r_{10})).$$

Figure 20.11.a shows the block b_{11} that represents the bridge depicted in Figure 20.10. Now, two series reductions can be applied. Blocks b_2 and b_3 can be represented by block b_{13} (see Figure 20.11.b) and its reliability is obtained by the

$$r_{13} = r_2 \times r_3.$$

The second set of blocks that can be serially combined is $\{b_5, b_{11}\}$. Figure 20.11.b shows the block b_{12}, which depicts such a composition. The reliability of the block b_{12} is expressed by

$$r_{12} = r_5 \times r_{11}.$$

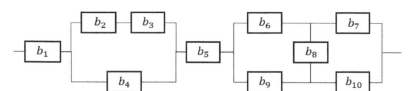

Figure 20.10 RBD before Reductions.

As the block b_4 depicts a subsystem configured in 2o3, so its reliability is

$$r_4 = 3r^2 - 2r^3,$$

where r is the reliability of each subsystem components at t. The RBD of Figure 20.11.b may now be transformed by applying the parallel reduction on blocks b_4 and b_{13}. Figure 20.11.c shows the resulting RBD, in which b_{14} is the resulting block. The reliability of the block b_{14} is depicted by

$$r_{14} = 1 - (1 - r_4)(1 - r_{13}).$$

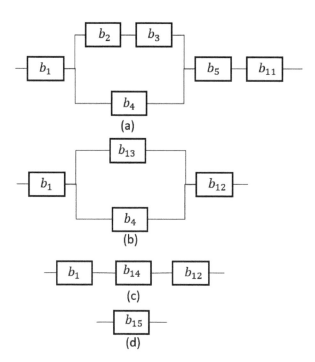

Figure 20.11 Reductions

Finally, the RBD shown in Figure 20.11.c can be reduced to one block by applying a series reduction on the blocks b_1, b_{12}, and b_{14}. The resulting RBD is depicted by only one block (b_5 - Figure 20.11.d), and its reliability is

$$r_{sys} = r_{15} = r_1 \times r_{12} \times r_{14}.$$

□

20.5 INCLUSION-EXCLUSION METHOD

This section presents how the inclusion-exclusion method (IEM) is applied to estimate reliability and availability of systems [224, 352]. The inclusion-exclusion principle is a counting method for obtaining the number of elements in the union of sets. Consider three events represented by the respective sets A, B, and C. The probability of the union of the sets A, B, and C is

$$P(A \cup B \cup C) = P(A) + P(B) + P(C) - P(A \cap B) \qquad (20.5.1)$$
$$- P(A \cap C) - P(B \cap C) + P(A \cap B \cap C).$$

More generally, consider the events represented by the finite sets A_1, ..., A_n. We have

$$P(\bigcup_{i=1}^{n} A_i) = \sum_{i=1}^{n} P(A_i) - \sum_{i,j=1\leq i\leq j\leq n} P(A_i \cap A_j) \qquad (20.5.2)$$

$$+ \sum_{i,j,k=1\leq i\leq j\leq k\leq n} P(A_i \cap A_j \cap A_k) - \dots + (-1)^{n-1} P(\bigcap_{i=1}^{n} A_i).$$

Let us consider the bridge model shown in Figure 20.9.a. This model has four minimal paths. The minimal paths are $MP_1 = \{c_1, c_2\}$, $MP_2 = \{c_4, c_5\}$, $MP_3 = \{c_1, c_3, c_5\}$, and $MP_4 = \{c_2, c_3, c_4\}$. Each minimal path is represented by the respective logical function:

$$\Psi_{MP_1}(c_1, c_2) = c_1 \wedge c_2,$$

$$\Psi_{MP_2}(c_4, c_5) = c_4 \wedge c_5,$$

$$\Psi_{MP_3}(c_1, c_3, c_5) = c_1 \wedge c_3 \wedge c_5,$$

$$\Psi_{MP_4}(c_2, c_3, c_4) = c_2 \wedge c_3 \wedge c_4.$$

As $MP_i \cap MP_i \equiv \Psi_{MP_i} \wedge \Psi_{MP_j}$, then

$$\Psi_{MP_1} \wedge \Psi_{MP_2} = c_1 \wedge c_2 \wedge c_4 \wedge c_5.$$

$$\Psi_{MP_1} \wedge \Psi_{MP_3} = c_1 \wedge c_2 \wedge c_3 \wedge c_5.$$

$$\Psi_{MP_1} \wedge \Psi_{MP_4} = c_1 \wedge c_2 \wedge c_3 \wedge c_4.$$

$$\Psi_{MP_2} \wedge \Psi_{MP_3} = c_1 \wedge c_3 \wedge c_4 \wedge c_5.$$

$$\Psi_{MP_2} \wedge \Psi_{MP_4} = c_2 \wedge c_3 \wedge c_4 \wedge c_5.$$

$$\Psi_{MP_3} \wedge \Psi_{MP_4} = c_1 \wedge c_2 \wedge c_3 \wedge c_4 \wedge c_5.$$

$$\Psi_{MP_1} \wedge \Psi_{MP_2} \wedge \Psi_{MP_3} = c_1 \wedge c_2 \wedge c_3 \wedge c_4 \wedge c_5.$$

$$\Psi_{MP_1} \wedge \Psi_{MP_2} \wedge \Psi_{MP_4} = c_1 \wedge c_2 \wedge c_3 \wedge c_4 \wedge c_5.$$

$$\Psi_{MP_1} \wedge \Psi_{MP_3} \wedge \Psi_{MP_4} = c_1 \wedge c_2 \wedge c_3 \wedge c_4 \wedge c_5.$$

$$\Psi_{MP_2} \wedge \Psi_{MP_3} \wedge \Psi_{MP_4} = c_1 \wedge c_2 \wedge c_3 \wedge c_4 \wedge c_5.$$

$$\Psi_{MP_1} \wedge \Psi_{MP_2} \wedge \Psi_{MP_3} \wedge \Psi_{MP_4} = c_1 \wedge c_2 \wedge c_3 \wedge c_4 \wedge c_5.$$

Now, consider the functioning probability of component i is p_i; then

$$P(MP_1) = P(\Psi_{MP_1}) = p_1 p_2.$$

$$P(MP_2) = P(\Psi_{MP_2}) = p_4 p_5.$$

$$P(MP_3) = P(\Psi_{MP_3}) = p_1 p_3 p_5.$$

$$P(MP_4) = P(\Psi_{MP_4}) = p_2 p_3 p_4.$$

$$P(MP_1 \cap MP_2) = P(\Psi_{MP_1} \wedge \Psi_{MP_2}) = p_1 p_2 p_4 p_5.$$

$$P(MP_1 \cap MP_3) = P(\Psi_{MP_1} \wedge \Psi_{MP_3}) = p_1 p_2 p_3 p_5.$$

$$P(MP_1 \cap MP_4) = P(\Psi_{MP_1} \wedge \Psi_{MP_4}) = p_1 p_2 p_3 p_4.$$

$$P(MP_2 \cap MP_3) = P(\Psi_{MP_2} \wedge \Psi_{MP_3}) = p_1 p_3 p_4 p_5.$$

$$P(MP_2 \cap MP_4) = P(\Psi_{MP_2} \wedge \Psi_{MP_4}) = p_2 p_3 p_4 p_5.$$

$$P(MP_3 \cap MP_4) = P(\Psi_{MP_3} \wedge \Psi_{MP_4}) = p_1 p_2 p_3 p_4 p_5.$$

$$P(MP_1 \cap MP_2 \cap MP_3) = P(\Psi_{MP_1} \wedge \Psi_{MP_2} \wedge \Psi_{MP_3}) = p_1 p_2 p_3 p_4 p_5.$$

$$P(MP_1 \cap MP_2 \cap MP_4) = P(\Psi_{MP_1} \wedge \Psi_{MP_2} \wedge \Psi_{MP_4}) = p_1 p_2 p_3 p_4 p_5.$$

$$P(MP_1 \cap MP_3 \cap MP_4) = P(\Psi_{MP_1} \wedge \Psi_{MP_3} \wedge \Psi_{MP_4}) = p_1 p_2 p_3 p_4 p_5.$$

$$P(MP_2 \cap MP_3 \cap MP_4) = P(\Psi_{MP_2} \wedge \Psi_{MP_3} \wedge \Psi_{MP_4}) = p_1 p_2 p_3 p_4 p_5.$$

$$P(MP_1 \cap MP_2 \cap MP_3 \cap MP_4) = P(\Psi_{MP_1} \wedge \Psi_{MP_2} \wedge \Psi_{MP_3} \wedge \Psi_{MP_4}) = p_1 p_2 p_3 p_4 p_5.$$

Therefore, applying Equation 20.5.2, we obtain

$$P(\bigcup_{i=1}^{4} MP_i) = P(MP_1) + P(MP_2) + P(MP_3) + P(MP_4) - P(MP_1 \cap MP_2) -$$

$$P(MP_1 \cap MP_3) - P(MP_1 \cap MP_4) - P(MP_2 \cap MP_3) - P(MP_2 \cap MP_4) -$$

$$P(MP_3 \cap MP_4) + P(MP_1 \cap MP_2 \cap MP_3) + P(MP_1 \cap MP_2 \cap MP_4)$$

$$+ P(MP_1 \cap MP_3 \cap MP_4) + P(MP_2 \cap MP_3 \cap MP_4) - P(MP_1 \cap MP_2 \cap MP_3 \cap MP_4) =$$

$$p_1 p_2 + p_4 p_5 + p_1 p_3 p_5 + p_2 p_3 p_4 - p_1 p_2 p_4 p_5 - p_1 p_2 p_3 p_5 - p_1 p_2 p_3 p_4$$
$$- p_1 p_3 p_4 p_5 - p_2 p_3 p_4 p_5 - p_1 p_2 p_3 p_4 p_5 + 4 p_1 p_2 p_3 p_4 p_5 - p_1 p_2 p_3 p_4 p_5 =$$
$$p_1 p_2 + p_4 p_5 + p_1 p_3 p_5 + p_2 p_3 p_4 - p_1 p_2 p_4 p_5 - p_1 p_2 p_3 p_5 - p_1 p_2 p_3 p_4$$
$$- p_1 p_3 p_4 p_5 - p_2 p_3 p_4 p_5 + 2 p_1 p_2 p_3 p_4 p_5.$$

If $p_i = p$, then

$$2p^2 + 2p^3 - 5p^4 + 2p^5$$

Considering $p = 0.9$, we obtain $P(\bigcup_{i=1}^{4} MP_i) = 0.97848^4$.

Example 20.5.1. A system is represented by the FT shown in Figure 19.22. The failure probability can be calculated by $P(\bigcup_{i=1}^{4} MC_i)$, where MC_i is a minimal cut set. The minimal cuts of this FT are $MC_1 = \{P_1, P_2\}$, $MC_2 = \{P_1, M_2, M_3\}$, $MC_3 = \{M_1, M_3, P_2\}$, and $MC_4 = \{M_1, M_2, M_3\}$. Each minimal cut is represented by the respective logical function:

$$MC_1 \Rightarrow \overline{\Psi}_{MC_1} = \overline{P_1} \wedge \overline{P_2},$$

$$MC_2 \Rightarrow \overline{\Psi}_{MC_2} = \overline{P_1} \wedge \overline{M_2} \wedge \overline{M_3},$$

$$MC_3 \Rightarrow \overline{\Psi}_{MC_3} = \overline{M_1} \wedge \overline{M_3} \wedge \overline{P_2},$$

and

$$MC_4 \Rightarrow \overline{\Psi}_{MC_4} = \overline{M_1} \wedge \overline{M_2} \wedge \overline{M_3}.$$

The terms $MC_1 \cap MC_2$, $MC_1 \cap MC_3$, $MC_1 \cap MC_4$, $MC_2 \cap MC_3$, $MC_2 \cap MC_4$, and $MC_3 \cap MC_4$ are represented by the respective logical functions

$$MC_1 \cap MC_2 \Rightarrow \overline{\Psi}_{MC_1 \cap MC_2} = \overline{P_1} \wedge \overline{P_2} \wedge \overline{M_2} \wedge \overline{M_3},$$

---

[4] Also see the results obtained using Equation 18.5.44 and in Section 20.4.

$$MC_1 \cap MC_3 \Rightarrow \overline{\Psi}_{MC_1 \cap MC_3} = \overline{P_1} \wedge \overline{P_2} \wedge \overline{M_1} \wedge \overline{M_3},$$

$$MC_1 \cap MC_4 \Rightarrow \overline{\Psi}_{MC_1 \cap MC_4} = \overline{P_1} \wedge \overline{P_2} \wedge \overline{M_1} \wedge \overline{M_2} \wedge \overline{M_3},$$

$$MC_2 \cap MC_3 \Rightarrow \overline{\Psi}_{MC_2 \cap MC_3} = \overline{P_1} \wedge \overline{P_2} \wedge \overline{M_1} \wedge \overline{M_2} \wedge \overline{M_3},$$

$$MC_2 \cap MC_4 \Rightarrow \overline{\Psi}_{MC_2 \cap MC_4} = \overline{P_1} \wedge \overline{M_1} \wedge \overline{M_2} \wedge \overline{M_3},$$

$$MC_3 \cap MC_4 \Rightarrow \overline{\Psi}_{MC_3 \cap MC_4} = \overline{M_1} \wedge \overline{M_2} \wedge \overline{M_3} \wedge \overline{P_2},$$

The terms $MC_1 \cap MC_2 \cap MC_3$, $MC_1 \cap MC_2 \cap MC_4$, $MC_1 \cap MC_3 \cap MC_4$, $MC_2 \cap MC_3 \cap MC_4$ are represented by the respective logical functions

$$MC_1 \cap MC_2 \cap MC_3 \Rightarrow \overline{\Psi}_{MC_1 \cap MC_2 \cap MC_3} = \overline{P_1} \wedge \overline{P_2} \wedge \overline{M_1} \wedge \overline{M_2} \wedge \overline{M_3},$$

$$MC_1 \cap MC_2 \cap MC_4 \Rightarrow \overline{\Psi}_{MC_1 \cap MC_2 \cap MC_4} = \overline{P_1} \wedge \overline{P_2} \wedge \overline{M_1} \wedge \overline{M_2} \wedge \overline{M_3},$$

$$MC_1 \cap MC_3 \cap MC_4 \Rightarrow \overline{\Psi}_{MC_1 \cap MC_3 \cap MC_4} = \overline{P_1} \wedge \overline{P_2} \wedge \overline{M_1} \wedge \overline{M_2} \wedge \overline{M_3},$$

$$MC_2 \cap MC_3 \cap MC_4 \Rightarrow \overline{\Psi}_{MC_2 \cap MC_3 \cap MC_4} = \overline{P_1} \wedge \overline{P_2} \wedge \overline{M_1} \wedge \overline{M_2} \wedge \overline{M_3},$$

The term $MC_1 \cap MC_2 \cap MC_3 \cap MC_4$ is represented by the respective logical function

$$MC_1 \cap MC_2 \cap MC_3 \cap MC_4 \Rightarrow \overline{\Psi}_{MC_1 \cap MC_2 \cap MC_3 \cap MC_4} = \overline{P_1} \wedge \overline{P_2} \wedge \overline{M_1} \wedge \overline{M_2} \wedge \overline{M_3}.$$

For a given component i, using the transformation rules shown in Table 18.3, from $\overline{b_i}$ we get $1 - x_i$, and $E(1 - x_i) = q_i$ which is the failure probability of the component i. Therefore

$$P(MC_1) = q_{p1} q_{p2},$$

$$P(MC_2) = q_{p_1} q_{m_2} q_{m_3},$$

$$P(MC_3) = q_{p_2} q_{m_1} q_{m_3},$$

$$P(MC_4) = q_{m_1} q_{m_2} q_{m_3},$$

$$P(MC_1 \cap MC_2) = q_{p_1} q_{p_2} q_{m_2} q_{m_3},$$

$$P(MC_1 \cap MC_3) = q_{p_1} q_{p_2} q_{m_1} q_{m_3},$$

$$P(MC_1 \cap MC_4) = q_{p_1} q_{p_2} q_{m_1} q_{m_2} q_{m_3},$$

$$P(MC_2 \cap MC_3) = q_{p_1} q_{p_2} q_{m_1} q_{m_2} q_{m_3},$$

$$P(MC_2 \cap MC_4) = q_{p_1} q_{m_1} q_{m_2} q_{m_3},$$

$$P(MC_3 \cap MC_4) = q_{p_2} q_{m_1} q_{m_2} q_{m_3},$$

$$P(MC_1 \cap MC_2 \cap MC_3) = q_{p_1} q_{p_2} q_{m_1} q_{m_2} q_{m_3},$$

$$P(MC_1 \cap MC_2 \cap MC_4) = q_{p_1} q_{p_2} q_{m_1} q_{m_2} q_{m_3},$$

$$P(MC_1 \cap MC_3 \cap MC_4) = q_{p_1} q_{p_2} q_{m_1} q_{m_2} q_{m_3},$$

$$P(MC_2 \cap MC_3 \cap MC_4) = q_{p_1} q_{p_2} q_{m_1} q_{m_2} q_{m_3},$$

and

$$P(MC_1 \cap MC_2 \cap MC_3 \cap MC_4) = q_{p_1} q_{p_2} q_{m_1} q_{m_2} q_{m_3}.$$

Assume the MTTF and the MTTR of each component is that specified in Table 19.3. Consider $q_i = MTTR_i/(MTTF_i + MTTR_i)$; then the failure probability of each term is calculated. The respective values are presented in Table 20.11.

Therefore, the failure probability (unavailability) is $P(\bigcup_{i=1}^{4} MC_i) = 8.72407 \times 10^{-5}$. Hence, as $A = 1 - P(\bigcup_{i=1}^{4} MC_i) = 0.999913^5$.

$\square$

---

[5] Also see the result shown in Example 19.3.3.

Table 20.11
Probabilities of the Terms

$P(MC_1)$	8.72334×10^{-5}
$P(MC_2)$	3.76714×10^{-9}
$P(MC_3)$	3.35226×10^{-9}
$P(MC_4)$	2.53485×10^{-10}
$P(MC_1 \cap MC_2)$	3.31907×10^{-11}
$P(MC_1 \cap MC_3)$	3.31907×10^{-11}
$P(MC_1 \cap MC_4)$	2.21124×10^{-14}
$P(MC_2 \cap MC_3)$	2.21124×10^{-14}
$P(MC_2 \cap MC_4)$	2.50975×10^{-12}
$P(MC_3 \cap MC_4)$	2.50975×10^{-12}
$P(MC_1 \cap MC_2 \cap MC_3)$	2.21124×10^{-14}
$P(MC_1 \cap MC_2 \cap MC_4)$	2.21124×10^{-14}
$P(MC_1 \cap MC_3 \cap MC_3)$	2.21124×10^{-14}
$P(MC_1 \cap MC_3 \cap MC_4)$	2.21124×10^{-14}
$P(MC_1 \cap MC_2 \cap MC_3 \cap MC_4)$	2.21124×10^{-14}

20.6   SUM OF DISJOINT PRODUCTS METHOD

This section presents the method for computing reliability and availability based on the sum of disjoint product (SDP) [2, 146, 419]. This method is based on the following set identity.

$$A \cup B = A \cup (A^c \cap B).$$

Consider the sets $A = \{a,b,c,d\}$ and $B = \{c,d,e,f\}$ in the universe $\Omega = \{a,b,c,d,e,f,g,h\}$; then we have

$$A^c = \{e,f,g,h\};$$

thus $A^c \cap B = \{e,f\}$. Therefore $A \cup (A^c \cap B) = \{a,b,c,d\} \cup \{e,f\} = \{a,b,c,d,e,f\}$.

Considering three sets, we have

$$A \cup B \cup C = A \cup (A^c \cap B) \cup (A^c \cap B^c \cap C).$$

For n sets, we have

$$\bigcup_{i=1}^{n} A_i = A_1 \cup (A_1^c \cap A_2) \cup (A_1^c \cap A_2^c \cap A_3) \cup ... \cup (A_1^c \cap A_2^c \cap A_3^c \cap ... \cap A_{n-1}^c \cap A_n).$$

$$(20.6.1)$$

Therefore, the probability of the union set of all sets is

$$P(\bigcup_{i=1}^{n} A_i) = P(A_1) + P(A_1^c \cap A_2) + P(A_1^c \cap A_2^c \cap A_3) + \ldots + P(A_1^c \cap A_2^c \cap A_3^c \cap \ldots$$

$$\cap A_{n-1}^c \cap A_n).$$

(20.6.2)

The RBD shown in Figure 18.1 is composed of three blocks, b_1, b_2, and b_3. This RBD has two minimal paths. They are $MP_1 = \{b_1, b_2\}$ and $MP_2 = \{b_1, b_3\}$. Each minimal path is depicted by the respective logical function:

$$\Psi_{MP_1} = b_1 \wedge b_2,$$

$$\Psi_{MP_2} = b_1 \wedge b_3.$$

The set MP_1^c is represented by the logical function

$$\overline{\Psi}_{MP_1} = \overline{b_1 \wedge b_2} = \overline{b_1} \vee \overline{b_2}.$$

The set $MP_1^c \cap MP_2$ are also represented by the logical function

$$\Psi_{MP_1^c \cap MP_2} = (\overline{b_1} \vee \overline{b_2}) \wedge (b_1 \wedge b_3).$$

$$\Psi_{MP_1^c \cap MP_2} = (\overline{b_1} \wedge b_1 \wedge b_3) \vee (\overline{b_2} \wedge b_1 \wedge b_3).$$

$$\Psi_{MP_1^c \cap MP_2} = \overline{b_2} \wedge b_1 \wedge b_3.$$

Using transformation rules shown in Table 18.3, from b_i we get x_1 and from $\overline{b_i}$ we get $1 - x_i$. As $E(x_i) = p_i$ and $E(1 - x_i) = 1 - p_i = q_i$, we have

$$P(MP_1) = P(\Psi_{MP_1}) = p_1 p_2.$$

$$P(MP_1^c \cap MP_2) = P(\Psi_{MP_1^c \cap MP_2}) = q_2 p_1 p_3.$$

Therefore

$$P(MP_1 \cup MP_2) = P(MP_1) + P(MP_1^c \cap MP_2)$$

$$P(MP_1 \cup MP_2) = p_1 p_2 + q_2 p_1 p_3.$$

Let $p_1 = p_2 = p_3 = 0.9$; then $P(MP_1 \cup MP_2) = 0.891$.

Example 20.6.1. The system represented by the RBD shown in Figure 20.12 is composed of the following minimal paths: $MP_1 = \{b_1, b_2\}$, $MP_2 = \{b_1, b_3, b_5\}$, and $MP_3 = \{b_2, b_3, b_4\}$.

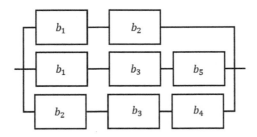

Figure 20.12   RBD – SDP.

The respective logic functions also depict the minimal paths, that is

$$MP_1 \Rightarrow \Psi_{MP_1} = b_1 \wedge b_2,$$

$$MP_2 \Rightarrow \Psi_{MP_2} = b_1 \wedge b_3 \wedge b_5,$$

$$MP_3 \Rightarrow \Psi_{MP_3} = b_2 \wedge b_3 \wedge b_4.$$

The complements of MP_i, MP_i^c, are also represented by the respective logical function $\overline{\Psi_{MP_i}}$; hence

$$MP_1^c \Rightarrow \overline{\Psi_{MP_1}} = \overline{(b_1 \wedge b_2)} = \overline{b_1} \vee \overline{b_2},$$

$$MP_2^c \Rightarrow \overline{\Psi_{MP_2}} = \overline{(b_1 \wedge b_3 \wedge b_5)} = \overline{b_1} \vee \overline{b_3} \vee \overline{b_5},$$

$$MP_3^c \Rightarrow \overline{\Psi_{MP_3}} = \overline{(b_2 \wedge b_3 \wedge b_4)} = \overline{b_2} \vee \overline{b_3} \vee \overline{b_4}.$$

Using the results above, we obtain

$$MP_1^c \cap MP_2 \Rightarrow \overline{(b_1 \wedge b_2)} \wedge (b_1 \wedge b_3 \wedge b_5).$$

$$= (\overline{b_1} \vee \overline{b_2}) \wedge (b_1 \wedge b_3 \wedge b_5).$$

$$= b_1 \wedge \overline{b_2} \wedge b_3 \wedge b_5.$$

$$MP_1^c \cap MP_2^c \cap MP_3 \Rightarrow \overline{(b_1 \wedge b_2)} \wedge \overline{(b_1 \wedge b_3 \wedge b_5)} \wedge (b_2 \wedge b_3 \wedge b_4).$$

$$= \overline{b_1} \wedge b_2 \wedge b_3 \wedge b_4.$$

Hence

$$P(MP_1) = p_1 \times p_2,$$

$$P(MP_1^c \cap MP_2) = q_2 \times p_1 \times p_3 \times p_5,$$

$$P(MP_1^c \cap MP_2^c, \cap MP_3 = q_1 \times p_2 \times p_3 \times p_4,$$

where $q_2 = 1 - p_2$ and $q_1 = 1 - p_1$.

Therefore

$$P(MP_1 \cup MP_2 \cup MP_3) = P(MP_1) + P(MP_1^c \cap MP_2) + P(MP_1^c \cap MP_2^c \cap MP_3) =$$

$$p_1 \times p_2 + (1 - p_2) \times p_1 \times p_3 \times p_5 + (1 - p_1) \times p_2 \times p_3 \times p_4.$$

For $p_i = p = 0.9$, $i = \{1, 2, 3, 4, 5\}$, we obtain $P(MP_1 \cup MP_2 \cup MP_3) = 0.9558$.

$\square$

Example 20.6.2. Assume the system represented by FT depicted in Figure 19.22. The minimal cuts are $MC_1 = \{P_1, P_2\}$, $MC_2 = \{P_1, M_2, M_3\}$, $MC_3 = \{M_1, M_3, P_2\}$, and $MC_4 = \{M_1, M_2, M_3\}$. Each minimal cut is represented by the respective logical function:

$$MC_1 \Rightarrow \overline{P_1} \wedge \overline{P_2},$$

$$MC_2 \Rightarrow \overline{P_1} \wedge \overline{M_2} \wedge \overline{M_3},$$

$$MC_3 \Rightarrow \overline{M_1} \wedge \overline{M_3} \wedge \overline{P_2},$$

and

$$MC_4 \Rightarrow \overline{M_1} \wedge \overline{M_2} \wedge \overline{M_3}.$$

The complements of MC_i, that is MC_i^c, $i = \{1,2,3,4\}$, are represented by

$$MC_1^c \Rightarrow \overline{\overline{P_1} \wedge \overline{P_2}} = P_1 \vee P_2,$$

$$MC_2^c \Rightarrow \overline{\overline{P_1} \wedge \overline{M_2} \wedge \overline{M_3}} = P_1 \vee M_2 \vee M_3,$$

$$MC_3^c \Rightarrow \overline{\overline{M_1} \wedge \overline{M_3} \wedge \overline{P_2}} = M_1 \vee M_3 \vee P_2,$$

and

$$MC_4^c \Rightarrow \overline{\overline{M_1} \wedge \overline{M_2} \wedge \overline{M_3}} = M_1 \vee M_2 \vee M_3.$$

From the above results, we obtain

$$MC_1^c \cap MC_2 \Rightarrow (P_1 \vee P_2) \wedge (\overline{P_1} \wedge \overline{M_2} \wedge \overline{M_3}) = \overline{P_1} \wedge P_2 \wedge \overline{M_1} \wedge \overline{M_3},$$

$$MC_1^c \cap MC_2^c \cap MC_3 \Rightarrow (P_1 \vee P_2) \wedge (P_1 \vee M_2 \vee M_3) \wedge (\overline{M_1} \wedge \overline{M_3} \wedge \overline{P_2}) =$$
$$P_1 \wedge P_2 \overline{M_1} \wedge \overline{M_3},$$

$$MC_1^c \cap MC_2^c \cap MC_3^c \cap MC_4 \Rightarrow (P_1 \vee P_2) \wedge (P_1 \vee M_2 \vee M_3) \wedge$$
$$= (M_1 \vee M_3 \vee P_2) \wedge (\overline{M_1} \wedge \overline{M_2} \wedge \overline{M_3}) P_1 \wedge P_2 \wedge \overline{M_1} \wedge \overline{M_2} \wedge \overline{M_3}.$$

Considering q_i and p_i as the failure and success probabilities of the component i, respectively, we have

$$Q(MC_1) = q_{p1} \times q_{p2},$$

$$Q(MC_1^c \cap MC_2) = q_{p1} \times p_{p2} \times q_{m2} \times q_{m3},$$

$$Q(MC_1^c \cap MC_2^c \cap MC_3) = p_{p1} \times q_{p2} \times q_{m1} \times q_{m3},$$

and

$$Q(MC_1^c \cap MC_2^c \cap MC_3^c \cap MC_4) = p_{p1} \times p_{p2} \times q_{m1} \times q_{m2} \times q_{m3}.$$

Hence, the failure probability is

$$Q = Q(MC_1) + Q(MC_1^c \cap MC_2) + Q(MC_1^c \cap MC_2^c \cap MC_3) +$$
$$Q(MC_1^c \cap MC_2^c \cap MC_3^c \cap MC_4).$$

Thus

$$Q = q_{p1} \times q_{p2} + q_{p1} \times p_{p2} \times q_{m2} \times q_{m3} +$$
$$p_{p1} \times q_{p2} \times q_{m1} \times q_{m3} + p_{p1} \times p_{p2} \times q_{m1} \times q_{m2} \times q_{m3}.$$

From Q, we obtain the success probability $P = 1 - Q$. The component i unavailability is $q_i = MTTR_i/(MTTF_i + MTTR_i)$ and the respective availability is $p_i = 1 - q_i$. Considering the components MTTFs and MTTRs depicted in Table 19.3, the system availability $(A = P)$ is 0.9999913^6.

□

20.7 METHODS FOR ESTIMATING BOUNDS

This section introduces some methods for estimating probability bounds ((un)reliability and (un) availability). Such methods can provide approximations to exact probabilities in a shorter time than the exact solution methods, especially when considering large models [224].

20.7.1 METHOD BASED ON INCLUSION AND EXCLUSION

As seen in Section 20.5, the Inclusion-Exclusion method (IEM) yields consecutive upper and lower reliability (and availability) bounds when minimal paths are adopted and the respective unreliability (and unavailability) bounds when minimal cuts are considered. Thus, for highly reliable (available) systems, the cuts are more useful than paths. On the other hand, if success probabilities are low, paths are better.

Consider the bridge depicted in Figure 20.10.a. This model has four minimal paths, $MP_1 = \{c_1, c_2\}$, $MP_2 = \{c_4, c_5\}$, $MP_3 = \{c_1, c_3, c_5\}$, and $MP_4 = \{c_2, c_3, c_4\}$, and for four minimal cuts, $MC_1 = \{c_1, c_4\}$, $MC_2 = \{c_2, c_5\}$, $MC_3 = \{c_1, c_3, c_5\}$, and $MC_4 = \{c_2, c_3, c_4\}$.

---

[6]See the result depicted in Example 20.5.1.

Let us first take the minimal cuts, and using the first term of Equation 20.5.2, we have

$$Q_1 = P(MC_1) + P(MC_2) + P(MC_3) + P(MC_4) = q_1q_4 + q_2q_3q_4 + q_2q_5 + q_1q_3q_5,$$

where $q_i = 1 - p_i$ is the failure probability of component i. If $q_i = q = 0.1$, $i \in \{1,2,3,4,5\}$, then

$Q_1 = 0.022$, and $P_1 = 1 - Q_1 = 0.978$. Using the second term of Equation 20.5.2, we obtain

$$Q_2 = Q_1 + P(MC_1 \cap MC_2) + P(MC_1 \cap MC_3) + P(MC_1 \cap MC_4) +$$
$$P(MC_2 \cap MC_3) + P(MC_2 \cap MC_4) +$$
$$P(MC_3 \cap MC_4) = Q_1 - q_1q_2q_3q_4 - q_1q_2q_5q_4 - q_1q_3q_5q_4 -$$
$$q_1q_2q_3q_5q_4 - q_2q_3q_5q_4 - q_1q_2q_3q_5.$$

Thus, $Q_2 = 0.02149$ and $P_2 = 1 - Q_2 = 0.97851$.

Now, take into account the third term of the Equation 20.5.2, so

$$Q_3 = Q_2 + P(MC_1 \cap MC_2 \cap MC_3) + P(MC_1 \cap MC_2 \cap MC_3) + P(MC_1 \cap MC_2 \cap MC_3) +$$
$$P(MC_1 \cap MC_2 \cap MC_3) = Q_2 + 4q_1q_2q_3q_4q_5.$$

Hence, we obtain $Q_3 = 0.02153$ and $P_3 = 1 - Q_3 = 0.97847$. Now, finally, consider the fourth term of Equation 20.5.2. Hence,

$$Q_4 = Q_3 + P(MC_1 \cap MC_2 \cap MC_3 \cap MC_4) = Q_3 - q_1q_2q_3q_4q_5.$$

Thus, we get $Q_4 = 0.02152$ and $P_4 = 1 - Q_4 = 0.97848$, where Q_4 and P_4 are the exact results.

Now consider the minimal paths and take into account the first term of the Equation 20.5.2. Therefore

$$P_1 = P(MP_1) + P(MP_2) + P(MP_3) + P(MP_4) = p_1p_2 + p_3p_4p_2 + p_1p_3p_5 + p_4p_5.$$

If $p_i = p = 0.9$, $i \in \{1,2,3,4,5\}$, then

$P_1 = 3.078$. This bound is, however, useless since it is higher than one. Now, adding the second term of Equation 20.5.2, we obtain

$$P_2 = P_1 + P(MP_1 \cap MP_2) + P(MP_1 \cap MP_3) + P(MP_1 \cap MP_4) + P(MP_2 \cap MP_3) +$$

$$P(MP_2 \cap MP_4) + P(MP_3 \cap MP_4) = P_1 - p_1 p_2 p_3 p_4 - p_1 p_2 p_5 p_4 - p_1 p_3 p_5 p_4 -$$

$$p_1 p_2 p_3 p_5 p_4 - p_2 p_3 p_5 p_4 - p_1 p_2 p_3 p_5.$$

Thus, $P_2 = 0.79299$.

Now, consider the third term of Equation 20.5.2. Hence

$$P_3 = P_2 + P(MP_1 \cap MP_2 \cap MP_3) + P(MP_1 \cap MP_2 \cap MP_3) + P(MP_1 \cap MP_2 \cap MP_3) +$$

$$P(MP_1 \cap MP_2 \cap MP_3) = P_2 + 3 p_1 p_2 p_3 p_4 p_5.$$

Thus, we get $P_3 = 1.56897$. Again, this bound is of no use because it is higher than one. Finally, take into account the fourth term of Equation 20.5.2. Thus,

$$P_4 = P_3 + P(MP_1 \cap MP_2 \cap MP_3 \cap MP_4) = P_3 - p_1 p_2 p_3 p_4 p_5.$$

Thus, we obtain $P_4 = 0.97848$, which is the exact result.

Now assume $p = 0.99$. The reliability bounds obtained through minimal cuts and paths are shown in Table 20.12 considering $i = \{1, 2, 3, 4\}$. Observe that the exact result is already reached when considering the minimal cuts and six decimal places when adopting the first term. On the other hand, the bounds obtained from minimal paths are all useless, except the final result.

Table 20.12
Reliability Bounds Computed from Minimal Cuts and Paths – Reliable System

i	P_i - Minimal Cuts	P_i - Minimal Paths
1	0.999798	3.9008
2	0.999798	-1.85317
3	0.999798	1.95079
4	0.999798	0.999798

For a very unreliable system, though, they are better; that is, when p is small (q is close to one), the minimal cuts would be less useful than the minimal paths. Assume, for instance, $q = 0.95$ ($p = 1 - q = 0.05$). Table 20.13 shows the unreliability bounds obtained through minimal cuts and paths. It is worth observing the bounds obtained through minimal cuts are useless since for $i \in \{1,2,3\}$ the bounds are either higher than one or smaller than zero. The only useful result is obtained when $i = 4$. This result is the exact result. When using the minimal path, though, the bounds are useful.

Table 20.13

Unreliability Bounds Computed from Minimal Cuts and Paths – Unreliable System

i	Q_i - Minimal Cuts	Q_i - Minimal Paths
1	3.51975	0.99475
2	-1.32656	0.994782
3	1.76856	0.99478
4	0.994781	0.994781

20.7.2 METHOD BASED ON THE SUM OF DISJOINT PRODUCTS

The SDP method calculates consecutive lower bounds on system reliability (availability) if minimal paths are adopted. Conversely, when minimal cuts are adopted, the method provides lower bounds on unreliability (unavailability) and consequently upper bounds on system reliability (availability). Unlike the IEM, which calculates consecutive upper and lower bounds by adding and subtracting terms, the SDP only adds terms when calculating the bounds.

Assume the bridge model depicted in in Figure 20.10.a. As already seen, this bridge has four minimal paths, $MP_1 = \{c_1, c_2\}$, $MP_2 = \{c_4, c_5\}$, $MP_3 = \{c_1, c_3, c_5\}$, and $MP_4 = \{c_2, c_3, c_4\}$. These minimal paths are represented by the respective logical functions:

$$MP_1 \Rightarrow b1 \wedge b2,$$

$$MP_2 \Rightarrow b4 \wedge b5,$$

$$MP_3 \Rightarrow b1 \wedge b3 \wedge b5,$$

and

$$MP_4 \Rightarrow b2 \wedge b3 \wedge b4.$$

Considering MP_1, we get

$$P_1 = V_1 = P(MP_1) = p_1 p_2.$$

The intersections $MP_1^c \cap MP_2$, $MP_1^c \cap MP_2^c \cap MP_3$, and $MP_1^c \cap MP_2^c \cap MP_3^c \cap MP_4$ are represented by

$$MP_1^c \cap MP_2 \Rightarrow \overline{b_1 \wedge b_2} \wedge b_4 \wedge b_5,$$

$$MP_1^c \cap MP_2^c \cap MP_3 \Rightarrow b_1 \wedge \overline{b_2} \wedge b_3 \wedge \overline{b_4} \wedge b_5,$$

and

$$MP_1^c \cap MP_2^c \cap MP_3^c \cap MP_4 \Rightarrow \overline{b_1} \wedge b_2 \wedge b_3 \wedge b_4 \wedge \overline{b_5}.$$

Hence, in the second iteration, we get

$$V_2 = P(MP_1^c \cap MP_2) = (1 - p_1 p_2) p_4 p_5,$$

and

$$P_2 = P_1 + V_2 = P_1 + (1 - p_1 p_2) p_4 p_5.$$

In the third iteration, we obtain

$$V_3 = P(MP_1^c \cap MP_2^c \cap MP_3) = p_1 (1 - p_2) p_3 (1 - p_4) p_5,$$

and

$$P_3 = P_2 + V_3 = P_2 + p_1 (1 - p_2) p_3 (1 - p_4) p_5.$$

In the last iteration, we get

$$V_4 = P(MP_1^c \cap MP_2^c \cap MP_3^c \cap MP_4) = (1 - p_1) p_2 p_3 p_4 (1 - p_5)$$

and

$$P_4 = P_3 + V_4 = P_3 + (1 - p_1) p_2 p_3 p_4 (1 - p_5).$$

Let us consider $p_j = p = 0.9$, $j \in \{1,2,3,4,5\}$, and compute the bounds P_i for $j \in \{1,2,3,4\}$. Table 20.14 depicts the results.

Table 20.14
Reliability Bounds - SDP

i	P_i
1	0.81
2	0.9639
3	0.97119
4	0.97848

20.7.3   MIN-MAX BOUND METHOD

Barlow and Proschan proposed a method for estimating success probability (reliability and availability) upper and lower bounds based on minimal path and minimal cuts [346] [224]. For example, assume a system composed of independent components with l minimal path and m minimal cuts, where ρ_i is the probability of the minimal path MP_i is operational, and γ_i is the failure probability of the cut MC_i.

As the system is at least as reliable as the most reliable minimal path, then we have

$$L = \max_{1 \le i \le l} \{\rho_i\}.$$

On the other hand, the system is at most as reliable as the least reliable minimal cuts. Thus,

$$U = \min_{1 \le i \le l} \{1 - \gamma_i\}.$$

Therefore, for the bridge model of Figure 20.10.a, we have

$$L = \max\{\rho_1, \rho_2, \rho_3, \rho_4\}$$

and

$$U = \min\{1 - \gamma_1, 1 - \gamma_2, 1 - \gamma_3, 1 - \gamma_4\}.$$

where $\rho_1 = p_1 p_2$, $\rho_2 = p_4 p_5$, $\rho_3 = p_1 p_3 p_5$, $\rho_4 = p_2 p_3 p_4$; $\gamma_1 = (1 - p_1)(1 - p_4)$, $\gamma_2 = (1 - p_2)(1 - p_5)$, $\gamma_3 = (1 - p_1)(1 - p_3)(1 - p_5)$, and $\gamma_4 = (1 - p_2)(1 - p_3)(1 - p_4)$. For $p_1 = p_2 = p_3 = p_4 = p_5 = 0.99$, we have $U = 0.9999$ and $L = 0.9801$.

20.7.4 ESARY-PROSCHAN METHOD

This section presents the Esary-Proschan method for estimating probabilities bounds [345] [224]. Assume a system composed of l minimal paths and m minimal cuts. A minimal path is functional if all of its components properly work; thus, if one component of a minimal path fails, the minimal path fails. Let ρ_i be the success probability (reliability or availability) of the minimal path MP_i.

Consider a parallel system with independent components. In such a system, the minimal paths do not share components. As for a parallel system, the system only fails if all minimal paths fail; hence the system fail probability (unreliability or unavailability) is $Q = \prod_{i=1}^{l}(1 - \rho_i)$. For a more general system, however, the paths share components; thus the failure probability is usually higher than $\prod_{i=1}^{l}(1 - \rho_i)$. Therefore, $\prod_{i=1}^{l}(1 - \rho_i)$ is a failure probability lower bound, and

$$U = 1 - \prod_{i=1}^{l}(1 - \rho_i) \qquad (20.7.1)$$

a success probability upper bound. Now consider the minimal cuts. Applying a similar argument, we obtain a success probability (reliability or availability) lower bound:

$$L = \prod_{j=1}^{m}(1 - \gamma_j), \qquad (20.7.2)$$

where γ_j is the failure probability of the minimal cut MC_j.

Let us assume the bridge model shown in Figure 20.10.a. As already seen, this bridge has four minimal paths, $MP_1 = \{c_1, c_2\}$, $MP_2 = \{c_4, c_5\}$, $MP_3 = \{c_1, c_3, c_5\}$, and $MP_4 = \{c_2, c_3, c_4\}$, and four minimal cuts, $MC_1 = \{c_1, c_4\}$, $MC_2 = \{c_2, c_5\}$, $MC_3 = \{c_1, c_3, c_5\}$, and $MC_4 = \{c_2, c_3, c_4\}$. Hence $\rho_1 = p_1 p_2$, $\rho_2 = p_4 p_5$, $\rho_3 = p_1 p_3 p_5$, $\rho_4 = p_2 p_3 p_4$; $\gamma_1 = (1 - p_1)(1 - p_4)$, $\gamma_2 = (1 - p_2)(1 - p_5)$, $\gamma_3 = (1 - p_1)(1 - p_3)(1 - p_5)$, and $\gamma_4 = (1 - p_2)(1 - p_3)(1 - p_4)$. Therefore,

$$U = 1 - (1 - \rho_1) \times (1 - \rho_2) \times (1 - \rho_3) \times (1 - \rho_4)$$

and

$$L = (1 - \gamma_1) \times (1 - \gamma_2) \times (1 - \gamma_3) \times (1 - \gamma_4).$$

For $p_1 = p_2 = p_3 = p_4 = p_5 = 0.9$, we have $U = 0.997349$ and $L = 0.978141$.

20.7.5 DECOMPOSITION

The reliability/availability evaluation of a large system is usually performed by first decomposing the system into a subsystem. Each subsystem is then decomposed into a smaller subsystem. This process stops when the analyst decides the subsystem is simple enough to be evaluated. Then, the smaller subsystems are evaluated and considered one component (reduction) into the higher-level subsystem. As already presented in Section 20.4, such an approach can be applied to obtain exact results or bounds.

To calculate bounds, after decomposing the system into smaller subsystems, the subsystems can be evaluated using any of those methods already introduced here to calculate bounds, and then reducing each subsystem and representing them as one component with the respective bounds obtained at the higher-level model.

Consider a system represented by the RBD depicted in Figure 20.13.a. This model is composed of twenty-one blocks, $\{b_i\}$, $i \in \{1, 2, ..., 21\}$. This model was decomposed into three subsystems, named S_1, S_2 and S_3, as shown in Figure 20.13. The subsystem S_1 has three minimal path and four minimal cuts. The minimal paths are

$$MP_1^1 \Rightarrow b_1 \wedge b_2,$$

$$MP_2^1 \Rightarrow b_1 \wedge b_3,$$

and

$$MP_3^1 \Rightarrow b_4 \wedge b_5.$$

The minimal cuts are

$$MC_1^1 \Rightarrow \overline{b_1} \wedge \overline{b_4},$$

$$MC_2^1 \Rightarrow \overline{b_1} \wedge \overline{b_5},$$

$$MC_3^1 \Rightarrow \overline{b_1} \wedge \overline{b_3} \wedge \overline{b_4},$$

and

$$MC_4^1 \Rightarrow \overline{b_1} \wedge \overline{b_3} \wedge \overline{b_5}.$$

Let us, for instance, apply the Esary-Proschan method introduced in Section 20.7.4, to calculate the probability bounds. Hence, using the minimal paths and the minimal cuts, we get $\rho_1^1 = p_1 p_2$, $\rho_2^1 = p_1 p_3$, $\rho_3^1 = p_4 p_5$, $\gamma_1^1 = (1 - p_4)(1 - p_5)$, $\gamma_2^1 = (1 - p_1)(1 - p_5)$, $\gamma_3^1 = (1 - p_1)(1 - p_3)(1 - p_4)$, and $\gamma_4^1 =$

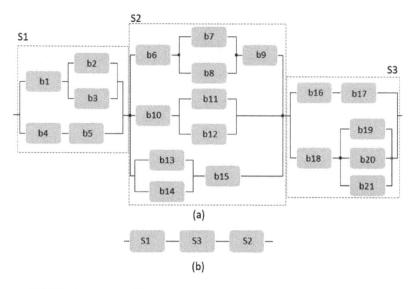

(a)

(b)

Figure 20.13   Decomposition.

$(1-p_1)(1-p_3)(1-p_5)$. Therefore we obtain the upper and lower probability bounds for the subsystem S_1:

$$L_1 = (1-\gamma_1^1) \times (1-\gamma_2^1) \times (1-\gamma_3^1) \times (1-\gamma_4^1)$$

and

$$U_1 = 1 - (1-\rho_1^1) \times (1-\rho_2^1) \times (1-\rho_3^1) \times (1-\rho_4^1)$$

For $p_1 = p_2 = p_3 = p_4 = p_5 = 0.95$, we obtain $L_1 = 0.987278$ and $U_1 = 0.999073$.

The subsystem S_2 has four minimal paths and four minimal cuts. The minimal paths are

$$MP_1^2 \Rightarrow b_{16} \wedge b_{17},$$

$$MP_2^2 \Rightarrow b_{18} \wedge b_{19},$$

$$MP_3^2 \Rightarrow b_{18} \wedge b_{20},$$

and

$$MP_4^2 \Rightarrow b_{18} \wedge b_{21}.$$

The minimal cuts are

$$MC_1^2 \Rightarrow \overline{b_{16}} \wedge \overline{b_{18}},$$

$$MC_2^2 \Rightarrow \overline{b_{17}} \wedge \overline{b_{18}},$$

$$MC_3^2 \Rightarrow \overline{b_{16}} \wedge \overline{b_{19}} \wedge \overline{b_{20}} \wedge \overline{b_{21}},$$

and

$$MC_4^2 \Rightarrow \overline{b_{17}} \wedge \overline{b_{19}} \wedge \overline{b_{20}} \wedge \overline{b_{21}}.$$

Applying the Esary-Proschan method to calculate the probability bounds, we get $\rho_1^2 = p_{16}p_{17}$, $\rho_2^2 = p_{18}p_{19}$, $\rho_3^2 = p_{18}p_{20}$, $\rho_4^2 = p_{18}p_{21}$, $\gamma_1^2 = (1 - p_{16})(1 - p_{18})$, $\gamma_2^2 = (1 - p_{17})(1 - p_{18})$, $\gamma_3^2 = (1 - p_{16})(1 - p_{19})(1 - p_{20})(1 - p_{21})$, and $\gamma_4^2 = (1 - p_{17})(1 - p_{19})(1 - p_{20})(1 - p_{21})$. Therefore, the upper and lower probability bounds for the subsystem S_2 are:

$$L_2 = (1 - \gamma_1^2) \times (1 - \gamma_2^2) \times (1 - \gamma_3^2) \times (1 - \gamma_4^2),$$

and

$$U_2 = 1 - (1 - \rho_1^2) \times (1 - \rho_2^2) \times (1 - \rho_3^2) \times (1 - \rho_4^2).$$

For $p_1 = p_2 = p_3 = p_4 = p_5 = 0.95$, we obtain $L_2 = 0.994994$ and $U_2 = 0.99991$.

The subsystem S_3 has six minimal paths and twelve minimal cuts. The minimal paths are

$$MP_1^3 \Rightarrow b_6 \wedge b_7 \wedge b_9,$$

$$MP_2^3 \Rightarrow b_6 \wedge b_8 \wedge b_9,$$

$$MP_3^3 \Rightarrow b_{10} \wedge b_{11},$$

$$MP_4^3 \Rightarrow b_{10} \wedge b_{12},$$

$$MP_5^3 \Rightarrow b_{13} \wedge b_{15},$$

and

$$MP_6^3 \Rightarrow b_{14} \wedge b_{15}.$$

The minimal cuts are

$$MC_1^3 \Rightarrow \overline{b_6} \wedge \overline{b_{10}} \wedge \overline{b_{13}} \wedge \overline{b_{14}},$$

$$MC_2^3 \Rightarrow \overline{b_6} \wedge \overline{b_{10}} \wedge \overline{b_{15}},$$

$$MC_3^3 \Rightarrow \overline{b_6} \wedge \overline{b_{11}} \wedge \overline{b_{12}} \wedge \overline{b_{13}} \wedge \overline{b_{14}},$$

$$MC_4^3 \Rightarrow \overline{b_6} \wedge \overline{b_{11}} \wedge \overline{b_{12}} \wedge \overline{b_{15}},$$

$$MC_5^3 \Rightarrow \overline{b_7} \wedge \overline{b_8} \wedge \overline{b_{10}} \wedge \overline{b_{13}} \wedge \overline{b_{14}},$$

$$MC_6^3 \Rightarrow \overline{b_7} \wedge \overline{b_8} \wedge \overline{b_{10}} \wedge \overline{b_{15}},$$

$$MC_7^3 \Rightarrow \overline{b_7} \wedge \overline{b_8} \wedge \overline{b_{11}} \wedge \overline{b_{12}} \wedge \overline{b_{13}} \wedge \overline{b_{14}},$$

$$MC_8^3 \Rightarrow \overline{b_7} \wedge \overline{b_8} \wedge \overline{b_{11}} \wedge \overline{b_{12}} \wedge \overline{b_{15}},$$

$$MC_9^3 \Rightarrow \overline{b_9} \wedge \overline{b_{10}} \wedge \overline{b_{13}} \wedge \overline{b_{14}},$$

$$MC_{10}^3 \Rightarrow \overline{b_9} \wedge \overline{b_{10}} \wedge \overline{b_{15}},$$

$$MC_{11}^3 \Rightarrow \overline{b_9} \wedge \overline{b_{11}} \wedge \overline{b_{12}} \wedge \overline{b_{13}} \wedge \overline{b_{14}},$$

and

$$MC_{12}^3 \Rightarrow \overline{b_9} \wedge \overline{b_{11}} \wedge \overline{b_{12}} \wedge \overline{b_{15}}.$$

Now we apply the Esary-Proschan method to calculate the probability bounds. Hence, $\rho_1^3 = p_6 p_7 p_9$, $\rho_2^3 = p_6 p_8 p_9$, $\rho_3^3 = p_{10} p_{11}$, $\rho_4^3 = p_{10} p_{12}$, $\rho_5^3 = p_{13} p_{15}$, $\rho_6^3 = p_{14} p_{15}$, $\gamma_1^3 = (1 - p_6)(1 - p_{10})(1 - p_{13})(1 - p_{14})$, $\gamma_2^3 = (1 - p_6)(1 - p_{10})(1 - p_{15})$, $\gamma_3^3 = (1 - p_6)(1 - p_{11})(1 - p_{12})(1 - p_{13})(1 - p_{14})$, $\gamma_4^3 = (1 - p_6)(1 - p_{11})(1 - p_{12})(1 - p_{15})$, $\gamma_5^3 = (1 - p_7)(1 - p_8)(1 - p_{10})(1 - p_{13})(1 - p_{14})$, $\gamma_6^3 = (1 - p_7)(1 - p_8)(1 - p_{10})(1 - p_{15})$, $\gamma_7^3 = (1 - p_7)(1 - p_8)(1 - p_{11})(1 - p_{12})(1 - p_{13})(1 - p_{14})$, $\gamma_8^3 = (1 - p_7)(1 - p_8)(1 - p_{11})(1 - p_{12})(1 - p_{15})$, $\gamma_9^3 = (1 - p_9)(1 - p_{10})(1 - p_{13})(1 - p_{14})$, $\gamma_{10}^3 = (1 - p_9)(1 - p_{10})(1 - p_{15})$, $\gamma_{11}^3 = (1 - p_9)(1 - p_{11})(1 - p_{12})(1 - p_{13})(1 - p_{14})$, and $\gamma_{12}^3 = (1 - p_9)(1 - p_{11})(1 - p_{12})(1 - p_{15})$. Therefore, the upper and lower probability bounds for the subsystem S_3 are:

$$L_3 = (1 - \gamma_1^3) \times (1 - \gamma_2^3) \times (1 - \gamma_3^3) \times (1 - \gamma_4^3) \times$$

$$(1 - \gamma_5^3) \times (1 - \gamma_6^3) \times (1 - \gamma_7^3) \times (1 - \gamma_8^3) \times$$
$$(1 - \gamma_9^3) \times (1 - \gamma_{10}^3) \times (1 - \gamma_{11}^3) \times (1 - \gamma_{12}^3),$$

and

$$U_3 = 1 - (1 - \rho_1^3) \times (1 - \rho_2^3) \times (1 - \rho_3^3) \times (1 - \rho_4^3) \times (1 - \rho_5^3) \times (1 - \rho_6^3).$$

For $p_1 = p_2 = p_3 = p_4 = p_5 = 0.95$, we obtain $L_3 = 0.999718$ and $U_3 = 0.999998$.

Now, reduce the RDB shown in Figure 20.13.a to the RDB presented in Figure 20.13.b. The subsystems are represented by one respective component. The reduced model (*rm*) has one minimal path, $MP_1^{rm} \Rightarrow s_1 \wedge s_2 \wedge s_3$, and three minimal cuts, $MC_1^{rm} \Rightarrow \overline{s_1}$, $MC_2^{rm} \Rightarrow \overline{s_2}$ and $MC_1^{rm} \Rightarrow \overline{s_3}$. Therefore

$$\rho_1^{rm} = U_1 U_2 U_3,$$

$$\gamma_1^{rm} = (1 - L_1),$$

$$\gamma_2^{rm} = (1 - L_2),$$

and

$$\gamma_3^{rm} = (1 - L_3),$$

Thus

$$L = (1 - \gamma_1^{rm}) \times (1 - \gamma_2^{rm}) \times (1 - \gamma_3^{rm}) = 0.989498$$

and

$$U = 1 - (1 - \rho_1^{rm}) = 0.998981.$$

EXERCISES

Exercise 1. Consider a RAID 50 with eight disks, each with time to failure exponentially distributed with rate $\lambda = 5.5 \times 10^{-5}$. Propose an RBD and calculate the reliability at $t = 7500\,h$ using the structure-function method.

Exercise 2. Assume a RAID 60 with ten disks, each with time to failure exponentially distributed with rate $\lambda = 5.5 \times 10^{-5}$. Propose an FT and obtain the reliability at $t = 7500\,h$ using the structure-function method.

Exercise 3. A system is composed of two servers (S_1 and S_2), each with its network-attached storage device (NAS_1 and NAS_2). The system is operational if both servers and their respective storage device are operational. Assume the MTTFs and the MTTRs of each component are depicted in Table 20.5. The steady-state availability of each component is calculated by $A_i = MTTF_i/(MTTF_i + MTTR_i)$. Propose an RBD and calculate the steady-state availability of the system using the enumeration method.

Exercise 4. Consider a RAID 5 with five disks, each with time to failure exponentially distributed with rate $\lambda = 4.5 \times 10^{-5}$. Propose an FT and calculate the reliability at $t = 2000\,h$ using the enumeration method.

Exercise 5. Calculate the reliability at $t = 3000\,h$ of the system represented by the RBD of Figure 20.14 using pivoting and the structure methods. Assume the reliability of each component is specified by $e^{-5 \times 10^{-5}t}$.

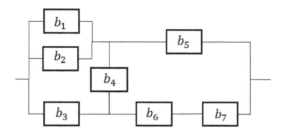

Figure 20.14 Pivoting and the Structure Methods.

Exercise 6. Calculate the reliability at $t = 3000\,h$ of the RBD of **Exercise 5.** by applying the inclusion-exclusion method.

Exercise 7. Consider the system of Example 19.3.3. Calculate the steady-state availability by applying the inclusion-exclusion method. The $MTTFs$ and $MTTRs$ of components are depicted in Table 19.3.

Exercise 8. Obtain the reliability at $t = 3000\,h$ of the RBD of **Exercise 5.** by applying the sum of disjoint products method.

Exercise 9. Consider the system of the Example 19.3.3. Calculate the reliability at $t = 2000\,h$ by applying the sum of disjoint products method. The $MTTFs$ of components are depicted in Table 19.3.

Exercise 10. Apply the reduction strategy to calculate the reliability at $t = 3000\,h$ of the system represented by the RBD of Figure 20.14.

Exercise 11. Calculate the reliability bounds of the system represented by the RBD shown in Figure 20.13 by applying decomposition and (a) inclusion and exclusion and (b) sum of disjoint products. Consider only two terms ($i = 2$). Assume $p_1 = p_2 = p_3 = p_4 = p_5 = 0.95$

Exercise 12. Obtain the reliability bounds of the system represented by the RBD shown in Figure 20.13 by applying decomposition and the min-max method. Assume $p_1 = p_2 = p_3 = p_4 = p_5 = 0.95$

Exercise 13. Compute the reliability bounds at $t = 2000\,h$ of Example 19.3.3 by applying the Esary-Proschan method. The $MTTFs$ of components are depicted in Table 19.3.

21 Modeling Availability, Reliability, and Capacity with CTMC

This chapter discusses reliability and availability modeling issues related to the system represented by state-space models. This chapter uses Markov chains to evaluate systems that combinatorial models do not represent well due to a complex interaction between components or an active-redundancy mechanism. Besides, hierarchical and heterogeneous modeling are also introduced to illustrate the adoption of different formalisms at distinct modeling levels.

This chapter presents a set of CTMC models for the availability and reliability evaluation of systems. First, we describe a single-component system, its availability model, and the respective reliability model. Then, from these basic models, a set of redundancy mechanisms and maintenance features is studied for estimating availability, reliability, and other related metrics.

21.1 SINGLE COMPONENT

Consider a single component repairable system (Figure 21.1.a). This system may either be operational or in failure. If the time to failure (TTF) and the time to repair (TTR) are exponentially distributed with rates λ and μ, respectively, the CTMC shown in Figure 21.1.b is its availability model. State U (Up) represents the operational state, and the state D (Down) denotes the faulty system. If the system is operational, it may fail. The system failure is represented by the transition from state U to state D. The faulty system may be restored to its operational state by a repair. The repair is represented by the transitions from state D to state U. The matrix rate, Q, is presented in Figure 21.1.c.

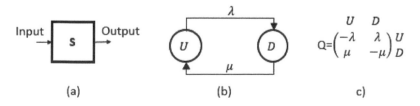

Figure 21.1 Single Component System - Availability Model.

The instantaneous probability of being in state U and D are respectively[1]

$$\pi_U(t) = \frac{\mu}{\lambda + \mu} + \frac{\lambda}{\lambda + \mu} e^{-(\lambda + \mu)t} \qquad (21.1.1)$$

and

$$\pi_D(t) = \frac{\lambda}{\lambda + \mu} - \frac{\lambda}{\lambda + \mu} e^{-(\lambda + \mu)t}, \qquad (21.1.2)$$

such that $\pi_U(t) + \pi_D(t) = 1$. The instantaneous availability is equal to $A(t) = \pi_U(t)$, and the instantaneous unavailability is equal to $UA(t) = \pi_D(t)$. Figure 21.2 shows $\pi_U(t)$ and $\pi_D(t)$ for $\lambda = 1\,fptu$ and $\mu = 3\,rptu$ in the interval $t \in (0,2)$.[2]

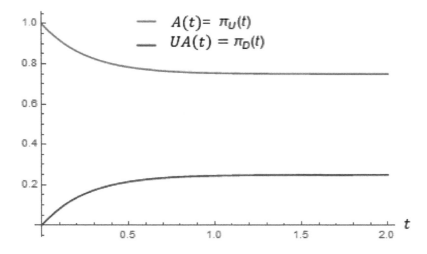

Figure 21.2 Instantaneous Availability.

If $t \to \infty$, then

$$\pi_U = \frac{\mu}{\lambda + \mu} \qquad (21.1.3)$$

and

$$\pi_D = \frac{\lambda}{\lambda + \mu}, \qquad (21.1.4)$$

---

[1] See Section 10.5.2 and Equation 16.3.13.
[2] $fptu$ denotes failure per time unit and $rptu$ represents repair per time unit.

such that $\pi_U + \pi_D = 1$. The steady-state measures can also be obtained by solving Equation 10.2.19[3]:

$$\Pi \cdot Q = 0, \quad \pi_U + \pi_D = 1,$$

where $\Pi = (\pi_U, \pi_D)$. The steady-state availability is equal to $A = \pi_U$, and the respective unavailability is equal to $UA = \pi_D$. The downtime in a period T is $DT = \pi_D \times T$. For time period of one year (365 days), the number of hours T is $8760h$ and $525,600\,min$.

Now assume a CTMC that represents the system failure (see Figure 21.3.a). This model has two states, U and D, and only one transition. This transition represents the system failure, that is, when the system is operational (U) it may fail, and this event is represented by the transition from the state U to state D, with failure rate (λ). The rate matrix is shown in Figure 21.3.b. Solving[4]

$$\frac{d\Pi(t)}{dt} = \Pi(t) \cdot Q,$$

where $\Pi(t) = (\pi_U(t), \pi_D(t))$ and $\pi_U(t) + \pi_D(t) = 1$, we obtain $\pi_U(t) = e^{-\lambda t}$ and $\pi_D(t) = 1 - e^{-\lambda t}$. The system reliability is

$$R(t) = \pi_U(t) = e^{-\lambda t} \tag{21.1.5}$$

and the unreliability is

$$UR(t) = \pi_D(t) = 1 - e^{-\lambda t}. \tag{21.1.6}$$

It is worth mentioning $UR(t) = F(t)$, where $F(t)$ is the cumulative distribution function of the time to failure (see Equation 16.2.2).

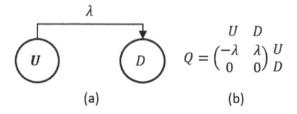

Figure 21.3 Single Component System – Reliability Model.

Consequently, as $MTTF = \int_0^\infty R(t)dt$, we have $MTTF = \int_0^\infty e^{-\lambda t}dt = 1/\lambda$.

---

[3] Also see Equation 16.3.12.
[4] See Equation 10.2.9.

21.2 HOT-STANDBY REDUNDANCY

A computational system is composed of two application servers configured in hot-standby. The application server S_1 is the main server, and S_2 is the hot-standby spare. Figure 21.4.a presents this system. When S_1 fails, S_2 immediately assumes the main server functions (perfect switching). Assume the times to failure of both servers are identically distributed with constant failure rates equal to λ. The time to repair of each server is also identically distributed according to an exponential distribution with rate μ. Let us first assume the number of repair facilities is infinite.

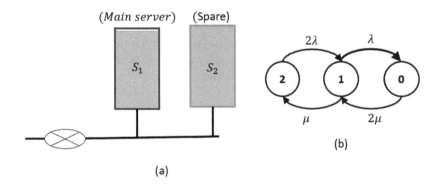

Figure 21.4 Hot-Standby Configuration.

The CTMC shown in Figure 21.4.b is the availability model. This model is composed of three states. State 2 represents both servers as operational. Although the spare server, S_2, is operational, it is processing the workload. It is ready to assume the main servers' activities as soon as S_1 fails. As both servers are turned on, both can fail. When one fails, the system transitions to state 1. In state 1, the spare server begins processing the system workload. Since both servers are turned on, the failure rate assigned to transition from state 2 to state 1 is 2λ. When in state 1, a repair may occur, which takes the system back to state 2. As in state 1, only one server fails; the rate from state 1 to state 1 is μ. When in state 1, another failure may occur, which takes the system to state 0. As in state 1, we have only one server operational; the transition rate from state 1 to state 0 is λ. When the system reaches state 0, both servers fail. As the number of repair facilities is infinite, the repair rate assigned to the transition from state 0 to state 1 is 2μ. The rate matrix is

$$Q = \begin{pmatrix} -2\lambda & 2\lambda & 0 \\ \mu & -\lambda-\mu & \lambda \\ 0 & 2\mu & -2\mu \end{pmatrix}.$$

The instantaneous availability is

$$A(t) = \pi_2(t) + \pi_1(t).$$

Solving $\Pi \cdot Q = 0$, $\pi_2 + \pi_1 + \pi_0 = 1$, where $\Pi = (\pi_2, \pi_1, \pi_0)$, we obtain

$$\pi_2 = \frac{\mu^2}{(\lambda + \mu)^2}, \ \pi_1 = \frac{2\lambda\mu}{(\lambda + \mu)^2}, \ \pi_0 = \frac{\lambda^2}{(\lambda + \mu)^2}.$$

The steady-state availability is $A = \pi_2 + \pi_1$; then

$$A = \frac{\mu(2\lambda + \mu)}{(\lambda + \mu)^2}. \tag{21.2.1}$$

The downtime in the period T is

$$DT = (1 - A) \times T.$$

The results presented above may also be obtained from RBDs and FTs (see Figure 21.5). For instance, consider the results presented in Example 18.5.3.

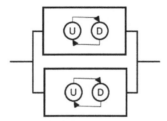

Figure 21.5 Hot-Standby Configuration RBD.

The availability of one component is

$$A_c = \frac{\mu}{\lambda + \mu},$$

and the hot-standby configuration is represented by an RBD with two components in parallel (see 18.5.29). Thus

$$A = 1 - (1 - \frac{\mu}{\lambda + \mu})^2.$$

After some algebra, we get

$$A = \frac{\mu(2\lambda + \mu)}{(\lambda + \mu)^2},$$

which is equal to the Equation 21.2.1.

Now, let us take into account the hot-standby configuration with only one repair facility. The CTMC shown in Figure 21.6 represents such a system. In this model, the transition rate from state 0 to state 1 is μ because there is only one repair facility.

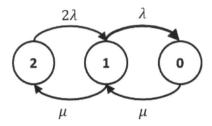

Figure 21.6   Hot-Standby Configuration with Only One Repair Facility

The rate matrix is

$$Q = \begin{pmatrix} -2\lambda & 2\lambda & 0 \\ \mu & -\lambda - \mu & \lambda \\ 0 & \mu & -\mu \end{pmatrix}.$$

The instantaneous availability is

$$A(t) = \pi_2(t) + \pi_1(t).$$

The steady-state availability is $A = \pi_2 + \pi_1$, which is

$$A = \frac{\mu(2\lambda + \mu)}{2\lambda^2 + 2\lambda\mu + \mu^2}. \tag{21.2.2}$$

This cannot be represented through standard RBD or FT. The downtime in the period T is

$$DT = (1 - A) \times T.$$

It is worth mentioning that the steady-state availability depicted by Equation 21.2.1 is larger than the availability expressed by Equation 21.2.2.

Example 21.2.1. Let us consider two servers configured in hot-standby as in Figure 21.4. Assume the time to failure of each server is independent and identically distributed according to an exponential distribution with the rate $\lambda = 5 \times 10^{-4} \, fph$. The time to repair the servers is exponentially distributed with the rate $\mu = 5 \times 10^{-2} \, rph$. The steady-state availability of the system when we consider two repair facilities (obtained from 21.2.1) is equal to one calculated from the RBD (calculated using Equation 18.5.29), $A = 0.999902$, and the respective yearly downtime in minutes is 51.5. The availability when the system has only one facility, calculated using Equation 21.2.2, is $A = 0.999804$, and the downtime in one year in minutes is 103.

$\square$

Now, consider the absorbing CTMC depicted in Figure 21.7.a. This CTMC is the reliability model of the system shown in Figure 21.4. State 2 denotes the system with two servers in operational condition, whereas state 1 represents the system with only one operational server. State 0 depicts a system with no operational server. As in state 2 two servers are available; the transition rate from state 2 to state 1 is λ. In state 1, the failed served may be repaired, which takes the system back to state 2. The repair rate is μ. In state 1, the second server may also fail, which takes the system to state 0, representing the system failure. The CTMC rate matrix is

$$Q = \begin{pmatrix} -2\lambda & 2\lambda & 0 \\ \mu & -\lambda-\mu & \lambda \\ 0 & 0 & 0 \end{pmatrix}.$$

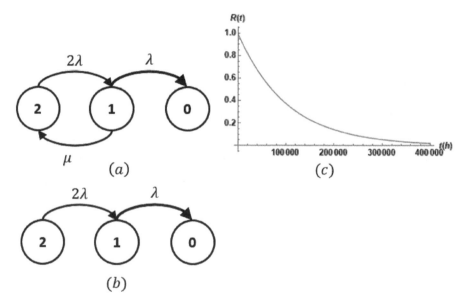

Figure 21.7   Reliability Model – Hot-Standby.

The reliability at t is obtained by

$$R(t) = 1 - \pi_0(t). \tag{21.2.3}$$

The mean time to failure can be calculated from

$$MTTF = \int_0^\infty R(t)\,dt = \int_0^\infty (1 - \pi_0(t))\,dt. \tag{21.2.4}$$

The MTTF may also be obtained using the method based on moments described in Section 10.6.1 (see Equation 10.6.4).

$$MTTF = \frac{(\lambda + \mu)(4\lambda + \mu)}{2\lambda^2(2\lambda + \mu)}. \tag{21.2.5}$$

The reliability calculated using this CTMC is higher than when calculated from the RBD as well as the mean time to failure. The reason for this is that the combinatorial models (RBD and FT) do not consider the repair of the first component that fails. It is worth noting that the system continues to provide the specified service even in the presence of one faulty server. The equivalent CTMC reliability model to the RBD is shown in Figure 21.7.b. The reliability for the RBD equivalent CTMC is

$$R(t) = 2e^{-\lambda t} - e^{-2\lambda t}$$

and the mean time to failure is

$$MTTF = \frac{3}{2\lambda}.$$

It is worth looking at Equation 18.5.24 and Equation 18.5.25.

Example 21.2.2. Let us consider the system depicted in Figure 21.4. Assume the time to failure of each server is independent and identically distributed according to an exponential distribution with the rate $\lambda = 5 \times 10^{-4}\,fph$. The time to repair the servers is exponentially distributed with the rate equal to $\mu = 5 \times 10^{-2}\,rph$. The system reliability at $t = 1000\,h$ calculated using Equation 18.5.24 is $R(1000\,h) = 0.8452$ and the mean time to failure is $3000\,h$[5]. The system reliability at $t = 1000\,h$ calculated using Equation 21.2.3 is $R(1000\,h) = 0.99$, and the mean time to failure is $102980\,h$ (computed using Equation 21.2.4 or Equation 21.2.5). Figure 21.7.c depicts the system reliability calculated from the CTMC for the time interval $(0, 400000\,h)$.

□

Example 21.2.3. An application server system, composed of two equivalent servers (Main Server - *MS* - and Standby Serve - *SS*), is configured in hot-standby. Figure 21.8.a depicts this system. Each application server is composed of a hardware infrastructure (HW), an operating system (OS), and a set of applications (APP). Each server has a hardware infrastructure (see Figure 21.8.b), which is composed of a motherboard (MB), a network controller (NC), a video controller (VC), a disk controller (VC), a disk (D), and a power source (S).

Each server may be represented by an RBD composed of three blocks (Figure 21.8.b). One block represents the application (App), another represents the operating system (OS), and a third block represents the hardware infrastructure. As the hardware infrastructure is decomposed into the motherboard (MB), network controller (NC), video controller (VC), disk controller (DC), disk (D), and power source,

---

[5]It can be calculated using Equation 18.5.25.

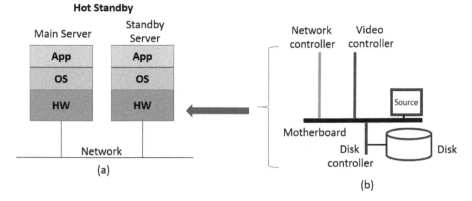

Figure 21.8 Application Servers – Hot-Standby.

the block that represents the hardware infrastructure is also represented by the respective RBD (Figure 21.8.c). Assume the time to failure of each component i is exponentially distributed with rate λ_i. Hence, the server reliability is

$$R_{Server}(t) = R_{App}(t) \times R_{OS}(t) \times R_{HW}(t),$$

$$R_{HW}(t) = R_{MB}(t) \times R_{NC}(t) \times R_{VC}(t) \times R_{DC}(t) \times R_D(t) \times R_S(t),$$

$$R_i(t) = e^{-\lambda_i t}, \quad i \in \{App, OS, MB, NC, VC, DC, D, S\}.$$

Therefore,

$$R_{Server}(t) = e^{-\Sigma_i \lambda_i t}, \quad i \in \{App, OS, MB, NC, VC, DC, D, S\},$$

where

$$\lambda_{Server} = \sum_i \lambda_i, \quad i \in \{App, OS, MB, NC, VC, DC, D, S\}, \tag{21.2.6}$$

and

$$MTTF_{Server} = \frac{1}{\lambda_{Server}}.$$

The failure rate of the server (λ_{Server}) is then assigned to the CTMC depicted in Figure 21.9.a, which is an availability model when considering only one repair facility. Assuming the server time to repair is exponentially distributed with rate μ, the CTMC can be used to estimate the system availability (Equation 21.2.2) and downtime in a period T. Hence

$$A = \frac{\mu(2\lambda_{Server} + \mu)}{2\lambda_{Server}^2 + 2\lambda_{Server}\mu + \mu^2}, \tag{21.2.7}$$

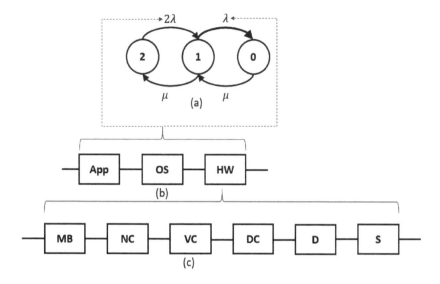

Figure 21.9 Availability Model – Hot-Standby.

and

$$DT = (1 - A) \times T. \qquad (21.2.8)$$

Table 21.1 presents the failure rates of each component. Hence, using Equation 21.2.6, we obtain $\lambda_{Server} = 1.24 \times 10^{-3}$.

Table 21.1
Failure Rates

i	$\lambda_i\ (h^{-1})$
App	5.56×10^{-4}
OS	5.00×10^{-4}
MB	1.67×10^{-5}
NC	2.00×10^{-5}
VC	2.22×10^{-5}
DC	1.82×10^{-5}
D	3.57×10^{-5}
S	6.67×10^{-5}

Therefore, using Equation 21.2.7, Equation 21.2.8, and assuming each server's $MTTR = 20h$ ($\mu = 1/MTTR = 5 \times 10^{-2}h^{-1}$), we calculate the steady-state availability and the respective yearly downtime:

$$A = 0.998838,$$

$$DT = 10.18\,h.$$

Using λ_{Server} as λ in the CTMC shown in Figure 21.7.a, the system reliability can de calculated. Figure 21.10 depicts the system reliability in the time interval $(0, 50000\,h)$. The system reliability at $t = 50000\,h$ is 0.0461325.

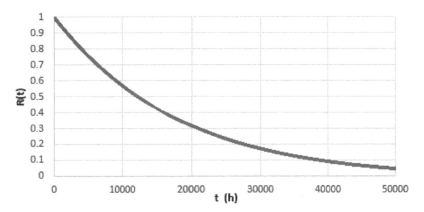

Figure 21.10   Reliability in $t \in (0, 50000\,h)$.

Using Equation 21.2.5 or numerically computing $\int_0^\infty R(t)\,dt$, the system mean time to failure is calculated:

$$MTTF = 17449.73\,h$$

$\square$

21.3   HOT-STANDBY WITH NON-ZERO DELAY SWITCHING

Consider again the system depicted in Figure 21.4. This system is composed of two servers in a hot-standby configuration. The time to failure of each server is assumed to be identically distributed with a constant rate equal to λ. The time to repair a server is exponentially distributed with a rate of μ. Only one repair facility is considered available. Now, however, assume that when the primary server fails, the standby server takes some time to take over the workload. The CTMC shown in Figure 21.11 is an availability model of such a system. The CTMC is composed of five states: 2,

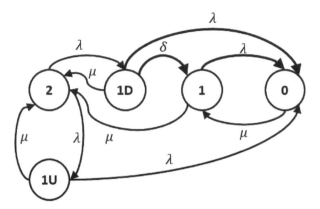

Figure 21.11 Hot-Standby Redundancy with Non-Zero Switching Delay – Availability Model.

$1U$, $1D$, 1, and 0. In state 2, the two servers are available. In-state 0, no server is available. In states $1U$, $1D$, and 1, only one server is operational.

In state 2, either the main server or the standby server may fail. If the standby server fails, the system transitions to state $1U$. It is worth noting that in state $1U$, the service is not interrupted since the failed server is not the server that is providing the service. In state $1U$, the standby server may be repaired, which takes the system back to state 2. In state $1U$, the primary server may fail. If this happens, the system transitions to state 0. As already mentioned, the main server may fail in state 2. If it fails, the system transitions to state $1D$. In this state, the service is interrupted unless the service requirement agreement states that short interruptions are allowed. The interruption occurs because the failed server is the main server (the server receiving the workload). In state $1D$, three events may occur. First, the primary server may be repaired. If this occurs, the system transitions back to state 2. Second, the standby server may also fail. If it fails, the system transitions to state 0. The third possible event is the standby server assuming the workload after a delay of $1/\delta$. The switching delay is considered exponentially distributed with a rate of δ. This event takes the system from state $1D$ to state 1. In state 1, two events are possible. First, the main server may be repaired, which takes the system back to state 2. Second, the standby server may also fail. If it does, the system transitions to state 0. Let us assume only one repair facility is available. In state 0, the server may be repaired. If this occurs, the system transitions to state 1. In this model, we assume the standby server is repaired first.

The system availability is specified by the expression

$$A = \pi_2 + \pi_1 + \pi_{1U}. \tag{21.3.1}$$

Solving $\Pi \cdot Q = 0$, $\sum_{\forall i} \pi_i = 1$, we obtain

$$A = \frac{\mu\left(\mu(\delta + 2\lambda) + 2\lambda(\delta + \lambda) + \mu^2\right)}{(2\lambda^2 + 2\lambda\mu + \mu^2)(\delta + \lambda + \mu)}. \qquad (21.3.2)$$

For $\lambda = 1.24 \times 10^{-3} h^{-1}$, $\mu = 2.5 \times 10^{-1} h^{-1}$ and $\delta = 240 h^{-1}$, we obtain $A = 0.999946$, and $DT = (1 - A) \times 525600$ minutes $= 28.2919$ minutes. Figure 21.12 presents the availability expressed in number of nines $(-\log(1 - A))$ against the switching rate, δ, depicted as $\log \delta$ in the interval $(10 h^{-1}, 240 h^{-1})$ (see Equation 16.2.26). Figure 21.13 shows the yearly downtime in minutes as a function of the switching rate.

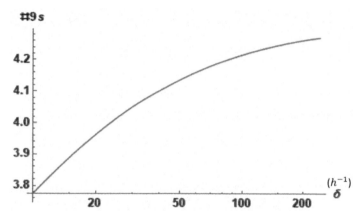

Figure 21.12 Availability in $\#9s \times \log \delta$.

Figure 21.14 is a reliability model of the hot-standby redundancy with non-zero switching delay. In state 2, both servers may fail. However, if the standby server fails, since it is not processing the workload, the service is not immediately interrupted. It transitions to state $1U$, which is still an operational state. In such a state, the spare server may be repaired, or the main server may fail. If it fails, the system becomes unavailable. If the primary server fails in state 2, the system immediately transitions to state 0. It is worth observing that in both states, 2 and $1U$, there is a transition with rate λ to state 0. The rate matrix is

$$Q = \begin{pmatrix} -2\lambda & \lambda & \lambda \\ \mu & -\lambda - \mu & \lambda \\ 0 & 0 & 0 \end{pmatrix}.$$

From Q, we obtain (see the Matrix Structure 10.6.3)

$$R = \begin{pmatrix} -2\lambda & \lambda \\ \mu & -\lambda - \mu \end{pmatrix}.$$

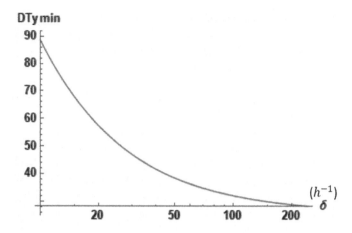

Figure 21.13   Downtime in Year in Minutes $\times \log \delta$.

Using Equation 10.6.7, we have

$$T R = -\Pi'(0).$$

Thus

$$(\tau_2, \tau_1) \begin{pmatrix} -2\lambda & \lambda \\ \mu & -\lambda - \mu \end{pmatrix} = - \begin{pmatrix} 1 \\ 0 \end{pmatrix},$$

where $\Pi'(0)^T = (1,0)$ (see Expression 10.6.1 and Expression 10.6.2). Solving this system of equation, we get

$$\tau_1 = \frac{1}{2\lambda + \mu}$$

and

$$\tau_2 = \frac{\mu}{\lambda(2\lambda + \mu)} + \frac{1}{2\lambda + \mu}.$$

As $MTTA = \sum_i^n \tau_i$ (see Equation 10.6.6), we obtain

$$MTTF = \tau_1 + \tau_2 = \frac{1}{\lambda}.$$

For $\lambda = 1.24 \times 10^{-3} h^{-1}$, we have $MTTF = 1/\lambda = 806.452\,h$. We may also solve[6]

$$\frac{d\Pi(t)}{dt} = \Pi(t) \cdot Q, \quad \sum_{\forall i} \pi_i(t) = 1,$$

---

[6]See the methods presented in Section 10.5.

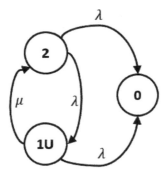

Figure 21.14   Hot-Standby Redundancy with Non-Zero Switching Delay – Reliability Model.

and calculate the system reliability, $R(t) = \pi_2 + \pi_{1U} = e^{-\lambda t}$, which is equal to the model shown in Figure 21.3. In state 2, both servers may fail, and both have the same failure rate λ. If the primary server fails, the system fails, which is represented by reaching State 0. On the other hand, in State 2, if the spare server fails, the system transition to State $1U$. In state $1U$, the primary server may also fail with rate λ. Hence, as the exponential distribution is memoryless, this model is equal to the CTMC depicted in Figure 21.3. From this result, we also obtain

$$MTTF = \int_0^\infty R(t)\,dt = \int_0^\infty e^{-\lambda t}\,dt = \frac{1}{\lambda}.$$

21.4   IMPERFECT COVERAGE

Coverage factor (c) was initially defined as the conditional probability that, given the existence of a failure in the operational system, the system can recover [56]. Since then, many authors have proposed refined notions of this concept. A typical strategy divides this notion into three phases: detection, location, and recovery. Each of these phases is associated with a probability of success. Therefore, the overall coverage probability, c, is obtained from the product of the success probabilities of the individual phases $c = c_d c_l c_r$. A component or subsystem failure may be covered, so the system continues to operate safely or be uncovered which may lead to a system failure.

Assume the application servers depicted in Figure 21.8. These servers are configured in hot-standby redundancy. The primary server processes all workload. If it fails, assuming the switching delay is zero, the standby server promptly takes over the workload processing (see CTMC shown in Figure 21.11); however, the transaction that was being processed in the primary server is lost. If the primary server is operational and the spare server fails, the failure detection mechanism may successfully perceive the spare server failure (the failure is covered) and start recovering mechanism. Nevertheless, the spare server failure may not be detected. In such a case, the spare server failure is hidden (the failure is uncovered) and will only be perceived (1) when the primary server fails, since the spare server will not be able to take over the workload processing or (2) by a later inspection. In this specific case, the coverage factor is represented by the probability of successfully detecting a failure, $c = c_d$ [22] [14].

The CTMC depicted in Figure 21.15 is an availability model of such a system. This CTMC is composed of five states, $\{2, 1, 1U, 0\}$. State 2 represents the two servers that are available; that is, the primary server is operational and processing the workload, whereas the standby is ready to take over the workload in case of the primary server failure. If the main server fails, the system transitions to state 1 with rate λ. If the standby server fails, it may not be detected. In such a case, it transitions to state $1U$ (Unsafe) with a rate of $\lambda(1-c)$ since its failure was undetected (uncovered). However, if the standby server failure is detected, the system transitions from state 2 to state 1 with the rate of λc. Therefore, the total rate from state 2 to state 1 is $\lambda + \lambda c = 2\lambda c$. In state 1, the server may be repaired, which takes the system back to state 0, or the other server may fail. We are considering the switching delay close to zero so that there is no service interruption in the case of the primary server failure since the standby server immediately takes over the workload processing. When in the unsafe state, $U1$, two events are possible. First, the main server may fail, and in such a case, the system becomes unavailable since it reaches state 0. The second possible event is that the system administrator may perceive the failure in the standby server (automatically or not). The perception delay is represented by the delay exponentially distributed with an average of $1/\beta$. After perceiving the standby uncovered failure, the system transitions to state 1, and in this state, the standby server may be repaired, which takes the system back to state 0.

The CTMC infinitesimal generator is

$$Q = \begin{pmatrix} -\mu & \mu & 0 & 0 \\ \lambda & -\lambda - \mu & \mu & 0 \\ 0 & 2c\lambda & -2(1-c)\lambda - 2c\lambda & 2(1-c)\lambda \\ \lambda & \beta & 0 & -\beta - \lambda \end{pmatrix}.$$

Solving $\Pi \cdot Q = 0$, $\sum_{\forall i} \pi_i = 1$, we obtain π_2, π_1, π_{1U}, and π_0. The steady-state availability is calculated by $A = \pi_2 + \pi_1 + \pi_{1U}$. Thus

$$A = \frac{\mu(2\lambda(\beta + \lambda) + \mu(\beta + (3 - 2c)\lambda))}{2\lambda^2(\beta + \lambda) + \mu^2(\beta + (3 - 2c)\lambda) + 2\lambda\mu(\beta - (c - 2)\lambda)}. \tag{21.4.1}$$

The probability of the system being in the unsafe state, $1U$, is

$$\pi_{1U} = \frac{2(c - 1)\lambda\mu^2}{\lambda(2(c - 2)\lambda\mu + (2c - 3)\mu^2 - 2\lambda^2) - \beta(2\lambda^2 + 2\lambda\mu + \mu^2)}, \tag{21.4.2}$$

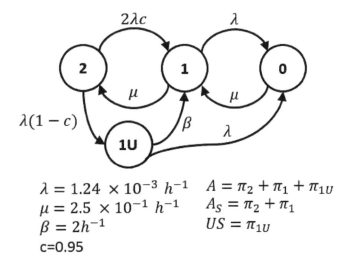

$$\lambda = 1.24 \times 10^{-3} \; h^{-1} \quad A = \pi_2 + \pi_1 + \pi_{1U}$$
$$\mu = 2.5 \times 10^{-1} \; h^{-1} \quad A_S = \pi_2 + \pi_1$$
$$\beta = 2h^{-1} \qquad\qquad US = \pi_{1U}$$
$$c = 0.95$$

Figure 21.15 Hot-Standby Redundancy with Imperfect Detection Coverage – Availability Model.

and the probability of being available and in a safe state is $A_S = \pi_2 + \pi_1$; hence

$$A_S = \frac{\mu(\beta + \lambda)(2\lambda + \mu)}{2\lambda^2(\beta + \lambda) + \mu^2(\beta + (3 - 2c)\lambda) + 2\lambda\mu(\beta - (c-2)\lambda)}. \qquad (21.4.3)$$

The downtime in a year in minutes, $T = 525600$ minutes, may be obtained from

$$DT = (1 - A) \times T.$$

$$DT = \frac{2\lambda^2(\beta - c\mu + \lambda + \mu)}{2\lambda^2(\beta + \lambda) + \mu^2(\beta + (3 - 2c)\lambda) + 2\lambda\mu(\beta - (c-2)\lambda)} \times 525600 \, minutes.$$
$$(21.4.4)$$

The period in a year, in minutes, that the system stays in the unsafe state, UST, is estimated from

$$UST = \pi_{1U} \times T.$$

$$UST = \frac{2(c-1)\lambda\mu^2 \times 525600}{\lambda\left(2(c-2)\lambda\mu + (2c-3)\mu^2 - 2\lambda^2\right) - \beta\left(2\lambda^2 + 2\lambda\mu + \mu^2\right)} minutes.$$
$$(21.4.5)$$

Figure 21.16 depicts some metrics against the detection (perception) rate, β. This allows the analyst to evaluate the impact of strategies and methods for implementing failure detection mechanisms. Figure 21.16.a presents the steady-state availability - A. Likewise, Figure 21.16.b shows the system availability disregarding the unsafe state (π_{1U}), that is when the system is available and in a failure covered state, A_S. Figure 21.16.c depicts the yearly downtime, DT, in minutes, and Figure 21.16.d presents the time period in one year the system stays in the uncovered state π_{1U}, UST. It is worth noting that the downtime, and the time spent in the uncovered states are of the same order.

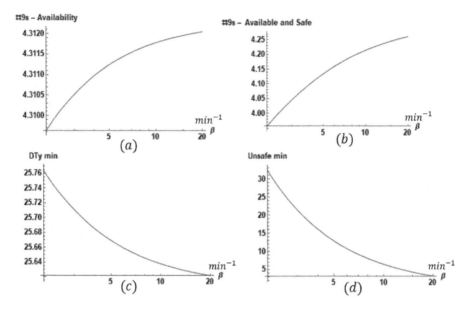

Figure 21.16 Availability, Unsafe State, Downtime, and Time in Unsafe State × β.

Similarly, Figure 21.17 depicts some metrics against the coverage factor (c). This also supports the analysis failure detection mechanisms on the metrics of interest. Figure 21.17.a shows the steady-state availability - A. Figure 21.17.b depicts the availability without considering the unsafe state (π_{1U}), that is A_S. Figure 21.17.c presents the yearly downtime, DT, in minutes, and Figure 21.17.d shows the period in one year the system stays in state π_{1U}, UST.

The CTMC depicted in Figure 21.18 is a reliability model of application servers depicted in Figure 21.8 considering the switching delay is zero and a coverage factor, c, assigned to the spare server. This mode is very similar to the CTMC shown in Figure 21.15. The system only interrupts the service when the state 0 is reached, which is an absorbing state. The system reliability is calculated by

$$R(t) = \pi_2(t) + \pi_1(t) + \pi_{1U}(t). \tag{21.4.6}$$

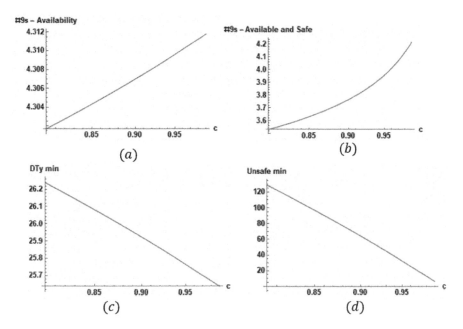

Figure 21.17   Availability, Unsafe State, Downtime, and Time in Unsafe State × c.

The Expression 21.4.7 allows estimating the system reliability disregarding the probability of being in the uncovered (unsafe) state $1U$.

$$R_S(t) = \pi_2(t) + \pi_1(t). \tag{21.4.7}$$

The MTTF can be calculated from

$$MTTF = \int_0^\infty R(t)\,dt = \int_0^\infty (\pi_2(t) + \pi_1(t) + \pi_{1U}(t))\,dt,$$

or using Equation 10.6.7, which leads to

$$MTTF =$$

$$\frac{4\lambda^2(\beta+\lambda)^2 + \mu^2\left(\beta^2 + 2\beta(3-2c)\lambda + (2c(2c-5)+7)\lambda^2\right) + \lambda\mu(\beta+\lambda)(5\beta + (13-8c)\lambda)}{2\lambda^2(\beta - c\mu + \lambda + \mu)(2\lambda(\beta+\lambda) + \mu(\beta+(3-2c)\lambda))}.$$

Assuming $\lambda = 1.24 \times 10^{-3}\,h^{-1}$, $\mu = 2.5 \times 10^{-1}\,h^{-1}$, $\beta = 2\,h^{-1}$, and $c = 0.95$, the MTTF is $81994.1\,h$. Figure 21.19 shows the system reliability in the time interval $(0, 100000\,h)$.

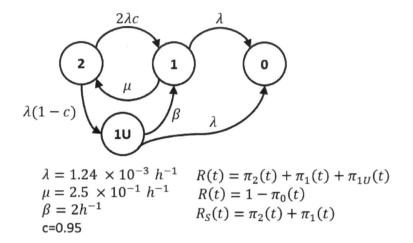

$$\lambda = 1.24 \times 10^{-3} \ h^{-1} \qquad R(t) = \pi_2(t) + \pi_1(t) + \pi_{1U}(t)$$
$$\mu = 2.5 \times 10^{-1} \ h^{-1} \qquad R(t) = 1 - \pi_0(t)$$
$$\beta = 2h^{-1} \qquad\qquad R_S(t) = \pi_2(t) + \pi_1(t)$$
$$c=0.95$$

Figure 21.18 Reliability Model.

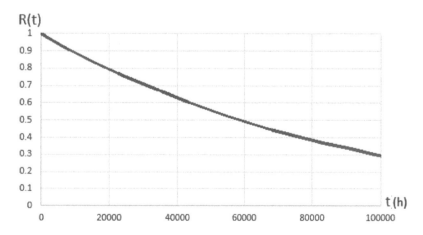

Figure 21.19 Reliability $\times\, t$ - $(0, 100000h)$.

21.5 COLD-STANDBY REDUNDANCY

Let us assume the system depicted in Figure 21.20. This system is composed of two routers configured in cold-standby. $Router_1$ (R_1) is the primary device, whereas $Router_2$ (R_2) is a spare unit. In normal operation, the arrival and departure traffic is routed by R_1, and $Router_2$ is offline. When R_1 fails, R_2 is switched on and assumes the traffic routing. Consider R_1 and R_2 are devices of the same brand and model, and assume the particular times to failure are exponentially distributed with a rate of λ. The delay required after switching one of the spare device until it gets operational is also assumed to be exponentially distributed with a rate of δ. The time to repair the routers is exponentially distributed with a rate of μ. Consider only one repair facility. It is also assumed that the router does not fail when switched off.

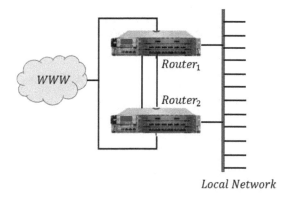

Local Network

Figure 21.20 Two Routers Configured in Cold-Standby.

The CTMC presented in Figure 21.21 is an availability model of the system shown in Figure 21.21. This model is composed of four states, 2, $1D$, 1, $1'$, and 0. In state 2, R_1 is operational and R_2 is turned off. The only event possible is a failure of the router R_1. It is worth mentioning that it is assumed that the switched-off device does not fail. If R_1 fails, the system transitions to state $1D$ with a rate of λ. In state $1D$, the system becomes unavailable since the spare router, R_2, requires time to become operational. As already mentioned, this delay is exponentially distributed with a rate of δ. From state $1D$, two events are possible: first R_2 can be switched on, and if it does occur, the system transitions from $1D$ to state 1, which is an operational state, with a rate of δ. The second possible event is the repairing of R_1, and if this happens, the system transitions back to state 2 with a rate of μ. In state 1, R_1 may be repaired, and so doing, the system returns to state 2 with a rate of μ. The second router, R_2, may also fail. When this occurs, the system transitions from state 1 to state 0 with a rate of λ. In state 0, the system is out of service; that is, both routers are out of order. It should be stressed that only one repair facility is available; hence, a repairing priority should be considered. In this example, R_1 is repaired first. When this occurs, the system transitions from state 0 to state $1'$. In state $1'$ (an operational state), R_1 may fail again, which takes the system back to state 0 with a rate of λ, or the R_2 may also be repaired. If this does occur, the system transitions from state $1'$ to state 2.

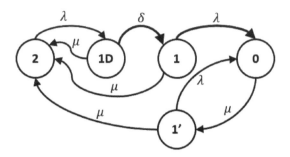

Figure 21.21 Availability Model – Cold-Standby.

Solving $\Pi \cdot Q = 0$, $\sum_{\forall i} \pi_i = 1$, we obtain π_2, π_1, π_{1D}, $\pi_{1'}$, and π_0. The steady-state availability is calculated by

$$A = \pi_2 + \pi_1 + \pi_{1'}. \tag{21.5.1}$$

$$A = \frac{\mu \left(\delta(\lambda + \mu) + \mu^2 \right)}{\delta \left(\lambda^2 + \lambda\mu + \mu^2 \right) + \mu^2(\lambda + \mu)}. \tag{21.5.2}$$

The availability expressed in a number of nines is

$$\#9s = -\log \left(\frac{\lambda \left(\delta\lambda + \mu^2 \right)}{\delta \left(\lambda^2 + \lambda\mu + \mu^2 \right) + \mu^2(\lambda + \mu)} \right). \tag{21.5.3}$$

The yearly downtime in hours is

$$DT = (\pi_{1D} + \pi_0) \times T \tag{21.5.4}$$

$$DT = \left(\frac{\lambda \left(\delta\lambda + \mu^2 \right)}{\delta \left(\lambda^2 + \lambda\mu + \mu^2 \right) + \mu^2(\lambda + \mu)} \right) \times T \tag{21.5.5}$$

where $T = 8760\,h$. The CTMC representing the reliability model is composed only of two states, 2 and $1D$. When R_1 fails, the system transitions to state $1D$ with a rate of λ. In state $1D$, the system is unavailable; hence, $1D$ is an absorbing state in the reliability model. Therefore, the system reliability is $R(t) = e^{-\lambda t}$ and $MTTF = 1/\lambda$.

Figure 21.22 depicts the system availability, expressed in number of nines, for $\lambda = 3.54 \times 10^{-4}$ and $\mu = 4.1666667 \times 10^{-2}$ and $\delta \in (0.5\,h^{-1}, 20\,h^{-1})$. For $\delta = 15\,h^{-1}$, the availability is 0.999991.

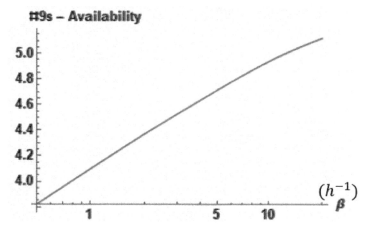

Figure 21.22 $\#9s \times \delta$ – Cold-Standby.

Example 21.5.1. Assume the hardware infrastructure of a router, R_i, is composed of a motherboard (MB), two interface cards (IC_1 and IC_2), and a power source (PS). This infrastructure is depicted in Figure 21.23.a. The router is operational if every hardware component is operational as well as its operational system (see Figure 21.23.b). Consider the times to failure of each of these components are exponentially distributed with rate λ_i, $i \in \{MB, IC_1, IC_2, PS\}$.

Figure 21.23.c shows an FT that represents a reliability model of the router. This model allows calculating the router reliability, its MTTF, and the respective failure rate.

The respective logical function of each fault tree is

$$\overline{\Psi} = \overline{MB} \vee \overline{IC_1} \vee \overline{IC_2} \vee \overline{PS} \vee \overline{OS}.$$

Hence,

$$\Psi = MB \wedge IC_1 \wedge IC_2 \wedge PS \wedge OS.$$

$$\Phi = x_{MB} \times x_{IC_1} \times x_{IC_2} \times x_{PS} \times x_{OS}.$$

Therefore,

$$R(t) = E(\Phi) = E(x_{MB} \times x_{IC_1} \times x_{IC_2} \times x_{PS} \times x_{OS}),$$

and as x_i, $i \in \{MB, IC_1, IC_2, PS\}$, are independent, then

$$R(t) = E(x_{MB}) \times E(x_{IC_1}) \times E(x_{IC_2}) \times E(x_{PS}) \times E(x_{OS}),$$

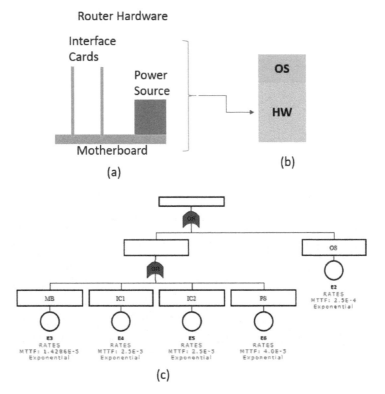

Figure 21.23 Router Infrastructure – Hardware and OS.

which is

$$R(t) = R_{MB}(t) \times R_{IC_1}(t) \times R_{IC_2}(t) \times R_{PS}(t) \times R_{OS}(t).$$

As $R_i(t) = e^{-\lambda_i t}$, $i \in \{MB, IC_1, IC_2, PS\}$, then $R(t) = e^{-\sum_{i \in \{MB, IC_1, IC_2, PS\}} \lambda_i t}$. Therefore the router failure rate is

$$\lambda_R = \sum_{i \in \{MB, IC_1, IC_2, PS\}} \lambda_i,$$

and the mean time to failure is

$$MTTF_R = 1/\lambda_R.$$

Table 21.2 shows the failure rates of each component. Considering these rates, router failure rates are $\lambda_R = 3.54 \times 10^{-4} \, fph$, and $MTTF_R = 2822.58 \, h$.

Table 21.2

Failure Rates – Router's Components

Component	Failure Rate h^{-1}
MB	1.43×10^{-5}
IC_1	2.50×10^{-5}
IC_2	2.50×10^{-5}
PS	4.00×10^{-5}
OS	2.50×10^{-4}

Using the router failure rate, $\lambda_R = \lambda$, calculated from FT in CTMC of the Figure 21.21, we obtain the availability and the respective yearly downtime: $A = 0.99991$ and $DT = 49.78$ minutes.

□

21.6 WARM-STANDBY REDUNDANCY

The system in Figure 21.24 is composed of two servers, server 1 (S_1) and server 2 (S_2), configured in warm-standby redundancy. This system hosts virtual machines for processing the workload demanded from users on the internet. The primary server, S_1, is readily available and provides two similar virtual machines, VM_1 and VM_2. server 1 infrastructure is composed of its hardware (HW), the host operating system (OS), a hypervisor (HP), besides the virtual machines. In normal operation, server 2 is in standby mode. However, it is not switched off. In standby mode, S_2 is turned on, and its host operating system and hypervisor are functional. The virtual machines, though, are not deployed. When S_1 fails, two virtual machines are mounted in S_2, and the workload is then assigned to them. Therefore, it is clear that the standby server takes a while to start processing (switching time) the workload that was being processed in S_1 since time is required to deploy the virtual machines in S_2. Consider that the switching time is exponentially distributed with a rate of δ. Assuming that when processing the workload, S_2's components are equivalent to S_1's components, and both MTTFs are equivalent. However, the S_2's MTTF, when in standby mode, is higher than when it is operating due to its smaller number of components. It is worth mentioning that S_2 in standby mode has no virtual machine deployed.

A server in standby mode may be decomposed into hardware (HW), an operating system (OS), and a hypervisor (HP). A server in operational mode, besides hardware, operating system, and hypervisor, also has two virtual machines, VM_1 and VM_2. Assume the time to failure of each component i is exponentially distributed with a rate of λ_i. If a server, in the respective operational mode, that is, operational (op) or standby (sb), requires all of its components in the respective mode to be functional

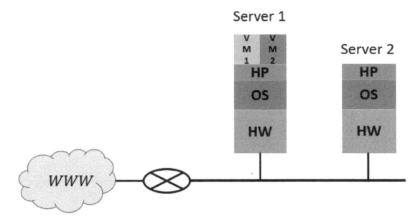

Figure 21.24 Two Servers Configured in Warm-Standby.

(not in failure), the server failure rate in operational mode[7] is

$$\lambda_{op} = \sum_{i \in \{HW,OS,HP,VM_1,VM_2\}} \lambda_i,$$

and the server failure rate in standby mode is

$$\lambda_{sb} = \sum_{i \in \{HW,OS,HP\}} \lambda_i.$$

The mean times to failure of the server in the respective failure modes are $MTTF_{op} = 1/\lambda_{op}$ and $MTTF_{sb} = 1/\lambda_{sb}$. The CTMC depicted in Figure 21.25 shows an availability model of the system depicted in Figure 21.24. This model is composed of five states, 2, 1D, 1′, 1, and 0. State 2 denotes that the primary server is operational, and the spare server is in standby mode. In this state, either server may fail. If the primary server fails, the system transitions to state 1D with a rate of λ_{op}.

On the other hand, if the spare server fails, the system transitions to state 1′ with a rate of λ_{sb}. In state 1′, two events may occur. First, the spare server may be repaired, which takes the system back to state 2. The time to repair is assumed to be exponentially distributed with a rate of μ. Second, the primary server may also fail, which transitions the system to state 0, where the system is unavailable. In state 1D, the service delivered is also unavailable since the spare device takes a while to mount the virtual machines. In this state, three events are possible. First, the primary server may be repaired, which takes the system back to state 2 with a rate of μ. Second, the spare server may also fail; hence taking the system to state 0 with a rate of λ_{sb}. The third possible event is the conclusion of the virtual machine mounting process. This

---

[7] Such modes can be represented by series RBD or with a single OR gate FT.

takes the system from state $1D$ to state 1 with a rate of δ. It is worth mentioning that the spare server is functional and that its hardware, operating system, hypervisor, and virtual machines are operating. Therefore, its failures rate is now λ_{op}. In state 1, two events may occur. The primary server may be repaired, represented by a transition to state 2 with a rate of μ. In such a case, the primary server reclaims the workload processing, and the spare server returns to standby mode. The other possible event in state 1 is the failure of the only operational server, which takes the system to state 0 with a rate of λ_{op}, in which the system is unavailable. In state 0, both servers are out of order. Only one repair facility is available. Therefore, a priority order should be assigned to which server should be repaired first. In this example, differently from the case shown in the CTMC of Figure 21.20, the spare server is repaired first. This event takes the system back to state 1 with a rate of μ.

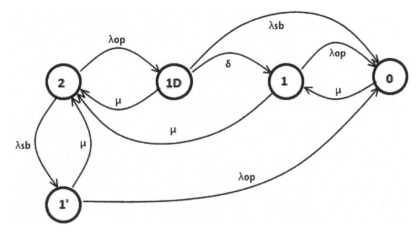

Figure 21.25   Two Servers Configured in Warm-Standby – Availability Model.

The CTMC rate matrix is

$$
Q = \begin{pmatrix}
-\mu & 0 & 0 & \mu & 0 \\
\lambda_{sb} & -\delta - \mu - \lambda_{sb} & \mu & \delta & 0 \\
0 & \lambda_{op} & -\lambda_{op} - \lambda_{sb} & 0 & \lambda_{sb} \\
\lambda_{op} & 0 & \mu & -\mu - \lambda_{op} & 0 \\
\lambda_{op} & 0 & \mu & 0 & -\mu - \lambda_{op}
\end{pmatrix}.
$$

The steady-state availability is calculated summing up the steady-state of the operational states, that is 2, 1, and $1'$. Therefore,

$$
A = \pi_2 + \pi_1 + \pi_{1'}.
$$

Solving $\Pi \cdot Q = 0$, $\sum_{\forall i} \pi_i = 1$, we get

$$A = \frac{\mu \left(\delta \left(\mu + \lambda_{op} + \lambda_{sb} \right) + \lambda_{op} \lambda_{sb} + \left(\mu + \lambda_{sb} \right)^2 \right)}{\delta \left(\lambda_{op}^2 + \lambda_{op} \left(\mu + \lambda_{sb} \right) + \mu \left(\mu + \lambda_{sb} \right) \right) + \left(\mu + \lambda_{op} \right) \left(\lambda_{op} \lambda_{sb} + \left(\mu + \lambda_{sb} \right)^2 \right)}.$$

The availability represented in the number of nines is $\#9s = -\log(1 - A)$, and the downtime in a period T is

$$DT = UA \times T.$$

Thus,

$$DT =$$

$$\left(\frac{\lambda_{op} \left(\delta \left(\lambda_{op} + \lambda_{sb} \right) + \lambda_{op} \lambda_{sb} + \left(\mu + \lambda_{sb} \right)^2 \right)}{\delta \left(\lambda_{op}^2 + \lambda_{op} \left(\mu + \lambda_{sb} \right) + \mu \left(\mu + \lambda_{sb} \right) \right) + \left(\mu + \lambda_{op} \right) \left(\lambda_{op} \lambda_{sb} + \left(\mu + \lambda_{sb} \right)^2 \right)} \right) \times T,$$

where $UA = 1 - A$ is unavailability. Figure 21.26 shows the reliability model of the system depicted in Figure 21.24. This model has three states: 2, 1', and 0. State 2 denotes that the two servers are operational. The primary server is processing the workload, and the spare server is in standby mode. Therefore, in state 2, the spare server fails; in such a case, the system transitions to state 1' with a rate of λ_{sb}. It is worth mentioning that state 1' is still operational because the failed server is not the one that is processing the workload. In state 1', two events are possible. First, the spare server may be repaired, which takes the system back to state 2 with a rate of μ. The second possible event is the failure of the primary server. Such an event takes the system from state 1' to state 0 with a rate of λ_{op}. In state 0, the system is in failure. In state 2, the primary server may also fail. If it does, the system transitions to state 0 with a rate of λ_{op} and fails to deliver the required service. The rate matrix is

$$Q = \begin{pmatrix} -\lambda_{op} - \lambda_{sb} & \lambda_{sb} & \lambda_{op} \\ \mu & -\mu - \lambda_{op} & \lambda_{op} \\ 0 & 0 & 0 \end{pmatrix}.$$

Therefore, the system reliability may be estimated by solving

$$\frac{d\Pi(t)}{dt} = \Pi(t) \cdot Q,$$

where $\Pi(t) = (\pi_2(t), \pi_{1'}(t), \pi_0(t))$ and $\pi_2(t) + \pi_{1'}(t) + \pi_0(t) = 1$ through the expression

$$R(t) = \pi_2(t) + \pi_{1'}(t).$$

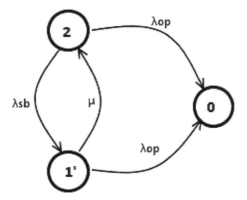

Figure 21.26 Two Servers Configured in Warm-Standby – Reliability Model.

The MTTF can be calculated from $\int_0^\infty R(t)\,dt$ or using Equation 10.6.7. Hence,

$$MTTF = \frac{1}{\lambda_{op}}.$$

Assume the components' failure rates are depicted in Table 21.3; the server repair rate is $\mu = 1.25 \times 10^{-1} h^{-1}$, and the rate of the switching time is $\delta = 30 h^{-1}$.

Table 21.3
Failure Rates

Components	Rate h^{-1}
HW	3.13×10^{-5}
OS	2.86×10^{-4}
HP	3.57×10^{-4}
VM1	2.86×10^{-4}
VM2	2.86×10^{-4}

Hence, $MTTF = 628.93\,h$ and $A = 0.999711$. The availability in number of nines for $\delta \in (0.5 h^{-1}, 20 h^{-1})$ is shown in Figure 21.27. The system reliability in the time interval $(0, 30000\,h)$ is depicted in Figure 21.28.

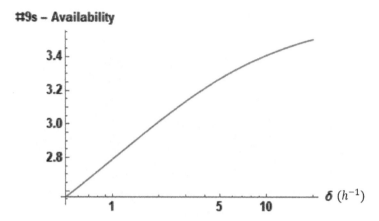

Figure 21.27 Availability × δ - Two Servers Configured in Warm-Standby

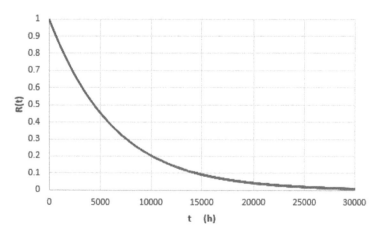

Figure 21.28 Reliability - Two Servers Configured in Warm-Standby.

21.7 ACTIVE-ACTIVE REDUNDANCY

Consider the system depicted in Figure 21.29. These servers share the workload processing that arrives at the system; that is, both servers are active and processing transactions. The system is considered available as long as at least one server is processing. However, if both servers are operational, the processing capacity is higher than if only one server is operational.

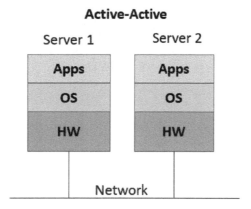

Figure 21.29 Active-Active Servers.

Assume the times to failure of both servers are independent and identically distributed according to an exponential distribution with a rate of λ. Also, consider that the time to repair a server is exponentially distributed with a μ. Hence, CTMC shown in Figure 21.6 can be adopted as a simple availability model of active-active configuration when considering only one repair facility. Likewise, the CTMC shown in Figure 21.4.b is an availability model when considering an unlimited number of repair facilities. For both models, the active-active configuration availability is estimated by

$$A = \pi_2 + \pi_1. \tag{21.7.1}$$

The availability expressions for both cases are represented by Expression 21.2.2 (one repair facility) and Expression 21.2.1 (unlimited repair facilities). They are shown here again for the sake of clarity. The availability of the active-active servers when considering only one repair facility is

$$A = \frac{\mu(2\lambda + \mu)}{2\lambda^2 + 2\lambda\mu + \mu^2},$$

and the availability when considering an unlimited repair facility is

$$A = \frac{\mu(2\lambda + \mu)}{(\lambda + \mu)^2}.$$

If we are interested in quantifying not only whether the probability of the system is available but to provide a figure of processing capacity that is available, the capacity-oriented availability (COA) could be an interesting metric [95, 437]. The capacity-oriented availability is represented by the mean number of available resources, $mnar = \sum_{i=1}^{n} i \pi_i$, (in this case, servers) normalized by the total number of resources (in this case servers). Therefore, consider a system with n equivalent servers; the capacity oriented availability can be formalized by

$$COA = \frac{\sum_{i=1}^{n} i \pi_i}{n}, \qquad (21.7.2)$$

where π_i is the probability of i servers being available, and n is the total number of servers. For the case shown in Figure 21.29, we have

$$COA = \frac{2 \times \pi_2 + \pi_1}{2}, \qquad (21.7.3)$$

which leads to

$$COA = \frac{\mu(\lambda + \mu)}{2\lambda^2 + 2\lambda\mu + \mu^2}, \qquad (21.7.4)$$

when considering only one repair facility. The COA, when considering two or more repair facilities, is

$$COA = \frac{\mu}{\lambda + \mu}. \qquad (21.7.5)$$

COA is a performability (performance + dependability) metrics since it combines the system processing capacity with availability.

Assume each server i (resource) sustains a throughput tp_i. Such a throughput may have been obtained through measurement, a performance model, or a specification. The average throughput – ATP 0- (another performability metric) is the weighted sum of throughputs in the system states. Consider a system with n resources (servers). Each server is able to sustain a throughput tp_i. The throughput could be in transactions per time units, $MIPS$, $MFLOPS$, Qph et alia. More formally:

$$ATP = \sum_{i=1}^{n} i \times tp_i \times \pi_i. \qquad (21.7.6)$$

Example 21.7.1. Consider the system depicted in Figure 21.29. The constant failure rate of each server is $\lambda = 10^{-4} h^{-1}$, and the constant repair rate is $\mu = 10^{-1} h^{-1}$. If only one repair facility is available, we have $A = 0.999999$ and $COA = 0.999$. If throughput delivered by one server is $tp = 1.2 \times 10^6\ tph$[8], the mean throughput provided by the system is $2 \times tp \times \pi_2 + tp \times \pi_1 = 2.3976 \times 10^6\ tph$.   □

---

[8] Transaction per hour - tph.

The reliability mode is equal to the CTMC depicted in Figure 21.7.a. Hence, the reliability at t is obtained by

$$R(t) = 1 - \pi_0(t),$$

and the mean time to failure can be calculated from

$$MTTF = \int_0^\infty R(t)\,dt = \int_0^\infty (1 - \pi_0(t))\,dt$$

or using the method based on moments described in Section 10.6.1, which leads to

$$MTTF = \frac{(\lambda + \mu)(4\lambda + \mu)}{2\lambda^2(2\lambda + \mu)}.$$

The system depicted in Figure 21.30 is an HTTP server system composed of two active-active computers. Now, however, other aspects neglected in the previous system are considered. Here, failure coverage, automatic switchover, and manual switchover mechanisms are analyzed. This system comprises two servers, a router, a switch, a load balancer, and the respective connections. However, the focus of this study is on the servers' failures, repair, failure detection, and switchover mechanisms. The computers (server 1 and server 2) are composed of a hardware system, an operating system, and an HTTP server application with the respective miscellaneous software required to make the system operational. These pieces of software are somewhat embedded in the HTTP server rectangles of the figures.

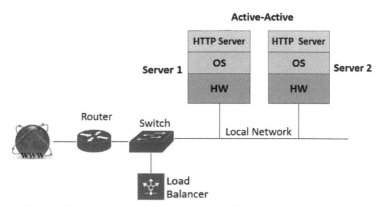

Analysis of Failure Coverage, Automatic and Manual Switchover Mechanisms.

Figure 21.30 Active-Active Servers.

Figure 21.31 shows the transaction flow in the components of the system. A request starts from a user on the internet; the request arrives in the router (1), then is directed to the network switch (2) that forwards the request to the load balancer (3). The load balancer delivers (4) the request to the least loaded server (5). The HTTP transaction is then processed in the server, and a reply (6) is sent to the user through the local network (7) and the internet (8). The load balancer periodically requests information related to resource usage from the servers (r_1 and r_2). If the server j is alive, it replies, providing the information requested (i_j, $j = \{1,2\}$).

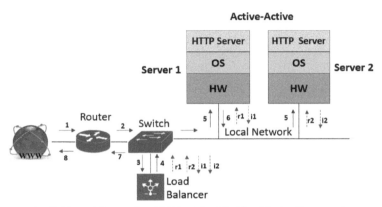

Two Servers Available and Processing 100% of the Workload Being Processed.

Figure 21.31   Active-Active Servers - Processing 100%.

When the server is unavailable, it does not reply (see Figure 21.32). The load balancer, however, waits for a reply during a specified period. In the time being, it keeps forwarding HTTP requests to the server. If the server is unavailable, these requests are lost. Assuming the load balancer evenly distributes the requests among both servers, 50% of the requests are lost.

After the specified delay, the load balancer understands the server is not available and stops forwarding HTTP requests to that server (see Figure 21.33). Now, 100% of the HTTP requests are handled by the only available server. It is worth stressing that although 100% of the requests are coped with, the processing capacity is reduced to only one server. The load balance resumes forwarding requests to the unavailable server when it replies to the information request. In this state, the system is again coping with 100% of the HTTP request, and it has two servers processing the requests (see Figure 21.31 again).

Figure 21.34 presents a CTMC that is an availability model of the system depicted in Figure 21.30. In state S_0 both servers are available and processing HTTP requests. A failure may occur with a rate of 2λ, and such a failure may be covered with probability c or may stay hidden with probability $(1 - c)$. It is worth noting that the probability c indeed represents the failure detection mechanism's capacity to sense a failure incident. If the failure is covered, the system transitions to state S_1 and otherwise, to state S_3. In both states, S_1 and S_3, only one server is available,

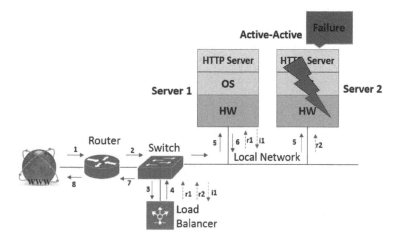

Figure 21.32 Active-Active Servers – Uncovered Failure – Processing 50% of the Workload is Lost.

but the failed server still receives requests to be processed. Such requests are lost; hence, only 50% of the requests are processed since half of them are lost. In state S_1, however, the load balancer is aware of the server failure and starts the automatic switchover to the available server. This process could be successful with probability a, which transitions the system to state S_2 with a rate of β multiplied by a or may be unsuccessful with probability $(1-a)$; thus reaching state $S5$ with a rate of β multiplied by $(1-a)$. In state S_2, only one server is available, but it is processing 100% of the arrived requests. In state S_5, on the other hand, the system is still processing only 50% of the requests since the automatic switchover failed. In state S_1, the failed server may also be repaired, which takes the system back to state S_0 with a rate of μ. In state S_1, the second server may also fail. If this happens, the system transitions to state S_7 with a rate of λ. In state S_3, a state in which the server failure is hidden, two events are possible. First, the second server may also fail. If it does occur, the system transitions to state S_7 with a rate of λ and becomes unavailable. The second event is failure detection. When it occurs, the system transitions to state S_4 with a rate of δ. In state S_4, four events are possible. First, the failed server may be repaired; thus taking the system back to state S_0 with a rate of μ. Second, the operational server may also fail; hence turning the system unavailable and reaching the state S_7 with a rate of λ. The third possible event is a successful automatic switchover. This takes the system to state S_2 with a rate $a \times \beta$. The fourth possible event is the unsuccessful automatic switchover, which takes the system to state S_5 with a rate $(1-a) \times \beta$. In state S_2, two events are possible. First, the failed server may be repaired. If it occurs, the system transitions back to state S_0 with a rate of μ. The other possible event is the failure of the second server. Such a failure turns the system unavailable and takes the system to state S_7 with a rate of λ. In state S_5 four events are also possible. The

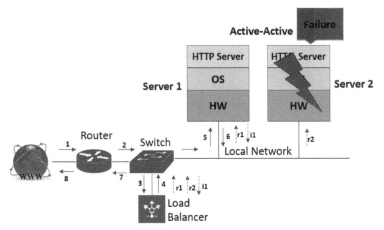

Failure Detected and Successful Switchover - 100% of the Workload Being Processed.

Figure 21.33 Active-Active Servers – One Server Available.

failed server may be repaired; thus taking the system back to state S_0 with a rate of μ. Thus, the second server may fail; thus reaching state S_7 with a rate of λ. The third event is the successful manual switchover, which takes the system to state S_2 with a rate of $m \times \alpha$. The last event is the unsuccessful manual switchover, which transitions the system to state S_6 with a rate of $(1 - m) \times \alpha$. In state S_6, the system only handles 50% of the HTTP requests. In state S_6, two events are possible. First, the failed server may be repaired. This event transitions the system back to state S_0 with a rate of μ. The other possible event is the second server failure, which turns the system unavailable by reaching state S_7 with a rate of λ. It is assumed there is only one repair facility. Therefore, a repair takes the system from state S_7 to state S_2.

The system availability is estimated from

$$A = 1 - \pi_{S_7},$$

which leads to

$$A = \frac{\mu(\mu((3-2c)\lambda+\delta)+2\lambda(\delta+\lambda))}{\mu^2((3-2c)\lambda+\delta)+2\lambda\mu(\delta-(c-2)\lambda)+2\lambda^2(\delta+\lambda)}. \quad (21.7.7)$$

The capacity oriented availability is calculated using

$$COA = \frac{2 \times \pi_{S_0} + \pi_{S_2} + 0.5 \times \sum_{i \in \{1,3,4,5,6\}} \pi_{S_i}}{2}, \quad (21.7.8)$$

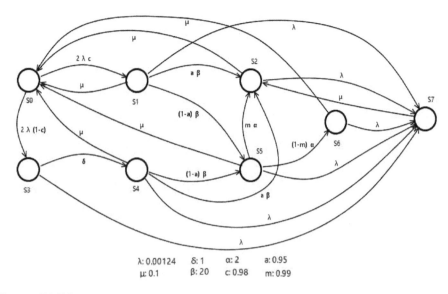

Figure 21.34   Active-Active Servers – Availability Model.

from which we obtain

$$COA = \frac{\mu\left(\lambda^2(\alpha+\lambda)\Lambda + \mu^2\Upsilon + \lambda\mu\Phi\right) + \mu^3\Delta + \mu^4\Theta)}{(\lambda+\mu)(\alpha+\lambda+\mu)(\beta+\lambda+\mu)\Omega}, \qquad (21.7.9)$$

where

$$\Lambda = \left(-0.5\beta\delta - 0.5\beta\lambda - 0.5\delta\lambda - 0.5\lambda^2\right),$$

$$\Upsilon =$$

$$(-0.5\alpha\beta\delta + \lambda^2\Sigma + \lambda((-0.25a - 1.25)\beta\delta + \alpha(\beta(0.25c - 0.75) - 1.25\delta)) +$$

$$(1.25c - 3.75)\lambda^3),$$

$$\Sigma = (\beta(-0.25ac + 0.75c - 2) + \alpha(0.75c - 2) - 2.5\delta),$$

$$\Phi = \left(\lambda^2\Xi + \lambda\Gamma + \alpha\beta\delta(a(0.25m - 0.25) - 0.25m - 0.75) + (0.5c - 2.25)\lambda^3\right),$$

$$\Xi = (\beta(-0.25ac + 0.5c - 1.75) + \alpha(0.5c - 1.75) - 1.75\delta),$$

$$\Gamma = ((-0.25a - 1.25)\beta\delta + \alpha(\beta(c(0.25am - 0.25a - 0.25m + 0.5) - 1.25) - 1.25\delta)),$$

$$\Delta = (\alpha((0.25c - 0.75)\lambda - 0.5\delta) + \beta(0.25c\lambda - 0.5\delta - 0.75\lambda) + \lambda$$

$$(c\lambda - 1.75\delta - 2.75\lambda)),$$

$$\Theta = ((0.25c - 0.75)\lambda - 0.5\delta),$$

and

$$\Omega = \left(\lambda \left((c-2)\lambda\mu + (c-1.5)\mu^2 - \lambda^2 \right) + \delta \left(-\lambda^2 - \lambda\mu - 0.5\mu^2 \right) \right).$$

A comment on the worth of the availability model shown in Figure 21.33 is required to support reaching a simpler model by removing some rare occurrence events. For instance, the likelihoods of repair events when in states S_1 and S_4 are rare since the rate β is much higher than μ. Hence, the availability model's analytics metrics may be significantly simplified at the expense of a slight loss of accuracy. Such a type of practical simplification may be fundamental to the process of reaching a closed-form solution.

Figure 21.35 presents the availability (in number of nines), the downtime, and the capacity-oriented availability considering the coverage probability interval $c \in (0.9, 0.99)$, considering $\lambda = 1.24 \times 10^{-3}\ h^{-1}$, $\mu = 0.1\ h^{-1}$, $\delta = 1\ h^{-1}$, $\alpha = 2(h^{-1})$, $\beta = 20(h^{-1})$, $a = 0.95$, and $m = 0.99$.

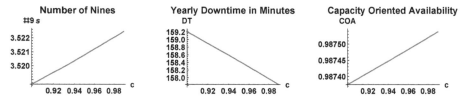

Figure 21.35   Availability (#9s), Yearly Downtime, $COA \times c$.

The detection delay is a key parameter for reducing the impact of hidden failure on system availability and processing capacity. Figure 21.36 presents the availability (in number of nines), the downtime, and the capacity-oriented availability considering the failure detection interval $\delta \in (1\,h^{-1}, 20\,h^{-1})$, assuming $\lambda = 1.24 \times 10^{-3}\ h^{-1}$, $\mu = 0.1\ h^{-1}$, $c = 0.98$, $\alpha = 2(h^{-1})$, $\beta = 20(h^{-1})$, $a = 0.95$, and $m = 0.99$.

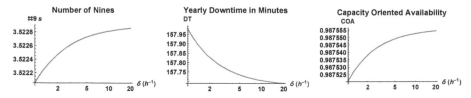

Figure 21.36   Availability (#9s), Yearly Downtime, $COA \times \delta$.

The automatic and manual switchover mechanisms do not affect the system availability and the respective downtime, but they have impact on the capacity-oriented availability. Figure 21.37 depicts the capacity-oriented availability considering the automatic (a) and the manual switchover (m) probability intervals $a, m \in (0.9, 0.99)$, considering $\lambda = 1.24 \times 10^{-3}\ h^{-1}$, $\mu = 0.1\ h^{-1}$, $\delta = 1\ h^{-1}$, $c = 0.98$, $\alpha = 2\ h^{-1}$, and $\beta = 20\ h^{-1}$.

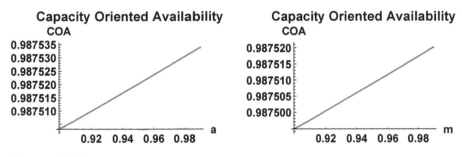

Figure 21.37 $COA \times a, m$.

Figure 21.38 shows the availability (in number of nines), the downtime and the capacity-oriented availability considering the repair rate interval $\mu \in (0.1\,h^{-1}, 0.25\,h^{-1})$, assuming $\lambda = 1.24 \times 10^{-3}\ h^{-1}$, $\delta = 1\ h^{-1}$, $c = 0.98$, $\alpha = 2\ h^{-1}$, $\beta = 20\ h^{-1}$, c=0.98, a=0.95, and m=0.99.

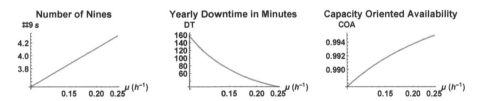

Figure 21.38 Availability (#9s), Yearly Downtime, $COA \times \mu$.

Efficient switchover mechanisms are critical to processing capacity. Figure 21.39 depicts the capacity-oriented availability considering the automatic (β) and the manual switchover (α) rates in the respective intervals $\beta \in (8h^{-1}, 20h^{-1})$ and $\alpha \in (0.5h^{-1}, 2h^{-1})$, assuming $\lambda = 1.24 \times 10^{-3}\ h^{-1}$, μ=0.1 h^{-1}, $\delta = 1\ h^{-1}$, c=0.98, a=0.95, and m=0.99.

The CTMC shown in Figure 21.40 is a reliability model of the system depicted in Figure 21.30. The only difference between this CTMC and the availability model is that there is no transition from state S_7 to state S_2. State S_7 is an absorbing state. Hence, the system is reliable as long as it does not reach state S_7. Therefore,

$$R(t) = 1 - \pi_{S_7}(t).$$

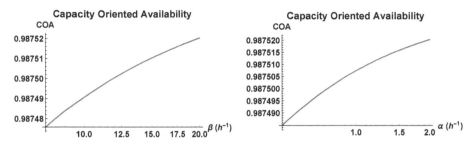

Figure 21.39 $COA \times \beta, \alpha$

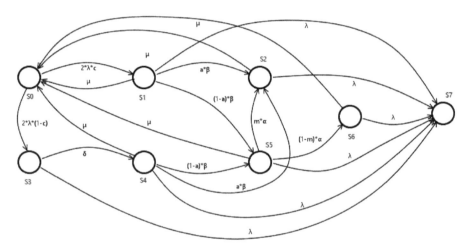

Figure 21.40 Reliability Model.

Assume $\lambda = 1.24 \times 10^{-3} \ h^{-1}$, $\mu = 1 \times 10^{-1} \ h^{-1} \ \delta = 1 \ h^{-1}$, $c = 0.98$, $\alpha = 2 \ h^{-1}$, $\beta = 20 \ h^{-1}$, c=0.98, a=0.95, and m=0.99. Figure 21.40 presents the system reliability in $t \in (0, 100000 \, h)$. The MTTF can be calculated from $\int_0^\infty R(t) \, dt = \int_0^\infty (1 - \pi_{S_7}(t)) \, dt$ or using Equation 10.6.4. The calculated mean time to failure is $MTTF = 33662.26 \, h$.

As previously suggested regarding the availability model, similar suppression of rare events may also be examined to support less complex reliability models at the expense of slight loss of accuracy.

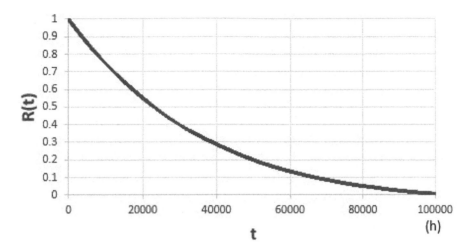

Figure 21.41 $R(t) \times t$.

21.8 MANY SIMILAR MACHINES WITH INDEPENDENT REPAIR FACILITIES

A system composed of M similar servers installed in a set of racks as is shown in Figure 21.42. Assume these servers are part of a cloud data center that provides $IaaS$[9] [65, 271, 331, 332]. Consider the time to failure of each server is independent and exponentially distributed with a rate of λ. Moreover, suppose each server has an independent repair facility and that the time to repair of each server is also independent and exponentially distributed with a rate of μ.

The system availability and reliability may be calculated using RBD or FT but may also be computed using a CTMC. The CTMC shown in Figure 21.43 is an availability model of such a system. State M denotes a system with M servers available. If one server fails, the system transitions to state $M-1$ with a rate of $M\lambda$. In state $M-1$, the failed server may be repaired, so the system transitions back to state M with a rate of μ, or a second server may fail, which transitions the system to state $M-2$ with a rate of $(M-2)\lambda$. Similar behavior is seen for the following states. In state 0, however, there is no available server; hence the only possible event is repairing a server, which transitions the system to state 1 with a rate of $M\mu$ since each server is supposed to have its repair facility. Solving $\Pi \cdot Q = 0$, $\sum_{\forall i} \pi_i = 1$, we get the probability of each state i by

$$\pi_i = \frac{M!}{i!\,(M-i)!} \times \frac{\lambda^{M-i}\mu^i}{(\lambda+\mu)^M}. \tag{21.8.1}$$

---

[9] Infrastructure as a Service - $IaaS$.

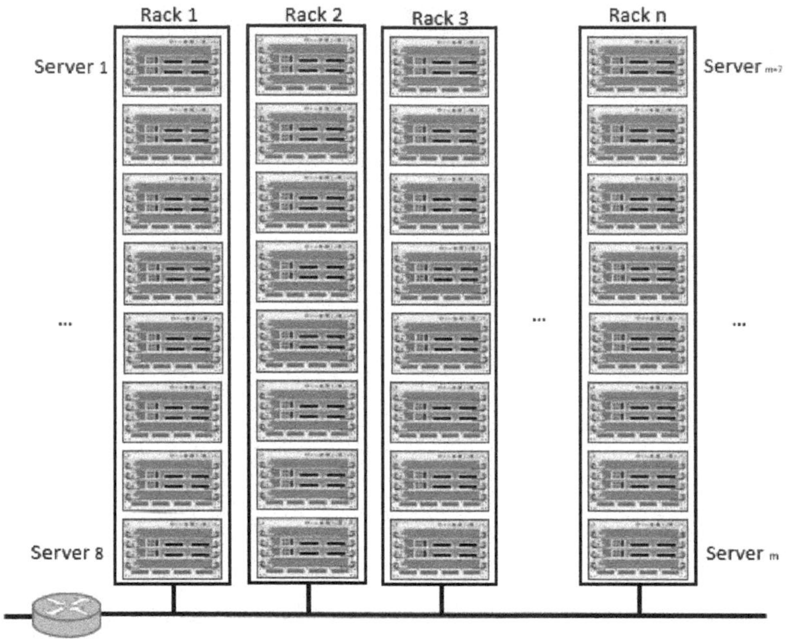

Figure 21.42 Racks of Servers.

The availability is $1 - \pi_0$, then

$$A = 1 - \left(\frac{\lambda}{\lambda + \mu}\right)^M, \tag{21.8.2}$$

which is equivalent to Expression 18.5.20. The unavailability $(UA = \pi_0)$ is represented by

$$UA = \left(\frac{\lambda}{\lambda + \mu}\right)^M, \tag{21.8.3}$$

The downtime in a period T is

$$DT = \left(\frac{\lambda}{\lambda + \mu}\right)^M \times T. \tag{21.8.4}$$

The average number of servers operational is calculated from

$$ANSO = \sum_{i=1}^{M} i\,\pi_i, \tag{21.8.5}$$

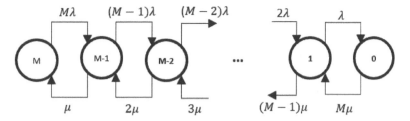

Availability Model

Figure 21.43 *M* Similar Machines with Independent Repair Facilities.

which leads to

$$ANSO = \sum_{i=1}^{M} i \left(\frac{M!}{i!\,(M-i)!} \times \frac{\lambda^{M-i}\mu^{i}}{(\lambda+\mu)^{M}} \right). \tag{21.8.6}$$

The capacity-oriented availability is calculated from

$$COA = \frac{\sum_{i=1}^{M} i\,\pi_{i}}{M}; \tag{21.8.7}$$

thus

$$COA = \frac{\sum_{i=1}^{M} i \left(\frac{M!}{i!(M-i)!} \times \frac{\lambda^{M-i}\mu^{i}}{(\lambda+\mu)^{M}} \right)}{M}. \tag{21.8.8}$$

The probability of *K* out of *M* servers to be operational (Number of Operational Servers - *NOS*) is obtained by

$$P(NOS \geq K) = \sum_{i=k}^{m} \left(\frac{M!}{i!\,(M-i)!} \times \frac{\mu^{i}\lambda^{M-i}}{(\lambda+\mu)^{M}} \right). \tag{21.8.9}$$

Example 21.8.1. A system is composed of $M = 8$ servers. The failure and repair rates are constants and equal to $\lambda = 1.24 \times 10^{-3}h^{-1}$ and $\mu = 2.5 \times 10^{-1}h^{-1}$, respectively. Furthermore, consider each server has an independent repair facility.

The system availability in a number of nines is obtained from

$$\#9s = -\log(\pi_{0}),$$

where

$$\pi_{0} = \frac{\lambda^{8}}{(\lambda+\mu)^{8}}.$$

Thus

$$\#9s = 18.4533.$$

Using 21.8.8, the capacity-oriented availability is obtained

$$COA = \frac{\sum_{i=1}^{8} i \left(\frac{8!}{i!(8-i)!} \times \frac{(1.24 \times 10^{-3})^{8-i}(2.5 \times 10^{-1})^{i}}{(1.24 \times 10^{-3} + 2.5 \times 10^{-1})^{8}} \right)}{8} = 0.995064.$$

Figure 21.44 presents the probability of K out of M servers being available in a number of nines, that is

$$-\log \left(1 - \left(\sum_{i=k}^{m} \left(\frac{M!}{i!(M-i)!} \times \frac{\mu^{i} \lambda^{M-i}}{(\lambda + \mu)^{M}} \right) \right) \right),$$

for $K = \{1, 2, 3, 4, 5, 6, 7, 8\}$.

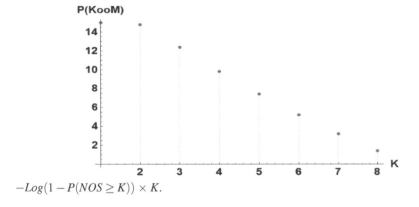

$-Log(1 - P(NOS \geq K)) \times K.$

Figure 21.44 M Similar Machines with Independent Repair Facilities.

☐

Example 21.8.2. Now consider that each of M servers of the Example 21.8.1 supports K virtual machines. Assume the time to failure and the time to restart (repair) a virtual machine are exponentially distributed with rates of λ_{vm} and μ_{vm}, respectively. Also, consider the server constant failure and repair rates are λ and μ. The availability model proposed represents an M servers system with K virtual machines for each server represented by two-level CTMCs as depicted in Figure 21.45. Figure 21.45.a is the servers' availability model as in as the CTMC depicted in Figure 21.43. However, as each server has K virtual machines, a CTMC representing the virtual machines available for each number of servers available is modeled. Therefore, when only one physical server is available, we may have up to K virtual machines available. Hence, the CTMC shown in Figure 21.45.d allows computing the availability and COA for a configuration when only one physical server is available. Thus, the probabilities of the CTMC of Figure 21.45.d must be multiplied by the probability of state 1 of the CTMC of Figure 21.45.a. Likewise, if two physical servers are available, up to $2K$ virtual machines may be available. It is worth noting that these CTMCs that denote the virtual machines' availability are similar to the CTMC presented in Figure 21.43 (and Figure 21.45). The CTMCs of Figure 21.45.b and 21.45.c are assigned to the states M and $M-1$ of the CTMC of the Figure 21.45.a. The number of states of the CTMC presented in Figure 21.45.b is $KM+1$ since KM virtual machines may be available in such a configuration. λ_{pm} denotes the constant failure rate of the physical server (hardware and software without their VMs). λ_{vm} is the constant failure rate of the virtual machines. μ_{pm} and μ_{vm} are the parameters of the exponentially distributed time to repair the physical server and the virtual machines, respectively.

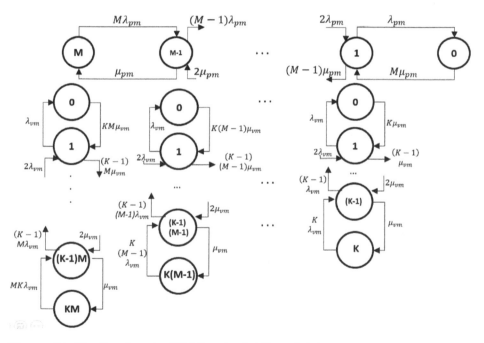

Figure 21.45   Two-Levels CTMCs - Availability Model

Solving the CTMCs and after some algebra, the expressions that allow calculating the availability, downtime in a period T, average number of virtual machines alive (operational), and respective capacity-oriented availability (considering a VM is the

Table 21.4

A, DT, $ANVMA$ **and** COA **- Two Server and Four VMs Depicted by Two-Level CTMCs**

Measure	Value
A	0.99985
DT (minutes)	78.8487
ANVMA	3.95087
COA	0.98772

resource provided) are:

$$A = \sum_{i=1}^{M} \frac{M! \, \mu^i \lambda vm^{iK} \lambda^{M-i} (\lambda + \mu)^{-M} (\lambda vm + \mu vm)^{-iK}}{i! \, (M-i)!} - \lambda^M (\lambda + \mu)^{-M} + 1,$$

(21.8.10)

$$DT = (1 - \sum_{i=1}^{M} \frac{M! \, \mu^i \lambda vm^{iK} \lambda^{M-i} (\lambda + \mu)^{-M} (\lambda vm + \mu vm)^{-iK}}{i! \, (M-i)!} - \lambda^M (\lambda + \mu)^{-M} + 1) \times T,$$

(21.8.11)

$$ANVMA = \sum_{i=1}^{M} \sum_{j=1}^{i \times K} \frac{j(iK)! \, \mu_{vm}^j \lambda_{vm}^{iK-j} (\lambda vm + \mu vm)^{-iK}}{j! \, (iK-j)!} \times \frac{M! \, \mu^i \lambda^{M-i} (\lambda + \mu)^{-M}}{i! \, (M-i)!},$$

(21.8.12)

and

$$COA = \frac{\sum_{i=1}^{M} \sum_{j=1}^{i \times K} \frac{j(iK)! \, \mu_{vm}^j \lambda_{vm}^{iK-j} (\lambda vm + \mu vm)^{-iK}}{j! \, (iK-j)!} \times \frac{M! \, \mu^i \lambda^{M-i} (\lambda + \mu)^{-M}}{i! \, (M-i)!}}{M \times K}.$$

(21.8.13)

Let us consider the specific case for two physical servers, each server hosting two VMs, where $\lambda_{pm} = 0.00124 \, h^{-1}$, $\lambda_{vm} = 0.000714286 \, h^{-1}$, $\mu_{pm} = 0.1 \, h^{-1}$ and $\mu_{vm} = 20 \, h^{-1}$. When a virtual machine fails, its repair is a reboot. The availability (A), the downtime in a year (DT), $ANVMA$, and COA were calculated and depicted in Table 21.4.

Assume each server hosts sixteen virtual machines. Figures 21.46 and 21.47 presents the average number of virtual machines alive and the respective capacity-oriented availability considering the number of physical machines $M = [1, 80]$. It is worth observing that although COA has a declining tendency, the actual changes observed are indeed tiny.

□

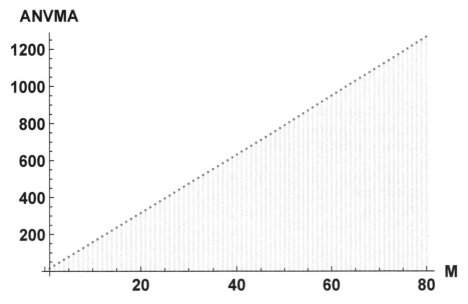

Figure 21.46   *ANVMA* × *M* - Each Server Hosting Up to 16 VMs.

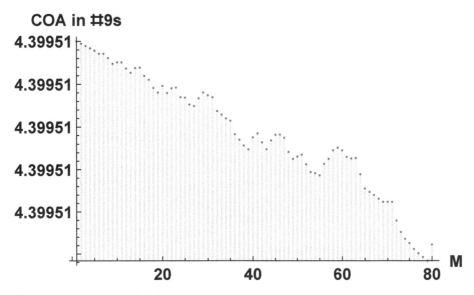

Figure 21.47   *COA* (#9s) × *M* - Each Server Hosting Up to 16 VMs.

21.9 MANY SIMILAR MACHINES WITH SHARED REPAIR FACILITY

As in the previous section, assume a system composed of M similar servers installed in a set of racks as is shown in Figure 21.42. Consider the time to failure of each server is independent and exponentially distributed with a rate of λ. Now, however, suppose there is only one repair facility, and the time to repair is exponentially distributed with a rate of μ.

The CTMC depicted in Figure 21.48 is an availability model of such a system. State M denotes a system with M servers available. If one server fails, the system transitions to state $M-1$ with a rate of $M\lambda$. In state $M-1$, the failed server may be repaired, so the system transitions back to state M with a rate of μ, or a second server may fail, which transitions the system to state $M-2$ with a rate of $(M-2)\lambda$. Similar behavior is seen for the following states. In state 0, however, there is no available server; hence, the only possible event is repairing a server, which transitions the system to state 1 with a rate of μ since there is only one repair facility.

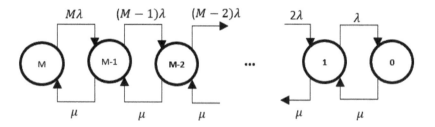

Figure 21.48 Availability Model – M Similar Machines with One Shared Repair Facility.

The state probabilities are obtained by finding a solution to the system of equations $\Pi \cdot Q = 0$, $\sum_{\forall i} \pi_i = 1$. The algebraic solution for the steady-state probability of state k, $k = M - j$, $j \in \{0, 1, 2, ..., M\}$, is

$$\pi_k = \frac{\frac{M! \mu^j \lambda^{M-j}}{j!}}{\sum_{i=0}^{M} \frac{M! \lambda^i \mu^{M-i}}{(M-i)!}}. \tag{21.9.1}$$

As the availability is $A = 1 - \pi_0$, then

$$A = 1 - \frac{M! \lambda^M}{\sum_{i=0}^{M} \frac{M! \lambda^i \mu^{M-i}}{(M-i)!}}, \tag{21.9.2}$$

and the downtime in a period T ($DT = \pi_0 \times T$) is

$$DT = \left(\frac{M! \lambda^M}{\sum_{i=0}^{M} \frac{M! \lambda^i \mu^{M-i}}{(M-i)!}} \right) \times T. \tag{21.9.3}$$

The average number of servers available ($ANSA$) and the capacity-oriented availability are specified by

$$ANSA = \sum_{j=1}^{M} j \times \frac{\frac{M! \mu^j \lambda^{M-j}}{j!}}{\sum_{i=0}^{M} \frac{M! \lambda^i \mu^{M-i}}{(M-i)!}}, \tag{21.9.4}$$

and

$$COA = \frac{\sum_{j=1}^{M} j \times \frac{\frac{M! \mu^j \lambda^{M-j}}{j!}}{\sum_{i=0}^{M} \frac{M! \lambda^i \mu^{M-i}}{(M-i)!}}}{M}. \tag{21.9.5}$$

The probability of K out of M servers to be operational (Number of Operational Servers - NOS) is obtained by

$$P(NOS \geq K) = \sum_{j=k}^{M} \frac{\frac{M! \mu^j \lambda^{M-j}}{j!}}{\sum_{i=0}^{M} \frac{M! \lambda^i \mu^{M-i}}{(M-i)!}}. \tag{21.9.6}$$

Example 21.9.1. A system is composed of $M = 8$ servers as in Example 21.8.1. The failure and repair rates are constants and equal to $\lambda = 1.24 \times 10^{-3} h^{-1}$ and $\mu = 2.5 \times 10^{-1} h^{-1}$, respectively. Now, however, only one repair facility is available.

The system availability in a number of nines is obtained from

$$\#9s = -\log(\pi_0),$$

where

$$A = -\log\left(\frac{M! \lambda^M}{\sum_{i=0}^{M} \frac{M! \lambda^i \mu^{M-i}}{(M-i)!}}\right) = 13.8481.$$

Using 21.9.4, the average number of servers available is

$$ANSA = 7.95912,$$

and the capacity-oriented availability is

$$COA = 0.99489.$$

Figure 21.44 presents the probability of K out of M servers being available in a number of nines, that is

$$-\log(1 - (\sum_{j=k}^{M} \frac{\frac{M! \mu^j \lambda^{M-j}}{j!}}{\sum_{i=0}^{M} \frac{M! \lambda^i \mu^{M-i}}{(M-i)!}})),$$

for $K = \{1,2,3,4,5,6,7,8\}$.

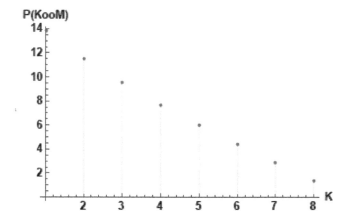

Figure 21.49 $-Log(1 - P(NOS \geq K)) \times K$ - M Similar Machines with One Shared Repair Facility

□

21.10 PHASE-TYPE DISTRIBUTION AND PREVENTIVE MAINTENANCE

Preventive maintenance has been acknowledged as a critical task for reducing maintenance costs and improving system reliability. Two main factors that must be considered in a preventive maintenance program are its cost compared with the reduction in the total costs of repair and the system performance improvement, and the utilization of the equipment maintained. If the cost of preventive maintenance is similar to the cost of repair after a failure, it may have little or no benefit. On the other hand, preventive maintenance should be considered if the fault can result in severe damage to the system and a much more expensive repair.

Preventive maintenance is used when the time to failure has an increasing failure rate over time. Preventive maintenance may be classified into classes, and perhaps the most important of them is the time-based preventive and condition-based maintenances (also called predictive maintenance). Time-based maintenance refers to replacing or renewing a system or its components to restore its reliability at a fixed time, interval, or usage regardless of its condition. Most failure modes provide some warning that the system or its components are in the process of failing or are about to fail. If evidence shows that such a phenomenon is progressing, actions may be taken to prevent it from falling and avoid more drastic consequences. Condition-based maintenance (predictive maintenance) is a strategy that looks for evidence that failure is developing or is about to occur [282].

In this section, let us consider time-based preventive maintenance. Assume a system (Figure 21.50.a) whose time to failure is distributed according to an Erlang distribution with four phases, each phase with a rate of λ. Such a distribution has an increasing failure rate; that is, the system ages. Also, let us consider that the time to repair is exponentially distributed with a rate of μ. An availability model without preventive maintenance is presented in Figure 21.50.b. In state 0, the system is as good as new. As the system ages, it transitions to state 1, 2, 3, and finally to 4, representing system failure. The system is then repaired (corrective maintenance), which transitions the system from state 4 to state 0 with a rate of μ. Therefore the system availability is obtained through the expression

$$A = 1 - \pi_4.$$

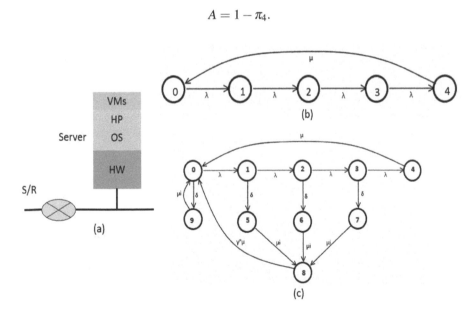

Figure 21.50 Preventive Maintenance.

Now, consider time-based preventive maintenance. Consider that the time between preventive maintenance is also exponentially distributed with a rate of δ, that is from

$1/\delta$; on average, preventive maintenance is started. The preventive maintenance is, here, subdivided into two sub-tasks, inspection and then repairing itself. Assume the inspection time is also exponentially distributed with a rate of μ_i. The preventive maintenance repairing time is assumed to be a submultiple of the corrective maintenance, but also exponentially distributed with a rate of $\gamma\mu$, where γ defines how much shorter is the preventive repair in comparison with the corrective repair. The CTMC shown in Figure 21.50.c is an availability model of such a system with both corrective and time-based preventive maintenance.

In state 0, two events are possible; first, the system may age and transition to state 1 with a rate of λ. The second possible event is the start of preventive maintenance. This event takes the system to state 9 with a rate of δ. In state 0, the system has not aged; hence, there will be an inspection but no repair. After the inspection, the system is taken back to state 0 with a rate of μ_i. In state 1 (the system has already aged), two events are also possible. First, the system may continue the aging process and transition to state 2 with a rate of λ. Preventive maintenance may also begin. This takes the system to state 5 with a rate of β. Then, the system is inspected, which transitions the system to state 8 with a rate of μ_i, and then the preventive repair is carried out with a rate of $\gamma\mu$ and takes the system back to state 0. The following states and transition work likewise. However, if the system reaches state 4 (a failure), the system is corrected (corrective maintenance) with a rate of μ, which takes the system back to state 0. The system is available in all states except states 4 and 8. Thus, solving the system of equations $\Pi \cdot Q = 0$, $\sum_{\forall i} \pi_i = 1$, we obtain the steady-state system probabilities, and the availability is expressed by

$$A = 1 - \sum_{i \in \{4,8\}} \pi_i.$$

Doing some algebra, we obtain

$$A = \qquad\qquad\qquad (21.10.1)$$

$$\frac{\gamma\mu(\delta+2\lambda)(\delta^2+2\delta\lambda+2\lambda^2)(\delta+\mu i)}{\gamma\delta\mu(\delta+2\lambda)(\delta^2+2\delta\lambda+2\lambda^2)+\gamma\mu i(\mu(\delta+2\lambda)(\delta^2+2\delta\lambda+2\lambda^2)+\lambda^4)+\delta\lambda\mu i(\delta^2+3\delta\lambda+3\lambda^2)}.$$

Example 21.10.1. Assume the system depicted in Figure 21.50.a, and consider the following rates: $\lambda = 2 \times 10^{-3}\,h^{-1}$, $\mu = 0.1\,h^{-1}$, $\mu_i = 1\,h^{-1}$, and $\delta = 1.428571 \times 10^{-3}\,h^{-1}$, and the multiple $\gamma = 4$. The steady-state availability without preventive maintenance (calculated from the CTMC shown in Figure 21.50.b) is $A = 0.99502$. The yearly downtime in hours in $DT = 1 - (1-A) \times T = 43.58\,h$, where $T = 8760\,h$ is the number of hours in a year.

The steady-state availability taking into account the preventive maintenance provides an availability of $A = 099626$ and the yearly downtime is $DT = 32.76\,h$. Figure 21.51 shows the availability in terms of the δ, considering the interval $\delta \in (10^{-5}\,h^{-1}, 5 \times 10^{-3}\,h^{-1})$.

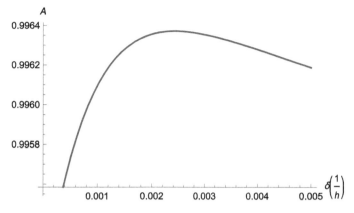

Figure 21.51 Availability $\times$ δ - Preventive Maintenance.

It is worth noting that a low rate (δ), which implies a long mean time between preventive maintenance (*mtbpm*), does not favor the availability. When δ is increased (reducing the *mtbpm*), the availability increases. However, when the preventive maintenance is too frequent, the availability decreases by stopping the system more than required. The *mtbpm* that maximizes the availability can be obtained by first deriving A in relation to δ

$$\frac{\partial A}{\partial \delta} = \gamma\lambda\mu\mu i$$

$$\left(2\delta^3\lambda^2(2(\gamma+4)\lambda-3\mu i)+3\delta^2\lambda^3((4\gamma+2)\lambda+(\gamma-6)\mu i)+4\delta\lambda^4(3\gamma\lambda+2\gamma\mu i-6\mu i)+2\lambda^5(2\gamma\lambda+3\gamma\mu i-6\mu i)+\delta^6+6\delta^5\lambda+\delta^4\lambda(15\lambda-\mu i)\right)/$$

$$\left(\gamma\left(\delta^4\mu+\delta^3\mu(4\lambda+\mu i)+2\delta^2\lambda\mu(3\lambda+2\mu i)+2\delta\lambda^2\mu(2\lambda+3\mu i)+\lambda^3\mu i(\lambda+4\mu)\right)+\delta\lambda\mu i\left(\delta^2+3\delta\lambda+3\lambda^2\right)\right)^2$$

and then finding out δ that solves

$$\gamma\lambda\mu\mu i$$

$$\left(2\delta^3\lambda^2(2(\gamma+4)\lambda-3\mu i)+3\delta^2\lambda^3((4\gamma+2)\lambda+(\gamma-6)\mu i)+4\delta\lambda^4(3\gamma\lambda+2\gamma\mu i-6\mu i)+2\lambda^5(2\gamma\lambda+3\gamma\mu i-6\mu i)+\delta^6+6\delta^5\lambda+\delta^4\lambda(15\lambda-\mu i)\right)/$$

$$\left(\gamma\left(\delta^4\mu+\delta^3\mu(4\lambda+\mu i)+2\delta^2\lambda\mu(3\lambda+2\mu i)+2\delta\lambda^2\mu(2\lambda+3\mu i)+\lambda^3\mu i(\lambda+4\mu)\right)+\delta\lambda\mu i\left(\delta^2+3\delta\lambda+3\lambda^2\right)\right)^2 = 0.$$

Hence, we obtain $\delta = 2.45257 \times 10^{-3}\, h^{-1}$. Thus, the optimal mean time between preventive maintenance for maximizing the availability is $mtbpm_{opt} = 1/\delta = 407.735h$.

21.11 TWO-STATES AVAILABILITY EQUIVALENT MODEL

Consider a system composed of two similar web-servers, one database server, and network infrastructure (Figure 21.52). This system is assumed to be operational as long as one web server and the database-server are functional. It is assumed that the network infrastructure is fault-free. It is assumed that the database-server repair has priority over the web-servers repair. The failure rates of the web-server and the database-server are constant and equal to λ_{ws} and λ_{db}, respectively. The time to repair web-servers and of the database-server are exponentially distributed with the respective rates μ_{ws} and μ_{db}. It is assumed that only one repair facility is available.

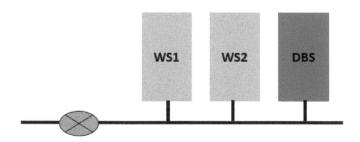

Figure 21.52 Two Web-Servers and One Database Server.

The CTMC depicted in Figure 21.53.a is an availability model of the system shown in Figure 21.52. The state $S0$ denotes the two web servers, and the database-server is operational. In this state, two events are possible; that is, one web-server may fail, which takes the system to states $S1$ with a rate of $2\lambda_{ws}$ or the database-server may fail. In such a case, the system transitions to state $S3$ with a rate of λ_{db}, in which the system becomes unavailable. In state $S1$ (the system is available), three possible events may occur. First, the failed web server may be repaired. This takes the system back to state $S0$ with a rate of μ_{db}. The second possible event is a failure on the second web-server, which takes the system to state $S2$ with a rate of λ_{ws}, and the system becomes unavailable. The third event is the database server, which transitions the system to state $S4$ with a rate of μ_{db}, and the system also becomes unavailable. The following states work likewise. The set of available states is $\{S0, S1\}$. Therefore, the system availability is obtained through

$$A = \pi_{S0} + \pi_{S1}.$$

Assume $\lambda_{ws} = 1.14 \times 10^{-4} h^{-1}$ and $\lambda_{db} = 2.28 \times 10^{-4} h^{-1}$, and $\mu_{ws} = \mu_{db} = 4.17 \times 10^{-2} h^{-1}$. The steady-state probability of each state is depicted in Table 21.5. Therefore, the system availability is $A = 0.99455$ and the yearly downtime in minutes is $DT = 2866\,minutes$.

Very often, it is interesting to obtain or consider a two-state availability model that allows computing the same availability of a multi-state model. In order to represent the equivalent two-state CTMC, the equivalent failure and repair rates should be properly defined. Consider a simple two-state model that represents the availability of the system depicted in Figure 21.52. This model is either in state U (UP) or in state D (Down) as shown in Figure 21.53.b. The steady-state availability of the system

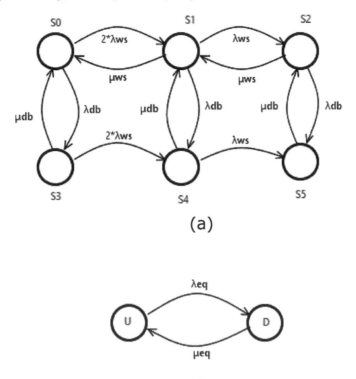

(a)

(b)

Figure 21.53 Two Web-Servers and One Database Server – Availability Model.

considering the two-state CTMC is represented by

$$A = \frac{\mu_{eq}}{\lambda_{eq} + \mu_{eq}},$$

where the equivalent failure rate, λ_{eq}, is defined by

$$\lambda_{eq} = \frac{\sum_{i \in S_{UD}} \pi_i \times \lambda_{id}}{\sum_{j \in S_U} \pi_j}, \qquad (21.11.1)$$

where S_U is the set of states (in the multi-state model) in which the system is operational, S_{UD} is the set of states of the multi-state CTMC in which the system is operational, and there is one a leaving arrow to a downstate. The rate assigned to such an arrow is named λ_{id}, and π_i and π_j are state probabilities. Finally, it is worth noting that the equivalent failure rate (λ_{eq}) is an output rate conditioned to the system having in an operational state.

Table 21.5

Steady-State Probabilities – Two Web-Servers and One Database Server

π_{S0}	0.9891095920
π_{S1}	0.0054374894
π_{S2}	0.0000150257
π_{S3}	0.0053786726
π_{S4}	0.0000589775
π_{S5}	0.0000002428

Similarly, the equivalent repair rate is also defined, that is

$$\mu_{eq} = \frac{\sum_{i \in S_{DU}} \pi_i \times \mu_{iu}}{\sum_{j \in S_D} \pi_j}, \tag{21.11.2}$$

where S_D is the set of states (in the multi-state model) in which the system is unavailable, S_{DU} is the set of states of the multi-state CTMC in which the system is unavailable, and there is one a leaving arrow to an up state. The rate assigned to such an arrow is named μ_{iu}, and π_i and π_j are state probabilities. It is worth mentioning that the equivalent repair rate (μ_{eq}) is an output rate conditioned to the system being failed. Therefore, $\sum_{i \in S_D} \pi_i = 5.45292 \times 10^{-3}$, $\sum_{j \in S_U} \pi_j = 0.99455$,

$$\lambda_{eq} = \frac{\pi_{s0} \times \lambda_{db} + \pi_{s1} \times \lambda_{db} + \pi_{s1} \times \lambda_{ws}}{\pi_{s0} + \pi_{s1}} = 2.28623 \times 10^{-4} h^{-1},$$

and

$$\mu_{eq} = \frac{\pi_{s2} \times \mu_{ws} + \pi_{s3} \times \mu_{db} + \pi_{s4} \times \mu_{db}}{\pi_{s2} + \pi_{s3} + \pi_{s4} + \pi_{s5}} = 4.16981 \times 10^{-2} h^{-1}.$$

Thus

$$A = \frac{\mu_{eq}}{\lambda_{eq} + \mu_{eq}} = \frac{4.16981 \times 10^{-2} h^{-1}}{2.28623 \times 10^{-4} h^{-1} + 4.16981 \times 10^{-2} h^{-1}} = 0.99455.$$

21.12   COMMON CAUSE FAILURE

As already mentioned in Section 18.7, Common Cause Failures (CCF) are one of the reasons why the reliability and availability models of a system may dangerously underestimate the probability of failure. CCFs occur when multiple components fail due to common causes, such as impact, vibration, temperature, power failure, and improper maintenance.

Consider a system composed of two identical servers (see Figure 21.8 and Figure 21.9). A server may fail due to the failures of its components. Assume the server failure is constant and equal to λ. The server may be repaired with a constant rate of repair μ. Let consider that only one repair facility is available. An external event may occur and results in failures in all servers at the same time. Consider this external event occurs with a constant rate of λ_c, which is denoted the common cause failure rate. The CTMC depicted in Figure 21.54 is an availability model of such a system and takes into account common cause failure.

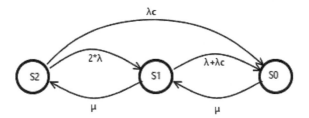

Figure 21.54 Two Web-Servers and Common Cause Failure – Availability Model.

The rate matrix is

$$Q = \begin{pmatrix} -\mu & \mu & 0 \\ \lambda + \lambda c & -\lambda - \lambda c - \mu & \mu \\ \lambda c & 2\lambda & -2\lambda - \lambda c \end{pmatrix}.$$

The availability can be obtained from

$$A = 1 - \pi_{s0},$$

which, solving the system of equations $\Pi \cdot Q = 0, \sum_{\forall i} \pi_i = 1$ and doing some algebra, we obtain

$$A = \frac{\mu(2\lambda + \lambda c + \mu)}{2\lambda^2 + \lambda(3\lambda c + 2\mu) + (\lambda c + \mu)^2}.$$

The availability may also be expressed in a number of nines by

$$\#9s = -\log(\pi_{s0}).$$

The downtime in a period T can be estimated from

$$DT = \pi_{s0} \times T = \left(\frac{2\lambda^2 + 3\lambda\lambda c + \lambda c(\lambda c + \mu)}{2\lambda^2 + \lambda(3\lambda c + 2\mu) + (\lambda c + \mu)^2} \right) \times T.$$

Figure 21.55.a and Figure 21.55.b show the availability and the respective number of nines as functions of the common cause failure rate in the interval $\lambda_c(10^{-5} h^{-1}, 10^{-3} h^{-1})$, assuming $\lambda = 1.24 \times 10^{-3} h^{-1}$ and $\mu = 5 \times 10^{-2} h^{-1}$.

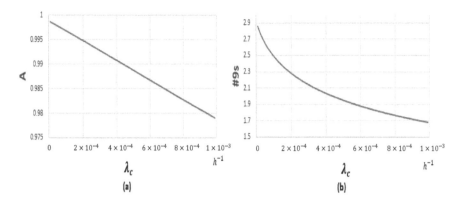

Figure 21.55   Common Cause Failure - $\lambda_c \times A$.

EXERCISES

Exercise 1. Assume a single-component system has the time to failure distributed according to an Erlang distribution with $\gamma = 2$ phases and each phase equal to $\lambda = 1.24 \times 10^{-3} h^{-1}$. Propose a CTMC that allows calculating the system reliability. (a) Calculate the MTTF of the system. (b) Plot the graph of the reliability, $R(t)$, in the interval $(0, 4000 h)$. If the repair rate is constant and equal to $\mu = 0.1 h^{-1}$, propose a CTMC that allows calculating the system availability and obtain the steady-state availability of the system.

Exercise 2. Consider two servers in hot-standby. Assume the time to failure of each server is independent and identically distributed with a constant rate of $\lambda = 4 \times 10^{-4} h^{-1}$. The time to repair the servers is exponentially distributed with a rate of $\mu = 0.1 h^{-1}$. If only one repair facility is available and using a CTMC (a) calculated the steady-state availability and the downtime in one year. Explain why these measures are different from those obtained from an FT or an RBD. (b) Obtain the system MTTF. (c) Calculate the reliability, $R(t)$, at $t = 10000 h$.

Exercise 3. Returning to the Example 21.2.3, if the failure rates are those shown in Table 21.6

and assuming each server has constant repair rate $\mu = 4 \times 10^{-2} h^{-1}$), calculate (a) the steady-state availability, (b) the respective yearly downtime, and (c) the reliability at $t = 4000 h$, and (c) the system $MTTF$.

Exercise 4. Now assume the hot-standby configuration of the previous exercise has a non-zero delay switching mechanism. Consider the switching rate is constant and equal to $\delta = 120 h^{-1}$. Calculate (a) the steady-state availability, (b) the respective yearly downtime, and (c) the reliability at $t = 4000 h$, and (c) the system $MTTF$.

Table 21.6
Failure Rates

i	$\lambda_i\ (h^{-1})$
App	5.00×10^{-4}
OS	4.50×10^{-4}
MB	1.80×10^{-5}
NC	2.32×10^{-5}
VC	2.42×10^{-5}
DC	1.52×10^{-5}
D	3.69×10^{-5}
S	5.97×10^{-5}

Exercise 5. Considering again the Exercise 3, now assume an imperfect detection mechanism. Let $c \in (0.9, 50.99)$. Plot (a) the steady-state availability, (b) the respective yearly downtime, and (c) the reliability at $t = 4000h$, and (c) the system $MTTF$ as a function of c.

Exercise 6. Looking back to the Example 21.5.1, assume the time to failure of each of its components is exponentially distributed with rates depicted in Table 21.7.

Table 21.7
Failure Rates – Router's Components

Component	Failure rate h^{-1}
MB	1.50×10^{-5}
IC_1	2.70×10^{-5}
IC_2	2.30×10^{-5}
PS	4.25×10^{-5}
OS	2.35×10^{-4}

(a) Obtain the steady-state availability, (b) the yearly downtime, (c) the MTTF and (c) and the system reliability at $t = 2000h$.

Exercise 7. Consider a two-component parallel-redundant system with distinct failure rates λ_1 and λ_2, respectively. Upon failure of a component, a repair process is invoked with the respective repair rates μ_1 and μ_2. Assume that a failure of a component while another is being repaired causes a system failure. Adopt CTMC for modeling. (a) Derive the reliability and the MTTF of the system. (b)Derive the steady-state availability of the system and the downtime.

Exercise 8. For a computer system composed by two servers (server sub-system: $S1$ and $S2$) operating in a hot-standby sparing configuration; a storage sub-system is composed of two disks ($D1$ and $D2$) configured in RAID 1 and controller (C). The system fails if the server sub-system or storage sub-system fails. Consider that the constant failure rates are $\lambda_{S1} = 1.14155 \times 10^{-4}h^{-1}$, $\lambda_{S2} = 7.61035 \times 10^{-5}h^{-1}$, $\lambda_C = 5.70776 \times 10^{-5}h^{-1}$, $\lambda_{D1} = \lambda_{D1} = 8 \times 10^{-5}h^{-1}$. The respective times to repair are exponentially distributed with rates $\mu_{S1} = \mu_{S2} = 20.833 \times 10^{-3}h^{-1}$, $\mu_{D1} = \mu_{D2} = 10.417 \times 10^{-3}h^{-1}$ and $\mu_C = 41.667 \times 10^{-3}h^{-1}$. Assume there is only one repair team. (a) Propose a CTMC model of the server sub-system and compute its availability. (b) Conceive an availability model of the whole system. (c) Compute the steady state availability of the system. (d) Calculate the respective system's downtime in minutes per year. (d) Conceive a reliability model of the whole system. (e) Calculate the system's MTTF. (f) Draw the reliability curve in the interval $[0, 1460\,h)$.

Exercise 9. Consider a system that has a time to failure obeying a 5-stage hypoexponentially distributed random variable with parameters $\lambda_1, \lambda_2, \lambda_3, \lambda_4, \lambda_5$, where $\lambda_1 = 5.1 \times 10^{-4}h^{-1}$ and $\lambda_2 = \lambda_3 = \lambda_4 = \lambda_5 = 5.88 \times 10^{-4}h^{-1}$. The system time to repair times is exponentially distributed with parameter $\mu = 2.0833 \times 10^{-2}h^{-1}$. (a) Compute the steady-state availability. (b) Present the equivalent two-state availability model and the respective availability. Explain.

Exercise 10. Consider a tiny-private cloud system composed of a cloud manager subsystem (CMSS), three servers (S_1, S_2, S_3) and a network-attached storage (NAS), which is composed by a NAS controller (NC) and six disks configured in RAID 5. Each computer hardware is composed of a motherboard (MB), memory (M), the network controller (NC), video controller (VC), an internal disk (HD), its disk controller (HDC), and the power source (PS). The cloud manager subsystem (CMSS)

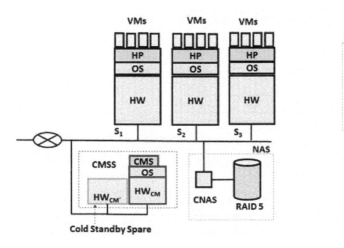

Figure 21.56 Tiny-Private Cloud System.

Table 21.8

Tiny-Private Cloud System Parameters

Component	MTTF (h)	MTTR (h)	MTTS (h)
Mother board (MB)	80000		
Memory (M)	40000		
Network Controller (NC)	60000		
Video controller (VC)	50000		
Hard disk controller (HDC)	45000		
Hard disk (HD)	35000		
Power source (PS)	20000		
Operational system (OS)	4000	1	
Hypervisor (HP)	5000	1	
Virtual Machine	4000	0.25	
NAS Controller (NASC)	50000	4	
Cloud Manager Software (CMS)	3000	2	
Server Hardware		24	
CM		8	
CM'		8	0.1

comprises two cloud managers (CM + CM') configured in cold-standby. Each cloud manager is operational if its hardware, its operating system, and the cloud manager software (CMS) are opertional. Each server is operational if its hardware, its operational system, the virtual machine manager (VMM), and at least one virtual machine (VM) are functional. Each server provides four VMs. The tiny-private cloud system is operational if at least one virtual machine is operational. Assume the times-to-failure and the times-to-repair are exponentially distributed. The time to start (TTS) the CM' is also exponentially distributed with rate δ. The MTTFs, the MTTRs, and the MTTS are depicted in Table 21.8. Consider only one repair team. (a) Compute the availability, (b) downtime, (c) capacity-oriented availability, and (d) mean number of operational VMs of the system. Hint: use RBDs or FT and CTMCs.

22 Modeling Availability, Reliability, and Capacity with SPN

This chapter discusses reliability and availability modeling issues related to the system represented by state-space models. This chapter uses stochastic Petri nets to evaluate systems not well represented by combinatorial models due to a complex interaction between components or an active-redundancy mechanism. In addition, hierarchical and heterogeneous modeling are also introduced to illustrate the adoption of different formalisms at distinct modeling levels. Section 22.12 presents some additional models.

This chapter presents a set of SPN models for the availability and reliability evaluation of systems [18, 169, 272]. We begin by describing a single-component system, its availability model, and the respective reliability model. Then, from these basic models, a set of redundancy mechanisms and maintenance features is studied for estimating availability, reliability, and other related metrics.

22.1 SINGLE COMPONENT

Consider a single component system named C. This component may be operational (*UP - U*) or in failure (*Down - D*). The SPN depicted in Figure 22.1.a represents this system. This net has two places, U and D, which represent the respective states of the component. Besides, there are two transitions, F and R, representing a component's fault and the respective repair. Both transitions have single-server semantics (*sss*). The component is initially operational; hence the initial marking vector is $M_0 = (m_U, m_D) = (1,0)$. In Mercury-like notation, the place marking is $\#U = 1$ and $\#D = 0$. Assume the failure and repair rates are λ and μ, respectively. The SPN may be evaluated either through numerical methods as described in Section 13.2) or by simulation as depicted in Section 14.2.

Figure 22.1.b shows the reachability graph and Figure 22.1.c presents the respective CTMC obtained from the SPN. It is worth looking at Section 21.1 and checking the instantaneous, steady-state availability, and the downtime metrics.

The steady-state availability is expressed as the probability of place U having one token, that is, $P(m_U = 1)$, which in Mercury notation is $P\{\#U = 1\}$. The predicate $\#U = 1$ ($m_U = 1$) is true only in marking $(1,0)$ (see Figure 22.1.b), which is mapped to state 1 of the CTMC (see Figure 22.1.c). Therefore, the steady-state availability is

$$A = P\{\#U = 1\} = \pi_1,$$

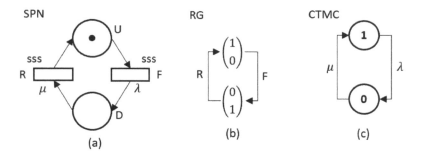

Figure 22.1   Single Component System – SPN Availability Model.

where π_1 is obtained by solving $\Pi \cdot Q = 0$, $\sum_{i=0}^{1} \pi_i = 1$ or by steady-state simulation of the SPN. The unavailability is

$$UA = P\{\#U = 0\} = P\{\#D = 1\} = \pi_0 = 1 - \pi_1.$$

The instantaneous availability is the probability of the component being operational at a specific time instant t, that is $P(m_U = 1)(t) = 1$. In Mercury-like notation it is $P\{\#U = 1\}(t)$. Solving $\partial \Pi / \partial t = \Pi(t)Q$, $\Pi = (1,0)$, $\sum_{i=0}^{1} \pi_i(t) = 1$, we obtain the instantaneous availability (see Section 21.1):

$$A(t) = P\{\#U = 1\}(t) = \pi_1 = \frac{\mu}{\lambda + \mu} + \frac{\lambda}{\lambda + \mu}\, e^{-(\lambda+\mu)t}.$$

The instantaneous unavailability is

$$UA(t) = P\{\#D = 1\}(t) = \pi_0 = \frac{\lambda}{\lambda + \mu} - \frac{\lambda}{\lambda + \mu}\, e^{-(\lambda+\mu)t}.$$

The downtime in a period T is obtained by

$$DT = P\{\#U = 0\} \times T.$$

Figure 22.2.a presents the reliability SPN model of the single-component system. The system reliability at t is the probability of not reaching the absorbing marking D, which is translated into state 0 of the CTMC (Figure 22.2.c) through the reachability graph (Figure 22.2.b). Solving $\partial \Pi / \partial t = \Pi(t)Q$, $\Pi = (1,0)$, $\sum_{i=0}^{1} \pi_i(t) = 1$, we obtain the reliability (see Section 21.1):

$$R(t) = P\{\#U = 1\}(t) = \pi_1 = e^{-\lambda t}.$$

Hence, the unreliability is

$$UR(t) = P\{\#D = 1\}(t) = \pi_0 = 1 - e^{-\lambda t}.$$

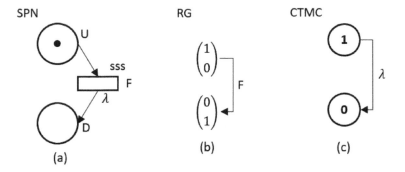

Figure 22.2 Single Component System - SPN Reliability Model.

The mean time to failure is then computed either by $MTTF = \int_0^\infty R(t)\,dt$ or by using Equation 10.6.4. The MTTF is

$$MTTF = \frac{1}{\lambda}.$$

22.2 MODELING TTF AND TTR WITH PHASE-TYPE DISTRIBUTION

This section presents a single-component system whose time to failure and time to repair are not exponentially distributed. Here, phase-type distributions were adopted to represent the TTF and TTR (see Section 13.3.8). In this specific case, the TTF is modeled by an Erlang distribution with K phases and with phase rate $\lambda = 1/ttfph$, where $ttfph$ is the respective mean value of each exponential phase of the Erlang distribution. A Cox-1 distribution represents the TTR. The Cox-1 distribution has three parameters: ω_1, ω_2, KC and $\mu = 1/ttrph$, where KC is the number of phases, $ttrph$ is the respective mean value of each exponential phase of the Cox-1 distribution (see Section 13.3.8). These parameters are depicted in Table 22.1

Figure 22.3.a is a high-level representation of such a system (transitions in gray). In this model, t_0 represents the event that causes the failure, and t_1 is the repair activity. A token in place P_0 denotes an operational component, whereas a token in P_1 represents a failure. Figure 22.3.b shows an SPN that refines both gray transitions, representing the TTF and the TTR, by the respective Erlang and Cox-1 subnets. These subnets are depicted inside dotted red rectangles. A detailed explanation of the Erlang and Cox-1 subnets is given in Section 13.3.8. Tokens in places P_0 and P_1

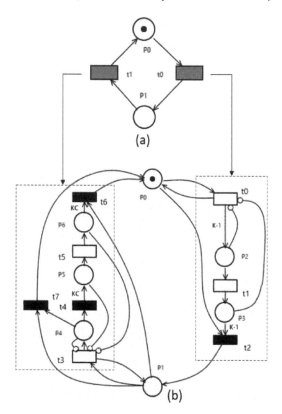

Figure 22.3   Single Component System – Erlang TTF and Cox-1 TTR.

of the SPN in Figure 22.3.b denote an operational or failed component. The steady-state system availability is obtained through

$$A = P\{\#P0 = 1\}.$$

The instantaneous availability is obtained by (in Mercury-like notation)

$$A(t) = P\{\#P0 = 1\}(t).$$

The downtime in a period T is obtained through

$$DT = P\{\#P1 = 1\} \times T.$$

Example 22.2.1. Assume the single-component system whose mode is shown in Figure 22.3. Consider the time to failure of such a component has been registered.

Table 22.1

Model Parameters

Transitions	Types	Priority	Weight	Server Semantics
t_0	timed	1	λ	sss
t_1	timed	1	λ	sss
t_2	immediate	1	1	
t_3	timed	1	μ	sss
t_4	immediate	1	ω_1	
t_5	timed	1	μ	sss
t_6	immediate	1	1	
t_7	immediate	1	ω_2	

The $MTTF = 2000\,h$ and $SD_{TTF} = 500\,h$. Applying the moment matching method depicted in Section 13.3.8, an Erlang distribution with the following parameter is presented as a suitable model: $ERL(K, \lambda)$, where $K = 16$ and $\lambda = 8 \times 10^{-2}\,h^{-1}$, so $ttfph = 1/\lambda = 125\,h$. The time to repair is suitably depicted by the following Cox-1 distribution: $Cox - 1(\omega_1, \omega_2, KC, \mu)$, where $\omega_1 = 0.01971$, $\omega_2 = 0.98029$, $KC = 7$, and $\mu = 0.34409$, so $ttrph = 1/mu = 2.906\,h$. The steady-state availability and yearly downtime in hours are $A = 0.99350$ and $DT = 56.91\,h$. Figure 22.4 shows the availability represented in number of nines for $ttfph \in (125\,h, 200\,h)$.

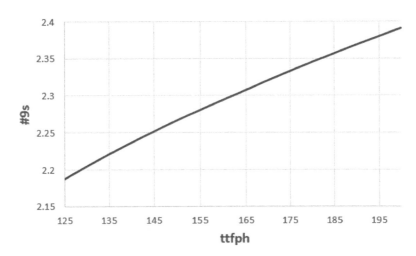

Figure 22.4 Single Component System - $\#9s \times ttfph \in (125h, 200h)$.

The reliability model (SPN) of the discussed component is depicted in Figure 22.5.b (Figure 22.5.a depicts a high-level model.). This model has an absorbing marking, $M = (m_0, m_1, m_2, m_3) = (0, 1, 0, 0)$. The system reliability is calculated through the expression (in Mercury-like notation):

$$R(t) = P\{\#P0 = 1\}(t).$$

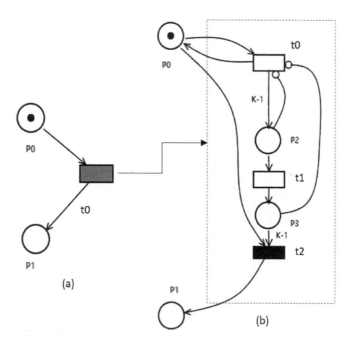

Figure 22.5   Phase-Type Distribution - Reliability Model.

Example 22.2.2. Considering the previous example, the system reliability in the interval $(0, 4000 h)$ is given in Figure 22.6

The calculated $MTTF = 2000 h$ and $MedTTF = 1958 h$. Since we have the $F_{ttf}(t) = 1 - R(t)$, many other statistics can be calculated.   □

It is worth mentioning that the other phase-type distributions introduced in Section 13.3.8 may also be applied to represent the delays specified in the availability and reliability models studied.

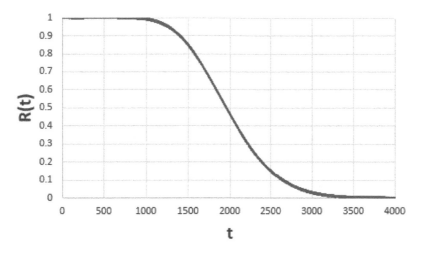

Figure 22.6   Phase-Type Distribution - $R(t) \times (0, 4000\,h)$.

22.3   HOT-STANDBY REDUNDANCY

This section presents an SPN model for hot-standby redundancies. As done with CTMCs is in Section 21.2, we consider a case in which only one repair facility is available and a case when the number of repair facilities available equals the number of system's components (also see Section 18.5 and Section 19.2). This system is composed of two equivalent servers configured in hot-standby redundancy (see Figure 22.7.a). The TTF and TTR of those servers are exponentially distributed with rates λ and μ, respectively. Hence, $MTTF = 1/\lambda$ and $MTTR = 1/\mu$.

First, consider a case in which only one repair facility is available. The SPN availability model is shown in Figure 22.7.b. This model comprises two places, COK and CF, two transitions F and R, and the respective arcs. The initial marking of place COK is $m_{COK} = 2$ (#$COK = 2$ in Mercury notation.) stating that both servers are available at time $t = 0$. The number of tokens in COK denotes the number of servers available, whereas the number of tokens in CF represents faulty servers. Transition F firing represents a server failure, and the transition R firing denotes a repairing. The server semantics of F is iss since both servers are concurrently operating and the server semantics of R is sss since, in this first case, we adopt only one repair facility. The arcs' weights are one.

As the system is properly working as long as there are at least one server is available, the steady-state availability is calculated through the expression

$$A = P\{\#COK > 0\},$$

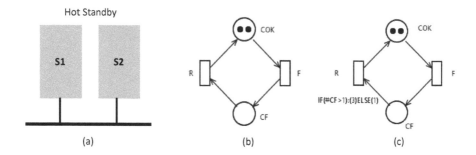

Figure 22.7 Hot-Standby Configuration – Availability and Reliability Models.

that is the probability of place *COK* having at least one token. The unavailability can be computed through

$$UA = P\{\#CF = 1\}$$

and the downtime in a period T is calculated through

$$DT = P\{\#CF = 1\} \times T.$$

The instantaneous availability is calculated through the expression

$$A = P\{\#COK > 0\}(t),$$

in Mercury-like notation. A reliability SPN model is proposed in Figure 22.7.c. This model is somewhat similar to the SPN (availability model) shown in Figure 22.7.b, but the arc that connects the place *CF* to transition *R* is marking dependent and has this expression:

$$IF(\#CF > 1) : (3)ELSE(1);$$

that is when both servers fail ($\#CF > 1$) the arc weight is three; otherwise it is one; thus, the repairing is impossible. In other words, the marking $M = (m_{COK}, m_{CF}) = (0, 2)$ is an absorbing marking. Therefore, the value of the metrics

$$R(t) = P\{\#COK > 0\}(t),$$

when analyzing this SPN (transient analysis - see Section 10.5) is the reliability at t.

Example 22.3.1. Assume the system above, that is, two servers configured in hot-standby redundancy. Let us define the servers' mean time to failure as $MTTF = 810h$ and their mean time to repair as $MTTR = 20h$. Assume both TTF and TTR are exponentially distributed, and there is only one repair facility. From the SPN depicted in Figure 22.7 the CTMC shown in Figure 21.6 is obtained. As already depicted in Equation 21.2.2, an analytic expression may be derived. Here, however, this model is numerically solved (see Section 10.4 and Section 10.5) using the Mercury tool. The steady-state availability calculated is $A = P\{\#COK > 0\} = 0.99883$, and the yearly downtime is $DT = 10.24h$. Figure 22.8 depicts the yearly downtime considering the $MTTF \in (800h, 16000h)$.

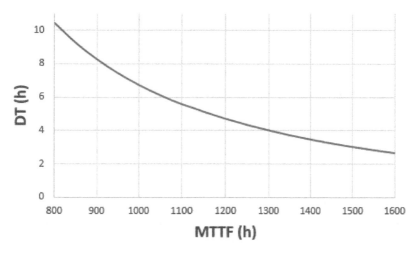

Figure 22.8   Hot-Standby Configuration – Downtime $\times MTTF$.

The reliability of this system in the interval $(0, 80000h)$ is shown in Figure 22.9; the mean time to failure is obtained by calculating the mean time to absorption, $MTTF = 17617.5h$.

□

If the semantics assigned to transition R is *iss*, the model is equivalent to one shown in Section 18.5, the *AND* gate depicted in Section 19.2 or the CTMC shown in Figure 21.5. In other words, this model has as many repair facilities as the number of faulty components.

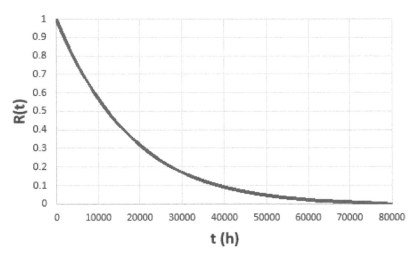

Figure 22.9   Hot-Standby Configuration – $R(t) \times t$.

22.4 IMPERFECT COVERAGE

Consider the system depicted in Figure 22.7.a. Now, however, assume the failure coverage is imperfect; that is, the system is configured in hot-standby, and one server may fail, and this failure may not be detected (a hidden failure). Such a failure may be later detected, or the second server available may also fail, and the service becomes unavailable. This aspect was already discussed in Section 21.4, and a CTMC model was presented.

This section proposes an availability and a reliability models specified in SPN (see Figure 22.10). The availability model is shown in Figure 22.10.a. It is composed of a set of places $P = \{COK, CF, CFS, HF\}$, a set of transitions $T = \{F, R, C, UC, D\}$, and their arcs (see Figure 22.10.a). Transition UC has a guard expression: $G(UC) := \#COK > 0 \rightarrow \{T, F\}$. The server semantics of F and R are *iss* and *sss*, respectively since only one repair facility is considered in this case. The weights assigned to C and UC are c and $1 - c$, respectively. Their priorities are equal to 1. The initial marking states that both servers are available, that is $M_0 = (m_{COK}, m_{CF}, m_{CFS}, m_{HF}) = (2, 0, 0, 0)$.

As both servers are initially available, the only possible event is a server failure. It is worth mentioning again that the server semantics of F is *iss*. One server failure is depicted by firing F, removing one token from COK, and storing one token in CF. The new marking is $M_1 = (1, 1, 0, 0)$, which is a vanishing marking. In this marking, C fires with probability c and UC fires with probability $1 - c$. If C fires, one token is removed from CF, and one token is stored in CFS. In this new marking, the system is aware of the server failure and demands its repair. The repair is represented by

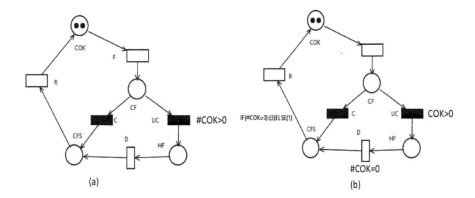

Figure 22.10 Hot-Standby with Imperfect Coverage - Availability (a) and Reliability (b) Models.

the firing of transition R. If, on the other hand, when in marking M_1, UC fires, this server failure is not detected by the system and becomes hidden. The hidden failure may be detected later on, after a detection time (DT) represented in transition D, and then be repaired, or the second server may fail before the detection of the first server failure. In such a case, the service becomes unavailable. Observe that the UC becomes disabled $(G(\#COK > 0) \to F)$ once a server is in failure because a second server failure is detected since the service is no longer provided. In this example, the time to failure, repair, and detection time are exponentially distributed with rates of λ, μ, and β, respectively. Hence, $MTTF = 1/\lambda$, $MTTR = 1/\mu$, and $MDT = 1/\beta$ (mean detection time).

The instantaneous system availability may de be calculated through

$$A(t) = P\{\#COK > 0\}(t).$$

The steady-state system availability may de be calculated through

$$A = P\{\#COK > 0\}.$$

The steady-state availability expressed in the number of nines may be calculated through

$$\#9s = -\log_{10} P\{\#COK = 0\}.$$

The probability of having a hidden failure is

$$PHF = P\{(\#COK > 0)AND(\#HF = 0)\}.$$

The probability that the system is available and safe (without hidden failure) is

$$AS = P\{(\#COK > 0)AND(\#HF = 0)\}.$$

The downtime in a period T is

$$DT = P\{\#COK = 0\} \times T,$$

and the time the system stays in an unsafe state (hidden failure) in a period T is

$$UST = P\{\#HF = 1\} \times T.$$

The reliability model is depicted in Figure 22.10.b. It is somewhat similar to the availability model but with essential adjustments. This SPN must have an absorbing marking, which states a condition when both servers are unavailable. Two changes were made in the SPN of Figure 22.10.a in order to obtain an SPN that allows calculating the reliability. First, when both servers are unavailable, system repair is not allowed. This condition denotes the service stopped; hence, the system ceased to provide its functions. This feature was obtained by including a marking dependent arc between place CFS and transition R. The expression is $IF(\#COK = 0)$: $(3)ELSE(1)$. Thus, when place $COK = 0$ (both servers have failed), the arc weight is set to three. As place CFS will never reach three tokens, this marking is absorbing. The second change was the assignment of a guard expression to transition D, $G(D) := \#COK = 0 \rightarrow \{T, F\}$; thus, when no token is in place COK, transition D becomes disabled. The system reliability is then calculated through

$$R(t) = P\{\#COK > 0\}(t),$$

and the probability of a system is reliable and safe (without hidden failure) is

$$RS(t) = P\{(\#COK > 0)AND(\#HF = 0)\}(t).$$

Example 22.4.1. Suppose we have the system depicted in Figure 22.7.a but with imperfect failure coverage. Consider the coverage probability is $c = 0.95$, and the TTF, TTR, and DT are exponentially distributed with $MTTF = 810h$, $MTTR = 20h$, and $MDT = 0.5$. Table 22.2 shows the results of the steady-state metrics presented above.

Figure 22.11 shows the availability (a), the availability without hidden failure (b), the yearly downtime (c), the period a hidden failure is present in a year (d), and the probability of having a hidden failure (e) for $d \in (0.05h, 0.95h)$. Figure 22.12 presents the availability (a), the availability without hidden failure (b), the yearly downtime (c), the period a hidden failure is present in a year (d), and the probability of having a hidden failure (e) for $c \in (0.58, 0.99)$. Figure 22.13 presents the reliability (a) and the reliability without hidden failure ($R(t)$ and Safe) in the interval $(0, 70000h)$. The mean time to failure calculated was $MTTF = 17596.53h$. The reliability at $t = 1000h$ is $R(1000h) = 0.9462788$. The probability of being operational (reliable) and not having a hidden failure at $1000h$ is $R(1000h)$ and Safe is 0.9462232.

□

Table 22.2

Steady-State Measures

Measures	Values
A	0.998838
A - #9s	2.93479
DT (h)	10.18
PHF	5.87517×10^{-5}
A & Safe	0.998779
A & Safe - #9s	2.91328
Unsafe time in a year(min)	30.88

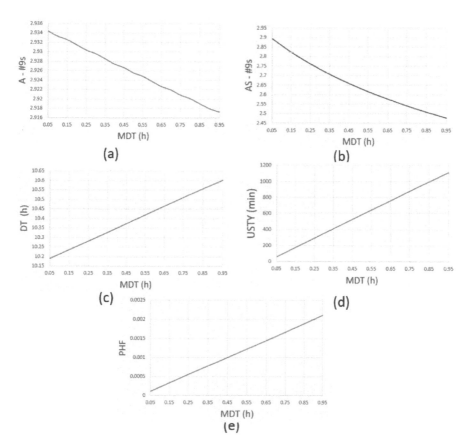

Figure 22.11 Hot-Standby with Imperfect Coverage - Measures × $MDT \in$ $(0.05\,h, 0.95\,h)$.

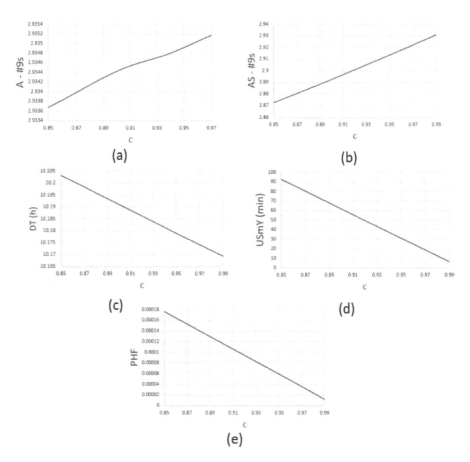

Figure 22.12 Hot-Standby with Imperfect Coverage - Measures $\times$ $c \in$ $(0.85\,h, 0.99, h)$.

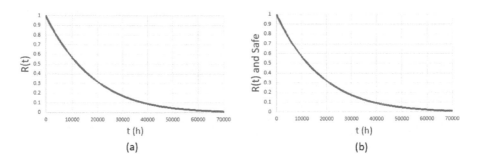

Figure 22.13 Hot-Standby with Imperfect Coverage - $R(t)$, $R(t)$ and Safe $\times$ $c \in$ $(0\,h, 70000, h)$.

22.5 COLD-STANDBY REDUNDANCY

This section depicts an SPN model for cold-standby redundancy. CTMC models for availability and reliability were already presented in Section 21.5. The system considered in this section is depicted in Figure 22.14.a. In the initial configuration, the server S_1 is operational, whereas S_2 is the cold spare. This system is considered operational if one web-server (WS_i) and one database-server (DB_i) are available. For these pieces of software to operate, the server's hardware (HW_i) and its operating system (OS_i) should be properly functioning, where $i \in 1,2$, is the index that represents each server. If one of the components (WS_i, DB_i, OS_i, and HW_i) of the server S_i fails, the system fails, and the spare-server should be activated as soon as possible to resume the service being delivered. The spare server is normally switched off; hence, when a failure occurs in the mains server, the spare server should be switched on, its operating system should be loaded, and the web-server and the database-server should be initiated in order to restore the system service (Figure 22.14.c). In the time being, arrival requests are lost (see Figure 22.14.b). In this model, only one repair facility is adopted, and when both servers are in failure, maintenance priority is given to S_1.

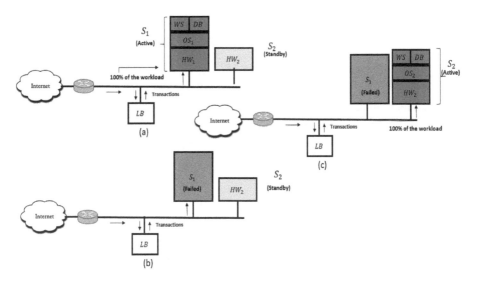

Figure 22.14 Cold-Standby System.

The SPN presented in Figure 22.15.b is an availability model. This SPN comprises six transitions, arcs, transitions' attributes, and the initial marking. One token in places S_iU and S_iD represents that servers S_i, $i \in \{1,2\}$, are operational (Up) or in failure ($Down$), respectively. One token in place $S2O$ represents the spare-server (S_2) turned off. Transitions F_i and R_i $i \in \{1,2\}$ denote the failure occurrence and the repair activity of the respective server. Transition D denotes the act of switching on the spare server, and the transition O_2 firing represents the acting of switching off the spare server. All transitions but O_2 are exponentially distributed. O_2 is an immediate transition. All timed transitions have server semantics sss and have the same priority level. Transition R_2 has a guard expression: $\#S_1D = 0$; that is, R_2 may only fire if place S_1D is unmarked. This was adopted to give repairing precedence to the main server (S_1) or its spare server (S_2) since only one repair facility is available. If this guard expression is not adopted, it is assumed that the number of repair facilities is equal to the number of servers. The arc connecting place S_1U to transition D is an inhibitor arc. This was adopted to represent the spare server switching on only when the main server (S_1) is down. When the spare server is available ($\#S_2U = 1$), and the main server is also available ($\#S_1U = 1$) - it is worth noting the inhibitor arc between place S_1D and transition O_2 - the spare server is switched off. This is depicted by firing transition O_2. The initial marking shows that S_1 is operational ($\#S_1U = 1$) and S_2 is turned off ($\#S_2O = 1$). An operational server is depicted by its hardware, operating system, web-server, and database-server available. If one of these components fails, the respective server (S_1 or S_2) becomes unavailable. The RBD shown in Figure 22.15.a may represent such a sub-system. As this RBD is a series of components, the reliability, is calculated by

$$R_{S_i}(t) = \prod_{j \in \{HW_i, OS_i, WS_i, DB_i\}} e^{-\lambda_j t} = e^{-t \sum_{j \in \{HW_i, OS_i, WS_i, DB_i\}} \lambda_j},$$

where $\lambda_{S_i} = \sum_{j \in \{HW_i, OS_i, WS_i, DB_i\}} \lambda_j$; hence $MTTF_{S_i} = 1/\lambda_{S_i}$. These $MTTF$s are assigned to transitions F_1 and F_2.

The $MTTR$s defined by the repairing facility team or specified in a service level agreement (SLA) are assigned to transitions R_1 and R_2. The mean time required to switch on ($MTTSO$) the spare server, considering starting all required pieces of software to make the service available, is assigned to transition D. The steady-state system availability is calculated through

$$A = P\{(\#S1U + \#S2U) > 0\},$$

and the downtime of period T is

$$DT = (1 - (P\{(\#S1U + \#S2U) > 0\})) \times T.$$

The reliability SPN model of such a system is shown in Figure 22.15.c and is equivalent to the SPN of the single-component (see Figure 22.2) system since once S_1 fails, the service stops being delivered. However, the reliability model may differ if a specified downtime is agreed upon between the partners. Therefore, the reliability at t is calculated through transient analysis and the expression:

$$R(t) = P\{\#S1U\}(t).$$

Example 22.5.1. Assume the system depicted in Figure 22.14. Consider the servers' $MTTF_{HW} = 16000h$, $MTTF_{OS} = 3000h$, $MTTF_{WS} = 1800h$, and $MTTF_{DB} =$

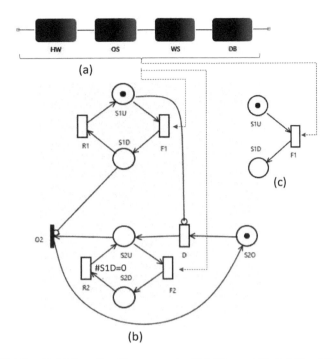

Figure 22.15   Cold-Standby System – Availability and Reliability Models.

$1500\,h$. As the TTF_j, $j \in \{HW, OS, WS, DB\}$ are exponentially distributed, then

$$MTTF_{S_i} = \cfrac{1}{\cfrac{1}{MTTF_{HW_i}} + \cfrac{1}{MTTF_{OS_i}} + \cfrac{1}{MTTF_{WS_i}} + \cfrac{1}{MTTF_{DB_i}}} = 618\,h.$$

Consider the $MTTR_{S_i} = 20\,h$, and $MTTSO_{S_i} = 0.06667\,h$. The steady-state availability is

$$A = P\{(\#S1U + \#S2U) > 0\} = 0.998886.$$

The yearly downtime in hours is

$$DT = 9.76\,h.$$

Figure 22.16.a and Figure 22.16.b, respectively, presents the system availability (in number of nines) and the yearly downtime against $MTTSO \in (0.05\,h, 0.2\,h)$. The system reliability at $t = 500\,h$ is $R(500\,h) = 0.4454068$. Figure 22.17 shows the system reliability in the interval $t \in (0, 2000\,h)$.

□

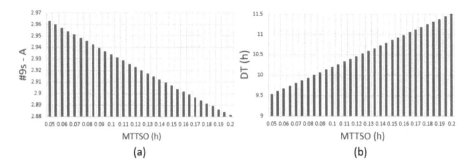

Figure 22.16 Availability and Downtime × *MTTSO*.

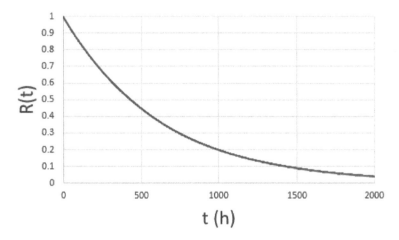

Figure 22.17 $R(t) \times t$.

22.6 WARM-STANDBY REDUNDANCY

This section presents SPN models for calculating the availability and reliability of systems configured in warm-standby redundancy. This system discussed in this section is similar to the one described in the previous section. The spare server (S_2), however, is not switched off. It is operational, but not fully operational; that is, it is switched on, running its operational system, but the web-server and the database-server are not in execution (see Figure 22.18.a). As both servers, S_1 and S_2, are executing their software systems, both may fail. However, as S_2 has fewer software components in execution, it is reasonable to assume its failure rate is lower than the failure rate of the primary server (S_1). It is worth mentioning that both servers (hardware, operating systems, etc.) are assumed to be equivalent.

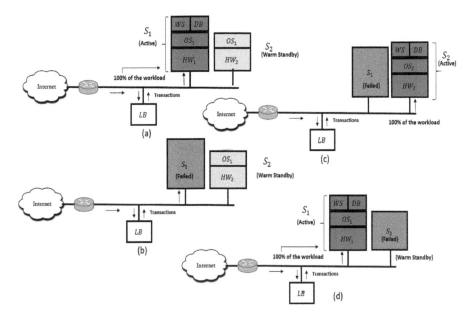

Figure 22.18   Warm-Standby System.

If S_1 is processing the workload and S_2 fails, nothing is lost, since S_2 is not processing the transactions (see Figure 22.18.d). Hence, it may be repaired and return to standby mode. Nevertheless, while S_1 is processing the workload, if S_1 fails, the standby server should be configured to process the workload; that is, the web-server and the database-server should be started (see Figure 22.18.b). This process takes a while, but the delay should be shorter than the time required to start up a cold-standby server as depicted in the previous section (see Figure 22.18.c).

The availability model shown in 22.19 is somewhat similar to the cold-standby model depicted in Figure 22.15.b. The difference is that the spare server may fail while in standby mode, and this feature is represented by places $S2O$ and $S2D2$, transitions $F22$ and $R22$, and their respective arcs. The server semantics of these two transitions are sss. The other features are equal to the cold-standby model represented in Figure 22.15. The steady-state system availability is estimated through

$$A = P\{(\#S1U = 1)OR(\#S2U = 1)\}. \qquad (22.6.1)$$

This expression is equivalent to

$$A = P\{(\#S1U + \#S2U) > 0\}, \qquad (22.6.2)$$

which was presented in the previous example. The instantaneous availability is computed through

$$A(t) = P\{(\#S1U = 1)OR(\#S2U = 1)\}(t)$$

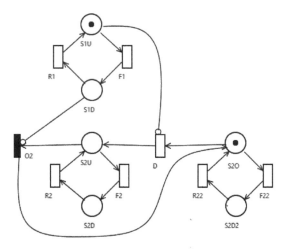

Figure 22.19 Warm-Standby - Availability Model.

or by

$$A(t) = P\{(\#S1U + \#S2U) > 0\}(t). \tag{22.6.3}$$

The downtime in a period T may, then, be estimated through

$$DT = 1 - (P\{(\#S1U + \#S2U) > 0\}) \times T$$

or by

$$DT = 1 - (P\{(\#S1U = 1)OR(\#S2U = 1)\}) \times T.$$

The reliability model of the warm-standby configuration is the same SPN adopted for calculating the reliability of the cold-standby configuration (see Figure 22.15.c). Therefore, the reliability at t may be calculated through

$$R(t) = P\{\#S1U\}(t).$$

Example 22.6.1. Consider the system depicted in Figure 22.18. Consider the servers' $MTTF_{HW_i} = 16000\,h, MTTF_{OS_i} = 3000\,h, MTTF_{WS_i} = 1800\,h$, and $MTTF_{DB_i} = 1500\,h, i \in \{1,2\}$. As the $TTF_j, j \in \{HW, OS, WS, DB\}$ are exponentially distributed, then the servers' mean time to failure when in active mode is

$$MTTF_{S_i} = \cfrac{1}{\frac{1}{MTTF_{HW_i}} + \frac{1}{MTTF_{OS_i}} + \frac{1}{MTTF_{WS_i}} + \frac{1}{MTTF_{DB_i}}} = 618\,h,$$

whereas the server S_2 mean time to failure when in standby mode is

$$MTTF_{S_2O} = \cfrac{1}{\frac{1}{MTTF_{HW_2}} + \frac{1}{MTTF_{OS_2}}} = 2526\,h.$$

Consider the $MTTR_{S_i} = 20h$, and $MTTSO_{S_i} = 0.017h$. The steady-state availability is

$$A = P\{(\#S1U + \#S2U) > 0\} = 0.99872.$$

The yearly downtime in hours is

$$DT = 11.19h.$$

It is worth noting that in this particular case, the availability is smaller than that obtained from the respective cold-standby redundancy. Likewise, the yearly downtime is higher. Figure 22.20 shows the availability and yearly downtime (in hours) for both the warm-standby and cold-standby (discussed in the previous section) configurations against the $MTTR \in (4h, 20h)$. The warm-standby configuration provides higher availability (and shorter downtime) than the cold-standby configuration for $MTTR$s shorter than $12h$.

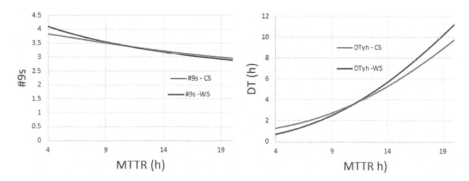

Figure 22.20　Warm-Standby vs Cold-Standby $\times$ $MTTR$- Availability ($\#9s$) and Downtime.

22.7　ACTIVE-ACTIVE REDUNDANCY

Suppose we have the system shown in Figure 21.29. As described in Section 21.7, the servers share the workload processing. It means both servers are active and processing transactions. The system is available if at least one server is processing. Nevertheless, if both servers are active, the processing capacity is higher than if only one server is operational. The basic SPN availability and reliability models are the same SPNs proposed to represent the hot-standby redundancy depicted in Figure 22.7. Therefore, using the SPN depicted in Figure 22.7.b, the steady-state availability can be obtained by

$$A = P\{\#COK > 1\},$$

as well as the instantaneous availability can be computed using

$$A(t) = P\{\#COK > 1\}(t),$$

and the downtime in a period T is calculated through

$$DT = P\{\#CF = 2\} \times T.$$

The reliability at t can be calculated using the SPN shown in Figure 22.7.c through

$$R(t) = P\{\#COK > 1\}(t).$$

Hence, the mean time to failure can be computed through

$$MTTF = \int_0^\infty R(t)\,dt.$$

The capacity oriented availability may also be calculated using the availability mode through

$$COA = \frac{E\{COK\}}{2},$$

where $E\{COK\}$ is the average number of servers available ($ANSA$).

Consider each server can sustain a throughput tp. The average throughput - ATP - is the weighted sum of throughputs. Consider a system with two servers, where each server can sustain a throughput tp. More formally:

$$ATP = P\{\#COK = 1\} \times tp + P\{\#COK = 2\} \times 2tp,$$

which is equal to

$$ATP = E\{COK\} \times tp.$$

Example 22.7.1. Supposed a system composed of two servers in a configuration active-active. Assume the times to failure and the time to repair are exponentially distributed with $MTTF = 810\,h$ and $MTTR = 20\,h$. Consider each server can sustain $5000\,tps$. Using the expression described above, the yearly downtime (DT), $ANSA$, COA, and ATP were numerically computed using the the Mercury tool:

Table 22.3
Measures: A, DT, COA, ANSA, ATP

Measures	Values
A	0.99884
DT (h)	10.17
COA	0.97534
ANSA	1.95067
ATP (tps)	9753.37

□

22.8 *KooN* REDUNDANCY

Consider a system composed of N similar servers in a set of racks, as shown in Figure 21.42. Assume the time to failure of each server is independent and exponentially distributed with a rate of $\lambda = 1/MTTF$. Also, suppose the time to repair of a server is exponentially distributed with a rate of $\mu = 1/MTTR$. Assume there is only one repair facility. A CTMC model of such a system was already presented in Section 21.9. This section presents an SPN model of this system. The availability model is depicted in Figure 22.21.a. This model is composed of two places, *UP* and *DW*, two transitions, *F* and *R*, and their respective arcs. The initial marking states that N servers are available, $M_0 = (m_{UP}, m_{DW}) = (20,0)$. The server semantics of transition *F* is *isss*, and the respective semantics of transition *R* is *sss* since only one repair facility is considered in the example. If the number of repair facilities was equal to the failed server, the server semantics of *R* would be *isss*. The *MTTF* is assigned to *F*, and the *MTTR* specifies the time of transition *R*.

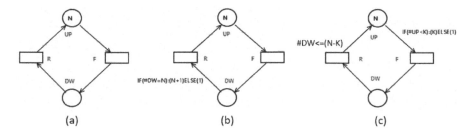

Figure 22.21 *KooN* Redundancy - Availability (a) and Reliability (b) (c) Models.

The steady-state availability is estimated through

$$A = P\{\#UP > 0\},$$

the downtime in the period T is computed using

$$DT = P\{\#UP = 0\} \times T,$$

and the instantaneous availability is estimated through

$$A(t) = P\{\#UP > 0\}(t).$$

The capacity-oriented availability is calculated using

$$COA = \frac{E\{\#UP\}}{N},$$

and the average number of servers available is estimated through

$$ANSA = E\{\#UP\}.$$

The probability of having K out of N servers available is computed using

$$P(NSA \geq K) = P\{\#UP >= K\},$$

where NSA is the number of servers available. If the system is considered available if at least K out of N servers are operational, then the steady-state availability would be

$$A = P(NSA \geq K) = P\{\#UP >= K\}.$$

The reliability model is depicted in Figure 22.21.b. It is worth mentioning the weight of the arc that connects place DW to transition R. It is marking dependent. When the number of tokens in place DW is N, the weight of the arc is $N + 1$; otherwise, it is one. Therefore the marking $(0, 20)$ is an absorbing marking. The system reliability at instant t may then be calculated through

$$R(t) = P\{\#UP > 0\}(t),$$

and the mean time to failure may be numerically calculated using

$$MTTF = \int_0^\infty R(t)\, dt,$$

or using the method presented in Section 10.6.1. Again, if the system is considered in failure if $N - (K - 1)$ servers fail, then the system reliability can be calculated from the SPN depicted in Figure 22.21.c. In this SPN, when $\#UP < K$, the weight of the arc between UP and F becomes $K + 1$; thus, F becomes disabled. If the initial marking is $(N, 0)$, $N > K$, and after a transition firing sequence, the SPN reaches the marking $(K - 1, K)$, F becomes disabled since $\#UP < K$, and the arc weight between UP and F is $K + 1$. This marking, $(K - 1, K)$, also disables transition R since its guard expression $(\#DW \leq (N - (K - 1)))$ is evaluated to false. Therefore, system reliability is obtained through

$$R(t) = (1 - P\{\#DW >= (N - (K - 1))\})(t).$$

Example 22.8.1. A system is composed of $M = 8$ servers. The failure and repair rates are constants, and the $MTTF = 810h$ and $MTTR = 20h$, respectively. Moreover, consider that only one repair facility is available. Also, assume the system is considered available as long as at least one server is available. The availability model was numerically solved using Mercury and through the expressions described above. Table 22.4 presents the respective results.

However, if the system is considered available if at least fifteen servers are available out of the twenty servers, the steady-state availability would be $A = P\{\#UP >= 15\} = 0.9949986$, which is $\#9s = -\log(1 - A) = 2.301$. Figure 22.22 shows the $P(NSA \geq K)$, for $K = \{1, 2, .., 20\}$.

□

Table 22.4

Measures: A, DT (s), ANSA, and COA

Measure	Values
A - #9s	14.00
DT (s)	2.868×10^{-7}
ANSA	19.16459
COA	0.95823

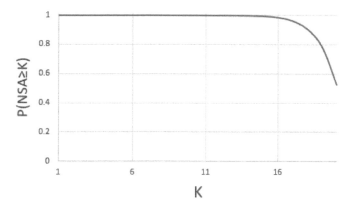

Figure 22.22 *KooN* Redundancy - $P(NSA \geq K) \times K = \{1, 2, .., 20\}$.

Example 22.8.2. Consider the system depicted in the previous example. However, the system is considered operational as long as at least six ($K = 6$) out of the eight ($N = 8$). Hence, the reliability is computed using.

$$R_{6oo8}(t) = (1 - P\{\#DW >= (N - (K - 1))\})(t) =$$

$$(1 - P\{\#DW >= (8 - (6 - 1))\})(t) = (1 - P\{\#DW >= 3\})(t).$$

The reliability at $t = 1000h$ is $R_{6oo8}(1000h) = 0.84332$. Figure 22.23 shows the reliability in the time interval $(0, 20,000h)$. The mean time to failure is obtained from $MTTF = \int_0^\infty R(t)\,dt = 5673.01\,h$.

$\square$

22.8.1 MODELING MULTIPLE RESOURCES ON MULTIPLE SERVERS

This subsection merges the content presented at the beginning of this section with the preceding section. The main concern here is to model multiple similar virtual machines (resources) hosted on multiple servers. Besides, we also consider a system that has either one repair facility or as many as are required.

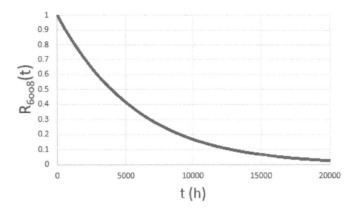

Figure 22.23 $R_{6008}(t) \times t$.

To exemplify such systems, suppose we have the rack of servers depicted in Figure 21.42; assume the number of servers is N, and that each server hosts M virtual machines. It is worth mentioning that this problem was already approached using CTMC in Section 21.8 and Section 21.9. Here, however, we represent this sort of system using SPN. Two SPN models are presented to evaluate availability and capacity. The first is a monolithic SPN, a model that depicts the servers and their respective virtual machines in one SPN. The second SPN represents such systems using a two-level SPN; an SPN represents the servers, and an SPN depicts the virtual machines for each number of servers available. These strategies are similar to those introduced in Section 21.8.

Figure 22.24 shows an SPN model that represents $N = 5$ servers, and each server hosts M virtual machines. This model allows calculating the availability, the average number of virtual machines alive, the average number of servers alive, as well as COA and downtime. Each server S_i is represented by two places (S_iU and S_iD), two transitions (FS_i and RS_i), and the respective arcs. One token in place S_iU represents the server S_i in the available state, whereas one token in place S_iD denotes the server S_i in failure. The event that represents the failure occurrence (in server S_i) is depicted by transition FS_i, and the server repair is represented by transition RS_i. The availability of virtual machines on server S_i is represented by the subnet depicted by places V_iU, V_iD, transitions FV_i, F_i, and RV_i, and their respective arcs. It is worth mentioning the inhibitor arc from place S_iU to transition F_i. Transition F_i is also guarded by $\#V_iU > 0$, and the weight of the arcs (V_iU, F_i) and (F_i, V_iD) are $\#V_iU$. Transition RV_i is guarded by $\#S_iU = 1$. The server semantics of transitions FV_i and RV_i (it is assumed a server has the capacity to startup its VMs in parallel) are $isss$ and the server semantics of transition FS_i and RS_i are sss. The immediate transitions priorities as well as their weight are equal to one.

Consider a server S_i is available and that it hosts eight VMs; hence, $\#S_iU = 1$ and $\#V_iU = M$. A VM may fail, which is represented by the firing of transition FV_i. If this

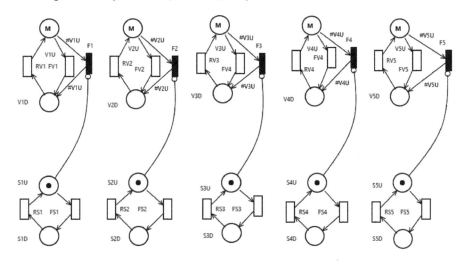

Figure 22.24 $N = 5$ Active Servers, Each Server Hosting M VMs.

does occur, the marking of V_iU becomes $\#V_iU = M - 1$, and the marking of V_iD is changed to $\#V_iD = 1$. In this new marking, another VM may fail, the server may also fail, and the failed VM may be restored. It is worth noting that the guard expression assigned to RV_i ($\#S_iU = 1$) is evaluated to true since the server S_i is available. If the server S_i fails, which is denoted by the firing of transition FS_i, one token is removed from S_iU, and one token is stored in S_iD. This new marking enables the immediate transition F_i. As the immediate transitions have higher priority than the timed one, F_i fires, and its firing removes all token from place V_iU and stores the same number in place V_iD. It is worth observing that in this new marking, F_i becomes disabled since its guard is evaluated to false because of $\#V_iU = 0$. The virtual machines of this server will only be enabled to restart when the server is repaired due to the guard expression assigned to RV_i ($\#S_iU = 1$).

The availability of this system, considering the system is available if at least one VM is available, is given by

$$A = P\{(\#V_1U + \#V_2U + \#V_3U + \#V_4U + \#V_5U) > 0\}.$$

If the system is considered available if at least K out of $N \times M$ virtual machines are available, then the availability is obtained through

$$A = P\{(\#V_1U + \#V_2U + \#V_3U + \#V_4U + \#V_5U) \geq K\}.$$

The average number of virtual machines alive (operational) is calculated through

$$ANVMA = E\{\#V_1U\} + E\{\#V_2U\} + E\{\#V_3U\} + E\{\#V_4U\} + (E\{\#V_5U\}.$$

The capacity-oriented availability is computed using

$$COA = \frac{E\{\#V_1U\} + E\{\#V_2U\} + E\{\#V_3U\} + E\{\#V_4U\} + E\{\#V_5U\}}{N \times M}.$$

Example 22.8.3. Suppose we have a system composed of five similar physical servers ($N = 5$), whose time to failure and time to repair are exponentially distributed with mean equal to $MTTF_s = 810\,h$ and $MTTR_s = 20\,h$. Each server hosts $M = 8$ virtual machines. Their time to failure and time to repair are also assumed to be exponentially distributed with means equal to $MTTF_v = 1000\,h$ and $MTTR_v = 0.05\,h$. The SPN representing this system is depicted in Figure 22.24. The net was numerically analyzed using the Mercury tool by applying the Gauss-Seidel iterative method. The state-space size was $100,000$. The average number of virtual machines alive was $ANVMA = 39.03179$, and the capacity-oriented availability was $COA = 0.97579$. Considering the system available if at least one VM is operational, its availability was $\#9s = 8$.

Figure 22.25 and Table 22.5 show the availability for a system with $N = 5$ servers and each server hosting $M = 4$ VMs when considering the system available for K out of 20 VMs, for $K = \{10, 11, 12, .., 20\}$.

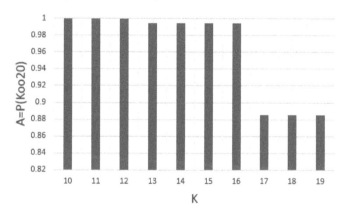

Figure 22.25 $A = P\{(\#V_1U + \#V_2U + \#V_3U + \#V_4U + \#V_5U) \geq K\} \times K \in \{10, 11, 12, ..., 20\}$.

Such a modeling approach would benefit from modeling using coloured stochastic Petri nets [170, 478] due to its regularity. However, the adoption of such a class of SPN would not reduce the state-space size. Therefore, the two-level SPN modeling strategy is better since the number of states generated is significantly smaller.

The model presented in Figure 22.26 is the two-level SPN availability model of the system studied above. Figure 22.26.a is a higher-level model which allows calculating the probability of having $i \in \{0, 1, 2, ..., N\}$ servers available (*PiSA*). This SPN is

Table 22.5

$A = P\{Koo20) \geq K\} \times K \in \{10, 11, 12, ..., 20\}$

K	P(Koo20″
10	0.999865
11	0.999864
12	0.99986
13	0.994462
14	0.994453
15	0.994439
16	0.994325
17	0.885118
18	0.885027
19	0.884889

composed of two places, UP and DW, two transitions, F_s and R_s, and their arcs. The server semantics of both transitions is *iss* since it is assumed that the number of re-pair facilities is equal to the number of failed servers. The number of tokens in place UP represents the number of servers available, whereas the number of tokens in DW denotes the number of servers in failure. $PiSA$ is obtained through the expression

$$PiSA = P\{\#UP = i\}, \tag{22.8.1}$$

which denotes the probability of having i servers available in steady-state. Figure 22.26.b presets a lower-level model. This model is represented by two places, UP_v and DW_v, two transitions, F_v and R_v, and their arcs. The server semantics of both transitions is *iss* since it is assumed that the server may restart its virtual machines concurrently. The number of tokens in place UP_v represents the number of virtual machines available, whereas the number of tokens in DW_v denotes the number of virtual machines in failure. This SPN allows computing the probability of having j virtual machines alive ($PjVMAi$) for a given number of servers, $j \in \{0, 1, 2, ..., M_i\}$, where M_i is the maximal number of virtual machines for a given number of servers i.

The SPN shown in Figure 22.26.a generates the CTMC depicted in Figure 21.45.a, whereas the SPN presented in Figure 22.26.b produces the other CTMCs of the Fig-ure 21.45. The probability of having j virtual machines alive, considering i servers are operational, is obtained through

$$PjVMAi = P\{\#UP_v = j\} \times P\{\#UP = i\}. \tag{22.8.2}$$

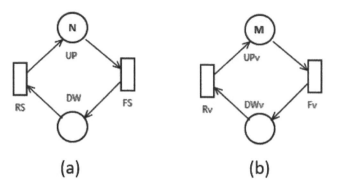

Figure 22.26 Two-level SPN Availability Model.

The average number of virtual machines alive (*ANVMA*) is obtained using

$$ANVMA = \sum_{j=1}^{M_i} \sum_{i=1}^{N} j \times P\{\#UP_v = j\} \times P\{\#UP = i\}, \quad (22.8.3)$$

in Mercury-like notation. The capacity-oriented availability is computed from

$$COA = \frac{\sum_{j=1}^{M_i} \sum_{i=1}^{N} j \times P\{\#UP_v = j\} \times P\{\#UP = i\}}{N \times M}. \quad (22.8.4)$$

Likewise, the probability of having at least *K* out of $N \times M$ virtual machines alive (*PKooNM*) is obtained from

$$PKooNM = \sum_{j=k}^{M_i} \sum_{i=1}^{N} P\{\#UP_v = j\} \times P\{\#UP = i\}. \quad (22.8.5)$$

Example 22.8.4. Now the model presented above is applied to solve the same problem introduced in Example 22.8.3. The system is composed of five equivalent servers ($N = 5$). Their time to failure and time to repair are exponentially distributed with $MTTF_s = 810\,h$ and $MTTR_s = 20\,h$. Each server hosts $M = 8$ virtual machines, whose $MTTF_v = 1000\,h$ and $MTTR_v = 0.05\,h$. The total number os state generated using this model was 131, that is, six states generated from the higher-level SPN, forty-one states generated from the configuration with five servers ($(N \times M) + 1 = (5 \times 8) + 1 = 41$), thirty-three states generated the configuration with four servers ($((N-1) \times M) + 1 = (4 \times 8) + 1 = 33$), twenty-five states generated from the configuration with three servers ($((N-2) \times M) + 1 = (3 \times 8) + 1 = 25$), seventeen states generated the configuration with two servers ($((N-3) \times M) + 1 = (2 \times 8) + 1 = 17$), and nine states generated from the configuration with one server ($((N-4) \times M) + 1 = (1 \times 8) + 1 = 9$). The system availability (at least one VM alive), the average number of VMs alive, the COA and the probability of at least twenty-two VMs alive out of forty ($P(22oo40$ - which may also be defined as the an available system) are depicted in Table 22.6.

Table 22.6

A, ANVMA, COA **and** *P(KooNM)* - *K* = 22 **and** *NM* = 40

A	0.999999031
ANVMA	38.93708115
COA	0.973427029
P(22oo40)	0.99916513

Figure 22.27 presents the probability of K out of NM virtual machines being operational for $K \in \{1, 2, ..., 40\}$.

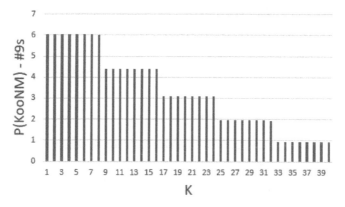

Figure 22.27 $P(Koo40)$ - in #9s - $K \in \{1, 2, ..40\}$.

□

22.9 CORRECTIVE MAINTENANCE

This section studies, in more detail, some aspects related to modeling corrective maintenance, such as the use of constrained repair facilities and priorities. The system depicted in Figure 22.28 serves as an example to study this topic. It is worth mentioning that corrective maintenance has already been discussed in this chapter, but the previously discussed scenarios do not fully cover the subject.

Assume times to failure of the eight servers in $Rack_1$ and $Rack_2$, that is S_i^j, $i \in \{1, 2, 3, 4\}$, $j \in \{1, 2\}$ are well represented by eight independent and identically distributed random variables, TTF_i^j. Consider TTF_i^j are distributed according to $Exp(\lambda)$. First, consider a case where the number of repair teams is equal to infinity

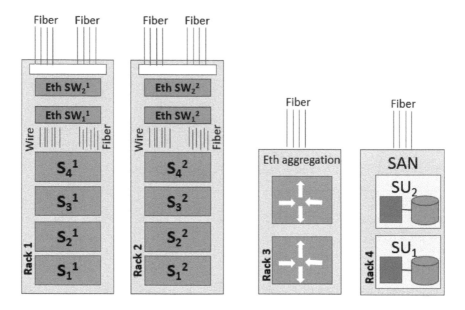

Figure 22.28 A Fragment of a Data Center Information Technology Infrastructure.

or the number of failed servers. In such a case, as soon as a server fails, one repair team is assigned to recover the respective server. Also, consider the times to repair the servers are independent and identically distributed random variables, TTR_i^j according to $Exp(\mu)$. As already seen in the chapter, such a system is well represented by the SPN shown in Figure 22.29.a. This net is composed of two places, S_{OK} and S_F, two transitions, F and R, and their respective arcs. Assume all eight servers are initially available, which is represented by #$S_{OK} = 8$. The server semantics of both transitions, F and R, are iss, all servers are operating, and the number of repair teams is infinity. Hence the enabling degree of R is only constrained by #S_F. A second case is when only one repair facility is available. This case is well depicted by the SPN shown in Figure 22.29.b. The only difference between this net and that presented in Figure 22.29.a is the server semantics of transitions R. A third model is presented in Figure 22.29.c. This net represents a configuration in which the number of repair teams is k. For representing such a case, one place was added to the previous models, RT, where #$RP = k$ denotes the number of repair teams, and the server semantics of R is iss. Thus, the maximal enabling degree of R is k.

Now, let us assume all devices depicted in Figure 22.28. This system is composed of eight servers ($Rach_1$ and $Rach_2$), four switches ($Rach_1$ and $Rach_2$), two aggregation routers ($Rach_3$), and two storage units ($Rach_4$) that composes a storage attached network (SAN). The repair facilities (repair teams) are shared to repair all these devices that compose the system. Figure 22.30 presents an availability model that

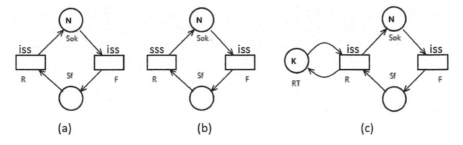

Figure 22.29 Basic Corrective Repair Models.

represents this system. The initial marking of place *RT*, *NRT*, represents the number of repair teams available for corrective maintenance. The sub-net represented by places *SUP* and *SD*, transitions *Fs*, *Rss* and *Res*, and their respective arcs and tokens represent the eight servers, their states (operational or in failure), their faults, and their respective repairs, where #*SUP* = *NS* = 8 is the number of servers available when the system started. Similarly, the sub-net depicted by places *SWUP* and *SWD*, transitions *Fsw*, *Rssw* and *Resw*, their respective arcs, and tokens represent the four switches, their states, their faults, and their respective repairs. #*SWUP* = *NSW* = 4 is the number of switches available in the initial configuration. Likewise, the aggregation routers and the SAN are similarly represented by specific sub-nets. The sub-net composed of places *RUP* and *RD*, transitions *Fr*, *Rsr* and *Rer*, their respective arcs, and tokens denote the two aggregation routers, their states, faults, and repairs, where #*RUP* = *NR* = 2 is the number of aggregation routers available when the system starts. Finally, the last sub-net is composed of places *SUUP* and *SUD*, transitions *Fsu*, *Rssu* and *Resu*, their arcs, and tokens represent the two storage units, their states, faults, and repairs. #*SUUP* = *NSU* = 2 is the number of aggregation storage units available in the initial state. The server semantics of every transition that represents a fault event (*Fs*, *Fsw*, *Fr*, and *Fsu*) is *iss* since for each of these device classes, there is more than one device. The timed transition adopted to represent the repair (*Res*, *Resw*, *Rer*, and *Resu*) also has server semantics *iss*. However, the enabling degree is constrained by the number of tokens is initially stored in place *RT*; hence their actual server semantics become *kss*, where *k* is their enabling degree (see Section 13.1). The immediate transitions represent the repair team allocation to a repair activity (repairing a system's component). Their weights define the allocation probability of a team to repair a system component (see probability choice in Section 13.1). The probability of firing the immediate transitions will depend on the respective weights, the number of tokens in *SD*, *SWD*, *RD*, *SUD*, and if place *RT* is marked. The immediate transition weights may be marking dependent to consider the number of devices of a specific class in failure. In this study, however, their weights were defined as constant and equal to one. The priorities assigned to the immediate transitions are also one. The repairing activities for each device class are represented by an immediate transition (*Rsi*, *i* ∈ {*s*, *sw*, *r*, *su*}), a place (*iUR*, *i* ∈ {*S*, *SW*, *R*, *SU*}) and a timed transition (*Rei, i* $\in \{s, sw, r, su\}$). A transition *Rsi* is only enabled if at least one device of the respective class *iD, i* $\in \{S, SW, R, SU\}$, and a repair team is available, #*RT* > 0. The time to failure and the time to repair of each component *i* are exponentially distributed with rates λ_i and μ_i, $i \in \{s, sw, r, su\}$, respectively.

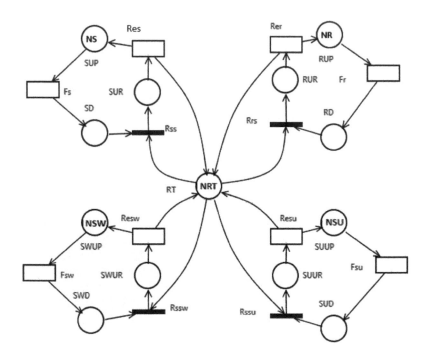

Figure 22.30 Shared Repair Facility – Corrective Maintenance.

Consider the system available if at least four servers, two switches, one router, and one storage unit are operational. Therefore, the steady-state availability is calculated through

$$A = P\{(\#SUP > 3)AND(\#SWUP > 1)AND(\#RUP > 0)AND(\#SUUP > 0)\}.$$

The availability expressed in number of nines is calculated by

$$\#9s = -\log UA,$$

where $UA = 1 - A$ is the steady-state unavailability. The downtime in the period T is computed through

$$DT = UA \times T.$$

Table 22.7

MTTF, MTTR, and Number of Resources of Each Type

Component	MTTF (h)	MTTR (h)	Number
Server	800	20	8
Switch	6000	40	4
Router	3000	40	2
Storage Units	8000	48	2

Assume the components' $MTTF$ and $MTTR$ are shown in Table 22.7.

The system availability and the yearly downtime are shown in Table 22.8 and Figure 22.31 considering the number of repairs as $NRT \in \{1,2,3,4,5,6\}$. It is worth mentioning the important impact of having two teams instead of one. The downtime reduction for three teams was far less significant, whereas four or more repair teams almost did not improve the system availability.

Table 22.8

Availability and Downtime - Shared Repair Facility

NRT	A	A - #9s	DT (min)
1	0.9992364	3.1171	401.349
2	0.99976391	3.6269	124.088
3	0.99978775	3.6732	111.559
4	0.99978948	3.6767	110.649
5	0.99978967	3.6771	110.548
6	0.99978968	3.6771	110.542

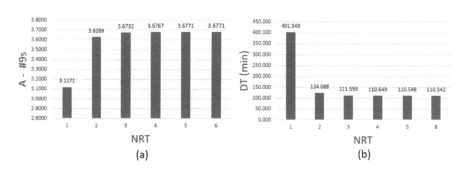

Figure 22.31 Availability and Downtime – Shared Repair Facility – Corrective Maintenance.

If the priorities assigned to Rsi, $i \in \{s, sw, r, su\}$, are $\pi(Rss) = \pi(Rssw) = 1$, $\pi(Rssu) = 2$ and $\pi(Rsr) = 3$, the availability is improved, and the respective downtimes reduced. Table 22.9 shows the availabilities and the respective downtimes when considering $NRT \in \{1, 2, 3, 4, 5, 6\}$.

Table 22.9

Availability and Downtime - Shared Repair Facility - Corrective Maintenance.

- $\pi(Rss) = \pi(Rssw) = 1$, $\pi(Rssu) = 2$ and $\pi(Rsr) = 3$

NRT	A	A - #9s	DTym
1	0.99924165	3.1201	397.446
2	0.99976553	3.6299	123.207
3	0.99978781	3.6733	111.524
4	0.99978948	3.6767	110.648
5	0.99978967	3.6771	110.548
6	0.99978968	3.6771	110.542

22.10 PREVENTIVE MAINTENANCE

Preventive maintenance was already discussed and modeled using CTMCs in Section 21.10. As mentioned in that section, preventive maintenance should be considered when the time to failure has an increasing failure rate over time. Preventive maintenance is an investment. Like anything we invest money and resources in, we expect benefits that outweigh our investment. Preventive maintenance analysis is used to determine if maintenance will be cost-effective, and if so, it is required to define the requirement and parameter values. This section introduces the SPN modeling of preventive maintenance of systems [282].

In computer systems, preventive maintenance is the task of regularly inspecting the computer hardware and software to help ensure that it continues to function correctly. The main activity when performing preventive maintenance on a computer system can be summarized by (1) cleaning up the hardware, (2) downloading the latest drivers, and updating the software, checking the antivirus updates, running the software utility disk, and erasing unused programs or other files. Also, if the computer is not regularly shut down, it may be useful to restart the computer from time to time since software aging may come to effect [168] [340] [430–432] .

A computer system composed of only one server with an increasing failure rate is first adopted to illustrate a basic availability model, represented in SPN, depicting failure, corrective and preventive maintenances. This system is composed of a hardware subsystem and its software subsystem (see Figure 22.32). The software subsystem comprises an operating system, a web-server, a database-server, and other software applications required for proper system service delivery. Assume the software subsystem is the one responsible for the increasing failure rate. The repair teams are responsible for the corrective maintenance as well as the preventive maintenance.

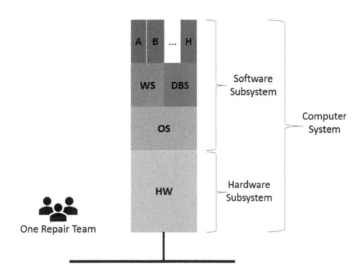

Figure 22.32   One Server – Corrective and Preventive Maintenances – One Repair Team.

The SPN shown in Figure 22.33 is an availability model of this system. This model is composed of eleven places, *SOK*, *SD*, *A*1, *A*2, *UR*, *W*, *AIR*, *UI*, *UPR*, *PME*, and *RT*; six exponentially timed transitions, *F*1, *F*2, *CR*2, *TBPR*, *I*, and *PR*; six immediate transitions, *C*1, *C*2, *F*3, *CR*1, *TA*, and *ATR*; and their arcs. Table 22.10 depicts the transitions' attributes. All transitions are marking independent and their server semantics are *sss*. All transitions' priorities are one, but the priority assigned to transition *ATR*. Its priority is zero.

A token in place *SOK* depicts the system as operational, whereas a token in place *SD* represents a system failure. Transitions *CR*1 and *CR*2, and place *UR* represent the corrective repairing process. The number of repair teams available is specified by the number of tokens in place *RT*. In this explanation, assume *#RT* = 1. Transition *R*1 represents the repair team allocation to recover the failed system, and the *MTTR* assigned to transition *CR*2 denotes the respective *mttr*. A token in place *UR* denotes the system is under repair. As soon as the repair is concluded (denoted by the transition *CR*2 firing), a token is stored in place *SOK*, which shows the system as operational, and stores a token in place *RT*, which states the repair team is again available for repairing activities. The system failure is denoted by the sub-net representing an Erlang distribution with k phase and phase rate equal to $\beta = 1/phttf$. The

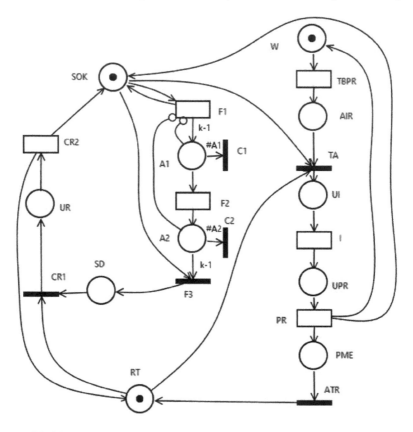

Figure 22.33 One Server SPN – Corrective and Preventive Maintenances.

sub-net denoted by places $A1$ and $A2$, the timed transitions $F1$ and $F2$, immediate transitions $C1$ and $C2$, their respective attributes, and arcs represent the failure rate increasing TTF, denoted by an Erlang distribution.

The time-base preventive maintenance (it is important again to stress the condition-based preventive maintenance is also called predictive maintenance) is represented by the sub-net depicted by places W, RSI, UI, UPR, and RT; timed transitions $TBPR$, I, and PR, immediate transition TA; the arcs and transition attributes. A token in place W represents the time between preventive maintenance has not elapsed. When it does, this is depicted by the transition $TBPR$ firing, whose mean time between preventive maintenance ($mtbpm$) is assigned. Such a firing removes a token from place W and stores a token in place AIR, which denotes the system is waiting for a maintenance team to become available to start the system inspection. It is worth mentioning that TA is an immediate transition, so as soon as a token is available in place RT, it does enable TA and then fires it. Its firing removes a token from place AIR and stores a token in place UI under inspection. The mean time required to perform the system inspection (*mit*) is assigned to transition I; its firing removes a token from place UI and stores one token in place UPR, under preventive maintenance. The transition I's priority is one since once the preventive maintenance starts, the computer stops operating; hence the wearing out process stops; thus disabling $F2$. The mean preventive maintenance time (*mpmt*) is assigned to transition PR (preventive maintenance). When PR fires, denoting the preventive maintenance was performed, a token is removed from place UPR and one token is stored in place W (waiting for another preventive maintenance cycle), and one token in place RT, which represents the release of the maintenance team.

As already mentioned, the time to failure with an increasing failure rate is depicted by the sub-net composed of places $A1$ and $A2$, the timed transitions $F1$ and $F2$, and immediate transitions $C1$ and $C2$, their respective attributes, and arcs, for $k > 1$. Tokens in places $A1$ and $A2$ represents wear-out effects (in the case of a software subsystem, it may also encompass software aging phenomena). When the preventive maintenance finishes, a token is removed from place UPR, and one token is stored in place PME (preventive maintenance end). This marking enables ATR, and $C1$ and $C2$ if places $A1$ and $A2$ are respectively marked. Look at the guard expressions of $C1$ and $C2$ in Table 22.10. If $A1$ and $A2$ have tokens, they are firable, whereas ATR is not since its priority is smaller than the priorities assigned to $C1$ and $C2$, $\pi(C1) = \pi(C2) = 2$, and $\pi(ATR) = 1$. Firing $C1$ and $C2$ removes all tokens from places $A1$ and $A2$, respectively. This means the system restores as new. After that, ATR fires and removes a token from PME and stores one token in place W, which denotes a new preventive cycle starts, and the repair team is deallocated from the preventive maintenance task by storing a token in place RT.

Table 22.10

Transitions' Attributes

Transition	Type	W	Guard Expression
F1	Timed	phttf	
F2	Timed	phttf	
F3	Immediate	1	
C1	Immediate	1	$(\#PME = 1)AND(\#A1 > 0)$
C2	Immediate	1	$(\#PME = 1)AND(\#A2 > 0)$
CR1	Immediate	1	
ATR	Immediate	1	
CR2	Timed	mttr	
TBPR	Timed	mtbpm	
TA	Immediate	1	
I	Timed	mit	
PR	Timed	mpmt	

The steady-state system availability is calculated through the expression

$$A = P\{\#SOK = 1\}, \tag{22.10.1}$$

the unavailability is obtained through

$$UA = 1 - P\{\#SOK = 1\}, \tag{22.10.2}$$

and the downtime in the period T is calculated from

$$DT = (1 - P\{\#SOK = 1\}) \times T. \tag{22.10.3}$$

Example 22.10.1. Assume the system described in Figure 22.33, whose transition attribute are depicted in Table 22.10 and the number of repair teams is one $\#RT = 1$. Consider the time to a corrective maintenance is exponentially distributed with mean $mttr = 20\,h$. Also assume the inspection time is exponentially distributed with mean $mit = 0.5\,h$. The time to perform preventive maintenance is distributed according to an exponential distribution with mean $mpmt = 1\,h$. The time between preventive maintenance is also exponentially distributed with mean $mtbpm$. The system time to failure is distributed according to an Erlang distribution with parameters $k = 5$ and $\beta = 1/phttf = 2.5 \times 10^{-3}h^{-1}$, which leads to $phttf = 400\,h$. Hence, the mean time to failure is $mttf = 2000\,h$.

The system availability and the respective yearly downtime when preventive maintenance is not applied are $A = 0.990099$ (in $\#9s = 2.004321$) and $DT = 86.73267\,h$, respectively.

Figure 22.34 presents the system availability considering $mtbpm \in (450\,h, 510\,h)$. The optimal mean time between preventive maintenance is $mtbpm = 498\,h$. Considering $mtbpm = 498\,h$, the system availability and the respective yearly downtime $(T = 8760\,h)$ are $A = 0.994782$ (in $\#9s = 2.282528$) and 45.7063, respectively. Hence, the yearly down time difference when comparing a system maintenance with and without preventive maintenance is $41.0264\,h$.

$\square$

Example 22.10.2. Now consider a system composed of two servers, where each server is similar to the server described in the previous example. The software subsystem of each server is composed of an operating system, a web-server, and a database-server required for the proper system service delivery. This system is assumed to be operational as long as two web-servers and two database-servers are properly functioning. Consider that the software subsystem of each server has an increasing failure rate. One repair team is responsible for the corrective maintenance as well as the preventive maintenance. The time parameters are also the same as depicted in the previous example. Hence, the time to corrective maintenance is exponentially distributed with mean $mttr = 20\,h$, the inspection time is exponentially distributed with mean $mit = 0.5\,h$, the time to perform a preventive maintenance is

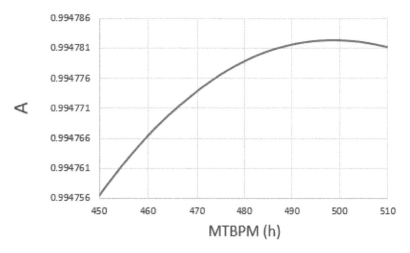

Figure 22.34   Availability $\times$ $mtbpm \in (450\,h, 510\,h)$.

distributed according to an exponential distribution with mean $mpmt = 1\,h$, the time between preventive maintenance is also exponentially distributed with mean $mtbpm$, and the system time to failure is distributed according to an Erlang distribution with parameters $k = 5$ and $\beta = 1/phttf = 2.5 \times 10^{-3}\,h^{-1}$, which leads to $phttf = 400\,h$. Hence, the mean time to failure is $mttf = 2000\,h$. The SPN shown in Figure 22.35 is an availability model for both servers, which considers the corrective and preventive maintenances of both servers since both have an increasing failure rate. In each preventive maintenance cycle, the preventive maintenance policy represented in this model performs maintenance of only one server. This is depicted by a choice structure represented by place W and transitions TA and $TA2$. If TA fires, the preventive maintenance is conducted on one server; on the other hand, if $TA2$ fires, the preventive maintenance is performed on the other server.

Table 22.11 depicts the transitions' parameter of the SPN shown in Figure 22.35. The system availability is calculated through

$$A = P\{(\#SOK = 1)AND(\#S2OK = 1)\},$$

and the downtime in a period T is obtained by

$$DT = (1 - (P\{(\#SOK = 1)AND(\#S2OK = 1)\})) \times T.$$

The steady-state system availability taking into account only corrective maintenance is $A = 0.9802$, and the respective yearly downtime is $DT = 173.45\,h$. Figure 22.36 shows the availability and the yearly downtime considering the mean time between preventive maintenance in the interval $mtbpm \in (220\,h, 289\,h)$. The optimal $mtbpm$ is $250\,h$. Considering $mtbpm = 250\,h$, the system steady-state availability is

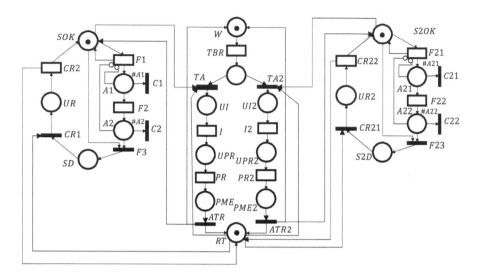

Figure 22.35 Two Server – Corrective and Preventive Maintenances.

$A = 0.98957219$, and the yearly downtime is $DT = 91.35$. The yearly downtime difference between the system with only corrective maintenance and the system with preventive maintenance, using the optimal, $mtbpm$, is $82.1\,h$. It is worth stressing that as in one preventive maintenance cycle, maintenance is performed in only one of the servers; the $mtbpm$ in this example is roughly half of the $mtbpm$ of the previous example.

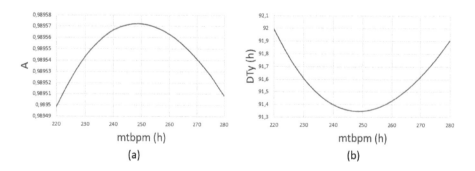

Figure 22.36 Two Server – Corrective and Preventive Maintenances – $A \times mtbpm$.

Table 22.11

Transitions' Attributes - Two Server SPN

Transition	Type	W	Guard Expression
F1, F21	Timed	phttf	
F2, F22	Timed	phttf	
F3, F23	Timed	1	
C1, C21	Immediate	1	$(\#UPR = 1)AND(\#A1 > 0)$ $(\#UPR2 = 1)AND(\#A21 > 0)$
C2, C22	Immediate	1	$(\#UPR = 1)AND(\#A2 > 0)$ $(\#UPR2 = 1)AND(\#A22 > 0)$
CR1, CR21	Immediate	1	
CR2, CR22	Timed	mttr	
TBPR, TBPR2	Timed	mtbpm	
TA, TA2	Immediate	1	
I, I2	Timed	mit	
PR, PR2	Timed	mpmt	

22.11 COMMON CAUSE FAILURE

This section shows how to represent a CCF using SPN. The system represented in this section is composed of two classes of servers, server-class 1 ($SC1$) and server-class 2 ($SC2$)). The number of servers of type $SC1$ is $NS1$, and the number of servers of type $SC2$ is $NS2$. The time to failure of each server class is exponentially distributed with the respective means $MTTF1 = 10000\,h$ and $MTTF2 = 15000\,h$. Two repair teams are available - so the server semantics of $RS1$ and $RS2$ are sss - and the time to repair is also exponentially distributed with mean $MTTR = 20\,h$. The common cause mean time to failure is assumed to be exponentially distributed with mean $MTTF_{ccf} = 100000\,h$.

An availability model of such a system is depicted by the SPN shown in Figure 22.37. The number of tokens in place $S1U$ denotes the number of servers of class $SC1$ in the operational state, whereas the number of tokens in place $S1D$ represents the number of servers of class $SC1$ in failure. Likewise, the number of tokens in place $S2U$ depicts the number of servers of class $SC1$ in the operational state, and the number of tokens in place $S2D$ represents the number of servers of class $SC2$ in failure. The server semantics of transitions $FS1$ and $FS2$ are $isss$, and the other transitions' server semantics are sss. Transition CCF represents the common cause of failure. The $MTTFS1$ is assigned to transition $FS1$, the $MTTFS2$ is assigned to transition $FS2$, and $MTTCF$ is associated with transition CCF. Transitions $RS1$ and $RS2$ have $MTTR$ as their delays. The arcs connecting $S1U$ to CCF are marking dependent, and the weight is equal to $\#S1U$. Similarly, the arcs connecting $S2U$ to CCF are marking dependent, and the weight is $\#S2U$. Likewise, the arcs connecting CCF to $S1D$ are also marking dependent, and the weight is $\#S1U$. The arcs connecting

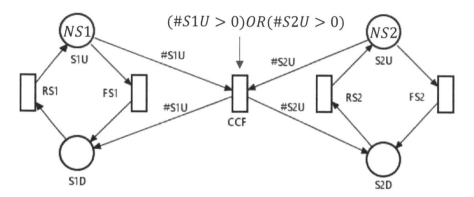

Figure 22.37 Two Web-Servers and Common Cause Failure – Availability Model.

$S2U$ to CCF is marking dependent too, and the weight is equal to $\#S2U$. Transition CCF has this guard expression: $(\#S1U > 0)OR(\#S2U > 0)$; that is to a CCF comes to effect if at least one server of any class should be operational. The steady-state system availability is defined by

$$A = P\{(\#S1U > 0)OR(\#S2U > 0)\};$$

hence the downtime in the period T is

$$DT = (1 - P\{(\#S1U > 0)OR(\#S2U > 0)\}) \times T.$$

Assuming the delays shown in the first paragraph, if $NS1 = 3$, $NS2 = 2$, and $T = 525600$ minutes, the steady-state system availability is $A = 0.9998999$, and the yearly downtime is 52.5986 minutes.

22.12 SOME ADDITIONAL MODELS

This section presents some additional practical applications of adopting the models introduced in this section. The first study concerns availability modeling for disaster-recovery. A second study concerns a stochastic model to evaluate IaaS cloud computing systems deployed into geographically distributed data centers [248].

22.12.1 DATA CENTER DISASTER RECOVERY

This system is composed of a primary data center and a disaster recovery cloud system (see Figure 22.38). The primary data center provides five virtual machines (VMs) that run a web application server. Three of these web-servers are active, while two are in a hot-standby state. An auto-scaling mechanism ensures that the correct number of active web-servers, which is three, never goes below or above this size. The web application deployed in those machines accesses a database-server running in the same data center. A load balancer (LB) distributes the user requests evenly among the active web application servers, avoiding a single VM becoming overloaded while the others are idle.

The disaster recovery cloud system has replicas of the web application and database-servers that are identical to those running in the primary data center. The storage volumes used by the primary and secondary database-servers are kept synchronized. Both web and database-servers are active in the disaster recovery cloud but do not process any user requests while the primary data center is online. Nevertheless, the auto-scaling mechanism is not considered for the web-servers in the disaster recovery cloud since only the minimum resources are used for this infrastructure. A disaster monitor located outside both sites is responsible for detecting when the primary data center has failed due to a disaster. When a disaster occurs, the disaster monitor notifies the secondary servers hosted in the cloud to assume the virtual IPs to which the load balancer transmits the users' requests. Using this mechanism makes the transition from the primary data center to the disaster recovery cloud seamless, avoiding users noticing the change of servers for the application.

The SPN model that represents the disaster recovery solution is composed of SPN submodels that represent web-servers, database-servers, data center, load balancers, cloud servers, and hot-standby redundancies. The top of Figure 22.39 presents the SPN models for the primary infrastructure. Figure 22.39.a represents the load balancer, while Figure 22.39.b models the database server. Figure 22.39.c and Figure 22.39.d represent, respectively, the web-server and the data center. The number "3" in the web server component means the number of active components, while the number "2" represents the total of hot-standby replicas. Note that the primary infrastructure automatically scales up or down the instances of web-servers according to predefined conditions. This work assumed that the primary infrastructure automatically scales up every time an active component fails and scales down whenever the number of active components exceeds three. The guard models this auto-scaling mechanism functions $G_{WEB1scDown}$ and $G_{WEB1scUp}$.

To represent the dependency between VMs and data centers, we included immediate transitions and guard functions for each component representing the virtual machines. As an example, if the data center goes down, the web-servers should also become unavailable. Such a behavior is modeled by two immediate transitions ($T_{WEB1dwDC}$ and $T_{WEB1dwHot}$) and three guard functions ($G_{WEB1dwDC}$, $G_{WEB1dwHot}$ and $G_{WEB1rep}$). The guard functions $G_{WEB1dwDC}$ and $G_{WEB1dwHot}$ enable, respectively, the transitions $T_{WEB1dwDC}$ and $T_{WEB1dwHot}$, which models the unavailability of the web servers. Since the web-servers cannot be recovered until the data center is up, the guard function $G_{WEB1rep}$ disables the transition $T_{WEB1rep}$. Table 22.12 summarizes the guard function definitions.

The bottom part of Figure 22.39 details the SPN models for the disaster recovery cloud. Figure 22.39.e models the load balancer, while Figure 22.39.f represents the

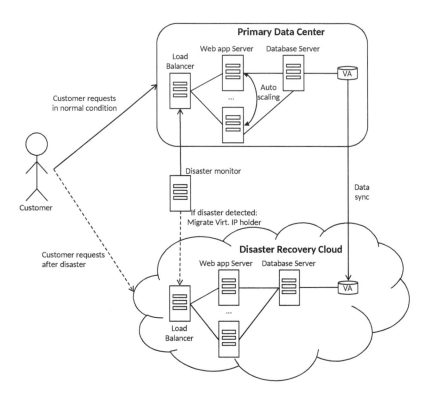

Figure 22.38 Adopted Disaster Recovery Solution

hot-standby component for the database server. Figure 22.39.g and Figure 22.39.h represent, respectively, the hot-standby component for the web-server and the cloud server. The number "3" in the hot-standby web server component represents the triple redundancy that exists for that component, similar to the redundancy already shown in the primary infrastructure. In order to represent the dependency between the hot-standby components and cloud infrastructure, we included two immediate transitions to each component and three guard functions. For example, if the disaster recovery cloud goes down, the database-server should also become unavailable. Such a behavior is modeled by the guard function $G_{DB2dwCS}$ and $G_{DB2dwCS}$. The guard function $G_{DB2dwCS}$ enables the transition $T_{DB2dwCS}$, which models the unavailability of the database-server from the hot-standby state, whereas the guard function $G_{DB2dwCS}$ enables the transition $T_{DB2dwCS}$, which represents the unavailability of the database-server from the up state. Since the database-server cannot be recovered until the cloud is operational, the guard function G_{DB2rep} disables the transition T_{DB2rep}. It is

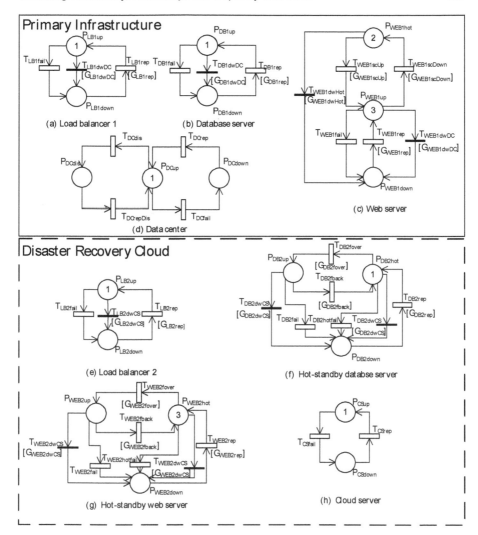

Figure 22.39 SPN for the Adopted Disaster Recovery Solution.

important to mention that the dependency between the load balancer and cloud sever is similar to the one explained before for the basic components.

Another existing dependency is between the primary infrastructure and the disaster recovery cloud. This dependency is represented by the failover and failback operations, which are triggered by the guard functions. For instance, the failover and failback operations of the database-server are triggered by the guard functions $G_{DB2fover}$ and $G_{DB2fback}$, respectively. The guard function $G_{DB2fover}$ enables the transition $T_{DB2fover}$ only if the disaster is detected (indicated by a token in P_{DCup}). The guard

Table 22.12

Guard Functions for the SPN Models Representing the Disaster Recovery Solution

Component	Guard	Function
Web server	$G_{WEB1dwDC}$	$(\#P_{DCup}=0)$
	$G_{WEB1rep}$	$(\#P_{DCup}=1)$
	$G_{WEB1scDown}$	$(\#P_{DCup} > 3)$
	$G_{WEB1scUp}$	$(\#P_{DCup} < 3)$
	$G_{WEB1dwHot}$	$(\#P_{DCup}=0)$
Database server	$G_{DB1dwDC}$	$(\#P_{DCup}=0)$
	G_{DB1rep}	$(\#P_{DCup}=1)$
Load balancer 1	$G_{LB1dwDC}$	$(\#P_{DCup}=0)$
	G_{LB1rep}	$(\#P_{DCup}=1)$
Load balancer 2	$G_{LB2dwCS}$	$(\#P_{CSup}=0)$
	G_{LB2rep}	$(\#P_{CSup}=1)$
Hot-standby web server	$G_{DB2fover}$	$(\#P_{DCdis}=1)$
	$G_{DB2fback}$	$(\#P_{DCup}=1)\text{AND}(\#P_{WEB1up}=3)\text{AND}$ $(\#P_{DB1up}=1)\text{AND}(\#P_{PLB1up}=1)$
	$G_{DB2dwCS}$	$(\#P_{CSdown}=1)$
	G_{DB2rep}	$(\#P_{CSup}=1)$
	$G_{DB2dwCS}$	$(\#P_{CSdown}=1)$
Hot-standby database server	$G_{WEB2fover}$	$(\#P_{DCdis}=1)$
	$G_{WEB2fback}$	$(\#P_{DCup}=1)\text{AND}(\#P_{WEB1up}=3)\text{AND}$ $(\#P_{DB1up}=1)\text{AND}(\#P_{PLB1up}=1)$
	$G_{WEB2dwCS}$	$(\#P_{CSdown}=1)$
	$G_{WEB2rep}$	$(\#P_{CSup}=1)$
	$G_{WEB2dwCS}$	$(\#P_{CSdown}=1)$

function $G_{DB2fback}$, on the other hand, enables the transition $T_{DB2fback}$ only if the entire infrastructure is operational after the disaster. That is, all the primary infrastructure is working properly. The definitions of guard functions are summarized in Table 22.12.

Table 22.13 shows the input parameters for the proposed disaster recovery model presented in Figure 22.39. These parameters were derived from [92, 183, 212, 245]. Note that we considered three classes of parameter settings: Very High Availability parameters (VHA), High Availability parameters (HA), and Medium Availability parameters (MA). These settings represent distinct reliability or maintainability conditions such as the existence of spare components on-site for speeding up the repairing activities or more careful choices of hardware and software that are reportedly more trustworthy. The SPN model was evaluated for each parameter setting, assuming that the disaster recovery (D/R) is enabled, and later, disabled. The Mercury tool was used for all analyses [274]. Table 22.14 presents the metrics employed in our analysis, which are the steady-state availability of the system for both cases: disaster recovery enabled (D/R enabled) and disaster recovery disabled (D/R disabled). These metrics are computed employing the respective expressions based on the probabilities of finding a given number of tokens in specific places of the SPN model. Table 22.15 presents numerical analysis results computed using the SPN models. As expected, VHA settings deliver the highest availability level. In addition, the steady-state system availability is larger when disaster recovery is enabled than when it does not exist for all parameter settings. This increased availability is also

Table 22.13
Model Input Parameters

Parameters	Transitions	Values (hours)		
		VHA	HA	MA
Mean time to failure of the Data Center (Disaster)	T_{DCdis}	21915	17532	13149
Mean time to repair of the Data Center (Disaster)	$T_{DCrepDis}$	8	12	16
Mean time to failure of the Data Center (Transient)	T_{DCfail}	13149	8766	4383
Mean time to repair of the Data Center (Transient)	T_{DCrep}	6	4	2
Mean time to failure of the LB (Data Center)	$T_{LB1fail}$	13149	8766	4383
Mean time to repair of the LB (Data Center)	T_{LB1rep}	6	4	2
Mean time to failure of the Web-Server (Data Center)	$T_{WEB1fail}$	2922	2199	1461
Mean time to repair of the Web-Server (Data Center)	$T_{WEB1rep}$	1	2	3
Mean time to scale up (Web-Server)	$T_{WEB1scUp}$	0.033	0.083	0.133
Mean time to scale down (Web-Server)	$T_{WEB1scDown}$	0.033	0.083	0.133
Mean time to failure of the Database (Data Center)	$T_{DB1fail}$	2922	2199	1461
Mean time to repair of the Database (Data Center)	T_{DB1rep}	1	2	3
Mean time to failure of the Cloud Server	T_{CSfail}	13149	8766	4383
Mean time to repair of the Cloud server	T_{CSrep}	6	4	2
Mean time to failure of the LB (Cloud)	$T_{LB2fail}$	13149	8766	4383
Mean time to repair of the LB (Cloud)	T_{LB2rep}	6	4	2
Mean time to failure of the Web-Server (Cloud)	$T_{WEB2fail}$	5844	4383	2922
Mean time to failure of the Hot-Standby Web Server (Cloud)	$T_{WEB2hotfail}$	2922	2199	1461
Mean time to repair of the Web-Server (Cloud)	$T_{WEB2rep}$	1	2	3
Failover operation of the Web-Server	$T_{WEB2fover}$	0.033	0.083	0.133
Failback operation of the Web-Server	$T_{WEB2fback}$	0.033	0.083	0.133
Mean time to failure of the Database (Cloud)	$T_{DB2fail}$	5844	4383	2922
Mean time to failure of the Hot-Standby Database (Cloud)	$T_{DB2hotfail}$	2922	2199	1461
Mean time to repair of the Database (Cloud)	T_{DB2rep}	1	2	3
Failover operation of the Database	$T_{DB2fover}$	0.033	0.083	0.133
Failback operation of the Database	$T_{DB2fback}$	0.033	0.083	0.133

noticed by comparing the annual downtime. For instance, in the HA settings, the system downtime decreases more than 72% due to introducing a disaster recovery solution.

Table 22.14

Steady-State Availability

Metrics Adopted to Compute of the Solution with and Without Disaster Recovery

Status	Availability
D/R enabled	$((\#P_{LB1up}==1)$ AND $(\#P_{WEB1up} >=3)$ AND $(\#P_{DB1up}==1))$ OR $((\#P_{LB2up}==1)$ AND $(\#P_{WEB2up} >=3)$ AND $(\#P_{DB2up}==1))$
D/R disabled	$(\#P_{LB1up}==1)$ AND $(\#P_{WEB1up} >=3)$ AND $(\#P_{DB1up}==1)$

The fifth column in Table 22.15 shows the downtime cost (D_{cost}) for each parameter setting. It was computed based on an hourly cost of 6,849.00 dollars, considering conditions tailored for small and medium businesses: $ 1,000,000 of annual revenue, 100% of the revenue from online activities, and 4 hours of high revenue per day. For the VHA settings, the difference in downtime-related costs per year between enabling a D/R or not enabling it is about 31,500.00 dollars, which is quite significant for the modeled scenario. If we consider the MA settings, this difference is even bigger (about 119,000.00 dollars). Furthermore, comparing the downtime-related costs between VHA and MA settings, whether enabling the D/R or not, the difference is close to half a million dollars.

To better estimate the financial advantage of a disaster recovery solution, it is necessary to consider the costs for purchasing and keeping such a computational environment ready for running. Therefore, we estimated the cost of the disaster recovery solution employing acquisition costs and energy consumption costs. For the sake of

Table 22.15

Results from the SPN Models

Class	Status	Availability	Downtime (h/yr)	D_{cost} ($)	L_q
VHA	D/R enabled	0.999038990	8.42	57,697.45	8,418.45
	D/R disabled	0.998513995	13.02	89,217.25	13,017.40
HA	D/R enabled	0.997220208	24.37	166,894.09	24,350.98
	D/R disabled	0.996144920	33.80	231,452.57	33,770.50
MA	D/R enabled	0.992429006	66.37	454,549.87	66,321.91
	D/R disabled	0.990448887	83.72	573,432.91	83,667.75

simplicity, and also for reasons of space, we considered that the disaster recovery solution is deployed in a private high available cloud environment (HA settings), which is described in [93]. This private cloud comprises five physical machines, where one machine runs the front-end, and four machines run the cluster. According to [93], the acquisition cost for such an infrastructure is US$ 14,248.80 and the power consumption cost for 12 months is US$ 1,936.80. Therefore, the total cost for deploying and keeping such an infrastructure during a year is estimated at US$ 16,185.60. This is an acceptable cost compared to the savings in downtime-related costs that the disaster recovery solution provides. If we consider a public cloud instead of a private one, the cost of the disaster recovery solution in a year would be even smaller, as demonstrated in [93]. A similar computational capacity could be rented in a public cloud with US$ 12,337.92 per year.

The last column in Table 22.15 presents the number of lost requests, L_q, in each scenario, computed using Equation (22.12.1), for a time interval T of one year (8760 hours), and an average arrival rate λ of 1000 transactions per hour, corresponding to 3.6 seconds of an interval between transaction arrivals. The results show that adopting a disaster recovery solution reduces considerably (64% for VHA, 72% for HA, and 79% for MA) the number of lost requests, so the company's reputation will be less affected than if there were no such solution. This result is very important, since a bad reputation due to service outages may lead to massive loss of customers, who may move to other competitor services.

$$L_q = (1-A) \times T \times \lambda. \tag{22.12.1}$$

22.12.2 DISASTER TOLERANT CLOUD SYSTEMS

This section presents a stochastic model to evaluate IaaS cloud computing systems deployed into geographically distributed data centers as well as taking into account disaster occurrence. The proposed model is based on SPN and supports performability evaluation. Using the proposed modeling approach, IaaS providers can evaluate the system distributed in different data centers and the impact of VM transmission time on performability metrics. Furthermore, the proposed strategy presents a tool that supports the evaluation by automatically creating the system models, namely Geoclouds [97, 152, 187].

Figure 22.40 presents a cloud architecture located in Brazil, which is composed of a data center located in Recife (Data Center 1), another in Rio de Janeiro (Data Center 2), and a backup server in São Paulo. Each data center consists of two physical machines, and each machine is capable of running up to two virtual machines. The evaluation will consider machine utilization in terms of the maximum number of VMs (U) and the probability of completing a task without error (P).

In this study, we assume all physical machines (PMs) are identical, in the sense that they adopt the same services and hardware/software components. PMs may share network-attached storage (NAS) or a storage area network (SAN) to provide distributed storage and to allow the migration of a virtual machine from one server to another in the same data center [79]. In case of failure, a VM must be instantiated in another physical machine. If there is no available PM, the VM image is migrated to another data center. Furthermore, a backup server (BS) is assumed to provide a backup of VM data. This component receives a copy of each VM image during data center operation. Hence, whenever a disaster makes one data center unavailable, BS periodically sends VM copies to an operational data center.

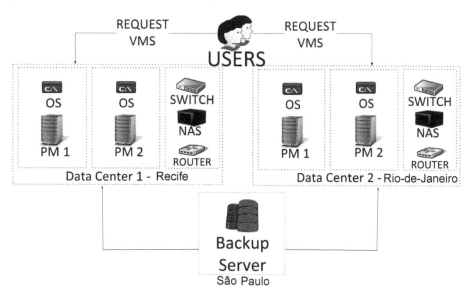

Figure 22.40 Cloud System Architecture.

Table 22.16 presents the dependability parameters associated with the devices, which were taken from [211], [420], [366], [398]. In this work, we consider the approach presented in [291] to assess the network throughput based on the distance between the communication nodes. We assume a transmission package loss ratio of 1%, maximum segment size per data package (MSS) 1460 of bytes, α as 0.45, and the size of VMs as 4GB. We considered the mean time between disasters to be 100 years and the data center to take 30 days to be repaired. Moreover, a VM takes five minutes to set up, and the mean time between requests is half an hour. The mean time for using a VM is 720 hours.

To perform the evaluation, the user should provide the parameters and execute the evaluation. The assessment process can be conducted transparently directly on the GeoClouds tool or creating the SPN models from scratch adopting Mercury [26] or TimeNET [428] tools. The SPN model related to the previous example is presented in Figure 22.41, which comprises four VM performability submodels, one transmission submodel, and several generic submodels. *OSPM_1* and *OSPM_2* represent the

Table 22.16

Dependability Parameters for Components of Figure 22.41

Component	MTTF(h)	MTTR(h)
Operating System (OS)	4000	1
Hardware of Physical Machine (PM)	1000	12
Switch	430000	4
Router	14077473	4
NAS	20000000	2
VM	2880	0.5
Backup Server	50000	0.5

physical machines of Data Center 1, and *OSPM_3* as well as *OSPM_4* are the models related to PMs of Data Center 2. *DISASTER1* and *DISASTER2* models disasters in Data Centers 1 and 2, respectively. *NAS_NET_1* and *NAS_NET_2* corresponds to network devices of Data Center 1 and 2.

The adopted modeling process considers first the evaluation of lower-level submodels, and then the individual results are applied to higher-level models. Finally, the basic SPN submodels are configured and combined to create the SPN final model. The generic component (Figure 22.1) is adopted to represent components that have no redundancy and might be in two states, either functioning or failed. In order to compute its availability, mean time to failure (*MTTF*) and mean time to repair (*MTTR*) are the only parameters needed.

The VM performability component represents VM requests on a single physical machine considering failures and repairs on the underlying infrastructure. Whenever a user request is performed, a new VM is started (considering that the infrastructure is operational) and becomes available for some time. This component interacts with three generic components: (i) one representing the occurrence of disasters (*DC*); (ii) the network infrastructure (*NAS_NET*); and (iii) the physical machine (*OSPM*).

If the external infrastructure or the VM fails during the virtual machine execution, the VM should be migrated to another physical machine. If there is no available physical machine in the system, the task is rejected, and a new request must be performed. Figure 22.42 presents the VM performability model, which is composed of three main parts: (i) *VM_PART* represents the VM behavior running on a single machine; (ii) *DC_PART* expresses the incoming requests to the data center; and (iii) *CLOUD_PART* models the requests generation.

A VM should migrate to another data center whenever the current data center is full or the underlying infrastructure has failed. Moreover, the backup server is responsible for transmitting the VM image in case of a disaster or network error. The transmission component represents the data transfer from one data center to another and from backup server to a data center.

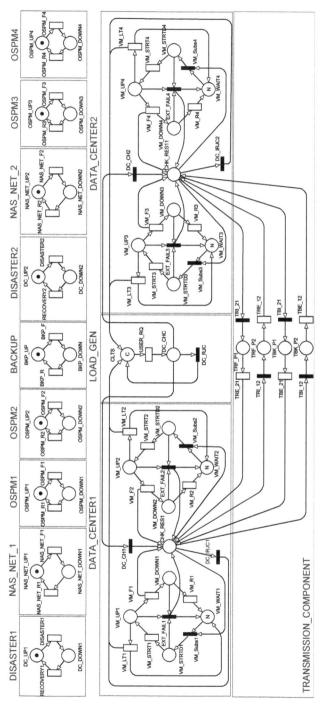

Figure 22.41 Case Study Output Model.

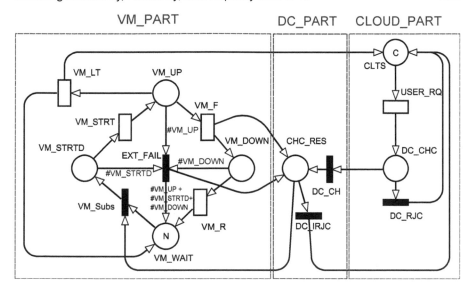

Figure 22.42   VM Performability SPN Model.

Whenever an external failure occurs, tokens of the input places are instantaneously eliminated, and the sum of removed tokens is inserted in *VM_WAIT*. *DC_PART* models the incoming requests to the data center and the failed VMs that should migrate to another machine. The *DC_PART* of different VM performability components are merged if the respective physical machines are located in the same data center. In other words, just one *DC_PART* is represented for each data center. Place *CHC_RES* represents the incoming requests to the current data center. In case of no available machine in the system, the request is canceled. The task cancellation is represented by the transition *DC_IRJC*. A task is rejected whenever one of the following conditions is satisfied: (i) the network infrastructure has failed *(#NAS_NET_UP=0)*, a disaster happened *(#DC_UP=0)*, the respective server cannot instantiate a new VM *(#VM_WAIT=0)*, the underlying physical machine is not operational *(#OSPM_UP=0)*. *DC_CH* represents the opposite idea, in the sense that a task is received only if the respective infrastructure is working. The guard expressions related to these transitions are represented in Table 22.17. *CLOUD_PART* represents the load generation and the rejection of requests when all data centers are unavailable. All the *CLOUD_PART*s of different VM performability submodels are merged; just one *CLOUD_PART* is represented for the whole system.

CLTS and *DC_CH* model clients that are about to perform requests and the requests that entered into the system, respectively. It is assumed that each client requests a single VM. The transition *USER_RQ* means the request process. Finally, *DC_RJC* denotes the request rejection when all data centers are unavailable. Both transitions have single-server semantics (sss). It is assumed that the data center is not available if

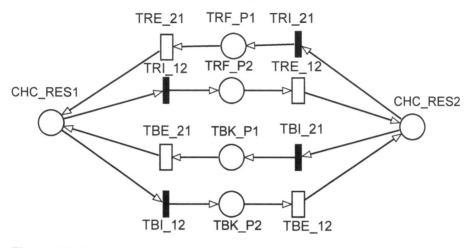

Figure 22.43 Transmission Component SPN Model.

Table 22.17

Guard Expressions for VM Performability Component

Transition	Condition	Description
EXT_FAIL	(#OSPM_UP=0) OR (#NAS_NET_UP=0) OR (#DC_UP=0) AND ((#VM_UP + #VM_DOWN + #VM_STRTD) > 0)	Failure of physical machine or infrastructure
VM_Subs	(#OSPM_UP>0) AND (#NAS_NET_UP>0) AND (#DC_UP>0)	Physical machine and infrastructure working
DC_IRJC	(#NAS_NET_UP=0) OR (#DC_UP=0) OR (#VM_WAIT=0) OR (#OSPM_UP=0)	Task rejection
DC_CH	(#NAS_NET_UP>0) AND (#DC_UP>0) AND (#VM_WAIT>0) AND (#OSPM_UP>0)	Request acceptance to data center
DC_RJC	(#NAS_NET_UP=0) OR (#DC_UP=0) OR (#VM_WAIT=0) OR (#OSPM_UP=0)	Task rejection

the underlying infrastructure is broken or the servers are full. It is important to stress that the guard expressions of *DC_IRJC*, *DC_CH*, and *DC_RJC* can vary depending on the number of physical machines and the number of data centers. In this case, we assume just one physical machine in one data center. However, this approach is generic enough to consider several machines in multiple data centers.

Table 22.18 presents the guard expressions of the transmission component. It is assumed that Data Center 1 contains the physical machines *OSPM_UP1* and *OSPM_UP2*, and Data Center 2 includes *OSPM_UP3* and *OSPM_UP4*. *(MTT)* represents the mean time to transmit one virtual machine from one location to another.

Table 22.18
Guard Expressions for Transmission Component

Transition	Condition
TRE_12	(#VM_WAIT1=0 OR #OSPM_UP1=0) AND (#VM_WAIT2=0 OR #OSPM_UP2=0) AND NOT((((#VM_WAIT3=0 OR #OSPM_UP3=0) AND (#VM_WAIT4=0 OR #OSPM_UP4=0)) OR #NAS_NET_UP2=0 OR #DC_UP2=0)
TRE_21	(#VM_WAIT3=0 OR #OSPM_UP3=0) AND (#VM_WAIT4=0 OR #OSPM_UP4=0) AND NOT((((#VM_WAIT1=0 OR #OSPM_UP1=0) AND (#VM_WAIT2=0 OR #OSPM_UP2=0)) OR #NAS_NET_UP1=0 OR #DC_UP1=0)
TBK_12	(#BKP_UP=1 AND #NAS_NET_UP1=0 OR #DC_UP1=0) AND NOT((((#VM_WAIT3=0 OR #OSPM_UP3=0) AND (#VM_WAIT4=0 OR #OSPM_UP4=0)) OR #NAS_NET_UP2=0 OR #DC_UP2=0)
TBK_21	(#BKP_UP=1 AND #NAS_NET_UP2=0 OR #DC_UP2=0) AND NOT((((#VM_WAIT1=0 OR #OSPM_UP1=0) AND (#VM_WAIT2=0 OR #OSPM_UP2=0)) OR #NAS_NET_UP1=0 OR #DC_UP1=0)

The *MTT* depends on the physical link speed, the distance between the data centers, and the VM size [259]. In this block, there are three *MTTs*: mean time to transmit a VM from the data center to another (*MTT_DCS*) and the mean times to transfer the VM image from backup server to Data Centers 1 and 2 (*MTT_BK1 and MTT_BK2*). The *MTT_DCS* parameter is associated to transitions *TRE_12* and *TRE_21*, while *MTT_BK1* and *MTT_BK2* are related to TBK_21 and TBK_12, respectively. It is worth mentioning that all transitions mentioned before have single server semantics (sss), and that the priorities and weights of all immediate transitions are equal to one.

To perform system evaluation, we consider provider and client-oriented metrics. The provider's oriented metric is the machine utilization in terms of a maximum number of VMs (*U*), and the user's oriented metric is the probability of a task being completed without error (*P*). The following operators are adopted for assessing the metrics: $P\{exp\}$ estimates the probability of the inner expression (*exp*); #*p* denotes the number of tokens in place *p*, and $E\{\#p\}$ estimates its expected number. *U* is calculated as follows:

$$U = \frac{\sum_{j=1}^{M} E\{\#VM\_UPj''}{M.N},$$
(22.12.2)

where M corresponds to the number of PMs and N is the maximum number of VMs per physical machine. P corresponds to:

$$P = \frac{(\sum_{j=1}^{Pm} E\{\#VM\_UPj^{\wedge}\}).(1/T)}{P\{\#CLTS > 0\}.(1/R)}, \tag{22.12.3}$$

in which T and R correspond to the times associated with transitions VM_LT and $USER\_REQ$ (Figure 22.42). This expression divides the throughput of completed requests by the incoming requests to compute the percentage of completed requests. Figure 22.44 shows VM utilization and the rejection probability for a different number of clients. It is assumed that each client can request a single VM. The results show that utilization increases with the number of clients. If the infrastructure is broken or the servers are full, the task is rejected; hence, it is possible to observe that the rejection probability increases due to an increase in system load. Therefore, we can conclude that the rejection probability is highly impacted by server utilization for this particular system and user loads.

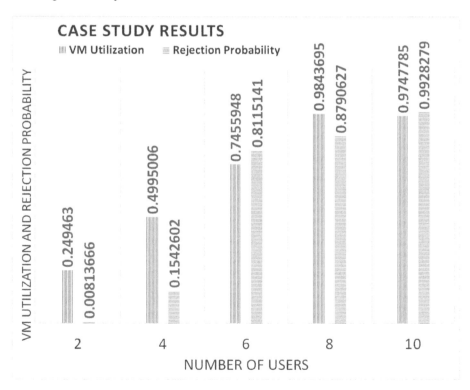

Figure 22.44 Case Study Results.

22.12.3 PERFORMABILITY EVALUATION OF AN MHEALTH SYSTEM CLOUD INFRASTRUCTURE

The proposed models aim to represent the behavior of an mHealth system monitoring of patient vital signs [189]. For this, some analytic models were created using RBD and Petri nets. The main objective is to estimate the probability of a message being delivered in a given time unit. The mHealth architecture is illustrated in Figure 22.45. It was considered that a monitoring device collects the **patient**'s vital signs and send them to a private **cloud infrastructure**. The cloud infrastructure is responsible for storing and processing data. The critical information about the patient is sent to the **mobile device** of the responsible medical doctor using the **4G connection** or **WiFi connection**.

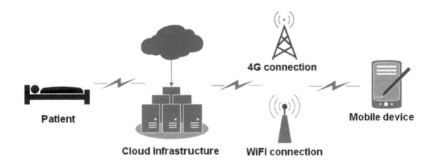

Figure 22.45 System Architecture.

Figure 22.46 shows a high-level model that represents the message flow from the patient to the mobile device. The token in the Send_message represents a message that needs to be delivered until the place Arrive_message.

The private cloud infrastructure is represented by an RBD model (Figure 22.47). This model is divided into three sub-models: Infrastructure Manager, Storage Manager, and Nodes. The cloud model represents a simple infrastructure, with just one Infrastructure Manager, one Storage Manager, and five Nodes. Note that at least one of five nodes must be available for the proper cloud operation. On the other hand, a single failure in the Infrastructure Manager or Storage Manager makes the private cloud unavailable. We consider that each component's time to failure and time to repair are exponentially distributed. The same assumption is used for the other models.

Another important component of the architecture is the mobile device. The Mobile_Device subsystem is represented by a series RBD, as shown in Figure 22.49. This subsystem is composed of the components Mobile_HW, Battery, Mobile_OS and App. Mobile_HW, which refers to the physical device; Battery is a common battery present in the mobile devices; Mobile_OS is the operating system running in the mobile device; App represents the application that communicates

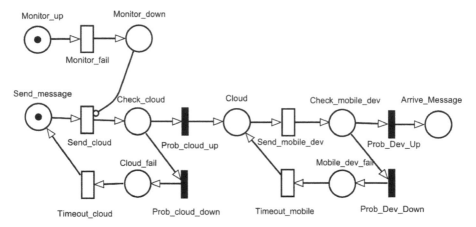

Figure 22.46 Message Delivery Model.

with the cloud to send information about the patient. A failure in any of the four components causes the unavailability of the mobile device. Figure 22.50 presents the communication model.

Then, the communication availability is calculated from Equation 22.12.4:

$$A_{Com} = P\{((\#wifi\_up = 1)AND(\#wifi\_nb = 1))OR \qquad (22.12.4)$$
$$((\#fourg\_up = 1)AND(\#fourg\_nb = 1)).\}$$

Distinct scenarios are presented to evaluate the mobile cloud according to the presented models. Our analysis aims at the availability of the mHealth system, considering three sets of scenarios, with different wireless communication, different battery discharge rates, and using different timeouts.

Figure 22.51.a shows the results considering different communication possibilities: a scenario with just WiFi technology; another with just 4G; another one with both technologies (WiFi and 3G); with WiFi signal more stable than 4G; and, finally, with 4G more stable than 4G. All these scenarios are being considered because the mobile device can go to different covered areas. The results show an overlap of red and green lines (just WiFi and just 4G). This means that when all mHealth architecture is considered, these scenarios have the same behavior.

The probability of a message being created in a monitoring device and immediately delivered to the mobile device is about 0.8063. Such a probability is 0.9999 if we consider a deliverer time equal to 1.8 minutes. Similar behavior can be observed when WiFi is more stable than 4G and when 4G is more stable than WiFi; in such cases, we observe an overlap of purple and light blue lines. Now, it is possible to observe better results. For example, the probability of a message being immediately delivered is about 0.8590, and 0.9999 for 1.6 minutes. Finally, we have results slightly

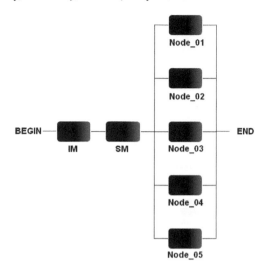

Figure 22.47   RBD Model for the Cloud Infrastructure.

better when WiFi and 4G are both available to use. In such a case, the probability of delivering a message in time close to 0 is 0.8637, and 0.9999 for 1.6 minutes.

Figure 22.51.b shows the results considering different battery discharge times: 9, 12, 15, 18, 21, and 24 hours. All these scenarios are being considered because the mobile device can have a different battery autonomy and use all phone features. Nine hours is the worst scenario when we have all devices resources activated [338]. As expected, the worst results are obtained when we have the lowest discharge times. With a discharge time of nine hours (red line), the probability of a message to be created from the monitoring device and immediately delivered to the mobile device is about 0.8637, and from 0.9999 in 1.6 minutes. With a discharge time of twenty-four hours (brown line), the probability of a message to be immediately delivered is about 0.9281 and 0.9999 in 1.3 minutes. We can observe a significant difference when comparing the best and worst scenarios. The immediate delivery probability to discharge times 12, 15, 18, and 21 hours are 0.8884, 0.9039, 0.9145, and 0.9222; and for probability 0.9999, is 1.5, 1.4, 1.4 and 1.3 minutes, respectively.

Figure 22.51.c shows the results considering different timeouts: 10, 20, 30, 40, 50, and 60 seconds. All these scenarios are being considered because the timeout for a delivery message is a project decision. Obviously, as the lower this time, the probability of delivering a message will be better. However, this can cause performance loss because more messages will be traveling on the network. As expected, the best results are obtained when we have the lowest timeouts. For a timeout of ten seconds (red line), the probability of a message being created from the monitoring device and immediately delivered to the mobile device is about 0.8637. The same probability is 0.9999 when the message is delivered by 1.6 minutes. Assuming a timeout

(a) Infrastructure Manager

(b) Storage Manager

(c) Nodes subsystem

Figure 22.48 Cloud Component Models.

Figure 22.49 RBD Model for the Mobile Device.

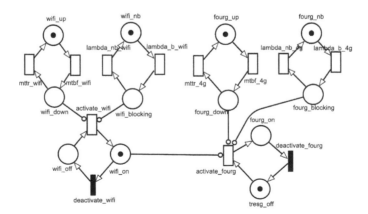

Figure 22.50 SPN model for Communication Technologies.

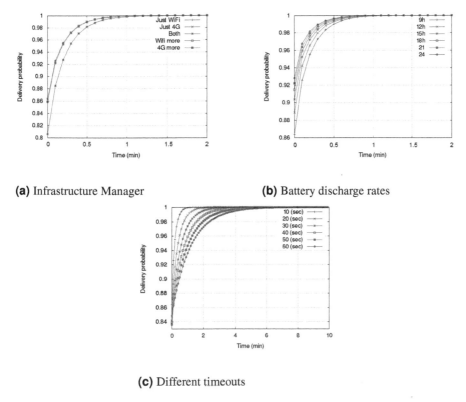

(a) Infrastructure Manager   (b) Battery discharge rates

(c) Different timeouts

Figure 22.51   Probability of delivering a message.

of twenty-four hours (brown line), the probability of a message being immediately delivered is about 0.8357. Likewise, it is 0.9999 for 8.8 minutes. We can observe an enormous difference when comparing the best and worst scenarios. The immediate delivery probability for timeouts of 20, 30, 40 and, 50 seconds is 0.8478, 0.8419, 0.8389, and 0.8370; and for probability 0.9999 is 3.0, 4.5, 5.9, and 7.3 minutes, respectively.

EXERCISES

Exercise 1. If you adopt SPN as the modeling formalism, provide the reasons for (a) adopting them as a modeling mechanism; (b) choosing either numerical analysis or simulation as the evaluation method; (c) choosing either steady-state or transient evaluation; (d) the model having specific qualitative properties, if you intend to adopt numerical analysis. What are those properties? Justify your answers.

Exercise 2. For a computer system composed of two servers (server sub-system: $S1$ and $S2$) operating in a cold-standby sparing configuration, a storage sub-system ($D1$ and $D2$) configured in RAID 1 and controller (C) – see Figure 22.52, the system fails if the server sub-system or storage sub-system or C fails. Consider that the constant failure rates are $\lambda_{S1} = 1.14155 \times 10^{-4} h^{-1}$, $\lambda_{S2} = 7.61035 \times 10^{-5} h^{-1}$, $\lambda_c = 5.70776 \times 10^{-5} h^{-1}$, $\lambda_{D1} = \lambda_{D2} = 8 \times 10^{-5} h^{-1}$. The respective times to repair are exponentially distributed with rate $\mu_{S1} = \mu_{S2} = 20.833 \times 10^{-3} h^{-1}$, $\mu_{D1} = mu_{D2} = 10.417 \times 10^{-3} h^{-1}$, and $\mu_{D2} = 41.667 \times 10^{-3} h^{-1}$. Assume the time to start the server is exponentially distributed with mean equal to 5 minutes. (a) Propose an SPN availability model of the system. (b) Compute the steady-state availability of the system. (c) Calculate the respective system's downtime in minutes per year. (d) Conceive a reliability model of the system. (e) Calculate the system's MTTF. (f) Draw the reliability curve in the interval $[0, 1460 h)$.

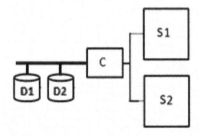

Figure 22.52 Database Server System.

Exercise 3. Assume the time to failure of a system is a five-stage hypoexponentially distributed random variable with parameters λ_1, λ_2, λ_3, λ_4, λ_5, where $\lambda_1 = 5.1 \times 10^{-4} h^{-1}$ and $\lambda_2 = \lambda_3 = \lambda_4 = \lambda_5 = 5.88 \times 10^{-4} h^{-1}$. Consider the repair times are exponentially distributed with parameter $\mu = 2.0833 \times 10^{-2}$ h^-1. Compute the steady-state availability and the yearly downtime.

Exercise 4. Figure 22.53 presents a tiny-private cloud system composed of a cloud manager (CM), three servers (S_1, S_2, S_3) and a storage sub-system, which is composed of an NAS controller (NASC), and six disks configured in RAID 5. Each computer hardware is composed of a motherboard (MB), memory (M), the network controller (NWC), video controller (VC), an internal disk (HD), its disk controller (HDC), and the power source (PS). The cloud manager is operational if their hardware and operating system and the cloud manager software (CMS) are operational. The server subsystem has two active servers and one operating in cold-standby. The spare server starts when one of the active servers fails. Each server is operational if its hardware and operating system, the virtual machine manager (VMM), and two virtual machines (VM) are functional. The tiny-cloud system is operational if at least one virtual machine is operational. Assume the times to failure and the times to repair are exponentially distributed. The MTTFs and the MTTRs are shown in Figure 22.53. Propose an availability model using the SPN and RBD of this system and calculate (a) the availability, (b) the yearly downtime, and (c) the capacity-oriented availability of the system.

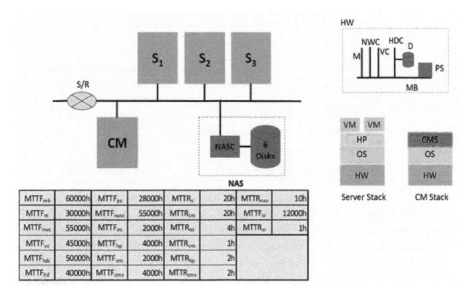

MTTF$_{mb}$	60000h	MTTF$_{ps}$	28000h	MTTR$_s$	20h	MTTR$_{nas}$	10h
MTTF$_m$	30000h	MTTF$_{nasc}$	55000h	MTTR$_{cm}$	20h	MTTF$_{sr}$	12000h
MTTF$_{nwc}$	55000h	MTTF$_{os}$	2000h	MTTR$_{os}$	4h	MTTR$_{sr}$	1h
MTTF$_{vc}$	45000h	MTTF$_{hp}$	4000h	MTTR$_{vm}$	1h		
MTTF$_{hdc}$	50000h	MTTF$_{vm}$	2000h	MTTR$_{hp}$	2h		
MTTF$_{hd}$	40000h	MTTF$_{cms}$	4000h	MTTR$_{cms}$	2h		

Figure 22.53 The Tiny-Cloud System Specification.

Exercise 5. For a computer system composed of two servers (server sub-system (*SS*): *S*1 and *S*2) operating in a cold-standby sparing configuration, a storage sub-system (*STS*) is composed of *D*1 and *D*2 configured in RAID 1 and a controller (*C*) – see Figure 22.54. The system fails if the server sub-system or storage sub-system or *C* fails. Each server is composed of the following hardware-software components: motherboard (*MB*), memory card (*MC*), network interface (*NI*), power source (*PS*), operating system (*OS*), and software applications (*A*). For each server to properly work, every one of its component should be correctly operating. Consider the *TTF*s and *TTR*s to be exponentially distributed. The components' *MTTF* are: $MTTF_{Di} = 15000h$, $MTTF_C = 22000h$, $MTTF_{MB} = 20000h$, $MTTF_{MC} = 12000h$, $MTTF_{NI} = 18000h$, $MTTF_{PS} = 6000h$, $MTTF_{OS} = 2000h$, $MTTF_A = 1500h$. Each server's $MTTR_{Si} = 48h$, and the storage sub-system's $MTTR_{Si} = 24h$. Assume the time to start a server is exponentially distributed with mean $MTTS = 0.1h$. (a) Identify the failure mode. (b) Propose an availability model of the system, considering a hierarchical modeling strategy based on SPN and FT. Take into account only one maintenance team. (c) Compute the steady-state availability of the system. (d) Calculate the respective system's downtime in minutes per year. (e) Conceive a reliability model based on the SPN and FT of the system. (f) Calculate the system's $MTTF$. (g) Draw the reliability curve in the interval $[0, 1460h)$.

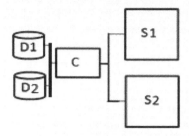

Figure 22.54   Computer System Specification.

Exercise 6. Consider again the system depicted in the previous exercise. Instead of adopting cold-standby redundancy, now consider a warm-standby sparing mechanism for the server subsystem. The standby server (when not operating) does not run software applications (A). Assume the time to start a server is exponentially distributed with mean $MTTS = 0.025\,h$. Propose an availability model of the system, considering a hierarchical model based on SPN and RBD. Consider only one maintenance team. (a) Compute the steady-state availability of the system. (b) Calculate the respective system's downtime in minutes per year.

Exercise 7. Assume the single-component system whose mode is shown in Figure 22.3. Consider the time to failure of such a component has been registered. The $MTTF = 3000\,h$ and $SD_{TTF} = 060\,h$. Applying the moment matching method depicted in Section 13.3.8, an Erlang distribution with the following parameter is presented as a suitable model: $ERL(K, \lambda)$, where $K = 25$ and $\lambda = 8.333 \times 10^{-3}\,h^{-1}$, so $ttfph = 1/\lambda = 120\,h$. The time to repair is suitably depicted by the following Cox-1 distribution: $Cox - 1(\omega_1, \omega_2, KC, \mu)$, where $\omega_1 = 0.0393$, $\omega_2 = 0.9607$, $KC = 3$, and $\mu = 0.1461\,h^{-1}$, so $ttrph = 1/mu = 6.8461\,h$. Propose an SPN availability model and (a) compute the steady-state availability and yearly downtime. b) Represent the availability in number of nines for $ttfph \in (120\,h, 200\,h)$. c) Using the reliability model (SPN) depicted in Figure 22.5.b (Figure 22.5.a depicts a high-level model.), plot the reliability in the time interval $(0, 4000\,h)$.

Exercise 8. Assume the system is composed of two servers configured in hot-standby redundancy. Let us define the servers' mean time to failure as $MTTF = 900\,h$ and their mean time to repair as $MTTR = 40\,h$. Assume both TTF and TTR are exponentially distributed, and there is only one repair facility. From the SPN depicted in Figure 22.7, (a) calculate the steady-state availability and the yearly downtime. (b) Calculate the yearly downtime considering the $MTTF \in (900\,h, 16000\,h)$. (c) Compute the reliability of this system in the interval $(0, 80000\,h$ using a similar model to the one shown in Figure 22.9. (d) Calculate the mean time to failure through the mean time to absorption of the SPN model.

Exercise 9. Suppose the system depicted in Figure 22.7.a but with imperfect failure coverage. Consider the coverage probability is $c = 0.97$, and the TTF, TTR, and DT are exponentially distributed with $MTTF = 900h$, $MTTR = 40h$, and $MDT = 0.5$. Propose an SPN availability model and calculate (a) the steady-state availability, (b) the steady-state availability expressed in number of nines, (c) the probability of having a hidden failure, (d) the probability of the system being available and safe (without hidden failure), (e) the downtime in a period T, (f) and the time the system stays in an unsafe state (hidden failure) in a period T, where $T = 8760h$.

Exercise 10. Assume the system depicted in Figure 22.14. As the TTF_j, $j \in \{HW, OS, WS, DB\}$ are exponentially distributed with $MTTF_{HW} = 20000h$, $MTTF_{OS} = 2800h$, $MTTF_{WS} = 2000h$, and $MTTF_{DB} = 1600h$. Also consider the servers' TTR being exponentially distributed with $MTTR_{S_i} = 40h$ as well as the time required to switching on ($TTSO$) the spare server is also exponentially distributed with $MTTSO_{S_i} = 0.06667h$. Propose an SPN availability model and (a) calculate the system steady-state availability, (b) the yearly downtime, (c) the system availability (in number of nines), (d) the yearly downtime against $MTTSO \in (0.05h, 0.2h)$, and (e) propose an SPN reliability model, and calculate the system reliability in the interval $t \in (0, 2000h)$.

Exercise 11. Consider the system depicted in Figure 22.18. As the TTF_j, $j \in \{HW, OS, WS, DB\}$ are exponentially distributed with $MTTF_{HW_i} = 20000h$, $MTTF_{OS_i} = 2800h$, $MTTF_{WS_i} = 2000h$, and $MTTF_{DB_i} = 1600h$, $i \in \{1,2\}$. Propose an SPN availability model and (a) calculate the servers' mean time to failure when in active mode, and the server's mean time to failure when in standby mode. As time required to switching on ($TTSO$) the spare server is also exponentially distributed with $MTTSO_{S_i} = 0.017h$, calculate (a) the system steady-state availability, (b) the yearly downtime, (c) the system availability (in number of nines), and (d) the yearly downtime.

Exercise 12. Assume a system composed of four servers in an active-active configuration. Assume the times to failure and to repairs is exponentially distributed with $MTTF = 700h$ and $MTTR = 20h$. Consider each server can sustain $45000tps$. Propose an SPN availability model and (a) calculate the steady-state system availability, (b) the yearly downtime, (c) $ANSA$, (d) COA, and (e) ATP using Mercury tool.

Exercise 13. Suppose a system is composed of six similar physical servers ($N = 6$). Each server is composed of a hardware infrastructure (HW), an operating system (OS), and a hypervisor (HP). In addition, six virtual machines are deployed in each server over the hypervisors as shown in Figure 22.55.a. The hardware infrastructure (see Figure 22.55.b) of each server is composed of a motherboard (MB), a network controller (NC), a video controller (VC), a disk controller (VC), a disk (D), and a power source (S). The components' failure rates are constant and presented in Table 22.19.

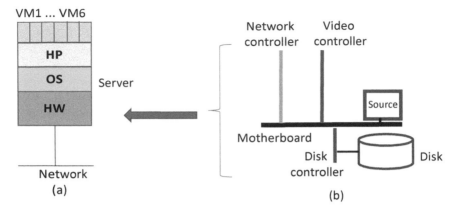

Figure 22.55   Servers' Software and Hardware Components.

Table 22.19
Failure Rates

i	$\lambda_i\ (h^{-1})$
HP	2×10^{-4}
OS and VMs	5.5×10^{-4}
MB	2×10^{-5}
NC	2.3×10^{-5}
VC	2.5×10^{-5}
DC	2×10^{-5}
D	3.8×10^{-5}
S	7×10^{-5}

The server time to repair is exponentially distributed with $MTTR_s = 20\,h$. Thus, each server hosts $M = 6$ virtual machines. The VMs' time to failure and time to repair are also assumed to be exponentially distributed with means equal to $MTTF_v = 800\,h$ and $MTTR_v = 0.05\,h$. Propose an availability model based on SPN and FT and (a) estimate each server $MTTF$, (b) calculate the system availability, considering that the system is available if twenty-eight VMs out of thirty-six VMs are operational, (c) calculate the yearly system downtime, (c) the COA, (d) and the average number of virtual machines in an operational state.

Exercise 14. Assume the system is composed of eight servers, four switches, two aggregation routers, and two storage units. The system is available if at least four servers, two switches, one router, and one storage unit are operational. The repair facilities (repair teams) are shared to repair all these devices that compose the system. Assume the components' $MTTF$ and $MTTR$ are shown in Table 22.20.

Table 22.20

MTTF, MTTR, and Number of Resources of Each Type

Component	MTTF (h)	MTTR (h)	Number
Server	900	40	8
Switch	7000	48	4
Router	5000	96	2
Storage Units	9000	48	2

Calculate the system availability and the yearly downtime, considering the number of repairs as $NRT \in \{1, 2, 3, 4, 5, 6\}$.

Exercise 15. Now consider a system composed of two servers, where each server is similar to the server described in Figure 22.33. Assume the number of repair teams is one $\#RT = 1$. Consider the time to corrective maintenance is exponentially distributed with mean $mttr = 10\,h$. Also, consider that the inspection time is exponentially distributed with mean $mit = 1\,h$. The time to perform preventive maintenance is distributed according to an exponential distribution with mean $mpmt = 2\,h$. The time between preventive maintenance is exponentially distributed with a mean equal to $mtbpm$. The system time to failure is distributed according to an Erlang distribution with parameters $k = 8$ and $\beta = 1/phttf = 2 \times 10^{-3}h^{-1}$, which leads to $phttf = 400\,h$. Calculate (a) the system availability and the respective yearly downtime when preventive maintenance is not adopted and (b) find out the $mtbpm$ that optimizes system availability.

Part IV

Measuring and Data Analysis

Performance evaluation is an essential task when planning or tuning a computer system. Such a workload could be observed during normal system operation or a test. The lack of suitable performance measures, models, and techniques can lead to bad decisions. A good performance evaluation study is dependent on the workload characterization since the performance results may only be as good as the quality of the workload [188] [238].

Computer system performance measurements are based on monitoring the system while subjected to a specific workload. Hence, for obtaining meaningful measurements, the workload should be carefully characterized, and to achieve such an aim, the analyst should consider different types of workloads and their suitability, how the system is monitored if the system is controlled or not, and how the measured data are summarized and presented [136].

Unlike performance, dependability is harder to be evaluated since system behavior is dependent on failure occurrences. Nevertheless, as the mean time between failures (MTBF) in a dependable system is usually in the order of years, the fault occurrence has to be artificially accelerated and injected into the system under test in order to analyze the faults' effects on the system behavior [41]. Therefore, reliability data analysis concerns the study of observed product lifetimes. Such lifetime data can be of products in the market or related to the system in operation. Hence, the data analysis and prediction are described as lifetime data analysis or reliability data analysis.

Chapter 23 introduces some fundamental notions related to performance measurement as well as strategies and techniques for computer system measurement and tools for performance data gathering of computer systems. It also addresses counters, timers and profiling methods and presents some measuring tools for the Linux operating system. Next, Chapter 24 presents some fundamental concepts related to workload generation and methods that support workload modeling. This chapter examines the subjects involved in selecting, using, and analyzing workloads for computer systems. Chapter 25 shows a set of methods for reliability or lifetime data analysis. These methods are classified as nonparametric and parametric methods. Parametric techniques assume the lifetime data obeys specific probability distributions; conversely, nonparametric techniques perform the reliability analysis data without assuming underlying probability distributions. Finally, Chapter 26 discusses failure monitoring and fault injection mechanisms.

23 Performance Measuring

This chapter introduces some essential concepts related to performance measurement and strategies and techniques for computer system measurement. It also presents some useful tools for performance data collection of computer systems. Section 23.1 presents some concepts on system measurement. Section 23.2 and Section 23.3 introduce some measuring strategies and basic metrics. Section 23.4 discusses counters and timers, which are fundamental instruments for computer performance measuring. Section 23.5 presents a strategy for measuring short-duration events. Section 23.6 discusses the program profiling process and types and introduces some profiling tools. Section 23.7 presents some system and process measuring tools for the Linux operating system, and finally, Section 23.8 closes the chapter.

23.1 BASIC CONCEPTS

Metrology is the science of measurement. A quantity is a property of phenomena or a system that can be measured. The first measurable quantities were probably length, mass, and time, that is, quantities used in everyday life. Later, with the development of science, measurable quantities were applied to study laws in physics, chemistry, biology, social sciences, electronics, and computing. Measurement is the process of determining the value of a quantity experimentally with the support of measuring instruments [347]. The term quantity may be used in a broad sense to represent a property of a system or may denote the specific measured value. For instance, the execution time of a task may denote a property of a system, or this term may also be adopted to represent the actual time required to execute a specific task (a value).

Measurement systems are a specific system or tool conceived to quantify a phenomenon or property; hence, each measurement is an experimental procedure. Measurement results cannot be accurate due to rounding, truncation, and the inability to capture values below or above a specified threshold, for instance. **Accuracy** of measurement represents how close a measurement result is to the true (real) value of a quantity. The true value of a quantity is usually not known. The true value of a quantity is often defined by standards that represent the ideal units; that is, the reference value is an agreed standard, such as the duration of a second, the length of a meter, the weight of one kilogram. Consider, for instance, a timer. The timer's accuracy is an indication of the closeness of the timer's measurement to that of a standard measurement of time defined by a recognized standards organization [238].

Accuracy adjustments are usually conducted by recalibrating the measurement system. From a practical point of view, the real value of a quantity is assumed to be known only when calibrating measurement instruments. In such cases, the real value is considered the value of the measurement standard used in the calibration, whose accuracy error must be negligible compared with the measurement instrument's accuracy error being calibrated.

Accuracy is a "Positive" characteristic of the measurement system, but it is usually expressed through its dual "negative" counterpart – inaccuracy (accuracy error) – of measurement. The **inaccuracy** reflects the unavoidable imperfection of a measurement process. More formally, **absolute accuracy error** (AE) may be defined as the absolute difference between a measured value ($\tilde{M}$) and the corresponding reference value (M).

$$AE = | \tilde{M} - M | . \tag{23.1.1}$$

The error may also be expressed as a **relative accuracy error**, that is

$$\varepsilon = \frac{| \tilde{M} - M |}{M}, \tag{23.1.2}$$

which may also be multiplied by 100 and presented in percentage.

Measurement errors may be classified into systematic errors and random errors. For instance, systematic errors usually result from an experimental mistake, such as incorrect procedure execution and changes in the system under evaluation. Random errors, on the other hand, are unpredictable. The characteristic of measurements that reflects the closeness of the results of measurements of the same quantity performed under the same conditions is called **repeatability**. Good repeatability indicates small random errors. **Reproducibility** is the quality of measurements that reflect the proximity of the results of measurements of the same quantity carried out under different conditions, that is, in different laboratories, using different equipment performed by different people. Good reproducibility indicates that both random and systematic errors are small. The dimensional **resolution** is the smallest measurable quantity of a measurement system. For example, interval timers are usually implemented using a counter driven by a signal derived from the system clock. Hence, the resolution of the timer limits the accuracy of its measurements to be no better than plus or minus one clock period. Figure 23.2.a shows two grid patterns that represent the smallest quantity that two measurement systems can measure. The pattern on the left represents a measurement system with higher resolution than a measurement system whose pattern is depicted on the right. In other words, the measurement system resolution is defined by the ratio between the maximal amplitude (A) that could be measured by the system and the maximal number subdivision supported by the measurement system. More formally,

$$r_D = \frac{A}{2^n - 1}. \tag{23.1.3}$$

Another related concept is the non-dimensional resolution, which is defined as

$$r_{ND} = \frac{1}{2^n - 1}, \tag{23.1.4}$$

which for a measurement system with large n, it may be approximated by

$$r \sim \frac{1}{2^n}. \tag{23.1.5}$$

As a simple example, consider a timer, whose clock frequency is specified as $f_1 = 1\,kHz$. Hence, the clock period is $T_c = 1\,ms$. If the number of bits of the timer is $n = 8$, then the maximal event duration that could be measured by the timer in the maximal count supported by the timer, that is, $2^n - 1 = 2^8 - 1 = 255$, multiplied by the clock cycle (T_c); thus $255 \times 1\,ms = 255\,ms$. Therefore, the shortest time that could be measured by the timer is this configuration is (see Equation 23.1.3)

$$r_D = \frac{255\,ms}{2^8 - 1} = 1\,ms.$$

Now, consider that the timer is configured on a different scale. In this new scale, the clock frequency is specified as $f_2 = 500\,Hz$. Hence, the new clock period is $T_c = 2\,ms$. As the number of bits of the timer is $n = 8$, then the maximal event duration that the timer could measure is $255 \times 2\,ms = 510\,ms$. However, the shortest time that this timer could measure in this new configuration is

$$r_D = \frac{510\,ms}{2^8 - 1} = 2\,ms.$$

The durations of events (T_e) are typically not an exact whole number; hence clock periods cause a round-up or down of the measured value by at most one clock period (T_c). Therefore, the measurement system resolution introduces a random **quantiz-ation error** into all measurements obtained using the timer. In general, the actual event duration is within the range $nT_c < T_e < (n+1)T_c$. Thus, we would like T_c to be as small as possible but constrained by the timer number of bits (n). Figure 23.1 shows an event duration that should be measured by two timers (Timer 1 and Timer 2), where each timer is configured with clock frequency equal to $f_1 = 1\,KHz$ and $f_2 = 500\,Hz$, respectively. We also assume the number of bits of counter used in the timer is $n = 8$. The duration of the event measured by Timer 1 is equal to $18\,ms$, whereas the event duration measured by Timer 2 is $19ms$.

The **precision** of a measurement system relates to the repeatability of the measure-ments obtained using a measurement system. Sometimes it may be easier to think of precision in terms of its complement, imprecision (precision error). Imprecision is the variability in the measurements obtained by making multiple measurements of a

Timers

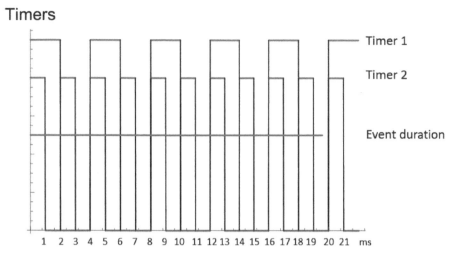

Figure 23.1   Resolution and Quantization Error.

particular quantity using the same measurement system. Statistics such as standard deviation, variance and range are possible functions to quantify the precision error. Highly precise measurements would be tightly clustered measures around a central value, whereas imprecise measurements would have a broader distribution.

The resolution of the measurement system affects its precision and its accuracy. Precision is often confused with accuracy, but these properties have very different meanings, as described above. Precision is related to resolution and variation, and accuracy refers to how close the measurement is to the true value. For example, Figure 23.2.b shows measurement systems with low precision and low accuracy, with low precision and high accuracy, with high precision and low accuracy, and high precision and high accuracy.

In general, quantifying the accuracy error is a complex task. Measuring this bias requires calibrating our measurement system, considering some standard values, and using expensive calibration measuring systems. Precision errors, however, may be quantified using statistics of variability and confidence intervals (see Chapter 3 and Chapter 6).

Calibration is usually costly, complex, and time-consuming. Thus, real calibration is mostly used for precision instruments. For other instruments, a simplified calibration is usually adopted. More precise lab instruments are adopted as a reference in simplified calibration but not certified calibration systems. For instance, consider a simplified calibration in which the complete check is performed by measuring the same quantity using a working standard accurate measuring system and the measuring system being checked.

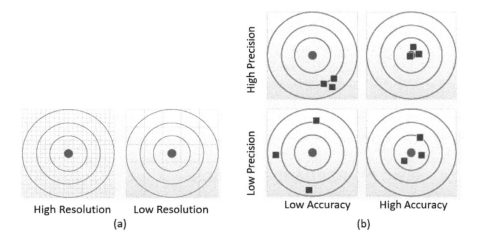

Figure 23.2 Resolution (a) Accuracy and Precision (b).

23.2 MEASUREMENT STRATEGIES

There are many types of performance metrics that we may wish to measure. The measuring strategies are usually based on the idea of the event. In this context, an event is some predefined change in the system state, such as a memory reading/writing, disk access, a network operation, a change in a processor's internal state, or a combination of subevents (simpler events).

One possible classification of measurement strategies classifies the strategies into two broad options: **passive** and **active measurement**. When adopting passive strategies, data is most readily available from accounting or activity logs. Such logs usually record selected attributes of all activities. For example, web-servers may be configured to record all transactions executed by the servers. However, if data is not readily available; we may apply active measurement strategies. Instrumenting a system to collect data at runtime can affect the system's behavior and performance. The active measurement may not be very troublesome for long-duration events, but it may be very problematic fine-grained events measurements [137].

Another possible characterization of computer measurement strategies adopts the following classes: **event-driven strategies** and **strategies based on sampling**. The event-driven strategies may also be divided into **direct measuring** and **indirect measuring**. An event-driven direct measurement strategy records the required information to calculate the performance metric whenever the predefined event occurs. For instance, an event-driven direct measuring method may be adopted to calculate the number of page faults during a program's execution. One drawback of such a strategy is that for high-frequency event occurrence, the overhead that may be introduced in the program execution could be significant. Therefore, event-driven measurement strategies are usually considered suitable for systems with low-frequency event occurrences. An event-driven indirect measuring strategy should be applied when the metric of interest is not directly accessible. For instance, the time demanded to execute a transaction in a system resource may be estimated using system throughput and the utilization of the resource (see Section 8.3).

Another general measuring strategy is based on **sampling measurement**. Sampling measuring periodically records the portion of the system state required to estimate the metric of interest. Thus, the overhead of such a strategy is independent of the number of occurrences of the event of interest.

23.3   BASIC PERFORMANCE METRICS

This section discusses some basic performance measures, from which other more complex measures may be derived. The fundamental measure observed in a computer system is the number of events that occurred during an observation period T, a counting. The period T is the delay between two events representing the beginning and the end of the observation period T. Many other measures could be obtained and derived from these two quantities (counting and T). Chapter 8 shown a set of quantities observed from a system composed of k devices during an observation period T. The fundamental quantities were the number of arrivals at resource i, A_i (transactions, operations, packets), the number of operations processed (concluded) by resource i, C_i (transactions, operations, packets, etc.), and the time the resource i was busy, B_i, during the period T. The number of arrivals and conclusions (jobs finished) performed by the system in the observation period T is denoted by A_0 and C_0, respectively.

From these fundamental quantities, the following metrics are obtained (already depicted in Chapter 8):

- The arrival rate of component i,

$$\lambda_i = \frac{A_i}{T},$$
(23.3.1)

- The throughput of component i,

$$X_i = \frac{C_i}{T},$$
(23.3.2)

- The utilization of component i,

$$U_i = \frac{B_i}{T},$$
(23.3.3)

- The mean service time of the component i,

$$S_i = \frac{B_i}{C_i},$$
(23.3.4)

- The system arrival rate,

$$\lambda_0 = \frac{A_0}{T}, \text{and} \tag{23.3.5}$$

- The system throughput,

$$X_0 = \frac{C_0}{T}. \tag{23.3.6}$$

The metrics depicted above are, in summary, (**1**) counts - A_i, C_i, A_0, and C_0 -, (**2**) delay - S_i -, which in the end is also a count, rates - λ_i, X_i, λ_0, and X_0 -, and (**3**) utilizations - U_i -, which are ratios between two delays (S_i and T, which, in turn, are also counts). Besides the metrics above, many other metrics could be estimated. Chapter 8 presents other many other metrics derived from the basic metrics depicted above.

23.4 COUNTERS AND TIMERS

Since the most fundamental metrics in a computer-based system is **event counting**, the most basic measuring tool in a computer's performance measurement is a **counter**. A counter measures the number of events that occurred in a period T (see Figure 23.3). Two typical implementations of counters are usually available: hardware counters and software counters.

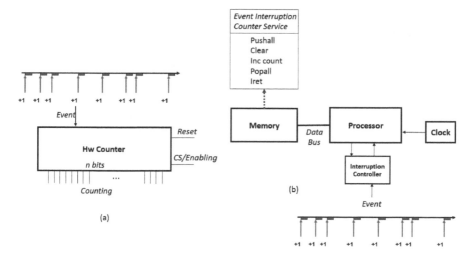

Figure 23.3 (a) Hardware Event-Counter (b) Software Event-Counter.

The **hardware-based counter** counts the number of events that occurred in an observation period T (see Figure 23.3.a). Such counters may also implement

hardware-based interval timers (see Figure 23.4). In such a case, the device counts the number of clock pulses since the system was enabled.

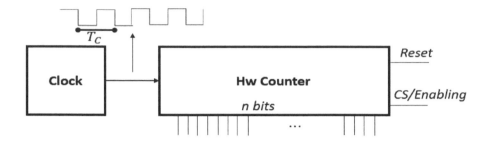

Figure 23.4   Hardware-Based Interval Timer.

It is worth mentioning that the counting resolution is limited by the clock period. A **software-based counter** is not directly incremented by events that are sensitive to hardware devices. Instead, a hardware interruption is usually generated, and, then, an interruption service is executed where a a variable (counter variable - *count*) is incremented (*Inc count*) or decremented (see Figure 23.3.b). A software-based counter may also be used to implement **software-based interval timers**. In such cases, the counter is incremented by a periodic time interruption (see Figure 23.5), in which a hardware counter generates a processor interruption at regular intervals (T_C), the processor suspends the execution of the current process (*application code*)[1], saves the flags and the return point onto the stack (see stack status at the bottom-center side of figure), and then, executes *time interruption service*, which calls a function (*SW counter code*) and saves the return point onto the stack (see stack status at the bottom-right side of figure). The *counter code* increments the variable *count*, and then the processor returns to the *time interruption service*. Then, when the interruption service finishes its execution, it returns to the *application code* process and executes the next instruction.

It is worth mentioning that the number of bits (n) of counters defines the longest interval that can be measured. An n-bits timer **rollover** occurs when the timer transitions from its maximum value ($2^n - 1$) to the zero. Consider the delay between two successive events e_1 and e_2 is expressed by

$$T_e = (c_2 - c_1)T_c, \tag{23.4.1}$$

where T_c is the clock period. However, when the difference $c_2 - c_1$ is negative, it reveals a **rollover** occurrence. Therefore, counter and timers should deal with this issue in order to avoid errors.

---

[1]SP - Stack Pointer. IP - Instruction Pointer.

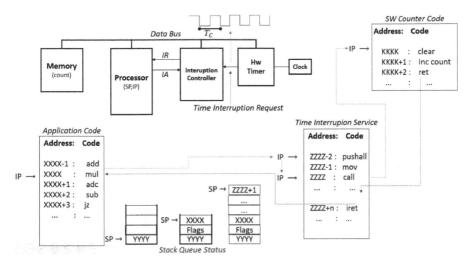

Figure 23.5   A Software-Based Interval Timer.

Overhead - The system under measurement determines how an interval timer should be used to measure the duration of an event. For instance, consider a portion of code depicted in Program 1 named *Piece of code being measured* as the event to be measured. We can think of this event as a method, function, procedure, block of instructions, or basic block, for example. The current time instant is captured by reading the software timer through *Start_count = read_timer()*. Executing this primitive function *read_timer()* reads the software time instant and stores the respective value on variable *Start_count*. After executing this primitive function, the event of interest (*Piece of code being measured*) starts its execution. After finishing the execution of the event, the software timer is read again, and its new current time instant is stored in variable *Stop_count*. The elapsed time of such an event (T_e) is estimated by subtracting the value in *Stop_count* from the value in *Start_count*. This difference specifies the number of clock cycles elapsed during the execution of the event. Multiplying such a difference by the delay of a clock cycle provides an estimation of the event duration. It is worth mentioning that the clock cycle here is considered a timing reference of the timer.

In Program 2, we have an example of how to measure the execution time of pieces of code (events) in Python programs. In this particular example, the execution times of three functions (three events) (*trig*, *factorial*, and *matrixops*) are measured by applying the *time.time()* function of Python *time* library. The functions call for recording the time stamps, the difference of time stamps, and the library that supports the *time.time()* function are written in red color.

In C language programs, the function *gettimeofday()* of library *<sys/time.h>* returns the time elapsed since 00:00:00 UTC[2] on January 1st, 1970 (UNIX epoch

---

[2]Universal Time Coordinated.

Algorithm 1 Measuring the Duration of a Piece Of Code in a Program

---

 1:

 2:

 3: $Start\_count = read\_timer();$

 4:          $\dots$

 5:              Piece of code being measured

 6:          $\dots$

 7: $Stop\_count = read\_timer();$

 8: $Elapsed\_time = (stop\_count - start\_count) \times clock\_period;$

 9:

10:

---

time). This function returns both the number of seconds and microseconds in separate *double* variables so that to obtain the total time, including microseconds, we need to sum both together accordingly. The piece of code depicted in red in Program 3 shows how to calculate the duration of a function. In this particular example, the execution time of function *func()* (the event of interest) is measured. The command lines in red depict the specific commands essential for estimating the execution time.

If fractions of seconds are not important, we can obtain the elapsed time by calculating *end.tv_sec − begin.tv_sec*. The second argument of *gettimeofday()* is used to specify the current *timezone*. Since we are calculating the elapsed time, *timezones* is irrelevant, provided that the same value is used both for begin and end. Thus, we used zero for both calls.

Estimating the event duration (T_e) using such an approach, the resulting measure includes more than the event duration itself (see Figure 23.6). It is important to stress that accessing the timer requires memory reading operations and may require a call to the operating system kernel. Besides, the value read from the timer is stored as a variable, which requires memory writing execution. Such a process is executed twice. First, it is executed at the beginning of the event, which has the overhead $T_1 + T_2$, and then again at the end of the event, causing the overhead T_3. These operations may add a significant amount of time (*overhead*) to the duration of the event itself.

$$overhead = T_1 + T_2 + T_3.$$

This overhead may be significant if *overhead* is of the order of the event duration (*ed*). If *overhead* $\ll T_e$, *overhead* could be disregarded. However, if *overhead* $\propto T_e$ or *overhead* $> T_e$, these operations add up to a significant delay to the duration of the event; thus, it is not suitable to measure an event of such a time order. Section 23.7 provides a quick view of the Linux performance counters and basic tools.

Algorithm 2 Measuring the Duration of Functions in Python Programs

```
1: import time
2: import pstats
3: import math
4: # importing NumPy for matrix operations
5: import numpy
6: #——————————————————————————————
7: def trig(a):
8:            print("Trigonometric Functions ", end= "\n"*2)
9:           print ("The converted value from radians to degrees is : ", end="")
10:          print (math.degrees(a))
11:          print ("The value of sine of pi/6 is : ", end="")
12:          print (math.sin(a))
13:          print ("The value of cosine of pi/6 is : ", end="")
14:          print (math.cos(a))
15:          print ("The value of tangent of pi/6 is : ", end="")
16:          print (math.tan(a),"\ n"*2)
17: #——————————————————————————————
18: def factorial(x):
19:           """"This is a recursive function to find the factorial of an integer"""""
20:           if x == 1:
21:                   return 1
22:           else:
23:                   return (x * factorial(x-1))
24: #——————————————————————————————
25: def matrixops(x,y):
26:          print ("The element wise square root is : ")
27:          print (numpy.sqrt(x))
28:          print ("he summation of all matrix element is : ")
29:          print (numpy.sum(y))
30:          print ("The column wise summation of all matrix is : ")
31:          print (numpy.sum(y,axis=0))
32:          print ("The row wise summation of all matrix is : ")
33:          print (numpy.sum(y,axis=1))
34:          print ("The transpose of given matrix is : ")
35:          print (x.T,"\ n"*2)
36: #——————————————————————————————
37: def main():
38:          rad = math.pi/6
39:          num = 50
40:          # initializing matrices
41:          b = numpy.array([[1, 2, 3, 4], [5, 6, 7, 8], [9, 10, 11, 12], [13, 14, 15, 16]])
42:          c = numpy.array([[17, 18, 19, 20], [21, 22, 23, 24], [25, 26, 27, 28], [29, 30, 31, 32]])
43:          start = time.time()
44:          trig(rad)
45:          end = time.time()
46:          print("trig(rad) function takes", end-start, "seconds", "\n"*2)
47:          start = time.time()
48:          factorial(num)
49:          end = time.time()
50:          print("The factorial of", num, "is", factorial(num),"\n"*2)
51:          print("factorial(num) function takes", end-start, "seconds", "\n"*2)
52:          start = time.time()
53:          matrixops(b,c)
54:          end = time.time()
55:          print("matrixops(x,y) function takes", end-start, "seconds", ""\n"*2)
56: if name__== "_main_" :
57:          main()
```

Algorithm 3 Measuring the Duration of Functions in C Programs

---

```
 1: /* Program to demonstrate time taken by function func() */
 2: #include <stdio.h>
 3: #include <sys/time.h>
 4: // A function that terminates when enter key is pressed
 5: void func() {
 6:          printf("func() starts \n");
 7:          printf("Press enter to stop fun \n");
 8:          while(1)     {
 9:                  if (getchar())
10:                  break;
11:          }
12:          printf("func() ends \n");
13:      }
14: // The main program calls func() and measures time taken by fun()
15: int main() {
16: // Calculate the time taken by func()
17:          double seconds, microseconds, elapsed;
18:          struct timeval begin, end;
19: // Start measuring time
20:          gettimeofday(&begin, 0);
21:          func();
22: // Stop measuring time
23:          gettimeofday(&end, 0);
24: // Calculate the elapsed time
25:          seconds = end.tv_sec - begin.tv_sec;
26:          microseconds = end.tv_usec - begin.tv_usec;
27:          elapsed = seconds + microseconds*1e-6;
28:          printf("Time measured: %.3f seconds.\n", elapsed);
29:          return 0;
30: }
```

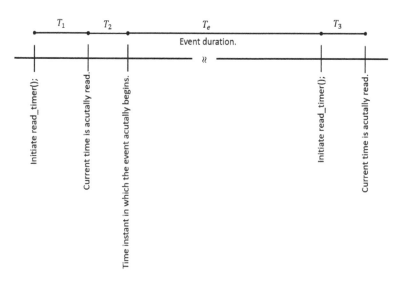

Figure 23.6   Overhead in Software-Based Interval Timer.

23.5   MEASURING SHORT TIME INTERVALS

Due to quantization error, we face difficulties when conducting direct measures of events whose durations (T_e) are shorter than the underlying clock period (T_c) related to the measurement system or even of the same order. In other words, direct measurement is not a suitable measuring approach when $T_e < T_c$ or even when $T_e > kT_c$ k, for small k. Nevertheless, we may apply a statistical-based method combined with multiple measurements to estimate the time of short-duration events. For illustrating this process, let us adopt a case in which the event's duration is shorter than the timer's clock period, that is $T_e < T_c$ as depicted in Figure 23.7.

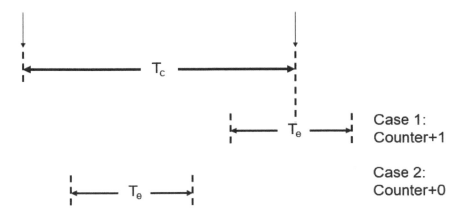

Figure 23.7   Short-Duration Events.

For instance, consider a C program that calls a function (the *event* of interest) written in assembly language (*int func_assembly(int a)*). Assume the time to execute this function is very short, that is $T_e < T_c$ or $T_e > kT_c$, and k is small. This system is composed of two modules (files) depicted in the Program List 4 and 5. The module shown in Program List 5 is a C program module that calls an external function implemented in x86 assembly language, which is presented in Program List 4.

The executable code is obtained by assembling[3] the *aseembly.asm* file, compiling the *main.c* file, and linking both object files (*main.o* and *assembly.o*) and generating the executable file (*main*) [51, 113]. This process is carried out by executing the three following command-lines:

```
> nasm -f elf assembly.asm
> gcc -c main.c -o main.o
> gcc main.o assembly.o -o main
```

---

[3]The Netwide Assembler (NASM) is an assembler that supports the x86-64 CPU architecture and Linux. NASM adopts the Intel assembly syntax. https://www.nasm.us/.

Algorithm 4 Assembly Module - assembly.asm

```
 1: [SECTION .text]                         ; Section containing code
 2:
 3: global func_assembly                     ; Required so linker can find entry point
 4:
 5: func_assembly:
 6:         push ebp                         ; Set up stack frame
 7:         mov ebp,esp
 8:         mov eax,[ebp+8]                  ; Passes the parameter to register eax
 9:         push ebx                         ; Program must preserve ebp, ebx, esi, and edi
10:         push esi
11:         push edi
12:         ...                              ; Functionality: few and fast assembly instructions
13:         pop edi                          ; Restore saved registers
14:         pop esi
15:         pop ebx
16:         pop eax                          ; Returning the integer through eax to variable c
17:                                          ; of the main function
18:         mov esp,ebp                      ; Destroy stack frame before returning
19:         pop ebp
20:         ret                              ; Return control to the caller
21:
22: [SECTION .data]                          ; Section containing initialized data
23:
24:         msg: db "Assembly Function",0
25:
26: [SECTION .bss]                           ; Section containing uninitialized data
```

Assume the program execution time on a given computer is about $2s$. Consider that the assembly function is responsible for a tiny portion of such a duration. Also assume the computer system timer interruption period is $T_c = 100\,\mu s$. We guess that the time to execute the assembly function (T_e) is shorter than T_c or about the same order. Hence, using the computer timer to directly measure the time required to execute the function *func_assembly()* would deliver a larger relative quantization error.

Therefore, we may resort to multiple-sampling and statistics to estimate T_e ($\tilde{T}_e$). For doing so, let us modify our *main* function on the C module for automatically executing the original code many times; let us say *n*. Hence, the modified *main* function may be implemented as the Program List 6, where the original main code is inserted into a *for* loop with the number of iterations equal to $k = 9340$. Hence, using this new version of the program, the assembly function is executed 9340 times, and the execution time of the new version of the program is about $9340 \times 2s = 18680\,s$ ($\approx 311.33\,min \approx 5.19\,h$). Let us also consider we know the address ranges of every function and variable of the program. This memory map would be obtained by analyzing the object file. The addresses of functions and variables may also be obtained by looking at the file *main_disassembly* obtained by executing the command

```
> objdump --disassemble -M intel main > main_disassembly
```

Algorithm 5 Main Module - main.c

```
 1: #include <stdio.h>
 2: extern int func_assembly(int a);
 3: double func1(double x)
 4: {
 5:          ...
 6:          return x;
 7: }
 8: double func2(double x)
 9: {
10:          double d;
11:          ...
12:          return d;
13: }
14: int main(void)
15: {
16:          double x, y, z;
17:          int a, b, c, d;
18:          ...
19:          x = func1(y);
20:          ...
21:          c = func_assembly(a);
22:          ...
23:          d = func2(x,z,a,b);
24:          ...
25:          return 0;
26: }
```

The command above generates the assembly mnemonics for the machine instructions for the input file (*main*) in Intel format (if you omit *-M intel*, the mnemonics are shown in ATT style), the address range of each function and variables.

After compiling the modified C source code and linking the corresponding object file with the object file obtained from the assembly code, we get a new executable file. Assume the first address of the assembly function is $3100030H$, and its final address is $3100261H$. The program was then executed. As already shown above, its execution lasted $18680s$. The time interruption service is executed at every $0.1ms$ (timer clock period). Hence, the program is interrupted at every $0.1ms$ for executing the time interruption service. Before changing the instruction pointer address register, the address of the next instruction (when the program is interrupted) is stored onto the system stack; then the first address of the time interruption service is stored in the instruction pointer register. Hence, the time interruption service is executed.

At the end of the interruption service, the program's execution is resumed by recovering the program's next instruction address from the stack. This process continues during the period the computer is functioning. As the program in execution is interrupted every $0.1ms$ for processing the interruption service, this service is an interesting location to insert a few instructions to check the program's interrupted address. This process is carried out by checking the stack top and recording the interrupted address in memory. For this reason, this measurement strategy is also

---

Algorithm 6 New Main Function - main.c

```
1:  ...
2:  int main(void)
3:  {
4:          double x, y, z;
5:          int a, b, c, d;
6:          int k = 9340;
7:          for(i=0; i< k; i++) {
8:            x = func1(y);
9:            ...
10:           c = func_assembly(a);
11:           ...
12:           d = func2(x,z,a,b);
13:           ...
14:         }
15:         return 0;
16: }
```

---

called *instruction-pointer sampling - ip-sampling(program-counter sampling - pc-sampling*). After that, the interruption service continues its execution. When the service is concluded, the program's execution is resumed by popping up the interrupted address and storing it in the instruction pointer register. When the program execution finishes, the program addresses where the program was interrupted are recorded in memory. Then, these addresses should be verified. Those addresses that belong to address range $3100030H : 3100261H$, should be counted. Let us consider that from $n = 186,800,000$ addresses recorded, $m = 9,340,000$ belong to the address range of the assembly function[4]. Therefore, the ratio between the total number of programs interruptions (due to time service) was

$$\hat{p} = \frac{m}{n} = \frac{9,340,000}{186,800,000} = 0.05.$$

As the execution time of the new version (modified) of the program lasted $T = 18680\,s$, the time estimated within the code portion related to the assembly function is

$$\tilde{T}_{me} = \hat{p} \times T = 0.05 \times 18680\,s = 934\,s.$$

As T_{me} is the time the system spent executing code related to the assembly function considering 9340 program's execution, the time spent in the assembly function code due to one program's execution is estimated by

$$\tilde{T}_e = \frac{\tilde{T}_{me}}{n} = \frac{934}{9340} = 0.1\,ms = 100\,ms.$$

---

[4]Figure 23.9 helps understanding this process since statistical profiling adopts such a technique.

It is worth comparing the point estimate of the event duration, $\tilde{T}_e = 100\,ms$, and the timer interruption period, $T_c = 100\,\mu s$, which constrains the resolution of the direct measurement system, thus not supporting the direct measuring of such a short event.

The confidence interval of the time to execute such a short event may be obtained by applying one of the two methods introduced in Section 6.3 or the approach discussed in Section 6.5. Here, we adopt the method depicted in Section 6.3.2. Using such a method, we calculated the confidence interval for execution time of the *func_assembly()* (the *event* of interest) considering a degree of confidence of $1 - \alpha = 95\%$.

Therefore, we should carry out the following steps:

- First, check if there is no evidence to refute the normal distribution as a suitable approximation to the binomial distribution.

The following steps can accomplish this:

- The procedure must have a fixed number of repetitions ($k = 9340$).

- Repetitions should be independent. We assume they are independent.

- Each repetition should have all results classified into two categories, in this case, **within** or **outside** the assembly function.

- The probabilities (p and q) must remain constant for each repetition. For this program, we assume they are constant. $\hat{p} = 0.05$.

- $n \times \hat{p} \geq 5$ or $n \times \hat{q} \geq 5$, where ($\hat{p} = 1 - \hat{q}$). In this case, we have: $186,800,000 \times 0.05 = 9,340,000 \geq 5$.

Then, execute the next steps:

- Find the critical value, $Z^* \left(Z_{\frac{\alpha}{2}} \right)$. Let us adopt $\alpha = 0.05$. Thus, $Z^* = 1.96$.

- Calculate the error interval, $\varepsilon = Z_{\frac{\alpha}{2}} \times \sqrt{\frac{\hat{p}\hat{q}}{n}}$. For this case, $\hat{p} = 0.05$, $\hat{q} = 0.95$, and $n = 186,800,000$. Therefore, $\varepsilon = 1.96 \times \sqrt{\frac{0.05 \times 0.95}{186,800,000}} = 31.255 \times 10^{-6}\,s$.

- Find $p \in (\hat{p} - \varepsilon, \hat{p} + \varepsilon)$. Thus, $(0.04997, 0.05442)$

- Find $T_e \in ((\hat{p} - \varepsilon) \times \frac{T}{k}, (\hat{p} + \varepsilon) \times \frac{T}{k})$. Hence, $T_e \in (99.97\,ms, 100.03\,ms)$ with 95% of confidence.

The main drawback of this approach is the time required to execute the experiment. In this case, the program's execution time, considering the 9340 iterations, was about $5.19\,h$. However, since we do not have a timer with a resolution that supports the direct measurement of such a short time, and if we afford the time, this is a suitable strategy.

23.6 PROFILING

Profilers are performance evaluation tools designed to analyze measures, such as frequency and duration of functions, procedures, methods, and blocks of code (portions of code) of programs. Besides, they are also adopted to evaluate the portions of code required for utilization of computing resources. Profilers produce program profiles, which can be adopted to determine the time the computer resources spend executing portions of codes of a program. Such information is useful for identifying bottlenecks and portions of the program that are critical for the program's execution performance. Once the critical parts of the program are identified, they can be tuned to improve the system performance.

Profiling methods are generally classified as deterministic or statistical profiling. Deterministic profilers are also known as block counting profilers or event-counting profilers, whereas statistical profilers are also called probabilistic profilers or sampling profilers. The profiler's output could be a statistical summary and streams of recorded events (traces).

23.6.1 DETERMINISTIC PROFILING

One might have the impression that deterministic profilers are better than statistical profilers. However, both classes have their advantages and drawbacks. Deterministic profiling aims at recording all events of interest (basic block[5], procedure, functions, methods); hence the aim is to gather the accurate duration of such events and the intervals between them. For probing the events, the deterministic profilers use hooks. Hooks could be implemented at the operating system level, at the programming language-interpreter level, and as language-specific features. Evaluating the program's performance with this class of profilers requires first instrumenting the program (inserting hooks) - see Figure 23.8 - on the specific parts of the program we are interested in analyzing. Therefore, it is an intrusive strategy since it must change the original program by inserting the hooks; hence changing the original code and its performance. After instrumenting the program, it is compiled, and executed, and a profile is generated and then analyzed.

Indeed, this profiler class is called deterministic because they probe events of interest and provide their exact counting (not the events' delays and durations). Some of these profiles may automatically insert hooks in many program points, which leads to high interference (overhead). Others provide the analysts with support for inserting the hooks where they are interested in probing, which may lead to significantly shorter overhead than the first approach when considering the original program performance. It is also worth mentioning that if the program has many events of interest, the profiler will generate a profile with many records. Furthermore, if these events are short, their execution time could be inaccurate due to overhead from the measurement system itself. Such overhead may not be a concern for small programs, but for large programs, the performance impact may be considerable.

---

[5]A basic block is a code sequence with no branches, except, possibly, at its entry and exit points.

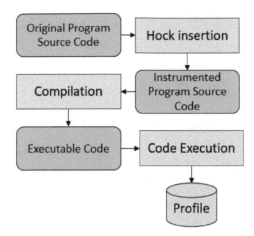

Figure 23.8   Deterministic Profiling.

Python programs can be evaluated through a built-in module called *cProfile* [91, 363]. This module supports deterministic profiling that analyzes how often and how long the program's parts are executed. The *cProfile* module can be invoked by executing the command line

```
> python -m cProfile [-s sort_order] program.py,
```

where *-s sort_order* specifies one of the *sort_stats()* (in red - see Program 7) sort values to sort the output. As a particular example, consider the following Python Program 7.

Executing the command line

```
> python3 -m cProfile -s cumtime fasdow_Cprof.py,
```

a profile is displayed on the standard output. This command-line executes Python 3 with a *cProfile* module for generating a deterministic profile of the Python program *fasdow˙Cprof.py*. The output profile is ordered considering the option *-s cumtime*. This option sorts the functions according to their cumulative time spent in each function and all their subfunctions. The output profile may also be sorted considering the following features:

- *ncalls* - for the number of calls,

- *tottime*- for the total time spent in the given function (and excluding time made in calls to sub-functions),

---

Algorithm 7 fasdow_Cprof.py

```
 1: import time
 2: import pstats
 3: #————————————————————————————————————————
 4: def fast():
 5:         """"""""""
 6:             print("Fast!")
 7: #————————————————————————————————————————
 8: def slow():
 9:         """"""""""
10:             time.sleep(3)
11:             print("Slow!")
12: #————————————————————————————————————————
13: def medium():
14:         """"""""""
15:             time.sleep(0.5)
16:             print("A little slowly...")
17: #————————————————————————————————————————
18: def main():
19:         """"""""""
20:             fast()
21:             slow()
22:             medium()
23: if name__== "_main_" :
24:             main()
```

- *percall* - is the quotient of *tottime* divided by *ncalls*,

- *cumtime* - is the cumulative time spent in this and all subfunctions, and

- *percall* - is the quotient of *cumtime* divided by primitive calls.

A primitive call denotes a function call not induced via recursion. If no output sorting option is defined, the profile is sorted considering the functions' standard names. A portion of the profile obtained is depicted below.

```
        265 function calls (264 primitive calls) in 3.504 seconds
   Ordered by: cumulative time
   ncalls  tottime  percall  cumtime  percall filename:lineno(function)
      2/1    0.000    0.000    3.504    3.504 {built-in method builtins.exec}
        1    0.000    0.000    3.504    3.504 fasdow_Cprof.py:1(<module>)
        1    0.000    0.000    3.504    3.504 fasdow_Cprof.py:21(main)
        2    3.503    1.752    3.503    1.752 {built-in method time.sleep}
        1    0.000    0.000    3.002    3.002 fasdow_Cprof.py:9(slow)
        1    0.000    0.000    0.502    0.502 fasdow_Cprof.py:15(medium)
        1    0.000    0.000    0.001    0.001 <frozen importlib._bootstrap>:
      966(_find_and_load)
            ...               ...              ...
        3    0.000    0.000    0.000    0.000 <frozen importlib._bootstrap_
   external>:34(_relax_case)
        4    0.000    0.000    0.000    0.000 {built-in method _imp.release_
```

```
lock}
1     0.000     0.000     0.000     0.000 <frozen importlib._bootstrap
>:310(__init__)
```

The first line shows that 265 calls were monitored. Of those calls, 264 were primitive calls. The program execution time was 3.504 s, considering a resolution of three decimal places. The next line informs that the next lines were ordered by their cumulative time (*cumtime*). It is worth noting that function *slow* took 3.002 s and function *medium* took 0.502 s. When there are two numbers in the first column (for example, 2/1), the function is recursed. The second value is the number of primitive calls, and the first is the total number of calls. When the function is not recursive, these two values are the same, and only one number is shown.

The *memory profiler* Python module gives support to program memory usage deterministic profiling. The most basic way to use it is with a decorator named *@profile* (a hook), which is added to the original Python code. Each decorator should be included before the definition of each Python function. When the command-line

```
> python -m memory_profiler program.py,
```

a memory profile related to the program *program.py* is generated on the standard output, which could be redirected to the file. As an example, consider the Program 8. The original program was modified by including decorators *@profile* (in red) before each user-function definition.

Executing the command-line

```
> python -m memory_profiler mempro.py
```

a profile is generated on the standard output. The profile obtained looks like the report below.

Memory Usage Profile - Function *load_1GB_of_data()*

```
Filename: mempro.py

Line #    Mem usage    Increment    Line Contents
================================================
    3   22.871 MiB   22.871 MiB    @profile(precision=4)
    4                              def load_1GB_of_data():
    5 1046.738 MiB 1023.867 MiB     return np.ones((2 ** 30), dtype=np.uint8)
```

Memory Usage Profile - Function *process_data()*

```
Filename: mempro.py

Line #    Mem usage    Increment    Line Contents
================================================
    7   22.871 MiB   22.871 MiB    @profile(precision=4)
    8                              def process_data():
    9 1046.738 MiB 1046.738 MiB     data = load_1GB_of_data()
   10 1046.875 MiB 1046.875 MiB     return modify(data)
```

Algorithm 8 Program *mempro.py*

```
1: import numpy as np
2: @profile(precision=4)
3: def load_1GB_of_data():
4:         return np.ones((2 ** 30), dtype=np.uint8)
5: @profile(precision=4)
6: def process_data():
7:         data = load_1GB_of_data()
8:         return modify(data)
9: @profile(precision=4)
10: def modify(data):
11:        return data * 2 +10
12: @profile(precision=4)
13: def mem():
14:        n = 100000
15:        a = [i for i in range(n)]
16:        b = [i for i in range(n)]
17:        c = list(range(n))
18:        d = list(range(n))
19:        e = dict.fromkeys(a, b)
20:        f = dict.fromkeys(c, d)
21: @profile(precision=4)
22: def main():
23:        mem()
24:        process_data()
25: if _name_== "_main_" :
26:        main()
```

Memory Usage Profile - Function *modify(data)*

```
Filename: mempro.py

Line #     Mem usage      Increment    Line Contents
================================================
    12 1046.738 MiB 1046.738 MiB    @profile(precision=4)
    13                              def modify(data):
    14 1046.875 MiB    0.137 MiB     return data * 2 +10
```

Memory Usage Profile - Function *mem()*

```
Filename: mempro.py

Line #     Mem usage      Increment    Line Contents
================================================
    16    20.934 MiB    20.934 MiB    @profile(precision=4)
    17                                def mem():
    18    20.934 MiB     0.000 MiB     n = 100000
    19    23.578 MiB     0.926 MiB     a = [i for i in range(n)]
    20    25.672 MiB     0.258 MiB     b = [i for i in range(n)]
    21    27.473 MiB     1.801 MiB     c = list(range(n))
    22    29.535 MiB     2.062 MiB     d = list(range(n))
    23    32.523 MiB     2.988 MiB     e = dict.fromkeys(a, b)
    24    35.527 MiB     3.004 MiB     f = dict.fromkeys(c, d)
```

Memory Usage Profile - Function *main()*

```
Filename: mempro.py

Line #    Mem usage      Increment    Line Contents
==================================================
    26   20.934 MiB    20.934 MiB    @profile(precision=4)
    27                               def main():
    28   22.871 MiB    22.871 MiB     mem()
    29 1046.875 MiB  1046.875 MiB     process_data()
```

For each decorated function, memory usage information is given for each function's command. Hence, in this particular case, memory consumption information for each command line is provided since we included decorators before the definition of functions *load_1GB_of_data()* (line 2), *process_data()* (line 5), *modify()* (line 9), *mem()* (line 12), and *main()* (line 21). The increment columns show the amount of memory each command of each function consumes. Looking at line 28, we see that function *mem()* increments 22.871 *MiB*[210] in memory usage, whereas *process_data()* adds 1046.875 *MiB*. The function *process_data()* memory usage is detailed from line 7 to 10. In line 9, we have the function call *load_1GB_of_data()*. It is worth noting the memory increment due to this function: 1023.867 *MiB*. The function call *modify(data)* increments only 0.137 *MiB*. Each command of function *mem()* increments the memory usage by the values on the increment column of the profile portion related to function *mem()*. The commands of lines 21, 22, 23, and 24 increment *1.801 MiB*, *2.062 MiB*, *2.988 MiB*, and *3.004 MiB*, respectively.

23.6.2 STATISTICAL PROFILING

The classical statistical profiling (also called sampling profiling) does not use hooks to probe events of a program as the deterministic profilers do. Instead, the program under analysis is compiled with the profiling option turned on, and the executable code is generated with a memory map of variables and labels defined on the program (see the top of Figure 23.9). Besides, a profiling module is attached to the program to check the addresses stored on the stack top (see the bottom center of Figure 23.9 in red). After compiling the source code (the program under analysis) and generating the executable code with the memory map, the executable code may be executed. During the code execution, the timer interruption interrupts the process related to the program under analysis periodically according to the time-frequency (f_s) defined for the time interruption. When the executable code is interrupted by the time interruption, the address of the executable code's next instruction is stored on the stack top (see the stack top in Figure 23.9 addressed by the stack pointer (SP)), and the time interruption service is executed (see bottom right of Figure 23.9). The instruction pointer (IP) is changed to address the first instruction of time interruption service. Inside the time interruption service, a call is executed to the profiling module (see

---

[6]The kibibyte (*KiB*) is a multiple of the unit byte. The kibibyte was conceived to replace the kilobyte since the interpretation of kilobyte to denote 1024 bytes conflicts with the International System of Units (SI) definition of the prefix kilo (1000). Likewise, mebibyte (*MiB*) replaces the megabyte (*MB*).

the upper right side of Figure 23.9); this is performed, by storing the next instruction address on the stack top, which decrements *SP* and changes the content of the *IP* to address the first instruction of profiling module.

The profiling module execution checks (see the line in red of the profiling module) the stack top and obtains the address of the next instruction to be executed (depicted red on the stack shown on the bottom center of Figure 23.9)[7] of the program under analysis. This process continues until the analyzed program finishes. After this process, the profiling module summarizes the set of samples obtained, which shows the address where the program under analysis was interrupted. Taking these addresses and the memory map shows the memory range addresses of functions, methods, or blocks of code and variables and generates a report stating if addresses of functions, methods, or blocks of code were visited during the program's execution.

Assuming the program under analysis has taken T as its execution time, and considering the sampling frequency ($f_s = 1/T_I$), where T_I is the time between time interruptions, we obtain the number of samples collected, $n_s = T/T_I$, during the process execution. Considering that the number of addresses sampled that belong to a function $f()$ address range is m, hence the time spent executing within the function $f()$ during the program's execution under analysis may be estimated by

$$T_f = \frac{m}{n_s} \times T. \tag{23.6.1}$$

Such a process is performed for every piece of code of interest (blocks, function, methods), considering the granularity adopted by the profiler.

The GNU Compiler Collection package[8] (*gcc* package) has a tool named *gprof* that supports profiling program codes written in C and C++, among other languages. The profiling method adopted by the *gcc* compiler and *gprof* is based on a statistical profiling strategy as well as the insertion of tiny pieces of extra code (hooks) into the beginning of each C function of the program under evaluation.

The main steps for profiling a C program written in two (or more) distinct files (*program.c* and *other_module.c*) with *gcc* and *gprof* are:

1. Compile the C program with profiling switch enabled:

```
>   gcc -Wall -pg program.c other_module.c -o
                                program -lm
```

---

[7]This figure is also useful for describing the process shown in Section 23.5.
[8]https://gcc.gnu.org/

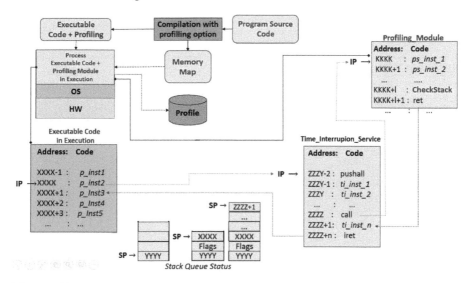

Figure 23.9   Statistical Profiling – Overview.

2. Run the respective program's executable code to generate profiling data (*gmon.out*):

```
>   program
```

3. Execute the *gprof* tool considering the profiling data file ((*gmon.out*)) to analyze and display the profiling information (*program_analysis.txt*):

```
>   gprof -b program gmon.out > program_analysis.txt
```

Before detailing the process above, let us consider a C program as an example to illustrate profiling using *gcc* and *gprof*. The aim of this program is only to *exercise* the computer functionalities, which demand time to carry out the respective functions. The source code is composed of two separate files depicted in the Program List 9 and 10.

The analysis result provided by *gprof* is divided into two parts, namely a *flat profile* and a *call graph*. The *flat profile* informs the time the program spent in each of its functions (itself and in it considering its children) and the percentage of the time spent in each function, taking into account the total program execution time.

Algorithm 9 Program *prog_m.c*

```c
 1: #include <stdio.h>
 2: #include <math.h>
 3: double new_func1(double x);
 4:
 5: double func1(double x)
 6: {
 7:         double b[10000];
 8:         int i = 0;
 9:         printf("\n Inside func1 \n");
10:         for(i=0;i<10000;i++) {
11:           b[i] = i*pow(x,3);
12:           x = x + b[i];
13:         }
14:         x = new_func1(x);
15:         return x;
16: }
17: static double func2(double x)
18: {
19:         double c[10000];
20:         double d;
21:         int i = 0;
22:         printf("\n Inside func2 \n");
23:         for(i=0;i<6000;i++){
24:           c[i] = i*sqrt(x);
25:           x = x + c[i];
26:         }
27:         d = new_func1(x);
28:         return d;
29: }
30: int main(void)
31: {
32:         int i = 0, j = 0;
33:         double x[15000];
34:         double z[5000];
35:         printf("\n Inside main()\n");
36:         for(i=0;i<5000;i++) {
37:           x[j] = 3*sqrt(i);
38:           j++;
39:           x[j] = func1(x[j-1]);
40:           j++;
41:           x[j] = func2(x[j-1]);
42:           z[i] = x[j-2]*x[j-1];
43:           j++;
44:         }
45:         for(i=0;i<5000;i++)
46:           z[i] = z[i] * z[i];
47:         return 0;
48: }
```

Algorithm 10 Program *prog.c*

```
 1: #include <stdio.h>
 2: #include <math.h>
 3: double new_func1(double x)
 4: {
 5:          int i = 0;
 6:          double a[20000];
 7:          printf("\n Inside func1 \n");
 8:          for(i=0;i<20000;i++) {
 9:             a[i] = i*sin(x);
10:             x = x + a[i];
11:          }
12:          return x;
13: }
```

More specifically, the *flat profile* has the following fields:

- *% time* is the percentage of the total execution time the program spent in this function. These should all add up to 100%.

- *cumulative seconds* is the cumulative total number of seconds the computer spent executing this function, plus the time spent in all the functions above this one in this table.

- *self seconds* is the number of seconds accounted for by this function alone. The flat profile listing is sorted first by this number.

- *calls* is the total number of times the function was called. If the function was never called, or the number of times it was called cannot be determined, the calls field is blank.

- *self ms/call* represents the average number of milliseconds spent in this function per call if this function is profiled.

- *total ms/call* represents the average number of milliseconds spent in this function and its children per call, if the function could not be profiled.

- *name* is the name of the function.

Before the column headers, a statement is shown indicating the sampling period (T_s). A time estimate (T_e) that is not much larger than the sampling period is not reliable since $ns = T_e/T_s$ is small (*ns* is the number of samples).

The call graph shows the time spent in each function and its children. It also displays, for each function, its function's callers, which functions are called by it, and how many times. There is also an estimate of the time spent in the children's functions of each function. Hence, such data can suggest places where we might optimize the code.

The lines full of dashes divide the data into entries, where each entry represents each function. Each entry has one or more lines. In each entry, the primary line is the one that starts with an index number in square brackets. At the end of this line, the function assigned to this entry is depicted. The preceding lines of the primary line of the entry describe the callers of this function. The following lines of the primary line of the entry describe its children's functions. The entries are sorted by time spent in the function and its children's functions.

For profiling the C program depicted in Program List 9 and 10, execute the command

```
> gcc -Wall -pg cf1.c cf1_n.c -o cf1 -lm
```

After that, run the executable code to generate the profile *gmon.out*. Then, execute the *gprof* to analyze the file *gmon.out* and display the profiling information on the file *program_analysis.txt*.

```
> gprof -b cf1 gmon.out > cf1_analysis.txt
```

The *flat profile* obtained for the program was

Flat Profile

```
Flat profile:

Each sample counts as 0.01 seconds.
  %   cumulative   self              self     total
 time   seconds   seconds    calls  ms/call  ms/call  name
73.24    75.30     75.30     10000    7.53     7.53    new_func1
15.95    91.70     16.40      5000    3.28    10.81    func1
10.80   102.80     11.10      5000    2.22     9.75    func2
 0.01   102.81      0.01                                main
```

The first information we obtain from the profile is the sampling period, $T_s = 0.01\,s$, where the profile states, "Each sample counts as 0.01 seconds.". Then, we have information related to each profiled function according to the fields described above. In this particular case, the function new_func1 is responsible for 73.24 % of the execution time of the whole program. The time spent only on this function was 75.30 s. It is worth mentioning that the sampling period is much shorter than the time spent executing the function ($0.01\,s \ll 75.30\,s$), which suggests 75.30 s as a reliable estimate. We also see that function new_func1 was called 10000 times during the program execution, and the mean time spent by executing this function per call was 7.53 ms.

The second most demanding function was $func1$, which was responsible for 15.95 % of the program's execution time, which demanded 16.40 s in its execution without considering its children functions. The time demanded by this function and its children's functions adds up to 91.70 s. This function was called 5000 times during the program execution, and the mean time spent by executing *func1* per call was 3.28 *ms*. Likewise, the *func2* function was the third most demanding function and was responsible for 10.80 % of the program's execution time. This function demanded 11.10 *s* in its execution without considering its children's functions. The function *func2* was called 5000 times during the program execution, and the mean time spent by this function per call was 2.22 *ms*. The program's execution time estimate was 102.81 *s* and is obtained from the column *cumulative* of line *main*.

The second part of the profile is the *call graph*. As already mentioned, the call graph depicts the time spent in each function and its children. Moreover, *call graph* also displays the callers of each function, the function called be each function, and the number of function's calls. Moreover, an estimate of the time spent in the children's functions of each function is also provided.

Call Graph Profile

```
Call graph

granularity: each sample hit covers 4 byte(s) for 0.01%
of 102.81 seconds

index % time    self  children    called     name
                                                     <spontaneous>
[1]     100.0   0.01  102.80                 main [1]
                16.40  37.65    5000/5000         func1 [3]
                11.10  37.65    5000/5000         func2 [4]
-----------------------------------------------------
                37.65   0.00    5000/10000        func1 [3]
                37.65   0.00    5000/10000        func2 [4]
[2]      73.2  75.30   0.00    10000        new_func1 [2]
-----------------------------------------------------
                16.40  37.65    5000/5000         main [1]
[3]      52.6  16.40  37.65    5000         func1 [3]
                37.65   0.00    5000/10000          new_func1 [2]
-----------------------------------------------------
                11.10  37.65    5000/5000         main [1]
[4]      47.4  11.10  37.65    5000         func2 [4]
                37.65   0.00    5000/10000          new_func1 [2]
-----------------------------------------------------

Index by function name

    [3] func1                    [1] main
    [4] func2                    [2] new_func1
```

The first entry of the *call graph* is [1], which is related to function *main*. The previous line shows that is not called by any other function (see the keyword "spontaneous"). The function *main* calls *func1* and *func2*. This is shown in the two subsequent lines of the primary line. The time spent in the main function itself denoted to the execution of the function *func1* was 16.40 *s*. Similarly, the time spent in the main function itself related to the execution of the function *func2* was 11.10 *s*. The time spent when executing each of these children's function was equal to 37.65 s for *func1* and *func2*, respectively. Adding up 16.40 s, 11.10 s, and 2 × 37.65 s totals 102.80, which was the program execution time estimate.

The second entry of the *call graph* is [2]. This entry focuses on function *new_func1*. The preceding lines of the primary line of this entry inform the functions that call *new_func1*. Therefore, we have *func1* and *func2*. The time spent executing *new_func1* due to function *func1* calls were 37.65 s. Likewise, the time spent executing *new_func1* due to function *func2* calls was also 37.65 s. Hence, summing them up, we obtain 75.30 s. The time spent by function *new_func1* children's functions was null. Indeed, function *new_func1* has no child function. Function *func1* calls function *new_func1* 5000 times of a total of 10000 calls. Similarly, function *func2* calls function *new_func1* 5000 of a total of 10000. Hence, no other function than *func1* and *func2* calls *new_func1*.

The third entry of the *call graph* is [3], which analyzes function *func1*. Function *func1* is called only by the *main* function. The time spent executing function *func1* itself was 16.40 s, and the time spent executing its children's functions was 37.65 s. Function *func1* was called 5000 times and also called function *new_func1* 5000 times. As we already seen, function *new_func1* is called 10000 times.

The last entry of the *call graph* is [4], which analyzes function *func2*. Function *func2* is also called only by the *main* function, and the time spent executing function *func2* itself was 11.10 s and the time spent executing its children functions was 37.65 s. Function *func2* was called 5000 times and also called function *new_func1* 5000 times.

23.7 COUNTERS AND BASIC PERFORMANCE TOOLS IN LINUX

The aim of this section is not to reference Linux counters and performance monitoring tools. Instead, the goal is to introduce some features and point out specific references more in-depth. The operating systems (OS) documentation is the best source to find out how you can collect performance metrics through its performance counters [443, 470]. The system performance measures are accessible to programmers via *system call services* (**syscalls** - , mostly using **Int 80h** for Intel-based Unix system), whose services are implemented in the Linux kernel [51, 113, 141, 306, 382, 397, 422]. When a program makes a system call, the arguments are handed to the kernel, which takes over the program's execution until the respective system call service finishes.

Linux provides a virtual filesystem **/proc**, also called a pseudo-filesystem, which contains a rich source of information about the hardware, kernel, and processes running on the system. It appears to the user as a common filesystem such as / or /home. The /proc virtual filesystem can be used with well-known Linux commands and tools such as *cat, more, grep, open, read, write, awk, printf, echo, cron* that can also be used in monitoring scripts.

The various entries in the */proc* virtual file system are described extensively in the */proc* man page five, which is obtained by executing *"man 5 proc"*. Below, we provide some useful entries of the content available in the */proc* virtual filesystem and briefly introduces some basic Linux monitoring tools.

23.7.1   SYSTEM INFORMATION

This section presents some important basic Linux monitoring tools. The monitoring tools usually get information from entries available in the virtual filesystem */proc*. This virtual filesystem may be regarded as an information and control center for the Linux kernel, and many monitoring and configuring utilities call files in */proc*. Some useful entries contained in */proc* are depicted below, and some of them are detailed further.

- ***/proc/sys/kernel/domainname*** holds the domain name.

- ***/proc/sys/kernel/hostname*** contains the computer's host name.

- ***/proc/cpuinfo*** carries data specifying processors and system architecture.

- ***/proc/meminfo*** holds statistics on memory usage.

- ***/proc/ostype*** contains the OS type.

- ***/proc/version*** carries the Linux kernel version number.

- ***/proc/osrelease*** holds the kernel Linux version revision.

- ***/proc/stat*** contains processors and memory usage information.

- ***/proc/loadavg*** holds information about the system load.

- ***/proc/uptime*** carries the idle duration since the boot.

- ***/proc/devices*** contains the character and block devices currently configured.

- ***/proc/diskstat*** holds the I/O statistics of block devices.

- ***/proc/iomem*** holds the current map of the system's memory for each physical device.

- ***/proc/ioports*** contains a list of currently registered ports used for input or output communication with a device.

Executing the command *"cat /proc/entry"* provides the respective content of the *entry*. Below, we display the content of ***/proc/cpuinfo*** and ***/proc/meminfo*** entries as examples.

Entry /proc/cpuinfo

The entry */proc/cpuinfo* provides a collection of data specifying the processors and system architecture dependent items. Two common entries are processor, which gives the processor number, and BogoMips[9], a system constant that is calculated during kernel initialization. Below we have a chunk of data provided through this entry.

```
processor : 0
vendor_id : GenuineIntel
cpu family : 6
model : 142
model name : Intel(R) Core(TM) i5-7200U CPU @ 2.50GHz
stepping : 9
microcode : 0x8e
cpu MHz : 2712.004
cache size : 3072 KB
...
bogomips : 5424.00
clflush size : 64
cache_alignment : 64
address sizes : 43 bits physical, 48 bits virtual
```

Entry /proc/meminfo

The entry */proc/meminfo* file reports statistics about the system's memory usage. The content provided, though, may slightly differ between different Linux systems. Below we have a portion of the data content commonly provided through this entry.

```
MemTotal:        2061512 kB
MemFree:          283080 kB
MemAvailable:     619608 kB
Buffers:           35512 kB
Cached:           506112 kB
SwapCached:         4512 kB
...
```

Command uname

The command **uname -a** also provides the kernel name, network host name, Linux kernel version number and its release, release date, hardware name, processor type, hardware platform, and operating system name.

Command top

The **top** command provides a dynamic view system. When the *top* command is executed, a report divided into two parts is dynamically generated. The first part

---

[9]BogoMips is a crude measurement of a processor's throughput calculated by the Linux kernel during its boot.

displays statistics on processes and resource usage, and the second part shows a list of running processes. If "*top*" is executed, the first part of the report is similar to the one in the screenshot below.

```
top - 12:58:59 up  8:02,  1 user,   load average: 0.01, 0.05, 0.01
Tasks: 228 total,   2 running, 226 sleeping,   0 stopped,   0 zombie
%Cpu(s):  0.7 us,   0.7 sy,   0.0 ni, 98.7 id,   0.0 wa,   0.0 hi,  0.0 si,  0.0 st
KiB Mem :  2061512 total,   734456 free,   701080 used,   625976 buff/cache
KiB Swap:   998396 total,   998396 free,        0 used.  1095772 avail Mem
```

At the top left of the screen, top displays the current time (12:58:59) in the format *hh* : *mm* : *ss*, followed by the system uptime expressed in a number of days, hours and minutes, which tells us the time the system has been running. In this specific case, the system has been running only for eight minutes and two seconds. Next comes the number of active user sessions. In this example, there is only one active user session. Finally, the average load over-represents the processors' utilization over the last minute, the last five minutes, and the last fifteen minutes, respectively. In this example, over the last one minute, the processors' utilization was 1% on average. Similarly, over the last five minutes, the processors' utilization was 5% on average. Likewise, over the last fifteen minutes, the processors' utilization was 1% on average.

For multiple processors or multi-core computers, a word of caution is required. If one has a load average of 1 on a single-processor (or single-core) computer, this means your processor (core) had utilization of 100% over the period. If one has a load average of 2 on a single-processor computer, this means the computer was overloaded by 100% over the entire period, that is (100% + 100 %). On a computer with two processors, a load average of 2 denotes the two processors were 100% in use each. Finally, on a system with four processors, a load average of 2 means that each processor has utilization of 50% over the entire period.

The second line shows the tasks' statistics regarding the processes running on a system. The "total" value is simply the total number of processes. For example, in the above screenshot, there are 228 processes, where 2 are *running* and 226 are *sleeping*. The third line has the processor's utilization details, where

- *us*, user : time running unniced user processes.

- *sy*, system : time running kernel processes.

- *ni*, nice : time running niced user processes.

- *id*, idle : time spent in the kernel idle handler.

- *wa*, IO-wait : time waiting for I/O completion.

- *hi* : time spent servicing hardware interruptions.

- *st* : time stolen from this vm by the hypervisor.

In this particular case, the processor is 98.7% idle (*id*). The processor's utilization percentage is obtained by adding up the user (*us*), system (*sy*), niced processes (*ni*), hardware interrupts (*hi*), and software interrupts (*si*). The *iowait* processes time (*wa*) and the stolen time (*st*) are not considered since they are waiting rather than being serviced.

As a default, the fourth line reflects physical memory, which is classified as: *total*, *free*, *used* and *buff/cache*. Likewise, the fifth line depicts the virtual memory[10], which is also classified as: *total*, *free* and *used*. The *avail* number on the fifth line is an estimation of physical memory available without swapping. This information is expressed in kibibytes (KiB) through exbibytes (EiB)[11] depending on the scaling factor.

Command *free*

The command *free* uses the */proc/meminfo* file to report the amount of free and used memory (both RAM and swap space on the system) as well as buffers used by the kernel. The command "*free*" with option *-m* presents the memory data in megabytes, such as

```
          total       used       free     shared  buff/cache   available
Mem:       2013       1173        241         25         598         570
Swap:       974         61        913
```

The first row would seem to say that this system has 2013 MB of total memory, 1173 MB used, and thus 241 MB free. This is because the Linux memory management system stores metadata recently accessed areas of the disk in buffers. Examples of metadata are permissions and the contents of a directory. Likewise, caches store recently accessed files. As these areas store transient content, they are considered available for use.

- *total* - The total amount of memory that can be used by the applications.

- *used* - Used memory, which is $used = total - free - buffers - cache$

- *free* - Unused memory.

- *buff/cache* - The combined memory used by buffers and cache.

- *available* - An estimate of the amount of memory available for new applications, without swapping.

---

[10]RAM (Random Access Memory) plus swap space is referred to as virtual memory. In Linux, the swap space is a disk area that copies RA pages when RAM fills up, and more space is required.

[11]The exbibyte (symbol EiB) is 2^{60} bytes. The exbibyte is approximately equal to 1.15 exabytes (EB).

Command *ipcs*

Each process running on the Linux system has its private memory area. One process is not allowed to access another process's memory. Besides, no user-level processes have access to memory used by the kernel processes. Linux, however, in order to support data sharing between processes, creates shared memory segments. Multiple processes can read and write to a common shared memory area. The Linux kernel manages the shared memory. The *ipcs* command provides a view of the shared memory segments on the system [51]. Below a chunk of data is provided by "*ipcs -m*". The *key* value is used to enable other users to gain access to the shared memory segment.

```
------ Shared Memory Segments --------
key         shmid      owner     perms    bytes      nattch    status
0x00000000  327680     prmm      600      4194304    2         dest
0x00000000  229377     prmm      600      524288     2         dest
0x00000000  4030466    prmm      600      1716224    2         dest
0x00000000  3997700    prmm      600      1716224    2         dest
0x00000000  7962629    prmm      600      278528     2         dest
0x00000000  4128774    prmm      600      385024     2         dest
0x00000000  4194311    prmm      600      118784     2         dest
0x00000000  4227080    prmm      600      385024     2         dest
0x00000000  7995401    prmm      600      278528     2         dest
0x00000000  4325386    prmm      600      118784     2         dest
0x00000000  7503884    prmm      600      4194304    2         dest
0x00000000  8093709    prmm      600      36864      2         dest
0x00000000  8126478    prmm      600      36864      2         dest
0x00000000  8257551    prmm      600      28672      2         dest
0x00000000  8290320    prmm      600      630784     2         dest
0x00000000  8224785    prmm      600      28672      2         dest
0x00000000  8323090    prmm      600      630784     2         dest
0x00000000  8355859    prmm      600      413696     2         dest
0x00000000  8388628    prmm      600      413696     2         dest
```

Execute "*man ipcs*" to see other options and the respective contents provided.

Command *vmstat*

The command name *vmstat* comes from "virtual memory statistics". However, this utility also provides other information. Besides reporting virtual memory statistics, *vmstat* presents kernel statistics about processes, block IO, disk, trap, and processor activity. The basic syntax of this command is *vmstat [options] [delay] [count]*, where

- *delay* is the delay between updates in seconds. If no delay is specified, only one report is printed with the average values since boot.

- *count* is the number of updates. In the absence of count, when a delay is defined, the default is infinite.

- *-a* - Displays active and inactive memory.

- *-f* - Displays the number of forks since boot. This is equivalent to the total number of tasks created. This display does not repeat.

- *-n* - Displays the header only once rather than periodically.

- *-s* - Displays a table of various event counters and memory statistics. This display does not repeat.

- *-d* - Reports disk statistics.

- *-D* - Reports some summary statistics about disk activity.

- *-p* - Displays detailed statistics about partition.

- *-S* - Switches outputs between 1000 (k), 1024 (K), 1000000 (m), or 1048576 (M) bytes. Note that this does not change the block (bi/bo) fields, always measured in blocks.

- *-t* - Appends *timestamp* to each line.

- *-w* - Displays wide output mode. The output is wider than 80 characters per line.

- *-V* - Displays version information.

- *-h* - Displays help.

As an example, consider executing "***vmstat -t 5 6***". *vmstat* is executed six (*count* = 6) times, the delay between samples is five seconds (*delay* = 5 s), and *-t* includes the time instant of each sample was collected. Below, an example of the output obtained is presented.

procs		memory				swap		io		system		cpu					timestamp
r	b	swpd	free	buff	cache	si	so	bi	bo	in	cs	us	sy	id	wa	st	
2	0	100600	281400	53520	523548	0	1	21	17	80	358	2	1	97	0	0	2020-05-05 15:33:12
1	0	100600	280896	53528	523548	0	0	0	10	88	472	1	1	98	0	0	2020-05-05 15:33:17
0	0	100600	280860	53536	523548	0	0	0	11	79	411	1	0	98	0	0	2020-05-05 15:33:22
0	0	100600	280648	53536	523548	0	0	0	15	71	410	1	0	99	0	0	2020-05-05 15:33:27
0	0	100600	280656	53544	523556	0	0	0	9	81	422	1	0	99	0	0	2020-05-05 15:33:32
0	0	100600	280688	53552	523556	0	0	0	15	80	406	1	1	99	0	0	2020-05-05 15:33:37

The *vmstat* output is divided into five sections: *procs*, *memory*, *swap*, *io*, *system*, and *cpu*. The *cpu* section has the following identifications:

- *r* - The number of processes in a wait state.

- *b* - The number of processes that were in sleep mode.

- *w* - The number of processes that have been swapped out by memory management and virtual memory subsystems and have yet to run.

The *memory* section has the following identifications:

- *swpd* - The total amount of physical virtual memory in use.
- *free* - The amount of free physical memory.
- *buff* - Memory that was being buffered when the measurement was taken.
- *cache* - Cache that is in use.

The *swap* section has the following identifications:

- *si* - Amount of memory transferred from swap space back into memory.
- *so* - Amount of memory swapped to disk.

The *io* section identifies *bi* disk blocks sent to disk devices in blocks per second. The *system* section has the following identifications:

- *in* - Displays the interrupts per second, including the CPU clocks.
- *cs* - Displays the number of context switches per second within the kernel.

The *cpu* section has the following identifications:

- *us* - Percentage of processor cycles spent on user processes.
- *sy* - Percentage of processor cycles spent on system processes.
- *id* - Percentage of unused processor cycles or idle time.

Entry */proc/loadavg*

The */proc/loadavg* file contains information about the system load. The first three numbers represent the number of active processes running on the system averaged over the last one, five, and fifteen minutes. The fourth entry shows the current number of scheduled processes and the total number of processes on the system. The final is the process ID of the process that most recently ran. Executing "*cat /proc/loadavg*", the following output is obtained as an example.

```
0.09 0.07 0.02 4/580 18347
```

Entry */proc/uptime* and Command *uptime*

The */proc/uptime* file contains the time duration since the system was booted, and the respective idle duration since the boot. Hence, the command "*cat /proc/uptime*" displays an output such as

```
98450.54 95394.98
```

The **uptime** command also can obtain the system's uptime. The *uptime* command also displays the load averages found in */proc/loadavg*. More precisely, *uptime* displays the current time, the time the system has been running, how many users are currently logged on, and the system load averages for the past one, five, and fifteen minutes. Thus, for example, executing the command "***uptime***" displays

```
22:20:35 up 1 day,  3:29,  1 user,  load average: 0.00, 0.05, 0.03
```

Command *iostat*

The *iostat* command generates processors, input/output devices, and partitions utilization statistics reports. Before discussing more details related to *iostat*, it is worth a word on the processor's states. A processor can be in one of four states, *user*, *sys*, *idle*, or *iowait*. Tools such as *iostat* provide the statistics based on the processor's counters the kernel periodically updates at 10 ms intervals. The kernel verifies if the processor is idle or not. If the processor is not idle, the kernel verifies if the executed instruction is in user or kernel space. If the instruction is in user space, the *user* counter is incremented by one. If the instruction is in kernel space, then the *sys* counter is incremented by one.

On the other hand, if the CPU is idle, the kernel verifies if there is at least one I/O disk in progress. If there is, then the *iowait* counter is incremented by one. If no I/O is in progress that was initiated from that processor, the *idle* counter is incremented by one. When a performance tool, such as *iostat*, is executed, it reads the current values from these four counters. Then, it (the process that represents the tool) sleeps for the specified delay (the user specifies the time interval) then rereads the counters. After that, the tool subtracts the previous values from the current values of counters to obtain the counters' variation during this sampling period. As *iostat* is aware that the counters are incremented at a fixed time interval (10 ms), it divides the difference (variation value) of each counter by the number increments in the sampling period. The basic syntax of this command is *iostat [options] [delay] [count]*, where *[delay]* and *[count]* have the same meaning as shown for *vmstat*, and the main options are

- *-c* - Displays the processor utilization report.

- *-d* - Displays the device utilization report.

- *-dec* = −0 | 1 | 2 ″ - Specifies the number of decimal places.

- *-g group_name* – device [...] | ALL ″ - Displays statistics for a group of devices.

- *-H* - This option must be used with option *-g* and indicates that only global statistics for the group are to be displayed.

- *-h* - Provides a utilization report easier to read by a human.

- *-k* - Displays statistics in kilobytes per second.

- *-m* - Displays statistics in megabytes per second.

- *-p* - This option displays statistics for block devices and all their partitions that are used by the system.

- *-s* - Displays a short version of the report that should fit in 80 characters wide screens.

- *-t* - Prints the time for each report displayed.

- *-V* - Prints version number.

- *-x* - Displays extended statistics.

- *-y* - Omits first report with statistics since system boot.

- *-z* - Omits output for any devices for which there was no activity.

The processor report displays the processor header row followed by a row of processor statistics. On multiprocessor systems, processors' statistics are calculated and averaged among all processors. The report has the following format:

- *% user* - Displays the percentage of processor utilization while executing at the user level (application).

- *% nice* - Displays the percentage of processor utilization while executing at the user level with nice priority.

- *% system* - Displays the percentage of processor utilization while executing at the system level (kernel).

- *% iowait* - Displays the percentage of time that the processor (or processors) were idle due to a disk I/O requests.

- *% steal* - Displays the percentage of time spent in involuntary wait by the virtual processor (or processors) while the hypervisor was servicing another virtual processor.

- *% idle* - Displays the percentage of time that the processor (or processors) was idle, and there is no disk I/O request initiated from that processor.

For instance, if this command "*iostat -t 5 3*" is executed, the following data is displayed. This command states that the utility *iostat* should be executed three times; the interval between each execution is five seconds, and *-t* states that the current time each sample is obtained should also be displayed (this is similar to what we have seen for *vmstat*). The first two of each sample summary consist of the system identification, data, and time the sample was collected. The third and the fourth lines of each sample summary displayed is a processor report. It is important to highlight that the first report generated by the *iostat* command provides statistics concerning the time since the system was booted unless the -*y* option is used. The next lines display the input/output device utilization report.

```
Linux 4.4.0-142-generic (ubuntu) 05/06/2020 _i686_ (1 CPU)
05/06/2020 09:39:38 PM
avg-cpu:  %user   %nice %system %iowait  %steal   %idle
           1.87    0.01    0.67    0.15    0.00   97.30
Device:            tps    kB_read/s    kB_wrtn/s    kB_read    kB_wrtn
loop0             0.00         0.00         0.00         56          0
sda               1.45        16.60        18.92    1841043    2098640
05/06/2020 09:39:43 PM
avg-cpu:  %user   %nice %system %iowait  %steal   %idle
           1.21    0.00    0.61    0.00    0.00   98.18
Device:            tps    kB_read/s    kB_wrtn/s    kB_read    kB_wrtn
loop0             0.00         0.00         0.00          0          0
sda               0.00         0.00         0.00          0          0
05/06/2020 09:39:48 PM
avg-cpu:  %user   %nice %system %iowait  %steal   %idle
           0.81    0.00    0.81    0.00    0.00   98.38
Device:            tps    kB_read/s    kB_wrtn/s    kB_read    kB_wrtn
loop0             0.00         0.00         0.00          0          0
sda               0.41         0.00         2.43          0         12
```

The input/output device utilization report provides statistics on a per physical device or partition. Block devices and partitions may be entered on the command line. If none is specified, the statistics for every device are displayed. Transfer rates are depicted in 1K blocks (default) for 512-byte blocks. The input/output device report displays the header row followed by a row of input/output device statistics. The report may show the following items, depending on the options adopted:

- *tps*
- *Blk_read/s* (kB_read/s, MB_read/s)
- *Blk_wrtn/s* (kB_wrtn/s, MB_wrtn/s)
- *Blk_dscd/s* (kB_dscd/s, MB_dscd/s)
- *Blk_read* (kB_read, MB_read)
- *Blk_wrtn* (kB_wrtn, MB_wrtn)
- *Blk_dscd* (kB_dscd, MB_dscd)
- *r/s*
- *w/s*

- *d/s*
- *f/s*
- *sec/s* (kB/s, MB/s)
- *rsec/s* (rkB/s, rMB/s)
- *wsec/s* (wkB/s, wMB/s)
- *dsec/s* (dkB/s, dMB/s)
- *rqm/s*
- *rrqm/s*
- *wrqm/s*

- *drqm/s*
- *% rrqm*
- *% wrqm*
- *% drqm*
- *areq-sz*
- *rareq-sz*
- *wareq-sz*
- *dareq-sz*

- *await*
- *r_await*
- *w_await*
- *d_await*
- *f_await*
- *aqu-sz*
- *%util.*

tps represents the number of I/O requests to the device per second. Multiple logical requests can be combined into a single I/O request to the device. A transfer is of indeterminate size. Hence, such a metrics only makes sense when comparing distinct measures or when combining it with I/O request average size measures, such as *areq-sz*, *rareq-sz*, *wareq-sz* and *dareq-sz*. *Blk_read/s* (kB_read/s, MB_read/s) represents the amount of data read from the device in of blocks (kilobytes, megabytes) per second. Blocks sizes are equal to 512 bytes. *Blk_wrtn/s* (kB_wrtn/s, MB_wrtn/s) is the amount of data written to the device expressed in a number of blocks per second. *Blk_dscd/s* (kB_dscd/s, MB_dscd/s) represents the amount of data discarded for the device specified in a number of blocks per second. *Blk_read* (kB_read, MB_read) is the total number of blocks read. Likewise, *Blk_wrtn* (kB_wrtn, MB_wrtn) is the total number of blocks (kilobytes, megabytes) written, and *Blk_dscd* (kB_dscd, MB_dscd) is the total number of blocks discarded.

r/s represents the number of read requests completed (after merges) per second for the device. Two requests can be merged if they are contiguous. *w/s* is the number of write requests completed (after merges) per second for the device. *d/s* denotes the number of discard requests completed (after merges) per second for the device, and *f/s* is the number of disks (partitions are not considered) flush requests completed (after merges) per second for the device.

sec/s (kB/s, MB/s) represents the number of sectors (kilobytes, megabytes) read from, written to, or discarded for the device per second. *rsec/s* (rkB/s, rMB/s) is the number of sectors read from the device per second. *wsec/s* (wkB/s, wMB/s) denotes the number of sectors written to the device per second, and *dsec/s* (dkB/s, dMB/s) represents the number of sectors discarded for the device per second. *rqm/s* denotes the number of merged I/O requests queued or being serviced by the device per second. *rrqm/s* is the number of merged read requests queued or being serviced by the device per second, and *wrqm/s* denotes the number of merged write requests queued or being serviced by the device per second.

drqm/s is the number of discard requests merged per second that were queued to the device. likewise, *% wrqm* represents the percentage of write requests merged before being sent to the device, and *% drqm* denotes the percentage of discard requests merged before being sent to the device. *areq-sz* is the average size (in kilobytes) of the I/O requests that were issued to the device. *rareq-sz* is the average size (in kilobytes) of the read requests that were issued to the device. Similarly, *wareq-sz* is the average size of the write requests that were issued to the device, and *dareq-sz* represents the average size of the discard requests that were issued to the device.

await is the average time (in milliseconds) for I/O requests issued to the device. This includes the time spent by the requests in queue and the time spent serving them. *r_await* is the average time for reading requests issued to the device. As with the previous metrics, this consists of the time spent by the requests in queue and the time spent servicing them. *w_await* denotes the average time for write requests issued to the device to be served, which also considers the time spent by the requests in queue and the service time. *d_await* is the average time for discard requests issued to the device to be served, which also consists of the queue and service times. *f_await* is the average time for flush requests issued to the device to be served. The block layer combines flush requests and executes at most one at a time.

aqu-sz is the average queue length of the requests that were issued to the device. Finally, *%util* is the percentage of elapsed time during which I/O requests were issued to the device (bandwidth utilization for the device). For requests serially sent to devices, the saturation occurs when this value is close to 100 %. However, 100 % does not reflect their performance limits for parallel requests to RAID arrays and SSDs[12].

Executing the command *"iostat -d -y 1800 48 > output"* generates an input/output device log file (*output*) with forty-eight samples with intervals between each sample of 1800 s (30 minutes). The report shows the *Device*, and basic standard metrics *tps*, *Blk_read/s*, *Blk_wrtn/s*, *Blk_dscd/s*, *Blk_read*, and *Blk_wrtn*. The respective values of each sample are presented in the following lines for each input/output device or partition. Below you have a chunk of data provided in file *output*.

```
Linux 4.4.0-142-generic (ubuntu)        05/08/2020      _i686_  (1 CPU)

Device:           tps   kB_read/s   kB_wrtn/s   kB_read    kB_wrtn
loop0            0.00        0.00        0.00          0          0
sda              0.00        0.00        0.00          0          0

Device:           tps   kB_read/s   kB_wrtn/s   kB_read    kB_wrtn
loop0            0.00        0.00        0.00          0          0
sda              0.41        0.00        5.69          0         28

Device:           tps   kB_read/s   kB_wrtn/s   kB_read    kB_wrtn
loop0            0.00        0.00        0.00          0          0
sda              0.40        0.00        3.23          0         16
```

If option *-x* were included, the other metrics depicted above would also be provided.

---

[12] A solid-state drive (SSD) replaces traditional mechanical hard disks by using flash-based memory.

Command *mpstat*

The **mpstat** command provides measures for each available processor as well as global average measures among all processors. The basic syntax of this command is *mpstat [options] [delay] [count]*, where *[delay]* and *[count]* are specified as we have defined for *vmstat* and *iostat*. The main options are

- *-u* reports processor utilization. *CPU* is the processor number. The keyword *all* indicates that statistics are calculated as averages among all processors. *%usr* shows the percentage of processor utilization that occurred while executing at the user level. *%nice* shows the percentage of processor utilization that occurred while executing at the user level with nice priority. *%sys* shows the percentage of processor utilization that occurred while executing at the system level (kernel). Note that this does not include time spent servicing hardware and software interrupts. *%iowait* shows the percentage of time that the processor or processors were idle due to disk I/O request. *%irq* shows the percentage of time spent by the processor or processors to service hardware interrupts. *%soft* shows the percentage of time spent by the processor or processors to service software interrupts. *%steal* shows the percentage of time spent in involuntary wait by the virtual processor or processors due to hypervisor. *%guest* shows the percentage of time spent by the processor or processors to run a virtual processor. *%gnice* shows the percentage of time spent by the processor or processors to run a niced guest. *%idle* shows the percentage of time that the processor or processors were idle and the system did not have disk I/O request.

- *-V* - Print version number then exit.

- *-I keyword [,...] — ALL* - Possible keywords are *CPU*, *SCPU*, and *SUM*. *CPU* reports the number of each individual interruption received per second by the processor or processors (see */proc/interrupts*). *SCPU* reports the number of each individual software interrupt received per second by the processor or processors. *SUM* reports the total number of interrupts per processor. *ALL* keyword is equivalent to specifying all the keywords above.

- *-P cpu [,...] — ON — ALL* - *cpu* is the processor number for which statistics are to be reported. Processor 0 is the first processor. *ON* indicates the report is for online processors. *ALL* indicates the report is for all processors.

- *-A* - This option is equivalent to specifying *-u -I ALL -P ALL*.

Executing the command "*mpstat -P cpu dbs ns > output*" generates the processor report log file (*output*) with *ns* samples with intervals between each sample of *dbs* seconds. As an example, consider "*mpstat -P 0 5 4 > output*". In this case, a report of processor 0 is generated. This report comprises four (4) samples, and the delay between samples was specified as five seconds (5 s). Below a data set is provided in file *output*. Besides the four samples, the averages of the samples are depicted in the last row.

```
02:10:20 PM  CPU    %usr   %nice    %sys %iowait    %irq   %soft  %steal  %gues$
02:10:25 PM    0    1.22    0.00    0.81    0.00    0.00    0.00    0.00    0.0$
02:10:30 PM    0    1.01    0.00    0.40    0.00    0.00    0.00    0.00    0.0$
02:10:35 PM    0    1.42    0.00    0.41    0.00    0.00    0.00    0.00    0.0$
02:10:40 PM    0    0.81    0.00    0.41    0.00    0.00    0.20    0.00    0.0$
Average:       0    1.12    0.00    0.51    0.00    0.00    0.05    0.00    0.0$
```

Network Time Protocol

The *Network Time Protocol* (*NTP*) is a protocol used to synchronize the computer system clock automatically over a network. Let us now configure a client computer to be time-synchronized with NTP servers. First, open */etc/ntp.conf* with the command "*sudo pico ntp.conf*" and include your list of *NTP* servers; for instance, add these lines in *ntp.conf*

```
NTP time.nist.gov iburst
NTP time.nist.gov iburst
server time.nist.gov iburst
server time.nist.gov iburst
```

Configuring with option *iburst*, the computer client sends eight packets to the *NTP* server for calibrating a system clock, but there are other options [315]. Save *ntp.conf* and restart the *NTP* service by executing "*sudo service ntp restart*". Executing "*ntpq -p*" or "*ntpq -pn*" you should be able to see the *NTP* servers. For instance,

```
     remote         refid      st t when poll reach   delay   offset  jitter
==============================================================================
time-e-wwv.nist .NIST.          1 u   49   64    1  213.551 -1406.2 631.967
time-a-g.nist.g .NIST.          1 u   54   64    1  223.910 -1426.1 634.623.
```

Check if the computer is synchronized by executing "*timedatectl status*". If the output is

```
Network time on: yes
NTP synchronized: no,
```

execute "*sudo service ntp stop*", then restart the *NTP* service by executing "*sudo service ntp restart*". After that, the command "*ntpstat*" may be executed. The output should look like

```
synchronized to NTP server (52.67.171.238) at stratum 4
time correct to within 1283 ms
polling server every 64 s
```

It is also possible to execute *"timedatectl status"* for checking the synchronization. The output should look like

```
Local time: Wed 2020-05-13 21:29:12 -03
Universal time: Thu 2020-05-14 00:29:12 UTC
RTC time: Thu 2020-05-14 00:29:11
Time zone: America/Maceio (-03, -0300)
Network time on: yes
NTP synchronized: yes
RTC in local TZ: no
```

Executing the command *"ntp-wait"* blocks until *ntpd* (*Network Time Protocol daemon*) is synchronized.

There are many other tools for infrastructure resource and software monitoring and analysis [299] such as Nagios [296], nmon [310] and Perfmon [333], for example.

Entry /proc/net/ and Command netstat

The entry **/proc/net/** provides an instant summary of various networking parameters and statistics. Its pseudo-files describe aspects and status of parts of the system networking layer, sockets, dbus communication, and communications between virtual and the desktop. These pseudo-files contain ASCII structures, and hence can be read by a text editor or *cat* command. Besides the pseudo-files, it contains some subdirectories that hold pseudo-files related to protocols, devices status. One may also use the command **netstat** to obtain the content of these pseudo-files. The *netstat* 's most common options are:

- *-t*, which shows only *TCP* connections,

- *-u*, which shows only *UDP connections,*

- *-a*, which depicts listening (waiting) sockets;

- *-n*, which displays the IP addresses, port numbers and user ids (no login names);

- *-p*, which lists the processes involved. It is valid only when *netstat* is executed as root, and

- *-c*, which continuously refreshes the list of connections.

Executing the command *"sudo netstat -tupan > netstat_dump"*, the first five options are activated. Typical results contained in the file *netstat dump* look like the following:

```
Active Internet connections (servers and established)
Proto Recv-Q Send-Q Local Address            Foreign Address      State        PID/Program name
tcp        0      0 127.0.0.1:631            0.0.0.0:*            LISTEN       821/cupsd
tcp        0      0 0.0.0.0:111              0.0.0.0:*            LISTEN       30985/rpcbind
tcp        0      0 192.168.61.128:34192     216.58.202.234:443  TIME_WAIT    -
tcp        0      0 192.168.61.128:54674     172.217.29.35:443   ESTABLISHED  4984/firefox
tcp        0      0 192.168.61.128:60552     172.217.29.78:443   TIME_WAIT    -
tcp        0      0 192.168.61.128:34194     216.58.202.234:443  TIME_WAIT    -
tcp        0      0 192.168.61.128:34322     172.217.30.14:443   ESTABLISHED  4984/firefox
tcp        0      0 192.168.61.128:56806     64.233.190.189:443  ESTABLISHED  4984/firefox
tcp        0      0 192.168.61.128:57048     44.233.50.225:443   ESTABLISHED  4984/firefox
tcp6       0      0 ::1:631                  :::*                LISTEN       821/cupsd
tcp6       0      0 :::111                   :::*                LISTEN       30985/rpcbind
udp        0      0 0.0.0.0:48086            0.0.0.0:*                        769/avahi-daemon: r
udp        0      0 0.0.0.0:68               0.0.0.0:*                        1195/dhclient
udp        0      0 0.0.0.0:111              0.0.0.0:*                        30985/rpcbind
udp        0      0 0.0.0.0:631              0.0.0.0:*                        822/cups-browsed
udp        0      0 0.0.0.0:633              0.0.0.0:*                        30985/rpcbind
udp        0      0 192.168.61.128:123       0.0.0.0:*                        3193/ntpd
udp        0      0 127.0.0.1:123            0.0.0.0:*                        3193/ntpd
udp        0      0 0.0.0.0:123              0.0.0.0:*                        3193/ntpd
udp        0      0 0.0.0.0:5353             0.0.0.0:*                        769/avahi-daemon: r
udp6       0      0 :::111                   :::*                             30985/rpcbind
udp6       0      0 :::633                   :::*                             30985/rpcbind
udp6       0      0 fe80:20c:29ff:fe95:123   :::*                             3193/ntpd
udp6       0      0 :::123                   :::*                             3193/ntpd
udp6       0      0 :::123                   :::*                             3193/ntpd
udp6       0      0 :::5353                  :::*                             769/avahi-daemon: r
udp6       0      0 :::41328                 :::*                             769/avahi-daemon: r
```

The output displays four established connections, *firefox* processes, and listening applications (listed as LISTEN), such as *cupsd*, which is the *Common Unix Printing ScheDuler,* and *rpcbind*, which is a server that converts *RPC*[13] program numbers into universal addresses.

---

[13]Remote Procedure Call.

Command *ss*

The command *ss* is a tool used to dump socket, *TCP UDP*, *DCCP*, *RAW*, Unix domain sockets, and the respective state statistics beyond what is provided by *netstat*. The standard syntax of the command is *"ss options filter"*. Some of the important options supported by this command are depicted below. For a detailed view of all options, please refer to *"man ss"*.

- *-n* does not resolve service names.

- *-r* tries to resolve numeric address/ports.

- *-a* displays both listening and non-listening sockets.

- *-l* displays only listening sockets.

- *-o* shows timer information.

- *-e* shows detailed socket information.

- *-m* shows socket memory usage.

- *-p* shows process using socket.

- *-i* shows internal *TCP* information.

- *-s* prints summary statistics.

- *-b* shows socket *BPF*[14] filters (It is allowed only for administrators).

- *-4* displays only *ipv4* sockets.

- *-6* displays only *ipv6* sockets.

- *-0* displays packet sockets.

- *-t* displays *TCP* sockets.

- *-u* displays *UDP* sockets.

- *-d* displays *DCCP* sockets.

- *-w* displays *RAW* sockets.

- *-x* displays Unix domain sockets.

- *-f* displays sockets of type *family: unix, inet (ipv4), inet6 (ipv6), link, netlink*.

If the command *ss* without options is executed, it shows information about all *TCP*, *UDP*, and Unix socket connections regardless of the state in which they are. The command *"ss -a"* retrieves a list of both listening and non-listening ports.

```
Netid  State    Recv-Q Send-Q Local Address:Port               Peer Address$
nl     UNCONN   0      0      rtnl:goa-daemon/2455      *                 $
nl     UNCONN   0      0      rtnl:mission-control/2463  *                $
       ...             ...                            ...
u_dgr  UNCONN   0      0      /run/user/116/systemd/notify 18218          $
u_str  LISTEN   0      128    /run/user/1000/systemd/private 21523        $
u_str  LISTEN   0      128    /run/user/116/systemd/private 18219         $
       ...             ...                            ...
u_str  LISTEN   0      10     @/tmp/ibus/dbus-m8neRU62 21830              $
u_str  ESTAB    0      0      * 526756                   * 526755
u_seq  ESTAB    0      0      * 525475                   * 525476
       ...             ...                            ...
u_str  ESTAB    0      0      * 23140                    * 23141
       ...             ...                            ...
udp    UNCONN   0      0      :::ntp                     :::*
udp    UNCONN   0      0      :::mdns                    :::*
tcp    LISTEN   0      5      127.0.0.1:ipp                  *:*          $
```

---

[14]Berkeley Packet Filter.

```
tcp    LISTEN    0    10    *:3000                              *:*
tcp    ESTAB     0    0     192.168.61.128:45690                216.58.222.$
tcp    ESTAB     0    0     192.168.61.128:39168                35.163.81.8$
tcp    ESTAB     0    0     192.168.61.128:60112                172.217.162$
       ...                  ...                          ...
```

The execution of the command line "*ss -l*" displays listening sockets only. We may collect more specific statistics, for instance by also specifying the type of connections, that is -*t* for *TCP*, -*u* for *UDP*, -*d* for *DCCP*, -*w* for *RAW*, and -*x* for *Unix* domains socket connections. Hence, by combining the options, we defining a command that collects listening sockets of each specific connection type, such as "*ss -lt*", "*ss -lu*", "*ss -ld*", "*ss -lw*", and "*ss -lx*". The first command ("*ss -lt*") may also be specified as "*ss -tl*" or "*ss -l -t*". Likewise, other combinations may also be represented using these alternative notations. If the options -*t*, -*u*, -*d*, -*w*, and -*x* are adopted alone, the respective commands display the respective connections that are established or connected. If we also need to collect information of connections that are listening, we also have to include the option -*a*. As an example, the execution of "*ss -a -t*" displays a portion of data similar to the following.

```
State      Recv-Q Send-Q Local Address:Port           Peer Address:Port
LISTEN     0      5      127.0.0.1:ipp                       *:*
LISTEN     0      10     *:3000                        *:*
ESTAB      0      0      192.168.61.128:58486          172.217.29.106:https
ESTAB      0      0      192.168.61.128:51124          216.58.202.225:https
ESTAB      0      0      192.168.61.128:41422          216.58.222.78:https
           ...                  ...                          ...
TIME-WAIT  0      0      192.168.61.128:58428          172.217.29.106:https
TIME-WAIT  0      0      192.168.61.128:43098          13.33.121.90:https
ESTAB      0      0      192.168.61.128:34450          13.33.121.58:https
ESTAB      0      0      192.168.61.128:53870          216.58.222.69:https
           ...                  ...                          ...
ESTAB      0      0      192.168.61.128:46412          216.58.202.227:https
ESTAB      0      0      192.168.61.128:53872          216.58.222.69:https
LISTEN     0      5      ::1:ipp                       :::*
```

The command *ss* with option -*p* displays the process identification (*pid*) related to socket connections. Thus, the execution of the command "*ss -tap*" shows all *TCP* socket connections with the respective *pid*.

```
State      Recv-Q Send-Q Local Address:Port           Peer Address:Port
LISTEN     0      5      127.0.0.1:ipp                       *:*
LISTEN     0      10     *:3000                        *:*
ESTAB      0      0      192.168.61.128:57714          172.217.29.99:https
                         users:(("firefox",pid=24148,fd=101))
ESTAB      0      0      192.168.61.128:51046          172.217.29.101:https
                         users:(("firefox",pid=24148,fd=88))
ESTAB      0      0      192.168.61.128:57228          172.217.192.189:https
                         users:(("firefox",pid=24148,fd=87))
ESTAB      0      0      192.168.61.128:48566          216.58.202.238:https
                         users:(("firefox",pid=24148,fd=76))
ESTAB      0      0      192.168.61.128:48816          216.58.222.74:https
                         users:(("firefox",pid=24148,fd=91))
ESTAB      0      0      192.168.61.128:42226          54.69.90.211:https
                         users:(("firefox",pid=24148,fd=169))
LISTEN     0      5      ::1:ipp                       :::*
```

As another example, the execution of the command line "*ss -tupan*" shows all *TCP* and *UDP* socket connections with the respective *pid* without resolving service names. The command line "*ss -s*" displays a summary of statistics such as the total number of established connections and counts of each socket type. A typical output display of the command line is

```
Total: 1212 (kernel 0)
TCP:   7 (estab 4, closed 0, orphaned 0, synrecv 0, timewait 0/0), ports 0

Transport Total  IP      IPv6
*         0      -       -
RAW       0      0       0
UDP       12     7       5
TCP       7      6       1
INET      19     13      6
FRAG      0      0       0
```

The command line "*ss -4 state FILTER*" provides the *TCP ipv4* sockets whereas "*ss -6 state FILTER*" displays the *TCP ipv6* sockets. We may also use the *ss* tool to display only sockets based on *TCP states*. The *TCP states* can be consulted by executing "*man ss*". As an example, the command line "*ss -4 state established*" outputs *TCP ipv4* sockets that are in state *established*.

```
Netid  Recv-Q Send-Q Local Address:Port     Peer Address:Port
tcp    0      0      192.168.61.128:59090   172.217.29.99:https
tcp    0      0      192.168.61.128:58992   52.13.228.162:https
tcp    0      0      192.168.61.128:47142   64.233.190.189:https
tcp    0      0      192.168.61.128:49990   216.58.202.238:https
```

The *ss* command also allows filtering of the output, taking into account socket port number. For example, the command line "*ss -etn sport = :47406*" shows all socket connections with the source port *47406*. Similarly, the command line "*ss -etn dport = :443*" shows all socket connections with the destination port *443*. A typical output displayed by the execution of this command line is

```
State Recv-Q Send-Q Local Address:Port     Peer Address:Port
ESTAB 0      0      192.168.61.128:47406   54.213.218.169:443
                                           timer:(keepalive,8min7sec,0)
                                           uid:1000 ino:628772 sk:468 <->
ESTAB 0      0      192.168.61.128:55054   172.217.29.42:443
                                           uid:1000 ino:628931 sk:469 <->
ESTAB 0      0      192.168.61.128:47230   64.233.190.189:443
                                           uid:1000 ino:628765 sk:46a <->
ESTAB 0      0      192.168.61.128:55056   172.217.29.42:443
                                           uid:1000 ino:628932 sk:46b <->
ESTAB 0      0      192.168.61.128:49990   216.58.202.238:443
                                           uid:1000 ino:625069 sk:45f <->
```

Similarly, the *ss* command also allows filtering of the output, taking into account the socket address. For example, the command line "*ss -etn dst 64.233.190.189*" shows all socket connections with the destination address *64.233.190.189*. Likewise, the command line "*ss -etn src 64.233.190.189*" shows all socket connections with the source address *64.233.190.189*. A typical display obtained by the execution of this command line is

```
State Recv-Q Send-Q Local Address:Port    Peer Address:Port
ESTAB 0      0      192.168.61.128:47406  54.213.218.169:443
                                          timer:(keepalive,4min42sec,0)
                                          uid:1000 ino:628772 sk:468 <->
ESTAB 0      0      192.168.61.128:36464  216.58.222.106:443
                                          uid:1000 ino:633068 sk:46f <->
ESTAB 0      0      192.168.61.128:47230  64.233.190.189:443
                                          uid:1000 ino:628765 sk:46a <->
ESTAB 0      0      192.168.61.128:49990  216.58.202.238:443
                                          uid:1000 ino:625069 sk:45f <->
ESTAB 0      0      192.168.61.128:59188  172.217.29.99:443
                                          uid:1000 ino:629634 sk:471 <->
ESTAB 0      0      192.168.61.128:55262  216.58.222.69:443
                                          uid:1000 ino:633562 sk:472 <->
```

Command *tcpdump*

The *tcpdump* is a powerful command-line tool for network traffic monitoring (sniffing) and analysis [426]. The command *tcpdump* is used to create "dumps" or "traces" of network traffic and can also be launched in the background or be scheduled by other tools. Monitoring network traffic through *tcpdump* requires high permission levels, so most commands are prefixed with the *sudo* command.

As already mentioned at the beginning of this section, our aim is not to reference network monitoring tools but rather introduce some features and simple examples and point out a specific reference on the subject. The *tcpdump* tool has many configuration options (parameters) that allow configuring and filtering specific types of classes of network traffic. This section discusses the most basic options that can be used as well as provides some basic but useful examples of using *tcpdump* for sniffing and analyzing network traffic.

Hence, let us start using the command "*tcpdump -D*" to find out which interfaces are available in the system. As a result, information such as depicted below is provided, which shows all the interfaces available. The particular interface *any* allows capturing in any active interface.

```
1.ens33 [Up, Running]
2.any (Pseudo-device that captures on all interfaces) [Up, Running]
3.lo [Up, Running, Loopback]
4.bluetooth0 (Bluetooth adapter number 0)
5.nflog (Linux netfilter log (NFLOG) interface)
6.nfqueue (Linux netfilter queue (NFQUEUE) interface)
7.usbmon1 (USB bus number 1)
8.usbmon2 (USB bus number 2)
```

A specific interface can be sniffed by using the *-i* option, followed by the interface name. The command "*sudo tcpdump -i ens33*" captures all packets in interface *ens33* until an interrupt signal is sent, which occurs by pressing *Ctrl+C*. Below, a chunk of data packets information is depicted as an example.

```
tcpdump: verbose output suppressed, use -v or -vv for full protocol
                                                              decode
listening on ens33, link-type EN10MB (Ethernet), capture size
                                                        262144 bytes
```

```
16:28:07.471548 IP ubuntu.ntp > a.st1.ntp.br.ntp: NTPv4, Client,
                                                   length 48
16:28:07.471974 IP ubuntu.ntp > time.cloudflare.com.ntp: NTPv4,
                                                   Client, length 48
16:28:07.472948 IP ubuntu.49396 > gateway.domain: 36848+ PTR?
                           186.7.160.200.in-addr.arpa. (44)
16:28:07.581837 IP gateway.domain > ubuntu.49396: 36848 1/0/0
                                   PTR a.st1.ntp.br. (70)
16:28:07.582096 IP ubuntu.47644 > gateway.domain: 27219+ PTR?
                           128.61.168.192.in-addr.arpa. (45)
16:28:07.627074 IP a.st1.ntp.br.ntp > ubuntu.ntp: NTPv4, Server,
                                                   length 48
16:28:07.629702 IP time.cloudflare.com.ntp > ubuntu.ntp: NTPv4,
                                                   Server, length 48
```

The command "*sudo tcpdump -i any*" may be adopted to listen on all interfaces. Now, let us use one of the lines shown above. Consider, for instance, the line

```
16:28:07.471548 IP ubuntu.ntp > a.st1.ntp.br.ntp: NTPv4, Client, length 48
```

This first field (*16:28:07.471548*) depicts the time that the packets were traveling, in this format: hh:mm:ss. The second field shows the source hostname, followed by the destination hostname, which is *ubuntu.ntp* > *a.st1.ntp.br.ntp*. The third field is *Network Time Protocol* version (*NTPv4*). The fourth field shows if the host is a client or a server. In this case, it is a client (*Client*), and the last field represents the *TCP* packet length in Bytes (*length 48*).

The flag *-n* translates hostnames into IP addresses. Hence, the command "*sudo tcpdump -in ens33*" captures all packets in interface *ens33* until an interrupt signal is sent and presents the output as the source and destination IP addresses instead of hostnames. It is worth mentioning that *-in* is a combination of option *-i* and option *-n*. Below, a piece of data packets information is shown as an example.

```
tcpdump: verbose output suppressed, use -v or -vv for full protocol decode
listening on ens33, link-type EN10MB (Ethernet), capture size 262144 bytes
17:27:19.034204 IP 192.168.61.128.123 > 200.186.125.195.123: NTPv4, Client,
                                                               length 48
17:27:19.201503 IP 200.186.125.195.123 > 192.168.61.128.123: NTPv4, Server,
                                                               length 48
17:27:21.034716 IP 192.168.61.128.123 > 54.232.82.232.123: NTPv4, Client,
                                                               length 48
17:27:21.180667 IP 54.232.82.232.123 > 192.168.61.128.123: NTPv4, Server,
                                                               length 48
```

As we did in the previous example, let us look at one of these lines shown above. As an example, assume the line

```
17:27:19.034204 IP 192.168.61.128.123 > 200.186.125.195.123: NTPv4, Client,
                                                               length 48
```

The main difference from the previous example is that the source host and destination hostnames are translated to the respective IP addresses and ports. Thus, the second field shows the source host address and port, followed by the destination host address and port, *192.168.61.128.123 > 200.186.125.195.123*.

The number of packets to be ready may also be specified by using the option *-c*, such as *"sudo tcpdump -ni any -c 10"*, where the number after *-c* denotes the number of packets. For example, in the command above, the *tcpdump* finishes the sniffing process as soon as it gets ten (10) packets. Below, a chunk of information collected is presented as an example.

```
tcpdump: verbose output suppressed, use -v or -vv for full protocol decode
listening on any, link-type LINUX_SLL (Linux cooked), capture size 262144 bytes
21:53:47.023515 IP 192.168.61.128.123 > 54.232.82.232.123: NTPv4, Client,
                                                                    length 48
21:53:47.176819 IP 54.232.82.232.123 > 192.168.61.128.123: NTPv4, Server,
                                                                    length 48
21:53:47.983129 IP 192.168.61.1.17500 > 255.255.255.255.17500: UDP, length 242
21:53:47.986708 IP 192.168.61.1.17500 > 255.255.255.255.17500: UDP, length 242
21:53:47.986729 IP 192.168.61.1.17500 > 255.255.255.255.17500: UDP, length 242
21:53:47.986960 IP 192.168.61.1.17500 > 192.168.61.255.17500: UDP, length 242
21:53:47.987383 IP 192.168.61.1.17500 > 255.255.255.255.17500: UDP, length 242
21:53:47.987524 IP 192.168.61.1.17500 > 255.255.255.255.17500: UDP, length 242
21:53:51.023942 IP 192.168.61.128.123 > 192.36.143.130.123: NTPv4, Client,
                                                                    length 48
21:53:51.024115 IP 192.168.61.128.123 > 192.99.2.8.123: NTPv4, Client,
                                                                    length 48
10 packets captured
10 packets received by filter
0 packets dropped by kernel
```

The option *-X* prints the data of each packet in hexadecimal and *ASCII*, besides the headers of each packet. For instance, consider the command line *"sudo tcpdump -ni any -c 3 -X"*. This command sniffs three packets from all interfaces, presents the source and destination IP addresses with the respective ports, and presents the content of each packet in hexadecimal and *ASCII* formats (option *-A* presents the content in *ASCII* only.). This option is useful when the administrator wants to analyze the content of the packets. Typical output looks like this:

```
tcpdump: verbose output suppressed, use -v or -vv for full protocol decode
listening on any, link-type LINUX_SLL (Linux cooked), capture size 262144 bytes
16:37:23.034792 IP 192.168.61.128.123 > 146.164.48.5.123: NTPv4, Client,
                                                                    length 48
0x0000:  45b8 004c 5e25 4000 4011 1af2 c0a8 3d80  E..L^%@.@.....=.
0x0010:  92a4 3005 007b 007b 0038 1fbc 2302 06e8  ..0..{.{.8..#...
0x0020:  0000 265d 0001 480e c8a0 07ba e26c 10ea  ..&]..H......l..
0x0030:  6618 9c88 e26c 10b4 f55d bdc1 e26c 10b5  f....l...]...l..
0x0040:  2cc4 fc08 e26c 10f3 08e7 00da            ,....l......
16:37:23.168734 IP 146.164.48.5.123 > 192.168.61.128.123: NTPv4, Server,
                                                                    length 48
0x0000:  4500 004c d2e6 0000 8011 a6e8 92a4 3005  E..L..........0.
0x0010:  c0a8 3d80 007b 007b 0038 0ae4 2401 06ec  ..=..{.{.8..$...
0x0020:  0000 0000 0000 0012 4750 5300 e26c 10ef  ........GPS..l..
0x0030:  241f 7404 e26c 10f3 08e7 00da e26c 10f2  $.t..l.......l..
0x0040:  e5fd 33d8 e26c 10f2 e5fd fe4f            ..3..l.....O
16:37:24.034421 IP 192.168.61.128.123 > 45.11.105.253.123: NTPv4, Client,
                                                                    length 48
```

```
0x0000:   45b8 004c e770 4000 4011 bd47 c0a8 3d80   E..L.p@.@..G..=.
0x0010:   2d0b 69fd 007b 007b 0038 87d3 2302 06e8   -.i..{.{.8..#...
0x0020:   0000 265d 0001 480f c8a0 07ba e26c 10ea   ..&]..H......l..
0x0030:   6618 9c88 e26c 10b5 f656 03e8 e26c 10b6   f....l...V...l..
0x0040:   30d8 da51 e26c 10f4 08ce 9afc             0..Q.l......
3 packets captured
3 packets received by filter
0 packets dropped by kernel
```

For instance, seeing the data shown above, after the header of the first packet,

```
16:37:23.034792 IP 192.168.61.128.123 > 146.164.48.5.123: NTPv4, Client,
                                                            length 48,
```

we get the packet's content:

```
0x0000:   45b8 004c 5e25 4000 4011 1af2 c0a8 3d80   E..L^%@.@.....=.
0x0010:   92a4 3005 007b 007b 0038 1fbc 2302 06e8   ..0..{.{.8..#...
0x0020:   0000 265d 0001 480e c8a0 07ba e26c 10ea   ..&]..H......l..
0x0030:   6618 9c88 e26c 10b4 f55d bdc1 e26c 10b5   f....l...]...l..
0x0040:   2cc4 fc08 e26c 10f3 08e7 00da             ,....l......
```

The command *tcpdump* is capable of monitoring many different protocols, such as *IP*, *TCP*, *UDP*, *ICMP*, and more. The aim here is not to explore them but to support the reader getting started. Details and formats of different protocols may be found in *tcpdump*'s manual. Assume the *TCP* packet header captured by *tcpdump* shown below:

```
17:14:06.396782 IP 150.161.2.9.80 > 192.168.61.128.50394: Flags [.],
                                                 seq 2921:4381, ack 430,

win 64240, length 1460: HTTP
```

The header's content may vary depending on the type of packet. However, in general, the *TCP* packet header has the first field,

```
17:14:06.396782,
```

that represents the *timestamp* of the received or sent packet. The field *IP* denotes the network layer protocol in (*IP* for IPv4 and *IP6* for IPv6 packets). In this particular case, we have *IP*. The next field is

```
150.161.2.9.80,
```

which is the source IP address and port (80). Port 80 is adopted for HTTP traffic. The next field is the destination IP address and port

```
192.168.61.128.50394,
```

Table 23.1
Typical *TCP* Flags

Value	Flag Type	Description
S	SYN	Connection Start
F	FIN	Connection Finish
P	PUSH	Data push
R	RST	Connection reset
.	ACK	Acknowledgment

where 50394 is the port number. After the source and destination addresses, the *TCP* flags are provided; in this specific case, it is *Flags [.]*. Table 23.1) shows some typical flags. This field can also be a combination of flags, such as *[S.]*, for a *SYN-ACK* packet.

Next is the sequence number of the data contained in the packet. For the first packet captured, this is an absolute number. Subsequent packets use a relative number to make it easier to follow. In this example, the sequence is *seq 2921:4381*, which means this packet contains bytes 2921 to 4381 of this flow. This is followed by the acknowledge number *ack*. In this specific case, the packet was received; hence, this field represents the next expected byte on this flow (*ack 430*). When sending a packet, the ack value is *ack 1*. Next, the window size (*win 64240*) specifies the number of bytes available in the receiving buffer followed by TCP options[15]. Finally, the packet length is the length (in bytes) of the payload data, which is the difference between the last (4381) and first (2921) bytes, that is $4381 - 2921 = 1460$.

The *tcpdump* allows the filtering of the captured packets using a variety of parameters, such as source and destination *IP* addresses, ports, protocols. Consider, for instance, we intend to capture only *ICMP* packets. The command line "*sudo tcpdump -i any icmp > tcpdum_test*" sniffers *ICMP* packets looking at every interface and writes the traffic headers in the file *tcpdum_test*. A typical chunk of data contained is shown below.

```
18:10:44.754016 IP ubuntu > ec2-54-204-39-132.compute-1.amazonaws.com: ICMP
                                                              echo request,

id 12648, seq 1, length 64

18:10:44.953102 IP ec2-54-204-39-132.compute-1.amazonaws.com > ubuntu: ICMP
                                                              echo reply,

id 12648, seq 1, length 64

18:10:45.753992 IP ubuntu > ec2-54-204-39-132.compute-1.amazonaws.com: ICMP
                                                              echo request,
```

---

[15]For details about TCP protocol options, consult Transmission Control Protocol (TCP) Parameters.

```
id 12648, seq 2, length 64

18:10:45.958080 IP ec2-54-204-39-132.compute-1.amazonaws.com > ubuntu: ICMP
                                                echo reply,

id 12648, seq 2, length 64

18:10:46.755299 IP ubuntu > ec2-54-204-39-132.compute-1.amazonaws.com: ICMP
                                                echo request,

id 12648, seq 3, length 64

18:10:46.935692 IP ec2-54-204-39-132.compute-1.amazonaws.com > ubuntu: ICMP
                                                echo reply,

id 12648, seq 3, length 64
```

Assume we intend to capture packets related to a specific host. The command line
"*sudo tcpdump -i any -c5 -n host 54.204.39.132 > tcpdum_test*" sniffers five packets
sent or coming from host *54.204.39.132* and writes the traffic headers in the file
tcpdum_test. A typical content of the file *tcpdum_test* is shown bellow.

```
18:41:33.385093 IP 192.168.61.128 > 54.204.39.132: ICMP echo request, id 14003,
                                                 seq 11, length 64
18:41:33.562817 IP 54.204.39.132 > 192.168.61.128: ICMP echo reply, id 14003,
                                                 seq 11, length 64
18:41:34.386068 IP 192.168.61.128 > 54.204.39.132: ICMP echo request, id 14003,
                                                 seq 12, length 64
18:41:34.553989 IP 54.204.39.132 > 192.168.61.128: ICMP echo reply, id 14003,
                                                 seq 12, length 64
18:41:35.387097 IP 192.168.61.128 > 54.204.39.132: ICMP echo request, id 14003,
                                                 seq 13, length 64
```

Likewise, we can sniffer packets based on the source or destination *IP* address or
hostname. The command line "*sudo tcpdump -i any -c4 -n src 54.204.39.132 >*
tcpdum_test" sniffers four packets coming from host *54.204.39.132* and writes the
traffic headers in the file *tcpdum_test*. A typical content of the file *tcpdum_test* is

```
19:10:02.273334 IP 54.204.39.132 > 192.168.61.128: ICMP echo reply, id 15168,
                                                 seq 1, length 64
19:10:03.286058 IP 54.204.39.132 > 192.168.61.128: ICMP echo reply, id 15168,
                                                 seq 2, length 64
19:10:04.757905 IP 54.204.39.132 > 192.168.61.128: ICMP echo reply, id 15168,
                                                 seq 3, length 64
19:10:05.463161 IP 54.204.39.132 > 192.168.61.128: ICMP echo reply, id 15168,
                                                 seq 4, length 64
```

Similarly, the command line "*sudo tcpdump -i any -c4 -n dst 54.204.39.132 >*
tcpdum_test" sniffers four packets sent to host *54.204.39.132* and writes the traffic
headers in the file *tcpdum_test*. The content of the file *tcpdum_test* would be similar
to this

```
20:37:27.179439 IP 192.168.61.128 > 54.204.39.132: ICMP echo request,
                                               id 18958, seq 1, length 64
20:37:28.180844 IP 192.168.61.128 > 54.204.39.132: ICMP echo request,
                                               id 18958, seq 2, length 64
20:37:29.182550 IP 192.168.61.128 > 54.204.39.132: ICMP echo request,
                                               id 18958, seq 3, length 64
20:37:30.184904 IP 192.168.61.128 > 54.204.39.132: ICMP echo request,
                                               id 18958, seq 4, length 64
```

Consider we need to capture packets related to a specific service or port. The command line "*sudo tcpdump -i any -c5 -n port 80 > tcpdum_test*" sniffers five packets related to port *80* (HTTP traffic) and writes the traffic headers in the file *tcpdum_test*. Below, a chunk of information collected is presented as an example.

```
20:55:56.878693 IP 192.168.61.128.51116 > 150.161.2.9.80: Flags [S],
                                                      seq 3926656975,

win 29200, options [mss 1460,sackOK,TS val 66984807 ecr 0,nop,wscale 7],
                                                      length 0

20:55:57.036618 IP 150.161.2.9.80 > 192.168.61.128.51116: Flags [S.],
                                                      seq 1039757299,

ack 3926656976, win 64240, options [mss 1460], length 0

20:55:57.036647 IP 192.168.61.128.51116 > 150.161.2.9.80: Flags [.], ack 1,

win 29200, length 0

20:56:00.920350 IP 192.168.61.128.51116 > 150.161.2.9.80: Flags [P.],
                                                      seq 1:460, ack 1,

win 29200, length 459: HTTP: GET /wp-content/uploads/thesis/Tese-Erico.pdf
                                                             HTTP/1.1

20:56:00.921007 IP 150.161.2.9.80 > 192.168.61.128.51116: Flags [.], ack 460,

win 64240, length 0

20:56:01.148625 IP 150.161.2.9.80 > 192.168.61.128.51116: Flags [.],
                                                      seq 1:1461, ack 460,

win 64240, length 1460: HTTP: HTTP/1.1 200 OK

20:56:01.148648 IP 192.168.61.128.51116 > 150.161.2.9.80: Flags [.], ack 1461,

win 32120, length 0
```

We can also find traffic in a range of ports by using the option *portrange*, for instance "*tcpdump portrange 21-23*". It is worth mentioning that the port numbers are divided into three ranges, named the *well-known ports*, the *registered ports*, and the *dynamic* or *private ports* [404]. The well-known ports are also known as system ports. These ports range from 0 through 1023. Some important system ports are depicted in Table 23.2.

Options can be combined by using the logical operators such as *and*, *or*, and *not* to create more filters. For example, the command "*sudo tcpdump -ni any -c10 src*

Table 23.2

Some System Ports

Port number	Assignment
20	File Transfer Protocol (FTP) Data Transfer
21	File Transfer Protocol (FTP) Command Control
22	Secure Shell (SSH) Secure Login
23	Telnet Remote Login Service, Unencrypted Text Messages
25	Simple Mail Transfer Protocol (SMTP) E-mail Routing
53	Domain Name System (DNS) Service
67, 68	Dynamic Host Configuration Protocol (DHCP)
80	Hypertext Transfer Protocol (HTTP) used in the World Wide Web
110	Post Office Protocol (POP3)
119	Network News Transfer Protocol (NNTP)
123	Network Time Protocol (NTP)
143	Internet Message Access Protocol (IMAP) Management of Digital Mail
161	Simple Network Management Protocol (SNMP)
194	Internet Relay Chat (IRC)
443	HTTP Secure (HTTPS) HTTP over TLS/SSL
631	The Internet Printing Protocol (IPP) Used to Printers (or Printer Servers) Located Remotely on the Network
3306	The Standard Port for MySQL

192.168.61.128 and port 80 > tcpdum_test" generates a dump-file *tcpdum_test* that contains only combined traffic from source *IP* address *192.168.61.128* and the port 80 (service *HTTP*). Even more complex filters can be created by grouping filter options by using parentheses and logical operators. For the command specified above, a typical content of the file *tcpdum_test* would be similar to this

```
12:25:28.713401 IP 192.168.61.128.51282 > 150.161.2.9.80: Flags [S],
                                                  seq 2199567800,

win 29200, options [mss 1460,sackOK,TS val 67957698 ecr 0,nop,wscale 7],
                                                  length 0

12:25:28.909354 IP 192.168.61.128.51282 > 150.161.2.9.80: Flags [.],
                                                  ack 2136435478,

win 29200, length 0

12:25:29.932347 IP 192.168.61.128.51282 > 150.161.2.9.80: Flags [P.],
                                                  seq 0:458, ack 1,

win 29200, length 458: HTTP: GET /wp-content/uploads/thesis/Tese-Joao.pdf
                                                  HTTP/1.1

12:25:30.186727 IP 192.168.61.128.51282 > 150.161.2.9.80: Flags [.],
                                            ack 1461, win 32120, length 0

12:25:30.186787 IP 192.168.61.128.51282 > 150.161.2.9.80: Flags [.],
                                            ack 2921, win 35040, length 0

12:25:30.186822 IP 192.168.61.128.51282 > 150.161.2.9.80: Flags [.],
                                            ack 4273, win 37960, length 0

12:25:30.200124 IP 192.168.61.128.51282 > 150.161.2.9.80: Flags [.],
                                            ack 5733, win 40880, length 0
```

```
12:25:30.200250 IP 192.168.61.128.51282 > 150.161.2.9.80: Flags [.],
                                          ack 7193, win 43800, length 0

12:25:30.200345 IP 192.168.61.128.51282 > 150.161.2.9.80: Flags [.],
                                          ack 8653, win 46720, length 0

12:25:30.200422 IP 192.168.61.128.51282 > 150.161.2.9.80: Flags [.],
                                          ack 9969, win 49640, length 0
```

The *tcpdump* utility can also generate a dump file in binary format by using the option -w. This option saves the output in a file *file-name.pcap*, which can be read by *tcpdump* with the -r option. It is worth noting that one cannot open a file with extension *pcap* with a text editor since it is in binary format.

These basic features will help you get started with this *tcpdump*. For a more detailed description of *tcpdump* options and filters, look at [426]. It is also important to mention that the analyst may not be restrained to the *tcpdump* utility. There are many other valuable tools for monitoring and analysis of network traffic such as Wireshark [467], NetworkMiner [303], SolarWinds [405], WinDump [466] and Ngrep [307], for instance.

Command *ping*

The ***ping*** utility is used to check the reachability of a host on the Internet. It is commonly used to check if a host is alive and verify if a host-to-host connection is performing. For instance the command "*ping -c5 108.61.13.174*" sends five (-*c5*) packets to the host address *108.61.13.174*. Following, we have a typical display of a *ping* session, which shows five packets of fifty-six bytes sent to the host address *108.61.13.174* and receiving five packets of sixty-four bytes sent from the host. The round trip time (*rtt*)[16] of each transaction is shown as well as a short statistical summary. Check *man ping* to see the options and other information about this command.

```
PING 108.61.13.174 (108.61.13.174) 56(84) bytes of data.
64 bytes from 108.61.13.174: icmp_seq=1 ttl=128 time=253 ms
64 bytes from 108.61.13.174: icmp_seq=2 ttl=128 time=248 ms
64 bytes from 108.61.13.174: icmp_seq=3 ttl=128 time=255 ms
64 bytes from 108.61.13.174: icmp_seq=4 ttl=128 time=252 ms
64 bytes from 108.61.13.174: icmp_seq=5 ttl=128 time=249 ms

--- 108.61.13.174 ping statistics ---
5 packets transmitted, 5 received, 0% packet loss, time 4006ms
rtt min/avg/max/mdev = 248.339/252.008/255.728/2.839 ms
```

Command *iperf*

The utility *iperf* is an open-source networking tool used to measure *TCP* and *UDP* throughput in a network. *Iperf* can be used in Linux, Windows, and other operating systems. The *iperf* tool works in the client-server model that one computer should

---

[16]*rtt* is the delay between the instant a request is made from a caller to a provider and the instant of the respective reception by the caller of the requested information.

configure as a server, and the other should be set up as a client to start traffic flow. The connection between the two computers can be wired or wireless. Let us explain its use by introducing a small example: the server is a Windows machine, and the client is a computer with Linux. The *IP* address of the server is *192.168.61.1* and the *IP* address of the client is *192.168.61.128*. It is worth mentioning that both *IP* addresses should be reachable. The analyst may check this by using the *ping* tool. Besides, it is wise to use the *iperf* of the same version in both computers (client and server).

The utility *iperf* supports some configuration options. The most important are

- *-s* configures the computer as an *iperf* server. Ex.:*192.168.61.1*.

- *-c* configures the computer as an *iperf* client. Ex.:*192.168.61.128*.

- *-u* configures the traffic as *UDP* (the default is *TCP*).

- *-b* defines the target bandwidth for *UDP* traffic. Ex.: *100M* (*M* - Mbit-s/s).

- *-i* specifies the output interval in seconds. Ex.: *-i1* - Interval of 1,*s*.

- *-p* specifies the port number. Ex.: *-p 5555*.

- *-w* defines the windows size. Ex.: *-w 1M* (*M* - Mbits).

- *-d* configures the traffic as bi-directional.

- *-l* defines the length. Ex.: *-l 1046* (Bytes).

- *-V* configures that an *IPv6* address is used instead of *IPv4* (the default).

The options above allow us to set many configurations. Here, we show two simple setups for testing *TCP* and *UDP* traffics. First, let us configure the client as well as the server to test *TCP* traffic. As mentioned above, our server is a Windows-based system. We configured it as a server using the following *Powershell* command line

```
> iperf -s -i1
```

As can be seen, *-s* defines it as a server and *-i1* defines the output interval as 1 *s*. The client computer is a Linux machine, which was configured as a client by executing the command line

```
> iperf -c 192.168.61.1 -i1 -t60
```

The client machine tries to access the server (*192.168.61.1*) sending *TCP* traffic for sixty seconds (*-t60*), and the output is refreshed every second (*-i1*). Below, a chunk of data displayed on the client and server standard output is shown as an example.

Client Screen

```
----------------------------------------------------------------
Client connecting to 192.168.61.1, TCP port 5001
TCP window size: 43.8 KByte (default)
----------------------------------------------------------------
[  3] local 192.168.61.128 port 58994 connected with 192.168.61.1
                                                          port 5001
[ ID] Interval        Transfer     Bandwidth
[  3]  0.0- 1.0 sec  23.6 MBytes   198 Mbits/sec
[  3]  1.0- 2.0 sec  28.0 MBytes   235 Mbits/sec
[  3]  2.0- 3.0 sec  15.8 MBytes   132 Mbits/sec
[  3]  3.0- 4.0 sec  19.5 MBytes   164 Mbits/sec
            ...            ...          ...
[  3] 55.0-56.0 sec  29.6 MBytes   249 Mbits/sec
[  3] 56.0-57.0 sec  21.2 MBytes   178 Mbits/sec
[  3] 57.0-58.0 sec  31.1 MBytes   261 Mbits/sec
[  3] 58.0-59.0 sec  29.2 MBytes   245 Mbits/sec
[  3] 59.0-60.0 sec  32.1 MBytes   269 Mbits/sec
[  3]  0.0-60.0 sec  1.65 GBytes   237 Mbits/sec
```

Server Screen

```
----------------------------------------------------------------
Server listening on TCP port 5001
TCP window size: 64.0 KByte (default)
----------------------------------------------------------------
[  4] local 192.168.61.1 port 5001 connected with 192.168.61.128
                                                          port 58994
[ ID] Interval        Transfer     Bandwidth
[  4]  0.0- 1.0 sec  23.6 MBytes   198 Mbits/sec
[  4]  1.0- 2.0 sec  28.0 MBytes   235 Mbits/sec
[  4]  2.0- 3.0 sec  15.6 MBytes   131 Mbits/sec
[  4]  3.0- 4.0 sec  19.6 MBytes   164 Mbits/sec
            ...            ...          ...
[  4] 55.0-56.0 sec  29.4 MBytes   247 Mbits/sec
[  4] 56.0-57.0 sec  21.3 MBytes   179 Mbits/sec
[  4] 57.0-58.0 sec  31.2 MBytes   262 Mbits/sec
[  4] 58.0-59.0 sec  29.1 MBytes   244 Mbits/sec
[  4] 59.0-60.0 sec  32.2 MBytes   270 Mbits/sec
[  4]  0.0-60.0 sec  1.65 GBytes   237 Mbits/sec
```

Now, let us configure the client and the server to test *UDP* traffic. We configured it as a server using the following *Powershell* command line

```
> iperf -s -i1 -u
```

As can be seen, *-s* defines it as a server, *-i1* defines the output interval as 1 *s*, and the option *-u* defines the *UDP* traffic. The client computer is (Linux machine) configured to execute the command line

```
> iperf -c 192.168.61.1 -i1 -t60 -u -b 1000M
```

The client machine tries to access the server (*192.168.61.1*) sending *UDP* traffic (*-u*) for sixty seconds (*-t60*); the output is refreshed every second (*-i1*) and defines the target bandwidth as *1000 Mbits/s*. Below, a chunk of data displayed on the client and server standard output is shown as an example.

Client Screen

```
--------------------------------------------------------------
Client connecting to 192.168.61.1, UDP port 5001
Sending 1470 byte datagrams
UDP buffer size:  160 KByte (default)
--------------------------------------------------------------
[   3] local 192.168.61.128 port 34970 connected with 192.168.61.1
                                                          port 5001
[ ID] Interval         Transfer      Bandwidth
[   3]   0.0- 1.0 sec  46.4 MBytes   390 Mbits/sec
[   3]   1.0- 2.0 sec  39.6 MBytes   332 Mbits/sec
[   3]   2.0- 3.0 sec  44.4 MBytes   372 Mbits/sec
[   3]   3.0- 4.0 sec  41.6 MBytes   349 Mbits/sec
            ...             ...          ...
[   3] 56.0-57.0 sec  49.6 MBytes   416 Mbits/sec
[   3] 57.0-58.0 sec  45.3 MBytes   380 Mbits/sec
[   3] 58.0-59.0 sec  49.5 MBytes   415 Mbits/sec
[   3] 59.0-60.0 sec  49.6 MBytes   416 Mbits/sec
[   3]   0.0-60.0 sec  2.65 GBytes   380 Mbits/sec
[   3] Sent 1939010 datagrams
[   3] Server Report:
[   3]   0.0-60.0 sec  2.65 GBytes   380 Mbits/sec    0.237 ms
                                                     0/1939009 (0%)
[   3]   0.0-60.0 sec  1 datagrams received out-of-order
```

Server Screen

```
-----------------------------------------------------------
Server listening on UDP port 5001
Receiving 1470 byte datagrams
UDP buffer size: 64.0 KByte (default)
-----------------------------------------------------------
[   3] local 192.168.61.1 port 5001 connected with 192.168.61.128 port 34970
[ ID] Interval       Transfer     Bandwidth        Jitter   Lost/Total Datagrams
[   3]  0.0- 1.0 sec  46.5 MBytes   390 Mbits/sec   0.012 ms    0/33169 (0%)
[   3]  1.0- 2.0 sec  39.6 MBytes   332 Mbits/sec   0.022 ms    0/28229 (0%)
[   3]  2.0- 3.0 sec  44.4 MBytes   372 Mbits/sec   0.020 ms    0/31643 (0%)
[   3]  3.0- 4.0 sec  41.6 MBytes   349 Mbits/sec   0.019 ms    0/29643 (0%)
         ...            ...           ...
[   3] 56.0-57.0 sec  49.6 MBytes   416 Mbits/sec   0.028 ms    0/35377 (0%)
[   3] 57.0-58.0 sec  45.3 MBytes   380 Mbits/sec   0.034 ms    0/32347 (0%)
[   3] 58.0-59.0 sec  49.4 MBytes   415 Mbits/sec   0.034 ms    0/35266 (0%)
[   3] 59.0-60.0 sec  49.6 MBytes   416 Mbits/sec   0.049 ms    0/35391 (0%)
[   3]  0.0-60.0 sec  2.65 GBytes   380 Mbits/sec   0.238 ms    0/1939009 (0%)
[   3]  0.0-60.0 sec  1 datagrams received out-of-order
```

Dstat Tool

dstat is a general-purpose system monitoring tool written in *Python* that combines many functionalities provided by *iostat*, *vmstat*, *netstat*, and *mpstat* [110, 111]. *dstat* provides information organized in columns and better formatted than the previous tools and commands. *dstat* default output is designed for being displayed on the screen in real-time. However, the output may also be exported to a CSV[17] output

---

[17]Comma-Separated Values.

file or directed to a text file. This section does not fully describe this tool but rather introduces some interesting options supported by *dstat* and compels the analyst to expand its features in specific documents.

The command line for executing *dstat* may be composed of the following fields:

```
> dstat [-options] [--advanced options] [delay] [count]
```

There are several standard monitoring options, besides external plugins the analyst can use. The argument *delay* specifies the delay in seconds between each measuring update. If no argument is explicitly provided in this field, the default value (one second) is adopted. The argument *count* specifies the number of updates to display before ending the measuring process. If no value is defined for this field, the monitoring process continues until a control-c command is executed. The list of options can be displayed by executing the command line:

```
> dstat -h
```

Some important options are depicted below:

- -c, −−cpu enables cpu stats,

- -C 0,3,total includes cpu0, cpu3 and total,

- -d, −−disk enables disk stats,

- -D total,hda includes hda and total,

- -g, −−page enables page stats,

- -i, −−int enables interrupt stats,

- -I 5,eth2 includes int5 and interrupt used by eth2,

- -l, −−load enables load stats,

- -m, −−mem enables memory stats,

- -n, −−net enables network stats,

- -N eth1,total includes eth1 and total,

- -p, −−proc enables process stats,

- -r, −−io enables io stats,

- -s, −−swap enables swap stats,

- -S swap1,total includes swap1 and total,

- -t, −−time enables time/date output,

- -T, −−epoch enables time counter (seconds),

- -y, −−sys enables system stats,

- -a, −−all equals -cdngy (default),

- -f, −−full expands -C, -D, -I, -N and -S discovery lists, and

- -v, −−vmstat equals -pmgdsc -D total;

and

- −−aio enables aio stats,

- −−fs, –filesystem enables fs stats,

- −−ipc enables ipc stats,

- −−lock enables lock stats,

- −−raw enables raw stats,

- −−socket enables socket stats,

- −−tcp enables tcp stats,

- −−udp enables udp stats,

- −−unix enables unix stats, and

- −−vm enables vm stats.

The list of options and external plugins can also be seen by executing the command line:

```
> dstat --list
```

A typical output shows the internal commands and the list of plugins as presented below.

internal:

```
aio, cpu, cpu24, disk, disk24, disk24old, epoch, fs, int,
    int24, io, ipc, load, lock, mem, net, page, page24,
    proc, raw, socket, swap, swapold, sys, tcp, time, udp,
    unix, vm
```

/usr/share/dstat:

```
/usr/share/dstat:
battery, battery-remain, cpufreq, dbus, disk-tps, disk-util,
    dstat, dstat-cpu, dstat-ctxt, dstat-mem, fan, freespace,
    gpfs, gpfs-ops, helloworld, innodb-buffer, innodb-io,
    innodb-ops, lustre, memcache-hits, mysql-io, mysql-keys,
    mysql5-cmds, mysql5-io, mysql5-keys, net-packets, nfs3,
    nfs3-ops, nfsd3, nfsd3-ops, ntp, postfix, power, proc-count,
    qmail, rpc, rpcd, sendmail, snooze, squid, test, thermal,
    top-bio, top-bio-adv, top-childwait, top-cpu, top-cpu-adv,
    top-cputime, top-cputime-avg, top-int, top-io, top-io-adv,
    top-latency, top-latency-avg, top-mem, top-oom, utmp,
vm-memctl, vmk-hba, vmk-int, vmk-nic, vz-cpu, vz-io,
    vz-ubc, wifi
```

Running the *dstat* command without any options and arguments is equivalent to adopting *-cdngy* (default) options or *-a* option. Executing this command displays

- **CPU stats**: cpu usage taking into account user-level (**usr**) processes, system-level (**sys**) processes, idle (**idl**) state, waiting (**wai**) state, hard interrupt (**hiq**) state, and soft interrupt (**siq**) state,

- **Disk stats**: total number of read (**read**) and write (**writ**) operations on disks,

- **Network stats**: total amount of bytes received (**recv**) and sent (**send**) on network interfaces,

- **Paging stats**: number of times information is copied into (**in**) and moved out (**out**) of memory, and

- **System stats**: number of interrupts (int) and context switches (**csw**).

As an example, a typical output looks like

```
> dstat
You did not select any stats, using -cdngy by default.
[71----total-cpu-usage---- -dsk/total- -net/total- ---paging-- ---system--
usr sys idl wai hiq siq| read  writ| recv  send|  in   out | int   csw
  1   1  97   1   0   0| 45k   19k|    0     0 |  6B 3363B|  65   231
 12   6  82   0   0   0| 120k    0 | 346B  333B|   0     0 | 409  2470
 12   4  81   3   0   0| 36k     0 | 180B  193B|   0     0 | 368  2812
 27  13  60   0   0   0|4096B    0 |3916B 4107B|   0     0 | 525  4615
 23   6  70   0   0   1|   0     0 |1778B  541B|   0     0 | 533  4626
 21  12  67   0   0   0| 116k  88k|5139B 2952B|   0     0 | 440  3765
 52  31  15   0   0   1| 236k 272k| 42k   10k|   0     0 | 679  7825
 22  15  60   1   0   1| 56k     0 | 11k 3994B|   0     0 | 624  6655
 75  17   7   0   0   1| 120k    0 | 32k   12k|   0     0 | 603  6500
 67  29   0   0   0   4|3352k    0 | 165k  14k|   0     0 | 701  5017
 76  23   0   0   0   1|1152k    0 | 20k   10k|   0     0 | 669  5125
      ...                   ...           ...            ...          ...
 85  13   0   0   0   2| 132k    0 | 27k   14k|   0     0 | 684  4160
 74  23   2   0   0   1| 192k 1568k| 57k   16k|   0     0 | 670  7111
 79  18   0   0   0   3| 60k   64k| 64k   14k|   0     0 | 769  9482
 72  24   0   0   0   3| 124k 8968k| 24k 5906B|   0     0 | 898  8253
```

```
62  38   0   0   0   0| 112k 1252k|  13k 7575B|    0 1252k| 437 3700
36  47   0   0   0  18|  84k   11M|  11k 3130B|    0   11M| 534 1966
69  31   0   0   0   0| 284k    0 | 625B  827B|    0    0 | 189  493
43  50   0   0   0   7|8192B 2268k|2510B 2562B|    0 5548k| 468  577
92   0   0   0   0   8| 192k 4440k|2274B 1111B|    0    0 |  66  197
71  21   0   0   0   7| 140k 4096k|7231B 2720B|    0 8196k| 438 1131
41  59   0   0   0   0| 408k 4172k| 835B 2998B|  96k  72k| 110  459
    ...              ...          ...          ...          ...
71  26   0   0   0   3|2356k    0 |1318B 2060B|    0    0 | 624 3338
71  16   0  14   0   0|3360k  476k|  11k 3077B|4096B    0 | 634 2926
62  36   0   0   0   2| 268k    0 | 270B  270B|8192B    0 | 409 2242
44  51   0   0   0   5| 112k 3040k|9655B 1926B|    0 3040k| 438 2749
48  52   0   0   0   0|   0     0 | 420B  504B|    0    0 | 291 1741
58  35   0   0   0   7|1880k 5048k| 862B 2616B| 348k 5148k| 477 1996
27  45   0   0   0  27|1304k 5296k|  35k 1821B|    0 5124k| 350  622
43  43   0   0   0  15|1440k 8192k| 699B  778B|    0 8196k| 462  843
48  34   0  18   0   0|2888k   76k|  10k 1782B|    0   72k| 347 1032
27  30  20  23   0   0| 836k    0 | 750B 2807B|  40k    0 | 312 1515
```

Execute the respective commands depicted below to get the CPU usage, the server's memory usage, and the network stats. The respective contents are stored text files formatted in columns.

```
> dstat -c > dstat_cpu_dump.txt
> dstat -m > dstat_mem_dump.txt
> dstat -n > dstat_net_dump.txt
```

Execute the commands shown below to obtain process stats using most of the CPU and stats of the process using most of the memory. The content of the files is formatted in columns.

```
> dstat -c --top-cpu > dstat_top_cpu_dump.txt
> dstat -d --top-mem > dstat_top_mem_dump.txt
```

The command-line shown below combines internal stats and external plugins to get information about top CPU, top memory, and top latency processes.

```
> dstat --top-cpu-adv --top-mem --top-latency
```

The command-line below collects a sample of the stats described above every thirty seconds of size one-hundred twenty and stores it in a text file.

```
> dstat --top-cpu-adv --top-mem --top-latency 30 120
                        >> top_dump_cpu_mem_lat.txt
```

The content depicted below is a chunk of the sample collected.

```
[7]--------most-expensive-cpu-process------- --most-expensive- --highest-total--
process        pid  cpu read write| memory process | latency process
firefox       3649 1.4%  21k  14k| firefox   3507G| gjs         9583
firefox       7892  31%  68B  68B| firefox   3493G| firefox      303
gnome-shell   2555  13%  37B 3987B| firefox   3485G| Xorg          34
gjs          18300 2.5%   0  6888B| firefox   3485G| gjs           29
Xorg          2358 2.4% 199B  23k| firefox   3485G| gjs           28
fairymax     17839 3.3%   0    4B| firefox   3485G| gjs           26
fairymax     17839  13%   0    4B| firefox   3485G| Xorg          56
gjs          18300 2.4%   0  6880B| firefox   3485G| gjs           29
gjs          18300 2.4%   0  6900B| firefox   3485G| gjs           27
firefox       3649 8.4% 655k 457k| firefox   3485G| gjs           28
gnome-shell   2555  14%1799B6148B| firefox   3485G| Xorg          58
```

23.7.2 PROCESS INFORMATION

As already mentioned, the virtual filesystem */proc* contains a rich source of information about the hardware, kernel, and processes running on the system. The previous section discussed some relevant entries of this filesystem related to hardware and operating system resources. This section focuses on information gathering related to processes running on the system.

The virtual filesystem */proc* has a collection of subdirectories */proc/[pid]*, each of which contains files and subdirectories related to information of processes running on the system. The name of each subdirectory */[pid]* is the process identification (*pid*), which is a unique number that is automatically assigned to each process when it is created. Details of the process can be obtained by looking at the associated files in the directory for this process. As an example, consider this entry */proc/22462* on a computer. Executing "*ls -l*", we get the list of files and subdirectories */proc/22462* contains. In this specific case, we have

```
dr-xr-xr-x   2 prmm prmm 0 May 21 16:53 attr
-rw-r--r--   1 prmm prmm 0 May 21 16:58 autogroup
-r--------   1 prmm prmm 0 May 21 16:58 auxv
-r--r--r--   1 prmm prmm 0 May 21 16:58 cgroup
--w-------   1 prmm prmm 0 May 21 16:58 clear_refs
-r--r--r--   1 prmm prmm 0 May 21 11:27 cmdline
-rw-r--r--   1 prmm prmm 0 May 21 16:58 comm
-rw-r--r--   1 prmm prmm 0 May 21 16:58 coredump_filter
-r--r--r--   1 prmm prmm 0 May 21 16:58 cpuset
lrwxrwxrwx   1 prmm prmm 0 May 21 16:48 cwd -> /home/prmm
-r--------   1 prmm prmm 0 May 21 16:58 environ
lrwxrwxrwx   1 prmm prmm 0 May 21 11:27 exe -> /usr/lib/firefox/firefox
dr-x------   2 prmm prmm 0 May 21 11:27 fd
dr-x------   2 prmm prmm 0 May 21 16:48 fdinfo
-rw-r--r--   1 prmm prmm 0 May 21 16:58 gid_map
-r--------   1 prmm prmm 0 May 21 16:58 io
-r--r--r--   1 prmm prmm 0 May 21 16:58 limits
-rw-r--r--   1 prmm prmm 0 May 21 16:58 loginuid
dr-x------   2 prmm prmm 0 May 21 16:58 map_files
-r--r--r--   1 prmm prmm 0 May 21 11:27 maps
-rw-------   1 prmm prmm 0 May 21 16:58 mem
-r--r--r--   1 prmm prmm 0 May 21 11:27 mountinfo
-r--r--r--   1 prmm prmm 0 May 21 16:58 mounts
-r--------   1 prmm prmm 0 May 21 16:58 mountstats
dr-xr-xr-x   6 prmm prmm 0 May 21 16:58 net
dr-x--x--x   2 prmm prmm 0 May 21 11:27 ns
-rw-r--r--   1 prmm prmm 0 May 21 16:58 oom_adj
-r--r--r--   1 prmm prmm 0 May 21 16:58 oom_score
-rw-r--r--   1 prmm prmm 0 May 21 16:58 oom_score_adj
-r--------   1 prmm prmm 0 May 21 16:58 pagemap
-r--------   1 prmm prmm 0 May 21 16:58 personality
-rw-r--r--   1 prmm prmm 0 May 21 16:58 projid_map
lrwxrwxrwx   1 prmm prmm 0 May 21 16:48 root -> /
-rw-r--r--   1 prmm prmm 0 May 21 16:58 sched
-r--r--r--   1 prmm prmm 0 May 21 16:58 schedstat
-r--r--r--   1 prmm prmm 0 May 21 16:58 sessionid
-rw-r--r--   1 prmm prmm 0 May 21 16:58 setgroups
-r--r--r--   1 prmm prmm 0 May 21 16:58 smaps
-r--------   1 prmm prmm 0 May 21 16:58 stack
-r--r--r--   1 prmm prmm 0 May 21 11:27 stat
-r--r--r--   1 prmm prmm 0 May 21 11:28 statm
-r--r--r--   1 prmm prmm 0 May 21 11:27 status
-r--------   1 prmm prmm 0 May 21 16:58 syscall
dr-xr-xr-x  66 prmm prmm 0 May 21 11:27 task
-r--r--r--   1 prmm prmm 0 May 21 16:58 timers
-rw-r--r--   1 prmm prmm 0 May 21 16:58 uid_map
-r--r--r--   1 prmm prmm 0 May 21 16:58 wchan
```

For a detailed description of each file and subdirectory contained in */proc/[pid]*, check *man proc*. Now, let us introduce some basic tools that support gathering data of processes by looking at the virtual filesystem */proc* and particularly its entries */proc/[pid]*.

Command *pidof*

The command **pidof** finds the *pid*'s a running program. For example, executing the command *pidof firefox* in my personal computer, the following message was shown 2685 2560 2525 2462. Likewise, when *pidof gnome-shell* was executed, these *pids* were shown: 2050 1293. **pgrep** finds the *pid*'s a running program based that matches a pattern. For instance, when the command *pgrep efox* was executed in my personal computer, the following message was shown: 2462.

Command *top*

The command **top** was partially discussed in the previous section. There, we mentioned that when command *top* is executed, two summaries are displayed. The first summary was already discussed and depicted the system resource information. Here, we discuss the second part of the report. This part presents a dynamic view of processes and threads currently being managed by the operating system. The default option when executing *top* displays the processes sorted by their processor utilization, which is refreshed every 5 seconds by default. The refresh period can be modified with the *-d*.

Before describing the second part, it is worth highlighting the first two lines of the first part again. At the top left of the screen, the current time (22:24:53) is displayed in the format *hh* : *mm* : *ss*. The system uptime depicts the duration the system has been running. In this case, the system has been running only for six minutes and twenty-six seconds. The next field depicts the number of active user sessions, which, in this case, is only one. The second line of the first part displays the tasks' statistics regarding the processes running on the system. The "total" value is simply the total number of processes. For example, in the above screenshot, there are 235 processes, where one is *running*, and 234 are *sleeping*. The average load represents the processors' utilization over the last minute, over the last five minutes, and over the last fifteen minutes, respectively. In this particular example, the processors' utilization was 8%, 7%, and 4% on average over the three observation periods, respectively.

First Part

```
top - 22:24:53 up  6:26,  1 user,  load average: 0.08, 0.07, 0.04
Tasks: 235 total,   1 running, 234 sleeping,   0 stopped,   0 zombie
%Cpu(s):  3.0 us,  1.1 sy,  0.0 ni, 95.4 id,  0.5 wa,  0.0 hi,  0.0 si,  0.0 st
KiB Mem : 2061512 total,  237068 free, 1157924 used,  666520 buff/cache
KiB Swap:  998396 total,  989208 free,    9188 used.  610784 avail Mem
```

Second Part

```
  PID USER      PR  NI    VIRT    RES    SHR S  %CPU %MEM     TIME+ COMMAND
 1832 prmm      20   0  157360  46528  35508 S  12.5  2.3   1:08.73 Xorg
    1 root      20   0   24096   4980   3816 S   0.0  0.2   0:03.51 systemd
    2 root      20   0       0      0      0 S   0.0  0.0   0:00.00 kthreadd
    3 root      20   0       0      0      0 S   0.0  0.0   0:04.02 ksoftirqd/0
    5 root       0 -20       0      0      0 S   0.0  0.0   0:00.00 kworker/0:0H
    7 root      20   0       0      0      0 S   0.0  0.0   0:03.55 rcu_sched
    8 root      20   0       0      0      0 S   0.0  0.0   0:00.00 rcu_bh
    9 root      rt   0       0      0      0 S   0.0  0.0   0:00.00 migration/0
   10 root      rt   0       0      0      0 S   0.0  0.0   0:00.10 watchdog/0
   11 root      20   0       0      0      0 S   0.0  0.0   0:00.01 kdevtmpfs
   12 root       0 -20       0      0      0 S   0.0  0.0   0:00.00 netns
   13 root       0 -20       0      0      0 S   0.0  0.0   0:00.00 perf
   14 root      20   0       0      0      0 S   0.0  0.0   0:00.02 khungtaskd
   15 root       0 -20       0      0      0 S   0.0  0.0   0:00.00 writeback
   16 root      25   5       0      0      0 S   0.0  0.0   0:00.00 ksmd
   17 root      39  19       0      0      0 S   0.0  0.0   0:00.00 khugepaged
   18 root       0 -20       0      0      0 S   0.0  0.0   0:00.00 crypto
```

This second part consists of a minimum of two lines. The first line shows the report header, and the following lines provide the respective information for each process, where *PID* is the process *id*. *USER* is the "effective" user who started the process. Linux assigns a real user *id* and an effective user *id* to processes. The latter allows a process acting on behalf of another user, such as a non-root user, to be elevated to root. *PR* field shows the scheduling priority of the process from the perspective of the kernel. *NI* field shows the "nice" value of a process. The *nice* value affects the priority of a process. *VIRT*, *RES*, *SHR* and *%MEM* are related to memory consumption of the processes. *VIRT* is the total amount of memory consumed by a process, considering its code, the data stored in memory, and memory that have been swapped to the disk. *RES* is the memory consumed by the process in RAM. *%MEM* is the percentage of the total RAM available, *SHR* is the amount of memory shared with other processes. *S* shows the process state. *TIME+* is the total processor time used by the process since it started with the resolution of hundredths of a second, and *COMMAND* shows the name of the processes. Check *man top* for a detailed explanation of options and display formats.

Command *ps*

The command ***ps*** shows information about a selection of the active processes. The general syntax for the ps command is *"ps [options]"*, where the options are specified by parameters (keywords) or a combination of parameters. Such combinations provide a vast number of options that can be used to show different information about a specific group of processes. Look at *man ps* for a detailed description of options supported by this command. It is worth mentioning that the *options* and combination of options may be preceded by a hyphen or not, and the use of hyphen may change the content of what is displayed about the process. Details on the use of hyphens and the respective semantics may be found in *man ps*.

Now, we present some simple examples of the use of *ps*; however, many more options are possible.

1. *"ps"* shows the *PID*, *TTY*, *TIME* and *CMD* of the processes of the current shell. *PID* is the process *ID*, *TTY* is the terminal that the user is logged in, *TIME* is the time in minutes and seconds that the process has been running, and *CMD* is the command that launched the process.

2. *"ps -A"* or *ps -e* displays *PID*, *TTY*, *TIME*, and *CMD* for all the running processes.

3. *"ps -T"* shows the *PID*, *TTY*, *TIME*, and *CMD* for all processes associated to the terminal.

4. *"ps -a"* displays *PID*, *TTY*, *TIME*, and *CMD* for all the running processes except those associated to the terminal.

5. *"ps -C command`name"* displays *PID*, *TTY*, *TIME*, and *CMD* for the process whose executable name is given in the *command`name*. Ex.: *"ps -C firefox"*

6. *"ps -p process`id"* shows the *PID*, *TTY*, *TIME*, and *CMD* for the process whose identification number is *process`id*. Ex.: *"ps -p 2437"*. Information of multiple processes may be obtained by specifying multiple process IDs separated by comma. Ex.: *"ps -p 2437,2525"*.

7. *"ps -u user`id"* displays the *PID*, *TTY*, *TIME*, and *CMD* of processes whose owner is *user`id*. Ex.: *"ps -u root"*, *"ps -u prmm"*.

8. *"ps u process`id"* displays the *USER*, *PID*, *%CPU*, *%MEM*, *RSS,TTY*, *STAT*, *START,TIME*, and *COMMAND* for the process whose identification number is *process`id*. Ex.: *"ps u 2825"*. *%CPU* is processor utilization related to the

process. *%MEM* is the ratio of the process's resident memory to the physical memory on the machine, expressed as a percentage. *RSS* resident sets size, the non-swapped physical memory that a task has used (in kiloBytes). *STAT* is the process state, and *START* is the time the command started.

9. *"ps u"* displays the information in the format depicted in item 8 for all processes associated with the user who started the terminal.

The information depicted below is a typical small chunk of data obtained when the command *"ps u"* is executed.

```
      PID  %CPU %MEM   VSZ   RSS  TTY  STAT START   TIME COMMAND
prmm  1830  0.0  0.2  28868  5184 tty2 Ssl+ 02:17   0:00

/usr/lib/gdm3/gdm-x-session --run-script gnome-session --session=gnome

prmm  1832  0.2  2.1 159376 45236 tty2 S+   02:17   1:59

/usr/lib/xorg/Xorg vt2 -displayfd 3 -auth /run/user/1000/gdm/Xauthority
                                                          -background none

prmm  1860  0.0  0.2   6560  4260 tty2 S+   02:17   0:01

dbus-daemon --print-address 4 --session

prmm  1863  0.0  0.6  92148 13436 tty2 Sl+  02:17   0:01

/usr/lib/gnome-session/gnome-session-binary --session=gnome

prmm  1955  0.0  0.2  46452  5932 tty2 Sl+  02:17   0:00

/usr/lib/gvfs/gvfsd

prmm  1960  0.0  0.2  43428  5480 tty2 Sl+  02:17   0:00

/usr/lib/at-spi2-core/at-spi-bus-launcher
```

Command *pstree*

The command ***pstree*** displays all running processes as a tree. The tree is rooted at either the *pid* specified in the command line or, if no *pid* is specified, *init*[18] if *pid* is omitted. If a user name is specified, all process trees rooted at processes owned by that user are shown. The command *pstree* supports many options. For a detailed view, refer to *man pstree*. As an example, consider the execution of the following command line *"pstree -p"*. The option *p* includes the process identification (*pid*) of each process in the tree of processes. A typical portion of the output when this command line is executed is

---

[18]The process *init* is the parent of all processes on the system and is executed by the kernel. It is responsible for starting all other processes and is also the parent of processes whose original parents have died.

```
systemd(1)-+-NetworkManager(902)-+-{gdbus}(1094)
           |                      `-{gmain}(1092)
           |-VGAuthService(881)
           |-accounts-daemon(875)-+-{gdbus}(1009)
           |                      `-{gmain}(1007)
           |-acpid(874)
           |-agetty(975)
           |-at-spi-bus-laun(1338)-+-dbus-daemon(1343)
           |                       |-{dconf worker}(1339)
           |                       |-{gdbus}(1342)
           |                       `-{gmain}(1340)
           |-at-spi-bus-laun(2180)-+-dbus-daemon(2187)
           |                       |-{dconf worker}(2182)
           |                       |-{gdbus}(2186)
           |                       `-{gmain}(2183)
           ...                     ...
           |                       |-{dconf worker}(2640)
           |                       |-{evolution-calen}(2641)
           |                       |-{gdbus}(2642)
           |                       `-{gmain}(2635)
           |-evolution-sourc(2434)-+-{dconf worker}(2435)
           |                       |-{gdbus}(2437)
           |                       `-{gmain}(2436)
           |-firefox(5217)-+-Web Content(5305)-+-{Chrome_~dThread}(5309)
           |               |                    |-{DOM File}(5316)
           |               |                    |-{DOM Worker}(5414)
           |               |                    |-{HTML5 Parser}(5342)
           ...             |                    ...
```

Consider, as an example, the command line "*pstree -p 5217*". This command line, besides specifying the option *-p*, which results in an output with *pid* attached to each process name, specifies a process. The specified process has *5217*. The number *5217* is the *pid* of the *firefox* process; hence the output is the process tree rooted in the process identified by *5217*. A typical portion of the output when this command line is executed is

```
firefox(5217)-+-Web Content(5305)-+-{Chrome_~dThread}(5309)
              |                    |-{DOM File}(5316)
              |                    |-{DOM Worker}(6323)
              |                    |-{HTML5 Parser}(5342)
              |                    |-{ImageBr~geChild}(5320)
              |                    |-{ImageIO}(5319)
              |                    |-{ImgDecoder #1}(5318)

              ...                  ...

              |                    `-{Worker Launcher}(5390)
              |-WebExtensions(5327)-+-{Chrome_~dThread}(5330)
              |                     |-{DOM File}(5338)
              |                     |-{HTML5 Parser}(5351)
              |                     |-{ImageBr~geChild}(5346)
              |                     |-{ImageIO}(5345)

              ...                  ...
```

Command *lsof*

The command *lsof* displays information about files that are opened by processes. An open file could be an ordinary disk file, directory, pseudo-file, pseudo-directory, library, device file[19], stream sockets, and network file systems. This command supports

---

[19]Devices handled as files. Device files are classified as character device files, block device files

several options. For an in-depth view of its options and formats, refer to *man lsof*. When no option is specified, *lsof* lists the open files of all active processes. As an example, consider the command line "*lsof -p 29003*", where *29003* is the *pid* of a process named *cwf*. When the command line was executed, the data below was displayed.

```
COMMAND   PID USER    FD    TYPE DEVICE SIZE/OFF    NODE NAME
cwf     29003 prmm    cwd    DIR    8,1    4096 943233 /home/prmm/Measuring/C
cwf     29003 prmm    rtd    DIR    8,1    4096      2 /
cwf     29003 prmm    txt    REG    8,1    7596 943238
                                          /home/prmm/Measuring/C/cwf
cwf     29003 prmm    mem    REG    8,1 1786484 130587
                                          /lib/i386-linux-gnu/libc-2.23.so
cwf     29003 prmm    mem    REG    8,1  147688 130563
                                          /lib/i386-linux-gnu/ld-2.23.so
cwf     29003 prmm     0u    CHR  136,2     0t0      5 /dev/pts/2
cwf     29003 prmm     1u    CHR  136,2     0t0      5 /dev/pts/2
cwf     29003 prmm     2u    CHR  136,2     0t0      5 /dev/pts/2
cwf     29003 prmm     3w    REG    8,1       0 943239
                                          /home/prmm/Measuring/C/file1.txt
```

In the content shows two open directories */home/prmm/Measuring/C* and */proc/2*, two libraries (*libc-2.23.so* and *ld-2.23.so*), three character-device files (*/dev/pts/2*), one file that contains the code of the process whose *pid = 29003* (*cwf*), and one data file (*file1.txt*).

Command */usr/bin/time*

The */usr/bin/time* command is used to calculate how long a given command takes to execute. It is useful to measure the execution time of scripts and commands. The analyst, however, should be aware that most Linux shells have their built-in versions of the time command. For instance, if the command line "*type time*" is executed in a bash shell, the display output is "*time is a shell keyword*". On the other hand, if the command line "*type /usr/bin/time*" is run, the display output is "*/usr/bin/time is /usr/bin/time*". Likewise, executing "*type time*" in a *zsh* shell, the display output is "*time is a reserved keyword*". Therefore, if one needs to execute the Gnu *time* command (*type /usr/bin/time*), the analyst must specify the full path to the *time* binary, which is usually */usr/bin/time*. The command *type /usr/bin/time* has configuration options. Check *man /usr/bin/time* for a detailed explanation about its options and display formats. The output format can be configured in a string specified with the *-f* option. The basic syntax for executing */usr/bin/time* with the output format option is */usr/bin/time string command*, where *command* is the utility whose execution time is to be measured. The *string* is an *ASCII* string with specified keywords depicted by a letter preceded by the symbol *%*. Therefore, when the command line "*/usr/bin/time -f "Elapsed real time (s) %e" gcc cwf.c -o cwf*" is executed, the display output is similar to

```
Elapsed Time (s) 0.05
```

The information shown by the execution of the command */usr/bin/time* is defined by the following keywords:

- *c* specifies the number of context switches due to time slicing.

- *C* specifies the name and arguments of the command being measured.

- *D* shows the average size of the unshared data area (KB).

- *e* shows the elapsed real time (s).

- *E* shows the elapsed time as *hours:minutes:seconds.*

- *F* depicts the number of input-output page faults.

- *I* depicts the number of filesystem inputs.

- *k* depicts the number of signals delivered to the process.

- *K* shows the average total (data+stack+text) memory use (KB).

- *M* depicts the maximum resident set size (KB).

- *O* depicts the number of filesystem outputs.

- *p* shows the average unshared stack size (KB).

- *P* shows the processor utilization.

- *r* depicts the number of socket messages received.

- *R* shows the number of recoverable page faults.

- *s* shows the number of socket messages sent.

- *S* shows the total processor time (in seconds) used by the system on behalf of the process.

- *t* presents the average resident set size (KB).

- *U* presents the total processor time (in seconds) used directly by the process.

- *w* presents the number of voluntary context switches.

- *W* depicts the number of times the process was swapped out of the main memory.

- *x* depicts the exit status of the command.

- *X* presents the average shared text size (KB).

- *Z* system page size (bytes).

As another example, consider the execution of the command line

```
usr/bin/time -f "Elapsed Time (s) %e, Maximum Resident Set Size (KB) %M"
                                                ~prmm/Measuring/C/cwf
```

This command displays the execution time, and the respective maximum resident memory size of the process whose code file is *cwf* during its lifetime.

```
Elapsed Time (s) 7.77, Maximum Resident Set Size (KB) 980
```

Command *date*

The command *date* is a widely used tool in Linux-based systems. This command displays or sets the date and time of the system. Nevertheless, there are many options for customizing its output, such as setting dates and times, presenting the information in various formats, calculating dates, and even setting the system clock. The standard syntax of the command is "> *date options format*". The *date* command supports many options and output formats. For a detailed view of the available options and formats, please refer to "> *man date*". Here, we present some useful options that supports measuring delays or duration of events or between events. Hence, instead of introducing its options and then depicting some examples, we present specific useful examples, and for them, we discuss the respective options and formats.

The command *date* without any options and arguments displays the current date and time, such as

```
Fri May 29 14:34:11 -03 2020
```

The output shows that it is Friday, May 29, 2020, and the command was executed on 14:34:11 PM, using a 24-hour format (*hh:mm:ss*)[20], and the time zone is GMT[21] -3.

For example, the four following commands display date and time in ISO 8601 format[22], where "hours", "minutes", "seconds", or "ns" (nanoseconds) defines the precision.

```
> date --iso-8601=hours (command line)
> 2020-05-29T16-03:00    (output),


> date --iso-8601=minutes (command line)
> 2020-05-29T16:52-03:00  (output),


> date --iso-8601=seconds    (command line)
> 2020-05-29T16:51:05-03:00 (output), and


> date --iso-8601=ns                      (command line)
> 2020-05-29T17:16:08,650258894-03:00    (output).
```

The next command displays date and time in RFC 3339 format[23], where "ns" defines the precision.

---

[20]*hh* - hour, *mm* - minutes, and *ss* - seconds.
[21]Greenwich Mean Time.
[22]https://www.iso.org/iso-8601-date-and-time-format.html.
[23]https://tools.ietf.org/html/rfc3339.

```
> date --rfc-3339=ns                    (command line)
> 2020-05-29 16:53:59.899910494-03:00 (output).
```

The execution of the next command line displays the time of the day in 24-hour format (*hh:mm:ss*).

```
> date +%T   (command line)
> 16:55:26   (output).
```

The execution of the command line below shows the time representation of the current place.

```
> date +%X        (command line)
> 04:56:17 PM     (output).
```

The command *date* tool also includes this interesting feature where it can represent the current time as a count of the number of seconds from the UNIX epoch time[24] to the current time. This is an attractive characteristic for calculating an event duration of the delay between two events. The following command line provides such information.

```
> date +%s   (command line)
> 1590782231 (output).
```

The command *date* can provide the fraction of a second in nanoseconds. The execution of the following command line depicts this counting.

```
> date +%N   (command line)
> 772361029  (output).
```

The next command provides the current time as a count of the number of seconds from the UNIX epoch time to the current time with the precision of nanoseconds.

```
> date +%s.%N            (command line)
> 1590782334.256798918   (output).
```

The following script allows one to obtain the Unix time epoch before executing the programs */Measuring/C/fork3* and */Measuring/C/fork2* and after their execution. The difference between *end* and *start* was the duration for executing both programs, that is $d = end - start = 1.00409944\,s$.

---

[24](00:00:00, Jan 1, 1970).

```
#!/bin/bash
#Filename: time_take.sh
start=$(date +%s.%N)
~/Measuring/C/fork3
~/Measuring/C/fork2
end=$(date +%s.%N)
echo Time Epoch Before $start seconds.
echo Time Epoch After $end seconds.
```

```
Time Epoch Before 1590788876.851077030 seconds.
Time Epoch After 1590788877.855176470 seconds.
```

Setting the system time and date manually with the *date* command is not recommended since most Linux platforms usually have the system clock is synchronized using the *ntp* or *systemd-timesyncd services*. Nevertheless, if one needs to set the system date and time manually, the option *–set=* may be useful. For example, if one is required to set the date and time to 6:03 pm, May 29, 2020, one may type

```
> date --set="20200529 18:03".
```

Command *pidstat*

The *pidstat* command is used for monitoring either specific processes (*PID*) or all processes being managed by Linux. The basic syntax of this command is *pidstat options delay count*, where *delay* and *count* have the same meaning as shown for *vmstat*. The *pidstat* supports many configuration options. For a detailed view of these options, refer to *man pidstat*. If the command is executed without an explicitly defined option, only processors' activities are reported. Some important options are depicted below.

- *-C comm* displays processes whose command names include the string *comm*.

- *-d* reports input-output statistics, where

    o *UID* is the real user identification,

    o *USER* is the name of the real user owning the process,

    o *PID* is the identification number of the process,

    o *kB_rd/s* is the number of kilobytes the process read from disk per second,

    o *kB_wr/s* is the number of kilobytes the process has written to disk per second,

    o *kB_ccwr/s* is the number of kilobytes whose the process has canceled writing to disk,

- ○ *iodelay* is the delay spent waiting for sync block I/O completion and swapping block I/O completion, and
- ○ *Command* is the command name of the process.

- *-G process_name* displays processes whose command names include the string *process_name*.

- *-h* displays all activities horizontally on a single line.

- *-I* indicates, in multiprocessing systems, that processes' related utilization processors should be divided by the number of processors.

- *-l* displays the process command name and its arguments.

- *-p* $\{pid_1, pid_2, ..., pid_n \mid SELF \mid ALL\}$ selects processes for which statistics are to be reported, where *pid* is the process identification number. The *SELF* keyword indicates that the reported statistics are related to the *pidstat*. The keyword *ALL* indicates that the statistics to be reported are for all the processes.

- *-R* reports realtime priority and scheduling policy information. The following values may be displayed:

- ○ *UID, USER, PID* - already described - and
- ○ *prio* is the realtime priority of the process,
- ○ *policy* is the scheduling policy of the process, and
- ○ *Command* is the command name of the process.

- *-r* reports page faults and memory utilization. When reporting statistics for an individual process, the following values may be displayed:

- ○ *UID, USER, PID* - already described - and
- ○ *minflt/s* is the number of faults the process has made per second, which have not required loading memory pages from disk[25],
- ○ *majflt/s* is the number of faults the process has made per second, which have required loading memory pages from disk[26],
- ○ *VSZ* is the virtual memory utilization of the entire process (Kbytes),
- ○ *RSS* is the non-swapped physical memory used by the process (Kbytes).
- ○ *%MEM* is the process currently used share of available physical memory.
- ○ *Command* is the command name of the process.

- When reporting global statistics (*-T All*) for processes and all their children, the following values are displayed:

---

[25] minor faults.
[26] major faults.

- o *UID* is the real user identification number of the process that is being monitored together with its children,

- o *USER* is the name of the real user owning the process that is being monitored together with its children,

- o *PID* is the identification number of the process that is being monitored together with its children,

- o *minflt-nr* is the number of faults[25] made by the process and its children during the time interval,

- o *majflt-nr* is the number of faults[26] made by the process and all its children during the time interval, and

- o *Command* is the command name of the process and its children.

- **•** *-s* reports the stack utilization. The following values may be displayed:

  - o *UID, USER, PID* - already described - and

  - o *StkSize* is the amount of memory reserved for the process as a stack (Kbytes).

  - o *StkRef* is the amount of memory used as a stack (Kbytes).

  - o *Command* is the command name of the process.

- **•** *-T {TASK|CHILD|ALL}* specifies what has to be monitored by the *pidstat* command. The keyword *TASK* indicates individual processes. The keyword *CHILD* indicates that statistics are related to processes and their children. The keyword *ALL* indicates that the statistics are reported for all individual processes and their children[27].

- **•** *-t* displays statistics for threads associated with selected processes. This option adds the following values to the reports:

  - o *TGID* is the identification number of the thread group leader and

  - o *TID* is the identification number of the thread being monitored.

- **•** *-U username* displays the real user name of the processes instead of the *UID*. If the username is specified, then only processes belonging to the user are displayed.

- **•** *-u* reports processor utilization. When reporting statistics for individual processes, the following values may be displayed:

  - o *UID, USER, PID* - already described - and

  - o *%usr* is the processor utilization by the process at the user level. This field does not include time spent running a virtual processor.

  - o *%system* is the processor utilization by the process at the system level.

---

[27] The statistics of a child process are collected when it finishes or is killed.

- ○ *%guest* is the processor utilization by the process in a virtual machine (virtual processor).

- ○ *%CPU* is the processor utilization by the process. In multiprocessor systems, the processor utilization related to the processes is divided by the number of processors (cores) if option *-I* is set on the command line,

- ○ *CPU* is the processor number to which the process is attached, and

- ○ *Command* is the command name of the process.

- • When reporting global statistics (*-T All*) for processes and their children, the following values are displayed:

  - ○ *UID* is the real user identification number of the process together with its children,

  - ○ *USER* is the name of the real user owning the process together with its children,

  - ○ *PID* is the identification number of the process together with its children,

  - ○ *usr-ms* is the number of milliseconds spent by the process and its children at the user level during the interval of time, without including time spent running a virtual processor,

  - ○ *system-ms* is the number of milliseconds spent by the process and its children at the system level (kernel) during the interval of time,

  - ○ *guest-ms* is the number of milliseconds spent by the process and its children in a virtual machine (virtual processor), and

  - ○ *Command* is the command name of the task which is being monitored together with its children.

- • *-V* prints version.

- • *-v* reports the values of some kernel tables. The following values may be displayed:

  - ○ *UID, USER, PID* - already described - and

  - ○ *threads* is the number of threads associated with the current process,

  - ○ *fd-nr* is the number of file descriptors associated with the current process, and

  - ○ *Command* is the command name of the process.

- • *-w* reports the processes switching activity. The following values may be displayed:

  - ○ *UID, USER, PID* - already described - and

  - ○ *cswch/s* is the number of context switches due to unavailable resources, o *nvcswch/s* is the number of context switches due to time slice duration, and

    o *Command* is the command name of the process.

In the following, we present a set of examples using *pidstat* and some simple combinations of options. As a first example, we executed the command without any explicit option. In such a case, its execution provides the processor's statistics for every process managed by the Linux kernel (equivalent to *-p ALL*).

```
> pidstat
```

Below, a typical chunk of data is obtained by executing the command line above.

```
03:59:41 PM   UID        PID    %usr %system  %guest    %CPU   CPU  Command
03:59:41 PM     0          1    0.00    0.01    0.00    0.01     0  systemd
03:59:41 PM     0          3    0.00    0.01    0.00    0.01     0  ksoftirqd/0
03:59:41 PM     0          7    0.00    0.01    0.00    0.01     0  rcu_sched
03:59:41 PM     0         10    0.00    0.00    0.00    0.00     0  watchdog/0
            ...                   ...                     ...
03:59:41 PM  1000      16757    0.00    0.00    0.00    0.00     0  bash
03:59:41 PM  1000      17198    0.00    0.00    0.00    0.00     0  pidstat
03:59:41 PM  1000      27935    0.22    0.07    0.00    0.28     0  Web Content
03:59:41 PM  1000      28477    0.00    0.00    0.00    0.00     0  gconfd-2
```

Adopting the *-p* followed by a process identification number *PID* provides processor performance statistics for a particular process, as shown below. For instance, consider the following command.

```
> pidstat -p 5217
```

The obtained output, when the above command line was executed, was this:

```
10:59:55 AM   UID        PID    %usr %system  %guest    %CPU   CPU  Command
10:59:55 AM  1000       5217    0.90    0.42    0.00    1.33     0  firefox
```

The following example displays the processor's performance statistics for all the processes that match the keyword "*firefox*".

```
> pidstat -C "firefox"
```

The output displayed when the command line was executed is

```
1:03:53 AM    UID        PID    %usr %system  %guest    %CPU   CPU  Command
11:03:53 AM  1000       5217    0.92    0.43    0.00    1.35     0  firefox
```

The following example displays sample performance statistics specified by the process identified by *pid* (process identification number), *-p 5217*. The time between samples is depicted by the delay field value, in this case, 2 *s*.

```
> pidstat -p 5217 2
```

A typical portion of data obtained by the execution of the command above is shown below.

```
11:06:06 AM   UID      PID    %usr %system  %guest    %CPU  CPU  Command
11:06:08 AM  1000     5217    1.05    0.00    0.00    1.05    0  firefox
11:06:10 AM  1000     5217    1.04    0.52    0.00    1.56    0  firefox
11:06:12 AM  1000     5217    1.05    0.00    0.00    1.05    0  firefox
11:06:14 AM  1000     5217    0.53    1.05    0.00    1.58    0  firefox
```

We can use *pidstat* to obtain input-output statistics about a process by adopting the option *-d*. Consider, as an example, the following command line. This command-line asks for samples of input-output statistics of the process specified by *-p 19635*, where the time between samples is 2 *s*.

```
> pidstat -p 19635 -d 2
```

A typical chunk of data obtained by the execution of the command is depicted below.

```
06:14:32 PM   UID      PID   kB_rd/s   kB_wr/s kB_ccwr/s iodelay  Command
06:14:37 PM  1000    19635     71.52      0.00     0.00       3  firefox
06:14:42 PM  1000    19635    147.57   2475.08     0.00      10  firefox
06:14:47 PM  1000    19635    266.67    141.41     1.35       0  firefox
06:14:52 PM  1000    19635     25.60    436.80     0.00       1  firefox
06:14:57 PM  1000    19635     99.31     49.66     1.84       2  firefox
06:15:02 PM  1000    19635      0.00     22.59     0.00       0  firefox
06:15:07 PM  1000    19635   1484.62    173.85     0.00      10  firefox
06:15:12 PM  1000    19635      0.00      3.77     0.00       0  firefox
06:15:17 PM  1000    19635      0.00      4.23     0.00       0  firefox
```

The command *pidstat* may be used to find a memory leak using the following command.

```
]
> pidstat -p 5217 -r 5
```

This command-line reports samples of page faults statistics of the process specified by *-p 5217*. The time between samples is 5 *s*. Such a command supports spotting the memory leaking problems.

```
11:11:42 AM  1000     5217     0.00     0.00 1209512  368116  17.86  firefox
11:11:47 AM  1000     5217     0.00     0.00 1209512  368116  17.86  firefox
11:11:52 AM  1000     5217     0.21     0.00 1209512  368116  17.86  firefox
11:11:57 AM  1000     5217   162.41    13.14 1213164  367872  17.84  firefox
11:12:02 AM  1000     5217   221.09    13.28 1219176  368016  17.85  firefox
11:12:07 AM  1000     5217  1373.02    31.75 1221104  372248  18.06  firefox
```

Likewise, the following command line reports five (count field - 5) samples of page faults statistics of the process specified by *-p 5217*, where the time between samples is 2 *s*.

```
> pidstat -p 5217 2 5
```

A typical chunk of data obtained by the execution of the command above is depicted below.

```
11:16:30 AM   UID      PID    %usr %system  %guest    %CPU  CPU  Command
11:16:32 AM   1000     5217   1.57   0.00    0.00     1.57    0  firefox
11:16:34 AM   1000     5217   1.05   0.00    0.00     1.05    0  firefox
11:16:36 AM   1000     5217   1.04   0.00    0.00     1.04    0  firefox
11:16:38 AM   1000     5217   1.57   0.00    0.00     1.57    0  firefox
11:16:40 AM   1000     5217   2.14   0.53    0.00     2.67    0  firefox
Average:      1000     5217   1.47   0.10    0.00     1.57    -  firefox
```

The execution of the following command line reports the processor's utilization statistics related to the process (*-T TASK*) specified by *-p 5217*.

```
> pidstat -p 5217 -T TASK
```

The above command line is equivalent to *pidstat -p 5217*. A typical portion of data obtained by the execution of the command is depicted below.

```
11:28:08 AM   UID      PID    %usr %system  %guest    %CPU  CPU  Command
11:28:08 AM   1000     5217   0.95   0.44    0.00     1.39    0  firefox
```

The execution of the following command line reports the number of milliseconds spent by the process specified by *-p 5217* and its children in each specific processor's state (*usr*, *system*, *guest*) during the time interval.

```
> pidstat -p 5217 -T CHILD
```

Typical output data obtained by the execution of the command is depicted below.

```
11:27:55 AM   UID      PID    usr-ms system-ms  guest-ms  Command
11:27:55 AM   1000     5217   1147300    534220        0  firefox
```

The execution of the following command line reports the processor's statistics represented in the last two command lines (*-T ALL*).

```
> pidstat -p 5217 -T ALL
```

```
11:28:20 AM   UID      PID    %usr %system  %guest    %CPU   CPU  Command
11:28:20 AM   1000     5217   0.95    0.44    0.00    1.39     0  firefox

11:28:20 AM   UID      PID    usr-ms system-ms  guest-ms  Command
11:28:20 AM   1000     5217  1147600    534390         0  firefox
```

The execution of the following command line reports the processor's utilization (*u*), input-output (*d*), and memory utilization and page faults (*r*) related to the process specified by *-p 19635*. The time between samples is *5t s*

```
> pidstat -p 19635 -dru 5
```

A typical portion of the output data collected by the execution of the command is depicted below. It is worth mentioning that each class of statistics (processor utilization, input-output, and memory) is depicted in different report lines.

```
06:30:05 PM   UID      PID    %usr %system  %guest    %CPU   CPU  Command
06:30:10 PM   1000    19635   7.69    0.00    0.00    7.69     0  firefox

06:30:05 PM   UID      PID  minflt/s  majflt/s      VSZ      RSS   %MEM  Command
06:30:10 PM   1000    19635   182.74     0.00   993840   272776  13.23  firefox

06:30:05 PM   UID      PID   kB_rd/s   kB_wr/s kB_ccwr/s iodelay  Command
06:30:10 PM   1000    19635    0.00      0.00      0.00       0   firefox

06:30:10 PM   UID      PID    %usr %system  %guest    %CPU   CPU  Command
06:30:15 PM   1000    19635  17.93    0.00    0.00   17.93     0  firefox

06:30:10 PM   UID      PID  minflt/s  majflt/s      VSZ      RSS   %MEM  Command
06:30:15 PM   1000    19635   173.84     0.00   992004   274140  13.30  firefox

06:30:10 PM   UID      PID   kB_rd/s   kB_wr/s kB_ccwr/s iodelay  Command
06:30:15 PM   1000    19635    0.00      0.00      0.00       0   firefox
```

23.8 FINAL COMMENTS

This chapter presented some fundamental concepts related to performance measurement and essential tools, strategies, and techniques for computer system measurement. It also introduced some tools for performance data collection of computer systems. Besides, we also described a general strategy for measuring short-duration events in computer systems, discussed the program profiling process, and introduced some profiling tools. Finally, a significant part of the chapter was devoted to discussing system and process measuring tools for the Linux operating system.

EXERCISES

Exercise 1. Explain the concepts of accuracy and accuracy error.

Exercise 2. Describe repeatability and reproducibility.

Exercise 3. What is measurement system resolution?

Exercise 4. Consider a time measurement system whose timer clock frequency is specified as $f = 2\,kHz$, and the counter number of bits is $n = 10$. Determine the maximum time that this measurement system can measure before the counter's rollover.

Exercise 5. Assuming the measurement system mentioned in Exercise 4: (a) Calculate the shortest time that this system could measure. (b) What is the non-dimensional resolution of the measurement system?

Exercise 6. Now consider that the measurement system of Exercise 4 has a timer clock frequency specified as $f = 3.5\,kHz$. In this new configuration, (a) what is the maximum duration measured by this measurement system before the counter's rollover? (b) What is the dimensional resolution of the measurement system in this new configuration?

Exercise 7. Considering the measurement system presented in Exercise 6, what is the maximal quantization error provided by the system?

Exercise 8. Now assume the measurement system of Exercise 6 was modified, and a counter of twelve bits is adopted instead of a ten-bit counter. Calculate (a) the dimensional resolution, (b) the maximal quantization error, (c) the non-dimensional resolution, and (d) the maximum time that can be measured by this measurement system before the counter's rollover.

Exercise 9. Explain the concepts of precision and precision error.

Exercise 10. Describe the relations between accuracy, precision, and resolution of a measurement system.

Exercise 11. Explain why reducing errors related to the measurement system's inaccuracy is usually harder to reduce and more costly than errors due to imprecision.

Exercise 12. What are the advantages and drawbacks of event-driven measuring strategies and sample-based strategies? Explain.

Exercise 13. Consider a server was monitored for thirty minutes. During this period, the server processed 3600 transactions. The server utilization was recorded every sixty seconds during the monitoring period. The sample is shown in Table 23.3.

(a) What is the average time a transaction demands from the server considering the scenario described above?

(b) How would you classify the measuring strategy to estimate the time demanded of the server per transaction?

Exercise 14. A system is composed of two servers (S_1 and S_2) and one storage system (ST). This system is monitored for $2\,h$. On average, each system transaction executed one request to S_1, two requests to S_2, and eight IO operations on ST. During this period, the number of transactions processed by the system was 8400. The servers' utilization measures were recorded at a frequency of 0.5 samples per second. The

Table 23.3

Server Utilization - Sample Frequency $= 2\,sample/min$

Utilization - U_i		
0.44	0.34	0.62
0.70	0.58	0.70
0.56	0.68	0.61
0.40	0.40	0.67
0.43	0.63	0.44
0.49	0.44	0.62
0.46	0.31	0.68
0.43	0.65	0.53
0.44	0.65	0.39
0.48	0.69	0.34

Table 23.4

Servers' Utilization Sample - Sample Frequency $= 0.5\,samples/s$

U_{S1}			U_{S2}		
0.36	0.38	0.32	0.62	0.41	0.70
0.41	0.38	0.35	0.61	0.66	0.50
0.30	0.30	0.41	0.73	0.74	0.66
0.32	0.39	0.41	0.58	0.50	0.40
0.30	0.39	0.40	0.46	0.40	0.68

utilization measures of each server are presented in Table 23.4. The IO operation takes, on average, $50\,ms$.

(a) What is the average time a transaction demands from each server and the storage system?

(b) Which component is the system bottleneck?

Exercise 15. Consider a C language program source that multiplies two 8×8 matrices and calculates the time required to multiply them by inserting time function calls inside the source code.

Exercise 16. Use a programming language of choice and implement a program that calculates the inverse of a matrix of 8×8. Insert time function calls inside the source code to calculate the time required to obtain the matrix inversion.

Exercise 17. Explain why and how the time measurement system overhead may be a restraint for adopting an event measuring strategy to quantify the events' duration.

Exercise 18. Why would the statistical measurement-based strategy be an alternative for measuring short-duration events? What are the pros and cons of methods based on this strategy? Comment.

Exercise 19. Consider a computer program composed of many functions (methods or routines), and assume the expected time to process a specific function, named f_1, is very short. In other words, the execution time of this function is about the same order (or shorter) as the smallest duration the direct measurement mechanism supported by the computer can quantify. Due to these constraints, the *instruction-pointer sampling* strategy is adopted to estimate the execution time of function f_1.

Let us consider that the timer interruption frequency is $10kHz$, and assume the system (program running on the computer) was monitored for $8h$. Then, from the total number of samples, $1,679,623$ addresses belong to the address range of function f_1.

(a) Obtain the point estimate of the time to execute f_1.

(b) Considering a degree of confidence of 95%, calculate the confidence interval of the time to execute f_1 by considering that the normal distribution approximates the binomial distribution.

Exercise 20. What is a deterministic profile? Explain.

Exercise 21. What is a statistical profile? Explain.

Exercise 22. What are the pros and cons of deterministic and statistical profiling strategies? Explain each characteristic.

Exercise 23. Use *gprof* to evaluate the C language code depicted in List 11. This program generates 1000 lists of 25 prime numbers. Each prime number is in the range $0 - 10000$. Besides, for each list, the largest prime is also shown.

(a) Present the flat, the call graph profiles, and interpret them.

(b) Adjust the code by adopting suitable programming practices for improving its performance. Check the performance of the new version of the program by using the *gprof*.

Exercise 24. Use a programming language of choice (different from C programming language) and implement the same functionality described by the program depicted in Exercise 23. In addition, use a profiling tool that supports the programming language.

(a) Generate a program profile and analyze the program's most demanding function (routines, methods, procedures, etc.).

(b) Adjust the original code for improving its performance.

Algorithm 11 C Program - Exercise 23

```
 1: #include <sys/time.h>
 2: #include <stdio.h>
 3: #include <stdlib.h>
 4: int * mra(int al2, int mn) {
 5:          struct timeval tv;
 6:          gettimeofday(&tv,NULL);
 7:          int * as = 0;
 8:          int i;
 9:          as = (int*)malloc(al2*sizeof(int));
10:          srand(tv.tv_usec);
11:          for(i=0; i < al2; ++i)
12:                  as[i] = (random() % (mn - 2)) + 2;
13:          return as;
14: }
15: int ip(int x) {
16:          int y;
17:          for(y=2; y < x; ++y)
18:                  if((x % y) == 0)
19:                  return 0;
20:          return 1;
21: }
22: int * fp(int al3, int * arr) {
23:          int * as = 0;
24:          int i;
25:          as = (int*)malloc(al3*sizeof(int));
26:          for(i=0; i < al3; ++i)
27:                  if(ip(arr[i]))
28:                          as[i] = 1;
29:          return as;
30: }
31: int fl(int al4, int * nums, int * ips) {
32:          if(al4==0)
33:                  return -1;
34:          if(!ips[al4-1])
35:                  return fl(al4-1,nums,ips);
36:          if(fl(al4-1,nums,ips) > nums[al4-1])
37:                  return fl(al4-1,nums,ips);
38:          nums[al4-1];
39: }
40: void po(int al5, int * nums, int * ips, int l) {
41:          int i;
42:          for(i=0; i < al5; ++i)
43:                  if(ips[i])
44:                          printf("%d ",nums[i]);
45:          printf("\n The largest prime is %d \n",l);
46: }
47: int main(void) {
48:          int i, l, al, al1, mn, mn1;
49:          int * ra = 0;
50:          int * pr = 0;
51:          int k = 1000;
52:          al1 = 25;
53:          al = al1;
54:          mn1 = 10000;
55:          mn = mn1;
56:          printf("Generate %d list(s) of size %d of prime numbers - Each prime is within (0, %d) \n",k,al,mn)
57:          for(i=0; i < k; i++) {
58:                  al = al1;
59:                  mn = mn1;
60:                  ra = mra(al,mn);
61:                  pr = fp(al,ra);
62:                  l = fl(al,ra,pr);
63:                  printf("\n List number %d \n",i+1);
64:                  po(al,ra,pr,l);
65:                  free(ra);
66:                  free(pr);
67:          }
68:          return 0;
69: }
```

Exercise 25. For a computer system with a Linux operating system, obtain the contents of the following entries and interpret them:

(a) */proc/cpuinfo* carries data specifying processors and system architecture.

(b) */proc/meminfo* holds statistics on memory usage.

(c) */proc/stat* contains processors and memory usage information.

(d) */proc/uptime* carries the idle duration since the boot.

(e) */proc/devices* contains the character and block devices currently configured.

(f) */proc/diskstat* holds the I/O statistics of block devices.

(g) */proc/iomem* holds the current map of the system's memory for each physical device.

(h) */proc/ioports* contains a list of currently registered ports used for input or output communication with a device.

Exercise 26. The Script 12 below collects a one hundred-sized sample of memory utilization through the command *free*. The delay between measures is sixty seconds. At each collect, capture the total memory used and the free memory in megabytes. The script produces a *txt* file organized in columns.

Algorithm 12 Memory Collection Script - Exercise 26

```
free -m | awk 'NR==1{printf "%s\t %s\t\n", $2, $3}' >> memfree.txt;
for i in {1..100}
do
        free -m | awk 'NR==2{printf "%d\t %d\t\n", $2, $3}' >> memfree.txt;
        sleep 60
done
```

(a) Write a short document defining the computer system's current state by specifying the computer model, the number of processors, the operating system, the applications under execution, and the performance policy, and execute Script 12.

(b) Provide a statistical summary for the collected sample and suitable graphs to support the data analysis.

(c) Write a textual summary describing and interpreting measured data.

(d) Use *dstat* to collect the sample instead of the script above.

(e) Comment on the pros and cons of adopting *dstat*.

Exercise 27. Script 13 collects a one hundred-sized sample of CPU utilization through command *top*. The delay between measures is one hundred and twenty seconds. At each collect, capture the CPU utilization in each specific state: *us*, *sy*, *ni*, *id*, *wa*, *hi*, and *st*. The script produces a *txt* file organized in columns.

Algorithm 13 CPU Utilization Considering the State Classes - Collection Script - Exercise 27

```
top -b -n 1 | awk 'NR==3{printf "%s\t %s\t %s\t %s\t %s\t %s\t %s\t %s\t\n", $3,
                             $5, $7, $9, $11, $13, $15, $17}' >> topcpu.txt;
for i in {1..100}
do
 top -b -n 1 | awk 'NR==3{printf "%.3f%%\t %.3f%%\t %.3f%%\t %.3f%%\t %.3f%%\t
                             %.3f%%\t %.3f%%\t %.3f%%\t\n", $2/100, $4/100,
                             $6/100, $8/100, $10/100, $12/100, $14/100,
                             $16/100}' >> topcpu.txt;
 sleep 120;
done
```

(a) Write a short document defining the computer system's current state by specifying the computer model, the number of processors, the operating system, the applications under execution, and the performance policy, and execute Script 13.

(b) Analyze the sample and provide its statistical summary and suitable graphs to represent the collected data.

(c) Write a summary describing and interpreting the sample and the possible features of the system.

(d) Use *dstat* to collect the sample instead of the script above.

(e) Comment on the pros and cons of adopting *dstat*.

Exercise 28. Through command *top*, Script 14 collects a one hundred-sized sample of CPU utilization. The delay between measures is sixty seconds. The script produces a *txt* file organized in columns.

(a) Write document defining the computer system's current state by specifying the computer model, the number of processors, the operating system, the applications under execution, and the performance policy, and execute Script 14.

Algorithm 14 CPU Utilization - Collection Script - Exercise 28

```
printf "CPU Utilization \n" >> cpu_util.txt;
for i in {1..100}
do
 top -b -n 1 | awk 'NR==3{printf "%.3f%% \n",
                          ($2+$4+$6+$12+$14+$16)/100}'
                        >> cpu_util.txt;
 sleep 60;
done
```

(b) Analyze the collected sample, provide its statistical summary and suitable and graphs to represent the sample.

(c) Write the summary interpreting the sample and the possible features of the system.

(d) Use *dstat* to collect the sample instead of the script above.

(e) Comment on the pros and cons of adopting *dstat*.

Exercise 29. Script 15 collects a one hundred-sized sample of CPU utilization through command *top*. The delay between measures is one hundred and twenty seconds. At each collect, capture the CPU utilization in each specific state: *us*, *sy*, *ni*, *id*, *wa*, *hi*, and *st*. The script produces a *txt* file organized in columns.

Algorithm 15 CPU Utilization Considering the State Classes Using Command *iostat* - Exercise 29

```
iostat | awk 'NR==3{printf "%s\t %s\t %s\t %s\t %s\t %s\t\n",
                     $2, $3, $4, $5, $6, $7}'
                   >> iostat_cpu_utilization.txt;
for i in {1..50}
do
 iostat | awk 'NR==4{printf "%.2f\t %.2f\t %.2f\t\t %.2f\t\t
                     %.2f\t %.2f\t\n", $2, $3, $4, $5, $6,
                     $7}' >> iostat_cpu_utilization.txt;
 sleep 60;
done
```

(a) Write a short description of the computer model, the computer system's current state, the number of processors, the operating system, the applications under execution, and the performance policy, and execute Script 15.

(b) Analyze the sample and provide the statistical summary and suitable graphs to represent the collected data.

(c) Write a summary describing and interpreting the sample and the possible features of the system.

(d) Use *dstat* to collect the sample instead of the script above.

(e) Comment on the pros and cons of adopting *dstat*.

Exercise 30. Adapt Script 16 (hint: adjust *NR* in line 4 of the script) and collect a one hundred-sized sample of *IO* traffic considering every block device of the system. The delay between measures is sixty seconds (see *iostat* command description). The sample is stored in a *txt* file.

Algorithm 16 IO Monitoring Using *iostat* - Exercise 30

```
iostat | awk 'NR==6{printf "%s\t %s\t %s\t %s\t %s\t %s\t\n", $1, $2, $3, $4,
                      $5, $6}' >> iostat_io_tps.txt;
for i in {1..10}
do
 iostat | awk 'NR==7,NR==8{printf "%s\t %.2f\t %.2f\t\t %.2f\t\t %d\t %d\t\n",
                      $1, $2, $3, $4, $5, $6}' >> iostat_io_tps.txt;
 sleep 5;
done
```

(a) Write a description of the system, such as the computer model, the computer system's current state, the number of processors, the operating system, the applications under execution, and the performance policy,

(b) Execute Script 16, analyze the sample, provide its statistical summary and graphs.

(c) Adopt a suitable method (see Chapter 6) and obtain the respective confidence intervals for each metric, assuming a degree of confidence of 95%.

(d) Write a summary interpreting the collected data and the system by which the data were collected.

(e) Use *dstat* to collect the sample instead of the script above.

(f) Comment on the pros and cons of adopting *dstat*.

Exercise 31. Write a script to collect a one hundred-sized sample of CPU utilization through the command *iostat*. The delay between measures should be two hundred and forty seconds. At each collect, capture the CPU utilization in each specific state: *user*, *nice*, *system*, *iowait*, *steal*, and *idle*. The script should produce a *txt* file organized in columns.

(a) Write a short description of the system, mentioning the computer model, the number of processors, the operating system, and the applications under execution,

(b) Execute the script, analyze the sample, and provide its statistical summary.

(c) Write a summary interpreting the collected data.

(d) Use *dstat* to collect the sample instead of the script above.

(e) Comment on the pros and cons of adopting *dstat*.

Exercise 32. Execute Script 17 and collect a sample of fifty measures of *pinging* time of a domain (ex.:www.google.com or other) The delay between measures is 10 seconds. The sample is stored in a *txt* file.

Algorithm 17 Collects a Sample of Pinging Time from a Domain - Exercise 32

```
printf "Ping Delay \n" >> pingtim.txt;
for i in {1..50}
do
    ping -c 1 www.google.com | awk -F"time=" 'NR==2{gsub(/ms/,X,$2);
                             print $2 }' >> pingtim.txt
    sleep 10
done
```

(a) Write a short description of the system, including location, computer model, operating system, and applications under execution,

(b) Analyze the sample, provide its statistical summary, and comment on the findings.

Exercise 33. The Script 18 (*tcpdumpscript.sh*) collects the network traffic on all interfaces of a computer for one hour. Store the network traffic on a raw data file (*any.pcap*). Afterward it kills the process that is executing the *tcpdump* command, generates a compressed file (*any.pcap.tar.gz*) from the raw data file, and deletes the raw data file (*any.pcap*). The script file was installed in the */usr/bin* directory using a root user. This script was scheduled to start running at 02:00 AM. The script was executed through the *cron* tool, and the scheduled time was defined executing the command #*crontab -e* through the root user. The scheduled time was defined through the command line below.

```
00 02 * * * /bin/tcpdumpscript.sh
```

It is worth noting that the first field in the command line specifies the minutes (00); the second field determines the hour (02); the third, fourth and fifth represent the day, month, and day of the week, respectively. The symbol $*$ denotes any value. For instance, if the field day has $*$, it defines that the command should be executed every day. In this particular case, the script */bin/tcpdumpscript.sh* should be run every day, every week at 02:00 AM.

Algorithm 18 This script collects one hour of network traffic of any interface of a computer. - Exercise 33

```
#!/bin/bash
/usr/sbin/tcpdump -i any -w /tmp/any.pcap 2>&1 &
PROCESS_ID=$!
sleep 3600
kill -15 $PROCESS_ID
if [ -f /tmp/any.pcap ]; then
    tar -cvzf /tmp/any.pcap.tar.gz /tmp/any.pcap
    rm /tmp/any.pcap
fi
```

After collecting the traffic, uncompress the file *any.pcap.tar.gz*, and read it using the command *tcpdump -r any.pcap*.

(a) Analyze the content of the file and define which *IP* addresses are responsible for the heaviest traffic.

(b) Generate a Pareto chart (see Section 3.1) to display them.

(c) Write a short summary interpreting the findings.

Exercise 34. Use Script 19 to collect one-hundred-sized sample of processor utilization related to a process such as, for instance, *firefox*. This script first finds out the *pid* that represents the *firefox* process, and, then, collects these metrics *%usr*, *%system*, *%guest*, *%CPU*, and the CPU core in which the process is executing. The time between samples is sixty seconds. Before starting the measurement process, access a browser exerciser web-page such as web.basemark.com/, and start the workload test. After finishing the measurement,

(a) analyze the data of the sample stored in the file *process-pid-$pid.txt*, and generate a statistical summary,

(b) write a short document interpreting the findings.

Exercise 35. Script 20 collects one-hundred-sized sample of memory usage related to the process analyzed in Exercise 34. The time between samples should be twelve seconds. As in the previous example, before beginning the measuring, access a

---

Algorithm 19 This script finds the *pid* of the process *firefox* and collects its processor utilization. - Exercise 34

```
#!/bin/bash
pid=$(pidstat -G firefox | awk 'NR==4{print $4}')
printf "Process Resource Utilization \n" > process-pid-$pid.txt
pidstat -u -p $pid | awk 'NR==3{printf "%s\t %s\t %s\t %s\t %s\t %s\t %s\n",
        $4, $5, $6, $7, $8, $9, $10}' >> process-pid-$pid.txt
for i in {1..100};
do
    pidstat -u -p $pid | awk 'NR==4{printf "%d\t %.2f\t %.2f\t\t %.2f\t %.2f\t
            %d\t %s\n", $4, $5, $6, $7, $8, $9, $10}' >> process-pid-$pid.txt
    sleep 60
done
```

---

browser exerciser web-page such as web.basemark.com/, and start the workload test. The collected measures are (*VSZ*) the virtual memory utilization of the entire process, (*RSS*) the non-swapped physical memory used by the process, and (*%MEM*) the process's currently used shared physical memory. After concluding the measurement,

(a) analyze the data of the sample stored in the file *process-mem-pid-$pid.txt*, and generate a statistical summary, and

(b) write a short document interpreting the findings.

Algorithm 20 This script finds the *pid* of the process *firefox* and collects its memory usage. - Exercise 35

```
#!/bin/bash
pid=$(pidstat -G firefox | awk 'NR==4{print $4}')
printf "Process Resource Utilization \n" > process-mem-pid-$pid.txt
ps -u -p $pid | awk 'NR==1{printf "%s\t %s\t %s\t %s\t %s\t %s\n", $2, $3, $4,
    $5, $6, $11}' >> process-mem-pid-$pid.txt
for i in {1..100}
do
    ps -u -p $pid | awk 'NR==2{printf "%d\t %.2f\t %.2f\t %d\t %.d\t %s\n",
        $2, $3, $4, $5, $6, $11}' >> process-mem-pid-$pid.txt
    sleep 12
done
```

Exercise 36. Adapt Script 19 to collect one-hundred-sized sample of reading and write disk rates related to the process analyzed in Exercise 34. The time between samples should also be sixty seconds. Before beginning the measuring, access a browser exerciser web-page such as web.basemark.com/, and start the workload test. After concluding the measurement,

(a) analyze the data of the sample stored in the file *process-diskrate-pid-$pid.txt*, and generate a statistical summary, and

(b) write a short document interpreting the findings.

Exercise 37. Write a shell script that collects a one-hundred-sized sample measuring the processor utilization, the respective disk reading and writing rate, the system total RAM used, the total reserved RAM for the buffer, and the cache. For example, besides the current workload, use a web browser to access four different web pages. This script should collect processor utilization, the disk reading and writing rates, the system total RAM used, the total reserved RAM for the buffer, and the cache.

(a) Define the computer system's current state by specifying the computer model, the number of processors, the operating system, which applications are under execution, the performance policy set in the system, etc.

(b) Execute the proposed script, collect the data, and save it to a *csv* file.

(c) Provide a statistical summary for each collected metrics and suitable graphs to support the data analysis.

(d) Write a textual summary for describing and interpreting the collected data through the statistical summary and the respective graphs.

Exercise 38. Write a shell script to capture 5000 TCP-type packets at port 22, considering the packet size is 60 bytes.

(a) Define the computer system's current state by specifying the computer model, the number of processors, the operating system, which applications are affecting the network traffic, etc.

(b) Execute the script, collect the data, and save it to a *csv* file.

(c) Provide a statistical summary and suitable graphs to support the data analysis.

(d) Write a text for describing and interpreting the collected data.

24 Workload Characterization

This chapter introduces some essential concepts related to workload generation and methods that support workload modeling. Workload may be defined as the amount of work carried out by a system in a specified period. Such a concept has been used in many areas of science and engineering. After some basic definitions, the types of workloads are introduced, and the issues involved in selecting, using, and analyzing workloads for computer systems [139] are discussed. After, we examine workload generation methods, benchmarks, and synthetic operational workload generation techniques. Later, we examine workload modeling.

In this context, the term workload refers to all inputs that affect the computer system's behavior, such as application programs, services, transactions, and data transfers submitted to a system [66]. When a computer system executes a specific workload, it uses the particular system resources such as processor, cache, bus, memory, storage, and network that composes the computer system [53]. Therefore, evaluating computer system performance is only meaningful when the workload context is defined [400]. Hence, for meaningful performance measurement, the workload should be carefully selected to achieve the aims required by the performance analyst [188].

Defining a suitable computer workload depends on the type of system being considered, such as a personal computer, a database server, a web-server, an application server accessible on the internet, a mainframe, and a supercomputer; and the type of application carried out by the system. Workloads are used, in general, for these primary purposes:

1. Evaluation of an existing system for diagnosis and improvements via reconfiguration and upgrade,

2. Selection of alternative systems, and

3. Analysis of new design proposals.

The level of detail required for workload characterization depends on the evaluation's aims. For instance, when evaluating an operating system scheduling strategy (**scheduling workload**), it may be required only to represent when processes are "running", "waiting" for some I/O response, and "blocked". However, when studying a processor's instruction set ((**instruction set workload**)), a much more elaborated depiction is needed, where the instruction mix is an essential aspect for discerning the effect of adding functional units. Instruction dependencies are vital for exploiting

445

the advantages of adopting pipelining, branch prediction, and out-of-order instruction execution. Workloads that exploit loop sizes are critical for evaluating the cost-benefit relation of instruction caching. Attributes such as I/O sizes (**I/O workload**), methods of file access, and read-write operations are of paramount importance when evaluating I/O devices. Virtual memory mechanisms support paging and segmentation activities; thus affecting the use of the main memory. Hence, when the number of executed programs uses many portions of scattered data, memory resource becomes a bottleneck for performance. **Memory workload** aims at exercising the memory use of the system for supporting memory management policies. A **database workload** binds resources consumed within a database to higher-level search-query-language commands, users, applications, and servers [434]. **Application-level workloads** may specify the sequences of transactions handled by a database to exploit the distinct behavior between a large bank database, and a database that provides data to a web-server. Such workloads are centered on application-specific transactions that depend on the application's functionality, and may include, for instance, entering and delivering orders, recording payments, checking the status of orders, and monitoring the level of resource usages [297, 298].

The internet is especially interesting in terms of the workload due to the temporal variation of the analyzed workload patterns. **Internet workloads** typically exhibit temporal changes when distinct patterns are observed at different hours of the day and different days of the week. Therefore, if we analyze the average workload throughout a period of great variability, the analysis will undoubtedly reflect the "average" behavior, but it will not describe the users' workload perception. Besides, internet applications and services are continually evolving. Assume, for instance, social networking, live-video, and video-on-demand applications. Such applications are inherently dynamic due to the content popularity evolution of given service or content [13].

Moreover, the workloads seen at two end nodes might be quite different. Clients usually interact with a limited number of servers, and servers typically interact with many clients at a time. Besides, caching proxies also modify the data streams between clients and servers [136]. In this context, a **web-server workload** may be characterized by the number of transaction requests (intensity) per time unit and the types of transactions since all transaction requests are not identical, and some web-servers may perform well when dealing with requests to objects, and not properly for requests that require database access [55].

24.1   TYPES OF WORKLOADS

This section discusses some important concepts related to computer systems' workloads. Classifying workloads is not easy due to many perspectives that may be considered [66, 136, 148, 188]. The classification discussed in this section also does not intend to cover all such perspectives. Instead, we aim to classify the several types of workloads we intend to discuss in this chapter.

In this chapter, we classify the computer workloads into three main classes, where the second is subdivided into two sub-classes:

- Real Workload

- Synthetic Workload

  - Benchmarks

  - Synthetic Operational Workload

- Performance Workload Model

A **real workload** is a timely ordered set of requests, transactions, program executions, and tasks carried out by a computer system during a production period of interest. By production period, we mean the time interval a computer system executes its ordinary, everyday, normal, common tasks during a time window of particular concern. This workload indeed represents the computer system real load demanded that occurred in that specific time interval. The computer load changes from hour to hour, weekday to weekday, and season to season; thus, a fundamental task for gathering representative data is the definition of the measuring period and the sampling frequency. The sampling frequency is a key concern when a sampling strategy is adopted instead of a complete trace recording of activities during the production period.

As an example, consider an application-level workload related to an online drugstore sales system. For the sake of simplicity, let us only focus on non-prescription medicines. From the perspective of customer sales, assume this system supports three sorts of transactions; the first consists of customers *consulting* the availability of the product. Customers are depicted in Figure 24.1. Second, suppose the medicine is not available (checked in the computer infrastructure database - see Figure 24.1). In that case, the online sales system replies informing that the drugstore does not have the required item.

On the other hand, the sales system shows the item, price, and number of items available in the stock. After that, the customer may add the item to its cart and start a new *consulting* transaction or leave the website. A second transaction type is *paying* transactions. Suppose the customer (after inserting items in its cart) decides to purchase the items. In that case, the customer should provide the card data (let us assume only this option for simplicity) and the delivery address. Then, the sales system processes the selling transaction by consulting the respective card flag company (see Figure 24.1). If the credit card institution allows the transaction, the drugstore receives proof of transaction and updates its product inventory. After that, the drugstore sends the customer a *proof of purchase* with the confirmed delivery address.

Each server of the system infrastructure (web-servers, application servers, database-server, load-balancer) supports their specific purpose applications (denoted by *App*); also, each has a set of monitoring applications (represented by *M*). The monitoring

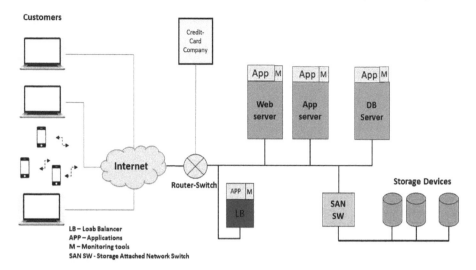

Figure 24.1 Online Drugstore Sales System.

application measures the transaction arrivals, transaction conclusions, resource utilization, number of packages, or bytes transferred between internal components and external agents. Figure 24.1 shows these components on the top of each server.

Assuming this online sales system and the particular point of view described, the workload in the period from 9 a.m. to 12 a.m. is the timely ordered set of transactions that occurred in this period. A critical aspect of this process is the amount of data transferred between the involved entities: customer, drugstore, and credit card company. Such a process may consider many other steps. However, the process described is sufficient to provide an overview of "a real" workload supported by online drugstore sales system websites considering the customer-drugstore perspective relation.

The monitoring tools running on the load-balancer gather the number of transactions of each type, the instant of each transaction request arrival, the number of packages related to the particular transaction, the instant the reply is at the customer, and the number of packages sent. Besides, it also registers the transactions issued to the credit card companies, the instants of each data transfer, and the number of packages sent and received from the credit card companies. The monitoring tools running on the other server record the resources utilization of each server and other events of interest.

Synthetic workloads are designed to mimic a particular behavior for the system under evaluation. In the classification depicted above, synthetic workloads are divided into two main sub-classes, that is **benchmarks** and **synthetic operational workloads**.

One important use of performance evaluation is for comparing systems. Performance comparisons of systems are relevant only if the systems are analyzed under similar conditions and the same workload. Comparing systems motivates the standardization of workloads that could be executed in different systems to compare the respective performances. Such standardized workloads are named **benchmarks**. Benchmarks have an enormous impact on computer business since they are regularly adopted to boost product sales. Therefore, the adoption of a specific benchmark has often been litigious. The main disputes and discussions are methodological issues, as marketing departments promote features that will show their products in a favorable light. This also forces the design departments to create excellent results when adopting the benchmark but not focusing on real applications. Hence, when adopting a specific benchmark, it is fundamental to define what the benchmark is supposed to represent, and the performance study's aim [136].

In this context, a benchmark is an artificial workload that exercises the important system features relevant for real workloads. A benchmark is usually a program or set of programs commonly adopted to compare the computer system's relative performance by executing several standard tests. Thus, benchmarking is the process of comparing performance computer systems under a benchmark.

However, benchmarks may not represent actual usage of computing systems since real workloads and computer system configurations may be significantly diverse in comparison to the benchmarks' behavior. Hence, computer system designers may be required to have the flexibility of generating **synthetic operational workload** that represents real workloads and their variation to exercise the computing systems' attributes. Such an approach may be pretty useful and be applied at several computing system levels. For instance, such an approach may be applied to tuning computer architecture features such as the number of processors and cores, the memory size, I/O capacity, bus bandwidth, etc. A **synthetic operational workload generator** is a controlled environment that aims at reproducing specific workload scenarios generated by real workloads that could be reproduced [53, 116, 117, 311, 312].

Such workload generators may generate the synthetic traces based on real traces, which are collected from existing systems, using a statistical summary of real traces or using probabilistic models that fit the real traces. This sort of workload generator allows us, for example, to reproduce original traces from the *Online Drugstore Sales System*, and generate distinct scenarios by changing the workload pattern. Such a flexible mechanism may be a useful tool for supporting tuning or planning the system capacity that represents future changes in the workload characteristics [148].

Assume, for instance, the system depicted in Figure 24.1 (Online Drugstore Sales System). In this system, traffic generated from one specific customer was gathered during a period of interest, as well as the aggregate traffic that is handled by the sales system. Figure 24.2 shows the data center as a high-level box (*Data Center*) and highlights only one customer of many depicted in Figure 24.1. All the system's customers are grouped in a box named *other customers*. Figure 24.2 aims at describing a synthetic operational workload generator for the Online Drugstore Sales System.

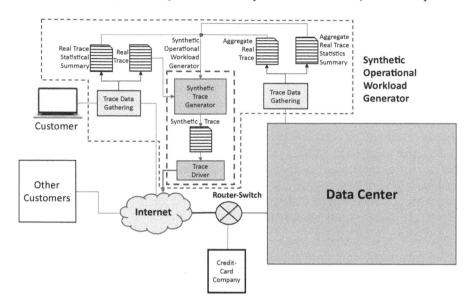

Figure 24.2   Synthetic Operational Workload.

The synthetic operational workload generator is mainly composed of three classes of modules. They are:

- Trace Data Gathering Modules,
- the Synthetic Trace Generator, and
- the Trace Driver.

The **Trace Data Gathering Modules** are responsible for gathering the ordered set of transactions between a particular customer (see the pink rectangles in Figure 24.2) and the computer infrastructure, as well as collecting the aggregate ordered set of transactions submitted to the data center. Adopting one or many trace data gathering modules on specific customers or an aggregate trace data gathering module (at the data center) depends on the type of performance study the analyst is willing to perform. The trace data gathering modules record the transaction submission and the respective replies received by a particular customer or the aggregated traffic at the data center border due to all customers interacting with the computing system. In addition, these modules also may provide statistical summaries related to each specific trace. The traces and the respective statistical summaries are shown as single snipped top corner striped rectangles.

The **Synthetic Trace Generator Module** works by interacting with trace data gathering modules and the trace driver (both are depicted as light gray rectangles at the center of Figure 24.2). The **Trace Driver** is the component that interacts with the computer infrastructure by emulating a real customer (or set of real customers) behavior by submitting transactions to the computing system and gathering the respective replies. The synthetic trace generator module depicted here is composed of a set of functions that analyze the raw traces generated by trace data gathering modules and use the respective statistical summaries associated with each specific trace, and generates synthetic traces:

1. These are equivalent to the gathered traces, which have the same transaction mix, the same transactions' frequencies, the same package sizes, and a similar number of packages related to each transaction. Such a type of workload generation aims to reproduce the transaction patterns statistically.

2. These are similar traces to the gathered traces but vary in one or more parameters aimed at exercising the computing system with variants of the real operational workload.

3. When the trace data contains sensitive information, using the original traces may not be possible due to information security issues. In such a case, the statistical summaries of each trace may support the analyst generating synthetic traces that are compatible with the real operational traces, at least in terms of their statistical summaries, that is, equivalent transaction mixes, frequencies, a number of packages sent and received, and the packages' sizes. Like the previous case, such functionality aims to exercise the computing system with variants of the real operational workload.

4. The last case uses the original traces or the statistical summaries by fitting probability distributions for generating synthetic traces. As in the two previous cases, the function option also aims to exercise the computing system with variants of the real operational workload but using probability distributions instead of simple statistical summaries.

24.2 WORKLOAD GENERATION

This section discusses in more detail some prominent benchmark systems and synthetic operational workload generation. First, we concentrate on some significant benchmarks due to historical aspects or their present-day importance in computational system performance evaluation. Later, we introduce some synthetic operational workload platforms.

24.2.1 BENCHMARKS

As already mentioned, standardized sets of workloads support comparing systems' performance. Such standardized workloads are named **benchmarks**. Benchmarks have an enormous impact on the computer business since they are regularly adopted to boost product sales. Hence, one should be very cautious when choosing a set of benchmarks to evaluate a system. It is fundamental to define what the benchmark is supposed to represent, and the performance study's aim for adopting a specific benchmark [456].

Before introducing the benchmarks, a word of caution should be said about some performance measures and scores usually adopted by some benchmarks. It is always important to stress that the main aims of benchmarks are comparing computer systems' performance. When the computer architects proposed reduced instruction-set computer architectures (*RISC* architectures), the meaning of the measure "millions of instructions per second" (*MIPS*) lost nearly all its significance. For instance, a high-level language instruction that may require only one *CISC* (complex instruction-set computer architectures) instruction to be executed, in *RISC* architectures, would require much more machine instruction to be executed. Hence, if the execution time of the high-level language instruction in both architectures is similar, the MIPS are much higher for *RISC* architectures since the number of machine instructions executed in the same period is much higher than the respective number of machine instructions executed in a *CISC* computer.

Another popular alternative to performance metrics is a million floating-point operations per second (*MFLOPS*). Floating-point operations are addition, subtraction, multiplication, and division operations, for example, applied to several high-level single-precision, double-precision, and floating-point instruction types. Such data is widely used in scientific calculations and specified in programming languages using high-level language data types, such as float, real, double, or double precision. However, *MFLOPS* is dependent on the program rate since different programs require different numbers of floating-point instructions. Also, as *MIPS* metrics, *MFLOPS* is a performance metric based on the instruction rate, which the compiler can strongly influence. Therefore, the classification *MFLOPS* changes according to the mixture of integer and floating-point operations and the mix of fast and slow floating-point operations. For example, a 100% floating-point instruction program will have a higher *MFLOPS* rate than a 100% floating-point instruction program.

Many benchmarks also produce their specific scores. The benchmarks development companies' general claim is that such scores allow a more straightforward comparison between computer performance since the end-user only needs to look at their specific scores. Nevertheless, these scores could be biased to specific vendors, computer lines and brands, compilers, or operating systems. Therefore, it is much safer to consider metrics such as execution time, memory usage, and energy consumption of programs in the distinct hardware-software platform we are interested in comparing since these are metrics of real interest to the end-user or take into account a set of benchmarks for getting a more balanced view of system performance.

One of the earliest attempts to use benchmarking was found in the Auerbach Standard EDP Reports published in 1962. These reports were adopted as specifications of the features of computers that vendors must offer. Besides, Auerbach described twelve standard configurations to support fair comparisons across vendor lines. The typical tasks of these seminal benchmarks were (a) file processing, (b) sorting, and (c) matrix inversion. These benchmarks gathered data at three levels: (1) basic central processor operations, (2) individual peripheral devices, and (3) specific system configurations [27, 237].

The method adopted by Auerbach was to implement a "routine" to estimate the specific computer system "speed" (unit of code by a unit of time.). In this early attempt, no stipulations were made that the benchmark should be executed in computer systems of specific features. This leads to biased implementations by vendors to check out their new products according to the benchmark problem at the expense of essential features [237].

In 1969, Bucholz described a synthetic program for measuring computer system performance. His approach was towards implementing a program that imitates the real application. The sample program introduced was a file maintenance program written in PL1. Such work was a mark for research on synthetic workload [61].

In 1976, a study group composed of the US government and industry was formed and implemented set benchmark programs that contained the required attributes for reproducible results for supporting product selections. However, the group concluded that although the benchmark library had been used successfully, there was still not enough information to support such a general platform.

Some of the benchmarks mentioned in this section are old applications that have been adopted for performance evaluation for a long time. These old benchmarks are the seminal work on benchmarking studies on computers. Other benchmarks described in this section are important due to their wide acceptance or standards for particular communities or groups. The term benchmark suite denotes a set of benchmarks together with a set of specific rules that govern the conditions and methods, such as the test platform environment, input data, output results, and evaluation metrics. A benchmark family is a set of benchmark suites [317]. Whenever the context is clear, we adopt the term benchmark for all of them, and when it is required, we apply these specific terms.

Given that different application domains have different execution characteristics, a wide variety of benchmarks has been developed to characterize these domains. Furthermore, different types of benchmarks must satisfy the different needs of many types of users. Designers of new computer systems, for example, often need benchmarks during the early stages of the design and implementation process. Since in the initial stages of a project, it is common to use simulators, emulators, and prototypes to estimate performance, benchmarks need to exercise the specific parts of interest of the new project instead of being a general benchmark that exploits many characteristics of the system since such a system may not yet be fully implemented.

On the other hand, a large organization that decides to purchase an expensive computer system from among several system candidates of different brands and prices can compromise large sums based on broader performance tests results. Consequently, these organizations need more complete benchmarks that more accurately characterize each system candidate's performance and thus provide reliable guidelines to decide which system to acquire.

Whetstone

Whetstone is a benchmark for evaluating computer performance focused on float-point instructions. Whetstone was based on work by Brian Wichmann from the National Physical Laboratory and implemented by H.J. Curnow of the HM Treasury Technical Support Unit. The first Whetstone benchmark was written in Algol 60 in 1972. The Fortran codes were published in 1973. The first results published were for IBM and ICL mainframes in 1973. The instruction rate was calculated in Kilo Whetstone Instructions Per Second or KWIPS. Later, Millions or MWIPS[1] was used. In 1980, facilities were added to time and produced speed ratings in MIPS (GMIPS and TIPS[2].), and MFLOPS (GFLOPS and TFLOPS). Afterward, the benchmark was also converted to Fortran 77, and later compatible non-official versions were implemented in Basic, Visual Basic, C, C++, Java, and Python programming languages [87, 243, 460].

As an example, we adopted the Whetstone C version, translated by Rich Painter [463] (see Appendix B). This version kept the look and feel of the FORTRAN version, and the major FORTRAN comment blocks were retained to minimize differences between versions. We changed the loop size to

```
loopstart = 100000;
```

and the function for measuring time. This last change aimed at improving the measurement system's precision. Hence, we included the following library.

```
#include <sys/time.h>
```

and two structure-variables were declared with structures type *timeval*:

```
struct timeval begin, end;
```

The command for starting measuring the execution time was substituted to

```
gettimeofday(&begin, 0);
```

and the command for getting the instant at the end of the piece of code we intend to measure was also substituted to

---

[1] Millions of Whetstone Instructions Per Second (MWIPS).
[2] M (Mega), G(Giga), T(Tera)

```
gettimeofday(&end, 0);
```

The execution time was, then, calculated by

```
long seconds = end.tv_sec - begin.tv_sec;
long microseconds = end.tv_usec - begin.tv_usec;
double elapsed = seconds + microseconds*1e-6;
```

The command $if \; (finisec - startsec <= 0)$ was substituted by

```
if (elapsed <= 0)
```

and the command lines

```
printf("Loops: %ld, Iterations: %d, Duration: %ld sec.\n",
       LOOP, II, finisec-startsec);
KIPS = (100.0*LOOP*II)/(float)(finisec-startsec);
```

were also changed to

```
printf("Loops: %ld, Iterations: %d, Duration: %.3f sec.\n",
       LOOP, II, elapsed);
KIPS = (100.0*LOOP*II)/(float)(elapsed);
```

Finally, the command line

```
printf("C Converted Double Precision Whetstones: %.1f MIPS\n",
       KIPS/1000.0);
```

was also substituted to

```
printf("C Converted Double Precision Whetstones: %.3f KIPS\n",
                                                   KIPS);
```

An script (*scriptwhetstone*) was also implemented to execute the benchmark *n* time (in the case below $n = 100.$). The script lines are

scriptwhetstone

```
printf "Whetstone Results \n" >> whetstone_result.txt;
for i in {1..100}
do
 whetstone >> whetstone_result.txt;
done
```

Table 24.1

Whetstone Execution Time (s)

Sample - Sample Size = 100									
5.938	5.198	5.188	5.424	8.751	5.165	5.811	5.195	5.128	5.236
6.19	6.005	5.202	5.158	5.311	5.224	5.676	5.444	5.141	5.272
5.535	6.024	5.216	5.385	5.272	5.35	5.378	5.262	5.244	5.238
5.564	5.372	5.206	5.273	5.211	5.206	5.419	5.649	5.202	5.204
5.289	5.175	5.467	5.539	5.211	5.382	5.172	5.905	5.195	5.149
6.098	5.157	5.44	5.314	5.283	5.35	5.278	6.48	5.854	5.173
5.53	5.379	5.183	5.414	5.211	5.29	5.119	5.239	5.425	5.314
5.407	5.22	5.151	5.569	5.181	5.864	5.124	5.104	5.337	5.569
5.486	5.231	5.23	5.514	5.564	5.595	5.102	5.108	5.255	5.736
5.431	5.258	5.383	5.741	5.51	5.184	5.094	5.275	5.256	5.274

Table 24.2

Whetstone - MIPs

Sample - Sample Size = 100									
1683.996	1923.697	1927.685	1843.689	1142.7	1936.192	1720.965	1925.104	1950.059	1909.686
1615.527	1665.152	1922.239	1938.776	1882.935	1914.332	1761.684	1836.737	1945.283	1896.654
1806.663	1660.106	1917.112	1857.076	1896.881	1869.283	1859.31	1900.436	1906.94	1909.291
1797.136	1861.357	1920.785	1896.317	1918.858	1920.794	1845.486	1770.243	1922.518	1921.67
1890.841	1932.305	1829.29	1805.472	1918.856	1858.101	1933.62	1693.587	1924.819	1942.138
1639.916	1939.292	1838.246	1881.819	1892.963	1869.048	1894.629	1543.126	1708.142	1932.928
1808.351	1859.077	1929.354	1847.106	1919.114	1890.382	1953.436	1908.789	1843.311	1881.842
1849.329	1915.63	1941.507	1795.694	1929.963	1705.45	1951.618	1959.134	1873.545	1795.663
1822.706	1911.543	1912.199	1813.725	1797.292	1787.359	1960.173	1957.633	1902.788	1743.225
1841.388	1901.907	1857.621	1741.85	1815.003	1929.004	1962.944	1895.723	1902.761	1896.269

such that *whetstone_result.txt* is the file where the execution times and instructions per second of each execution were stored. This experiment was executed in a small Linux virtual machine deployed as a guest on a personal computer. Table 24.1 depicts the execution times (in seconds) of the sample and Table 24.2 shows the respective MIPs.

The statistical summary for the execution time and MIPs is shown in Table 24.3.

The confidence interval, the mean execution time (*met*), and the average MIPs (*amips*) with 95% degree of confidence were calculated using the nonparametric bootstrap. These confidence intervals are depicted below:

$$met \in (5.3408\,s, 5.5116\,s)$$

Table 24.3

Whetstone Statistical Summary - Execution Times and MIPs

Execution Times (s)		MIPs	
Mean (s)	5.1435	Mean (MIPs)	1950.005
SD (s)	0.1412	SD (MIPs)	119.6115
Variance (s^2)	0.0199	Variance ($MIPs^2$)	14306.9025
CoV (%)	2.7444	CoV (%)	6.1339
Q1 (s)	5.0523		
Median (s)	5.0845		
Q3 (s)	5.1928		
IIQ (s)	0.1405		
Minimal (s)	4.995	Minimal (MIPs)	1666.7
Maximal (s)	5.944	Maximal (MIPs)	2000
Range (s)	0.949	Range (MIPs)	333.3
Skewness	2.5927	Skewness	-1.990374
Kurtosis	10.1346	Kurtosis	2.0012

and

$$amips \in (1830.7399\,MIPs, 1874.2690\,MIPs),$$

respectively.

Linpack

The original LINPACK Benchmark was, in some sense, an accident since it was initially designed to support the Linpack package's users by providing information on the execution times required to solve a system of linear equations.

The first version of the Linpack Benchmark report appeared as an appendix in the Linpack Users' Guide in 1979 [107]. Results were provided for a matrix problem of size 100 on a collection of widely used computers. This was done so users could estimate the time required to solve their matrix problem by extrapolation. Its performance is represented in MFLOPS (GFLOPS, TFLOPS). Over the years, additional performance data was added, and today the collection includes a vast number of computer systems. Besides, the scope of the benchmark has also expanded. The original version was produced in Fortran, but a C programming language version appeared later. Nowadays, there are many variants and extensions of Linpack. For instance, the Intel Optimized Linpack Benchmark for Linux is a generalization of the Linpack 1000 Benchmark, which handles matrices of order 1000 [108]. It calculates a dense linear equations system, estimates the time it takes to solve the system, converts that time into a performance rate, and tests its accuracy. It is worth highlighting that the number of equations (N) is not limited to 1000 as some previous versions [185].

As an example, we adopted the Linpack_BENCH, which is a C program that drives the single and double precision Linpack benchmark program [240] (see Appendix C). Thus, the C source adopted here embodies both single and double precision specified at compilation time. Furthermore, we may also use a compiler option to allow "rolled loops" (default) or "unrolled loops".

We included the library *sys/time.h* for improving the measurement system's precision. Thus, we added the following line.

```
#include <sys/time.h>
```

and two structure-variables were declared with structures type *timeval*:

```
struct timeval begin, end;
```

The command for starting measuring the execution time was substituted to

```
gettimeofday(&begin, 0);
```

and the command for getting the instant at the end of the piece of code we intend to measure was also substituted to

```
gettimeofday(&end, 0);
```

The execution time was, then, calculated by

```
long seconds = end.tv_sec - begin.tv_sec;
long microseconds = end.tv_usec - begin.tv_usec;
double elapsed = seconds + microseconds*1e-6;
printf("Time measured: %.3f seconds.\n", elapsed);
```

Hence a macro-view of the C code main function is shown below.

```
struct timeval begin, end;

int main ( );
{
    // Start measuring time
    // gettimeofday(&begin, 0);

    Code

    // Stop measuring time and calculate
```

```
    // the elapsed time

    gettimeofday(&end, 0);
    long seconds = end.tv_sec - begin.tv_sec;
    long microseconds = end.tv_usec - begin.tv_usec;
    double elapsed = seconds + microseconds*1e-6;
    printf("Duration: %.3f sec.\n \n",elapsed);
    return 0;
}
```

where the execution time of the Linpack executable file is registered in variable *elpased* and displayed on the screen as its "Duration". The script file depicted later redirects this output to the text file "Linpack_result.txt". Besides, the three pieces of codes shown below were commented. They are:

Piece of Code 1

```
/*  printf ( "\n" );
    printf ( "Linpack_BENCH\n" );
    printf ( "  C version\n" );
    printf ( "\n" );
    printf ( "  The Linpack benchmark.\n" );
    printf ( "  Language: C\n" );
    printf ( "  Datatype: Double precision real\n" );
    printf ( "  Matrix order N              = %d\n", N );
    printf ( "  Leading matrix dimension LDA = %d\n", LDA );
*/
```

Piece of Code 2

```
//  printf ( "     Norm. Resid      Resid           MACHEP
              X[1]            X[N]\n" );
//  printf ( "\n" );
//  printf ( "  %14f  %14f  %14e  %14f  %14f\n", residn, resid_max,
              eps, b[0], b[N-1] );
//  printf ( "\n" );
```

and

Piece of Code 3

```
//  printf ( "\n \n" );
//  printf ( "Linpack_BENCH\n" );
//  printf ( "  Normal end of execution.\n" );
```

An script (*scriptlinpack*) was also implemented to execute the benchmark *n* time (in the case below $n = 100$.). The script lines are *scriptlinpack*

```
printf "Linpack Results \n" >> Linpack_result.txt;
for i in {1..100}
do
 Linpack >> Linpack_result.txt;
done
```

such that *Linpack_result.txt* is the file where the execution times and the float-point instructions per second of each execution were stored. This experiment was executed in a small Linux virtual machine deployed as a guest on a personal computer. The general format of the *Linpack_result.txt* text file is

```
Linpack Results

        Factor Solve Total MFLOPS Unit Cray-Ratio

0.876013 0.002379 0.878392 761.239477 0.002627 15.685571

Duration: 1.047 sec.


        Factor Solve Total MFLOPS Unit Cray-Ratio

0.871313 0.002381 0.873694 765.33279 0.002613 15.601679

Duration: 1.014 sec.



                        . . .



        Factor Solve Total MFLOPS Unit Cray-Ratio

0.917287 0.002389 0.919676 727.067648 0.002751 16.422786

Duration: 1.128 sec.
```

It is worth noting the duration of each run of the script. Table 24.4 summarizes the execution times (in seconds) of the sample and Table 24.5 shows the respective MFLOPs.

The statistical summary for the execution time and MFLOPs are shown in Table 24.6.

Table 24.4
Execution Times (s) - Sample

1.026	1.176	1.011	1.05	0.971	0.976	0.971	0.975	0.993	1.039
1.022	0.991	0.984	1.057	0.968	0.98	0.979	0.968	0.983	1.008
1.094	1.164	1.162	1.23	1.044	1.009	0.978	0.979	0.994	1.121
1.054	0.991	1.007	1.194	1.006	1.048	0.975	0.97	0.98	1.017
1.006	1.002	0.986	1.079	0.986	0.99	1.068	1.063	0.979	1.035
0.997	1.006	0.982	1.129	0.98	0.997	0.967	0.988	1.029	1.116
1.278	1.000	0.986	1.024	0.987	0.971	0.979	0.975	1.036	1.092
1.117	1.138	1.153	1.093	0.989	0.972	0.964	0.973	0.973	1.152
1.004	0.997	1.074	0.987	1.04	1.078	0.996	0.976	0.985	
0.992	1.009	1.107	0.974	0.986	0.969	1.245	1.083	0.979	

Table 24.5
MFLOPs - Sample

788.010	796.221	780.648	700.904	811.560	805.568	812.502	778.932
778.046	783.746	782.745	753.855	814.900	809.610	813.576	816.090
776.614	796.433	801.115	741.579	819.267	805.452	806.487	815.964
717.150	718.996	677.170	637.622	764.267	805.484	813.273	808.413
778.305	795.794	800.420	700.841	799.033	743.131	811.583	
797.236	790.672	802.999	745.268	799.125	798.122	759.108	
790.276	792.810	805.858	692.535	808.349	808.532	815.769	
782.594	789.785	805.110	765.752	803.973	813.903	812.309	
736.026	703.503	683.327	726.113	801.124	813.473	819.274	
790.624	793.091	736.269	802.781	754.608	727.001	790.083	

Table 24.6
Statistical Summary - Execution Time (s) and MFLOPS

	Mean	SD	Var	CoV (%)	Min	Q1	Med
MFLOPS	779.12	40.44	1635.02	5.19	637.62	759.11	795.79
Execution Time (s)	1.0292	0.0693	0.00481	6.74	0.964	0.9798	0.9985
	Q3	Max	Range	IIQ	Skewness	Kurtosis	
MFLOPS	808.35	819.27	181.65	49.24	-1.44	1.51	
Execution Time (s)	1.0585	1.278	0.314	0.0787	1.57	2.02	

The confidence interval, the mean execution time (*met*), and the average MFLOPs (*amflops*) with 95% of confidence were calculated using the nonparametric bootstrap. These confidence intervals are depicted below:

$$met \in (1.0166\,s, 1.0430\,s)$$

and

$$amflops \in (768.9516\,MFLOPs, 787.2465\,MFLOPs),$$

Similar exercise can be performed for the open-source benchmarks as some of the following.

Livermore Loops

The Livermore Kernel loops is a benchmark, originally written in Fortran, composed of twenty-four kernels. McMahon implemented the Livermore loops at Lawrence Livermore National Laboratories [268]. This benchmark executes the 24 kernels three times at different loop spans to produce short, medium, and long vector performance measurements. Besides, each loop implements a specific common type of scientific programming constructs applied at the laboratory. The performance measurements are depicted in MFLOPS (or multiples of that), and statistics such as are reported for minimum, maximum, and three means: arithmetic, geometric, and harmonic are provided. Since the original implementation, the Livermore Kernels were also implemented in many other languages such as C, C++, and SISAL.

We implemented a C program (*livermore.c*) that sequentially executed twenty-three out of twenty-four kernels of the Livermore loops available at [242]. Kernel 13 was not considered. The time to execute the program was measured by adopting the same function and structure considered when evaluating Whetstone and Linpack. The C program was executed one hundred times, and each execution time (in seconds) was stored in a *livermore_result.txt* file (See Appendix D). For performing the measurement, we adopted the script (*scriptlivermore*) below.

scriptlivermore

```
printf "Livermore Results \n" >> livermore_result.txt;
for i in {1..100}
do
  livermore >> livermore_result.txt;
done
```

The execution times of the sample are shown in Table 24.7. In addition, Table 24.8 shows the statistical summary for the execution times measured.

Table 24.7
Livermore Loops - Execution Time (s) - Sample Size = 100.

Execution Time (s)									
1.6475	1.7330	1.9164	1.6553	1.6220	1.7002	1.6535	1.6623	1.6750	2.0213
1.6772	2.0070	1.9102	1.6303	1.6116	1.6100	1.6926	1.6216	1.7082	1.8907
1.6362	1.9237	1.8715	1.6449	1.6822	1.6585	1.6180	1.6073	1.7872	1.8362
1.6887	1.9817	1.8311	1.8270	1.7110	1.6209	1.6187	1.6733	1.8434	2.1401
1.6761	1.8616	1.7787	1.6160	1.6202	1.8410	1.6988	1.6728	1.7011	1.9049
1.6253	2.2834	1.7739	1.6104	1.6394	2.0386	1.0600	1.6117	2.0276	1.8762
1.6222	1.9232	1.9019	1.6771	1.6431	1.8624	1.7094	1.6396	1.6811	1.9521
1.7626	2.1220	1.9437	1.6272	1.6153	1.8295	1.6784	1.6330	1.6601	1.8233
1.6307	1.9953	1.8822	1.6288	1.6197	1.8011	1.7038	1.6581	1.6482	1.6694
1.6252	2.0549	1.6760	1.6814	1.6707	1.6963	1.6290	1.6249	1.6857	1.6559

Table 24.8
Statistical Summary - Execution Time (s) - Livermore Loops

	Mean	SD	Var	CoV (%)	Min	Q1	Med
Execution Time (s)	1.7431	0.1615	0.0261	9.26	1.0600	1.6338	1.6813
	Q3	Max	Range	IIQ	Skewness	Kurtosis	
Execution Time (s)	1.8428	2.2834	1.2234	0.2091	0.27	3.35	

The confidence interval of the mean execution time ($met(s)$) with 95% degree of confidence was calculated using the nonparametric bootstrap. The confidence interval estimated was

$$met \in (1.7109\,s, 1.7725\,s).$$

Dhrystone

The Dhrystone benchmark was implemented by Reinhold P. Weicker and published in 1984 using a subset of the ADA program language (the Pascal subset of ADA) [459]. Later on, it was also translated to PASCAL, Fortran, and C. Among all these implementations, the C implementation is the most popular [317]. Dhrystone consists of 12 procedures included in one measurement loop with 94 statements; during one loop (one Dhrystone), 101 statements (103 in the C version) are executed dynamically [460]. It aimed to measure computer systems' performance focusing on integer instruction performance since, in that era, many computers mainly used integer instruction, and the Whetstone benchmark already focused on floating-point instruction. The basis for the Dhrystone benchmark was a literature survey on the distribution of source language features, taking into account non-numeric, system-type programming. As a result, Dhrystone has a lower nesting depth. For each function call executed, the number of instructions performed is usually low.

Moreover, most of the execution time is spent handling strings, characters, and comparing them. At that time, many computers mainly used integer instruction. Nowadays, however, Dhrystone may not be very useful since it is too short so that it fits in on-chip caches, and fails to stress the memory system. Besides, due to its size, it does not exercise read and write files.

Sieve

Jim Gilbreath had been examining the possibility of writing a small benchmarking program wanting it to be portable between languages, small enough to fit on a code page, and not dependent on specific features like multiplication or hardware division. The algorithm mainly emphasizes array search performance and basic logic and branching capabilities. It also does not require any advanced language features, such as recursion or advanced collection types. The algorithm's implementation calculates only the odd primes so that the array of elements 8191 represented primes less than 16385. The benchmark was first named Sieve, and the first results were introduced in the September 1981 issue of BYTE in an article entitled "A High-Level Language Benchmark." [157]. The paper presented recommendations for implementations in ten languages, including BASIC, C, Pascal, COBOL, and FORTRAN, and some lesser-known examples.

In the January 1983 edition of BYTE, Jim Gilbreath and his brother, Gary, returned the code and removed most of the less popular languages, leaving Pascal, C, FOR-TRAN IV, COBOL, and added Ada and Modula-2. Newer versions of the benchmark keep on being implemented in new languages [319].

PassMark

PassMark Software Pty. Ltd. is a company focused on developing benchmarks for the Windows operating system. The first benchmark was delivered in 1998 [471]. Since then, the initial benchmark evolved into a family of benchmark suites. One benchmark suite of this family is the PerformanceTest suite. The PerformanceTest suite conducts 32 standard benchmark tests across five test suites and calculates the PassMark rating system results. The standard test suites are composed of **CPU suite**, **Memory suite**, **2D suite**, **3D suite**, and **Disk suite**.

The **CPU suite** consists of mathematical operations, compression, encryption, sorting, and physics-related functions. The **Memory suite** is composed of database operations, uncached memory reading, cached memory reading, memory write, memory latency (the time it takes for a single byte of memory to be transferred to the CPU for processing.), and memory threaded. The memory threaded test is nearly identical to the uncached memory reading, but separate threads perform them simultaneously to check how well memory copes with concurrent accesses. The **2D suite** contains several tests that exercise the standard Windows graphics functions, dependent on how fast the video card can carry out 2D graphics operations and the color depth.

The 2D graphics test checks vectors, bitmaps, fonts, text, PDF rendering, how fast, scalable vector graphics are displayed, zoomed and rotated, and other GUI elements. The **3D suite** graphics test consists of

1. a full screen 1920×1080, $8\times$ anti-aliasing, and methods for generating water as well as ground based on the height above the water;

2. a full screen 1920×1080, $8\times$ anti-aliasing, using geometry shader;

3. a full screen 1920×1080, $4\times$ anti-aliasing, unordered transparency technique, and Tessellation technique used to produce terrain; and

4. a full screen 3840×2160, $8\times$ anti-aliasing, $2\times$ anti-aliasing, compute shader for bloom and warp effect with support for multi-GPU, and multithreading.

Finally, the **Disk suite** exercises the mass storage units.

1. sequential readings;

2. sequential writings;

3. random reading and writing in files assuming $32\,KB$ blocks with a queue depth of 20; and

4. random reading and writing in files assuming $2\,KB$ blocks with a queue depth of 1.

After running the tests, the PerformanceTest suite provides an overall PassMark rating. Users have provided their performance results to the company's benchmark website that stores their results. Such results are made available to users, and cover many systems and many different processor types [472]. Besides the standard test suites, PassMark also provides advanced tests that exercise CPU, memory, disk, graphics functions, network and internet, and GPU (Graphical Processor Unit).

3DMark and PCMark

The FutureMark benchmark family is a set of benchmarks implemented by Futuremark Corporation, founded in 1997. Regardless of the company's acquisition and merging, two of the most well-known benchmarks that are part of their product line are 3DMark and PCMark. PCMark evaluates the system and 3iDMark is centered on the graphics features. 3DMark focuses on rendering games and consists of a set of tests that generates a set of specific scores, such as graphics test score, physics test score, combined test score, which are then adopted to compose the 3DMark score by combining these specific scores using a weighted harmonic mean.

One of the specific scores produced by 3DMark is the graphics test score (S). The S score is calculated by executing graphics tests, which produce results in frames per second, and from these specifics, the S score is calculated by multiplying the harmonic mean of each test result with a scaling constant [1].

The PCMark suite consists of tests that exercise individual workloads at a time in sequence; each test gives a specific score. A workload stresses one or more components of the system under evaluation. The most important workloads include storing pictures, gaming, video playback and transcoding, image manipulation, web-browsing, and decrypting. A PCMark score is a number describing the overall performance of the system [326].

Sandra

SiSoft Sandra is a benchmark utility for Windows; the first version was launched in 1997 by SiSoftware. Since then, Sandra (and its free version - Sandra Lite) has become widely used. Sandra displays, among other data, information about hardware devices, processors, BIOS, energy consumption, buses, video, memory, drives, ports, and processes. In addition, the benchmark supports performance evaluation of file systems, network traffic, multimedia processing, float precision arithmetic, and other features.

The test execution provides the overall test results and individual test results such as virtual machine performance, processor power management, network, memory, and storage devices. The overall score includes benchmarks of CPU, GPU, memory bandwidth, and file system performance. After completing the test, graphs may be displayed for comparing the results of each test with reference results from other computers [369].

SPEC Suite

SPEC stands for the Standard Performance Evaluation Corporation. This organization was created to define, implement, and validate standardized benchmarks to evaluate computing systems' performance and energy consumption. SPEC has implemented many benchmark suites, reviews, and published submitted results from their organization members and others [410].

SPEC was founded in 1988 by workstation vendors who recognized that the marketplace demanded practical, standardized performance experiments. Since then, SPEC expanded from a small group with a single benchmark to become a successful performance standardization group with more than one hundred members with a family of benchmarks composed of dozens of specific benchmark suites.

The original Open Systems Group (OSG) focuses on benchmarks for desktop systems, high-end workstations, and servers running open systems environments. This group is currently divided into subgroups with specific concerns, such as OSG-Cloud, OSG CPU, OSG-Java, OSG-Power, OSG-Storage, and OSG-Virtualization sub-committees.

Nowadays, two of the most important benchmark suites supported by SPEC are SPEC Cloud IaaS and SPEC CPU. The SPEC CPU benchmark suite includes CPU benchmarks for measuring and comparing computer performance by stressing the system's processor, memory subsystem, and compiler. SPEC CPU 2017 has 43 benchmarks, organized into four groups, that is (1) single copy execution of integer benchmarks, (2) single copy execution floating-point benchmarks, (3) concurrent execution of integer benchmark copies, and (4) concurrent execution of floating-point of benchmarks copies. These benchmarks are written in C, C++, and Fortran programming languages.

The essential metrics supported by SPEC CPU are (a) time to complete a workload and (b) the throughput, that is, the work completed per unit of time, such as jobs per hour. Besides, the SPEC CPU also incorporates the capacity to measure and report power and energy used.

TPC Family

The Transaction Processing Performance Council (TPC) was founded in 1988, aiming at setting standards for transaction processing performance measurement. The two major organizational activities are (1) creating benchmarks and (2) creating a process for reviewing and monitoring those benchmarks. In 1989, the TPC published its first benchmark, TPC Benchmark A (TPC-A) [433].

The TPC-A benchmark implemented a DebitCredit online transaction processing (OLTP) applications characterized by multiple online sessions, disk input/output, application execution time, and transaction integrity. The workload was intended to reflect an OLTP application and measures how many transactions per second a system can perform when driven from multiple terminals. However, it does not support multiple transaction types of varying complexities. The second benchmark implemented by the TPC was TPC-B, a batch version of DebitCredit, without the network and user interaction, focused mainly on the batch transaction processing. However, TPC-B was not as successful as TPC-A.

In 1991, TPC announced its Fair Use policies, which were required to be adopted when TPC results are used in publicity aiming at avoiding misuse or misappropriation of the TPC's trademark. In addition, a group of certified TPC auditors was also created to review and approve the TPC benchmark test and results before being submitted to the TPC as an official benchmark result or publicized.

The TPC-C benchmark was approved in 1992, and like TPC-A, it was an online transaction processing (OLTP) benchmark. Nevertheless, TPC-C is a much more complex benchmark than its predecessors since it supported multiple concurrent transaction types either executed online or queued for deferred execution. As a result, TPC-C is ranked in transactions per minute (tpmC).

Since then, many other benchmarks have been announced and superseded by new versions or new benchmarks, such as TCP-DI, TPC-VMS, TPCx-IoT, and many others. TCP-DI combines and transforms data extracted from an OTLP system and other data sources, and loads them into a data warehouse. The source and destination models, transformations, and implementation instructions are specified to support integration requirements. The TPC-VMS is a benchmark focused on a Virtualization Environment. This benchmark manages three database workloads, consolidates them onto one server, and runs the benchmark workload in three virtual machines (VMs) on the system under test. The TPC-IoT was designed to verify performance, price-performance, and availability metrics of systems that gather vast data from large numbers of devices while running real-time analytic queries. The workload aims at typical activities in IoT systems.

The number of benchmark suites and families available nowadays is extensive. Furthermore, this field is in continuous evolution due to technological advances and new market players. Therefore, this section provides a glimpse of the benchmark arena.

24.2.2 SYNTHETIC OPERATIONAL WORKLOAD GENERATION

One difficulty when using benchmarks for evaluating computer system performance is that benchmarks only support evaluating cases that benchmark designers envisaged in advance. Specifically, there is no guarantee that the benchmarks indeed cover all engaging scenarios the planner may need. Therefore, another approach consists of creating a software (tool) that automatically creates or injects workloads to the system under evaluation or an emulator or simulator.

Indeed, many authors use the terms traffic injector, trace generator, traffic generators, and workload generators indistinguishably. On the other hand, some authors employ the term traffic injector for tools that only replay traffic (traces) on the computer system. Others adopt the term trace generator for tools that generate synthetic workloads recorded into a trace file. Many authors use the terms traffic injector, trace generator, traffic generators, and workload generators indistinguishably. Some authors use traffic injectors for tools that only replay traffic (traces) on the computer system. Others adopt the term trace generator for tools that generate synthetic workloads recorded into a trace file. However, some author uses the terms traffic generators or workload generator to refer to software systems that generate synthetic workloads based on traces or a mathematical model to drive a load into a system, benchmark, system-emulator or simulator. Therefore, we will use the term Workload Automation Software (WAS) or Workload Automation Tool (WAT) as a generic term. Whenever required, however, a more specific term may be adopted with a specific explanation.

In general terms, implementing a workload automation software requires gathering data from real workloads, analyzing the collected data, generating statistics, creating patterns or models, generating traces, and storing them for later use or injecting the traffic into the system or its emulator or simulator. Hence, the traffic to be injected or stored may express both the original workload or variants that may express other engaging scenarios. Therefore, such software should be carefully implemented to emulate similar users' behavior or specific scenarios. Figure 24.2 somewhat reflects these cases. This class of workload automation software may also be considered as a generalization of the concept of benchmarks. However, we prefer classifying such types as a distinct software class [136].

httperf

This software system is a tool implemented in the C programming language at HP Research Labs for generating HTTP workloads and measuring server performance. The initial focus of httperf was providing facilitates to build benchmarks. The httperf is logically divided into three parts: the core HTTP engine, workload generation, and statistics analyzer [182, 292].

The HTTP engine handles the communication with the server and takes care of connection management and HTTP requests and replies handling. The workload generation initiates the HTTP calls at the appropriate times, so a particular workload is induced into the server. The statistics analyzer estimates various performance statistics.

Let us show some performance workloads generated by HTTP by looking at some examples. Executing the command

```
> httperf --server www.google.com
```

creates one connection, and this only connection makes one call. This can be seen in the field *Total*.

```
Maximum connect burst length: 0
Total: connections 1 requests 1 replies 1 test-duration 0.238 s
Connection rate: 4.2 conn/s (238.4 ms/conn, <=1 concurrent connections)
Connection time [ms]: min 238.4 avg 238.4 max 238.4 median 238.5 stddev 0.0
Connection time [ms]: connect 72.7
Connection length [replies/conn]: 1.000
Request rate: 4.2 req/s (238.4 ms/req)
Request size [B]: 67.0
Reply rate [replies/s]: min 0.0 avg 0.0 max 0.0 stddev 0.0 (0 samples)
Reply time [ms]: response 160.4 transfer 5.3
Reply size [B]: header 732.0 content 12567.0 footer 2.0 (total 13301.0)
Reply status: 1xx=0 2xx=1 3xx=0 4xx=0 5xx=0
CPU time [s]: user 0.02 system 0.20 (user 6.7% system 85.6% total 92.3%)
Net I/O: 54.8 KB/s (0.4*10^6 bps)
Errors: total 0 client-timo 0 socket-timo 0 connrefused 0 connreset 0
Errors: fd-unavail 0 addrunavail 0 ftab-full 0 other 0
```

The field *Connection Rate* tells the input connection rate in connections per second format. The first *Connection Time* field shows the lifetime of a TCP connection, that is, the time between the connection initiation and connection closure. The second *Connection Time* field depicts the average connection time if multiple connections were initiated. The field *Connection Length* tells us the average number of replies each connection has received. The *Request Rate* shows the request rate at which the HTTP requests were issued by httperf. The *Request Size* depicts the request size in bytes. The field *Reply Rate* informs the rate at which the server replies to the requests. *Reply Time* shows the time taken by the web-server to respond to the request and the time taken to receive this reply. The field *Reply Size* is similar to the request size; thus shows the reply size in bytes. Finally, the *Reply Status* shows the status code of the reply that httperf received from the server. The rest of the two sections are for CPU and resources the client spends in carrying out the tests and errors encountered during the test.

The following command is similar to the previous one, but instead of providing the *URL*, the IP address is specified.

```
> httperf --server 172.217.30.36
```

The following command, besides the IP address, the connection rate (*–rate 600* requests per second) and the number of sessions are specified (*–num-conns 20* - twenty sessions). The default number of calls per session is one; each connection (session) executes one HTTP call and, if it succeeds, gets the respective reply.

```
> httperf --hog --server 172.217.30.36

        --rate 600 --num-conns 20
```

The option *–hog* uses as many TCP ports as required. Without this option, httperf is typically limited to using ports in the range of 1024 to 5000, which can become a bottleneck. This option must also be specified when measuring NT servers since it avoids a TCP incompatibility between NT and UNIX machines.

The command below, besides the information specified in the previous command, also defines the port, which is 80. The option *–port* defines the number of ports (*N*) on which the web-server is listening for HTTP requests. Its default value is 80.

```
> httperf --server 172.217.30.36 --port 80

        --rate 600 --num-conns 20
```

```
Maximum connect burst length: 3
Total: connections 20 requests 20 replies 20 test-duration 0.454 s
Connection rate: 44.1 conn/s (22.7 ms/conn, <=20 concurrent connections)
Connection time [ms]: min 419.8 avg 432.5 max 443.9 median 432.5 stddev 8.1
Connection time [ms]: connect 240.4
Connection length [replies/conn]: 1.000
Request rate: 44.1 req/s (22.7 ms/req)
Request size [B]: 66.0
Reply rate [replies/s]: min 0.0 avg 0.0 max 0.0 stddev 0.0 (0 samples)
Reply time [ms]: response 192.1 transfer 0.0
Reply size [B]: header 309.0 content 219.0 footer 0.0 (total 528.0)
Reply status: 1xx=0 2xx=0 3xx=20 4xx=0 5xx=0
CPU time [s]: user 0.03 system 0.39 (user 6.2% system 86.4% total 92.5%)
Net I/O: 25.6 KB/s (0.2*10^6 bps)
Errors: total 0 client-timo 0 socket-timo 0 connrefused 0 connreset 0
Errors: fd-unavail 0 addrunavail 0 ftab-full 0 other 0
```

The line *Total* shows the number of connections (sessions), 20 connections, the total number of calls and replies, 20 each since each connection makes only one call - default, and the test duration, 454 *ms*. After that, we get the connection rate (in connections per second), the minimal, the average, the median, the maximal, and the standard deviation of the connection times. Then, we get the request rate (in requests per second), the request size in bytes, the reply rates (replies per second), the reply time, and subsequent data as in the previous examples.

The following specifies two hundred sessions, each session makes thirty calls, and a timeout of 5 *s* for each call is defined.

```
> httperf --hog --server 172.217.30.36 --rate 600

          --num-conns 200 --num-calls 30 --timeout 5
```

After executing this command above, the following reports are provided.

```
Maximum connect burst length: 3
Total: connections 20 requests 600 replies 600 test-duration 18.916 s
Connection rate: 1.1 conn/s (945.8 ms/conn, <=20 concurrent connections)
Connection time [ms]: min 16073.9 avg 17611.3 max 18897.6 median 17725.5
                                                           stddev 618.6
Connection time [ms]: connect 67.7
Connection length [replies/conn]: 30.000
Request rate: 31.7 req/s (31.5 ms/req)
Request size [B]: 66.0
Reply rate [replies/s]: min 32.6 avg 33.5 max 34.6 stddev 1.0 (3 samples)
Reply time [ms]: response 584.8 transfer 0.0
Reply size [B]: header 417.0 content 324.0 footer 0.0 (total 741.0)
Reply status: 1xx=0 2xx=0 3xx=600 4xx=0 5xx=0
CPU time [s]: user 1.09 system 17.46 (user 5.8% system 92.3% total 98.0%)
Net I/O: 25.0 KB/s (0.2*10^6 bps)
Errors: total 0 client-timo 0 socket-timo 0 connrefused 0 connreset 0
Errors: fd-unavail 0 addrunavail 0 ftab-full 0 other 0
```

As twenty sessions were specified, and each session makes twenty calls, the total number of calls is six hundred. The system also received six hundred replies, and no error was observed. The fields of the report are the same as depicted in the previous example.

The command line bellow creates fifty sessions; each session makes ten calls to the server specified by the http://www.google.com/index.html. The request rates specified two hundred requests per second, and the timeout is of each call is five seconds. The default port is eighty.

```
> httperf --server www.google.com --uri /index.html
                                        --num-conn 50

          --num-call 10 --rate 200 --timeout 5
```

The command line below generates a total of five sessions at a rate of 600 sessions per second. Each session consists of twenty calls spaced out by two seconds, and a timeout of $5\,s$ for each call.

```
> httperf --hog --server www.google.com --uri /index.html

          --wsess=5,20,2 --rate 600 --timeout 5
```

The option *–period=[D]T1[,T2]* specifying "interarrival time" can alternatively be specified by the option *–rate*. However, more alternatives are is available with *– period*. The *D* parameter specifies the interarrival time distribution. If omitted or set to "d", a deterministic period is specified by parameter *T1* seconds. If *D* is set to "e", the exponential distribution is used with a mean interarrival time of *T1*. Finally, if *D* is set to "u", the period distribution is uniform over the interval $[T1, T2)$. If "d", "e" or "u" are omitted, it is equivalent to "d", and the period is specified by the parameter $T1$ in units of seconds. The default value for the period is 0. In such a case, sessions are generated sequentially without any delay. Hence, it is worth noting that specifying, for instance, *–rate=5* is equivalent to specifying *–period=d0.2* or *– period=0.2*. The following three command lines show examples adopting these three possible configurations ('d", "e" or "u").

```
> httperf --hog --server www.google.com --uri /index.html

          --wsess=5,20,2 --period=d0.0017 --timeout 5
```

```
> httperf --hog --server www.google.com --uri /index.html

          --wsess=5,20,2 --period=e0.0017 --timeout 5
```

```
> httperf --hog --server www.google.com --uri /index.html

          --wsess=5,20,2 --period=u0.0017,0.0024 --timeout 5
```

A Workload for Multiplayer Online Gaming

A group from Universität Mannheim and Technische Universität Darmstadt proposed a WAS for online gaming infrastructures [235, 435]. Their proposal generates workload independently from the network infrastructure by using only game logic inputs (e.g., steering, throttling, shooting) instead of direct communication with the underlying network. Their framework allows us to conduct real multi-player gaming sessions with humans and to create detailed trace files. In a simulator mode, synthetically created sessions can be carried out in a controlled environment by supporting reproducible simulation, mainly achieved by setting the seed values wherever random numbers are generated.

The evaluation framework is composed of three major components: (1) the game Planet PI4, a 3D space shooter for multiple players connected via an exchangeable P2P overlay network. The players can fly space ships through a virtual asteroid field and shoot each other—the game bases or repair points are incentives for players to gather at specific locations. Players can either battle in a free-for-all fashion or as opposing teams. (2) A discrete event game simulator provides an environment that can simulate peers playing the game and the underlying network. (3) A monitoring server is used to monitor and trace all the game data from the human players as the game progresses. Human players can generate the workload in an entire gaming session or synthetically, either by simple mobility models or AI (artificial intelligence) players.

Fanban

Fanban is a Java open-source performance workload creation, and execution framework [134]. Fanban has two major components, the Fanban Driver Framework and the Fanban Harness. The Fanban Driver Framework is an API-based framework that aims at helping develop workload generators. The driver framework controls the workload lifecycle execution and the stochastic model adopted to simulate users' behavior. It is implemented by adopting a distributed architecture that allows distributing the workload drivers to multiple machines. Fanban Harness is a mechanism for supporting implementing servers that deal with the transaction requests submitted by Fanban drivers. Fanban Harness also supports implementing servers for non-Fanban workload generators.

Fanban infrastructure provides built-in support for servers such as Apache HTTPd, Sun Java System Web, Portal and Mail Servers, Oracle RDBMS, Memcached. It also provides a web interface for execution control, queueing, statistics and data analysis, and viewing results.

Fanban allows us to vary the workload scale by providing load variation files to a run at submission time. This feature, coupled with the runtime reporting, allows us to monitor the response times and stability as the load varies.

Workload Cloud-System Generation - Osmania University

Sudha Pelluri and Keerti Bangari presented a research initiative that implemented a workload generator that creates the synthetic session-based requests to application [329]. Their workload generator comprises two modules: Module 1 is responsible for characterizing the real workloads, and Module 2 is for synthetic workload Generation.

Module 1 downloads real workload trace files and subjects them to statistical analysis, in which statistics and plots are generated. First, the trace file contains the mean

CPU usage and the memory usage by each job. Then, using the findings of the statistics, the workload characteristics are defined. The probability distributions for real workloads can, then, be used to generate the synthetic workloads.

Module 2 is the actual workload generator. This module adopts Fanban[134], which is an open-source workload generation tool. Fanbanis adopted as a programmed Java driver to generate the synthetic workload reflecting the behavior of the real workload. The system setup was implemented in a virtual environment created using four virtual machines (VMs) each. These VMs act as clients that generate the workloads to the System Under Test (SUT). The SUT was implemented as another virtual machine and Apache web-server.

NoWog

NoWog (Not only Workload Generator) is an open-source synthetic-workload database generator able to exercise the NoSQL database. NoWog also mimics real-world database applications and has language for describing workload characteristics and the storage model. In addition, NoWog language supports probability distributions for reading and writing data types such as numbers, texts, arrays, and nested documents [15]. NoWog language is less expressive than SQL or NoSQL query languages but suitable to specify, create, read, update, and delete (CRUD) operations and define the distribution of those operations in time intervals. However, a mapper function translates NoWog language to a targeted database system.

This platform allows us to specify the total number of each read and write operation and the distributions of that operations over a time interval. Hence, the analyst can define the total number of operations; the throughput of a database application can also be mimicked by NoWog. The operations' variance depends on the number of rules that the users define and on the values obtained by the random value generator.

GT-CWSL

The Georgia Tech Cloud Workload Specification Language (GT-CWSL) provides a structured way to specify application workloads. GT-CWSL combines benchmark and workload features to create workload specifications used by a synthetic workload generator to generate synthetic workloads for performance evaluation of cloud computing applications.

The author also proposes a workload generation methodology that allows control over the workload attributes such as think time, inter-session interval, session length, workload mix, and sensitivity analysis. They implemented a workload generator based upon the Fanban Harness by extending it to accept GT-CWSL specifications [34].

WGCap

The Workload Generator for HP (Hewlett Packard) Capacity Advisor (WGCap) is a synthetic workload generator that creates traces imported into the Capacity Advisor. The Capacity Advisor then simulates the resource consumption by looking at CPU demand, memory size, disk data rate, and network data rate [147] based on the generated traces. The Capacity Advisor [68] is a capacity planning tool of the HP Virtual Server Environment (VSE) [454].

The VSE is a virtualization solution implemented by HP that manages and monitors virtual servers. The VSE is a unified set of multi-platform products and technologies to maximize the use of server resources. VSE Management provides visualization, configuration, workload policy, application management, and capacity planning tools to improve system resource utilization. VSE provides an integrated graphical environment, through HP SIM1, for managing physical servers, logical servers, virtual machines, server blades, partitions, applications, and workloads [452, 453].

The Capacity Advisor is a component of the VSE that acts as a capacity planning tool. It aims to enable capacity planners to analyze historical workload utilization data to plan workload migrations or new workload undertakings. For VSE, the workload is a set of processes within an OS image running on a system whose performance is conducted as a single unit. The Capacity Advisor collects workload utilization from each system and stores it on the HP Systems Insight Manager.

The Capacity Advisor has two methods for gathering data traces from systems. The first method adopts agents at the systems to collect historical data related to resource utilization. The historic data traces are obtained for CPU utilization, memory utilization, disk I/O capacity utilization, and network I/O capacity utilization at a specified sample frequency. The second method imports the data directly to the Capacity Advisor Database.

The WGCap works with two types of input data for generating the synthetic traces: real traces (collected from existing systems) or statistical data (estimated from the resources). The output produced by WGCap is a CSV file with the same structure as the files exported by Capacity Advisor with each resource's values synthetically generated, so the synthetic traces generated can be imported (see Figure 24.3). The format header is structured as follows:

```
#Profile: name
#Host: hostname
#CPU: CPU count@CPU speedGHz
#Memory: MEM sizeMB
#OS: platform
#Model: model
#Version: version number
[YYYYMMDDhhmm,] UTIS, metric [, metric, ...]
```

The last header line contains the comma-separated list of labels for the date and gathered metrics, where the fields are defined as:

1. *YYYYMMDDhhmm* - Timestamp in local time, given in units of

   YYYY (year),

   MM (month, as 01 to 12),

   DD (day, as 01 to 31),

   hh (hours, as 00 to 23), and

   mm (minutes, as 00 to 59).

2. UTIS - Universal Time (GMT) in seconds (standard UNIX time in seconds since 1 January 1970).

3. metric - At least one of the following:

   CPU ALLOC,

   CPU UTIL,

   DISK UTIL,

   MEM ALLOC,

   MEM UTIL,

   NET UTIL,

   PHYS CPUS,

   PHYS MEM.

The workload is generated considering three methods: (1) generating synthetic traces from real traces, (2) generating synthetic traces from statistical summaries, and (3) generating statistical summaries and synthetic traces from real traces.

The first method allows the workload generator to create synthetic traces from actual traces. The user can generate synthetic traces through real traces following the empirical distribution function's behavior that represents the real trace provided in the period. The second method generates synthetic traces receiving as input the statistical summaries provided by the user. Probability distribution in a trace represents each resource (IO, disk, memory, CPU). After calculating the statistical summaries, the user must choose a probability distribution that fits the statistical summary to determine each resource's behavior. The third method addresses the situation where the customer can not provide or arrange the real traces to be directly used to generate synthetic traces. However, the traces can be used for the generation of statistical summaries and finding suitable theoretical distributions. In this method, the synthetic traces are generated from the theoretical distributions.

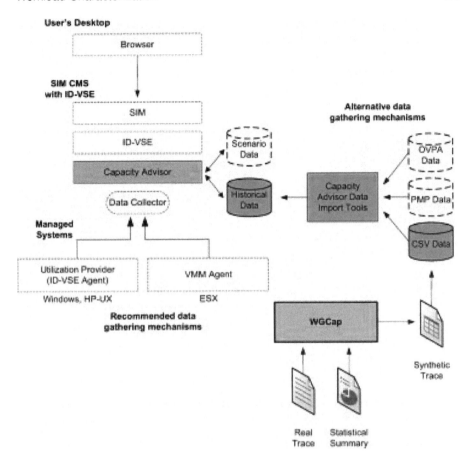

Figure 24.3 WGCap-Capacity Advisor Interaction.

24.3 WORKLOAD MODELING

A computer system workload model represents a workload of the computer system. Such a model may be adopted to analyze scenarios of interest that the performance analyst is required to evaluate via closed-form formulas, numerical analysis, or simulation. Such a model may also be adapted to generate actual system workloads or generate synthetic workloads. However, workload characterization is not always straightforward due to the required level of detail in which the workload should be represented and which aspects of the workload are significant.

Workloads can be described by their

- **(a) intended work** or can be described by the
- **(b) impact** on the computer system resources

Figure 24.4 shows these perspectives highlighted above. In the latter case, the impact of the workload on the system is represented by statistical summaries and probabilistic distributions of the system's resource utilization, throughput, and time required for resources to process the computer system *demand* (see Section 8.3).

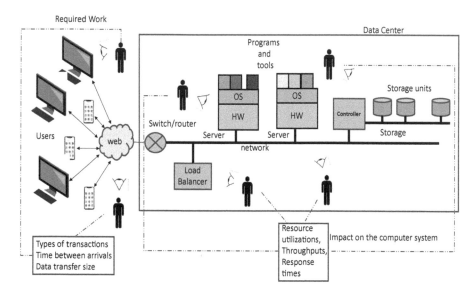

Figure 24.4   Workload Point of Views: **Intended Work** or **Impact on Resources**.

The workload may also be represented by the intended work, that is, by what, when, and how often the system should perform the related activities. However, let us first consider the case in which the workload is described by its **impact** on the computer system (descriptive models).

24.3.1   MODELING WORKLOAD IMPACT

Statistical and probabilistic modeling of the workload impact of system infrastructure involves sampling the usage, throughput, discard rates, delays related to the selected resources of interest, obtained statistical summaries, and probability distributions that represent the representative samples. We illustrate this general approach by using a set of examples.

Example 24.3.1. Assume a computer system with a Linux operating system executes the following script (already shown when studying *Linpack* benchmark):

scriptlinpack

```
printf "Linpack Results \n" >> Linpack_result.txt;
for i in {1..100}
do
 Linpack >> Linpack_result.txt;
done,
```

where *Linpack* is the executable file of the *Linpack* benchmark (see Section 24.2.1 and Appendix C). Each execution of the file *Linpack* provides the respective execution time and the float-point instructions per second of each execution, among other data.

The script *scriptlinpack* executes the *Linpack* benchmark one hundred times and writes the benchmark's results in the file *Linpack_result.txt*. After starting the script's execution, the following command was executed in another command-line interface (shell):

```
> pidstat -u -C "Linpack" 1 >> Linpack_uti_result.txt
```

The execution of the command-line above looks up any process whose filename is *linpack* and measures its processor utilization. The utilization measures are obtained with a delay between measures equal to one second. The utilization measures are stored in the file *Linpack_uti_result.txt*. When the script ends its execution, the monitoring may be finished by executing the command *Control* + *C*. As the monitoring system started after the *scriptlinpack* begins, only eighty-one ($C0 = 81$ - The number of completed tasks according to the notation introduced in Chapter 8) out of one hundred *Linpack* executions were measured. The content of the file *Linpack_uti_result.txt* is shown in Table 24.9.

Table 24.9

Content of the File *Linpack_uti_result.txt*

Time	PM	PID	%usr	%system	%guest	%CPU	CPU	Command
3:12:59	PM	25432	53.47	0	0	53.47	0	Linpack
3:13:00	PM	25433	48.35	0	0	48.35	0	Linpack
3:13:01	PM	25434	47	0	0	47.00	0	Linpack
3:13:02	PM	25435	43	0	0	43.00	0	Linpack
3:13:03	PM	25436	47	0	0	47.00	0	Linpack
3:13:04	PM	25437	49.5	0	0	49.50	0	Linpack
3:13:05	PM	25438	53.06	0	0	53.06	0	Linpack
3:13:06	PM	25439	55	1	0	56.00	0	Linpack
3:13:07	PM	25440	56	1	0	57.00	0	Linpack
3:13:08	PM	25441	53	0	0	53.00	0	Linpack
3:13:09	PM	25442	51	0	0	51.00	0	Linpack
3:13:10	PM	25443	36.96	0	0	36.96	0	Linpack

(Continued)

Table 24.9

Content of the File *Linpack_uti_result.txt*

Time	PM	PID	%usr	%system	%guest	%CPU	CPU	Command
3:13:11	PM	25444	38	0	0	38.00	0	Linpack
3:13:12	PM	25445	31	0	0	31.00	0	Linpack
3:13:13	PM	25446	21	0	0	21.00	0	Linpack
3:13:14	PM	25447	24	0	0	24.00	0	Linpack
3:13:15	PM	25448	27	0	0	27.00	0	Linpack
3:13:16	PM	25449	29.7	0	0	29.70	0	Linpack
3:13:17	PM	25450	34.34	0	0	34.34	0	Linpack
3:13:18	PM	25451	28.71	0	0	28.71	0	Linpack
3:13:19	PM	25452	31	2	0	33.00	0	Linpack
3:13:20	PM	25453	33.68	0	0	33.68	0	Linpack
3:13:21	PM	25454	34	1	0	35.00	0	Linpack
3:13:22	PM	25455	23.76	0	0	23.76	0	Linpack
3:13:23	PM	25456	11.11	0	0	11.11	0	Linpack
3:13:37	PM	25469	89.11	0.99	0	90.10	0	Linpack
3:13:38	PM	25470	93	0	0	93.00	0	Linpack
3:13:39	PM	25471	84	0	0	84.00	0	Linpack
3:13:40	PM	25472	72.73	0	0	72.73	0	Linpack
3:13:41	PM	25473	68.32	0	0	68.32	0	Linpack
3:13:42	PM	25474	68.37	0	0	68.37	0	Linpack
3:13:43	PM	25475	65	0	0	65.00	0	Linpack
3:13:44	PM	25476	71	0	0	71.00	0	Linpack
3:13:45	PM	25477	69	0	0	69.00	0	Linpack
3:13:46	PM	25478	74	0	0	74.00	0	Linpack
3:13:47	PM	25479	78	0	0	78.00	0	Linpack
3:13:48	PM	25480	80	1	0	81.00	0	Linpack
3:13:49	PM	25481	86	0	0	86.00	0	Linpack
3:13:50	PM	25482	80.81	0	0	80.81	0	Linpack
3:13:51	PM	25483	85	0	0	85.00	0	Linpack
3:13:52	PM	25484	89.9	0	0	89.90	0	Linpack
3:13:57	PM	25490	14	0	0	14.00	0	Linpack
3:13:58	PM	25491	16.33	0	0	16.33	0	Linpack
3:13:59	PM	25492	20	0	0	20.00	0	Linpack
3:14:00	PM	25493	15	0	0	15.00	0	Linpack
3:14:01	PM	25494	19.8	0	0	19.80	0	Linpack
3:14:02	PM	25495	26.26	0	0	26.26	0	Linpack
3:14:04	PM	25500	51.06	0	0	51.06	0	Linpack
3:14:05	PM	25500	82.14	7.14	0	89.29	0	Linpack
3:14:15	PM	25501	75	0	0	75.00	0	Linpack
3:14:19	PM	25508	10	0	0	10.00	0	Linpack
3:14:20	PM	25509	14	0	0	14.00	0	Linpack
3:14:21	PM	25510	10.89	0	0	10.89	0	Linpack
3:14:22	PM	25511	16	0	0	16.00	0	Linpack

(Continued)

Table 24.9

Content of the File *Linpack_uti_result.txt*

Time	PM	PID	%usr	%system	%guest	%CPU	CPU	Command
3:14:23	PM	25512	19.19	0	0	19.19	0	Linpack
3:14:24	PM	25513	22.77	0	0	22.77	0	Linpack
3:14:25	PM	25514	27	0	0	27.00	0	Linpack
3:14:26	PM	25515	30	0	0	30.00	0	Linpack
3:14:27	PM	25516	20	0	0	20.00	0	Linpack
3:14:29	PM	25517	95.05	0	0	95.05	0	Linpack
3:14:30	PM	25518	91	0	0	91.00	0	Linpack
3:14:31	PM	25519	91	1	0	92.00	0	Linpack
3:14:32	PM	25520	82	0	0	82.00	0	Linpack
3:14:33	PM	25521	81.32	0	0	81.32	0	Linpack
3:14:34	PM	25522	77	0	0	77.00	0	Linpack
3:14:35	PM	25523	78	0	0	78.00	0	Linpack
3:14:36	PM	25524	84.85	0	0	84.85	0	Linpack
3:14:37	PM	25525	88.12	0	0	88.12	0	Linpack
3:14:38	PM	25526	84.27	0	0	84.27	0	Linpack
3:14:39	PM	25527	69.31	0	0	69.31	0	Linpack
3:14:40	PM	25528	61	1	0	62.00	0	Linpack
3:14:41	PM	25529	58	0	0	58.00	0	Linpack
3:14:42	PM	25530	52.53	0	0	52.53	0	Linpack
3:14:43	PM	25531	44.55	0	0	44.55	0	Linpack
3:14:44	PM	25532	34	1	0	35.00	0	Linpack
3:14:45	PM	25533	30	0	0	30.00	0	Linpack
3:14:46	PM	25534	24	0	0	24.00	0	Linpack
3:14:47	PM	25535	22.77	0	0	22.77	0	Linpack
3:14:48	PM	25536	14	0	0	14.00	0	Linpack
3:14:49	PM	25537	16.16	0	0	16.16	0	Linpack
3:14:50	PM	25538	21.21	0	0	21.21	0	Linpack

The statistical summary of the processor total utilization (in range $(0, 1)$) is depicted in Table 24.10. It is worth mentioning that the mean and the median are close, and the interquartile range is 0.51. The kurtosis value of -1.4040 shows that the data sample is much flatter than a normal distribution. The skewness value of 0.1751 indicates the very light right tail.

Figure 24.5 shows the histogram of the collected sample, and Figure 24.6 depicts the respective empirical cumulative distribution function.

We considered the uniform distribution as a possible theoretical probability distribution for representing the data set. The uniform distribution with parameters $min = 0.1000$ and $max = 0.9505$ was not rejected by the Kolmogorov-Smirnov

Table 24.10

Statistical Summary

Mean	Standard Error	Median	Mode	SD	CoV	Variance	Kurtosis
0.4965	0.0297	0.4835	0.1400	0.2676	0.5389	0.0716	-1.4040
Skewness	**Range**	**Minimum**	**Maximum**	**Q1**	**Q3**	**IQR**	**Count**
0.1751	0.8505	0.1000	0.9505	0.2400	0.7500	0.5100	81

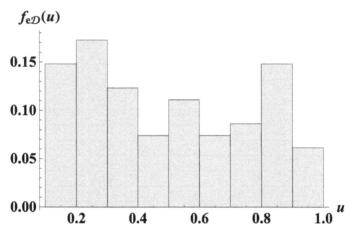

Figure 24.5 Histogram.

goodness of fit test with $\alpha = 0.05$ degree of significance. The probability density function and the respective cumulative distribution function of this theoretical distribution are depicted in Figure 24.7 and Figure 24.8, respectively. It is also worth noting that the coefficient of variation of the data sample is 0.5389. This mesure is close to the coefficient of variation of the distribution $U(0.1000, 0.9505)$, which is $CoV_{U(0.1000, 0.9505)} = 0.46743$.

The confidence interval of the mean utilization with 95% degree of confidence calculated using the nonparametric bootstrap by considering ten thousand re-samples was

$$\bar{u} \in (0.439748, 0.55552).$$

Likewise, the confidence interval of the mean utilization with 95% degree of confidence calculated using the semi-parametric bootstrap by considering ten thousand re-samples was

$$\bar{u} \in (0.472043, 0.578624).$$

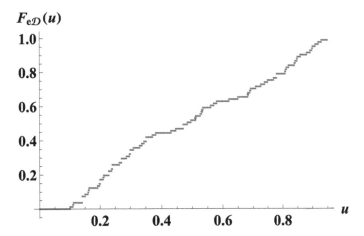

Figure 24.6   Empirical Cumulative Distribution Function.

The time measured for carrying out the eighty-one *Linpack* executions was estimated by subtracting the time instant of the last measure (3h 14min 50s) from the time instant when the first detected execution started (3h 12min 58s). This measured delay was $T = 112\,s$. This information is obtained from Table 24.9. Therefore, the system throughput[3] (see Chapter 8) for this workload was

$$X0 = \frac{C0}{T} = \frac{81\ executions}{112\,s} = 0.7232\,eps.$$

Using the demand law (see Section 8.3), we may estimate the time demanded from the processor for one execution of the *Linpack* benchmark by

$$D_{CPU} = \frac{\overline{U_{CPU}}}{X_0} = \frac{0.4965}{0.7232\,eps} = 686.51\,ms.$$

At the end of each *scriptlinpack* execution, the script duration is stored in the text file *Linpack_result.txt*. Details on that process were depicted when we described the *Linpack* benchmark. As in that case, Table 24.11 shows the durations of each *scriptlinpack* execution, totaling eighty-one durations.

```
Linpack Results

     Factor Solve Total MFLOPS Unit Cray-Ratio

0.876013 0.002379 0.878392 761.239477 0.002627 15.685571
```

---

[3] *eps* stands for executions per second.

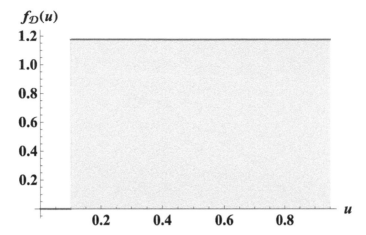

Figure 24.7   Uniform Density Function - $U(0.1, 0.9505)$.

```
Duration: 1.047 sec.


    Factor Solve Total MFLOPS Unit Cray-Ratio

0.871313 0.002381 0.873694 765.33279 0.002613 15.601679

Duration: 1.014 sec.



                         ...



    Factor Solve Total MFLOPS Unit Cray-Ratio

0.917287 0.002389 0.919676 727.067648 0.002751 16.422786

Duration: 1.128 sec.
```

It is worth noting the duration of each run of the script. Table 24.11 summarizes the eighty-one durations.

Table 24.12 depicts a statistical summary of the data content shown in Table 24.11. It is worth highlighting the mean value, that is, $\overline{D} = 1.1472\,s$. The time demanded to execute the *linpack* executable file was $686.51\,ms$. The difference $1147.20\,ms - 686.51\,ms = 460.70\,ms$ is related to the other commands of the *scriptlinpack*, in particular, related to the file write operation related to the standard output writing redirection.

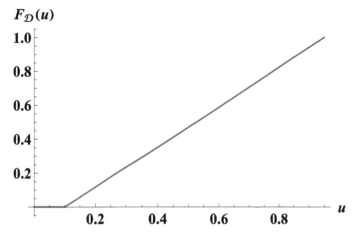

Figure 24.8   Uniform Cumulative Distribution Function - $U(0.1, 0.9505)$.

Table 24.11
Durations of Each Eighty-One Runs of the Script *scriptlinpack*

Durations (s)								
0.961	1.066	0.989	0.948	1.024	2.468	0.954	0.977	1.090
0.963	0.953	1.083	0.958	0.948	10.646	0.951	0.970	1.105
1.028	0.943	1.125	0.953	0.943	0.987	0.962	0.946	1.053
1.100	0.954	1.040	1.062	0.971	0.992	1.101	0.952	1.056
1.128	0.956	1.020	0.940	0.956	0.955	1.216	1.031	1.008
1.048	1.042	1.000	0.940	1.059	0.954	1.066	1.153	1.092
1.009	1.162	0.954	0.962	0.947	1.031	0.995	1.081	0.969
1.050	1.010	1.011	0.953	0.944	0.947	1.105	1.043	0.959
0.944	1.010	0.959	0.950	1.204	0.972	0.971	1.043	0.951

Table 24.12
Measured Duration of Each *scriptlinpack* **Execution (s)**

Mean	Median	Mode	SD	Var	Kurt	Skew
1.1472	0.9920	0.9540	1.0829	1.1726	76.6919	8.6709
Range	**Min**	**Max**	**Count**	**Q3**	**Q1**	**IQR**
9.7060	0.9400	10.6460	81	1.0430	0.9560	0.0870

☐

It is worth noting that for representing the impact of a workload on the computer system resources, the respective resource utilization must also be evaluated, adopting a similar approach considered in the study for processor resources. We may stress I/O devices such as mass data storage, memory, and network among critical system resources.

Characterizing the distribution of a workload attribute in isolation may not be enough for an efficient and thorough representation of the workload on a system. Therefore, an important aspect that should be carefully looked at is possible correlations between distinct workload attributes and between samples. Hence, analyzing the correlation between workload parameters (see Section 4.6) and samples' autocorrelation (see Autocorrelation in Section 14.4.2) are aspects that should not be overlooked.

Example 24.3.2. We executed the *stress* program with the following options

```
>> sudo stress --cpu 1 --hdd 1 --timeout 180s,
```

which spawn one threads (*worker*) spinning on *sqrt*() and writing one *GB*. The *stress* program was configured to be executed for 180 *s*.

After starting the execution of the *stress*, we executed *iostat* (see Section 23.7.1) to monitor the system resources. The sample consists of 24 measures collected every five seconds. Hence, the collecting process was 120*s*. It is worth mentioning that the execution of the *iostat* program finished before the *stress* process finishes. The command line for executing the *iostat* command was

```
>> iostat -t 5 24 > cpuiostat.txt
```

The sample is stored in the file *cpuiostat.txt*. Below, we have a chunk of the sample stored in the file. We removed the first set of measures from the sample generated by *iostat* because it provides statistics concerning the period since the system was started (in red).

```
Linux 4.4.0-142-generic (ubuntu)  01/08/2021 _i686_ (1 CPU)

01/08/2021 05:18:25 PM
avg-cpu:  %user   %nice %system %iowait  %steal   %idle
           6.00    0.00    2.40    2.04    0.00   89.56
Device:            tps    kB_read/s    kB_wrtn/s    kB_read    kB_wrtn
sda               7.80        54.80      2223.87     898623   36465032
01/08/2021 05:18:30 PM
avg-cpu:  %user   %nice %system %iowait  %steal   %idle
          88.00    0.00   12.00    0.00    0.00    0.00
Device:            tps    kB_read/s    kB_wrtn/s    kB_read    kB_wrtn
sda             114.00         0.00     92798.40          0     463992
01/08/2021 05:18:35 PM
avg-cpu:  %user   %nice %system %iowait  %steal   %idle
          88.58    0.00   11.42    0.00    0.00    0.00
Device:            tps    kB_read/s    kB_wrtn/s    kB_read    kB_wrtn
sda             125.45         0.00     98555.51          0     491792
                            ...
```

```
01/08/2021 05:20:20 PM
avg-cpu:   %user   %nice %system %iowait  %steal   %idle
           92.59    0.00    7.41    0.00    0.00    0.00
Device:             tps   kB_read/s   kB_wrtn/s   kB_read   kB_wrtn
sda              107.82        0.00    82457.72         0    411464
```

Table 24.13 shows the statistical summary the sample measures %*user*, %*system*, *tps*, *kB_wrtn/s* and *kB_wrtn*. The *io_read* operation numbers were not significant; hence we do not present them. Figure 24.9 depicts the individual plot of each set of collected measures.

Table 24.13

Statistical Summary of %*user* %*system tps kB_wrtn/s kB_wrtn*.

Metric	%user	%system	tps	kB_wrtn/s	kB_wrtn
Total	23	23	23	23	23
Mean	90.23	9.77	107.88	81101.00	405527.00
SD	1.94	1.94	20.27	17370.00	86953.00
Var	3.78	3.78	411.04	301702659	7560898745
CoV	0.02	0.20	0.19	0.21	0.21
Min	87.20	4.80	52.60	40431.00	202156.00
Q_1	88.58	8.60	99.80	74317.00	371584.00
Med	90.18	9.82	114.00	84964.00	424820.00
Q_3	91.40	11.42	124.95	91607.00	458952.00
Max	95.20	12.80	135.20	103670.00	518352.00
Range	8.00	8.00	82.60	63239.00	316196.00
IQR	2.82	2.82	25.15	17290.00	87368.00
Skew	0.64	-0.64	-1.18	-1.22	-1.21
Kurt	0.46	0.46	1.33	0.82	0.80

The empirical cumulative distribution of each set of measures of the sample is shown in Figure 24.10. Figure 24.11 shows the linear relationship between the system utilization (%*system*) and the *io throughput* (*tps*), the disk writing rate (*kB_wrtn/s*), and the bytes written to the disk (*kB_wrtn*) by setting each intercept to zero. In all those cases, we notice a a strong linear relationship between each measure and the system utilization since $\rho^2_{tps,\%system} = 0.98$, $\rho^2_{kB\_wrtn/s,\%system} = 0.975$, and $\rho^2_{kB\_wrtn/s,\%system} = 0.9749$.

Besides, we took, for instance, the twenty-three measures of the *tps* and applied the Kolmogorov-Smirnov goodness of fit for checking if the normal distribution with mean $\mu = 107.88 tps$ and standard deviation $\sigma = 20.27 tps$ is a suitable distribution to represent the sample. Similarly, the Kolmogorov-Smirnov goodness of fit does not

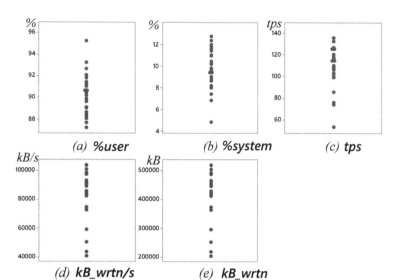

Figure 24.9 Individual Plots of %*user*, %*system*, *tps*, *kB_wrtn/s* and *kB_wrtn*.

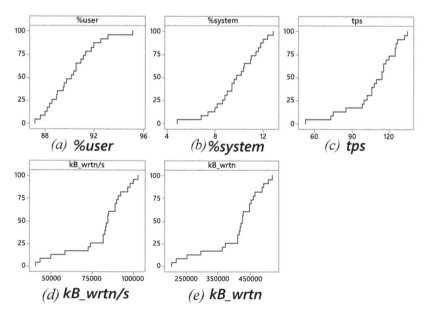

Figure 24.10 *ECD* of %*user*, %*system*, *tps*, *kB_wrtn/s* and *kB_wrtn*.

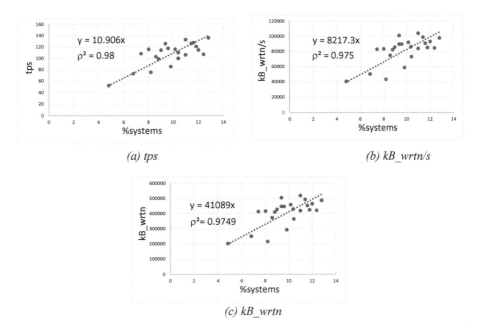

(a) tps   (b) kB_wrtn/s

(c) kB_wrtn

Figure 24.11 Correlations between %*system* and *t ps*, *kB_wrtn/s* and *kB_wrtn*.

reject normal distribution with mean $\mu = 9.77\%$, and the standard deviation $\sigma = 1.94\%$ is a suitable distribution to represent %*system*. The Kolmogorov-Smirnov goodness of fit also failed to reject the triangular distributions $Tr(40.431 \times 10^3 \, kB/s,$ $103.67 \times 10^3 \, kB/s, 99.201 \times 10^3 \, kB/s)$, and $Tr(202.160 \times 10^3 \, kB, 518.350 \times 10^3 \, kB, 496.07 \times 10^3 \, kB)$ for representing *kB_wrtn/s* and *kB_wrtn*, respectively. For all goodness of fit tests, we found no evidence to reject the distribution even considering a degree of confidence of 80%. Figure 24.12 shows the respective probability density function of each random variable.

□

Example 24.3.3. Suppose a web client access a web-server in a data center to execute a set of webservices. The client requested one hundred and twenty services' execution. The time the web-server took to process each service required in each request is shown in Table 24.14. The statistical summary of the sample is shown in Table 24.15. The histogram of the sample, depicted in Figure 24.13, shows a multimodal data set. The Coefficient of Range (*CoR*) (see Definition 3.3.2) is

$$CoR = \frac{M - m}{M + m} =$$

$$CoR = \frac{415.24 - 38.75}{415.24 + 38.75} = 0.83,$$

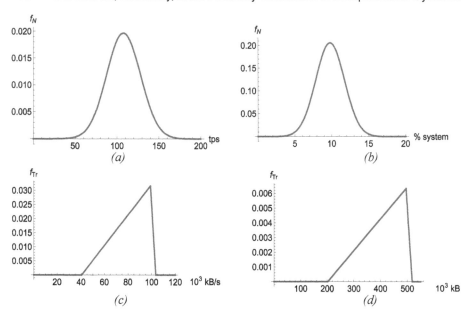

Figure   24.12 Probability   Density   Functions $N(107.88\,tps, 20.27\,tps)$, $N(9.77\%, 1.94\%)$, $Tr(40.431, 103.67, 99.201)$ $(10^3\,kB/s)$ and $Tr(202.160, 518.350, 496.07)\,(10^3\,kB)$.

Table 24.14

Time to Process the Web-Services (ms)

Time to Process the Web-Services (ms)							
79.64	80.54	192.37	179.34	178.59	369.49	92.89	204.91
68.36	87.02	182.82	159.90	159.21	349.93	66.16	173.15
54.55	95.64	165.40	101.96	133.65	415.24	82.11	172.20
91.32	79.83	168.11	154.74	178.78	394.52	97.12	156.22
97.32	69.18	197.71	195.89	157.41	374.03	81.13	147.62
96.27	101.25	168.13	156.31	137.62	292.46	179.32	166.99
98.04	75.28	221.44	189.21	176.00	298.33	147.42	159.13
98.76	82.02	201.08	138.45	177.28	354.87	155.25	293.95
83.97	187.29	195.40	174.78	294.54	327.20	171.52	334.99
73.76	167.51	174.27	140.36	377.36	377.57	192.19	337.18
78.62	165.81	173.95	186.52	353.59	387.83	161.02	
97.68	165.53	178.57	165.38	298.93	261.05	181.62	
73.91	199.97	181.23	185.32	381.67	353.62	139.32	
331.82	370.15	354.70	349.68	398.14	349.86	347.34	

Table 24.15
Statistical Summary - Time to Process the Web-Services (*ms*)

Mean (ms)	193.56	Skewness	0.72
SD (ms)	99.64	Kurtosis	2.37
CoV	0.51	Min (ms)	38.75
Q1 (ms)	101.85	Max (ms)	415.24
Med (ms)	173.26	Sample Size	120
Q3 (ms)	241.25		

which is not negligible, even though the coefficient of variance is $CoV = 0.51$ (see Table 24.15). The sample was checked against over forty random variable distributions, but none failed to be rejected with 80% of degree of confidence, which means we have pretty much evidence for not accepting them as good fits.

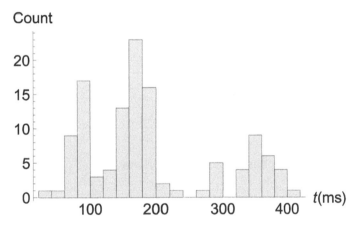

Figure 24.13 Histogram - Time to Process the Web-Services (*ms*).

Looking at the histogram, we may guess the existence of data clusters around 80 *ms*, 150 *ms*, 180 *ms*, and 340 *ms*. Hence, we applied the *K-Means* clustering method (see Section 7.5) for dividing the original sample into four clusters around the above values. Using Mathematica, we carried out the K-Means clustering considering the Euclidean distance, aiming to reduce each cluster's standard deviation and consider 81.13 *ms*, 139.32 *ms*, 174.27 *ms*, and 341.01 *ms* as the initial centroids. As a result, we obtained the four clusters shown in Table 24.16, Table 24.17, Table 24.18, and Table 24.19, respectively.

Table 24.16

Cluster 1 - Time to Process the Web-Services (*ms*)

101.74	97.32	78.62	97.12	95.64
38.75	96.27	97.68	81.13	79.83
79.64	98.044	73.91	95.47	69.18
68.36	98.76	92.89	94.51	101.25
54.55	83.97	66.16	80.54	75.28
91.32	73.76	82.11	87.02	82.02
				101.96

Table 24.17

Cluster 2 - Time to Process the Web-Services (*ms*)

187.29	192.37	174.27	173.15	186.52	178.78
199.97	182.82	173.95	185.05	185.32	176.00
179.32	197.71	178.57	179.34	172.20	177.28
171.52	221.44	181.23	195.89	173.37	261.05
192.19	201.08	181.62	189.21	196.70	
190.70	195.40	204.91	174.78	178.59	

Table 24.18

Cluster 3 - Time to Process the Web-Services (*ms*)

165.81	168.11	154.74	156.22	133.65
165.53	168.13	156.31	147.62	157.41
147.42	161.02	138.45	166.99	137.62
155.25	139.32	140.36	159.13	
145.65	150.79	165.38	159.21	

The statistical summary of each cluster is depicted in Table 24.20. It is worth mentioning the variability reduction of each cluster compared to the original data set (look at the *CoV* of each cluster). The goodness of fit of each data set (cluster) was applied to check if the normal distribution would fit each data set well. The Kolmogorov-Smirnov goodness of fit method fail to reject the suitability of following normal distributions for each cluster with even for 80% of confidence, respectively: $N(84.35\,ms, 14.86\,ms)$, $N(187.93\,ms, 17.15\,ms)$, $N(155.11\,ms, 10.77\,ms)$, and $N(351.37\,ms, 33.21\,ms)$.

□

Table 24.19

Cluster 4 - Time to Process the Web-Services (*ms*)

294.54	334.99	369.49	298.33	398.14
377.36	337.18	349.93	354.87	331.82
353.59	347.34	415.24	327.20	370.15
298.93	349.86	394.52	377.57	354.70
381.67	379.61	374.03	387.83	349.68
293.95	341.01	292.46	353.62	

Table 24.20

Statistical Summary of Clusters

Statistics	Cluster 1	Cluster 2	Cluster 3	Cluster 4
Mean (ms)	84.35	187.93	155.11	351.37
SD (ms)	14.86	17.15	10.77	33.21
CoV	0.18	0.09	0.07	0.09
Q1 (ms)	76.12	177.28	147.42	334.2
Med (ms)	83.97	183.94	156.86	353.59
Q3 (ms)	96.91	195.4	165.4	377.41
Skewness	-1.08	2.5	-0.52	-0.3
Kurtosis	4.15	10.97	2.03	2.4
Min (ms)	38.75	171.52	133.65	292.46
Max (ms)	101.96	261.06	168.13	415.24
Sample Size	31	34	26	29

24.3.2   MODELING INTENDED WORKLOAD

As already mentioned, workloads may also be characterized by the **intended** work to be executed on the system. The aspects and parameters of workloads depend on each system's business process. Hence, we may need to know what each authentication can request and how such requests are made, what keys should be pressed, what outcomes are expected, what error messages might be delivered, and so on. Besides, it may also be useful to represent the distinct sources that require the transactions' executions. Usually, modeling the intended workload is set forth by adopting two classes of models:

- **descriptive** models and

- **generative** models.

The **descriptive** models represent the observed phenomena and describe them using statistics and probability, whereas the **generative** models aim to mimic the workload generation process. The **descriptive** models usually represent the **intended** workload presenting statistical summaries, time series, and distributions of

1. **classes of transactions** executed by the computer system,

2. **time between transactions** of each transaction class, and

3. **the data size** handled in each transaction class.

Example 24.3.4. Assume a simple online bookstore system where customers (clients) access the bookstore services deployed in a data center information technology (IT) infrastructure. The customer starts interacting by using the online bookstore service by the first login in with his/her credentials, which are stored in the bookstore database. Next, the data center load balancer delivers the respective transactions on the specific web-server. Next, the web-server accesses the database-server for data transactions. Finally, the application server interprets the request, returns the required data to the bookstore business logic, and delivers it to the customer. Figure 24.14 depicts a broad view of the data center infrastructure that supports the bookstore IT services.

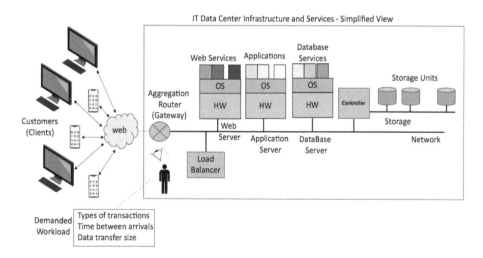

Figure 24.14   Bookstore Information Technology Data Center Subsystem.

The data traffic between the internet and the data center may be measured at the aggregation router (gateway). The measuring system[4] monitors the income-outgo

---

[4]The measuring system is depicted the man and eye side icons shown in the figure.

traffic at this device. The aggregation router's income-outgo traffic was monitored for thirty-two minutes and twelve seconds ($32\,min$ and $12\,s$). The transaction arrivals and replies (delivered results) are recorded in seconds, and the respective number of bytes is transferred in each event. Table 24.21 shows the timely-ordered event (arrival and replies) occurrence instants and the respective number of bytes transferred by the execution of the respective transaction.

This aggregated traffic (a time series) is shown in Figure 24.15.

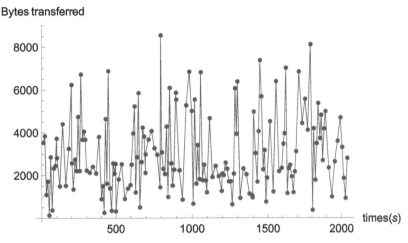

Figure 24.15   Arrival/Reply Times (s) $\times$ Bytes Transferred.

This time series' autocorrelation (see Equation 14.4.38 and Equation 4.6.4) implies a long-range dependence between observations since the autocorrelation is high for large lags. Figure 24.16 and Table 24.22 show the autocorrelation for lags in the interval of integers defined by $[1, 22]$. This graph shows the long-memory dependence between observations. The autocorrelation for lag size equal to 1 is 0.9813, which is very high. The autocorrelation slowly decreases for the following lag sizes, but for the lag size equal to 22, the autocorrelation is still 0.5946, stressing a long-range autocorrelation.

The time between events - TBE - (arrivals and replies) are shown in Table 24.23, the histogram (Figure 24.17) presents its distribution and its empirical cumulative distribution function ($ECDF$) is depicted in Figure 24.18. The histogram clearly shows a data set with three modes. These distinct modes are also reflected on the $ECDF$.

The statistical summary of TBE is presented in Table 24.24. As the mean is smaller than the median, it is an indication of the right tail. The skewness points to a heavier tail beyond the mean. The third quartile and the maximal values are $18.9612\,s$ and $22.0094\,s$. Hence, this interval contains 25% of the data. This finding stresses the

Table 24.21

Transaction Arrivals and Replies Instants and the Respective Bytes Transferred

Time (s)	Bytes	Time (s)	Bytes	Time (s)	Bytes	Time (s)	Bytes
9.99	3556	497.38	2560	1006.06	684	1495.43	1894
20.03	3866	498.43	338	1016.91	5564	1515.90	4538
29.91	1114	517.66	1835	1027.04	1626	1537.10	1244
39.75	1734	538.75	2544	1036.63	3430	1557.67	6413
49.13	152	559.26	919	1047.16	1837	1576.10	2197
58.88	2875	580.12	1404	1056.78	6837	1595.19	2354
69.35	393	597.06	1568	1068.45	1784	1607.03	3487
79.56	2356	604.39	2524	1079.29	2508	1615.29	3971
90.59	2476	616.00	3983	1090.49	1768	1625.45	7037
98.72	3748	625.09	5250	1097.14	1218	1633.33	1171
100.73	2838	631.78	1220	1115.53	4682	1642.97	2342
119.96	1513	641.34	2871	1133.69	1932	1652.78	2499
139.36	4428	651.13	5872	1154.12	2454	1663.70	1957
160.06	1544	660.08	522	1174.04	1977	1674.35	1210
180.24	3272	671.08	2646	1193.32	1281	1684.28	2189
199.51	6263	678.32	4254	1196.74	2087	1694.22	3130
201.57	2596	688.44	3839	1206.84	2021	1714.36	6864
211.17	1368	696.70	2137	1218.56	2603	1735.59	4446
222.88	2767	697.72	3001	1229.03	2318	1756.27	5585
233.02	2234	717.66	3694	1239.68	1728	1774.11	4133
243.43	4767	737.82	4096	1251.02	1730	1794.18	8128
253.45	2234	757.14	3290	1261.69	652	1805.24	384
263.14	6744	775.54	2985	1271.66	2088	1814.76	4203
272.87	3692	795.17	1463	1280.54	6080	1824.89	1795
282.52	4078	797.51	8566	1289.88	3951	1834.20	3510
291.72	3696	805.97	3097	1295.48	6398	1844.74	5389
300.91	2250	815.55	2323	1314.05	948	1856.13	3746
322.16	2147	825.47	2084	1334.38	2327	1865.65	4837
342.40	2428	836.21	4305	1355.07	2054	1874.28	2712
364.21	2115	846.44	1007	1374.98	1149	1883.53	4194
383.92	3825	855.02	6107	1394.47	1060	1894.19	5007
400.07	911	866.07	2579	1395.87	971	1915.01	2366
409.81	1518	874.87	1542	1405.26	4987	1936.20	1007
418.91	272	883.77	2283	1416.50	3047	1956.11	2656
429.50	4663	893.70	5878	1428.90	1708	1975.67	3622
438.07	1638	896.06	5561	1438.78	4070	1994.77	4711
448.34	6898	917.37	2248	1448.45	7391	2006.28	3329
457.74	1419	937.60	872	1458.42	5702	2016.29	1879
468.79	366	959.61	5291	1468.86	2286	2027.88	941
479.57	2582	980.02	6861	1478.98	3184	2040.14	2816
489.17	2102	996.61	5027	1487.71	773		

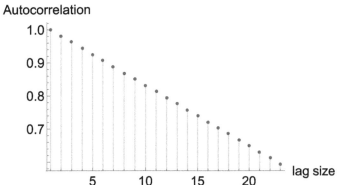

Figure 24.16 Autocorrelations for Lag Sizes $\in [1, 22]$.

Table 24.22

Lag Size $\times$ Autocorrelation (AC)

Lag Size	AC	Lag Size	AC	Lag Size	AC
1	0.9813	9	0.8313	17	0.6856
2	0.9626	10	0.8130	18	0.6674
3	0.9438	11	0.7945	19	0.6491
4	0.9248	12	0.7761	20	0.6308
5	0.9059	13	0.7579	21	0.6126
6	0.8870	14	0.7397	22	0.5946
7	0.8683	15	0.7217		
8	0.8497	16	0.7038		

presence of some peaks in this region. Indeed, all these findings are also observed in the histogram shown in Figure 24.17. Fifty percent of the data lay between the $Q1 = 9.53118\,s$ and $Q3 = 18.9612\,s$. As this interval is not wide, it also highlights another peak, which is also confirmed in the histogram. At the histogram, we observe three groupings of different sizes. The $ECDF$ also suggests these data concentrations by the sharp rising around $10\,s$ and $20\,s$. The coefficient of variation ($CoV = 0.4217$) shows that the data are not dispersed around the central tendency.

The sample was compared with sixty-five random variable distributions, but none failed to be rejected with 80% of degree of confidence. Thus, we have substantial evidence for not recognizing them as good fits. The histogram depicted in Figure 24.17 suggests three possible data groupings. The first largest group seems to be centralized around $8\,s$. The second largest group looks disposed of about $20\,s$, and the smallest grouping is around $2\,s$. Observing the data set, we found the following measures close to these numbers; they are $2.0132\,s$, $8.2110\,s$, and $20.0698\,s$. Then, we

Table 24.23

Time Between Events (Arrivals/Replies) - (s)

TBE (s)	TBE (s)	TBE (s)	TBE (s)	TBE (s)	TBE (s)
10.1931	89.5144	97.8848	104.6833	117.0302	199.1403
10.4639	90.9112	98.0995	105.2704	117.2631	199.2262
14.0707	91.0457	98.3645	105.4577	118.4272	199.3244
20.1324	91.8760	98.7733	105.9073	122.5929	200.6983
20.6307	91.9632	98.8196	106.4179	123.9676	201.3779
23.4328	92.4646	99.1418	106.4451	161.4718	201.6161
23.6311	93.1125	99.2316	106.5989	165.8783	201.7147
34.2176	93.4803	99.3689	106.6585	169.3683	202.2334
55.9738	93.8422	99.3976	107.4584	178.3988	202.3985
66.4565	93.9197	99.6752	107.8231	181.6187	203.3030
66.8478	93.9868	99.7173	108.3644	183.9152	204.1887
72.3412	94.5050	100.0639	108.4560	184.0203	204.2581
73.3463	95.1728	100.2161	109.2460	184.2598	204.7415
77.1604	95.2208	100.3569	109.8072	185.7212	205.1146
78.8207	95.5848	101.0011	110.0552	190.9094	205.7387
81.2633	95.8814	101.1981	110.3096	191.0399	206.8178
82.1098	95.9512	101.2112	110.4684	192.2536	206.8507
82.5995	96.0143	101.2891	110.4697	192.2546	206.9965
82.6721	96.0209	101.2922	110.6003	192.7332	208.2693
84.5438	96.1983	101.4513	112.0575	192.7362	208.5504
85.6186	96.3900	101.5681	112.3852	193.2159	210.9642
85.8493	96.5447	102.1191	113.4699	194.0946	211.8112
86.2736	96.7535	102.2413	113.8750	194.8679	211.9522
87.2938	96.8380	102.7766	115.1334	195.5594	212.2561
87.9488	97.3274	104.0937	115.9414	196.2714	212.5500
88.7509	97.3884	104.4237	116.1352	197.0920	213.1436
89.0693	97.4959	104.6816	116.7282	199.1356	218.1027
					220.0938

Table 24.24

Time Between Events (Arrivals and Replies) TBE **- Statistical Summary**

Mean (s)	12.5223	Q3 (s)	18.9612
SD (s)	5.2805	Sk	0.3367
Var (s^2)	27.8832	Kur	2.2312
CoV	0.4217	Min (s)	1.0193
Q1 (s)	9.5312	Max (s)	22.0094
Med (s)	10.4683	Sample Size	163

applied the *K-Means* clustering to reduce the standard deviation and adopt the above measures as the initial centroids. As a result, we obtained three clusters: *Cluster 1*, *Cluster 2*, and *Cluster 3*.

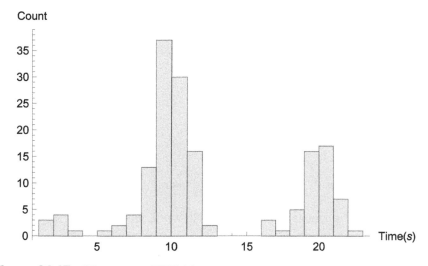

Figure 24.17   Histogram - *TBE* (s).

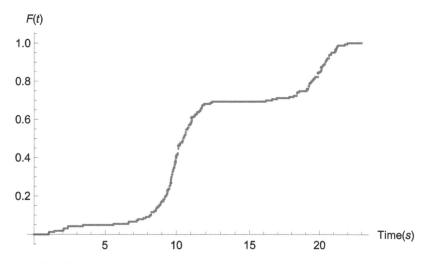

Figure 24.18   *ECDF - TBE* (s).

The three clusters are shown in Table 24.25, Table 24.26, and Table 24.27, respectively. *Cluster 1* has 104 measures, *Cluster 2* is composed of 50 measures, and *Cluster 3* has only 9 elements. The data distributions of each cluster are shown in Figure 24.20. The statistical summary of each cluster is shown in Table 24.27. We found similar characteristics for all clusters; the mean values are close to the median values. The respective data are somewhat close to the central tendency measures. Observe each interquartile range and the respective kurtosis. Their kurtosis and the skewness are similar to normal distributions. *Cluster 3* has statistics that have a larger deviation from normal distributions. However, the respective cluster size is small. The *KS* goodness of fit does not reject normal distributions for any of the clusters, even for 80% degree of confidence.

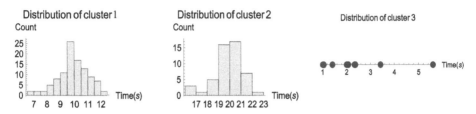

Figure 24.19   Histograms of *Cluster 1* and *Cluster 2*. Individual Plot of *Cluster 3*.

Table 24.25

Time Between Events (*TBE* - s) - Cluster 1

Cluster 1 - *TBE* (*s*)							
10.0357	10.0216	10.7823	8.2672	10.1289	10.6658	7.7160	10.1292
9.8820	9.6838	9.6021	8.4544	9.5951	9.9717	11.8427	9.3113
9.8364	9.7327	8.2110	9.5881	10.5270	8.8751	8.2600	10.5458
9.3842	9.6545	7.3346	9.9142	9.6198	9.3480	10.1568	11.3875
9.7496	9.1963	11.6135	10.7458	11.6728	9.3920	7.8821	9.5221
10.4683	9.1876	9.0911	10.2241	10.8364	11.2385	9.6390	8.6274
10.2119	9.7388	6.6848	8.5849	11.2058	12.3968	9.8099	9.2465
11.0310	9.1046	9.5585	11.0470	6.6456	9.8773	10.9246	10.6599
8.1263	10.5907	9.7885	8.7949	10.1001	9.6753	10.6418	11.5133
9.6014	8.5619	8.9514	8.9069	11.7263	9.9675	9.9369	10.0064
11.7030	10.2777	11.0055	9.9232	10.4682	10.4424	9.9398	11.5941
10.1451	9.3987	7.2341	9.4505	10.6445	10.1211	11.0600	12.2593
10.4094	11.0468	10.1198	10.8456	11.3470	8.7294	9.5173	10.9807

Table 24.26
Time Between Events (*TBE* - s) - Cluster 2.

Cluster 2 - *TBE* (*s*)				
19.2254	20.5115	16.5878	21.1952	19.5559
19.4095	20.8550	18.3915	20.5739	19.1040
20.6996	16.9368	18.1619	18.4260	
20.1715	19.9324	20.4258	19.0909	
19.2733	20.1616	19.9226	20.1378	
21.2550	19.3216	19.2736	21.2256	
20.2398	18.4020	18.5721	20.6851	
21.8103	19.6271	20.3303	17.8399	
19.7092	21.3144	20.6818	20.0698	
16.1472	20.2233	19.9136	20.8269	
19.2255	22.0094	19.4868	21.1811	
21.0964	20.4189	20.4741	19.9140	

Table 24.27
Time Between Events (*TBE* - s) - Cluster 3.

Cluster 3 - *TBE* (*s*)		
2.0132	2.0631	1.0464
1.0193	2.3433	2.3631
3.4218	5.5974	1.4071

Estimating the distribution parameters for each cluster (see 25.3), we obtained the following normal distributions for each cluster, respectively: $N(9.9022 s, 1.1325 s)$, $N(19.8005, s, 1.2571 s)$, and $N(2.3639 s, 1.4251 s)$. *Cluster 1* represents 63.80%, *Cluster 2* has 30.67%, and *Cluster 3* contains only 5.52% of the original sample, respectively. Figure 24.20 shows the respective cumulative distribution functions.

Figure 24.21 and Figure 24.22 present both the histogram and the *ECDF* of the bytes transferred per the transactions observed. Table 24.29 shows the statistical summary for the collected sample of bytes transferred. As we see, the median is smaller than the mean, which suggests a tail to the right. The intervals (Q_1, Med) and (Med, Q_3) a data concentration of data before the median. The skewness (0.81853) confirms a tail to the right. The kurtosis shows a flatness closer to a normal distribution. The histogram suggests a unimodal data distribution.

Table 24.28

Statistical Summary of Each Cluster

	Cluster 1	Cluster 2	Cluster 3
Mean (s)	9.9022	19.8005	2.3639
SD (s)	1.1325	1.2571	1.4251
Var (s^2)	1.2825	1.5804	2.0309
CoV	0.1144	0.0635	0.6029
Q1 (s)	9.3661	19.2255	1.3169
Med (s)	9.9300	20.0011	2.0631
Q3 (s)	10.6522	20.6818	2.6278
SK	-0.4459	-0.8988	1.3435
Kurt	3.4400	3.8206	4.0133
Min (s)	6.6457	16.1472	1.0193
Max (s)	12.3968	22.0094	5.5974
Cluster Size	104	50	9

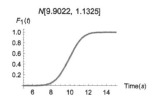
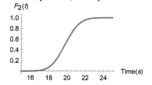
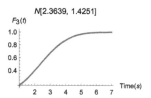

Figure 24.20 *CDF* of Time Between Events (s) - *Cluster 1, Cluster 2,* and *Cluster 3.*

The *KS* goodness of fit does not reject the Weibull distribution $Weibull(\alpha, \beta)$ - for $\alpha = 1.6951$, and $\beta = 3394.2684$ bytes even when adopting 80% degree of confidence. Figure 24.23 shows the Weibull cumulative distribution function.

Table 24.29

Bytes Transferred per Transaction - Statistical Summary

Mean $(bytes)$	3010.27	Q3 $(bytes)$	4075.86
SD $(bytes)$	1798.16	SK	0.81853
Var $(bytes^2)$	3233379	Kurt	3.0988
CoV	0.597343	Min $(bytes)$	152.272
Q1 $(bytes)$	1730.57	Max $(bytes)$	8566.27
Med $(bytes)$	2524.34	Sample Size	163

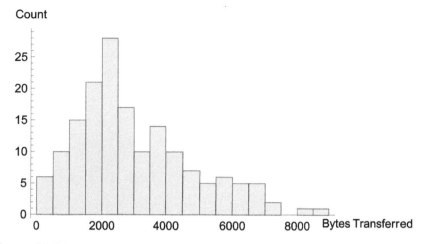

Figure 24.21   Histogram - Bytes Transferred.

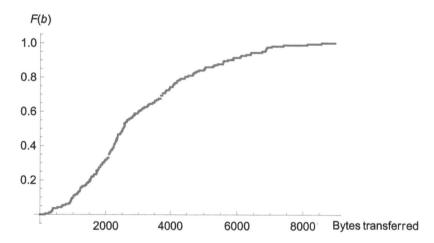

Figure 24.22   *ECDF* - Bytes Transferred.

☐

The **Generative** models. There are many circumstances in which the generative rules may be required to represent workloads. A generative workload approach may be adopted to exercise real operative systems, system prototypes, or system simulators or be adopted as part of a numerical or analytic model. Depending on the context, a suitable abstraction should be adopted to specify the workload. However, in any circumstance, a generative workload representation's fundamental characteristic resembles the temporal processes' execution that produces the workloads. In other words, generative workload mechanisms devise or execute the timely ordered events

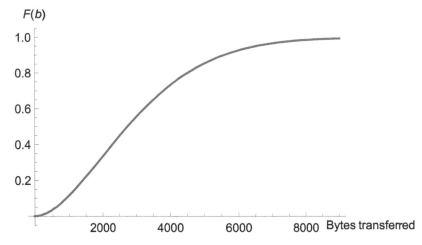

Figure 24.23 *Weibull*(1.6951, 3394.2684 *bytes*) *CDF* - Bytes Transferred.

and activities the workload process must carry out.

For instance, consider that we need to devise a generative workload generator that exercises a stochastic simulator (see Chapter 14). For instance, assume a workload generator representing a set of customers who access an online sales system over the web. The workload generator should generate timely ordered events to exercise the simulator that executes the online sales system's simulation model. The equivalent transaction instance (i), type of transaction (tr), arrival time (at), and generated byte transferred size (bg) distributions may be created by generating timely-ordered tuples (i, tr, tbt_i, bt_i) using the respective empirical or theoretical distributions.

Besides, consider workload demands occur in bursts in varying time scales; each burst is portrayed by modal distributions, usually centered around a value. The broader distributions characterizing the entire workload are sequences of activity bursts of distinct modal distributions. Therefore, the joint distribution does not apprehend the workload dynamics unless we adopt sampling locality, in which we first sample from one part of the broader distribution, then from another, and so on.

Example 24.3.5. Let us adopt the online bookstore system depicted in Example 24.3.4 as a particular instance of the generic selling system introduced above. As previously described, the customers interact with the online bookstore system by logging in and then yielding requests, devised as transactions, to be performed on the specific set of servers required to accomplish the required service. After processing each customer query, the servers deliver the data required to the customers. Figure 24.14 shows a high-level view of the infrastructure that supports the bookstore services.

Figure 24.24 presents a flowchart that specifies the activities that generate the sequence of customers' online bookstore transactions, whose implementation is written in Mathematica shown in Program 21. The distributions' parameters specified are the same as those estimated in Example 24.3.4.

Block A represents the declaration of variables and data structures depicted from Line 1 to Line 11 of the program. The number of generated transactions (GT, n) mentioned in the first decision block (Block B) is defined as 1000 in the program (see the upper limit of the structure). Block C, which specifies the number of bytes transferred (bytes generated - btg) in the transaction occurrence i, is implemented by Line 14. The byte transferred in each transaction is obtained by

$$btg = Weibull^{-1}(1.6951, 3394.2684\, bytes)\, bytes.$$

The transaction type (tr), specified in Block D, is implemented by Line 15 according to

$$tr = \begin{cases} 3, & \text{if } u \leq 0.0552; \\ 2, & \text{if } 0.0552 < u \leq 0.3067; \\ 1, & \text{if } u > 0.3067. \end{cases}$$

Depending on the transaction type (1, 2, or 3) (see Block E), the new time between transactions (tbt) is generated (see Line 17, Line 19, and Line 21) as specified by

$$tbt = \begin{cases} N^{-1}(2.3639\, s, 1.4251\, s), & \text{if } tr = 3; \\ N^{-1}(9.9022\, s, 1.1325\, s), & \text{if } tr = 2; \\ N^{-1}(9.9022\, s, 1.1325\, s), & \text{otherwise } tr = 1. \end{cases}$$

5

The blocks that represent these functions are Block F, Block G, and Block H. It is important to highlight that $F_{btg}^{-1}(\Theta_{btg})$ denotes $Weibull^{-1}(1.6951, 3394.2684\, bytes)$, and $F_{at_i}^{-1}(\Theta_{at_i})$, $i \in \{1, 2, 3\}$, represents $N^{-1}(\mu_i\, s, \sigma_i\, s)$, where μ_i and σ_i are estimated by the respective values of lines *Mean* and *SD* of Table 24.28.

Hence, a tuple (i, tr, at, btg) that represents a transaction is composed, where i is the transaction occurrence that is first (1), second (2), third (3), and so forth. The arrival time $(at$ - see Line 25) of the transaction occurrence i is obtained using tbt according to

$$at_i = at_{i-1} + tbt_i,$$

$a_0 = 0\, s$.

Line 27 appends each new tuple representing a transaction to a structure that represents a transaction trace. Likewise, Line 26 also appends each new tbt to the tbt

---

[5] $F_{tr}^{-1}(\Theta_{tr})$ denotes the tr's *CDF*.

timely-ordered trace structure (Block I). Line 29 (Block I) stores the transaction trace to a CSV file. Similarly, Line 30 (Block I) stores the byte transferred trace to a CSV file. As mentioned, the flowchart (Figure 24.24) summarizes the set of steps required to generate a transaction sample trace.

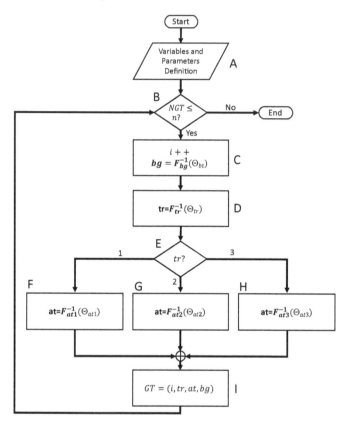

Figure 24.24   Flowchart that Represents the Customers' Online Bookstore Transactions Trace.

Executing Program 21, a sample trace of one thousand (1000) transactions was generated. The respective time series is shown in Figure 24.25. Figure 24.26 shows the autocorrelation, a long-range dependence between observations since the autocorrelation is high for large lags. The autocorrelation for lag size equal to 1 is 0.99696 and slowly decreases for the following lag sizes. Even for a lag size equal to 22, the autocorrelation is still 0.932967.

Table 24.30 presents the statistical summary of the time between transactions of the generated workload and the respective bytes transferred in each transaction. The results shown in Table 24.30 are pretty much similar to the statistics shown in Table

Algorithm 21 The Online Bookstore Transactions' Generation

```
 1: Clear[n1]; Clear[n2]; Clear[n3]; Clear[at];
 2: Clear[p1]; Clear[p2]; Clear[p3]; Clear[i];
 3: Clear[tbt]; Clear[tr]; Clear[btg]; Clear[datag];
 4: ClearAll;
 5: n1=104; n2=50; n3=9; n=163; at=0;
 6: p1 = N[n1/n];
 7: p2 = N[n2/n];
 8: p3 = N[n3/n];
 9: datag = {}; datatbt = {};
10: datag = Append[datag, { " ", "Transaction Type", "Time Between Arrivals","Bytes Transfered" }];
11: datatbt = Append[datatbt, { "Time Between Transactions" }];
12: For[i = 1, i <= 1000, i++,
13:        tr = 0; at = 0;
14:        btg = Extract[RandomVariate[WeibullDistribution[1.6951, 3394.2684], 1],1];
15:        tr = Extract[RandomChoice[ { p1, p2, p3} − > {1, 2, 3 }, 1], 1];
16:        If[tr == 1,
17:               tbt = Extract[RandomVariate[NormalDistribution[9.9022, 1.1325], 1],1],
18:                  If[tr == 2,
19:                        tbt = Extract[RandomVariate[NormalDistribution[2.3638, 1.4251],1],1],
20:                           If[tr == 3,
21:                              tbt = Extract[RandomVariate[NormalDistribution[19.8005,1.2571],1],
   1];
22:                  ]
23:               ]
24:        ];
25:        at = at + tbt;
26:        datatbt = Append[datatbt, tbt];
27:        datag = Append[datag, { i, tr, at, btg }];
28: ]
29: Export["dattraf.csv", datag];
30: Export["datatbt.csv", datatbt];
31: Print["End"]
```

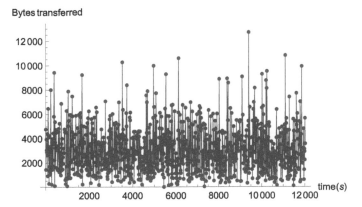

Figure 24.25   One-Thousand-Transaction Generated Time Series.

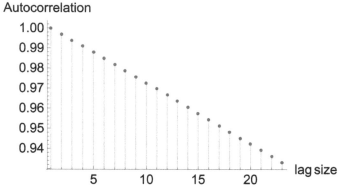

Figure 24.26 Generated Time Series - Autocorrelations for Lag Sizes $\in [1, 22]$.

24.24 and Table 24.29, which strongly indicates both samples were obtained from a process with similar *tbt* and *bt* distributions.

Table 24.30

Statistical Summaries - Time Between Transactions (*tbs*) and Bytes Transferred (*bt*)

Statistics	*tbt* (s)	Statistics	*bt* (bytes)
Mean (s)	12.0138	**Mean (bytes)**	3076.7590
SD (s)	5.1422	**SD (bytes)**	1899.2918
CoV	0.4280	**CoV**	0.6173
Q1 (s)	9.2002	**Q1 (bytes)**	1650.5
Med (s)	10.2506	**Med (bytes)**	2815
Q3 (s)	17.7132	**Q3 (bytes)**	4159
IQR (s)	8.5130	**IQR (bytes)**	2508.5
Skewness	0.4395	**Skewness**	1.0117
Kurtosis	2.6139	**Kurtosis**	4.5102
Sample Size	1000	**Sample Size**	1000

Figure 24.28 shows the *CDF* of the time between transactions of the generated workload. Likewise, Figure 24.30 depicts the *CDF* of the bytes transferred for each transaction of the generated workload. It is worth noting the resemblance between the distributions presented in Figure 24.28 and Figure 24.18 and between the distributions presented in Figure 24.30 and Figure 24.22, as expected since the generated workload follows the theoretical distributions the time between transactions and the transferred bytes per transaction of the online bookstore system presented in Example 24.3.4.

□

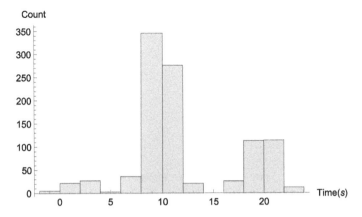

Figure 24.27 Histogram of Time Between Transactions (s).

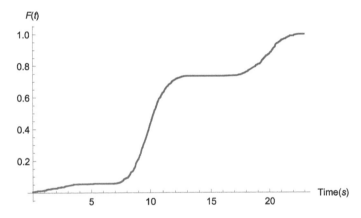

Figure 24.28 *CDF* of Time Between Transactions (s).

Some workload classes are far from steady. In some cases, the workload exhibits high variability, irregular congestion spikes, and burstiness. For instance, Internet traffic shows multifaceted burstiness and correlated structure over wide time scales. If the workload model did not account for burstiness, the accuracy and precision of the performance models' evaluation results would be deeply affected [21, 194, 209, 219, 308, 322, 323, 368, 476]. Let us now consider modeling a bursty workload by adopting the Markov Modulated Process (*MMP*) to describe unsteady transaction request rounds.

Example 24.3.6. This example shows a stochastic model for plain bursty workload traffic. Bursty workload traffic denotes long-term highly variable transaction requests; the arrival rates differ by orders of magnitude. Nevertheless, it is also highly likely that the arrival rate does not vary much in the short term. The Markov chain

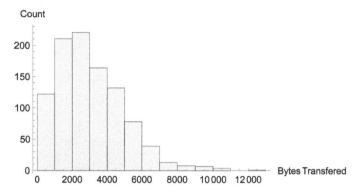

Figure 24.29   Histogram of Generated Bytes Transferred.

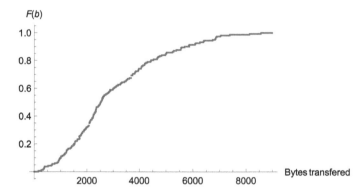

Figure 24.30   *CDF* of Generated Bytes Transferred.

adequately reproduces such long and short-term changes with multiple workload states, where each state generates an arrival rate.

The workload is characterized by two sets of long periods. During each period, the traffic requests are sent to the computational system, taking a distinct probability function into account. In this specific case, the two long period durations are obtained from random variables T_α and T_β that are exponentially distributed according to $Exp(\alpha)$ and $Exp(\beta)$. The time between transaction, tbt, requests to the computational system in each period is also exponentially distributed with parameters μ and λ, respectively, which characterize two transaction types, $tr = 1$ and $tr = 2$. Besides, the number of bytes transferred, bt_1 and bt_2, to the system by each transaction type are distributed according to $Exp(\omega_1)$ and $Exp(\omega_2)$, respectively.

Figure 24.31 shows the CTMC that generates this traffic. A simulator[6] of this CTMC was implemented using Mathematica for generating traces of transactions (see Appendix E). Each transaction record is specified by the tuple (i, tr, gt, bg, tbt), where

---

[6]For more details about simulation look at Chapter 14.

i denotes the transaction instance, that is a first transaction, second, third..., tr, as we already are aware, represents the transaction type ($tr = 1$ and $tr = 2$), gt denotes the global time registered during the trace generation. It is a cumulative time that starts at $gt = 0$ and is incremented by the winning event (shortest delay) assigned to $ta = F_\alpha^{-1}$ and $tl = F_\lambda^{-1}$ or $tb = F_\beta^{-1}$ and $tm = F_\mu^{-1}$. The variable bg is the number of bytes transferred in each transaction. Whenever states s_0 and s_1 are reached, a value is generated and assigned to bt_1, which is then assigned to bg. Likewise, when states s_2 and s_3 are reached, a number is generated and assigned to bt_2, and then to bg. Finally, tbt is a variable that records the time between each transaction. Such values are obtained from those values generated and assigned to $tl = F_\lambda^{-1}$ and $tm = F_\mu^{-1}$. In this particular case, the time units adopted are seconds (s), and the simulator finishes its execution when a one-thousand-length trace ($nt = 1000$ transactions) is generated.

As a specific case, let us define $\alpha = 5tps$, $\beta = 10tps$, $\lambda = 350tps$, and $\mu = 700tps$. Besides, let us also specify $\omega_1 = 400 \times 10^{-6} bytes^{-1}$ and $\omega_2 = 200 \times 10^{-6} bytes^{-1}$.

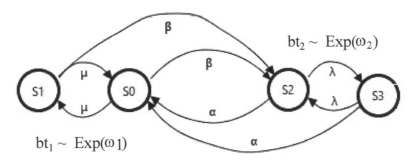

Figure 24.31   Bursty Workload Model - MMP.

After executing the workload generator (see Appendix E) represented by the model shown in Figure 24.31, the traffic depicted in Figure 24.32 was generated. This time series shows the transaction request occurrence instants versus the number of bytes transferred in the respective transaction. The autocorrelation test with a degree of confidence equal to 90 % was executed for a lag-size equal to seven (7). The test obtained enough evidence to reject the hypothesis of uncorrelated data. Besides, Figure 24.33 shows high autocorrelation even for a lag-size as large as twenty-two.

The generator also calculated the global time gt and the time proportion the model spends in each state, that is s_0, s_1, s_2, and s_3, that is $\hat{P}(s_0)$, $\hat{P}(s_1)$, $\hat{P}(s_2)$, and $\hat{P}(s_3)$, where $SJ(s_0)$, $SJ(s_1)$, $SJ(s_2)$, $SJ(s_3)$ are the sojourn time of each state s_i, respectively, and

$$\hat{P}(s_i) = \frac{SJ(s_i)}{gt}, \quad i \in \{0, 1, 2, 3\}.$$

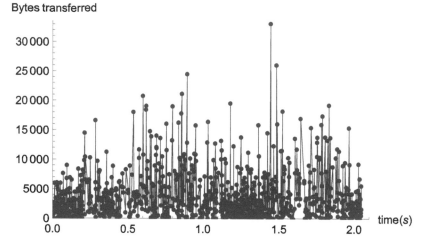

Figure 24.32   Time-Series: Bytes Transferred × Transaction Request Occurrence Instants.

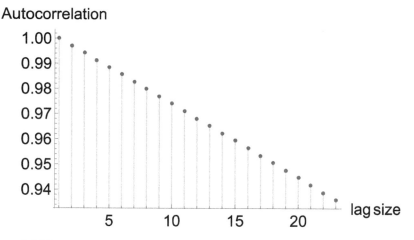

Figure 24.33   Autocorrelation Graph.

These measures are depicted in Table 24.31. The throughput is calculated by

$$\hat{tp} = \frac{nt}{gt}.$$

Hence, as the number of transaction requests is $nt = 1000$ and the global time (see Table 24.31), then throughput is estimated by $\hat{tp} = 1000/2.04952\,s = 487.918\,tps$.

The steady-state probability of each state calculated from the CTMC shown in Figure 24.31 (see Section 10.4) were $\pi_{s_0} = 0.167848$, $\pi_{s_1} = 0.165484$, $\pi_{s_2} = 0.335698$, and $\pi_{s_3} = 0.330969$. The throughput may be estimated from the CTMC by

$$tp = (\pi_{s_2} + \pi_{s_3})\lambda + (\pi_{s_0} + \pi_{s_1})\mu.$$

Thus, $tp = 466.666tps$. It is worth stressing that the time proportion the model spends in each state and the throughput calculated from the generator (considering the trace length generated) are close enough to the steady-state results obtained from the CTMC.

Table 24.31

Traces Duration (gt) - Sojourn Time for State (SJ) - Time Proportion in Each State ($\hat{P}$)

Global Time (s) - gt	2.04952	$\hat{P}(s_0)$	0.170164
$SJ(s_0)$ (s)	0.348756	$\hat{P}(s_1)$	0.169026
$SJ(s_1)$ (s)	0.346423	$\hat{P}(s_2)$	0.301147
$SJ(s_2)$ (s)	0.617208	$\hat{P}(s_3)$	0.359663
$SJ(s_3)$ (s)	0.737138	$\sum_{i=0}^{3}\hat{P}(s_i)$	1

The statistical summary of the Time Between Transactions (tbt) and Bytes Transferred (bg) per transaction are shown in Table 24.32. It is worth noting the coefficient of variation of both data sets. The coefficient of variation of tbt is close to one (1), whereas the respective statistic for bg is close to 1.2. This feature is statistically supported since the tbt distribution kurtosis is much spikier than the bg distribution. The kurtosis of the tbt distribution is 19.1329, and the respective measure of bg distribution is 9.6995

Figure 24.34 shows the histogram and the Weibull cumulative distribution of the Time Between Transactions. The KS goodness of fit test was applied to both data sets. The test did not reject the Weibull distribution with form parameter $\alpha = 0.9386$ and scale parameter equal to $\beta = 2.0757 \times 10^{-3}$ s for representing tbt distribution, taking into account a degree of confidence of 90%. Figure 24.35 presents the histogram and exponential cumulative distribution for the Bytes Transferred per transaction. The KS goodness of fit test also did not reject the exponential distribution with parameter equal to $\lambda = 270.634 \times 10^{-6}$ b^{-1}.

□

It is worth stressing that the Discrete Time Markov Chain (See Chapter 9) and Semi-Markovian Chains (See Section 10.7) may also be used to generate workload traffic. Besides, more sophisticated modulation may also be represented by such models.

Table 24.32

Statistical Summary - Time Between Transactions (s) and Bytes Transferred (bytes)

Mean (s)	2.0287×10^{-3}	Mean (bytes)	3695.03
SD (s)	2.3839×10^{-3}	SD (bytes)	4000.32
CoV	1.1751	CoV	1.08262
Q1 (s)	496.577×10^{-6}	Q1 (bytes)	952.948
Med (s)	1.3451×10^{-3}	Med (bytes)	2393.37
Q3 (s)	2.6488×10^{-3}	Q3 (bytes)	4919.32
IQR (s)	2.15221×10^{-3}	IQR (bytes)	3966.38
Skewness	3.1250	Skewness	2.1727
Kurtosis	19.1329	Kurtosis	9.6995
Sample Size	1000	Sample Size	1000

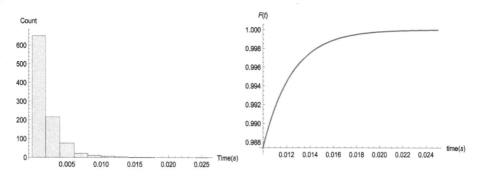

Figure 24.34 Histogram and $Weibull(0.9386, 2.0757 \times 10^{-3} \, s)$ Cumulative Distribution of tbt.

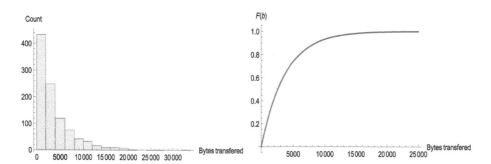

Figure 24.35 Histogram and $Exp(270.634 \times 10^{-6} \, b^{-1})$ Cumulative Distribution of bg.

As depicted in Section 13.3.2, SPN is a formalism well suited to represent modulated workload traffic. Such a model may be adopted to generate authentic and synthetic workloads and be suitable for evaluation via numerical analysis and simulation. For example, the Markov chain specified in Example 24.3.6 is well represented by the SPN shown in Figure 24.36.

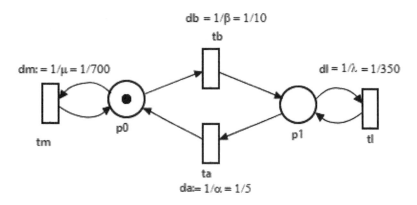

Figure 24.36 Bursty Workload SPN - MMP.

The net is composed of two places, $P = \{p_0, p_1\}$, four transitions, $T = \{t_a, t_b, t_l, t_m\}$, and their respective arcs shown in Figure 24.36. The initial marking is defined as $M_0^T = (1, 0)$. Exponentially distributed time random variables are assigned to each of these transitions with rates α, β, λ, and μ, respectively. The transfer transaction rate of type 1 ($tr = 1$) is assigned to transition t_l whereas transfer transaction rate of type $tr = 2$ is assigned to transition 2 (t_m). When using this model to generated a real synthetic workload, when t_l fires, a set of bytes is generated to be transferred according to the distribution $Exp(\omega_2)$. Likewise, when t_m fires, a set of bytes is generated to be transferred according the distribution $Exp(\omega_1)$.

At the initial marking, t_m and t_b are the only transitions enabled. As $\mu \gg \beta$, t_m is much more likely to fire than t_b. Firing t_m the SPN reaches the initial marking again. When t_b fires, the SPN reaches marking $M_1^T = (0, 1)$. M_1 enables t_l and t_a. As $\lambda \gg \alpha$, t_l is likely to fire. Firing t_l the SPN reaches M_1^T again. When t_a fires, the SPN reaches marking $M_0^T = (1, 0)$.

The throughput related to transaction type 1 is calculated from the SPN model by

$$tp_1 = P(\#p_0 > 0) \times \lambda,$$

where $P(\#p_0 > 0)$ denotes the probability of place p_0 having a marking larger than zero, that is $m_0 > 0$[7]. Similarly, the throughput related to transaction type 2 is calcu-

---

[7] See Section 13.3.1 about the SPN-Mercury tool notation.

lated from the SPN model by

$$tp_2 = P(\#p_1 > 0) \times \mu.$$

The total throughput is calculated by

$$tp = P(\#p_0 > 0) \times \lambda + P(\#p_1 > 0) \times \mu.$$

Example 24.3.7. Adopting $\alpha = 5tps$, $\beta = 10tps$, $\lambda = 350tps$, and $\mu = 700tps$, and obtaining the steady-state solution for the SPN shown in Figure 24.36, we obtain $tp_1 = 233.3333$, $tp_2 = 233.3333$, and $tp = 466.6666$ as the results calculated from the CTMC in Example 24.3.6. It is worth mentioning the throughput calculated from the trace generated was $\hat{tp} = 487.918tps$, which is close to the value obtained for the SPN when considering a trace-length of 1000 transaction requests.

□

This chapter presented some essential concepts related to workload generation and modeling, besides discussing issues involved in selecting, usage, and workload analysis for computer systems. We covered three important categories: actual workload, synthetic workload (benchmarks and synthetic operational workload), and workload modeling.

EXERCISES

Exercise 1. What are the primary purposes for workload characterization?

Exercise 2. Classify computer workload into types and explain them.

Exercise 3. What do you understand by synthetic operational workload?

Exercise 4. Explain what the workload type called benchmark is.

Exercise 5. Specify a methodology to evaluate and compare the performance of two personal computers (see Section 6.4 and Section 6.5) considering as workload the benchmarks **Whetstone**, **Linpack**, **Livermore Loops**, and **Dhrystone**. Describe the methodology activities through an activity diagram and a document that explains them, the tools needed to execute each activity, the inputs, the outcomes, and the statuses that indicate the conclusion of each of the process's activities. Adopt the execution time of the programs as the prime metric for comparing the computer's performance.

Execute all the proposed methodology steps, present the respective statistical summaries, box-plot, histogram or individual dot diagrams, empirical cumulative distribution, theoretical distribution, and a document that interprets them and stresses the comparison result.

Exercise 6. Generate an HTTP workload to exercise a server and measure the server's performance. Explain the findings of your experiment.

Exercise 7. What is a workload model?

Exercise 8. Workload models may be described by their **intended work** or their **impact**. Explain what do you understand from each of these perspectives.

Exercise 9. Use a benchmark program to exercise a given server over a period. Present the workload impact on the server's resources by presenting the respective statistical summary, box-plot, histogram or individual dot diagrams, and empirical cumulative distribution for each metric.

Exercise 10. Consider an online drugstore sale system where customers reach the drugstore services deployed in a data center. The customer begins interacting with the sales system by login in with his/her credentials. The data center load balancer delivers the respective transactions to be executed on the specific web-server. The web-server starts the corresponding business transaction by initiating interactions with the application server. The application server interprets the request, interacts with the database-server, returns the data content to the drugstore business logic, delivers the required digital content to the customer, and (if products are purchased) delivers products to the customer's address.

The data traffic between customers on the internet and the data center where the drugstore sale system is deployed is measured at the aggregation router (gateway). The measuring system monitors the income-outgo traffic at this device. The aggregation router's income-outgo traffic was monitored, and the event occurrence instant (in seconds) and the number of bytes transferred in each transaction event are shown in Table 24.33. Table 24.34 presents the time between events (*tbe*). Obtain the descriptive model that represents aggregation traffic (workload) by providing the following:

(a) The time series plot is represented by event occurrence instant (*et*) versus bytes transferred (*bt*) per event.

(b) Obtain the sequence of time between events (*tbe*).

(c) Present the statistical summary, the histogram or the individual plot, the box-plot, and the empirical cumulative distribution of *tbe*.

(d) Present the statistical summary, the histogram or the individual plot, the box-plot, and the empirical cumulative distribution of *bt*.

(e) Find out theoretical distributions that fit *tbe*. If required, use clustering to support this task.

(f) Find out theoretical distributions that fit *bt*. If required, use clustering to support this task.

Table 24.33

Transaction Event Instants (et) and the Respective Bytes Transferred (bt)

et (s)	bt (bytes)	et (s)	bt (bytes)	et (s)	bt (bytes)	et (s)	bt (bytes)
0.1200	2740	3.3007	594	6.3823	145	9.0435	884
0.2617	1303	3.4108	2365	6.4293	2075	9.0493	346
0.3170	97	3.4432	204	6.4350	17	9.0621	1889
0.3928	2131	3.4494	1188	6.4544	2796	9.2650	684
0.3955	744	3.4544	3741	6.5231	659	9.2719	438
0.5067	126	3.4668	2125	6.5831	2123	9.2940	857
0.5304	257	3.4848	2422	6.6720	1976	9.3865	5249
0.5350	777	3.5050	838	6.6775	176	9.5284	47
0.5453	5423	3.5628	2096	6.7753	1564	9.6365	430
0.5639	900	3.5643	753	6.7817	486	9.7373	2780
0.5875	761	3.6592	140	6.7891	664	9.7906	4048
0.6049	1346	3.6941	516	6.8364	4460	9.8110	763
0.8042	3129	3.8604	1324	6.8512	2009	9.8793	938
1.0496	835	3.8735	968	6.8722	702	10.1100	218
1.0802	89	3.9691	6	6.8740	2058	10.3092	189
1.1803	352	3.9847	209	6.8882	3012	10.3699	509
1.4463	974	4.0683	1212	6.9671	865	10.4001	557
1.4942	2714	4.3119	127	7.0189	1739	10.4196	430
1.5928	3919	4.3251	331	7.0373	1227	10.4497	350
1.6299	11	4.3401	451	7.0875	4568	10.4935	65
1.6314	841	4.3503	76	7.1703	3918	10.7219	1077
1.6382	1734	4.4704	2525	7.1907	6761	11.0806	815
1.6557	3581	4.5673	204	7.3243	822	11.1017	1535
1.6699	645	4.5793	1318	7.4248	845	11.3439	1269
1.6844	1512	4.6076	2952	7.4663	3345	11.9945	133
1.7339	378	4.7603	527	7.4862	1840	12.0448	1032
2.0104	520	4.7647	2545	7.5094	3645	12.1035	7903
2.0874	185	4.8466	577	7.6111	204	12.5683	468
2.1512	311	4.9189	892	7.6361	147	12.6067	89
2.1619	1869	4.9545	2203	7.6827	1918	12.7058	1305
2.2077	1224	4.9839	1094	7.7632	609	12.8066	1670
2.2283	1026	5.1661	914	7.9162	2381	13.5426	3189
2.2351	1756	5.1765	2134	7.9212	2997	13.8904	648
2.3011	780	5.2331	18	7.9353	1871	14.1392	1047
2.3863	1626	5.2777	151	7.9382	1618	14.4505	1506
2.4291	891	5.3282	312	7.9423	2661	14.5485	4495
2.5166	31	5.3376	1639	8.1330	2411	14.6085	534
2.5207	133	5.3716	690	8.2460	1171	14.6172	672
2.6264	2672	5.4377	1000	8.2636	4746	14.9729	200
2.6819	584	5.4473	3567	8.3960	1426	15.0903	328
2.6898	859	5.4519	1367	8.3996	3143	15.3077	283
2.7228	108	5.4684	587	8.4177	331	15.4877	128
2.7820	50	5.4822	1882	8.4824	112	15.5546	3174
2.7842	1605	5.6830	522	8.5872	287	15.6439	97
2.8081	3102	5.7065	3402	8.6284	2316	15.6671	1301
2.8405	1104	5.9383	334	8.6446	470	15.8142	146
2.9302	306	5.9539	948	8.6749	122	16.0631	133
3.0038	999	6.0793	435	8.7076	470	16.0694	133
3.1675	4542	6.0971	459	8.9732	2678	16.1310	1581
3.2211	1961	6.1318	306	9.0155	1651	16.2218	4023

Table 24.34

Time Between Events - (s)

tbe (s)	tbe (s)	tbe (s)	tbe (s)
0.1417	0.1101	0.0470	0.0058
0.0554	0.0324	0.0057	0.0129
0.0758	0.0062	0.0195	0.2029
0.0027	0.0050	0.0686	0.0069
0.1112	0.0123	0.0600	0.0221
0.0237	0.0180	0.0889	0.0925
0.0046	0.0202	0.0055	0.1419
0.0103	0.0579	0.0977	0.1081
0.0186	0.0015	0.0064	0.1008
0.0236	0.0949	0.0074	0.0533
0.0174	0.0349	0.0472	0.0204
0.1993	0.1663	0.0148	0.0683
0.2454	0.0131	0.0210	0.2306
0.0306	0.0956	0.0018	0.1992
0.1001	0.0156	0.0143	0.0607
0.2660	0.0836	0.0788	0.0302
0.0479	0.2436	0.0518	0.0196
0.0987	0.0132	0.0184	0.0301
0.0371	0.0150	0.0502	0.0438
0.0015	0.0101	0.0828	0.2284
0.0068	0.1201	0.0204	0.3588
0.0174	0.0969	0.1335	0.0210
0.0142	0.0119	0.1006	0.2423
0.0145	0.0283	0.0415	0.6506
0.0495	0.1527	0.0198	0.0503
0.2765	0.0044	0.0233	0.0587
0.0770	0.0819	0.1017	0.4649
0.0639	0.0723	0.0250	0.0384
0.0106	0.0356	0.0466	0.0991
0.0458	0.0294	0.0806	0.1008
0.0207	0.1822	0.1530	0.7361
0.0067	0.0103	0.0050	0.3477
0.0660	0.0567	0.0141	0.2488
0.0852	0.0445	0.0029	0.3113
0.0428	0.0505	0.0041	0.0980
0.0875	0.0094	0.1907	0.0599
0.0041	0.0341	0.1130	0.0087
0.1057	0.0661	0.0176	0.3557
0.0555	0.0095	0.1324	0.1174
0.0079	0.0046	0.0037	0.2175
0.0331	0.0165	0.0180	0.1800
0.0592	0.0138	0.0647	0.0669
0.0022	0.2008	0.1048	0.0893
0.0239	0.0235	0.0412	0.0233
0.0323	0.2318	0.0161	0.1471
0.0897	0.0156	0.0303	0.2489
0.0736	0.1254	0.0328	0.0064
0.1638	0.0178	0.2656	0.0616
0.0536	0.0348	0.0423	0.0907
0.0796	0.2505	0.0279	

Exercise 11. The data traffic between internet customers on and a data center is measured at the aggregation router (gateway). The aggregation router's income traffic was monitored, the arrival instant (in seconds - *at*) and the number of bytes transferred in each arrival are shown in Table 24.35. Figure 24.36 depicts the time between arrivals (*tba*). Present the descriptive model that represents aggregation traffic (workload) by providing:

(a) The time series plot is represented by arrival time (*at*) versus bytes transferred (*bt*) per arrival.

(b) Obtained the sequence of time between arrivals (*tba*).

(c) Present the statistical summary, the histogram or the individual plot, the box-plot, and the empirical cumulative distribution of *tba*.

(d) Present the statistical summary, the histogram or the individual plot, the box-plot, and the empirical cumulative distribution of *bt*.

(e) Find out theoretical distributions that fit *tba*. If required, use clustering to support this task.

(f) Find out theoretical distributions that fit *bt*. If required, use clustering to support this task.

Exercise 12. Adjust the workload simulator presented in Example 24.3.5 to record the transaction traces in time order of their occurrence.

(a) Propose a flow-chart[8] that represents the new solution.

(b) Adopt your programming language of choice and implement the workload simulator.

(c) Using the workload simulator implemented, generate a one-thousand length workload request trace.

(d) Plot the time series $bt \times at$.

(e) Calculate autocorrelation for the following lag-sizes:1 to 20.

(f) Obtained the sequence of time between arrivals (*tba*).

(g) Present the statistical summary, the histogram or the individual plot, the box-plot, and the empirical cumulative distribution of *tba*.

(h) Present the statistical summary, the histogram or the individual plot, the box-plot, and the empirical cumulative distribution of *bt*.

---

[8]Hint: Adopt the flowchart depicted in Figure 24.24 as the start point.

Table 24.35
Arrival Time and Bytes Transferred

bt (bytes)	at (s)	bt (bytes)	at (s)	bt (bytes)	at (s)	bt (bytes)	at (s)
1639	0.1200	1833	3.3007	1852	6.3823	1890	9.2746
1152	0.2617	1367	3.4108	1822	6.4293	2967	9.3173
1308	0.3170	1924	3.4432	1093	6.4350	862	9.4048
993	0.3928	981	3.4494	1719	6.4544	1241	9.4090
1128	0.3955	1916	3.4544	2120	6.5231	2337	9.5146
1428	0.5067	2067	3.4668	1557	6.5831	2357	9.5701
1420	0.5304	2001	3.4848	1297	6.6720	1450	9.5780
1143	0.5350	1374	3.5050	1078	6.6775	1131	9.6111
1156	0.5453	1359	3.5628	1157	6.7753	1489	9.6703
1130	0.5639	1738	3.5643	1344	6.7817	2169	9.6724
2069	0.5875	1347	3.6592	1451	6.7891	1198	9.6964
2107	0.6049	1856	3.6941	1561	6.8364	1353	9.7287
1678	0.8042	1458	3.8604	1131	6.8512	1828	9.8184
952	1.0496	1768	3.8735	1392	6.8722	1455	9.8920
1630	1.0802	1763	3.9691	1303	6.8740	1654	10.0558
1156	1.1803	750	3.9847	858	6.8882	1764	10.1094
1830	1.4463	1186	4.0683	1262	7.0082	1262	10.1889
2098	1.4942	1435	4.3119	2127	7.1499	1101	10.2990
1672	1.5928	1209	4.3251	1402	7.2053	1830	10.3314
1655	1.6299	1626	4.3401	1828	7.2810	1390	10.3376
1791	1.6314	1072	4.3503	1345	7.2837	1501	10.3427
1891	1.6382	1985	4.4704	1885	7.3949	1768	10.3550
617	1.6557	1080	4.5673	1443	7.4186	2348	10.3730
2030	1.6699	1135	4.5793	1411	7.4232	1748	10.3932
1700	1.6844	1218	4.6076	1653	7.4335	1464	10.4511
1181	1.7339	1271	4.7603	1359	7.4521	1846	10.4525
1732	2.0104	1977	4.7647	1981	7.4758	1218	10.5474
1407	2.0874	1188	4.8466	724	7.4932	1893	10.5823
2165	2.1512	1332	4.9189	1981	7.6925	2594	10.7487
1271	2.1619	1526	4.9545	1729	7.9379	1208	10.7618
1526	2.2077	924	4.9839	1754	7.9684	1152	10.8573
1192	2.2283	1297	5.1661	1411	8.0685	1369	10.8729
2265	2.2351	1860	5.1765	1886	8.3345	2363	10.9565
1396	2.3011	1683	5.2331	1786	8.3824	1179	11.2002
569	2.3863	1424	5.2777	1312	8.4811	1255	11.2134
1194	2.4291	1141	5.3282	1351	8.5182	1584	11.2284
1814	2.5166	1407	5.3376	1401	8.5197	1555	11.2385
2234	2.5207	1142	5.3716	1469	8.5265	1252	11.3586
2071	2.6264	1043	5.4377	1021	8.5439	1676	11.4556
1732	2.6819	1046	5.4473	1728	8.5581	890	11.4675
1288	2.6898	1187	5.4519	1568	8.5727	1996	11.4958
1260	2.7228	1468	5.4684	1772	8.6221	1448	11.6485
1948	2.7820	1257	5.4822	1379	8.8986	2134	11.6529
732	2.7842	1354	5.6830	1216	8.9756	1597	11.7348
1690	2.8081	1608	5.7065	882	9.0395	1902	11.8072
2204	2.8405	1909	5.9383	443	9.0501	1078	11.8427
2393	2.9302	1072	5.9539	1659	9.0959	1644	11.8722
836	3.0038	1800	6.0793	1645	9.1166	1911	12.0544
1789	3.1675	1053	6.0971	1222	9.1233	2143	12.0647
1448	3.2211	1393	6.1318	1027	9.1894	1608	12.1214

Table 24.36

The Time Between Arrivals - (s)

tba (s)	tba (s)	tba (s)	tba (s)
0.1417	0.1101	0.0470	0.0428
0.0554	0.0324	0.0057	0.0875
0.0758	0.0062	0.0195	0.0041
0.0027	0.0050	0.0686	0.1057
0.1112	0.0123	0.0600	0.0555
0.0237	0.0180	0.0889	0.0079
0.0046	0.0202	0.0055	0.0331
0.0103	0.0579	0.0977	0.0592
0.0186	0.0015	0.0064	0.0022
0.0236	0.0949	0.0074	0.0239
0.0174	0.0349	0.0472	0.0323
0.1993	0.1663	0.0148	0.0897
0.2454	0.0131	0.0210	0.0736
0.0306	0.0956	0.0018	0.1638
0.1001	0.0156	0.0143	0.0536
0.2660	0.0836	0.1200	0.0796
0.0479	0.2436	0.1417	0.1101
0.0987	0.0132	0.0554	0.0324
0.0371	0.0150	0.0758	0.0062
0.0015	0.0101	0.0027	0.0050
0.0068	0.1201	0.1112	0.0123
0.0174	0.0969	0.0237	0.0180
0.0142	0.0119	0.0046	0.0202
0.0145	0.0283	0.0103	0.0579
0.0495	0.1527	0.0186	0.0015
0.2765	0.0044	0.0236	0.0949
0.0770	0.0819	0.0174	0.0349
0.0639	0.0723	0.1993	0.1663
0.0106	0.0356	0.2454	0.0131
0.0458	0.0294	0.0306	0.0956
0.0207	0.1822	0.1001	0.0156
0.0067	0.0103	0.2660	0.0836
0.0660	0.0567	0.0479	0.2436
0.0852	0.0445	0.0987	0.0132
0.0428	0.0505	0.0371	0.0150
0.0875	0.0094	0.0015	0.0101
0.0041	0.0341	0.0068	0.1201
0.1057	0.0661	0.0174	0.0969
0.0555	0.0095	0.0142	0.0119
0.0079	0.0046	0.0145	0.0283
0.0331	0.0165	0.0495	0.1527
0.0592	0.0138	0.2765	0.0044
0.0022	0.2008	0.0770	0.0819
0.0239	0.0235	0.0639	0.0723
0.0323	0.2318	0.0106	0.0356
0.0897	0.0156	0.0458	0.0294
0.0736	0.1254	0.0207	0.1822
0.1638	0.0178	0.0067	0.0103
0.0536	0.0348	0.0660	0.0567
0.0796	0.2505	0.0852	0.0445

(i) Find out theoretical distributions that fit *tba*. If required, use clustering to support this task.

(j) Find out theoretical distributions that fit *bt*. If required, use clustering to support this task.

Exercise 13. Adopt your programming language of choice and implement the workload simulator specified by the model depicted in Figure 24.37, which represents a Markov Modulated Process. This process sends requests whose time between transactions, *tbt*, are specified by $Exp(\mu)$ (transaction type tr_1) and $Exp(\lambda)$ (transaction type tr_2), respectively. The request transaction rate is λ and μ depending on which state the workload simulator is. If the simulator is on states *one*, the rate is μ. If the simulator is on states *two*, the rate is λ. The sojourn time in states *one* is specified by $Exp(\alpha)$. Likewise, the sojourn time in states *two* is specified by $Exp(\beta)$. When a transaction type tr_1 is generated, the number of bytes transferred (*bt*) to the computer system is specified by $N(2000\,bytes, 500\,bytes)$ (Normal distribution. $N(m, \sigma)$, *m* is mean, and σ is the standard deviation.). Similarly, when a transaction type tr_2 is submitted, the number of bytes transferred to the computer system is specified by $W(2, 2000\,bytes)$ (Weibull distribution. $W(s, f)$, *s* is the shape parameter, and *f* is the form parameter.). Assume $\alpha = 2\,tps$, $\beta = 8\,tps$, $\lambda = 500\,tps$, and $\mu = 700\,tps$[9]. The simulator generates traces of time-ordered event, where each event is represented by a record in trace. A record is specified by a tuple (i, tr, gt, bg, tbt), where *i* denotes the transaction instance, that is a first transaction, second, third..., *tr*, as we already are aware represents the transaction type ($tr = 1$ and $tr = 2$), *gt* denotes the global time registered during the trace generation. It is a cumulative time that starts at $gt = 0$ and is incremented by the winning event (shortest delay) assigned to $ta = F_\alpha^{-1}$ and $tl = F_\lambda^{-1}$ or $tb = F_\beta^{-1}$ and $tm = F_\mu^{-1}$. The variable *bg* is the number of bytes transferred in each transaction[10].

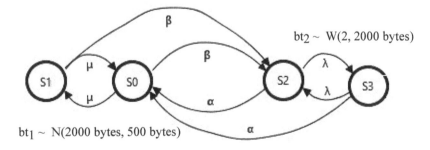

Figure 24.37 Markov Modulated Workload Traffic.

(a) Adopt your programming language of choice and implement the workload simulator.

(b) Using the simulator, obtain a two-thousand length workload request trace.

(c) Plot the time series $bt \times at$.

(d) Calculate autocorrelation for the following lag-sizes:1 to 20.

(e) Obtained the sequence of time between arrivals (tba).

(f) Using the generated trace, calculate the percentage of time spent in each state.

(g) Using the generated trace, calculate the arrival rate (the number of transaction arrivals divided by the trace time duration).

(h) Adopt the CTMC and calculate the steady-state probability of each state. Compare these results with the respective estimates obtained in (f).

(i) Adopt the CTMC and calculate the arrival rate. Compare these results with the respective estimate obtained in (g).

(j) Present the statistical summary, the histogram or the individual plot, the box-plot, and the empirical cumulative distribution of tba.

(k) Present the statistical summary, the histogram or the individual plot, the box-plot, and the empirical cumulative distribution of bt.

(l) Find out theoretical distributions that fit tba. If required, use clustering to support this task.

(m) Find out theoretical distributions that fit bt. If required, use clustering to support this task.

Exercise 14. Adopt your programming language of choice and implement the workload simulator specified by the SPN depicted in Figure 24.38. The simulator should generate three types of transaction requests, that is tr_1, tr_2, and tr_3. The workload simulator sends requests whose time between transactions, tbt, is specified by $Exp(\lambda)$ (transaction type tr_1), $Exp(\mu)$ (transaction type tr_2), and $Exp(v)$ (transaction type tr_3), respectively. The workload has three modulating states at which event arrivals follow the rates λ, μ, and v. Each of these states has the sojourn time defined by $Exp(\alpha)$, $Exp(\beta)$, and $Exp(\delta)$, respectively. An event arrival is represented by the firings of transitions t_l, t_m, and t_n, whose rates are λ, μ, and v. The sojourn time of each modulating state is specified by assigning the rates α, μ, and v to ta_1 and ta_2, tb_1 and tb_2, and tc_1 and tc_2, respectively. When a transaction of type 1 arrives (represented by transition t_l), the number of bytes transmitted is specified by $Exp(1/1800\,bytes)$. Similarly, when transaction of type 2 arrives (represented by transition t_m), the number of bytes transmitted is specified by

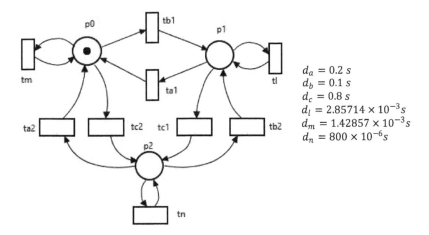

Figure 24.38 Modulated Workload Traffic - SPN.

$N(1200\,bytes, 300\,bytes)$. Likewise, when transaction of type 3 arrives (represented by transition t_n), the number of bytes transmitted is specified by $W(4, 2000\,bytes)$.

(a) Adopt your programming language of choice and implement the workload simulator[11].

(b) Using the simulator, obtain a two-thousand length workload request trace.

(c) Plot the time series $bt \times at$.

(d) Calculate autocorrelation for the following lag-sizes:1 to 10.

(e) Obtained the sequence of time between arrivals (*tba*).

(f) Using the generated trace, calculate the percentage of time spent in each state.

(g) Using the generated trace, calculate the arrival rate (the number of transaction arrivals divided by the trace time duration).

(h) Consider the SPN and calculate the steady-state probability of each state. Compare these results with the respective estimates obtained in (*f*).

(i) Adopt the SPN and calculate the arrival rate. Compare these results with the respective estimate obtained in (*g*).

---

[11]Hint: a possible strategy to implement the workload simulator consists of first generating the reachability graph of the SPN shown in Figure 24.38, which is isomorphic to a CTMC, and then adopt the strategy applied to implement the workload simulator shown in Appendix E.

(j) Present the statistical summary, the histogram or the individual plot, the box-plot, and the empirical cumulative distribution of *tba*.

(k) Present the statistical summary, the histogram or the individual plot, the box-plot, and the empirical cumulative distribution of *bt*.

(l) Find out theoretical distributions that fit *tba*. If required, use clustering to support this task.

(m) Find out theoretical distributions that fit *bt*. If required, use clustering to support this task.

25 Lifetime Data Analysis

The nonparametric techniques are straightforward to use since they are distribution-free. However, these methods' restrictions are that their results cannot accurately be extrapolated beyond the last failure. On the other hand, parametric methods can assess the system's reliability for its entire lifespan. Nevertheless, they require first fitting the failure data (and the repair data) to a statistical distribution. This chapter presents a set of methods for what is usually referred to as reliability or lifetime data analysis. These methods may be classified as nonparametric and parametric methods. The nonparametric techniques are straightforward to use since they are distribution-free. Nonparametric allows analysis of data reliability (and maintainability) without assuming an underlying time distribution.

On the other hand, parametric methods assume the lifetime (failure time or repair time) data obeys a specific probability distribution. One of the advantages of non-parametric methods is evaluating lifetime data without taking an underlying lifetime distribution, which avoids errors brought up assuming unsuitable distributions. However, these methods' restrictions are that their results cannot accurately be extrapolated beyond the last failure. On the other hand, parametric methods can assess the system's reliability for its entire lifespan. Yet, they require first fitting the failure data (and the repair data) to a statistical distribution. However, once the distribution is known, the probability knowledge of such distribution may be applied to extract information on the reliability data.

On the other hand, such methods tend to provide less accurate estimates than parametric methods when a specific distribution is known to represent the data failure [41, 115, 123, 230, 232, 233, 269, 349, 352, 401, 429]. The chapter is divided into three main sections. Section 25.1 introduces some fundamental concepts required throughout the chapter. Section 25.2 describes some important nonparametric methods and illustrates them through examples. Finally, Section 25.3 depicts a set of parametric methods and applies them to some specific examples.

25.1 INTRODUCTION

This section introduces a set of fundamental concepts related to lifetime data [40, 115, 123, 230, 232, 233, 269, 429]. These concepts are required to understand and apply the methods described in the chapter. First, however, we provide a few widely known reliable data sources. Lifetime data may be classified in many ways depending on whether it is obtained from an **operational** system or generated in a reliability test. The lifetime data obtained in a test (**test generated failures**) is likely to be accurate since it is carefully observed.

On the other hand, operational data may not be accurate due to the delay between the actual failure and the instant the failure is detected. In such cases, the lifetime data may be grouped into time intervals since the monitoring system cannot define when a failure occurred precisely. Such class of data is called **grouped** data, whereas data sets representing the system or components' failure time accurately are called **ungrouped**. Furthermore, the sample size of test generated failures is likely to be much smaller than the lifetime obtained from operational systems; hence the analyst may face a case where the sample size is small (**small sample size**) and cases where the sample size is large (**large sample size**). Another important aspect to be considered when analyzing reliability data is related to the availability of the time to failure (time to repair) of every device, system, or component in the study. The data set is **complete** when we know the exact failure times for all the units we are studying; otherwise, the data set is **censored**. Summarizing the concepts discussed, the data set taxonomy may be:

- **Operational** and **Test generated failures**,

- **Grouped** and **Ungrouped** data,

- **Large** and **Small** sample, and

- **Complete** and **Censored** data.

25.1.1 RELIABILITY DATA SOURCES

As we have seen, lifetime data may be obtained from operational systems or reliability tests. Device manufacturers may also carry reliability tests of their products and make the corresponding lifetime data available as handbooks, data books, databases, and some in-house data collections that are not generally available. This section provides a few widely known reliability data sources.

Such lifetime data sources can be categorized as Company-specific, Industry-specific, and Generic lifetime data sets. Company-specific lifetime data are collected from comparable or similar systems or components manufactured by the company. Industry-specific reliability data comes from data books of distinct companies that produce similar products. Generic lifetime data sets are assembled from extensive data sources that combine multiple assets and sources. Company-specific data should be used in preference to Industry-specific data, which, in turn, should be used in preference to Generic data. It is worth noting that reliability data are strongly related to specific modes of failure. Unfortunately, few lifetime data sources specify the failure modes. Some of these data sources are published as handbooks and databases [10].

The US Military Handbook 217 (MIL-HDBK-217) is a well-known source of generic electro-electronic device data for military and commercial enterprises. MIL-HDBK-217F fosters a predictive process comprising of two parts: (1) **part count method** and (2) **part stress method**. The part count method assumes typical operating conditions, i.e., complexity, temperature, stresses, operating mode, and environment. More formally:

$$\lambda_p = \sum_{i=1}^{n} \lambda_{ref,i},\qquad(25.1.1)$$

where $\lambda_{ref,i}$ is the component i's failure rate under the reference conditions, and n is the number of elements that compose the part p. Since the parts may not operate under the reference conditions, the actual operating conditions will result in failure rates different from those given by the parts count method. Therefore, the part stress method requires the specific component's factors so that

$$\lambda = \sum_{i=1}^{n} \lambda_{ref,i} \times \pi_S \times \pi_T \times \pi_E \times \pi_Q \times \pi_A, \qquad (25.1.2)$$

where π_S, π_T, π_E, π_Q, and π_A are the stress, temperature, environment, quality and adjustment factors, respectively.

OREDA is a project constituted of oil and gas corporations that, among other objectives, aims to produce and maintain a reliability database to sustain reliability information interchange among associate members. This project started in 1981 as an initiative of the Norwegian Petroleum Directorate (Petroleum Safety Authority). Non-members may access the reliability data by purchasing OREDA handbook licenses [320, 321, 406].

Reliability prediction methods have a long and distinguished history of application inside and outside the telecommunications business. The Bellcore/Telcordia standards - SR-332 - support reliability prediction models for components in commercial applications. SR-332 methodology is similar to the MIL-HDBK-217. SR-332 employs a series of models for several classes of electronic, electrical, and electromechanical parts to predict infant mortality and steady-state failure rates, considering environmental circumstances, quality levels, electrical stress factors, and several other parameters affected. It is worth stating that Bellcore (a spin-off of AT&T Bell Labs) was the research branch of the Bell Operating Companies purchased by SAIC and became Telcordia Technologies. Later on, Ericsson acquired Telcordia [425]. SR-332 Issue 4 provides hardware reliability prediction process developed from prominent industries [411].

FARADIP reliability data is represented as ranges. Overall, the lower values in these ranges are employed as predictions when assessing reliability design. In other words, these estimates might reasonably represent the devices' failure rates after some field experience and presumed reliability growth. Failure mode percentages are also considered as well as impact factors. This database includes microelectronics, discrete electronics, passive instruments and analyzers, connections, electromechanical, power, mechanical, pneumatics, hydraulics, computers, communication, alarms, and fire protection devices. The data supplied are for a typical ground-fixed environment[1]. Variation due to other environments and quality arrangements is dealt with employing multiplying factors [401, 402].

---

[1]Typical ground-fixed environments are those moderately controlled settings such as devices in permanent racks, boxes, and shelves, with satisfactory cooling air and unheated buildings and communications facilities. The term cooling air denotes airflow over devices at or below the devices' temperature to draw heat away and cool down or stabilize the temperature to that of the air [402].

SN 29500 was conceived and has been supported and updated by Siemens company. This standard is adopted by Siemens and its associates as the source for reliability predictions of electronic and electromechanical components. It gives component reference failure rates expressed in FIT^2 for a list of device classes regarding a reference state.

The process for estimating the failure rate (in FIT unities) of a device begins with looking up the device's failure rate (in FIT) at reference state (rs) from a table. The SN 29500 standard also provides a method for estimating the failure rate at operating state (λ_{os} - in FIT) from the failure rate at reference state (λ_{rs} - in FIT.):

$$\lambda_{os} = \lambda_{rs} \times f_{temp} \times f_v \times f_c \times f_{stress}, \tag{25.1.3}$$

where f_{temp} is the temperature factor, f_v is the voltage factor, f_c is the current factor, and f_{stress} is the stress factor [348].

The British Handbook of Reliability Data for Electronic Components used in Telecommunication Systems (HRD-5) provides definitions, and failure rates and outlines a methodology for assessing system (sub-systems, circuit) reliability from electro-electronic and electromechanical component failure information. This handbook has strived in the light of components' field data gathered by British Telecom, France Telecom, and laboratory-derived data. The reliability data estimation has been adopted to (1) afford a basis for estimating the reliability of devices, (2) identify critical reliability components, and (3) to provide means of assessing the reliability impact on system design and analyzing alternative options [402].

The Automotive Electronics Council (AEC) was initially established by Chrysler, Ford, and GM to establish common part-qualification and quality-system standards. The AEC Technical Committee is responsible for establishing standards for pursuing highly reliable systems. The reliability data produced are primarily concerned with electronic parts employed in military, transport, manufacturing, integrated circuits, discrete semiconductors, passive electronic components, computers, telecommunication, and information systems. The documents produced by AEC are available on the website [5, 10].

Xilinx publishes reports to pursue reliable product manufacturing. Xilinx executes reliability programs in response to internal requirements for either supporting reliability qualifications of new devices or adjusting the manufacturing processes to sustain quality standards. The manufacturing process is supervised by a reliability monitor that considers the maturity of the manufacturing process, the number of device hours, and the failure in time rate. The reliability tests are periodically conducted, but the number of tests can be reduced or eliminated based on the maturity of the process [473].

---

^{2}Failure in Time (FIT) is of failure rate unity expressed as the number of failures in one billion hours ($10^9 h$). Hence, $1\,FIT$ represents one observed failure in a period of one billion hours [348].

Information Technology Intelligence Consulting Corporation (ITIC) has provided reliability data of mainstream server manufacturers, operating systems, and virtualization platforms. The ITIC 2020 Global Server Hardware, Server OS Reliability Report considers the systems' reliability by weighing metrics and policies such as (1) automated and manual patch management, (2) Tier 1, Tier 2, and Tier 3 help desk calls, (3) inherent server OS reliability, (4) inherent server availability, (5) unavailability due to planned outages and upgrades, (6) security issues, (7) human error, (8) server virtualization reliability, (10) vendor technical services, (11) overworked, understaffed information technology departments, (12) servers' hardware aging, (13) integration and interoperability issues [186, 457].

Electronic Parts Reliability Data (ERPD) document presents failure rates on electronic components obtained from historically observed empirical failures on the field. Data comprised in this document presents industry average failure rates and the respective confidence intervals. The failure rate report was obtained by combining various failure rates on similar parts from various sources [127]. Likewise, the Nonelectronic Parts Reliability Data (NPRD) document provides failure rates on diverse electrical, mechanical, electromechanical, and microwave parts based on observed field failures [314].

Backblaze is a cloud storage and data backup company. Backblaze has been providing yearly reliability data of its storage systems and devices [33]. The approach adopted by Backblaze is to take a daily snapshot of each operational storage device of their datacenters. This snapshot includes basic drive information along with statistics related to that drive. All of the drive snapshots for a given day are collected into a "CSV" format file. The initial row of each file holds the column names, and the additional rows are the actual data. The columns record the data collection date, serial numbers, manufacturer-assigned serial numbers of the drives, models, capacities, and if the device is functional or in failure. Backblaze makes these datasets freely available, and they can be accessed on the Internet.

A final warning is needed when using reliability data from sources mentioned above and others. Failure rate data combines many inherent parameters that may drastically modify the results of the most basic figures over which predictions are to be assessed. Therefore, failure rates as primary parameters should be adopted from those sources with caution. Hence, it is prudent to state that in many circumstances, reliability estimates obtained from models that adopt such data should be assumed:

- as approximations of the reliability, the design is qualified in the field,

- to produce relative comparisons to support decisions, and

- as a basis for contractual requirements.

Hence, a relevant recommendation is to adopt a conservative view of data provided by manufacturers, companies-consortia, general data sources.

25.1.2 CENSORING

This section provides more details about the censoring process. Censoring arises when the data are incomplete because units were withdrawn from consideration prior to failure or units were functioning when the observation period started, but we do not know how long these units have been operating. In addition, units may be removed, for instance, when they fail because of other failure modes than the one being estimated.

The data set is said to be **Left-Censored** when we do not know when all the units were placed into operation. In this case, we know that a unit is operating when the observation period starts, but not how long the unit has been functioning. The data set is said to be **Right-Censored** when observation of a lifetime may be terminated before the item fails. For example, assume a set of n similar servers are under a lifetime test. The time required to observe the lifetime (time to failure) of all servers in the study may be large enough that, due to practical constraints, it may prevent the failure observation of all servers. Thus, these servers that do not fail during the observation are said to be right-censored.

A lifetime data set is singly censored when all censoring times are the same. On the other hand, in multiply censored data, the censoring times occur at many different times. For example, figure 25.1 depicts three data sets: complete data set (a), singly censored data set (b), and multiply censored data set (c).

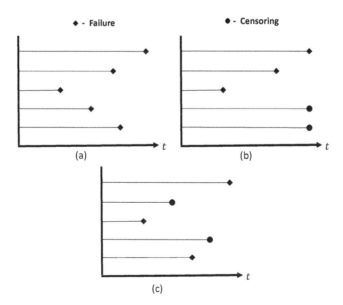

Figure 25.1 Complete Data Set (a) Singly Censored Data (b), and Multiply Censored Data.

Now assume a specific case where five servers (S_1, S_2, S_3, S_4, and S_5) are under a reliability test that lasts T hours (see Figure 25.2.a). During the test, S_2, S_4, and S_5 failed, whereas the servers S_1 and S_3 did not fail. Hence, S_1 and S_3 are censored. This class of censoring is termed **Right-Censoring Type 1**.

Consider now that the reliability test is finished when k servers out of n ($k \leq n$) servers fail. For instance, assume, as in the previous case, that five servers (S_1, S_2, S_3, S_4, and S_5) are allocated to a reliability test. Now, however, assume the test is finished when three out of the five serves fail. As an example, Figure 25.2.b shows five servers. During the test, the first server to fail was S_1, the second server that failed was S_5, and the third server that failed was S_1. As the test finishes, when three out of five servers fail, the servers S_2 and S_4 are censored. This type of censoring is named **Right Censoring Type 2**.

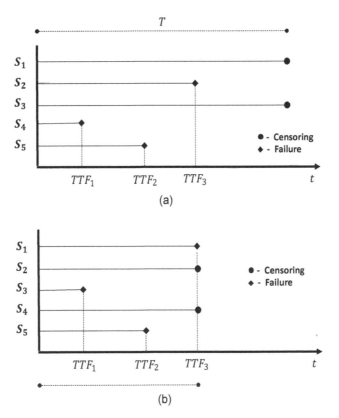

Figure 25.2 Right-Censoring (a) Type 1 and (b) Type 2 - Ungrouped Data.

Interval Censoring occurs when a failure is known to have occurred between the times of readout i and readout $i+1$ (grouped data). For example, in Figure 25.3, servers S_5, S_1 and S_6, and S_3 were censored in the second, third, and fourth readout since they failed between the respective readout and the previous, but the exact failure time is unknown.

Figure 25.3 shows a reliability experiment in which the failure time are grouped. The reliability experiment lasted T. One server (S_4) has already failed in the first readout. This is left censorship since it occurred before the first readout. It is an interval censoring when considering the first readout (first interval). When the experiment finished, the server S_2 was still working; hence, S_2 is considered a right censoring type 1. As already mentioned, in the second readout, one failure was observed (S_5). We know that it failed between the first and second readouts, but we did not know the precise time when it failed. At the third readout, two servers were considered in failure (S_1 and S_6). Server S_3's failure was observed in the fourth readout. In these last three cases (S_5, S_1 and S_6, and S_3), we have interval censoring.

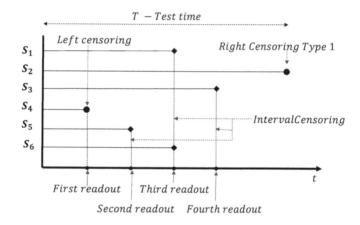

Figure 25.3 Left, Right and Interval Censoring - Grouped Data.

In the most general case, each unit in a test may have a specified interval during which it is known to have failed or a past censorship time is known to have survived. These intervals and censorship times may differ from each other. In the testing, each unit rarely has a different censorship time. However, when considering field data, it is likely to occur. For instance, consider a data center where several similar servers are operational. These servers would most likely be installed at different times. Therefore, each server would have different operating times on a given reference date, resulting in different censorship times.

25.2 NON-PARAMETRIC METHODS

Nonparametric lifetime data analysis is based on the empirical time to failure distribution (and time to repair), the respective empirical reliability (and maintainability), and the empirical hazard function. This section presents five nonparametric methods for reliability data analysis.

25.2.1 UNGROUPED COMPLETE DATA METHOD

The first method presented may be applied to complete ungrouped data; that is, it can be adopted when the times to failure of all observed devices are exact. Assume n servers were observed, and the time to failure (t_i) of each server was exactly recorded. Consider the set of t_is was sorted in ascending order and is shown in Column t_i of Table 25.1, where $i = 1, 2, ..., n$ denotes the ith failure; hence $t_i < t_{i+1}$ and so forth.

Table 25.1

Ungrouped Complete Data

i	t_i	$\hat{R}(t_i)$	$\hat{F}(t_i)$	$\hat{f}(t_i)$	$\hat{\lambda}(t_i)$
1					
2					
...	...	...	...	...	...
$n-1$					
n					

The reliability at t_i may be estimated by

$$\hat{R}(t_i) = \frac{n-i}{n}, \tag{25.2.1}$$

where $n - i$ is the number of surviving servers at t_i and n is the total number of servers at the beginning of the observation period. Therefore, as $F(t) = 1 - R(t)$ (see Equation 16.2.2), then

$$\hat{F}(t_i) = 1 - \frac{n-i}{n} \tag{25.2.2}$$

$$\hat{F}(t_i) = \frac{i}{n}.$$

As $f(t_i) = dF(t_i)/dt$ (see Equation 16.2.1), we estimate of the probability density function using

$$\hat{f}(t_i) = \frac{1}{n(t_i - t_{i-1})}. \tag{25.2.3}$$

Since $\lambda(t) = f_t(t)/R(t)$ (see Equation 16.2.6), then

$$\hat{\lambda}(t_i) = \frac{1}{(n-i)(t_i - t_{i-1})}. \tag{25.2.4}$$

It is worth observing that for t_n, $\hat{F}(t_n) = 1$; hence $\hat{R}(t_i) = 0$, which denotes that the probability of surviving t_n is null. Since it is unlikely any sample has the longest time to failure (time to repair), the Equation 25.2.1 tends to underestimate the reliability.

An alternative is to adopt

$$\hat{F}(t_i) = \frac{i}{n+1},$$ (25.2.5)

which leads to

$$\hat{R}(t_i) = \frac{n+1-i}{n+1}.$$ (25.2.6)

Hence,

$$\hat{f}(t_i) = \frac{1}{(n+1)(t_i - t_{i-1})}$$ (25.2.7)

and

$$\hat{\lambda}(t_i) = \frac{1}{(n+1-i)(t_i - t_{i-1})}.$$ (25.2.8)

$\hat{R}(t_i)$, $\hat{F}(t_i)$, $\hat{f}(t_i)$, and $\hat{\lambda}(t)$ are provided in the respective columns of Table 25.1. Another alternative is based on medians. The medians are usually numerically calculated. The following formula is often adopted as an approximation of the median [40, 42].

$$\hat{F}(t_i) = \frac{i - 0.3}{n + 0.4},$$ (25.2.9)

$$\hat{R}(t_i) = \frac{n + 0.7 - i}{n + 0.4},$$ (25.2.10)

$$\hat{f}(t_i) = \frac{1.}{(n + 0.4)(t_i - t_{i-1})}$$ (25.2.11)

and

$$\hat{\lambda}(t_i) = \frac{1}{(n + 0.7 - i)(t_i - t_{i-1})}.$$ (25.2.12)

The mean time to failure is estimated by

$$\widehat{MTTF} = \frac{\sum_{i=1}^{n} t_i}{n}.$$ (25.2.13)

Other statistics such as standard deviation, variance, skewness, kurtosis, and quantile may also be calculated from the sample (see Chapter 3). The confidence interval of the mean time to failure may also be estimated using bootstrap (see Section 6.5).

Example 25.2.1. Consider a set of fifty servers ($n = 50$) was set for an accelerate reliability test. The test finished when all servers presented a failure. Table 25.2, Column

Table 25.2
Ungrouped Complete Lifetime Data

i	t_i	$\hat{R}(t_i)$	$\hat{F}(t_i)$	$\hat{f}(t_i)$	$\hat{\lambda}(t_i)$
1	2.9	1.0000	0.0000	0.0068	0.0069
2	41.1	0.9861	0.0139	0.0005	0.0005
3	42.3	0.9663	0.0337	0.0162	0.0172
4	43.6	0.9464	0.0536	0.0159	0.0171
5	60.2	0.9266	0.0734	0.0012	0.0013
6	86.4	0.9067	0.0933	0.0008	0.0009
7	88.5	0.8869	0.1131	0.0095	0.0110
8	101.7	0.8671	0.1329	0.0015	0.0018
9	120.7	0.8472	0.1528	0.0010	0.0013
10	160.2	0.8274	0.1726	0.0005	0.0006
11	187.2	0.8075	0.1925	0.0007	0.0009
12	219.4	0.7877	0.2123	0.0006	0.0008
13	271.0	0.7679	0.2321	0.0004	0.0005
14	273.7	0.7480	0.2520	0.0073	0.0101
15	281.3	0.7282	0.2718	0.0026	0.0037
16	388.0	0.7083	0.2917	0.0002	0.0003
17	396.9	0.6885	0.3115	0.0022	0.0033
18	557.8	0.6687	0.3313	0.0001	0.0002
19	560.0	0.6488	0.3512	0.0088	0.0140
20	626.6	0.6290	0.3710	0.0003	0.0005
21	665.0	0.6091	0.3909	0.0005	0.0009
22	704.2	0.5893	0.4107	0.0005	0.0009
23	757.5	0.5694	0.4306	0.0004	0.0007
24	774.8	0.5496	0.4504	0.0012	0.0022
25	920.1	0.5298	0.4702	0.0001	0.0003
26	1072.1	0.5099	0.4901	0.0001	0.0003
27	1113.0	0.4901	0.5099	0.0005	0.0010
28	1143.9	0.4702	0.5298	0.0006	0.0014
29	1169.7	0.4504	0.5496	0.0008	0.0018
30	1378.5	0.4306	0.5694	0.0001	0.0002
31	1453.2	0.4107	0.5893	0.0003	0.0007
32	1507.2	0.3909	0.6091	0.0004	0.0010
33	1529.4	0.3710	0.6290	0.0009	0.0025
34	1688.1	0.3512	0.6488	0.0001	0.0004
35	1762.7	0.3313	0.6687	0.0003	0.0009
36	1940.3	0.3115	0.6885	0.0001	0.0004
37	2022.0	0.2917	0.7083	0.0002	0.0009
38	2174.7	0.2718	0.7282	0.0001	0.0005
39	2187.5	0.2520	0.7480	0.0016	0.0067
40	2260.5	0.2321	0.7679	0.0003	0.0013
41	2353.0	0.2123	0.7877	0.0002	0.0011
42	2388.0	0.1925	0.8075	0.0006	0.0033
43	2759.8	0.1726	0.8274	0.0001	0.0003
44	3020.9	0.1528	0.8472	0.0001	0.0006
45	3172.9	0.1329	0.8671	0.0001	0.0012
46	3251.1	0.1131	0.8869	0.0003	0.0027
47	3355.4	0.0933	0.9067	0.0002	0.0026
48	3803.7	0.0734	0.9266	0.0000	0.0008
49	4555.9	0.0536	0.9464	0.0000	0.0008
50	7847.7	0.0337	0.9663	0.0000	0.0004

t_i, presents the time to failure of the servers in ascending order. Columns $\hat{R}(t_i)$, $\hat{F}(t_i)$, $\hat{f}(t_i)$, and $\hat{\lambda}(t_i)$ depict the reliability, the cumulative time distribution, the density, and the failure rate estimate at t_i, respectively. In this specific study the Functions 25.2.10, 25.2.9, 25.2.11 and 25.2.12 were adopted. From this table, the reliability at $2022\,h$ is estimated as $\hat{R}(2022\,h) = 0.2917$. Likewise, $\hat{F}(t)$, $\hat{f}(t)$, and $\hat{\lambda}(t)$ are estimated. The estimated mean time to failure was $MTTF = 1384.85\,h$. Adopting bootstrap, a confidence interval for the $MTTF$ was estimated. The confidence interval obtained considering 95% degree of confidence was $MTTF \in (1016.57\,h, 1811.27\,h)$.

The reliability function $\hat{R}(t_i)$ and the cumulative function $\hat{F}(t_i)$ estimate are a step functions that decreases and increases, respectively, after each observed failure time. Consequently, some authors graph the reliability and cumulative function estimate as step functions. The density function estimate $(\hat{f}(t_i))$ is well represented by kernel density estimates or the empirical density function, closely related to histograms. Likewise, we plotted the hazard function estimate $(\hat{\lambda}(t_i))$. Here, however, for each of these functions $(\hat{R}(t_i), \hat{F}(t_i), \hat{f}(t_i), \text{and } \hat{\lambda}(t_i))$, we plot each point and connect them with line segments. Figure 25.4 shows the graphs of $\hat{R}(t_i)$, $\hat{F}(t_i)$, $\hat{f}(t_i)$, and $\hat{\lambda}(t_i)$.

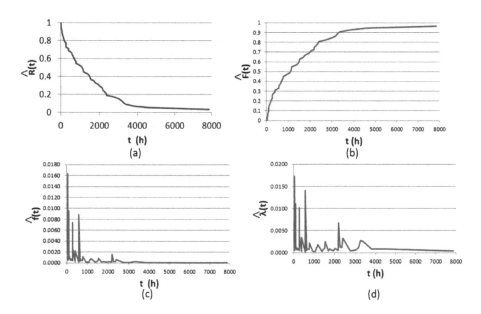

Figure 25.4 $\hat{R}(t_i)$, $\hat{F}(t_i)$, $\hat{f}(t_i)$ and $\hat{\lambda}(t_i)$ - Ungrouped Complete Data.

Assume one is interested in estimating the reliability at t_j, where t_j is not a failure time recorded and $t_i < t_j < t_{i+1}$. Consider t_i and t_{i+1} are failure time during the observation. One of the simplest approaches is adopting a linear interpolation between the points $(t_i, \hat{R}(t_i)$ and $(t_{i+1}, \hat{R}(t_{i+1})$ and, then estimating $R(t_j)$ by

$$\hat{R} = (t_j) = a \times t_j + b,$$ (25.2.14)

such that

$$a = \frac{\hat{R}(t_{i+1}) - \hat{R}(t_i)}{t_{i+1} - t_i}$$ (25.2.15)

$$b = \hat{R}(t_i) - a \times t_i.$$ (25.2.16)

Other interpolation or regression methods (see Section 6.7) may also be applied and provide more accurate estimates [316, 357].

Example 25.2.2. Consider the lifetime data set depicted in Table 25.2. Assume we need to estimate the reliability at $t_j = 2200\,h$. This value is recorded in the table. Hence, an alternative is estimating the reliability using Function 25.2.14. It is worth noting that $2187.52\,h < t_j < 2260.55\,h$. Therefore

$$a = \frac{\hat{R}(t_{i+1}) - \hat{R}(t_i)}{t_{i+1} - t_i} = \frac{0.23214 - 0.25198}{2260.55 - 2187.52} = -2.717 \times 10^{-4}$$

and

$$b = \hat{R}(t_i) - a \times t_i = 0.25198 - (-2.717 \times 10^{-4} \times 2187.52) = 0.84633.$$

Therefore $\hat{R}(2200\,h) = -2.717 \times 10^{-4} \times 2200 + 0.84633 = 0.24859$. As $F(t) = 1 - R(t)$, then $\hat{F}(2200\,h) = 0.75141$.

$\square$

25.2.2   GROUPED COMPLETE DATA METHOD

Assume the set of computers in a reliability test. Consider the test protocol specifies that an inspection should be carried out every day to find failed computers. Therefore, the computers' failure times are placed into time intervals of twenty-four hours. Such a sort of failure data is called grouped, as already mentioned at the beginning of the chapter. This chapter introduces a method for lifetime data analysis of grouped and complete data; that is, the time to failure of the computers is not exact, and the time to failure of every computer in the test is available.

Now consider the observation time was subdivided into k intervals, where $t_1, t_2, ..., t_k$ are the time instants that represent the end of the respective time interval. Hence, $t_1 < t_2 < ... < t_k$. Let n be the number of observed computers at the beginning of the test, and n_i be the number of surviving computers at the end of interval i, $i \in \{1, 2, 3, ..., k\}$ (see Figure 25.5). Therefore, the reliability estimate at t_i can be calculated through

$$\hat{R}(t_i) = \frac{n_i}{n},$$ (25.2.17)

that is the ratio between the number of surviving devices at t_i, considering n devices at the start of the observation. This method is usually applied to large samples; more precise data plots are usually unnecessary, as depicted in the previous method.

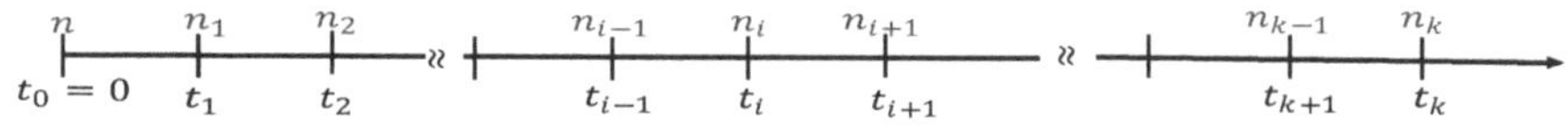

Figure 25.5   Failure Times - Grouped Complete Data.

As $F(t) = 1 - R(t)$, the failure time cumulative distribution function is estimated by

$$\hat{F}(t_i) = \frac{n - n_i}{n};$$ (25.2.18)

$n - n_i$ is the number of devices that has failed by t_i. Likewise, an estimate of the probability density function at t_i is calculated by

$$\hat{f}(t_i) = \frac{\hat{F}(t_{i+1}) - \hat{F}(t_i)}{t_{i+1} - t_i} = \frac{\hat{R}(t_i) - \hat{R}(t_{i+1})}{t_{i+1} - t_i} =$$

$$\hat{f}(t_i) = \frac{\frac{n_i}{n} - \frac{n_{i+1}}{n}}{t_{i+1} - t_i} =$$

$$\hat{f}(t_i) = \frac{n_i - n_{i+1}}{n\,(t_{i+1} - t_i)}.$$ (25.2.19)

Since $\hat{\lambda}(t_i) = \hat{f}(t_i)/\hat{R}(t_i)$, we get

$$\hat{\lambda}(t_i) = \frac{\frac{n_i - n_{i+1}}{n\,(t_{i+1} - t_i)}}{\frac{n_i}{n}}.$$

Thus,

$$\hat{\lambda}(t_i) = \frac{n_i - n_{i+1}}{n_i\,(t_{i+1} - t_i)}.$$ (25.2.20)

The mean time to failure can be estimated by

$$\widehat{MTTF} = \frac{\sum_{i=0}^{k-1} \bar{t}_i\,(n_i - n_{i+1})}{n},$$ (25.2.21)

where $\bar{t}_i = (t_i + t_{i+1})/2$, $n_0 = n$, and $t_0 = 0$. The confidence interval for the MTTF can be estimated using nonparametric bootstrap (see Section 6.5) through the failure times observed, such that for each time interval i the overall sample contains $(n_i - n_{i+1})$ equal TTF_is, where $TTF_i = \bar{t}_i\,(n_i - n_{i+1})$, $i \in \{0,1,2,...,k-1\}$.

A linear interpolation, as adopted in the previous section, may be applied to estimate $\hat{R}(t_j)$ and $\hat{F}(t_i)$) at t_j, for $t_{i-1} < t_j < t_i$, $i \in \{1,2,...,k\}$. Other interpolation methods may also be applied.

Example 25.2.3. Fifty servers ($n = 50$) were placed in an accelerated reliability test. The test protocol specifies that an inspection should be carried out every $400\,h$. The test finished when all server failed. Table 25.3 shows the time intervals (Column t_i), the number of failed servers in the respective interval (Column $n_{i-1} - n_i$) - $n_0 = n$, the number of surviving devices at t_i (Column n_i), the reliability estimate at t_i (Column $\hat{R}(t_i)$), the cumulative time to failure distribution estimate (Column $\hat{F}(t_i)$) at t_i, the estimate of the time to failure density function at t_i (Column $\hat{f}(t_i)$), and the estimate of the failure rate at t_i (Column $\hat{\lambda}(t_i)$).

Table 25.3
Grouped Complete Lifetime Data

t_i	$n - n_i$	n_i	$\hat{R}(t_i)$	$\hat{F}(t_i)$	$\hat{f}(t_i)$	$\hat{\lambda}(t_i)$
0	Not used	50	1.0000	0.0000	0.0009	0.0009
400	17	33	0.6600	0.3400	0.0004	0.0005
800	7	26	0.5200	0.4800	0.0003	0.0005
1200	5	21	0.4200	0.5800	0.0002	0.0005
1600	4	17	0.3400	0.6600	0.0002	0.0004
2000	3	14	0.2800	0.7200	0.0003	0.0011
2400	6	8	0.1600	0.8400	0.0001	0.0003
2800	1	7	0.1400	0.8600	0.0001	0.0007
3200	2	5	0.1000	0.9000	0.0001	0.0010
3600	2	3	0.0600	0.9400	0.0001	0.0008
4000	1	2	0.0400	0.9600	0.0000	0.0000
4400	0	2	0.0400	0.9600	0.0001	0.0013
4800	1	1	0.0200	0.9800	0.0000	0.0000
5200	0	1	0.0200	0.9800	0.0000	0.0000
5600	0	1	0.0200	0.9800	0.0000	0.0000
6000	0	1	0.0200	0.9800	0.0000	0.0000
6400	0	1	0.0200	0.9800	0.0000	0.0000
6800	0	1	0.0200	0.9800	0.0000	0.0000
7200	0	1	0.0200	0.9800	0.0000	0.0000
7600	0	1	0.0200	0.9800	0.0001	0.0025
8000	1	0	0.0000	1.0000	0.0000	Not used

The reliability at $t_i = 2000\,h$ is estimated as $\hat{R}(2000\,h) = 0.28$. Therefore, the cumulative time distribution of the $TTFs$ is at $t_i = 2000\,h$ is $\hat{F}(2000\,h) = 0.72$. The $\widehat{MTTF} = 1368\,h$. Adopting bootstrap, a confidence interval for the $MTTF$ was estimated. The sample used to perform the resampling was composed of a multiset of $TTFs$ in which the midpoint, $\bar{t}_i$, of each interval i is repeated $n_i - n_{i-1}$. $n_i - n_{i-1}$ is the number of failures in each interval. The original sample from which the resamples are obtained is shown in Table 25.4. Applying nonparametric bootstrap, one thousand

Table 25.4

Grouped TTFs - Replicated Interval's Midtimes

TTFs (h)				
200	200	600	1400	2200
200	200	600	1400	2200
200	200	600	1400	2600
200	200	600	1800	3000
200	200	1000	1800	3000
200	200	1000	1800	3400
200	200	1000	2200	3400
200	600	1000	2200	3800
200	600	1000	2200	4600
200	600	1400	2200	7800

resamples were generated, and the respective resamples' means were computed and ordered. After, the quantiles 25% and 97.5% were selected to obtain a confidence interval of the MTTF, considering 95% degree of confidence. The obtained confidence interval was $MTTF \in (1000h, 1800h)$.

The reliability at $t = 2100h$ can be interpolated by using $\hat{R}(t) = -3 \times 10^{-4}t + 0.88$, which is the line equation for interpolating between points $(2000h, 0.28)$ and $(2400h, 0.16)$. Therefore, $\hat{R}(2000h) = 0.25$. Figure 25.6 shows the graphs $\hat{R}(t) \times t$, $\hat{F}(t) \times t$, $\hat{f}(t) \times t$, and $\hat{\lambda}(t) \times t$.

$\square$

25.2.3   UNGROUPED MULTIPLY CENSORED DATA METHOD

This section presents a method for reliability analysis of ungrouped multiply censored data. Let n be the number of devices, such as servers, routers, switches, that were observed. During the observation period, a device may either fail or be censored at any moment. Figure 25.7 shows an observation timeline in which the failure or censored times are represented. It is worth stressing that the data set is ungrouped; hence, the time intervals between events (failure or censoring) vary.

The probability of a device failure occurs after t_i, given it did not fail by t_{i-1}, is

$$P(T > t_i | T > t_{i-1}) = \frac{P((T > t_i) \cap (T > t_{i-1}))}{P(T > t_{i-1})} =$$

$$P(T > t_i | T > t_{i-1}) = \frac{P(T > t_i)}{P(T > t_{i-1})} =$$

$$P(T > t_i | T > t_{i-1}) = \frac{R(t_i)}{R(t_{i-1})}.$$

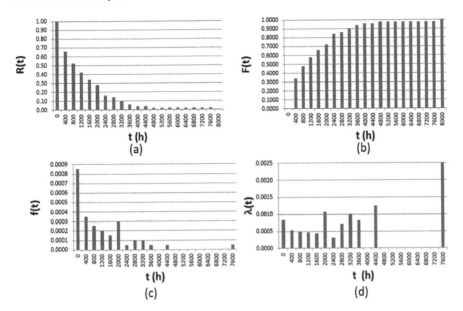

Figure 25.6 $\hat{R}(t) \times t$, $\hat{F}(t) \times t$, $\hat{f}(t) \times t$, and $\hat{\lambda}(t) \times t$.

As $P(T > t_i | T > t_{i-1}) = R(\triangle t_i)$, which denotes the probability of surviving $\triangle t_i$, given it survived t_{i-1}, then

$$R(\triangle t_i) = \frac{R(t_i)}{R(t_{i-1})},$$

thus

$$R(t_i) = R(\triangle t_i) \times R(t_{i-1}). \qquad (25.2.22)$$

Assume

$$\hat{F}(t_i) = \frac{i}{n+1}$$

and

$$\hat{R}(t_i) = 1 - \hat{F}(t_i),$$

then

$$\hat{R}(t_i) = 1 - \frac{i}{n+1} = \frac{n+1-i}{n+1}$$

and

$$\hat{R}(t_{i-1}) = \frac{n+1-(i-1)}{n+1} = \frac{n+2-i}{n+1}.$$

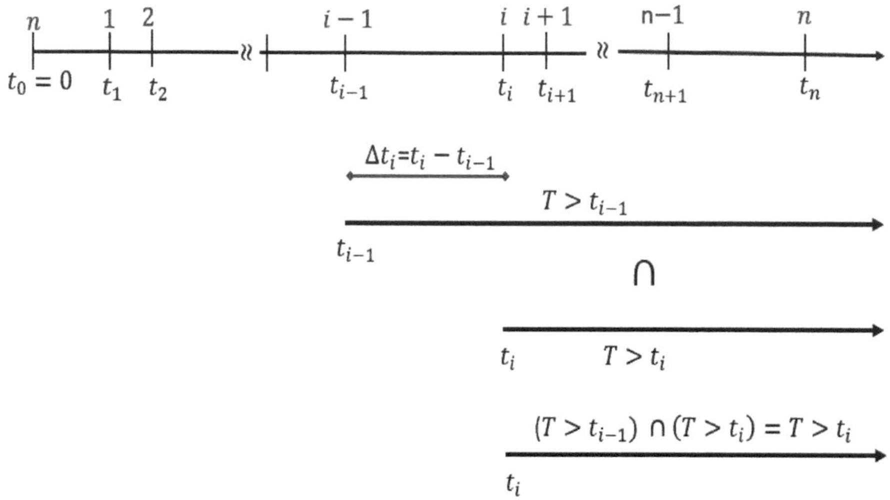

Figure 25.7 Failure or Censored Times - Ungrouped Multiply Censored Data.

Using Equation 25.2.22, we obtain

$$\hat{R}(t_i) = \hat{R}(\triangle t_i) \times \hat{R}(t_{i-1}),$$

hence

$$\hat{R}(\triangle t_i) = \frac{\frac{n+1-i}{n+1}}{\frac{n+1-(i-1)}{n+1} = \frac{n+2-i}{n+1}},$$

$$\hat{R}(\triangle t_i) = \frac{n+1-i}{n+2-i}. \qquad (25.2.23)$$

As two sorts of events may occur at t_i, that is a failure or a censoring, let

$$\delta_i = \begin{cases} 1 & \text{if a failure occurs at } t_i \\ 0 & \text{if a censoring occurs at } t_i. \end{cases} \qquad (25.2.24)$$

Therefore,

$$\hat{R}(t_i) = \hat{R}(\triangle t_i)^{\delta_i} \times \hat{R}(t_{i-1}), \qquad (25.2.25)$$

thus

$$\hat{R}(t_i) = \left(\frac{n+1-i}{n+2-i}\right)^{\delta_i} \times \hat{R}(t_{i-1}). \qquad (25.2.26)$$

Hence

$$\hat{F}(t_i) = \left(\frac{i}{i-1}\right)^{\delta_i} \times \hat{F}(t_{i-1}), \qquad (25.2.27)$$

and

$$\hat{f}(t_i) = \frac{1}{(n+1)(t_i - t_{i-1})}, \tag{25.2.28}$$

$$\hat{\lambda}(t_i) = \frac{1}{(n+1-i)(t_i - t_{i-1})}. \tag{25.2.29}$$

As the data set is censored, the formulas for computing $MTTF$ and standard deviation are no longer valid since the respective values would be too pessimistic. Interpolation may be applied to estimate $\hat{R}(t_j)$ and $\hat{F}(t_i)$) at t_j, for $t_{i-1} < t_j < t_i$, $i \in \{1,2,...,k\}$.

Example 25.2.4. Fifty servers ($n = 50$) went through an accelerated reliability test. However, not all servers were kept until the end of the test; that is, some of them were removed (censored) from the test when they were still operational. Table 25.5 shows the event times (Column t_i) - failure or censoring. Column δ_i represents failures (1) or censoring (0). Columns $\hat{R}(t_i)$, $\hat{F}(t_i)$, $\hat{f}(t_i)$, and $\hat{f}(t_i)$ present the reliability, the cumulative time to failure distribution, the failure density function, and the failure rate functions at t_i, respectively. Column $t_i - t_{i-1}$ presents the time interval between two consecutive events, and Column i specifies the event order. Figure 25.8 shows the graphs $\hat{R}(t) \times t$, $\hat{F}(t) \times t$, $\hat{f}(t) \times t$, and $\hat{\lambda}(t) \times t$.

$\square$

25.2.4 KAPLAN-MEIER METHOD

This section introduces the Kaplan-Meier nonparametric method for reliability data analysis [203]. First, we consider grouped and censored reliability data. Afterward, the method is also applied to grouped and complete, ungrouped and complete, and ungrouped and censored data sets.

Grouped and Censored Data

Assume the set of n computers in a university campus. Consider, the maintenance management policy specifies that an inspection should be carried out every week ($\triangle t_i$) to find failed computers. Therefore, the time to failure of computers is place into time intervals of one week. Such a sort of failure data is called grouped, as already mentioned in the beginning of the chapter. Some computers may also be removed from the campus before failure occurrence (censoring). Figure 25.9 shows the timeline divided into equal intervals $\triangle t_i = t_i - t_{i-1}$, $i \in \{1,2,...,n\}$. The observation period started at $t_0 = 0$ with n computers. In the beginning of each time interval ($\triangle t_i$), $i \in \{1,2,...,n\}$, we have n_i surviving computers since $t_0 = 0$, where $n_i = n_{i-1} - c_{i-1} - r_{i-1}$, where n_{i-1} is surviving computers up to t_{i-1}, c_{i-1} is the number of censored computers in the interval $\triangle t_{i-1}$, and r_{i-1} is the number of failed computer in the same interval, $\triangle t_{i-1}$. Likewise, n_{i+1} is the number of surviving

Table 25.5
Ungrouped Multiply Censored Lifetime Data

$t_i - t_{i-1}$	i	t_i	δ_i	$\hat{R}(t_i)$	$\hat{F}((t_i)$	$\hat{f}((t_i)$	$\hat{\lambda}((t_i)$
2.91	1	2.91	0	1.0000	0.0000	0.0067	0.0069
38.18	2	41.08	1	0.9800	0.0200	0.0005	0.0005
1.22	3	42.31	1	0.9600	0.0400	0.0161	0.0171
1.25	4	43.55	1	0.9400	0.0600	0.0157	0.0170
16.61	5	60.17	1	0.9200	0.0800	0.0012	0.0013
26.25	6	86.42	1	0.9000	0.1000	0.0007	0.0008
2.08	7	88.50	1	0.8800	0.1200	0.0094	0.0109
13.19	8	101.70	1	0.8600	0.1400	0.0015	0.0018
19.05	9	120.75	0	0.8600	0.1400	0.0010	0.0012
39.43	10	160.18	0	0.8600	0.1400	0.0005	0.0006
27.07	11	187.24	1	0.8390	0.1610	0.0007	0.0009
32.19	12	219.43	1	0.8180	0.1820	0.0006	0.0008
51.61	13	271.04	1	0.7971	0.2029	0.0004	0.0005
2.70	14	273.74	1	0.7761	0.2239	0.0073	0.0100
7.58	15	281.32	0	0.7761	0.2239	0.0026	0.0037
106.71	16	388.04	1	0.7545	0.2455	0.0002	0.0003
8.89	17	396.92	1	0.7330	0.2670	0.0022	0.0033
160.84	18	557.76	1	0.7114	0.2886	0.0001	0.0002
2.26	19	560.02	0	0.7114	0.2886	0.0087	0.0138
66.60	20	626.62	1	0.6892	0.3108	0.0003	0.0005
38.40	21	665.02	1	0.6670	0.3330	0.0005	0.0009
39.14	22	704.16	1	0.6447	0.3553	0.0005	0.0009
53.37	23	757.53	1	0.6225	0.3775	0.0004	0.0007
17.22	24	774.75	1	0.6003	0.3997	0.0011	0.0022
145.31	25	920.07	1	0.5780	0.4220	0.0001	0.0003
151.99	26	1072.06	1	0.5558	0.4442	0.0001	0.0003
40.98	27	1113.03	1	0.5336	0.4664	0.0005	0.0010
30.87	28	1143.91	1	0.5113	0.4887	0.0006	0.0014
25.77	29	1169.68	1	0.4891	0.5109	0.0008	0.0018
208.84	30	1378.51	1	0.4669	0.5331	0.0001	0.0002
74.67	31	1453.19	1	0.4446	0.5554	0.0003	0.0007
53.98	32	1507.16	1	0.4224	0.5776	0.0004	0.0010
22.21	33	1529.38	1	0.4002	0.5998	0.0009	0.0025
158.75	34	1688.13	0	0.4002	0.5998	0.0001	0.0004
74.62	35	1762.75	1	0.3766	0.6234	0.0003	0.0008
177.59	36	1940.34	0	0.3766	0.6234	0.0001	0.0004
81.64	37	2021.98	1	0.3515	0.6485	0.0002	0.0009
152.75	38	2174.73	1	0.3264	0.6736	0.0001	0.0005
12.79	39	2187.52	1	0.3013	0.6987	0.0015	0.0065
73.03	40	2260.55	1	0.2762	0.7238	0.0003	0.0012
92.49	41	2353.03	1	0.2511	0.7489	0.0002	0.0011
34.97	42	2388.00	1	0.2260	0.7740	0.0006	0.0032
371.78	43	2759.78	1	0.2009	0.7991	0.0001	0.0003
261.09	44	3020.87	1	0.1758	0.8242	0.0001	0.0005
152.03	45	3172.89	1	0.1507	0.8493	0.0001	0.0011
78.20	46	3251.09	1	0.1255	0.8745	0.0003	0.0026
104.33	47	3355.42	1	0.1004	0.8996	0.0002	0.0024
448.33	48	3803.75	0	0.1004	0.8996	0.0000	0.0007
752.11	49	4555.86	0	0.1004	0.8996	0.0000	0.0007
3291.80	50	7847.66	1	0.0502	0.9498	0.0000	0.0003

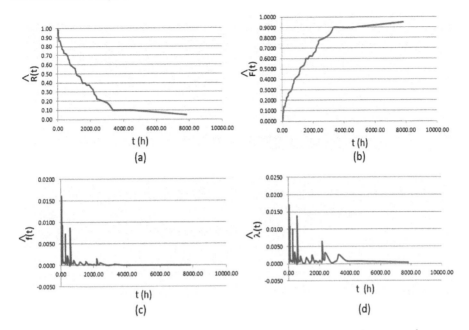

Figure 25.8   Ungrouped Multiply Censored Data - $\hat{R}(t) \times t$, $\hat{F}(t) \times t$, $\hat{f}(t) \times t$, and $\hat{\lambda}(t) \times t$.

computers at t_{i+1}, where $n_{i+1} = n_i - c_i - r_i$, where n_i is surviving computers up to t_i, c_i is the number of censored computers in the interval $\triangle t_i$, and r_i is the number of failed computers in the same interval, $\triangle t_i$. It is assumed the censors in $\triangle t_i$ occurs in the beginning of the interval and the failures occur at the end of each interval. Figure 25.9 stresses these assumptions, where in this particular case, at the beginning of $\triangle t_i$, we have two censors (two little upward red arrows) and one failure (one red arrow) at the end of $\triangle t_i$.

As the method is described in Section 25.2.3, we get (see Equation 25.2.22):

$$\hat{R}(t_i) = \hat{R}(\triangle t_i) \times \hat{R}(t_{i-1}),$$

where now

$$\hat{R}(\triangle t_i) = 1 - \frac{r_i}{n_i} \qquad (25.2.30)$$

and

$$n_{i+1} = n_i - c_i - r_i. \qquad (25.2.31)$$

Therefore,

$$\hat{R}(t_1) = \hat{R}(\triangle t_0) \times \hat{R}(t_0),$$

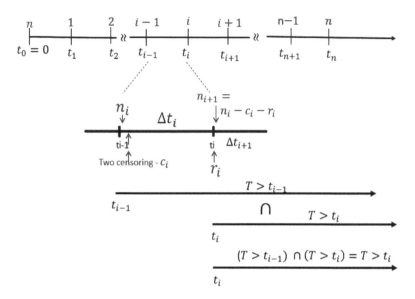

Figure 25.9   Failure or Censored Times - Kaplan-Meier Applied to Grouped Censored Data.

$$\hat{R}(t_1) = \hat{R}(\triangle t_0) \times (1 - \frac{r_1}{n_1}),$$

$$\hat{R}(t_1) = (1 - \frac{r_1}{n_1}),$$

since $\hat{R}(\triangle t_0) = 1$. Besides, as $n_1 = n$, then

$$\hat{R}(t_1) = (1 - \frac{r_1}{n})$$

Likewise,

$$\hat{R}(t_2) = \hat{R}(\triangle t_2) \times \hat{R}(t_1).$$

Hence,

$$\hat{R}(t_2) = (1 - \frac{r_1}{n_1}) \times (1 - \frac{r_2}{n_2}),$$

where $n_2 = n_1 - c_1 - r_1$.

Generalizing, we obtain

$$\hat{R}(t_i) = \prod_{j=1}^{i}(1 - \frac{r_j}{n_j}), \tag{25.2.32}$$

where $n_j = n_{j-1} - c_{j-1} - r_{j-1}$.

As the data set is not complete, the formulas for computing $MTTF$ and standard deviation are not valid because the respective values would be too pessimistic. Interpolation may be applied to estimate $\hat{R}(t_j)$ and $\hat{F}(t_i)$) at t_j, for $t_{i-1} < t_j < t_i$,

$i \in \{1, 2, ..., n\}$.

Example 25.2.5. Consider eighty servers ($n = 80$) were observed during sixteen weeks. Inspections were to be carried out every week ($168\,h$). The observation finished at the end of the sixteenth week. Table 25.6 shows the time instants that represent the end of each of the sixteen intervals (Column t_i), the number of failed servers in the respective interval (Column r_i), the number of censored devices at each interval (Column c_i), the reliability estimate at t_i (Column $\hat{R}(t_i)$), the cumulative time to failure distribution estimate (Column $\hat{F}(t_i)$) at t_i, the estimate of the time to failure density function at t_i (Column $\hat{f}(t_i)$), and the estimate of the failure rate at t_i (Column $\hat{\lambda}(t_i)$). Figure 25.10 shows the graphs $\hat{R}(t) \times t$, $\hat{F}(t) \times t$, $\hat{f}(t) \times t$, and $\hat{\lambda}(t) \times t$.

Table 25.6

Kaplan-Meier - Grouped and Censored Data

i	t_i (h)	r_i	c_i	n_{i+1}	$t_i - t_{i-1}$ (h)	$1 - r_i/n_i$	$\hat{R}(t_i)$	$\hat{F}(t_i)$	$\hat{f}(t_i)$	$\hat{\lambda}(t_i)$
0	0			80		1	1	0	7.35×10^{-5}	7.44×10^{-5}
1	168	0	0	80	168	1	1	0	7.35×10^{-5}	7.53×10^{-5}
2	336	0	0	80	168	1	1	0	7.35×10^{-5}	7.63×10^{-5}
3	504	0	2	78	168	1	1	0	7.53×10^{-5}	7.94×10^{-5}
4	672	1	0	77	168	0.9872	0.9872	0.0128	7.63×10^{-5}	8.15×10^{-5}
5	840	1	1	75	168	0.9870	0.9744	0.0256	7.83×10^{-5}	8.50×10^{-5}
6	1008	0	0	75	168	1	0.9744	0.0256	7.83×10^{-5}	8.63×10^{-5}
7	1176	2	1	72	168	0.9733	0.9484	0.0516	8.15×10^{-5}	9.16×10^{-5}
8	1344	1	1	70	168	0.9861	0.9352	0.0648	8.38×10^{-5}	9.60×10^{-5}
9	1512	0	1	69	168	1	0.9352	0.0648	8.50×10^{-5}	9.92×10^{-5}
10	1680	2	1	66	168	0.9710	0.9081	0.0919	8.88×10^{-5}	1.06×10^{-4}
11	1848	0	1	65	168	1	0.9081	0.0919	9.02×10^{-5}	1.10×10^{-4}
12	2016	0	0	65	168	1	0.9081	0.0919	9.02×10^{-5}	1.12×10^{-4}
13	2184	2	1	62	168	0.9692	0.8802	0.1198	9.45×10^{-5}	1.21×10^{-4}
14	2352	1	2	59	168	0.9839	0.8660	0.1340	9.92×10^{-5}	1.32×10^{-4}
15	2520	1	0	58	168	0.9831	0.8513	0.1487	1.01×10^{-4}	1.38×10^{-4}
16	2688	1	1	56	168	0.9828	0.8366	0.1634	1.04×10^{-4}	1.49×10^{-4}

□

Grouped and Complete Data

Now assume the data set has no censoring, that is, the data set is complete. In other words, the time to failure of all devices is available but is grouped into intervals. The analysis of such a data set is a particular case of the method shown above in which $c_i = 0$ for every interval i (see Figure 25.11). Therefore, the Equation 25.2.33 becomes

$$n_{i+1} = n_i - r_i. \quad (25.2.33)$$

The other estimate functions remain the same but considering the new calculation of n_{i+1}. Besides, as the data set is complete, estimates of the $MTTF$, variance, and

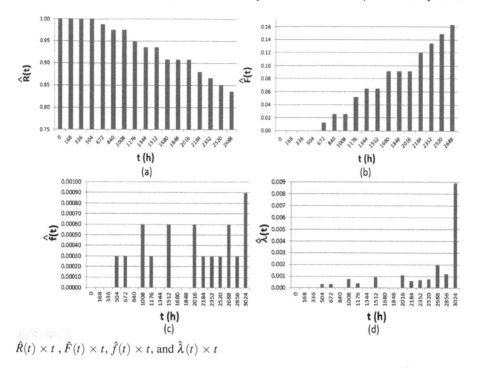

$\hat{R}(t) \times t$, $\hat{F}(t) \times t$, $\hat{f}(t) \times t$, and $\hat{\lambda}(t) \times t$

Figure 25.10 Kaplan-Meier Applied to Grouped Censored Data.

standard deviation are possible. The Equation 25.2.21 can be adopted to estimate the mean time to failure, that is

$$\widehat{MTTF} = \frac{\sum_{i=0}^{k-1} \bar{t}_i (n_i - n_{i+1})}{n},$$

$$\widehat{MTTF} = \frac{\sum_{i=0}^{k-1} \bar{t}_i r_i)}{n},$$

where $\bar{t}_i = (t_i + t_{i+1})/2$. The confidence interval for the MTTF can be estimated using nonparametric bootstrap (see Section 6.5) through the failure times observed, such that for each time interval i the overall sample contains $(n_i - n_{i+1})$ equal TTF_is, where $TTF_i = \bar{t}_i (n_i - n_{i+1})$, $i \in \{0, 1, 2, ..., k-1\}$.

Example 25.2.6. Twenty routers ($n = 20$) were observed under stress workload for $3528\,h$, that is twenty weeks (20). The maintenance management protocol defines an inspection routine that should be carried out every week, that is every $168\,h$. After $3528\,h$, all routers failed. Table 25.7 shows the time instant of the end of each interval (Column t_i), the number of failed routers in the respective interval i (Column r_i), the reliability estimate at t_i (Column $\hat{R}(t_i)$), the cumulative time to failure distribution estimate (Column $\hat{F}(t_i)$) at t_i, the estimate of the time to failure density function at t_i (Column $\hat{f}(t_i)$), and the estimate of the failure rate at t_i (Column $\hat{\lambda}(t_i)$).

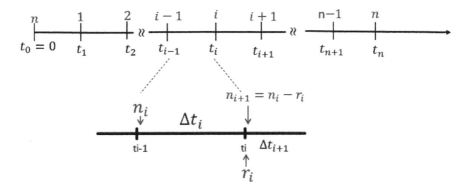

Figure 25.11   Failure Times - Kaplan-Meier Applied to Grouped Complete Data.

Table 25.7

Kaplan-Meier - Grouped and Complete Data

i	t_i (h)	r_i	n_{i+1}	$t_i - t_{i-1}$ (h)	$1 - r_i/n_i$	$\hat{R}(t)$	$\hat{F}(t)$	$\hat{f}(t)$	$\hat{\lambda}(t)$
1	168	0	20	168	1	1	0	0	0
2	336	0	20	168	1	1	0	0	0
3	504	0	20	168	1	1	0	0	0
4	672	1	19	168	0.9500	0.95	0.05	0.00030	0.00031
5	840	1	18	168	0.9474	0.9	0.1	0.00030	0.00033
6	1008	0	18	168	1	0.9	0.1	0	0
7	1176	2	16	168	0.8889	0.8	0.2	0.00060	0.00074
8	1344	1	15	168	0.9375	0.75	0.25	0.00030	0.00040
9	1512	0	15	168	1	0.75	0.25	0	0
10	1680	2	13	168	0.8667	0.65	0.35	0.00060	0.00092
11	1848	0	13	168	1	0.65	0.35	0	0
12	2016	0	13	168	1	0.65	0.35	0	0
13	2184	2	11	168	0.8462	0.55	0.45	0.00060	0.00108
14	2352	1	10	168	0.9091	0.5	0.5	0.00030	0.00060
15	2520	1	9	168	0.9	0.45	0.55	0.00030	0.00066
16	2688	1	8	168	0.8889	0.4	0.6	0.00030	0.00074
17	2856	2	6	168	0.75	0.3	0.7	0.00060	0.00198
18	3024	1	5	168	0.8333	0.25	0.75	0.00030	0.00119
19	3192	3	2	168	0.4	0.1	0.9	0.00089	0.00893
20	3360	2	0	168	0	0	1		

Figure 25.12 shows the graphs $\hat{R}(t) \times t$, $\hat{F}(t) \times t$, $\hat{f}(t) \times t$, and $\hat{\lambda}(t) \times t$. The reliability at $t = 2016 h$ is $\hat{R}(2016 h) = 0.65$. Interpolation may also be adopted to estimate $\hat{R}(t_j)$ and $\hat{F}(t_i)$ at t_j, for $t_{i-1} < t_j < t_i$, $i \in \{1, 2, ..., n\}$.

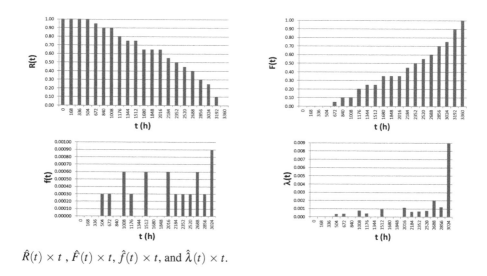

$\hat{R}(t) \times t$, $\hat{F}(t) \times t$, $\hat{f}(t) \times t$, and $\hat{\lambda}(t) \times t$.

Figure 25.12 Kaplan-Meier Applied to Grouped Complete Data.

The estimated mean time to failure is $\widehat{MTTF} = 2276.4 h$. Confidence interval for the $MTTF$ was estimated using nonparametric bootstrap. The sample used to perform the resampling was composed of a multiset of $TTFs$ in which the midpoint, $\bar{\tau}_i$, of each interval i is repeated r_i, which is the number of failures in the interval i. The original sample from which the resamples are obtained is the multiset $\{672, 840, 1176, 1176, 1344, 1680, 1680, 2184, 2184, 2352, 2352, 2520, 2688, 2856, 2856, 3024, 3192, 3192, 3192, 3360\}$. The estimated confidence interval of the MTTF, considering 95% degree of confidence was $MTTF \in (1844.4 h, 2605.6 h)$.

$\square$

Ungrouped and Complete Data

Consider a complete lifetime data set of devices. Also, assume that the times to failure are exact, which is ungrouped. The analysis of such a data set is a particular case of the Kaplan-Meier method in which $r_i = 1$ and $c_i = 0$ for t_i (see Figure 25.13). Indeed, every t_i is a time to failure since there is no censoring. Therefore, the Equation 25.2.31 becomes

$$n_{i+1} = n_i - 1. \tag{25.2.34}$$

Therefore,

$$\hat{R}(t_i) = \prod_{j=1}^{i} (1 - \frac{1}{n_j}),$$ (25.2.35)

and the other estimate functions remain basically the same but computed, taking into account a new calculation of n_{i+1}. As the data set is complete, the $MTTF$, the variance, the standard deviation, and other statistics may also be calculated.

The other estimate functions remain basically the same but take into account a new calculation of n_{i+1}. As the data set is complete, the $MTTF$, the time to failure variance, the standard deviation, and other statistics may also be calculated from the sample. Nonparametric bootstrap may also be adopted to estimate confidence intervals.

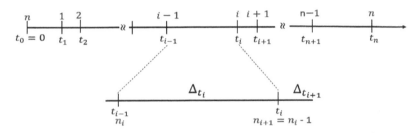

Figure 25.13 Failure Times - Kaplan-Meier Applied to Ungrouped and Complete Data.

Example 25.2.7. Forty eight ($n = 48$) servers were observed in a reliability accelerated test that lasted until all servers failed. The exact time to failure of each server was recorded. Table 25.8 summarizes the conducted reliability analysis. Column t_i) shows i^{th} time to failure. Column n_{i+1} depicts the number of surviving devices at the beginning of the $i+1$ time interval ($\triangle t_{i+1}$). The reliability estimate at t_i, the cumulative time to failure distribution estimate at t_i, the estimate of the time to failure density function at t_i, and the estimate of the failure rate at t_i are presented in the respective columns.
From Table 25.8, the reliability at $2027.21\,h$ is estimated as $\hat{R}(2027.21\,h) = 0.29167$. Likewise, $\hat{F}(2027.21\,h) = 0.70833$, $\hat{f}(2027.21\,h) = 1.565 \times 10^{-3}$ and $\hat{\lambda}(2027.21\,h) = 5.37, \times 10^{-3}$ are estimated. The estimated mean time to failure was $MTTF = 1789.14\,h$. Adopting bootstrap, a confidence interval for the $MTTF$ was estimated. The confidence interval obtained considering 95% degree of confidence was $MTTF \in (1423.72\,h, 2183.88\,h)$. Interpolation may be adopted for estimating the statistics at t_j, for $t_{i-1} < t_j < t_i, i \in \{1, 2, ..., n\}$. Figure 25.14 depicts the reliability function and cumulative distribution function of the time to failure.

□

Table 25.8

Kaplan-Meier - Ungrouped and Complete Data

i	t_i (h)	n_{i+1}	$1 - r_i/n_i$	$\hat{R}(t_i)$	$\hat{F}(t_i)$	$\hat{f}(t_i)$	$\hat{\lambda}(t_i)$
	0	48	1	1	0		
1	30.04	47	0.97917	0.97917	0.02083	0.000694	0.00071
2	245.07	46	0.97872	0.95833	0.04167	0.000097	0.00010
3	305.49	45	0.97826	0.93750	0.06250	0.000345	0.00037
4	357.54	44	0.97778	0.91667	0.08333	0.000400	0.00044
5	446.86	43	0.97727	0.89583	0.10417	0.000233	0.00026
6	462.06	42	0.97674	0.87500	0.12500	0.001371	0.00157
7	521.41	41	0.97619	0.85417	0.14583	0.000351	0.00041
8	522.82	40	0.97561	0.83333	0.16667	0.014775	0.01773
9	525.27	39	0.97500	0.81250	0.18750	0.008503	0.01047
10	525.47	38	0.97436	0.79167	0.20833	0.104167	0.13158
11	533.38	37	0.97368	0.77083	0.22917	0.002634	0.00342
12	614.24	36	0.97297	0.75000	0.25000	0.000258	0.00034
13	682.11	35	0.97222	0.72917	0.27083	0.000307	0.00042
14	706.65	34	0.97143	0.70833	0.29167	0.000849	0.00120
15	728.22	33	0.97059	0.68750	0.31250	0.000966	0.00140
16	776.81	32	0.96970	0.66667	0.33333	0.000429	0.00064
17	983.08	31	0.96875	0.64583	0.35417	0.000101	0.00016
18	1122.82	30	0.96774	0.62500	0.37500	0.000149	0.00024
19	1162.18	29	0.96667	0.60417	0.39583	0.000529	0.00088
20	1240.12	28	0.96552	0.58333	0.41667	0.000267	0.00046
21	1274.35	27	0.96429	0.56250	0.43750	0.000609	0.00108
22	1352.68	26	0.96296	0.54167	0.45833	0.000266	0.00049
23	1400.67	25	0.96154	0.52083	0.47917	0.000434	0.00083
24	1479.84	24	0.96000	0.50000	0.50000	0.000263	0.00053
25	1487.85	23	0.95833	0.47917	0.52083	0.002601	0.00543
26	1570.43	22	0.95652	0.45833	0.54167	0.000252	0.00055
27	1577.28	21	0.95455	0.43750	0.56250	0.003041	0.00695
28	1683.28	20	0.95238	0.41667	0.58333	0.000197	0.00047
29	1701.61	19	0.95000	0.39583	0.60417	0.001137	0.00287
30	1822.66	18	0.94737	0.37500	0.62500	0.000172	0.00046
31	1911.96	17	0.94444	0.35417	0.64583	0.000233	0.00066
32	1958.93	16	0.94118	0.33333	0.66667	0.000444	0.00133
33	2013.9	15	0.93750	0.31250	0.68750	0.000379	0.00121
34	2027.21	14	0.93333	0.29167	0.70833	0.001565	0.00537
35	2113.3	13	0.92857	0.27083	0.72917	0.000242	0.00089
36	2164.79	12	0.92308	0.25000	0.75000	0.000405	0.00162
37	2235.64	11	0.91667	0.22917	0.77083	0.000294	0.00128
38	2487.26	10	0.90909	0.20833	0.79167	0.000083	0.00040
39	2883.53	9	0.90000	0.18750	0.81250	0.000053	0.00028
40	3057.72	8	0.88889	0.16667	0.83333	0.000120	0.00072
41	3305.78	7	0.87500	0.14583	0.85417	0.000084	0.00058
42	3389.78	6	0.85714	0.12500	0.87500	0.000248	0.00198
43	4011.22	5	0.83333	0.10417	0.89583	0.000034	0.00032
44	4138.45	4	0.80000	0.08333	0.91667	0.000164	0.00196
45	4870.55	3	0.75000	0.06250	0.93750	0.000028	0.00046
46	4939.94	2	0.66667	0.04167	0.95833	0.000300	0.00721
47	5047.31	1	0.50000	0.02083	0.97917	0.000194	0.00931
48	5479.37	0	0	0	1	0.000048	

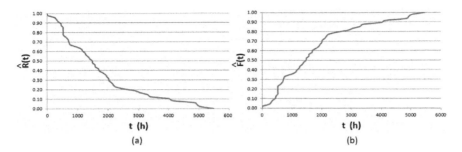

Figure 25.14   Kaplan-Meier Applied to Ungrouped Complete Data - $\hat{R}(t) \times t$ and $\hat{F}(t) \times t$.

Ungrouped and Censored Data

Now, the Kaplan-Meier method is applied to an ungrouped and censored lifetime data set. Such a data set has exact event times. The events may be of two types: failure or censoring. Hence, as the times are exact, that is, are not grouped, in each time interval $\triangle t_i$ either $r_i = 1$ or $c_i = 1$, such that

$$n_{i+1} = n_i - 1.$$

Thus, in time intervals $\triangle t_i$ in which occurs a censoring, the term $1 - r_i/n_i = 1 - 0/n_i = 1$. Therefore,

$$\hat{R}(t_i) = \prod_{j=1}^{i}(1 - \frac{r_i}{n_j}). \qquad (25.2.36)$$

From the above, we have $\hat{R}(t_i) = \hat{R}(t_{i-1}) \times (1 - \frac{r_i}{n_i})$.

Example 25.2.8. Assume that forty eight ($n = 48$) servers were observed in operation. The server may fail (Column $r_1 = 1$) or be censored (Column $c_i = 1$). The exact time of each event (failure or censoring) of each server was recorded. Table 25.9 summarizes the recorded data and reliability analysis. Column t_i) shows i^{th} time to failure. Column n_{i+1} depicts the number of surviving devices at t_{i+1}. The reliability estimate at t_i , the cumulative time to failure distribution estimate at t_i, the estimate of the time to failure density function at t_i, and the estimate of the failure rate at t_i are presented in the respective columns. Column $1 - 1/n_i$ shows the impact on the reliability due to the type of event, failure or censoring, in the interval $\triangle t_i = t_{i+1} - t_i$. It is worth observing that if the event i is a censoring, $1 - 1/n_i = 1$.

Table 25.9
Kaplan-Meier - Ungrouped and Censored Data

i	t_i (h)	r_i	c_i	n_{i+1}	$1 - 1/n_i$	$\hat{R}(t_i)$	$\hat{F}(t_i)$	$\hat{f}(t_i)$	$\hat{\lambda}(t_i)$
0	0			48	1.00000	1.00000	0.00000		
1	1157.5	1	0	47	0.97917	0.97917	0.02083	0.00002	0.00002
2	1582.5	1	0	46	0.97872	0.95833	0.04167	0.00005	0.00005
3	1745.6	1	0	45	0.97826	0.93750	0.06250	0.00013	0.00014
4	2187.7	0	1	45	1.00000	0.93750	0.06250	0.00000	0.00000
5	2534.3	1	0	44	0.97778	0.91667	0.08333	0.00006	0.00007
6	2671	1	0	43	0.97727	0.89583	0.10417	0.00015	0.00017
7	2735.5	0	1	43	1.00000	0.89583	0.10417	0.00000	0.00000
8	2773.3	0	1	43	1.00000	0.89583	0.10417	0.00000	0.00000
9	2952.1	1	0	42	0.97674	0.87500	0.12500	0.00012	0.00013
10	3288.7	1	0	41	0.97619	0.85417	0.14583	0.00006	0.00007
11	3501	1	0	40	0.97561	0.83333	0.16667	0.00010	0.00012
12	3820.8	0	1	40	1.00000	0.83333	0.16667	0.00000	0.00000
13	3988.7	0	1	40	1.00000	0.83333	0.16667	0.00000	0.00000
14	4109.6	0	1	40	1.00000	0.83333	0.16667	0.00000	0.00000
15	4335.3	1	0	39	0.97500	0.81250	0.18750	0.00009	0.00011
16	4657	1	0	38	0.97436	0.79167	0.20833	0.00006	0.00008
17	4870.3	1	0	37	0.97368	0.77083	0.22917	0.00010	0.00013
18	4968	1	0	36	0.97297	0.75000	0.25000	0.00021	0.00028
19	4968.3	1	0	35	0.97222	0.72917	0.27083	0.06944	0.09524
20	5015.3	1	0	34	0.97143	0.70833	0.29167	0.00044	0.00063
21	5191.6	1	0	33	0.97059	0.68750	0.31250	0.00012	0.00017
22	5199.9	1	0	32	0.96970	0.66667	0.33333	0.00251	0.00377
23	5223.1	0	1	32	1.00000	0.66667	0.33333	0.00000	0.00000
24	5440.7	1	0	31	0.96875	0.64583	0.35417	0.00010	0.00015
25	5445.8	1	0	30	0.96774	0.62500	0.37500	0.00408	0.00654
26	5662.6	1	0	29	0.96667	0.60417	0.39583	0.00010	0.00016
27	5729.9	0	1	29	1.00000	0.60417	0.39583	0.00000	0.00000
28	6126.4	1	0	28	0.96552	0.58333	0.41667	0.00005	0.00009
29	6270.5	1	0	27	0.96429	0.56250	0.43750	0.00014	0.00026
30	6307.3	1	0	26	0.96296	0.54167	0.45833	0.00057	0.00105
31	6332.9	0	1	26	1.00000	0.54167	0.45833	0.00000	0.00000
32	6396.2	1	0	25	0.96154	0.52083	0.47917	0.00033	0.00063
33	6477.2	1	0	24	0.96000	0.50000	0.50000	0.00026	0.00051
34	6617.3	1	0	23	0.95833	0.47917	0.52083	0.00015	0.00031
35	6711.5	0	1	23	1.00000	0.47917	0.52083	0.00000	0.00000
36	7497.2	1	0	22	0.95652	0.45833	0.54167	0.00003	0.00006
37	8005.1	1	0	21	0.95455	0.43750	0.56250	0.00004	0.00009
38	8239.7	1	0	20	0.95238	0.41667	0.58333	0.00009	0.00021
39	8380.4	1	0	19	0.95000	0.39583	0.60417	0.00015	0.00037
40	8456.7	1	0	18	0.94737	0.37500	0.62500	0.00027	0.00073
41	9071.2	0	1	18	1.00000	0.37500	0.62500	0.00000	0.00000
42	10272.1	0	1	18	1.00000	0.37500	0.62500	0.00000	0.00000
43	10559.1	1	0	17	0.94444	0.35417	0.64583	0.00007	0.00020
44	10894.1	1	0	16	0.94118	0.33333	0.66667	0.00006	0.00019
45	12015.9	1	0	15	0.93750	0.31250	0.68750	0.00002	0.00006
46	12084	1	0	14	0.93333	0.29167	0.70833	0.00031	0.00105
47	12540.9	1	0	13	0.92857	0.27083	0.72917	0.00005	0.00017
48	15183.3	1	0	12	0.92308	0.25000	0.75000	0.00001	0.00003

From Table 25.9, we have, for instance, the reliability estimate at $t_i = 3501\,h$, that is $\hat{R}(3501\,h) = 0.8333$. Interpolation may be adopted for estimating the statistics at t_j, for $t_{i-1} < t_j < t_i$, $i \in \{1, 2, ..., n\}$. As the data set is censored, the formulas for computing $MTTF$ and standard deviation are not valid since the respective values would be too pessimistic. Figure 25.15 depicts the graphs $\hat{R}(t) \times t$ and $\hat{F}(t) \times t$.

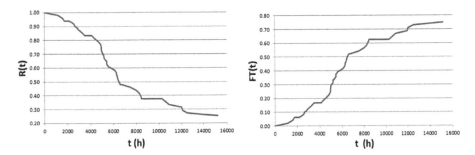

Figure 25.15   Kaplan-Meier Applied to Ungrouped and Censored Data - $\hat{R}(t) \times t$ and $\hat{F}(t) \times t$.

☐

There are other nonparametric methods for reliability data analysis such as the Actuarial Simple and Standard methods [88]. The interested readers are referred to [88, 115, 229].

25.3   PARAMETRIC METHODS

The last section introduced some fundamental nonparametric strategies for lifetime data analysis. Now, theoretical distributions are adopted for evaluating reliability and other related metrics based on collected lifetime data. Therefore, estimating the distribution parameters is a decisive activity for accomplishing such a task.

This section introduces three main strategies for estimating probability distribution parameters:

- Graphical methods (Section 25.3.1),

- Methods based on moments (Section 25.3.2), and

- Maximum likelihood methods (Section 25.3.3).

The general process for estimating distribution parameters for reliability data analysis consists of the following:

1. Carry out an exploratory data analysis (see Chapter 3) and rule out distributions that clearly do not hold the attributes of the data set. For instance, check the data statistics of centrality, variability, skewness, flatness, percentiles, moments, failure rate (see Section 16.2 and Section 25.2) as well as construct graphs such as histograms, dot-plots, box-plots, and cumulative empirical distributions and compare with the respective measures and graphs of the candidate theoretical distributions. Those distributions that are not rejected in this preliminary analysis are considered for the next two steps.

2. Estimate the theoretical distribution parameters using one of those strategies depicted above, and

3. Perform goodness of fit, aiming at finding evidence to reject the theoretical distribution as a good fit to the empirical data (see Section 6.6).

25.3.1 GRAPHICAL METHODS

This section introduces a set of specific graphical methods adopted to estimate parameters of probability distributions. These methods are mainly presented for specific probability distributions. Nevertheless, such a strategy may also be applied to other probability distributions not covered in this section.

Exponential Distribution

Let us first adopt the graphical method for estimating the parameter (λ) of an exponential distribution. Consider T a random variable exponentially distributed random with parameter λ representing the time to failure of a specific class of devices. Assume a time to failure sample of size n was collected from a population that follows an exponential distribution with parameter λ; and sort the sample in ascending order such that $S = \{t_1, t_2, ..., t_i, ... t_n\}$, where $t_1 < t_2 < ... < t_i < ... < t_n$.

The cumulative distribution function of T is

$$F(t) = 1 - e^{-\lambda t},$$

where $t \leq 0$, and $\lambda \in \mathbb{R}$. From the equation above we obtain

$$e^{-\lambda t} = 1 - F(t).$$

Applying the natural logarithm to both sides of the above expression, we get

$$-\lambda t \ln(e) = \ln(1 - F(t))$$

$$\lambda t \ln(e) = -\ln(1 - F(t)).$$

Since $\ln(e) = 1$ and $ln(a/b) = ln(a) - ln(b)$, and if $a = 1$, then $ln(a) - ln(b) = -ln(b) = ln(1/b)$, then

$$\lambda t = ln\left(\frac{1}{1 - F(t)}\right). \tag{25.3.1}$$

Now plot the graph

$$\left(t_i, ln\left(\frac{1}{1-F(t_i)}\right)\right), \forall t_i \in S.$$

Hence, since the straight-line equation is defined as $y = ax + b$, where a is the angular coefficient, and b is the linear coefficient (also called the intercept), we have from the above equation

$$ln\left(\frac{1}{1-F(t)}\right) = \lambda t,$$

where, $a = \lambda$ and $b = 0$. An estimate of a and b may be obtained by applying linear regression (see Section 6.7.1) using the dots plotted, such that $\hat{a}$ and $\hat{b}$ are estimates of a and b, respectively. Thus,

$$y = \hat{a}t + \hat{b}. \tag{25.3.2}$$

If $\lambda = 1$, then $MTTF = E(T) = 1/1 = 1$. Hence, a $F(t) = 1 - e^{-\lambda t}$, then $F(MTTF) = F(1) = 1 - e^{-11} = 0.63212$. Therefore, using the Equation 25.3.2 (obtained using linear regression), we get

$$\hat{\lambda} = \hat{a}. \tag{25.3.3}$$

It is expected that $\hat{b} \approx 0$, and the correlation coefficient (obtained in the linear regression) $r^2 \to 1$.

Example 25.3.1. Assume fifty routers ($n = 50$) were observed in an accelerated reliability test. The test finished when all routers failed. The times each router failed were recorded in ascending order. The times to failure are depicted in Table 25.10. According to the process introduced at the beginning of this section, the first step to be carried out is an exploratory analysis.

The exploratory analysis of the reliability data set depicted in Table 25.10 is summarized in Table 25.11 and through the graphs presented in Figure 25.17. The histogram, the box plot is shown in Figure 25.16, and the skewness statistics clearly show a data set with a long right tail. The standard deviation and the mean are close; hence, the coefficient of variance is close to one. The histogram and the kurtosis also confirm a leptokurtic data sample. All this evidence does not allow us to reject the exponential distribution as a suitable probability distribution to represent this data set.

The next steps are estimating the distribution parameter, and, then, performing goodness of fit. Figure 25.17 depicts the graph $\left(t_i, ln\left(\frac{1}{1-F(t_i)}\right)\right), \forall t_i \in S, |S| = 50$. Applying a linear regression, we get

$$g(t) = 9.41 \times 10^{-4} t + 0.0702,$$

Table 25.10

Accelerated Reliability Test - Graphical Method - Exponential Distribution

i	t_i (h)	$ln(1/(1-F(t_i)))$	i	t_i (h)	$ln(1/(1-F(t_i)))$
1	55.13	0.0198	26	589.74	0.7129
2	60.30	0.0400	27	607.52	0.7538
3	67.72	0.0606	28	662.78	0.7963
4	79.26	0.0817	29	687.83	0.8408
5	85.23	0.1032	30	705.79	0.8873
6	136.80	0.1252	31	767.32	0.9361
7	224.48	0.1476	32	896.23	0.9874
8	247.39	0.1706	33	938.90	1.0415
9	248.97	0.1942	34	975.09	1.0986
10	279.49	0.2183	35	1018.11	1.1592
11	313.73	0.2429	36	1199.00	1.2238
12	316.06	0.2683	37	1393.77	1.2928
13	329.03	0.2942	38	1532.19	1.3669
14	331.67	0.3209	39	1533.68	1.4469
15	339.86	0.3483	40	1538.12	1.5339
16	343.51	0.3765	41	1659.30	1.6292
17	350.85	0.4055	42	1839.23	1.7346
18	385.08	0.4353	43	2015.29	1.8524
19	413.06	0.4661	44	2039.53	1.9859
20	437.54	0.4978	45	2069.30	2.1401
21	451.11	0.5306	46	2097.77	2.3224
22	489.88	0.5645	47	2347.56	2.5455
23	520.41	0.5996	48	2676.02	2.8332
24	526.72	0.6360	49	3884.70	3.2387
25	548.65	0.6737	50	4166.57	3.9318

$g(t) = 1/(1 - F(t))$ and $r^2 = 0.9794$. Therefore, using Equation 25.3.3, we obtain

$$\hat{\lambda} = \hat{a} = 9.41 \times 10^{-4} h^{-1},$$

and

$$\widehat{MTTF} = \frac{1}{\hat{\lambda}} = \frac{1}{9.41 \times 10^{-4} h^{-1}} = 1063.2 h.$$

Using $\hat{\lambda} = 9.41 \times 10^{-4} h^{-1}$, we conduct a graphical goodness of fit (see Figure 25.18), where we obtain

$$y = \alpha t + \beta = 0.9595t - 0.006,$$

Table 25.11

Statistical Summary - Reliability Data Set

Sample Size, n	50
Mean	948.47
Median	569.2
Variance	875297.39
Standard Deviation	935.57
Skewness	1.7072
Kurtosis	3.0554
Range	4111.5
Coefficient of Variance	0.9864
Minimum	55.1
1st Quartile	329
3rd Quartile	1532.2
Maximum	4166.6

and

$$r^2 = 0.9782,$$

from which we observed that $\hat{\alpha} = 0.9596$, and $\hat{\beta} = -0.006$; hence, the linear regression provided an angular coefficient that approaches one and the intercept is close to zero. Besides, the linear correlation coefficient is also close to 1. Besides, we applied the KS goodness of fit. The calculated $D_{calc} = 0.115$ and the $D_{critical,0.05} = 0.1921$. As $D_{calc} < D_{critical,0.05}$ the KS goodness of fit test fails to reject the exponential distribution with $\lambda = 9.41 \times 10^{-4} h^{-1}$ as suitable distribution to represent the reliability data set with 95% degree of confidence.

$\square$

Normal Distribution

Consider T a random variable normally distributed with parameters μ and σ representing the time to failure of a class of devices. Assume a time to failure sample of size n was collected from a population that follows a normally distributions with parameter μ and σ, and sort the sample in ascending order such that $S = \{t_1, t_2, ..., t_i, ... t_n\}$, where $t_1 < t_2 < ... < t_i < ... < t_n$.

The first step in this process consists of normalizing the times to failure of the sample S, that is, generating another ordered list $S_N = \{z_1, z_2, ..., z_i, ... z_n\}$, where

$$z_i = \frac{t_i - \mu}{\sigma} = \frac{t_i}{\sigma} - \frac{\mu}{\sigma}.$$

Now plot the points (t_i, z_i), $\forall i$. If the data is normally distributed, the plot would present a linear correlation between the two data sets. Applying a linear regression,

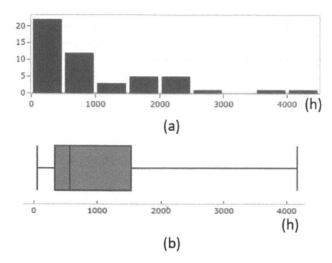

Figure 25.16   Histogram and BoxPlot - Reliability Data Set.

we get $y = \hat{\alpha}x + \hat{\beta}$, we have the intercept

$$\hat{\beta} = -\frac{\mu}{\sigma}$$

and the angular coefficient

$$\hat{\alpha} = \frac{1}{\sigma}.$$

Therefore, the estimates of σ and μ are

$$\hat{\sigma} = \frac{1}{\hat{\alpha}} \qquad (25.3.4)$$

and

$$\hat{\mu} = -\hat{\beta} \times \hat{\sigma}. \qquad (25.3.5)$$

Example 25.3.2. Consider fifty servers ($n = 50$) were observed in an accelerated reliability test. The test finished when all servers failed. The times each server failed is depicted in Table 25.12 in ascending order. The first step is to perform exploratory analysis.

The exploratory analysis statistics are summarized in Table 25.13 and Figure 25.19. The histogram, the box plot, the skewness and the kurtosis are somewhat similar to data that comes from normally distributed population. The mean and the median are

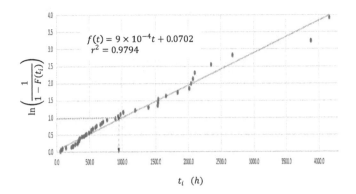

Figure 25.17 $ln\left(\frac{1}{1-F(t_i)}\right) \times t_i$ - Parameter Estimation.

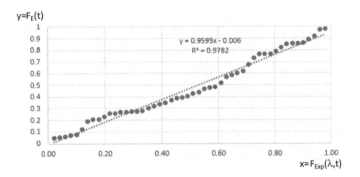

Figure 25.18 $F_E(t) \times F_{Exp}(t)$ - Graphical Goodness of Fit.

also close. 70% of the data is between $(\mu - \sigma, \mu + \sigma)) = (847.71, 1256.16)$, 96% of the data is between $(\mu - 2\sigma, \mu + 2\sigma)) = (643.47, 1460.38)$. Besides, if a data set is normally distributed $IIQ \approx (4/3) \times SD$. As $IIQ = 276$ and $(4/3) \times 204.22 = 272.30$, which are characteristics similar to normal distributions. All this evidence does allow us to reject the normal distribution as suitable to represent the data set.

The next steps are estimating the distribution parameter, and, then, performing goodness of fit. Figure 25.20 depicts the plot (t_i, z_i), $\forall t_i \in S$, $|S| = 50$.
Applying a linear regression, we get

$$g(t) = 4.9 \times 10^{-3}t - 5.1509,$$

Table 25.12

Accelerated Reliability Test - Graphical Method - Normal Distribution

i	t_i	z_i	i	t_i	z_i
1	636.48	-2.03	26	1092.69	0.20
2	655.59	-1.94	27	1109.97	0.28
3	686.07	-1.79	28	1113.08	0.30
4	724.69	-1.60	29	1121.29	0.34
5	766.42	-1.40	30	1140.09	0.43
6	777.75	-1.34	31	1140.22	0.43
7	777.98	-1.34	32	1152.21	0.49
8	797.59	-1.25	33	1158.12	0.52
9	809.10	-1.19	34	1159.89	0.53
10	847.18	-1.00	35	1177.00	0.61
11	859.46	-0.94	36	1180.88	0.63
12	867.44	-0.90	37	1185.52	0.65
13	913.13	-0.68	38	1189.06	0.67
14	932.18	-0.59	39	1196.93	0.71
15	939.88	-0.55	40	1201.42	0.73
16	946.88	-0.51	41	1204.95	0.75
17	968.99	-0.41	42	1217.67	0.81
18	990.92	-0.30	43	1224.61	0.85
19	1005.05	-0.23	44	1240.62	0.92
20	1009.45	-0.21	45	1247.78	0.96
21	1019.82	-0.16	46	1324.45	1.33
22	1049.60	-0.01	47	1334.81	1.39
23	1065.90	0.07	48	1335.96	1.39
24	1070.28	0.09	49	1455.52	1.98
25	1070.53	0.09	50	1503.57	2.21

As

$$\hat{\sigma} = \frac{1}{\hat{\alpha}} = \frac{1}{4.9 \times 10^{-3}} = 204.22$$

and

$$\hat{\mu} = -\hat{\beta} \times \hat{\sigma} = -(-5.1509) \times 204.22 = 1051.93.$$

We apply the KS goodness of fit. The calculated $D_{calc} = 0.092$ and the $D_{critical,0.05} = 0.1921$. As $D_{calc} < D_{critical,0.05}$ the KS test fails to reject the normal distribution with $\mu = 1051.93\,h$ and $\sigma = 204.22\,h$ as suitable distribution to represent the reliability data set with 95% degree of confidence.

□

Table 25.13
Statistical Summary - Exploratory Analysis

Sample Size, n	50
Mean	1051.96
Median	1082.00
Variance	41735.67
Standard Deviation	204.29
Skewness	-0.18
Kurtosis	-0.42
Range	868.00
Coefficient of Variance	0.1942
Minimum	636.00
1st Quartile	913.00
3rd Quartile	1189.00
Maximum	1504.00

Weibull Distribution

Assume T a random variable distributed according to a Weibull distribution with parameters β (scale)) and α (shape) representing the time to failure of class of components. Consider a time to failure ordered sample of size n was obtained from a population that follows a Weibull distribution , $S = \{t_1, t_2, ..., t_i, ... t_n\}$, such that $t_1 < t_2 < ... < t_i < ... < t_n$.

The cumulative distribution function of T is

$$F(t) = 1 - e^{-(\frac{t}{\beta})^\alpha},$$

where $t \leq 0$, $\beta \leq 0$ and $\alpha > 0$. From the equation above we obtain

$$1 - F(t) = e^{-(\frac{t}{\beta})^\alpha},$$

then

$$\ln(1 - F(t)) = \ln(e^{-(\frac{t}{\beta})^\alpha}),$$

$$\ln(1 - F(t)) = -\left(\frac{t}{\beta}\right)^\alpha \ln(e),$$

$$-\ln(1 - F(t)) = \left(\frac{t}{\beta}\right)^\alpha,$$

$$\ln(1) - \ln(1 - F(t)) = \left(\frac{t}{\beta}\right)^\alpha,$$

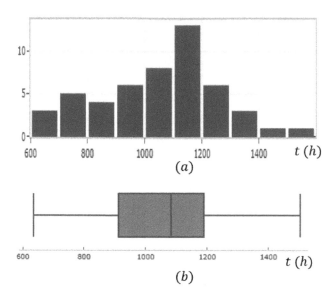

Figure 25.19   Histogram and BoxPlot - Lifetime Data Set.

$$-\ln\left(\frac{1}{1-F(t)}\right) = \left(\frac{t}{\beta}\right)^{\alpha},$$

$$\ln\left(\frac{1}{1-F(t)}\right) = -\left(\frac{t}{\beta}\right)^{\alpha},$$

$$\ln(\ln\left(\frac{1}{1-F(t)}\right)) = \ln\left(-\frac{t}{\beta}\right)^{\alpha},$$

$$\ln(\ln\left(\frac{1}{1-F(t)}\right)) = \alpha\ln\left(\frac{t}{\beta}\right),$$

$$\alpha\ln\left(\frac{t}{\beta}\right) = \ln(\ln\left(\frac{1}{1-F(t)}\right)),$$

$$\alpha(\ln(t) - \ln(\beta)) = \ln(\ln\left(\frac{1}{1-F(t)}\right))$$

and

$$\alpha\ln(t) - \alpha\ln(\beta)) = \ln(\ln\left(\frac{1}{1-F(t)}\right)).$$

Considering the straight line equation $at + b = y$, we have

$$a = \alpha,$$

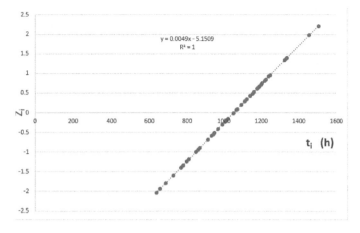

Figure 25.20 $z_i \times t_i$ - Parameter Estimation.

and

$$b = -\alpha \ln(\beta).$$

Therefore

$$\hat{\alpha} = \hat{a}, \tag{25.3.6}$$

and

$$-\frac{b}{\alpha} = \ln(\beta),$$

$$e^{-\frac{b}{\alpha}} = e^{\ln(\beta)};$$

thus,

$$\beta = e^{-\frac{b}{\alpha}}.$$

Therefore

$$\hat{\beta} = e^{-\frac{\hat{b}}{\hat{\alpha}}}. \tag{25.3.7}$$

Example 25.3.3. Let us consider fifty switches ($n = 50$) were observed in an acceler-ated reliability test. The test ended when all switches failed. The times each switches failed is shown in Table 25.14. The times to failure are presented in ascending order. Table 25.14 also depicts $\ln(t_i)$, $F(t_i)$ and $\ln(\ln(1/(1 - F(t_i)))$.

The exploratory analysis statistics are summarized in Table 25.15 and Figure 25.21. The histogram, the box plot, the skewness, and the kurtosis show a long right tail

Table 25.14

Accelerated Reliability Test - Graphical Method - Weibull Distribution

i	t_i	ln ti	$F(t_i)$	$\ln(\ln(1/(1-F(t_i))))$	i	t_i	ln ti	$F(t_i)$	$\ln(\ln(1/(1-F(t_i))))$
1	3.28×10^{-4}	-8.02	0.02	-3.92	26	910.58	6.81	0.51	-0.34
2	0.12	-2.11	0.04	-3.22	27	1090.43	6.99	0.53	-0.28
3	1.56	0.45	0.06	-2.80	28	1164.06	7.06	0.55	-0.23
4	2.47	0.90	0.08	-2.50	29	1419.43	7.26	0.57	-0.17
5	6.22	1.83	0.10	-2.27	30	1671.05	7.42	0.59	-0.12
6	8.59	2.15	0.12	-2.08	31	1855.10	7.53	0.61	-0.07
7	9.61	2.26	0.14	-1.91	32	2697.31	7.90	0.63	-0.01
8	17.21	2.85	0.16	-1.77	33	2897.99	7.97	0.65	0.04
9	24.65	3.20	0.18	-1.64	34	3456.24	8.15	0.67	0.09
10	49.36	3.90	0.20	-1.52	35	3499.52	8.16	0.69	0.15
11	76.59	4.34	0.22	-1.41	36	3782.63	8.24	0.71	0.20
12	95.13	4.56	0.24	-1.32	37	4992.07	8.52	0.73	0.26
13	121.50	4.80	0.25	-1.22	38	6044.74	8.71	0.75	0.31
14	147.24	4.99	0.27	-1.14	39	6740.84	8.82	0.76	0.37
15	151.17	5.02	0.29	-1.05	40	7202.70	8.88	0.78	0.43
16	213.86	5.37	0.31	-0.98	41	7909.20	8.98	0.80	0.49
17	235.65	5.46	0.33	-0.90	42	19703.65	9.89	0.82	0.55
18	248.85	5.52	0.35	-0.83	43	21868.86	9.99	0.84	0.62
19	262.00	5.57	0.37	-0.76	44	23635.18	10.07	0.86	0.69
20	286.72	5.66	0.39	-0.70	45	23962.06	10.08	0.88	0.76
21	363.96	5.90	0.41	-0.63	46	45766.82	10.73	0.90	0.84
22	390.03	5.97	0.43	-0.57	47	66616.55	11.11	0.92	0.93
23	522.95	6.26	0.45	-0.51	48	94174.38	11.45	0.94	1.04
24	593.85	6.39	0.47	-0.45	49	95334.56	11.47	0.96	1.18
25	634.55	6.45	0.49	-0.39	50	143343.92	11.87	0.98	1.37

and a highly concentrated time to failure on the left-hand side of the distribution. The coefficient of variance of 2.40 stresses that the long right tail is larger than an exponential distribution. The mean and the median also confirm the right-skewness of the data distribution. The first and third quartiles also ratify such a feature. All these features show time to failure distribution concentrated on low values; that is, the populations seem to be prone to early failure. A Weibull distribution with a shape parameter in this range $0 < \alpha < 1$ may be suitable for representing the devices' lifetime.

The next steps are estimating the distribution parameter, and, then, performing goodness of fit. Figure 25.22 depicts the plot for the set of dots $(\ln(t_i)$, $\ln(\ln(1/(1-F(t_i))))$, $\forall t_i \in S$. Applying a linear regression, we obtain $y = 0.3118x - 2.5046$ and $r^2 = 0.9668$. The correlation coefficient stresses the fit of the dots to the straight line model, where $\hat{a} = 0.3118$ and $b = -2.5046$.

Therefore,

$$\hat{\alpha} = \hat{a} = 0.3118,$$

and

$$\hat{\beta} = e^{-\frac{b}{\hat{a}}} = e^{-\frac{2.5046}{0.3118}} = 3081.89.$$

Table 25.15
Statistical Summary

Sample Size, n	50
Mean	11924.07
Median	772.57
Variance	820740348.76
Standard Deviation	28648.57
Skewness	3.22
Kurtosis	10.62
Range	143343.92
Coefficient of Variance	2.40
Minimum	0.0003
1st **Quartile**	114.90
3rd **Quartile**	6218.77
Maximum	143343.92

The last step is applying goodness of fit. In this case, again, we adopted the KS method. The calculated $D_{calc} = 0.081$ and the $D_{critical,0.05} = 0.1921$. As $D_{calc} < D_{critical,0.05}$ the KS test fails to reject the Weibull distribution with $\alpha = 0.3118\,h$ and $\beta = 3081.89\,h$ as suitable distribution to represent the reliability data set with 95% degree of confidence.

$\square$

Although the reasoning behind the graphical method is simple, the process, in some cases, could be quite laborious. Besides, the linearization process adopted to estimate the distribution parameters may not always be possible. The interested reader is referred to [232, 269] for the application of graphical methods to other distributions.

25.3.2   METHOD OF MOMENTS

This section introduces the method of moments to estimate parameters of probability distributions. Let us assume $\mu_k = E(X^k)$ is the kth moment about the origin of a random variable X, if it exists, and consider $m_k = (\sum_{i=1}^{n} x_i^k)/n$ as the kth moment about the origin of a data sample.

The method of moments is based on matching the sample moments with the corresponding distribution moments. This method equates as many moments as the number of distribution parameters to be estimated and then solves the equation system for the distribution parameters. The process of estimating the distribution parameters ($\Theta = \{\theta_1, \theta_2, ...\theta_q\}$) may be summarized in the following steps:

1. Find the algebraic expressions of the q moments, $\mu_1, \mu_2, ...\mu_q$, of the theoretical distribution with q parameters.

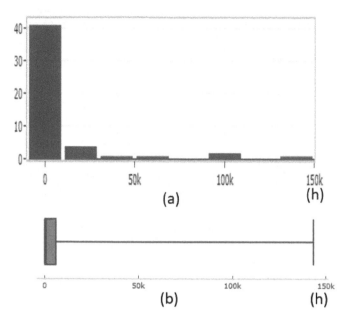

Figure 25.21   Histogram and BoxPlot.

2. Find the q moments, $m_1, m_2, ...m_q$, of the sample.

3. Solve the system of equations $\mu_1 = m_1$, $\mu_2 = m_2$, ..., $\mu_q = m_q$ for the parameters $\theta_1, \theta_2, ...\theta_q$.

The result of this process provides $\hat{\theta}_1$, $\hat{\theta}_2$, ..., $\hat{\theta}_q$ as estimates of θ_1, θ_2, ..., θ_q.

Bernoulli Distribution

Assume X is a random variable distributed according to a Bernoulli distribution with parameters p. As the Bernoulli distribution has only one parameter, we need only one moment. The Bernoulli first moment about the origin is $\mu_1 = p$, and the sample first moment is given by $(\sum_{i=1}^{n} x_i)/n$, where n is the sample size. Hence

$$\hat{p} = \frac{\sum_{i=1}^{n} x_i}{n}. \tag{25.3.8}$$

Example 25.3.4. Assume a test was carried out in one hundred similar and independent devices. After the test, each device is either in an operational state ($x_i = 1$) or in failure ($x_i = 0$). This sort of random experiment with only two results is represented by a Bernoulli distribution. Table 25.16 shows the test results for each device i. Applying Equation 25.3.8, we get $\hat{p} = (\sum_{i=1}^{50} x_i)/50 = 44/50 = 0.88$.

□

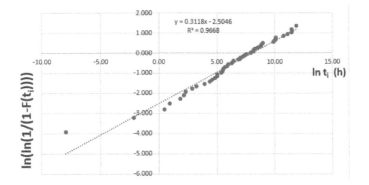

Figure 25.22 $\ln(t_i) \times \ln(\ln(1/(1 - F(t_i))))$- Parameter Estimation.

Table 25.16
Test Result - Fifty Devices - Success: 1 Failure:0

i	x_i	i	x_i	i	x_i	i	x_i	i	x_i
1	0	11	1	21	1	31	1	41	1
2	1	12	0	22	1	32	1	42	1
3	0	13	1	23	1	33	1	43	1
4	0	14	1	24	1	34	1	44	1
5	0	15	1	25	1	35	1	45	1
6	1	16	1	26	1	36	1	46	1
7	1	17	1	27	1	37	1	47	1
8	1	18	1	28	1	38	1	48	0
9	1	19	1	29	1	39	1	49	1
10	1	20	1	30	1	40	1	50	1

Normal Distribution

Assume T is a random variable normally distributed random variable with parameters μ and σ that specifies the time to failure of a class of computers. Assume a time to failure sample of size n was collected from a population distributed according to T. As the normal distribution has two parameters, the expressions of the first two moments about the origin should first be obtained. These moments could be derived from the normal moment generating function:

$$M_T(t) = e^{\frac{\sigma^2 t^2}{2} + \mu t}. \tag{25.3.9}$$

Taking the first derivative of $M_T(t)$ in relation to t, we obtain

$$\frac{dM_T(t)}{dt} = e^{\frac{\sigma^2 t^2}{2} + \mu t} \left(\mu + \sigma^2 t\right);$$

then for $t = 0$, we get

$$\mu_1 = \mu.$$

Now, calculating the second derivative of $M_T(t)$ for t, we obtain

$$\frac{d^2 M_T(t)}{dt^2} = e^{\frac{\sigma^2 t^2}{2} + \mu t} \left(\mu^2 + \sigma^2 + \sigma^4 t^2 + 2\mu\sigma^2 t \right);$$

then for $t = 0$, we get

$$\mu_2 = \mu^2 + \sigma^2.$$

Now consider a sample of size n obtained from a population normally distributed. Obtain the first two moments about the origin

$$m_1 = \frac{\sum_{i=1}^{n} x_i}{n}$$

and

$$m_2 = \frac{\sum_{i=1}^{n} x_i^2}{n}.$$

Then, since $\mu_1 = \mu$ and $\mu_2 = \mu^2 + \sigma^2$, we obtain

$$\hat{\mu} = m_1 \tag{25.3.10}$$

and from

$$\mu_2 = \mu^2 + \sigma^2 = m_2,$$

we get

$$\hat{\sigma} = \sqrt{m_2 - \hat{\mu}^2}. \tag{25.3.11}$$

Example 25.3.5. Consider one hundred mobile phones ($n = 100$) were observed in an accelerated reliability test. The test finished when all devices failed. The times each cell phone failed is depicted in Columns (X_i) of Table 25.17. According to the methodology introduced at the beginning of the section, the first step consists of performing the exploratory analysis. The exploratory analysis did not reject the normal distribution (not shown here). Then, the next step is estimating the normal distribution parameters, μ, and σ, and adopting the method of moments presented.

From Columns (X_i) of Table 25.17, we get

$$m_1 = \frac{\sum_{i=1}^{100} x_i}{100} = \frac{203944.39}{100} = 2039.44 \, h.$$

Likewise, from Columns (X_i^2) of Table 25.17, we obtain

$$m_2 = \frac{\sum_{i=1}^{100} x_i^2}{100} = \frac{433335291.14}{100} = 4333352.91 \, h^2.$$

Table 25.17

Reliability Data - Method of Moments - Normal Distribution

i	X (h)	X^2 (h^2)	X (h)	X^2 (h^2)	X (h)	X^2 (h^2)	X (h)	X^2 (h^2)	X (h)	X^2 (h^2)
1	1932.41	3734196.07	2779.88	7727757.45	2000.63	4002510.60	2278.45	5191355.07	1751.54	3067892.88
2	2543.30	6468385.68	1343.91	1806080.85	1735.15	3010741.28	1726.79	2981786.65	1955.83	3825279.63
3	1989.76	3959159.33	2625.11	6891194.33	1779.09	3165176.16	2897.16	8393547.39	1742.95	3037863.49
4	1370.60	1878550.89	2165.88	4691028.34	2355.40	5547885.88	2338.33	5467766.90	2587.04	6692750.99
5	2534.88	6425613.02	2085.70	4350155.32	1775.38	3151968.66	2268.75	5147227.59	2102.09	4418787.56
6	2381.49	5671504.62	1778.45	3162893.46	1927.19	3714047.07	2286.86	5229729.05	1775.92	3153874.29
7	2229.08	4968789.04	1376.75	1895447.13	2267.41	5141146.44	2071.94	4292947.17	1910.91	3651589.16
8	1889.29	3569401.01	2151.97	4630975.73	2284.85	5220519.21	2365.82	5597120.01	1502.08	2256235.66
9	1234.54	1524098.38	1263.58	1596639.82	2203.85	4856967.07	2479.97	6150239.49	1952.44	3812037.13
10	2150.00	4622493.18	1897.31	3599777.81	2308.12	5327440.93	1761.41	3102566.72	2241.34	5023590.17
11	1628.61	2652369.42	1823.22	3324136.69	2681.86	7192368.19	2329.27	5425485.20	2162.98	4678486.79
12	1106.21	1223709.61	1641.32	2693945.76	1889.73	3571083.42	1810.38	3277460.58	1247.32	1555808.12
13	2760.74	7621672.92	2821.84	7962767.45	2573.71	6623979.34	2044.85	4181392.57	2138.76	4574308.99
14	2641.28	6976365.72	1478.01	2184508.38	1499.95	2249835.79	2433.91	5923908.63	2000.44	4001775.53
15	1688.82	2852113.08	2844.03	8088481.81	2376.46	5647557.17	1752.25	3070362.55	2373.51	5633573.09
16	1431.29	2048604.75	2526.76	6384517.27	2053.29	4216012.99	1937.59	3754235.70	2212.79	4896435.24
17	1630.21	2657576.95	1220.12	1488682.00	1586.37	2516555.33	2469.75	6099680.39	1657.15	2746129.73
18	1681.18	2826379.33	2077.11	4314392.22	1654.62	2737768.33	2371.86	5625726.79	2335.36	5453905.40
19	1995.67	3982698.33	2685.95	7214337.17	2059.20	4240287.45	1795.31	3223139.74	2421.60	5864163.73
20	2336.49	5459191.18	2601.33	6766911.49	1968.53	3875098.30	1390.10	1932383.43	1736.75	3016289.30
j	1	1	2	2	3	3	4	4	5	5

Adopting Equation 25.3.10 and 25.3.11, the normal distribution parameters are estimated:

$$\hat{\mu} = m_1 = 2039.44\,h$$

and

$$\hat{\sigma} = \sqrt{m_2 - \hat{\mu}^2} = \sqrt{4333352.91 - 2039.44^2} = 417.16\,h.$$

Applying the KS goodness of fit, we obtain $D_{cal} = 0.054$ and the $D_{critical,5\%} = 0.1358$. As $D_{cal} < D_{critical,5\%}$, the test fails to reject the normal distribution with parameters $\mu = 2039.44\,h$ and $\sigma = 417.16\,h$ as suitable distribution to represent the mobile phones' lifetime data with 95% degree of confidence.

□

Uniform Distribution

Let T be a random variable uniformly distributed with parameters a and b that specify the time to failure of a specific system class. The times to failure of a sample of size n were collected from a population distributed according to T. As the uniform distribution has two parameters, the expressions of the first two moments about the origin should be obtained. These moments could be obtained from the uniform moment generating function, but they are readily available:

$$\mu_1 = \frac{a+b}{2}. \tag{25.3.12}$$

$$\mu_2 = \frac{1}{3}\left(a^2 + ab + b^2\right). \tag{25.3.13}$$

Using the time to failure sample, obtain the first two data moments about the origin

$$m_1 = \frac{\sum_{i=1}^{n} x_i}{n}$$

and

$$m_2 = \frac{\sum_{i=1}^{n} x_i^2}{n}.$$

As

$$\mu_1 = \frac{a+b}{2} = m_1$$

and

$$\mu_2 = \frac{1}{3}\left(a^2 + ab + b^2\right) = m_2,$$

we get

$$\hat{a} = \hat{m}_1 - \sqrt{3}\sqrt{\hat{m}_2 - \hat{m}_1{}^2} \tag{25.3.14}$$

and

$$\hat{b} = \hat{m}_1 + \sqrt{3}\sqrt{\hat{m}_2 - \hat{m}_1{}^2}. \tag{25.3.15}$$

Example 25.3.6. Consider one hundred hard disks ($n = 100$) were observed in an accelerated lifetime test. The test finished when all hard disks failed. The times each device failed is depicted in Columns (X_i) of Table 25.18. The exploratory analysis did not reject the uniform distribution (not shown here). Then, we can estimate the uniform distribution parameters, a and b, adopting the method of moments presented.

From Columns X_i and X_i^2 of Table 25.18, we get

$$m_1 = \frac{\sum_{i=1}^{100} x_i}{100} = \frac{201284.46}{100} = 2012.84\,h.$$

and

$$m_2 = \frac{\sum_{i=1}^{100} x_i^2}{100} = \frac{443259330.98}{100} = 4432593.31\,h^2.$$

Adopting Equation 25.3.14 and 25.3.15, the uniform distribution parameters are estimated:

$$\hat{a} = \hat{m}_1 - \sqrt{3}\sqrt{\hat{m}_2 - \hat{m}_1{}^2} = 943.66\,h,$$

and

$$\hat{b} = \hat{m}_1 + \sqrt{3}\sqrt{\hat{m}_2 - \hat{m}_1{}^2} = 3082.03\,h.$$

Table 25.18
Reliability Data - Method of Moments - Uniform Distribution

i	X_i	X_i^2	X_i	X_i^2	X_i	X_i^2	X_i	X_i^2	X_i	X_i^2
1	2856.62	8160300.92	1672.02	2795642.78	2635.36	6945147.89	1640.34	2690713.24	1035.77	1072814.71
2	1727.87	2985522.47	2137.97	4570933.60	2339.64	5473917.63	1249.89	1562213.90	2374.61	5638794.99
3	2865.72	8212342.86	1085.82	1179000.83	1038.09	1077624.83	1175.60	1382043.60	2325.91	5409844.13
4	2028.35	4114210.60	2958.37	8751969.35	1933.44	3738186.87	2982.06	8892652.72	2587.45	6694901.58
5	2319.19	5378656.59	2933.59	8605960.40	2000.58	4002319.74	2272.19	5162868.24	2400.68	5763252.51
6	2589.71	6706593.53	2005.83	4023350.12	1362.62	1856735.80	2893.73	8373699.65	1334.42	1780681.61
7	1910.43	3649735.81	1466.14	2149565.66	2116.37	4479009.60	2692.80	7251175.52	1911.65	3654401.57
8	1866.85	3485120.50	1041.02	1083716.14	1744.71	3044022.29	1885.83	3556355.75	1547.38	2394384.82
9	2295.51	5269369.50	1486.71	2210304.21	2963.62	8783054.98	2792.29	7796889.17	1029.54	1059956.56
10	2954.65	8729953.64	2524.52	6373209.42	2677.85	7170862.49	2845.76	8098346.86	2941.04	8649705.93
11	1625.57	2642472.65	1629.54	2655386.97	1374.89	1890320.78	2678.82	7176093.77	2553.51	6520434.80
12	1217.35	1481947.90	2630.91	6921682.94	2907.65	8454434.28	1264.84	1599819.28	1412.85	1996157.54
13	1978.55	3914642.25	2762.20	7629747.59	1007.14	1014333.66	2054.35	4220368.16	1532.18	2347580.97
14	1033.45	1068015.36	1707.66	2916113.60	2907.77	8455144.19	2631.64	6925537.46	2717.89	7386909.19
15	1008.61	1017286.51	1617.82	2617330.89	2732.17	7464750.51	1296.03	1679692.57	2623.16	6880954.98
16	1197.82	1434775.10	2353.50	5538942.93	1308.42	1711963.04	1414.01	1999435.87	1242.13	1542896.51
17	2683.58	7201623.59	1630.21	2657575.58	2547.35	6488989.31	1826.99	3337894.54	1215.28	1476899.56
18	1874.05	3512063.82	1703.33	2901331.62	1578.88	2492846.54	1985.87	3943679.38	2300.03	5290126.35
19	2936.52	8623158.52	1710.78	2926754.82	2285.26	5222397.31	1220.95	1490728.69	1548.17	2396841.08
20	2115.88	4476943,01	2198.22	4832161.14	1625.39	2641877.36	1664.33	2769984.08	2752.86	7578244.29
j	1	1	2	2	3	3	4	4	5	5

Applying the KS goodness of fit, we obtained $D_{cal} = 0.045$ and the $D_{critical,5\%} = 0.1358$. As $D_{cal} < D_{critical,5\%}$, the test fails to reject the uniform distribution with parameters $a = 943.66\,h$ and $b = 3082.03\,h$ as suitable distribution to represent the hard disks' lifetime data with 95% degree of confidence.

□

Gamma Distribution

Assume T is a gamma random variable with parameters α and β that specifies the time to failure of a type of server. Assume a time to failure sample of size n was obtained from the population distributed according to T. As the gamma distribution has two parameters, the two first moments about the origin should be obtained. These moments could be derived from the gamma moment generating function:

$$M_T(t) = e(1 - \beta t)^{-\alpha}. \tag{25.3.16}$$

Taking the first derivative of $M_T(t)$ in relation to t, and setting $t = 0$, we get

$$\mu_1 = \alpha\beta.$$

Now, calculating the second derivative of $M_T(t)$ for t, and setting $t = 0$, we obtain

$$\mu_2 = \alpha(\alpha + 1)\beta^2.$$

Now consider a sample obtained from the population and calculate the first two moments about the origin

$$m_1 = \frac{\sum_{i=1}^{n} x_i}{n}$$

and

$$m_2 = \frac{\sum_{i=1}^{n} x_i^2}{n}.$$

then, let $\mu_1 = m_1$ and $\mu_2 = m_2$ and solve this system. As a result, we get

$$\hat{\alpha} = \frac{m_1}{\beta} \tag{25.3.17}$$

and

$$\hat{\beta} = \frac{m_2 - m_1^2}{m_1}. \tag{25.3.18}$$

Example 25.3.7. Consider one hundred servers ($n = 100$) were monitored in an accelerated lifetime test. The test finished when all servers failed. The times each server failed is depicted in Columns (X_i) of Table 25.19. The exploratory analysis did not reject the gamma distribution (not shown here). Then, the next step is estimating the gamma distribution parameters, α, and β.

Table 25.19
Reliability Data - Method of Moments - Gamma Distribution

i	X (h)	X^2 (h^2)	X (h)	X^2 (h^2)	X (h)	X^2 (h^2)	X (h)	X^2 (h^2)	X (h)	X^2 (h^2)
1	4195.92	17605779.41	1746.02	3048600.14	1300.81	1692106.18	2214.98	4906124.06	2090.18	4368840.61
2	1190.14	1416435.90	2038.79	4156679.55	1941.21	3768297.23	2857.16	8163357.64	2790.39	7786276.17
3	2234.14	4991361.07	2564.35	6575879.71	1790.60	3206238.03	1611.54	2597073.60	2671.41	7136440.41
4	2523.00	6365529.06	2086.50	4353464.71	1960.12	3842061.94	1903.24	3622327.89	1531.43	2345276.16
5	2409.63	5806316.77	1636.87	2679357.17	1432.29	2051447.36	1595.11	2544378.10	1403.19	1968949.04
6	1960.41	3843200.63	1418.13	2011079.23	1728.36	2987235.40	2079.64	4324901.25	1804.30	3255481.71
7	2382.73	5677380.75	1094.11	1197080.34	2155.39	4645705.34	2958.03	8749929.80	1818.84	3308178.69
8	3917.29	15345152.86	3365.21	11324635.45	2853.05	8139917.35	1902.73	3620365.13	1305.41	1704085.43
9	2364.80	5592288.36	905.68	820257.99	3930.69	15450329.10	2459.02	6046769.65	1530.36	2342012.12
10	2746.54	7543494.67	1133.86	1285642.77	2478.42	6142542.39	3940.48	15527353.37	4119.24	16968179.17
11	3173.21	10069266.24	2596.85	6743641.97	1823.81	3326272.11	2882.11	8306533.30	1692.25	2863712.92
12	3202.53	10256192.96	1727.47	2984153.49	2487.21	6186205.75	1446.72	2092986.44	1562.77	2442248.77
13	2020.45	4082201.77	2553.14	6518520.35	2703.02	7306315.63	3031.93	9192587.05	1979.02	3916534.13
14	2054.05	4219111.15	2117.49	4483746.56	4535.91	20574451.39	1877.18	3523796.57	1303.20	1698336.76
15	2249.76	5061439.08	2639.86	6968859.18	2228.87	4967879.31	1481.10	2193659.71	1119.80	1253956.84
16	1315.16	1729639.68	2984.36	8906398.57	1337.68	1789374.99	4227.25	17869680.64	2956.08	8738434.57
17	2318.19	5373987.16	2773.01	7689559.98	1669.84	2788363.97	1601.80	2565753.17	2068.08	4276935.02
18	2523.54	6368232.70	1376.74	1895409.06	1043.14	1088143.25	1142.26	1304757.54	2773.37	7691567.00
19	609.57	371572.41	2394.18	5732102.78	1069.94	1144762.41	2341.68	5483463.16	645.74	416977.94
20	2270.96	5157253.79	1515.85	2297797.84	1704.44	2905109.65	3107.05	9653760.41	1449.79	2101882.33
j	1	1	2	2	3	3	4	4	5	5

From Columns (X_i) of Table 25.19, we get

$$m_1 = \frac{\sum_{i=1}^{100} x_i}{100} = \frac{215781.09}{100} = 2157.81\,h.$$

Likewise, from Columns (X_i^2) of Table 25.19, we obtain

$$m_2 = \frac{\sum_{i=1}^{100} x_i^2}{100} = \frac{531425326.31}{100} = 5314253.26\,h^2.$$

Hence, using Equation 25.3.17 and 25.3.18, the parameters are estimated:

$$\hat{\alpha} = \frac{m_1}{\beta} = 7.08$$

and

$$\hat{\beta} = \frac{m_2 - m_1^2}{m_1} = 304.99\,h.$$

Applying the KS goodness of fit, we obtained $D_{cal} = 0.033$ and the $D_{critical,5\%} = 0.1358$. As $D_{cal} < D_{critical,5\%}$, the test fails to reject the gamma distribution with parameters $\hat{\alpha} = 7.08$ and $\hat{\beta} = 304.99\,h$ with 95% degree of confidence.

□

Poisson Distribution

Assume X is a random variable distributed according to a Poisson distribution with parameters λ. As the Poisson distribution has only one parameter, we need only one moment. The Poisson first moment about the origin is $\mu_1 = \lambda$, and the sample first moment is given by $(\sum_{i=1}^{n} x_i)/n$, where n is the sample size. Hence

$$\hat{\lambda} = \frac{\sum_{i=1}^{n} x_i}{n}. \qquad (25.3.19)$$

Example 25.3.8. Customers call a small help center according to a Poisson distribution. The mean number of calls per hour is constant and equal to λ. The help center was monitored for one hundred hours ($n = 100$ h), and the number of calls in each hour was recorded in Table 25.20. Applying Equation 25.3.19, we get $\hat{\lambda} = (\sum_{i=1}^{100} x_i)/100 = 993/100 = 9.93$ calls per hour.

□

25.3.3   MAXIMUM LIKELIHOOD ESTIMATION

This section introduces the Maximum Likelihood Estimation (MLE) approach for estimating parameters of a distribution. Such a strategy is appealing because it estimates values of the parameters that would have most likely produced the observed data.

For instance, let us guess a set of data is distributed according to $f(\Theta,t)$ (density function). Such a distribution may assume several particular shapes depending on the parameters' values. Figure 25.23 shows, for example, some possible formats of such a distribution.

For the distribution $f(\Theta,t)$, let us consider $\Theta = \{\theta_1, \theta_2\}$. These two parameters are what define the density function curve, as depicted in Figure 25.23. In order to adopt MLE, data must be independent and identically distributed (i.i.d.). In other words, for a data set to be i.i.d., it is required that any given data point does not depend on

Table 25.20

Number of Calls per Hour in a Period of 100 Hours

Time Intervals are Equal to One Hour

i (h)	X_i	X_i	X_i	X_i	X_i	X_i	X_i	X_i	X_i	X_i
1	4	6	7	8	9	10	11	11	12	14
2	5	6	7	8	9	10	11	11	12	14
3	6	6	7	8	9	10	11	11	12	14
4	6	7	8	8	9	10	11	12	12	14
5	6	7	8	9	9	10	11	12	12	16
6	6	7	8	9	9	10	11	12	13	16
7	6	7	8	9	9	10	11	12	13	17
8	6	7	8	9	10	10	11	12	13	17
9	6	7	8	9	10	10	11	12	13	18
10	6	7	8	9	10	11	11	12	14	19
j	1	2	3	4	5	6	7	8	9	10

any other data point and that each data point is generated from the same distribution with the same parameters.

This problem is set up as a conditional probability of which the aim is to maximize the probability of obtaining our data given Θ. Therefore, for a data sample of size n, mathematically, this looks like:

$$P(t_1, t_2, ..., t_n \mid \Theta).$$

The aim is to maximize this probability of observing our data as a function of Θ. In other words, we want to find θ_1 and θ_2 values such that $P(t_1, t_2, ..., t_n \mid \Theta)$ is as high as it can possibly be.

We are used to t being the independent variable. However, in this case θ_1 and θ_2 are the independent variable(s), and t_1, t_2, ..., t_n are constant since the observed data do not change.

We know that the probability of multiple independent events is termed joint probability. We can treat each data point (observation) as one single event. If the events are i.i.d., we can treat the observations of our data sample as a series of independent events, such that the joint probability follows:

$$P(t_1, t_2, ..., t_n \mid \Theta) = P(t_1 \mid \Theta) P(t_2 \mid \Theta) ... P(t_n \mid \Theta),$$

$$P(t_1, t_2, ..., t_n \mid \Theta) = \prod_{i=1}^{n} P(t_i \mid \Theta).$$

$$f(\Theta, t) \times t$$

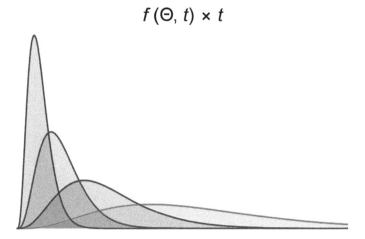

Figure 25.23 $f(\Theta, t) \times t$ for Different Values of θ_1 and θ_2.

It is worth stressing again; our goal is to maximize this probability term by finding the optimal θ_1 and θ_2. Hence, we seek the "argmax" of this term concerning θ_1 and θ_2. Therefore

$$\hat{\theta}_1 = arg_{\theta_1} max \prod_{i=1}^{n} P(t_i | \Theta)$$

and

$$\hat{\theta}_2 = arg_{\theta_2} max \prod_{i=1}^{n} P(t_i | \Theta).$$

Hence, find θ_1 and θ_2 by finding the roots of the derivatives of $\prod_{i=1}^{n} P(t_i | \Theta)$ with respect to each component of Θ, in this case, θ_1 and θ_2.

$$\frac{\partial (\prod_{i=1}^{n} P(t_i | \Theta))}{\partial \theta_1} = 0$$

and

$$\frac{\partial (\prod_{i=1}^{n} P(t_i | \Theta))}{\partial \theta_2} = 0.$$

However, obtaining a derivative to calculate the parameter value, θ_j, that maximizes $\prod_{i=1}^{n} P(t_i | \Theta)$ is often not an easy task. It usually is easier to obtained the derivative of

$$\ln(\prod_{i=1}^{n} P(t_i | \Theta)).$$

$$\sum_{i=1}^{n} \ln(P(t_i | \Theta))).$$

In such cases, we solve

$$\frac{\partial\left(\sum_{i=1}^{n}\ln(P(t_i\,|\,\Theta))\right)}{\theta_1} = 0$$

$$\Leftrightarrow$$

$$\sum_{i=1}^{n}\frac{\partial\left(\ln(P(t_i\,|\,\Theta))\right)}{\theta_1} = 0$$

and

$$\frac{\partial\left(\sum_{i=1}^{n}\ln(P(t_i\,|\,\Theta))\right)}{\theta_2} = 0$$

$$\Leftrightarrow$$

$$\sum_{i=1}^{n}\frac{\partial\left(\ln(P(t_i\,|\,\Theta))\right)}{\theta_2} = 0$$

to find θ_1 and θ_2. Obviously, $\ln(\prod_{i=1}^{n}P(t_i\,|\,\Theta))$ is a different value from $\prod_{i=1}^{n}P(t_i\,|\,\Theta)$, but both functions have the same global maximum with respect to Θ since $\ln f(t)$ does not change the curvature of $f(t)$. Figure 25.24 shows three density functions, $f(\Theta,t)$, $g(\Theta,t)$, and $h\Theta,t)$, and the respective $\ln(f(\Theta,t))$, $\ln(g(\Theta,t))$, and $\ln(h\Theta,t))$ for different values of their parameters. It it worth stressing that although

$$f(\Theta,t) \neq \ln(f(\Theta,t)),$$

$$g(\Theta,t) \neq \ln(g(\Theta,t)),$$

and

$$h\Theta,t) \neq \ln(h\Theta,t)),$$

and

$$\max(f(\Theta,t)) \neq \max(\ln(f(\Theta,t))),$$

$$\max(g(\Theta,t)) \neq \max(\ln(g(\Theta,t))),$$

and

$$\max(h(\Theta,t)) \neq \max(\ln(h(\Theta,t))),$$

the argument (t) that maximize $f(\Theta,t)$ and $\ln(f(\Theta,t))$, $g(\Theta,t)$ and $\ln(g(\Theta,t))$, and $h(\Theta,t)$ and $\ln(h(\Theta,t))$ are the same, that is

$$\arg_t(\max(f(\Theta,t))) = \arg_t(\max(\ln(f(\Theta,t)))),$$

$$\arg_t(\max(g(\Theta,t))) = \arg_t(\max(\ln(g(\Theta,t)))),$$

and

$$\arg_t(\max((h\Theta,t))) = \arg_t(\max(\ln(h(\Theta,t)))).$$

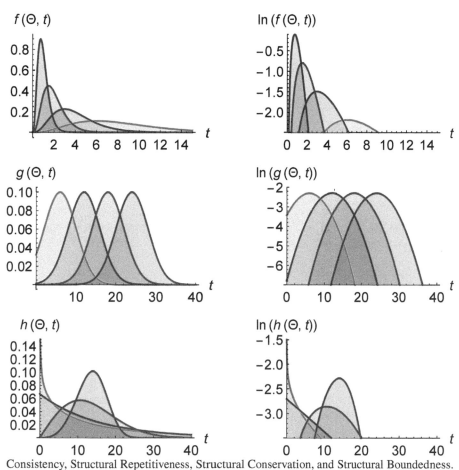

Consistency, Structural Repetitiveness, Structural Conservation, and Structural Boundedness.

Figure 25.24 $f(\Theta,t)$, $\ln(f(\Theta,t))$, $g(\Theta,t)$, $\ln(g(\Theta,t))$, and $h(\Theta,t)$, $\ln(h(\Theta,t))$.

Normal Distribution

Now, let us think about a distribution with two parameters we want to infer, μ and σ, rather than the symbolic representation θ. Assume a sample of only one data point was collected from a normal population with μ and σ as its true, but unknown, parameter values. Assume the likelihood function is the density function of normal distribution; hence

$$L(\mu,\sigma|t_1) = N(\mu,\sigma,t_1) = \frac{1}{\sigma\sqrt{2\pi}}e^{-\frac{(t_1-\mu)^2}{2\sigma^2}}.$$

Figure 25.25 shows the value of the likelihood L given the data point t_1.

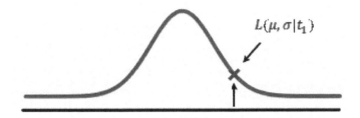

Figure 25.25 $L(\mu,\sigma|t_1)$ for Data Sample of Only One Point $\{t_1\}$.

Now assume $\{t_1,t_2,...,t_n\}$ as independent data points collected from a population normally distributed with the unknown parameters μ and σ. Therefore,

$$L(\mu,\sigma|t_1,t_2,...,t_n) = L(\mu,\sigma|t_1) \times L(\mu,\sigma|t_2) \times ... \times L(\mu,\sigma|t_n),$$

since the points are i.i.d. Thus,

$$L(\mu,\sigma|t_1,t_2,...,t_n) = \frac{1}{\sigma\sqrt{2\pi}}e^{-\frac{(t_1-\mu)^2}{2\sigma^2}} \times \frac{1}{\sigma\sqrt{2\pi}}e^{-\frac{(t_2-\mu)^2}{2\sigma^2}} \times ... \times \frac{1}{\sigma\sqrt{2\pi}}e^{-\frac{(t_n-\mu)^2}{2\sigma^2}}.$$

Now, let us solve $L(\mu,\sigma|t_1,t_2,...,t_n)$ for the maximum likelihood for μ and σ. Hence, we have to calculate two derivatives of $L(\mu,\sigma|t_1,t_2,...,t_n)$, one with respect to μ, and the other with respect to σ. Hence, take

$$\frac{\partial L(\mu,\sigma|t_1,t_2,...,t_n)}{\partial \mu} = 0$$

and

$$\frac{\partial L(\mu,\sigma|t_1,t_2,...,t_n)}{\partial \sigma} = 0.$$

and solve for μ and σ.

But before taking the derivative of $L(\mu,\sigma|t_1,t_2,...,t_n)$, let us consider the $\ln(L(\mu,\sigma|t_1,t_2,...,t_n))$ since it transforms the products into summations and $\ln e = 1$, which makes taking the derivative much easier. Thus,

$$\ln(L(\mu,\sigma|t_1,t_2,...,t_n)) =$$

$$\ln(\frac{1}{\sigma\sqrt{2\pi}}e^{-\frac{(t_1-\mu)^2}{2\sigma^2}} \times \frac{1}{\sigma\sqrt{2\pi}}e^{-\frac{(t_2-\mu)^2}{2\sigma^2}} \times ... \times \frac{1}{\sigma\sqrt{2\pi}}e^{-\frac{(t_n-\mu)^2}{2\sigma^2}}).$$

Hence,

$$\ln(L(\mu, \sigma | t_1, t_2, ..., t_n)) =$$

$$\ln(\frac{1}{\sigma\sqrt{2\pi}} e^{-\frac{(t_1-\mu)^2}{2\sigma^2}}) + \ln(\frac{1}{\sigma\sqrt{2\pi}} e^{-\frac{(t_2-\mu)^2}{2\sigma^2}}) + ... + \ln(\frac{1}{\sigma\sqrt{2\pi}} e^{-\frac{(t_n-\mu)^2}{2\sigma^2}}).$$

Let us take one of these terms above, for instance,

$$\ln(\frac{1}{\sigma\sqrt{2\pi}} e^{-\frac{(t_i-\mu)^2}{2\sigma^2}});$$

hence,

$$\ln(\frac{1}{\sigma\sqrt{2\pi}} e^{-\frac{(t_i-\mu)^2}{2\sigma^2}}) = \ln(\frac{1}{\sigma\sqrt{2\pi}}) + \ln(e^{-\frac{(t_i-\mu)^2}{2\sigma^2}}).$$

Thus,

$$\ln(\frac{1}{\sigma\sqrt{2\pi}} e^{-\frac{(t_i-\mu)^2}{2\sigma^2}}) = \ln((2\pi\sigma^2)^{-\frac{1}{2}}) - \frac{(t_i-\mu)^2}{2\sigma^2} \ln e.$$

$$\ln(\frac{1}{\sigma\sqrt{2\pi}} e^{-\frac{(t_i-\mu)^2}{2\sigma^2}}) = \ln((2\pi\sigma^2)^{-\frac{1}{2}}) - \frac{(t_i-\mu)^2}{2\sigma^2}.$$

$$\ln(\frac{1}{\sigma\sqrt{2\pi}} e^{-\frac{(t_i-\mu)^2}{2\sigma^2}}) = -\frac{1}{2}\ln(2\pi\sigma^2) - \frac{(t_i-\mu)^2}{2\sigma^2}.$$

$$\ln(\frac{1}{\sigma\sqrt{2\pi}} e^{-\frac{(t_i-\mu)^2}{2\sigma^2}}) = -\frac{1}{2}\ln(2\pi) - \frac{1}{2}\ln(\sigma^2) - \frac{(t_i-\mu)^2}{2\sigma^2}.$$

$$\ln(\frac{1}{\sigma\sqrt{2\pi}} e^{-\frac{(t_i-\mu)^2}{2\sigma^2}}) = -\frac{1}{2}\ln(2\pi) - \ln(\sigma) - \frac{(t_i-\mu)^2}{2\sigma^2}.$$

Now, take

$$\ln(\frac{1}{\sigma\sqrt{2\pi}} e^{-\frac{(t_1-\mu)^2}{2\sigma^2}}) + \ln(\frac{1}{\sigma\sqrt{2\pi}} e^{-\frac{(t_2-\mu)^2}{2\sigma^2}}) + ... + \ln(\frac{1}{\sigma\sqrt{2\pi}} e^{-\frac{(t_n-\mu)^2}{2\sigma^2}}) =$$

$$-\frac{1}{2}\ln(2\pi) - \ln(\sigma) - \frac{(t_1-\mu)^2}{2\sigma^2} - \frac{1}{2}\ln(2\pi) - \ln(\sigma) - \frac{(t_2-\mu)^2}{2\sigma^2} ...$$

$$-\frac{1}{2}\ln(2\pi) - \ln(\sigma) - \frac{(t_n-\mu)^2}{2\sigma^2} =$$

$$-\frac{n}{2}\ln(2\pi) - n\ln(\sigma) - \frac{(t_1-\mu)^2}{2\sigma^2} - \frac{(t_2-\mu)^2}{2\sigma^2} - ... -$$

$$\frac{(t_n-\mu)^2}{2\sigma^2} =$$

$$-\frac{n}{2}\ln(2\pi) - n\ln(\sigma) - \sum_{i=1}^{n}\frac{(t_i-\mu)^2}{2\sigma^2}.$$

Therefore, we started from

$$\ln(L(\mu,\sigma|t_1,t_2,...,t_n)) = \ln(\frac{1}{\sigma\sqrt{2\pi}}e^{-\frac{(t_1-\mu)^2}{2\sigma^2}} \times \frac{1}{\sigma\sqrt{2\pi}}e^{-\frac{(t_2-\mu)^2}{2\sigma^2}} \times ... \times$$

$$\frac{1}{\sigma\sqrt{2\pi}}e^{-\frac{(t_n-\mu)^2}{2\sigma^2}})$$

and arrived at

$$\ln(L(\mu,\sigma|t_1,t_2,...,t_n)) = -\frac{n}{2}\ln(2\pi) - n\ln(\sigma) - \sum_{i=1}^{n}\frac{(t_i-\mu)^2}{2\sigma^2}. \qquad (25.3.20)$$

Now, let us take

$$\frac{\partial\ln(L(\mu,\sigma|t_1,t_2,...,t_n))}{\partial\mu} = -0 - 0 + \sum_{i=1}^{n}\frac{(t_i-\mu)}{\sigma^2}.$$

Hence,

$$\frac{\partial\ln(L(\mu,\sigma|t_1,t_2,...,t_n))}{\partial\mu} = \sum_{i=1}^{n}\frac{(t_i-\mu)}{\sigma^2} =$$

$$\frac{\partial\ln(L(\mu,\sigma|t_1,t_2,...,t_n))}{\partial\mu} = \frac{1}{\sigma^2}\sum_{i=1}^{n}(t_i-\mu).$$

Therefore

$$\frac{\partial\ln(L(\mu,\sigma|t_1,t_2,...,t_n))}{\partial\mu} = \frac{1}{\sigma^2}(\sum_{i=1}^{n}t_i-n\mu). \qquad (25.3.21)$$

Now, taking the Equation 25.3.20, that is

$$\ln(L(\mu,\sigma|t_1,t_2,...,t_n)) = -\frac{n}{2}\ln(2\pi) - n\ln(\sigma) - \sum_{i=1}^{n}\frac{(t_i-\mu)^2}{2\sigma^2}$$

and deriving it with respect to σ

$$\frac{\partial\ln(L(\mu,\sigma|t_1,t_2,...,t_n))}{\partial\sigma} = \frac{\partial(-\frac{n}{2}\ln(2\pi) - n\ln(\sigma) - \sum_{i=1}^{n}\frac{(t_i-\mu)^2}{2\sigma^2})}{\partial\sigma},$$

we obtain

$$\frac{\partial\ln(L(\mu,\sigma|t_1,t_2,...,t_n))}{\partial\sigma} = 0 - \frac{n}{\sigma} + \sum_{i=1}^{n}\frac{(t_i-\mu)^2}{\sigma^3}.$$

Therefore

$$\frac{\partial \ln(L(\mu,\sigma|t_1,t_2,...,t_n))}{\partial \sigma} = -\frac{n}{\sigma} + \frac{1}{\sigma^3}\sum_{i=1}^{n}(t_i-\mu)^2. \tag{25.3.22}$$

Now, take the Equation 25.3.21 and let

$$\frac{\partial \ln(L(\mu,\sigma|t_1,t_2,...,t_n))}{\partial \mu} = 0,$$

then,

$$\frac{1}{\sigma^2}\left(\sum_{i=1}^{n}t_i - n\mu\right) = 0,$$

thus

$$\hat{\mu} = \frac{\sum_{i=1}^{n}t_i}{n}. \tag{25.3.23}$$

Likewise, take the Equation 25.3.22 and let

$$\frac{\partial \ln(L(\mu,\sigma|t_1,t_2,...,t_n))}{\partial \sigma} = 0,$$

then,

$$-\frac{n}{\sigma} + \frac{1}{\sigma^3}\sum_{i=1}^{n}(t_i-\mu)^2 = 0,$$

$$-n + \frac{1}{\sigma^2}\sum_{i=1}^{n}(t_i-\mu)^2 = 0.$$

Thus

$$\sigma^2 = \frac{\sum_{i=1}^{n}(t_i-\mu)^2}{n}.$$

Hence

$$\hat{\sigma} = \sqrt{\frac{\sum_{i=1}^{n}(t_i-\mu)^2}{n}}. \tag{25.3.24}$$

Example 25.3.9. Consider the experiment depicted in Example 25.3.5. As described, the times each cell phone failed is depicted in Columns (X_i) of Table 25.17. As already seen, the exploratory analysis did not reject the normal distribution. Applying Equation 25.3.23 and Equation 25.3.24, the normal distribution parameters are estimated:

$$\hat{\mu} = \frac{\sum_{i=1}^{n}t_i}{n} = \frac{203944.39}{100} = 2039.44\,h$$

$$\hat{\sigma} = \sqrt{\frac{\sum_{i=1}^{n}(t_i-\mu)^2}{n}} = \sqrt{\frac{17402129.24}{100}} = 417.16h.$$

The KS goodness of fit test fails to reject the normal distribution with parameters $\mu = 2039.44\,h$ and $\sigma = 417.16h$ as suitable distribution to represent the times to failure with 95% degree of confidence.

Exponential Distribution

Now let us assume a an independent set of measures, a sample, $\{t_1, t_2, \ldots, t_n\}$, was collected from an exponentially distributed population with true but unknown parameter λ.

$$f(t) = \lambda e^{-\lambda t}, \ t \geq 0.$$

The likelihood function considered to estimate the distribution parameter is represented by joint distribution with a λ that maximizes likelihood function for the sample $\{t_1, t_2, \ldots, t_n\}$. Therefore, as the set of measures of the sample are i.i.d., then

$$L(\lambda, |t_1, t_2, \ldots, t_n) = f(t_1) \times f(t_2) \times \ldots \times f(t_n).$$

$$L(\lambda, |t_1, t_2, \ldots, t_n) = \lambda e^{-\lambda t_1} \times \lambda e^{-\lambda t_2} \times \ldots \times \lambda e^{-\lambda t_n}.$$

$$L(\lambda, |t_1, t_2, \ldots, t_n) = \prod_{i=1}^{n} \lambda e^{-\lambda t_i}.$$

$$L(\lambda, |t_1, t_2, \ldots, t_n) = \lambda^n e^{-\lambda \sum_{i=1}^{n} t_i}. \tag{25.3.25}$$

Now let us take the $\ln(L(\lambda, |t_1, t_2, \ldots, t_n))$; thus

$$\ln(L(\lambda, |t_1, t_2, \ldots, t_n)) = \ln(\lambda^n e^{-\lambda \sum_{i=1}^{n} t_i}).$$

$$\ln(L(\lambda, |t_1, t_2, \ldots, t_n)) = \ln \lambda^n + \ln e^{-\lambda \sum_{i=1}^{n} t_i}.$$

$$\ln(L(\lambda, |t_1, t_2, \ldots, t_n)) = n \ln \lambda - \lambda \sum_{i=1}^{n} t_i \ln e.$$

$$\ln(L(\lambda, |t_1, t_2, \ldots, t_n)) = n \ln \lambda - \lambda \sum_{i=1}^{n} t_i. \tag{25.3.26}$$

Now, take the derivative of $\ln(L(\lambda, |t_1, t_2, \ldots, t_n))$ with respect to λ:

$$\frac{\partial \ln(L(\lambda, |t_1, t_2, \ldots, t_n))}{\partial \lambda} = \frac{\partial (n \ln \lambda - \lambda \sum_{i=1}^{n} t_i)}{\partial \lambda},$$

thus

$$\frac{\partial \ln(L(\lambda, |t_1, t_2, \ldots, t_n))}{\partial \lambda} = \frac{\partial n \ln \lambda}{\partial \lambda} - \frac{\partial \lambda \sum_{i=1}^{n} t_i}{\partial \lambda}.$$

$$\frac{\partial \ln(L(\lambda, |t_1, t_2, \ldots, t_n))}{\partial \lambda} = \frac{n}{\lambda} - \sum_{i=1}^{n} t_i.$$

In order to find the parameter λ that maximizes $\ln(L(\lambda, t_1, t_2, \ldots, t_n))$, set

$$\frac{\partial \ln(L(\lambda, |t_1, t_2, \ldots, t_n))}{\partial \lambda} = 0$$

and solve for λ. Therefore

$$\hat{\lambda} = \frac{n}{\sum_{i=1}^{n} t_i}. \qquad (25.3.27)$$

Example 25.3.10. Consider the experiment introduced in Example 25.3.1, in which fifty routers ($n = 50$) were observed in an accelerated reliability test. The time to failure of each device is recorded in Table 25.10. The exploratory analysis did not rule out the exponential distribution as a possible fit to represent the time to failure. Using Equation 25.3.27 to estimate λ, we get

$$\hat{\lambda} = \frac{50}{\sum_{i=1}^{50} t_i} = \frac{50}{47423.25} = 1.054 \times 10^{-3} \, h^{-1}.$$

As $D_{cal} = 0.091$ and $D_{critical,5\%} = 0.1921$ ($D_{cal} < D_{critical,5\%}$), the KS test fails to reject the exponential distribution with $\lambda = 1.054 \times 10^{-3} \, h^{-1}$ to represent the reliability data set with 95% degree of confidence.

Geometric Distribution

Consider a sample $\{x_1, x_2, \ldots, x_n\}$ of n independent measures, collected from a geometrically distributed population with true but unknown parameters p, $0 \leq p \leq 1$. As the geometric distribution is a discrete random variable, the likelihood function is the joint probability mass function (pmf). As the pmf of a geometric random variable is

$$p(x, p) = p(1-p)^{x-1}, \quad 0 \leq p \leq 1, \quad x = 1, 2, 3, \ldots$$

Thus, the likelihood function is

$$L(p \mid x_1, x_2, \ldots, x_n) = \prod_{i=1}^{n} p(1-p)^{x_i-1}.$$

$$L(p \mid x_1, x_2, \ldots, x_n) = p^n \prod_{i=1}^{n} (1-p)^{x_i-1}.$$

$$L(p \mid x_1, x_2, \ldots, x_n) = p^n (1-p)^{(\sum_{i=1}^{n} x_i)-n}.$$

Now, take $\ln(L(p \mid x_1, x_2, \ldots, x_n))$; hence

$$\ln(L(p \mid x_1, x_2, \ldots, x_n)) = \ln(p^n (1-p)^{(\sum_{i=1}^{n} x_i)-n}).$$

$$\ln(L(p \mid x_1, x_2, \ldots, x_n)) = \ln(p^n) + \ln((1-p)^{(\sum_{i=1}^{n} x_i)-n}).$$

$$\ln(L(p \mid x_1, x_2, \ldots, x_n)) = n \ln p \,(-n + \sum_{i=1}^{n} x_i) \ln(1-p).$$

Now, take the derivative of $\ln(L(p \mid x_1, x_2, ..., x_n))$ with respect to p:

$$\frac{\partial \ln(L(p \mid x_1, x_2, ..., x_n))}{\partial p} = \frac{\partial(n \ln p(-n + \sum_{i=1}^{n} x_i) \ln(1-p))}{\partial p}$$

$$\frac{\partial \ln(L(p \mid x_1, x_2, ..., x_n))}{\partial p} = \frac{n}{p} - \frac{-n + \sum_{i=1}^{n} x_i}{1-p}.$$

Let us set

$$\frac{\partial \ln(L(p \mid x_1, x_2, ..., x_n))}{\partial p} = 0,$$

then

$$\frac{n}{p} - \frac{-n + \sum_{i=1}^{n} x_i}{1-p} = 0$$

and solve for p

$$\hat{p} = \frac{n}{\sum_{i=1}^{n} x_i}. \tag{25.3.28}$$

Example 25.3.11. Consider a set of electronic gadgets was placed under a stress test until failure. For each device, the test procedure is repeated until the device fails. Table 25.21 shows the number of trials before each device i fails.

Table 25.21
Number of Trials until Failure

i	X_i	X_i	X_i	X_i	X_i	X_i	X_i	X_i	X_i	X_i
1	19	21	3	12	8	10	11	11	8	13
2	3	7	14	24	26	1	6	11	1	7
3	8	2	6	9	8	8	4	30	3	12
4	8	5	8	5	6	16	3	7	1	9
5	3	23	20	32	32	23	1	5	23	7
6	7	9	3	2	27	2	6	4	6	14
7	8	11	4	6	49	10	10	10	10	8
8	2	18	16	18	3	8	4	26	8	15
9	3	2	1	4	3	9	15	2	3	11
10	8	2	38	11	7	3	25	8	12	29

The exploratory analysis shows the statistics depicted in Table 25.22, and Figure 25.26 shows the histogram and the boxplot. The data set is right-skewed, and the standard deviation is not much smaller than the mean. These are characteristics of geometric distributions. Hence, the next step is estimating the geometric distribution parameter, p.

Table 25.22

Statistical Summary

Mean	SD	Var	CoV	Q1	Med	Q3	IQR	Min	Max	R	SK	Kurt
10.63	9.09	82.70	0.86	4.00	8.00	13.75	9.75	1.00	49.00	48.00	1.64	3.02

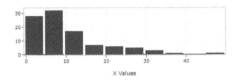 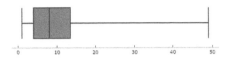

Figure 25.26 Histogram and Boxplot.

Using Equation 25.3.28, we estimate the parameter of the geometric distribution

$$\hat{p} = \frac{100}{\sum_{i=1}^{100} x_i} = \frac{100}{1063} = 0.09.$$

Applying the KS goodness of fit, the geometric distribution with parameter $p = 0.09$ was not rejected with 95% confidence. □

Poisson Distribution

A Poisson distribution specifies a random variable representing the probability of a given number of events taking place in a defined time interval. Thus, assume a sample $\{x_1, x_2, ..., x_n\}$ of n independent measures, collected from a Poisson distributed population with true but unknown parameters λ. The Poisson distribution is a discrete random variable; the likelihood function is the joint probability mass function (pmf). As the pmf of the Poisson random variable is

$$p(x, \lambda) = \frac{\lambda^x e^{-\lambda}}{x!},$$

thus, the likelihood function is

$$L(\lambda \,|\, x_1, x_2, ..., x_n) = \prod_{i=1}^{n} \frac{\lambda^{x_i} e^{-\lambda}}{x_i!}.$$

$$L(\lambda \,|\, x_1, x_2, ..., x_n) = \frac{\prod_{i=1}^{n} \lambda^{x_i} e^{-\lambda}}{\prod_{i=1}^{n} x_i!}.$$

Hence,

$$L(\lambda \,|\, x_1, x_2, ..., x_n) = \frac{\lambda^{\sum_{i=1}^{n} x_i} e^{-n\lambda}}{\prod_{i=1}^{n} x_i!}. \tag{25.3.29}$$

Then, taking the natural logarithm, we get

$$\ln(L(\lambda \,|\, x_1, x_2, ..., x_n)) = \ln\left(\frac{\lambda^{\sum_{i=1}^{n} x_i} e^{-n\lambda}}{\prod_{i=1}^{n} x_i!}\right),$$

$$\ln(L(\lambda \,|\, x_1, x_2, ..., x_n)) = \ln(\lambda^{\sum_{i=1}^{n} x_i} e^{-n\lambda}) - \ln(\prod_{i=1}^{n} x_i!),$$

$$\ln(L(\lambda \,|\, x_1, x_2, ..., x_n)) = \ln(\lambda^{\sum_{i=1}^{n} x_i}) + \ln(e^{-n\lambda}) - \ln(\prod_{i=1}^{n} x_i!),$$

$$\ln(L(\lambda \,|\, x_1, x_2, ..., x_n)) = \sum_{i=1}^{n} x_i \ln\lambda - n\lambda \ln e - \ln(\prod_{i=1}^{n} x_i!),$$

Thus,

$$\ln(L(\lambda \,|\, x_1, x_2, ..., x_n)) = \sum_{i=1}^{n} x_i \ln\lambda - n\lambda - \ln(\prod_{i=1}^{n} x_i!). \qquad (25.3.30)$$

Taking the derivative of $\ln(L(\lambda \,|\, x_1, x_2, ..., x_n))$ with respect to λ, we get

$$\frac{\partial \ln(L(\lambda \,|\, x_1, x_2, ..., x_n))}{\partial \lambda} = \frac{\partial \left(\sum_{i=1}^{n} x_i \ln\lambda - n\lambda - \ln(\prod_{i=1}^{n} x_i!)\right)}{\partial \lambda},$$

$$\frac{\partial \ln(L(\lambda \,|\, x_1, x_2, ..., x_n))}{\partial \lambda} = \frac{\partial \sum_{i=1}^{n} x_i \ln\lambda}{\partial \lambda} - \frac{\partial n\lambda}{\partial \lambda} - \frac{\partial \ln \prod_{i=1}^{n} x_i}{\partial \lambda}.$$

Hence,

$$\frac{\partial \ln(L(\lambda \,|\, x_1, x_2, ..., x_n))}{\partial \lambda} = \frac{\sum_{i=1}^{n} x_i}{\lambda} - n. \qquad (25.3.31)$$

Now let set

$$\frac{\partial \ln(L(\lambda \,|\, x_1, x_2, ..., x_n))}{\partial \lambda} = 0$$

and solve for λ. Then, we obtain

$$\hat{\lambda} = \frac{\sum_{i=1}^{n} x_i}{n}. \qquad (25.3.32)$$

Example 25.3.12. Consider the study depicted in Example 25.3.8. In that example, customers called a help center according to a Poisson distribution with true but unknown parameter λ, which denoted the mean number of calls per hour. The help center was monitored for one hundred hours ($n = 100$ h), and the number of calls in each hour was presented in Table 25.20. Applying Equation 25.3.32, we have an estimate of λ:

$$\hat{\lambda} = \frac{\sum_{i=1}^{100} x_i}{100} = \frac{993}{100} = 9.93$$

calls per hour.

$\square$

Dealing With Censoring

Above, we illustrated the maximum likelihood method for complete lifetime data sets. Often, however, these sets contain censored data. For example, consider an experiment where n devices are observed, which finishes as soon as r failures occur. In such a case, we are dealing with the right-censored of type II. Hence, lifetime data consider another term in its likelihood function. As mentioned earlier, the term for the complete data uses the density function. The second term for representing the censoring takes into account the complementary cumulative density function. This extended likelihood function has the form:

$$L(\theta, |x_1, x_2, ..., x_n) = \prod_{i=1}^{r} f(\theta|x_i) \times \prod_{j=r+1}^{n} (1 - F(x_j|\theta)), \qquad (25.3.33)$$

where $n - r$ is the number of censored data points, x_j is the jth suspension, and $F(x_i|\theta)$ is the cumulative distribution function, and θ is the set parameters of the distribution. The complementary cumulative density function, the second term of the likelihood function, is the survival function at t, and we can think of it as a weighting function applied to the density function. It is worth noting that the survival function at $t = 0$ is one.

With this new likelihood function, the analysis process proceeds as described previously: take the likelihood function and its partial derivatives concerning the parameters. The likelihood function for the censored lifetime data highlights some of the advantages the maximum likelihood method analysis has over other parameter estimation techniques.

Assume the TTFs are exponentially distributed with rate λ_i; thus, we may adopt

$$L(\lambda, |x_1, x_2, ..., x_n) = \prod_{i=1}^{r} \lambda e^{-\lambda t_i} \times \prod_{j=r+1}^{n} e^{-\lambda t_r}. \qquad (25.3.34)$$

Thus, we get

$$L(\lambda, |x_1, x_2, ..., x_n) = \lambda^r \prod_{i=1}^{r} e^{-\lambda t_i} \times \prod_{j=r+1}^{n} e^{-\lambda t_r}$$

$$L(\lambda, |x_1, x_2, ..., x_n) = \lambda^r e^{-\lambda^r \sum_{i=1}^{r} t_i} e^{-\lambda^{n-r} t_r}$$

$$L(\lambda, |x_1, x_2, ..., x_n) = \lambda^r e^{-\lambda^{n-r} t_r - \lambda^r \sum_{i=1}^{r} t_i}$$

as the likelihood function. Differentiating $L(\lambda, |x_1, x_2, ..., x_n)$ with respect to λ

$$\frac{\partial L(\lambda, |x_1, x_2, ..., x_n)}{\partial \lambda} = \frac{\partial (\lambda^r e^{-\lambda^{n-r} t_r - \lambda^r \sum_{i=1}^{r} t_i})}{\partial \lambda}$$

and setting it equal to zero,

$$\frac{\partial(\lambda^r e^{-\lambda^{n-r}t_r - \lambda^r \sum_{i=1}^r t_i})}{\partial \lambda} = 0,$$

we obtain

$$\hat{\lambda} = \frac{r}{\sum_{i=1}^r t_i + (n-r)t_r}. \tag{25.3.35}$$

Hence, the estimate of the mean time to failure is

$$\widehat{MTTF} = \frac{\sum_{i=1}^r t_i + (n-r)t_r}{r}. \tag{25.3.36}$$

Example 25.3.13. Consider sixty servers were observed during their operations. The times to failure are assumed to be independent and identically distributed according to an exponential distribution. Thus, the experiment finishes when thirty-five ($K = 35$) servers fail out of sixty ($N = 60$). Table 25.23 shows the particular times to failure of the thirty-five servers.

Table 25.23

Time to Failure Exponentially Distributed with Right-Censoring Type II

Parameter Estimation

TTF (h)	19.13	34.99	37.46	180.00	368.14	371.45	386.44	445.64	449.78	485.93
TTF (h)	582.15	622.88	663.82	714.09	739.94	788.03	950.67	983.90	1008.97	1132.58
TTF(h)	1136.15	1207.51	1241.35	1300.74	1370.45	1414.29	1578.61	1602.37	1687.14	1748.39
TTF(h)	1760.31	1823.25	1889.51	2170.34	2225.88					

The summation of such times is obtained by the summation of each time to failure, that is $\sum_{i=1}^r t_i = 44048.63\,h$. The maximal time to failure of these thirty-five servers is $t_r = t_{35} = 2225.88\,h$, and the number of censored servers was $n - r = 25$; hence $(n - r) \times t_r = 55647.08\,h$, such that $\sum_{i=1}^r t_i + (n-r) \times t_r = 35157.27\,h$. Therefore

$$\hat{\lambda} = \frac{r}{\sum_{i=1}^r t_i + (n-r)t_r} = \frac{35}{35157.27\,h} = 9.96 \times 10^{-4}\,h^{-1},$$

and

$$\widehat{MTTF} = \frac{1}{\hat{\lambda}} = 1009.49\,h.$$

□

Now assume an experiment in which n devices are observed for a period of T. Consider that during the observation, r devices failed; hence $(n-r)$ were right-censored because they survived the observation period. In such a case, we are dealing with the right-censored of type I. Therefore Equation 25.3.35 and Equation 25.3.36 may be adapted to estimate the distribution parameter:

$$\hat{\lambda} = \frac{r}{\sum_{i=1}^{r} t_i + (n-r)T}.$$

(25.3.37)

Thus, the estimate of the mean time to failure is

$$\widehat{MTTF} = \frac{\sum_{i=1}^{r} t_i + (n-r)T}{r}.$$

(25.3.38)

Example 25.3.14. Assume again sixty servers ($n = 60$) were observed for a period $T = 13000\,h$. The times to failure are assumed to be independent and identically distributed according to an exponential distribution. At the end of the observation period (T), $r = 42$ servers have failed. Thus, $(n-r) = 18$ servers were censored. Table 25.24 shows the times to failure of the forty-two failed servers.

Table 25.24

Time to Failure Exponentially Distributed with Right-Censoring Type I

Parameter Estimation

TTF (h)				
31.32	353.41	1230.39	2639.87	9266.99
91.00	368.63	1266.36	2700.43	12377.70
131.81	671.81	1350.85	2758.79	
139.65	681.83	1455.53	2829.03	
159.92	758.35	1739.20	3260.55	
160.95	859.26	1957.75	4114.70	
246.19	907.43	1966.66	5159.89	
247.87	981.33	2245.22	5329.46	
302.91	1082.50	2570.87	5818.41	
346.96	1199.17	2609.79	7455.63	

The summation of the time to failure is $\sum_{i=1}^{42} t_i = 91826.38\,h$. The observation period is $T = 13000\,h$, and the number of censored servers was $n - r = 18$; hence $(n-r) \times T = 92877.99\,h$, such that $\sum_{i=1}^{42} t_i + (n-r) \times T = 184704.37\,h$. Therefore

$$\hat{\lambda} = \frac{r}{\sum_{i=1}^{r} t_i + (n-r)t_r} = \frac{42}{184704.37\,h} = 2.27 \times 10^{-4}\,h^{-1},$$

and

$$\widehat{MTTF} = \frac{1}{\hat{\lambda}} = 4397.72\,h.$$

□

Now, let us consider an experiment in which n devices are observed for a period of T (Right-Censoring Type 1), but the devices may also be taken away before finishing the observation period and without failing (Left Censoring). The number of devices that failed during the observation is r; the number of devices that were still operating at the end of the observation period (T) is rc devices failed. The number of devices that were censored before finishing the observation period is lc. Therefore, the total number of censored devices is $(rc + lc)$. In such a case, we are dealing with the multiply censored reliability data. Therefore Equation 25.3.35 and Equation 25.3.36 may be adapted to estimate the distribution parameter:

$$\hat{\lambda} = \frac{r}{\sum_{i=1}^{r} t_i + \sum_{j=1}^{lc} t_j + rc \times T}, \tag{25.3.39}$$

where t_i is a time to failure, and t_j is a left-censoring time. Thus, the estimate of the mean time to failure is

$$\widehat{MTTF} = \frac{\sum_{i=1}^{r} t_i + \sum_{j=1}^{lc} t_j + rc \times T}{r}. \tag{25.3.40}$$

Example 25.3.15. Consider once again that sixty servers $(n = 60)$ were observed for a period $T = 8000\,h$. The times to failure are assumed to be independent and identically distributed according to an exponential distribution. At the end of the observation period (T), $r = 49$ servers have failed, and seven were left-censored $(lc = 7)$ - $\delta = 0$, that is, were taken away before presenting any failure. After the observation period, $rc = 4$ servers were still operating (right-censoring). Thus, $(cr + lc) = 11$ servers were censored. Table 25.24 shows the times to failure $(\delta = 1)$ of the forty-two failed servers as well as those that were censored.

Hence, as $r = 49$, $\sum_{j=1}^{lc} t_j = 16904.44\,h$ and $rc \times T = 32000.00\,h$.

$$\hat{\lambda} = \frac{r}{\sum_{i=1}^{r} t_i + \sum_{j=1}^{lc} t_j + rc \times T} = \frac{49}{16904.44 + 32000.00} = 5.04 \times 10^{-4} h^{-1},$$

and

$$\widehat{MTTF} = \frac{\sum_{i=1}^{r} t_i + \sum_{j=1}^{lc} t_j + rc \times T}{r} = \frac{1}{\hat{\lambda}} = 1985.52\,h.$$

□

Table 25.25
Time to Failure Exponentially Distributed.

Right-Censoring Type I and Left Censoring - Parameter Estimation.

Event	TTF (h) - Input	$\delta = 0$ and $\delta = 1$	Event	TTF (h) - Input	$\delta = 0$ and $\delta = 1$
1	122.58	1	31	2189.07	1
2	156.77	1	32	2218.00	1
3	235.83	1	33	2490.93	1
4	280.09	1	34	2538.60	1
5	292.17	0	35	2542.83	1
6	360.66	1	36	2574.39	1
7	406.39	1	37	2781.96	1
8	443.42	1	38	2914.31	0
9	556.43	1	39	2927.24	1
10	572.07	1	40	3563.35	1
11	793.91	1	41	3637.54	0
12	801.65	1	42	3749.42	0
13	831.43	1	43	3950.42	1
14	834.62	1	44	4084.52	1
15	837.44	1	45	4308.15	1
16	838.65	0	46	4476.51	1
17	864.63	1	47	4721.39	1
18	879.01	1	48	4868.94	1
19	886.98	1	49	5026.22	1
20	919.37	1	50	5267.14	1
21	937.83	1	51	5443.13	1
22	952.14	1	52	5472.35	0
23	1099.93	1	53	5552.04	1
24	1206.23	1	54	6685.09	1
25	1228.13	1	55	6821.95	1
26	1228.17	1	56	6836.19	1
27	1639.41	1	57		0
28	1776.60	1	58		0
29	1805.49	1	59		0
30	1902.25	1	60		0

25.3.4   CONFIDENCE INTERVALS

This section briefly discusses some alternatives for computing distribution parameters' confidence intervals. Before starting, it is worth noting that confidence intervals for samples obtained from normal and binomial distribution have already been discussed in Chapter 6. In that chapter, nonparametric and semi-parametric bootstraps have also been introduced.

Estimating Confidence Interval for Distribution Parameters Using Semi-Parametric Bootstrap

The previous sections presented three parametric approaches for distribution parameters' point estimation. A reasonably general strategy can be adopted for estimating distribution parameters' confidence interval by adopting semi-parametric bootstrap methods introduced in Section 6.5.3. The general steps of this strategy are shown in the Method 22.

Algorithm 22 Distribution Parameters' Confidence Interval based on Semi-Parametric Bootstrap

---

1: Obtain a sample of n independent measures from a population distributed according to $F(t, \Theta)$ ($f(t, \Theta)$ - density function - or $p(t, \Theta)$ - probability mass function), $\Theta = \{\theta_1, \theta_2, ..., \theta_n\}$, where the values of Θ are unknown.
2: Obtain the distribution parameters's point estimation, $\hat{\Theta} = \{\hat{\theta}_1, \hat{\theta}_2, ..., \hat{\theta}_n\}$, using one of the parametric methods introduced in this chapter.
3: Generate random variates using the probability distribution with the point estimates, $\hat{\Theta} = \{\hat{\theta}_1, \hat{\theta}_2, ..., \hat{\theta}_n\}$, obtained in step 2, to generate a resample of size n.
4: For each resample, calculate a distribution parameters's point estimates, $\hat{\Theta}^j = \{\hat{\theta}_1^j, \hat{\theta}_2^j, ..., \hat{\theta}_n^j\}$, using the same method adopted in step 2.
5: Repeat steps 3 and 4 m times. Adopt a "big" number, (say $m = 1000$ or $10,000$).
6: For each parameter θ_i, sort the point estimates obtained in the resamples, $\{\hat{\theta}_i^1, \hat{\theta}_i^2, ..., \hat{\theta}_i^m\}$, in ascending order.
7: Considering the desired degree of confidence, $(1 - \alpha)$, for each parameter θ_i, determine the percentiles $\alpha/2 \times 100\%$ and $(1 - \alpha/2) \times 100\%$. These values are the lower and upper limits of the parameter θ_i confidence interval.

Example 25.3.16. Consider the study depicted in Example 25.3.7, in which one hundred servers ($n = 100$) were monitored in a lifetime test. The times each server failed is depicted in Table 25.19. As already seen, the exploratory analysis did not reject the gamma distribution. In that study, the method of moments was adopted to obtain point estimates of the gamma distribution parameters, α, and β. The estimates were $\hat{\alpha} = 7.08$ and $\hat{\beta} = 304.99 \, h$.

The Mathematica code depicted below is a specific implementation of Steps $3 - 7$ of Method 22.

The clause RandomVariate[GammaDistribution[$\hat{\gamma}$, $\hat{\beta}$],ss] generates a *resample$_i$* of size ss (equal to the original sample size), based on a gamma distribution with parameters $\hat{\gamma}$ and $\hat{\beta}$. These parameters were estimated from the original sample using the method of moments. The clause FindDistributionParameters [*resample$_i$*,GammaDistribution[γ, β] estimates the gamma parameters for the

Algorithm 23 Gamma Distribution Parameters' Confidence Interval based on Semi-Parametric Bootstrap

1: nors = 1000, ss=100;
2: $\alpha = 0.1$;
3: $\hat{\gamma} = 7.08$, $\hat{\beta} = 304.99$;
4: parest = { γ, β } /. Table[FindDistributionParameters[RandomVariate [GammaDistribution[$\hat{\gamma}$, $\hat{\beta}$],ss], GammaDistribution[γ, β], ParameterEstimator− >"MethodOfMoments"], { *nors* }];
5: Print["degree of confidence = ", N[1 - α], " - $\gamma \in$ ",Quantile[$\hat{\gamma}$, { $\alpha/2$, (1 - ($\alpha/2$)) }]]
6: Print["degree of confidence = " , N[1 - α], " - $\beta \in$ ",Quantile[$\hat{\beta}$, { $\alpha/2$, (1 - ($\alpha/2$)) }]]

resample$_i$. The number of resamples obtained is specified in *nors*. The command $\{\gamma, \beta\}/.$ removes the symbols γ and β from the list *parest*. Quantile[parest[[All,1]], $\alpha/2$, (1 - ($\alpha/2$))]] and Quantile[parest[[All, 2]], $\alpha/2$, (1 - ($\alpha/2$))]] find the quantile $\alpha/2$ and 1 - $\alpha/2$ for γ and β, respectively, where α is the degree of significance.

Executing this Mathematica code, a confidence interval was generated for the distribution parameters. The confidence intervals obtained were $\gamma \in (5.6, 9.2)$ and $\beta \in (233.35\,h, 386.96\,h)$ with 90% degree of confidence. ☐

Example 25.3.17. Consider the study depicted in Example 25.3.8, in which customers call a help center according to a Poisson distribution. The mean number of calls per hour is constant and equal to λ. As already mentioned, the number of calls in each hour was recorded in Table 25.20. The Mathematica code depicted below is a specific implementation of the Steps $3 - 7$ of the Method 22.

Algorithm 24 Poisson Distribution Parameters' Confidence Interval based on Semi-Parametric Bootstrap

1: nors = 1000, ss=100;
2: $\alpha = 0.1$;
3: $\hat{\lambda} = 9.93$;
4: parest = λ /. Table[FindDistributionParameters[RandomVariate[PoissonDistribution[$\hat{\lambda}$],ss], PoissonDistribution[λ],ParameterEstimator $- >$ "MaximumLikelihood"],{ *nors* }];
5: Print["degree of confidence = ", N[1 - α], " - $\lambda \in$ ",Quantile[parest[[All]], { $\alpha/2$, (1 - ($\alpha/2$))}]]

The Mathematica Code 23 is pretty much similar to Code 23. The difference is only related to the distribution adopted. In this particular case, we also adopted the MLE (see "MaximumLikelihood") for estimating the distribution parameter instead of the Method of Moments, which was adopted in Code 23. In one execution of the code, we obtained this result: $\lambda \in (9.41, 10.47)$ with 90% degree of confidence.

Confidence Interval for the Mean and Rate of Exponentially Distributed Data

As the exponential distribution plays a very important role in performance and reliability modeling, this section presents a parametric method for estimating the confidence interval for the distribution parameter and its expected value. Assume a random variable T follows an exponential distribution with parameter λ; thus its density function is $f_T(t) = \lambda e^{-\lambda t}$. Also consider the following ordered failure time $\{t_1, t_2, \ldots t_n\}$; and $Y = t_1 + t_2 + \ldots + t_n$, where each t_i is a failure time value assigned to a random variable T_i, where every T_i is independent and identically distributed according to $f_{T_i}(t) = \lambda e^{-\lambda t}$. Therefore $Y = \sum_{i=1}^{n} T_i$ is a gamma distribution with parameters n and λ, that is $Gamma(n, \lambda)$[3]. The second parameter of the gamma distribution is a rate; then multiplying Y by a constant gives another gamma random variable, W, with the same shape and rate divided by that constant [207, 254, 461]. We choose to multiply by 2λ; thus

$$W = 2\lambda Y$$

and then

$$W = 2\lambda (T_1 + T_2 + \ldots + T_n). \tag{25.3.41}$$

Thus,

$$W = 2n\lambda \overline{T}, \tag{25.3.42}$$

where $\overline{T} = (\sum_{i=1}^{n} T_i)/n$. The random variable $\overline{T}$ is distributed according to $Gamma(n, \lambda))$. Hence, the random variable $W = n2\lambda\overline{T}$ is distributed according to $Gamma(n, \lambda/(2\lambda)) = Gamma(n, \lambda/(2\lambda))$, that is

$$W = 2n\lambda\overline{T} \sim Gamma(n, \frac{\lambda}{2\lambda})$$

$$W = 2n\lambda\overline{T} \sim Gamma(n, \frac{1}{2}).$$

Since

$$Gamma(n, \frac{1}{2}) = \chi^2_{2n},$$

then,

$$W = 2n\lambda\overline{T} \sim \chi^2_{2n}. \tag{25.3.43}$$

---

[3] In this particular case, it is an Erlang distribution with parameter n and λ.

Therefore, the confidence interval for λ can be estimated by

$$P(\chi^2_{2n,\alpha/2} < W < \chi^2_{2n,1-(\alpha/2)}) = 1 - \alpha.$$

$$P(\chi^2_{2n,\alpha/2} < 2n\lambda\overline{T} < \chi^2_{2n,1-(\alpha/2)}) = 1 - \alpha.$$

Hence the confidence interval for λ is estimated by

$$\frac{\chi^2_{2n,\alpha/2}}{2n\overline{T}} < \lambda < \frac{\chi^2_{2n,1-(\alpha/2)}}{2n\overline{T}}, \tag{25.3.44}$$

considering $1 - \alpha$ degree of confidence.

As the expected value of W $(\widehat{MTTF})$ is $E(W) = 1/\hat{\lambda}$, then the confidence interval for the mean is estimated by

$$\frac{2n\overline{T}}{\chi^2_{2n,1-(\alpha/2)}} < MTTF < \frac{2n\overline{T}}{\chi^2_{2n,\alpha/2}}. \tag{25.3.45}$$

Consider the experiment finishes when k out of n devices fail, that is, a **right-censoring type-2 data**; the respective confidence interval can be estimated by the above equations, but $n\overline{T}$ should be changed by

$$n\overline{T} = \sum_{i=1}^{k} T_i + (n-k)T_k,$$

so

$$\frac{\chi^2_{2n,\alpha/2}}{2\left(\sum_{i=1}^{k} T_i + (n-k)T_k\right)} < \lambda < \frac{\chi^2_{2n,1-(\alpha/2)}}{2\left(\sum_{i=1}^{k} T_i + (n-k)T_k\right)}, \tag{25.3.46}$$

and

$$\frac{2\left(\sum_{i=1}^{k} T_i + (n-k)T_k\right)}{\chi^2_{2n,1-(\alpha/2)}} < MTTF < \frac{2\left(\sum_{i=1}^{k} T_i + (n-k)T_k\right)}{\chi^2_{2n,\alpha/2}} \tag{25.3.47}$$

where considering T_k is the time of failure of the k device. $1 - \alpha$ is the degree of confidence. These expressions may also be adopted to provide a reasonable estimate for **right-censoring type-1 data**. In such a case, $n\overline{T}$ is changed to

$$n\overline{T} = \sum_{i=1}^{j} T_i + (n-k)T_k,$$

where T_j is the closest, but smaller or equal, value to T_k, where T_k is the time duration of the experiment. Therefore,

$$\frac{\chi^2_{2n,\alpha/2}}{2\sum_{i=1}^{j} T_i + (n-j)T_k} < \lambda < \frac{\chi^2_{2n,1-(\alpha/2)}}{2\sum_{i=1}^{j} T_i + (n-j)T_k}, \tag{25.3.48}$$

and

$$\frac{2 \sum_{i=1}^{j} T_i + (n-j) T_k}{\chi^2_{2n,1-(\alpha/2)}} < MTTF < \frac{2 \sum_{i=1}^{j} T_i + (n-j) T_k}{\chi^2_{2n,\alpha/2}}. \tag{25.3.49}$$

Example 25.3.18. Assume the reliability experiment described in Example 25.3.1, in which fifty routers ($n = 50$) were observed in an accelerated reliability test. The times each router failed were recorded in Table 25.10 (complete data). The exploratory analysis does not allow us to reject the exponential distribution as a suitable probability distribution to represent this data set. Then, the parameter point estimation was obtained, $\lambda = 9.41 \times 10^{-4} h^{-1}$, and the KS goodness of fit test fails to reject the exponential distribution as suitable to represent the reliability data set with 95% degree of confidence.

We adopted Equation 25.3.44 to estimate the confidence interval for the exponential distribution parameter, λ, that is

$$\lambda \in \left(\frac{\chi^2_{2n,\alpha/2}}{2n\overline{T}}, \frac{\chi^2_{2n,1-(\alpha/2)}}{2n\overline{T}} \right),$$

$$\lambda \in \left(\frac{74.22}{250948.46}, \frac{129.56}{250948.46} \right),$$

$$\lambda \in \left(7.83 \times 10^{-4} h^{-1}, 1.37 \times 10^{-3} h^{-1} \right),$$

considering 95% degree of confidence. Adopting Equation 25.3.45, the confidence interval of the MTTF is estimated:

$$MTTF \in \left(\frac{2n\overline{T}}{\chi^2_{2n,1-(\alpha/2)}}, \frac{2n\overline{T}}{\chi^2_{2n,\alpha/2}} \right),$$

$$MTTF \in (732.06 h, 1277.88 h),$$

and the point estimate of the $MTTF = 948.46 h$.

□

Example 25.3.19. Now, also consider a test in which 60 units have been tested. The test finished when 37 failures occurred. The observed failure times are recorded in Table 25.26. Function δ shows if the event i is a failure ($\delta=1$) or a censoring ($\delta=0$).

Assuming the times to failure are exponentially distributed, the point estimate for λ and the $MTTF$ are $\hat{\lambda} = 1.46 \times 10^{-4} h^{-1}$ and $\widehat{MTTF} = 6858.46 h$. The confidence interval for λ and $MTTF$ are

$$\frac{\chi^2_{2n,\alpha/2}}{2 \sum_{i=1}^{k} T_i + (n-k) T_k} < \lambda < \frac{\chi^2_{2n,1-(\alpha/2)}}{2 \sum_{i=1}^{k} T_i + (n-k) T_k},$$

Table 25.26

Time to Failure Exponentially Distributed with Right-Censoring Type 2

i	δ	$TTF(h)$	δ	$TTF(h)$	δ	$TTF(h)$	δ	$TTF(h)$	δ	$TTF(h)$	δ	$TTF(h)$
1	1	31.32	0		1	2564.12	1	346.96	0		1	3432.90
2	1	91.00	1	907.43	0		1	353.41	1	1481.06	1	3666.17
3	1	131.81	0		0		1	368.63	1	1739.20	0	
4	1	139.65	1	1002.30	0		0		1	1770.10	0	
5	1	159.92	0		1	2700.43	0		1	1957.75	1	5159.89
6	1	160.95	1	1095.70	0		1	671.81	1	1966.66	0	
7	0		1	1199.17	1	2829.03	0		0		0	
8	1	246.19	1	1230.39	1	2947.40	0		1	2106.44	1	7455.63
9	1	247.87	0		1	2985.47	0		0		0	
10	1	302.91	1	1350.85	1	3260.55	0		1	2245.22	1	12377.70
j		1		2		3		4		5		6

$$\frac{\chi^2_{120,0.025}}{2\sum_{i=1}^{37} T_i + (60-37)\,12377.70} < \lambda < \frac{\chi^2_{120,0.975}}{2\sum_{i=1}^{37} T_i + (60-37)\,12377.70},$$

$$\frac{40.48}{2 \times 126820.73 + (60-37)\,12377.70} < \lambda < \frac{83.30}{2 \times 126820.73 + (60-37)\,12377.70}.$$

$$\lambda \in (1.11 \times 10^{-4}\,h^{-1}, 1.85 \times 10^{-4}\,h^{-1}),$$

and

$$\frac{2\sum_{i=1}^{37} T_i + (n-k)\,T_k}{\chi^2_{2n,1-(\alpha/2)}} < MTTF < \frac{2\sum_{i=1}^{37} T_i + (n-k)\,T_k}{\chi^2_{2n,\alpha/2}},$$

$$\frac{2 \times 126820.73 + (60-37)\,12377.70}{\chi^2_{120,0.975}} < MTTF < \frac{2 \times 126820.73 + (60-37)\,12377.70}{\chi^2_{120,0.025}},$$

$$MTTF \in (5407.06\,h, 8987.57\,h).$$

□

If T is the time to repair, the method introduced above provides the confidence intervals for the mean time to repair ($MTTR$) and for the repair rate (μ).

Confidence Interval for Availability - TTF and TTR Exponentially Distributed

This section presents a parametric method for estimating the confidence interval for availability when assuming the time to failure (TTF) and time to repair (TTR) are exponentially distributed [207].

The steady-state availability is defined (see Equation 16.2.18) as

$$A = \frac{MTTF}{MTTF + MTTR}.$$

If $TTF \sim Exp(\lambda)$ and $TTR \sim Exp(\mu)$, then we have (see Equation 16.3.12)

$$A = \frac{\frac{1}{\lambda}}{\frac{1}{\lambda} + \frac{1}{\mu}},$$

$$A = \frac{1}{1 + \frac{\frac{1}{\mu}}{\frac{1}{\lambda}}},$$

$$A = \frac{1}{1 + \frac{\lambda}{\mu}} = \frac{1}{1 + \rho},$$

where $\rho = \lambda/\mu$. Therefore, the availability point estimate is obtained by

$$\hat{A} = \frac{1}{1 + \hat{\rho}},$$

and

$$\hat{\rho} = \frac{\hat{\lambda}}{\hat{\mu}}.$$

We have seen that $Y \sim \chi^2_{2n}$, if $Y = \sum_{i=1}^{n} TTF_i$, for each TTF_i distributed according to $f(t) = \lambda\, e^{-\lambda t}$. Likewise, if $D = \sum_{i=1}^{n} TTR_i$, for each TTR_i distributed according to $f(t) = \mu\, e^{-\mu t}$; hence $D \sim \chi^2_{2n}$. Therefore,

$$\rho = \frac{\lambda}{\mu} \sim F(2n, 2n),$$

where $F(2n, 2n)$ is the Snedecor-Fisher F cumulative distribution function, and $f(2n, 2n)$ is the respective density function. Since

$$\hat{\rho} = \frac{\hat{\lambda}}{\hat{\mu}} = \frac{\frac{n}{Y}}{\frac{n}{D}} = \frac{D}{Y},$$

then

$$\rho \in (\hat{\rho}_l, \hat{\rho}_u) = \left(\frac{\hat{\rho}}{f_{2n,2n,1-\frac{\alpha}{2}}}, \frac{\hat{\rho}}{f_{2n,2n,\frac{\alpha}{2}}} \right), \tag{25.3.50}$$

where α is the degree of significance,

$$f_{2n,2n,1-\frac{\alpha}{2}} = \arg f\left(2n, 2n, 1 - \frac{\alpha}{2}\right)$$

and

$$f_{2n,2n,\frac{\alpha}{2}} = \arg f\left(2n, 2n, \frac{\alpha}{2}\right).$$

Therefore

$$A \in (\hat{A}_l, \hat{A}_u) = \left(\frac{1}{1 + \hat{\rho}_u}, \frac{1}{1 + \hat{\rho}_l} \right). \tag{25.3.51}$$

Table 25.27

Time to Repair Exponentially Distributed

i	TTR (h)	TTR (h)	TTR (h)	TTR (h)
1	4.78	1.92	10.86	7.12
2	42.77	15.13	20.41	0.34
3	2.70	0.59	18.74	15.85
4	56.63	11.98	6.00	7.20
5	7.28	67.39	5.47	31.01
6	5.43	7.56	2.55	10.41
7	27.75	2.99	10.35	34.33
8	10.83	37.68	4.71	
9	7.36	16.79	29.69	
10	36.76	8.41	32.88	
j	1	2	3	4

Example 25.3.20. Consider the experiment depicted in Example 25.3.19. Also assume the repair time of each failure is depicted in Table 25.27. The exploratory analysis of the time to repair data set does not reject the exponential distribution as suitable to represent the repair time. The repair rate point estimate was obtained by applying the MLE method. The rate point estimate is $\hat{\mu} = 5.96 \times 10^{-2} h^{-1}$, and the $MTTR$ point estimate is $\widehat{MTTR} = 16.77 h$. As $\hat{\lambda} = 1.46 \times 10^{-4} h^{-1}$ and $\widehat{MTTF} = 6858.46 h$ (see Example 25.3.19), we get

$$\hat{\rho} = \frac{\hat{\lambda}}{\hat{\mu}} = \frac{1.46 \times 10^{-4} h^{-1}}{5.96 \times 10^{-2} h^{-1}},$$

$$\hat{\rho} = 2.45 \times 10^{-3}.$$

Applying Equation 25.3.50 and Equation 25.3.51, the confidence intervals for ρ and the availability (A) are estimated:

$$\rho \in (\hat{\rho}_l, \hat{\rho}_u) = \left(\frac{\hat{\rho}}{f_{2n,2n,1-\frac{\alpha}{2}}}, \frac{\hat{\rho}}{f_{2n,2n,\frac{\alpha}{2}}} \right),$$

$$\rho \in \left(\frac{2.45 \times 10^{-3}}{f_{74,74,0.975}}, \frac{2.45 \times 10^{-3}}{f_{74,74,0.025}} \right),$$

$$\rho \in \left(\frac{2.45 \times 10^{-3}}{1.5828}, \frac{2.45 \times 10^{-3}}{0.6318} \right),$$

$$\rho \in (1.55 \times 10^{-3}, 3.87 \times 10^{-3}),$$

and

$$A \in (\hat{A}_l, \hat{A}_u) = (\frac{1}{1 + \hat{\rho}_u}, \frac{1}{1 + \hat{\rho}_l}),$$

$$A \in (\frac{1}{1 + 3.87 \times 10^{-3}}, \frac{1}{1 + 1.55 \times 10^{-3}}),$$

$$A \in (0.99614, 0.99846),$$

with 95% degree of confidence.

$\square$

It is worth mentioning that the confidence interval for availability may also be obtained through nonparametric and semi-parametric bootstrap methods (see Section 6.5). Besides, if the requirements are satisfied, the parametric method for proportion may also be adopted (see Section 6.3.1 and Section 6.3.2).

EXERCISES

Exercise 1. Describe the main aspects that distinguish nonparametric and parametric reliability data analysis, and the respective advantages and disadvantages.

Exercise 2. What should be the concerns when using a reliability data set provided by manufacturers, companies-consortia, or general data sources for estimating reliability-related measures of a system? Comment.

Exercise 3. Comment upon your understanding of a) grouped and ungrouped data set, b) complete and censored data, and c) operational data and test generated data.

Exercise 4. Explain the following concepts: a) left-censoring, b) right-censoring type 1 and type 2, c) interval censoring, and d) multi-censored data.

Exercise 5. Assume a set of sixty servers ($n = 60$) were place in an accelerated reliability test. The test finished when all servers presented a failure. Table 25.28, Column t_i, presents the time to failure of the servers in ascending order. Use the method depicted in Section 25.2.1 and calculate a) $\hat{R}(t)$, b) $\hat{F}(t)$, c) $\hat{f}(t)$, d) $\hat{\lambda}(t)$ at $t = 1800.82\,h$, e) draw $\hat{R}(t_i) \times t_i$, f) $\hat{F}(t_i) \times t_i$, g) $\hat{f}(t) \times t$, g) $\hat{\lambda}(t) \times t$, i) $\widehat{MTTF}$, and g) estimate the confidence interval using nonparametric bootstrap.

Exercise 6. Sixty server ($n = 60$) were placed in an accelerated reliability test. The test protocol specifies that an inspection should be carried out every $500\,h$. The test finished when all server failed. Table 25.29 shows the time intervals (Column t_i), the number of failed servers in the respective interval (Column $n_{i-1} - n_i$) and the number of surviving devices at t_i (Column n_i). Adopt a nonparametric method to calculate a) $\hat{R}(t)$ and b) $\hat{F}(t)$ at $t = 3500\,h$, c) draw $\hat{R}(t_i) \times t_i$, and $\hat{F}(t_i) \times t_i$, estimate d) $MTTF$, and e) adopt bootstrap to estimate a confidence interval for the $MTTF$.

Exercise 7. Sixty servers ($n = 60$) went through an accelerated reliability test. However, not all servers were kept until the end of the test, that is, some of them were

Table 25.28
Time to Failure - Complete Data

i	TTF_i (h)	TTF_i (h)	TTF_i (h)	TTF_i (h)	TTF_i (h)	TTF_i (h)
1	1088.55	1808.22	2295.93	2677.00	3715.81	4262.82
2	1421.70	1808.77	2368.95	2734.39	3716.82	4362.63
3	1501.50	1835.81	2438.96	2795.40	3770.61	4500.37
4	1534.56	1859.16	2509.08	2968.35	3808.22	4658.01
5	1611.89	1889.69	2592.39	3106.45	3823.24	4775.04
6	1629.61	2044.81	2601.27	3282.68	3844.85	4798.53
7	1665.32	2065.61	2629.69	3601.69	3943.01	4958.32
8	1740.20	2179.10	2635.79	3623.20	3988.39	5260.35
9	1799.39	2249.68	2660.02	3627.13	4118.64	5508.57
10	1800.82	2261.86	2674.43	3631.10	4216.89	6968.88
j	1	2	3	4	5	6

Table 25.29
Grouped Complete Data

i	t_i (h)	$n_i - n_{i-1}$	n_i	i	t_i (h)	$n_i - n_{i-1}$	n_i
1	500	0	60	8	4000	12	12
2	1000	0	60	9	4500	4	8
3	1500	2	58	10	5000	5	3
4	2000	13	45	11	5500	1	2
5	2500	8	37	12	6000	1	1
6	3000	11	26	13	6500	0	1
7	3500	2	24	14	7000	1	0

removed (censored) from the test when they were still operational. Table 25.30 shows the event times (Column t_i) - failure or censoring. Column δ_i represents failures (1) or censoring (0). Column $t_i - t_{i-1}$ presents the time interval between two consecutive events, and Column i specifies the event order. Using a nonparametric method draw the graphs a) $\hat{R}(t) \times t$, b) $\hat{F}(t) \times t$, c) $\hat{f}(t) \times t$, d) $\hat{\lambda}(t) \times t$ and e) estimate $\hat{R}(3088.73 h)$.

Exercise 8. Adopt the Kaplan-Meier method to analyze the lifetime data depicted in Table 25.28. Calculate a) $\hat{R}(t)$, b) $\hat{F}(t)$, c) $\hat{f}(t)$, d) $\hat{\lambda}(t)$ at $t = 1800.82 h$, e) draw $\hat{R}(t_i) \times t_i$, f) $\hat{F}(t_i) \times t_i$, g) $\hat{f}(t) \times t$, g) $\hat{\lambda}(t) \times t$ and h) $\widehat{MTTF}$.

Exercise 9. Use the Kaplan-Meier method to evaluate the reliability data depicted in Table 25.29. Calculate a) $\hat{R}(t)$ and b) $\hat{F}(t)$ at $t = 3500 h$, c) draw $\hat{R}(t_i) \times t_i$, d) $\hat{F}(t_i) \times t_i$, e) $\hat{f}(t) \times t$, f) $\hat{\lambda}(t) \times t$ and estimate g) $MTTF$.

Table 25.30

Ungrouped Multiply Censored Reliability Data

i	t_i (h)	δ	$t_i - t_{i-1}$ (h)	t_i (h)	δ	$t_i - t_{i-1}$ (h)	t_i (h)	δ	$t_i - t_{i-1}$ (h)
1	19.11	0	19.11	1544.00	1	54.31	4196.34	0	217.43
2	25.62	1	6.51	1558.04	1	1503.73	4278.78	1	4061.36
3	269.48	1	262.97	1947.92	0	444.19	4623.43	1	562.08
4	431.81	1	168.84	2115.51	1	1671.32	4668.51	0	4106.43
5	520.48	0	351.64	2307.92	1	636.60	4862.93	0	756.50
6	533.40	1	181.76	2347.95	0	1711.35	5120.96	1	4364.45
7	684.16	1	502.40	2413.24	0	701.89	5400.25	1	1035.79
8	709.78	0	207.38	2509.03	1	1807.15	5693.01	0	4657.22
9	830.20	1	622.82	2782.08	1	974.93	6120.47	1	1463.25
10	861.62	0	238.80	3088.73	1	2113.80	6656.40	1	5193.15
11	897.72	1	658.91	3153.86	1	1040.06	8042.32	1	2849.17
12	915.40	1	256.49	3156.66	0	2116.60	8893.73	1	6044.55
13	939.79	0	683.30	3162.79	1	1046.19	9022.43	1	2977.88
14	1037.99	0	354.68	3276.37	0	2230.17	9216.15	0	6238.27
15	1113.06	0	758.37	3313.52	1	1083.35	9301.77	1	3063.49
16	1276.45	0	518.08	3323.28	1	2239.93	9379.77	1	6316.28
17	1283.82	1	765.75	3492.84	1	1252.91	9681.48	1	3365.21
18	1353.88	1	588.13	3559.71	1	2306.80	10351.36	1	6986.15
19	1425.11	1	836.98	3966.95	0	1660.15	10993.42	1	4007.27
20	1489.69	0	652.71	3978.91	0	2318.77	13496.11	0	9488.83
j	1	1	1	2	2	2	3	3	3

Exercise 10. Consider the Kaplan-Meier method to analyze the reliability data depicted in Table 25.30. Draw the graphs a) $\hat{R}(t) \times t$, b) $\hat{F}(t) \times t$, c) $\hat{f}(t) \times t$, d) $\hat{\lambda}(t) \times t$ and e) estimate $\hat{R}(3088.73\,h)$.

Exercise 11. Adopt the Kaplan-Meier method to evaluate the lifetime data depicted in Table 25.31 ($n = 60$). Draw the graphs a) $\hat{R}(t) \times t$, b) $\hat{F}(t) \times t$, c) $\hat{f}(t) \times t$, d) $\hat{\lambda}(t) \times t$ and e) estimate $\hat{R}(3000\,h)$.

Exercise 12. Describe and explain the set of main steps required to conduct a parametric reliability data analysis.

Exercise 13. What are the pros and cons of the following parametric reliability data analysis: a) graphical methods, b) methods of moments, and c) maximum likelihood estimation methods?

Exercise 14. Adopt the parametric graphical method to estimate a) the parameters of the respective distribution of the time to failure depicted in Table 25.32. Then, calculate b) reliability at 1500 h, c) the MTTF, d), and the probability of failure occuring before 2000 h. Next, use a semi-parametric bootstrap to estimate e) the distribution parameters' confidence intervals and f) the confidence interval for the

Table 25.31
Grouped and Censored Lifetime

i	t_i (h)	r_i	c_i	i	t_i (h)	r_i	c_i
1	500	0	0	15	7500	0	0
2	1000	0	0	16	8000	0	0
3	1500	5	0	17	8500	3	0
4	2000	2	0	18	9000	0	3
5	2500	0	0	19	9500	3	0
6	3000	1	0	20	10000	0	0
7	3500	0	0	21	10500	0	0
8	4000	0	1	22	11000	4	0
9	4500	0	0	23	11500	2	0
10	5000	0	0	24	12000	0	2
11	5500	3	0	25	12500	1	0
12	6000	0	0	26	13000	1	0
13	6500	0	0	27	13500	1	1
14	7000	0	3				

MTTF, both taking into account a degree of confidence of 95%. Finally, follow the steps of the process introduced at the beginning of Section 25.3.

Exercise 15. Follow the steps of the process introduced at the beginning of Section 25.3, and use the method of moments to estimate a) the parameters of the respective distribution of the time to failure depicted in Table 25.32. Then, calculate b) reliability at 2000 h, c) the MTTF, d), and the probability of failure occuring before 1500 h. Finally, use a semi-parametric bootstrap to estimate e) the distribution parameters'

Table 25.32
Complete Lifetime Data 1

i	i	t_i (h)	i	t_i (h)	i	t_i (h)
1	1491.69	2012.44	2177.31	2304.81	2526.19	2623.42
2	1658.64	2019.12	2191.58	2314.00	2526.29	2638.32
3	1675.79	2084.55	2194.35	2324.13	2542.23	2647.35
4	1682.47	2149.75	2201.15	2325.86	2553.81	2649.69
5	1738.15	2155.84	2202.14	2384.41	2555.57	2655.05
6	1757.47	2157.88	2224.74	2431.54	2562.97	2726.43
7	1757.75	2163.99	2246.18	2440.51	2582.93	2852.27
8	1759.99	2167.58	2246.74	2442.32	2584.48	2860.86
9	1965.29	2171.39	2255.70	2485.58	2610.54	2971.95
10	1999.42	2173.28	2275.81	2496.99	2619.31	2993.84
j	1	2	3	4	5	6

confidence intervals and f) the confidence interval for the MTTF, both taking into account a degree of confidence of 95%.

Exercise 16. Use the steps of the process introduced at the beginning of Section 25.3, and adopt the method of moments to estimate a) the parameters of the respective distribution of the time to failure depicted in Table 25.33. Calculate b) reliability at 1800 h, c) the MTTF, d), and the probability of failure occuring before 2000 h. Use a semi-parametric bootstrap to estimate e) the distribution parameters' confidence intervals and f) the confidence interval for the MTTF, both taking into account a degree of confidence of 95%.

Table 25.33
Complete Lifetime Data 2

i	t_i (h)	t_i (h)	t_i (h)	t_i (h)	t_i (h)	t_i (h)
1	181.08	658.83	1221.34	1845.80	3194.77	5841.50
2	240.86	694.08	1244.88	1851.42	3497.30	5850.43
3	263.06	756.13	1337.23	1935.93	3604.04	6311.20
4	264.17	786.60	1393.94	2454.37	3760.59	6379.18
5	265.68	888.89	1410.33	2472.42	4152.82	7812.82
6	269.54	935.89	1432.05	2692.20	4232.05	7885.99
7	275.38	946.92	1443.58	2762.68	4322.29	9631.08
8	421.45	1016.55	1466.69	2832.03	5419.60	9744.26
9	486.90	1116.88	1677.79	2838.51	5444.05	11362.94
10	600.91	1206.65	1827.14	2864.39	5703.44	12203.88
j	1	1	2	2	3	3

Exercise 17. Adopting the steps of the process presented at the beginning of Section 25.3, and using the MLE method to estimate a) the parameters of the respective distribution of the time to failure depicted in Table 25.34. Then, calculate b) reliability at 1200 h, c) the MTTF, d) the probability of failure occuring before 2100 h, and estimate e) the confidence interval for the MTTF, taking into account a degree of confidence of 95%.

Exercise 18. Sixty electronic devices were placed in a burnout test. Table 25.35 presents the number of days each device i took to present a failure. Use the steps of the process introduced at the beginning of Section 25.3, and adopt the MLE method to estimate a) the parameters of the respective distribution of the time to failure (in number of days), and estimate b) the confidence interval for the MTTF (in days), taking into account a degree of confidence of 90%.

Exercise 19. Consider sixty servers were observed, and the times to failure are assumed to be independent and identically distributed according to an exponential distribution. The experiment finishes when thirty-five ($K = 40$) out of sixty ($N = 60$) servers fail (right-censored type 2). Table 25.36 shows the particular times to failure

Table 25.34

Complete Lifetime Data 3

i	t_i (h)	t_i (h)	t_i (h)	t_i (h)	t_i (h)	t_i (h)
1	1164.47	1879.51	2149.23	2461.07	2687.37	2998.00
2	1335.07	1886.57	2240.11	2474.16	2703.08	3064.88
3	1552.69	1897.95	2242.40	2495.14	2732.45	3077.69
4	1629.10	1912.29	2249.53	2500.40	2746.86	3081.54
5	1643.89	2000.63	2276.01	2522.37	2760.66	3202.92
6	1650.58	2006.88	2316.41	2527.72	2828.27	3218.80
7	1690.51	2038.23	2336.91	2560.14	2840.78	3328.58
8	1756.71	2047.01	2343.17	2599.07	2911.08	3540.94
9	1832.27	2092.11	2379.02	2618.26	2927.73	3782.06
10	1841.94	2144.63	2405.44	2680.06	2962.52	3980.04
j	1	2	3	4	5	6

Table 25.35

Number of Days Required to Each Device to Fail

i	t_i (days)	i	t_i (days)	i	t_i (days)	i	t_i (days)	i	t_i (days)	i	t_i (days)
1	33	11	3	21	7	31	1	41	27	51	1
2	1	12	5	22	2	32	10	42	15	52	5
3	2	13	8	23	1	33	5	43	9	53	3
4	1	14	3	24	5	34	6	44	8	54	3
5	2	15	2	25	4	35	12	45	18	55	2
6	5	16	15	26	6	36	6	46	17	56	6
7	2	17	3	27	1	37	1	47	3	57	7
8	10	18	6	28	2	38	12	48	4	58	3
9	1	19	6	29	5	39	5	49	15	59	15
10	7	20	16	30	1	40	2	50	6	60	1

of the thirty-five servers. Estimate a) the parameter distribution, b) its confidence interval, c) the MTTF with its respective d) confidence interval. Adopt 95% degree of confidence.

Exercise 20. Assume the reliability experiment in which sixty servers ($n = 60$) were observed in an accelerated reliability test. The times each server failed were recorded in Table 25.37 (complete data). a) Conduct an exploratory analysis and check the suitability of an exponential distribution, and provide the respective arguments to reject or not reject it. b) Obtain a point estimate of distribution parameter λ, c) Conduct a goodness of fit. d) Obtain a point estimate of the MTTF. e) Estimate the parameter confidence interval. f) Estimate the MTTF confidence interval. Adopt 5% degree of significance.

Table 25.36

Right-Censored Type 2 Reliability Data

i	t_i (h)	t_i (h)	t_i (h)	t_i (h)
1	8.95	467.27	1096.39	1950.93
2	33.32	592.06	1126.06	2075.53
3	91.09	601.69	1156.91	2319.03
4	131.16	652.75	1214.78	2333.53
5	253.39	681.88	1262.18	2359.06
6	271.13	737.38	1266.85	2493.80
7	315.78	853.69	1453.09	2648.68
8	317.38	952.50	1511.67	3543.60
9	380.30	1033.08	1632.25	5714.21
10	398.49	1048.36	1693.86	7427.04
j	1	2	3	4

Table 25.37

Complete Reliability Data

i	t_i (h)	i	t_i (h)	i	t_i (h)	i	t_i (h)	i	t_i (h)	i	t_i (h)
1	765.32	11	1822.54	21	515.21	31	4569.68	41	408.16	51	338.18
2	736.36	12	2026.03	22	5400.53	32	4104.01	42	1509.31	52	197.89
3	4688.02	13	211.91	23	1460.71	33	728.45	43	434.26	53	584.37
4	2181.27	14	1109.13	24	1672.60	34	1188.55	44	2005.96	54	86.76
5	4085.90	15	1189.89	25	640.21	35	640.83	45	924.12	55	2204.17
6	9044.38	16	1348.37	26	711.69	36	5613.10	46	1510.17	56	6591.52
7	3573.45	17	389.56	27	190.62	37	247.44	47	2548.00	57	6023.71
8	7201.78	18	3563.30	28	4266.00	38	1647.28	48	157.32	58	398.62
9	1237.32	19	2082.53	29	1087.26	39	500.76	49	399.17	59	4064.59
10	740.13	20	3322.64	30	489.08	40	3510.87	50	2020.38	60	2467.03

Exercise 21. Considering the servers' time to failure depicted in Table 25.37, and assuming the time to repair each server was recorded in Table 25.38: a) Conduct an exploratory analysis and check the suitability of an exponential distribution and provide the respective arguments to reject or not reject it; b) Obtain a point estimate of the distribution parameter μ; c) Conduct a goodness of fit test; d) Obtain a point estimate of the MTTR; e) Estimate the parameter confidence interval; f) Estimate the MTTR confidence interval; g) Obtain a point estimate of the availability, and h) estimate the availability confidence interval. Adopt 95% degree of confidence.

Exercise 22. Consider the reliability experiment in which sixty servers ($n = 60$) were observed in an accelerated reliability test. The times each server failed were recorded in Table 25.37 (complete data). Using a nonparametric method, calculate a) $\hat{R}(t)$, b)

Table 25.38

Time to Repair

i	t_i (h)	i	t_i (h)	i	t_i (h)	i	t_i (h)	i	t_i (h)	i	t_i (h)
1	37.22	11	0.55	21	77.86	31	19.38	41	75.61	51	48.76
2	139.50	12	48.81	22	47.11	32	182.35	42	157.60	52	118.03
3	24.32	13	58.16	23	4.40	33	86.26	43	8.66	53	65.51
4	14.23	14	25.52	24	56.38	34	4.94	44	41.18	54	42.57
5	10.52	15	32.71	25	18.90	35	40.57	45	58.78	55	26.96
6	39.32	16	9.54	26	2.72	36	55.67	46	4.96	56	14.14
7	64.19	17	18.39	27	0.19	37	76.56	47	5.34	57	102.39
8	34.35	18	39.92	28	21.85	38	38.61	48	2.17	58	16.45
9	45.10	19	162.43	29	287.06	39	82.61	49	107.50	59	8.61
10	124.29	20	51.72	30	105.93	40	18.60	50	39.75	60	140.42

$\hat{F}(t)$, c) $\hat{f}(t)$, d) $\hat{\lambda}(t)$ at $t = 1000h$, e) draw $\hat{R}(t_i) \times t_i$, f) $\hat{F}(t_i) \times t_i$, g) $\hat{f}(t) \times t$, h) $\hat{\lambda}(t) \times t$, i) $\widehat{MTTF}$, and j) estimate the confidence interval using nonparametric bootstrap.

26 Fault Injection and Failure Monitoring

Dependable systems are designed to cope with faults through mechanisms that constrain errors' propagation and avoid system failures. Therefore, obtaining statistical data from the operational environment after implementing the system or from an equivalent system already operating on the field may not be a suitable alternative due to the time required to obtain such data.

Indeed, fault injection has two main aims: system validation and system evaluation. The first objective concerns comparing the specified behavior with the implemented system's behavior and gaining confidence if the system behaves as expected in the presence of faults [32, 70]. The second objective aims to check if the implemented system copes with faults appropriate as specified. In other words, fault injection methods provide means for measuring the impact of faults in the systems' functions and performance and for evaluating how effective fault-tolerant mechanisms are on models, working prototypes, or systems in the field. Hence, fault injection tools provide means to improve the confidence in the systems' ability to deliver the proper service [20, 109].

Already by 1972 fault-injection was adopted to test the *Self-Testing And Repairing computer* (JPL-STAR) [28]. A major concern when adopting fault injection for a system is to assure that the generated faults represent actual faults to obtain meaningful results [251]. Fault injection literature is prolific in efforts aiming to study fault injection techniques. Fault injection methods range, for instance, from voltage glitches to electromagnetic interference, encompassing light attack, heavy-ion radiation, and software injected faults [60, 70, 82, 135, 217, 231, 262, 266, 300, 309, 399, 408].

This chapter aims first to characterize some important fault injection procedures and then introduce the concept of fault acceleration and some fault acceleration models. Later, some noteworthy fault injection tools are briefly discussed, and finally, we examine a generic architecture of a software-based fault injection tool.

The fault injections may be applied in an existing system or functional system prototype or in a system model [85, 181]. This classification takes into account two perspectives: 1) the aim target to which faults are to be injected or 2) the implementation mechanism. The aim target could be: a) specifications (models) or b) systems (actual systems or system-functional prototypes). The implementation mechanism may be divided as a) hardware-based, b) software-based, and c) hardware-software-based fault injection mechanisms. Hardware-implemented fault injection is accomplished by disturbing the hardware with fluctuations in the environment parameters' values. Such variations may be produced by heavy-ion radiation, electromagnetic interference, voltage glitches at the system's specific points, power supply disturbances, luminous exposures, etc. Hardware fault injection mechanisms are only be applied to existing systems or functional hardware prototypes. Software-based fault injection mechanisms, on the other hand, may be employed **i)** to inject actual software faults in a system, functional prototype, **ii)** to emulate hardware faults on existing systems or functional prototypes, and **iii)** to simulate hardware and software faults in the models. Hybrid strategies combine two or more fault injection methods to exercise the system under analysis. For example, employing hardware and software fault injection techniques may improve the model's validation process and support verifying how effective a fault-tolerant mechanism is by joining the versatility of software fault injection and the accuracy of hardware monitoring. Figure 26.1 shows the hardware-based fault injection mechanisms, software-based fault injection mechanisms, and the target where each strategy may be applied, that is, a functional system (or even an operation prototype) or a model.

	Hardware Fault Injection	Software Fault Injection
System	• Voltage glitches. • Electromagnetic interference. • Light attack. • Heavy-ion radiation etc.	• For emulating harware faults. • At the software layers' stack.
Model	X	Simulation.

Figure 26.1 Fault Injection Characterization.

Fault injection may also be classified as **invasive** or **non-invasive** methods. For example, optical discharge such as laser-shooting on a particular hardware module may require depacking the device to direct the laser beam to the device's surface. In such a case, clear evidence of depacking and packing are likely to be unavoidable. On the other hand, lowering the power voltage or increasing the hardware module's clock rate may not require depacking the module; thus, it does not damage the device covering. A software fault may also be injected by changing variables or memory location's value or might be emulated by disabling communication interfaces between systems' components and the environment.

26.1 FAULT ACCELERATION

The reliability of physical devices is greatly subject to the working environment. Consequently, testing such devices should take the environmental factors into account. The testing times are usually considerably shorter than the devices' expected lifetimes. Environmental stressing promotes stimuli to the device's system to hasten faults that are presumed to evolve to failures during the operational phase regarding the intended working environment attributes [60, 115, 160, 204, 269, 279, 337, 429].

There are numerous accelerated stress models. Most of these models are either statistical or physics-based models [124, 269, 469].

Environmental stresses are generally related to (1) natural stress, circumscribed by the geographic area, meteorological conditions, and (2) induced stress situations. The latter may be either directly or indirectly shaped to mimic stress exposures due to environmental conditions. These environmental stimuli back the creation of harsh circumstances that lead to changes in time to failure or lifetime under a normal state. The most common scenarios of interest are those that represent failure accelerations. For example, if corrosion failures occur at typical temperatures and humidities, then identical corrosion is likely to arise much faster in a humidified laboratory at high temperatures. The testing activity that resembles the environmental factors for the accelerating fault phenomenon is called fault acceleration. It is worth stressing that physical models might be appealing choices for representing well-known failure phenomena. However, the relations between accelerating factors and the actual failure are usually complex. In many practical cases, simpler approximation models may suffice when a set of plausible constraints are adopted. On the other hand, empirical models may be an attractive modeling approach when the chemical or physical failing processes are not well known. However, the analyst should be careful when adopting such models for extrapolation.

Failure scaling factors (usually called acceleration factors AF) or its inverse, time scaling factors (usually called compression factors $CF = 1/AF$), are functions that assign to faults' events values that represent primary parameters to accelerated life testing. The acceleration factors speed up systems' or devices' degradation and allow one to estimate the failure rate - λ - (or the time to failure - TTF) under stress circumstances due to temperature, voltage, humidity, mechanical wear-out, memory leaking, etc. A suitable choice of such factors, AF or CF, supports extrapolating the failure rate (or the time to failure) to a given specific operational state. The acceleration factor is defined as the ratio between the average failure rate at state condition 1 - stress (λ_1 or λ_s) and average failure rate at state condition 2 - possibly normal operational condition (λ_2 or λ_o); hence

$$AF = \frac{\lambda_2}{\lambda_1} = \frac{\lambda_s}{\lambda_o}, \tag{26.1.1}$$

which is equivalent to

$$AF = \frac{TTF_1}{TTF_2} = \frac{TTF_o}{TTF_s}, \tag{26.1.2}$$

where TTF_1 (TTF_o) and TTF_2 (TTF_s) are time to failure at condition 1 (possibly normal operation condition) and the time to failure at condition 2 (stress), respectively.

Constant Scaling

In many practical cases, simple **constant scaling factors** represent the environment's dynamics that affect the fault events for reasonable value ranges. Hence, as the time to failure of an event in stress conditions may be estimated from

$$TTF_s = TTF_o \times CF,$$

where CF is constant, the cumulative distribution function is obtained from

$$F_s(t) = F_o\left(\frac{t}{CF}\right). \tag{26.1.3}$$

As $f(t) = dF(t)/dt$, then

$$f_s(t) = \frac{1}{CF} \times f_o\left(\frac{t}{CF}\right). \tag{26.1.4}$$

As the hazard function (see Equation 16.2.6) is

$$\lambda(t) = \frac{f(t)}{R(t)} = \frac{f(t)}{1 - F(t)},$$

then

$$\lambda_s(t) = \frac{\frac{1}{CF} \times f_o\left(\frac{t}{CF}\right)}{1 - F_o\left(\frac{t}{CF}\right)}.$$

Therefore

$$\lambda_s(t) = \frac{1}{CF} \times \lambda_o(t). \tag{26.1.5}$$

Thus, applying transformation factor CF (constant), the Equations 26.1.3, 26.1.4, and 26.1.5 do not change their respective shapes. On the other hand, if the scaling factor (AF, CF) is not constant, then the shape of the distribution TTF_s may change with relation to the shape of the distribution TTF_o.

As the mean time to failure may be calculated from (see Equation 16.2.11)

$$MTTF = \int_0^\infty (1 - F(t))\, dt,$$

then, the mean time to failure ($MTTF_s$) may be obtained from

$$MTTF_s = \int_0^\infty \left(1 - F_o\left(\frac{t}{CF}\right)\right) dt, \tag{26.1.6}$$

Table 26.1
Linear Relations

Measures	Normal	Stress
Time	TTF_o	$TTF_s = TTF_o \times CF$
CDF	$F_o(t)$	$F_s(t) = F_o\left(\frac{t}{CF}\right)$
Density function	$f_o(t)$	$f_s(t) = \frac{1}{CF} \times f_o\left(\frac{t}{CF}\right)$
Hazard Function	$\lambda_o(t)$	$\lambda_s(t) = \frac{1}{CF} \times \lambda_o(t)$
MTTF	$MTTF_o$	$MTTF_s = MTTF_o \times CF$

which is equal to

$$MTTF_s = MTTF_o \times CF, \tag{26.1.7}$$

when CF is constant. Hence, let us summarize these results in Table 26.1.

Example 26.1.1. Assume a stress experiment was executed and a sample of one hundred times to failure was collected. The mean time to failure calculated from the sample was $MTTF_s = 548.3\,h$. If the acceleration factor is $AF = 12$, then the mean time to failure at normal operation condition may be estimated using Equation 26.1.2. Hence,

$$MTTF_o = AF \times MTTF_s$$

$$MTTF_o = 12 \times 548.3\,h$$

$$MTTF_o = 6579.6\,h.$$

$\square$

There is a subtle assumption when multiplying test lifetime data by a constant factor since it assumes the lifetime distribution of the system under stress conditions is the same as the lifetime distribution of the system in normal operating conditions. Consequently, the two distributions are considered to have the same shape, which may not be the case [469].

Non-Constant Scaling

For **non-constant scaling factors**, the failure rate (and the time to failure) changes according to the stresses' parameters represented in the model. Failure rate increases are commonly related to aging, environmental condition changes, and operation stress levels. Assume the following very general model

$$AF = \sum_{i=1}^{n} B_i \times A_i^{(D_i - F_i \times s_i)^{E_i}} + C_i, \tag{26.1.8}$$

where B_i, C_i, D_i, and F_i are constant values, and s_i is a stress parameter, such that $s_i \in [0, D_i]$. Besides, A_i and E_i are functions of the stress parameter s_i, which may also be constant, and n is the number of stress factors. Such a model may configured to represent many scaling factors' dynamics.

Example 26.1.2. Consider the failure acceleration factor model defined in Expression 26.1.8 of a specific device customized with $n = 1$, $A_1 = B_1 = E_1 = F = 1$, $C_1 = 0$, and $D_1 = 2$. Thus, the specific scaling factor is

$$AF = A_0^{2-s},$$

where $A_{1_0} = A_0 = 4$; hence

$$AF = 4^{2-s},$$

where $s \in [0, 2]$ denotes the stress level, and A_0 is the failure factor when no failure acceleration is applied. The maximal stress level is two ($s = 2$) and when no stress is applied $s = 0$. An accelerated experiment was conducted for a sample of similar devices and the mean time to failure considering the stress level $s = 2$ was $MTTF_s = 548.3\,h$. Thus, the mean time to failure at normal operation conditions ($s = 0$) is estimated by

$$MTTF_o = MTTF_s \times AF,$$

$$MTTF_o = MTTF_s \times A_0^{2-s},$$

$$MTTF_o = 548.3\,h \times 4^2,$$

$$MTTF_o = 8772.38\,h.$$

Figure 26.2.a and Figure 26.2.b depict the failure rate and the mean time to failure as function of $AF = A_0^{2-s}$ for $A_0 = 4$ and $s \in [0, 2]$.

□

A power law is a relationship between quantities where a change in one quantity is inversely proportional to the power of another quantity. In a mechanical system, the lifetime of a component is expected to decrease as stress increases. One of the most widely used models for reliability stress analysis of mechanical systems is the **Inverse Power Law (IPL)** [377]. The *IPL* model may be represented by customizing the Model 26.1.8. For instance, assuming $n = 1$, and $B_1 = B$ is a real positive constant, $A_i = s$, $C_1 = D_1 = 0$, $E_1 = 1$ and $F_1 = n$, we obtain

$$TTF = Bs^{-n}, \tag{26.1.9}$$

which is an *IPL* model for the time to failure (*TTF*).

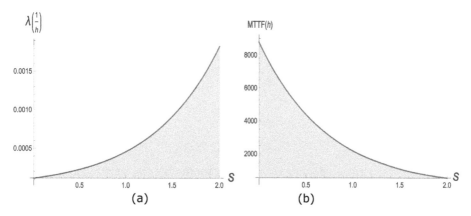

Figure 26.2   a) $\lambda(AT) \times AF$ and b) $MTTF(AT) \times AF$.

Example 26.1.3. Assume a mechanical system whose time to failure is dependent on electrical tension, V, provided by the power supplier, and obeys the *IPL*

$$TTF = BV^{-2},$$

where B is the dimensional constant equal to $10^8 \, hV^2$. If the mean time to failure, $MTTF_2$, for $V_2 = 120V$ is $7000\,h$, the mean time to failure, $MTTF_1$ (and the respective failure rate, assuming it is constant at that respective voltage) taking into account the electrical tension at $V_1 = 140V$ may estimated using

$$MTTF_1 = BV_1^{-2},$$

and

$$MTTF_2 = BV_2^{-2}.$$

Hence,

$$\frac{MTTF_1}{MTTF_2} = \frac{BV_1^{-2}}{BV_2^{-2}},$$

$$MTTF_1 = MTTF_2 V_1^{-2} V_2^2, \qquad (26.1.10)$$

$$MTTF_1 = 120h \times 140^{-2} V^{-2} \times 120^2 V^2 = 5142.86h,$$

and

$$\lambda_1 = \lambda_2 V_1^2 V_2^{-2}, \tag{26.1.11}$$

$$\lambda_1 = \frac{1}{120\,h} \times 140^2 V^2 \times 120^{-2} V^{-2} = 1.944 \times 10^{-4} h^{-h}.$$

□

Regression

An alternative strategy is adopting **curve fitting methods** as those introduced in Section 6.7 to estimate parameters (failure rates, time to failure statistics, etc.) at several different high-stress levels, and then fitting the respective model, and extrapolating the found parameter values to the normal stress level. Hence, such a strategy aims to find out trends that allow having predictive analytic functions through the available data set to estimate failure parameters at normal operating conditions.

Example 26.1.4. Let us consider five samples of ten similar devices that were tested under distinct stress levels. The stress levels adopted in the experiment accelerate the devices' failures by 10, 12, 14, 16, and 18. The whole experiment finished when every device of each sample failed. We assume the failure rate is constant for each stress level. The mean failure rate and the respective mean time to failure for each stress level are depicted in Table 26.2.

Table 26.2
Stress Levels (s) × Mean Failure Rates (λ) and MTTF

s (stress level)	λ (fph)	$MTTF$ (h)
10	8.55×10^{-3}	116.98
12	1.13×10^{-2}	88.31
14	1.56×10^{-2}	64.15
16	2.36×10^{-2}	42.42
18	3.21×10^{-2}	31.13

Figure 26.3.a shows the set of points, each represented by $(s, \lambda(s))$, where $\lambda(s)$ is the mean failure rate, obtained from the sample evaluated considering the specific stress level, $s \in \{10, 12, 14, 16, 18\}$. Likewise, Figure 26.3.b shows the set of points $\{(s, MTTF(s))\}$, where $MTTF(s)$ is the mean time to failure obtained from the sample evaluated at the stress level s.

Applying exponential regression (see Section 6.7.3) to the data set $\{(s, \lambda(s))\}$, we obtain

$$\lambda(s) = 1.4638 \times 10^{-3} e^{171.891 \times 10^{-3} s} \; fph.$$

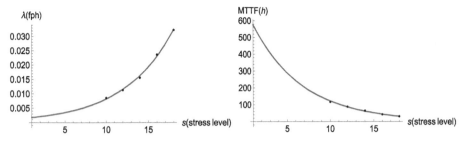

Figure 26.3   a) $\lambda(s) \times s$ and b) $MTTF(s) \times s$,

The root mean square error for the model shown above and the respective data points is $RMSE = 4.66 \times 10^{-4}$. Extrapolating s to normal operation conditions, $s = 1$, we obtain $\lambda = 1.776 \times 10^{-3}$ *fph* (a constant failure rate at normal condition.); thus $MTTF = 575.26\,h$. Regression models are one of the most popular statistical procedures employed for forecasting, and many of such models could be applied to data sets according to their trends.

□

Arrhenius Model

In 1889, Svante August Arrhenius[1] proposed an equation that combines the concepts of temperatures and rates of chemical reactions [23, 378]. More precisely, Arrhenius' model relates the concepts of activation energy and the Boltzmann probability distribution. The Boltzmann distribution (also called Gibbs distribution) provides the probability of a specific system state as a function of the state's energy and temperature [122]; that is

$$p_i = \frac{e^{\frac{E_i}{kT}}}{\sum_{j=1}^{m} e^{\frac{E_j}{kT}}},$$

where p_i is the probability of the system being in state i, E_i is the energy of that state, m is the number of all accessible states in the system, and a constant kT of the distribution is the product of Boltzmann's constant ($k = 8.62 \times 10^{-5}\,eV/K$) and thermodynamic temperature T (in Kelvin).

The Arrhenius formula formalizes the dependency between the reaction rates (r), the system temperature, and the activation energy (E_a).

$$r = F \times e^{\frac{-E_a}{kT}}, \qquad (26.1.12)$$

---

[1]A Swedish physicist who received the Nobel Prize for Chemistry in 1903 [378].

where F is the pre-exponential factor (also called the frequency factor), which denotes the frequency of collisions between reactant molecules at a standard concentration and a specific temperature, and E_a is the activation energy. The activation energy is the threshold energy that the reactant(s) must gain before entering a transition state. Assuming Equation 26.1.12 to represent failures in electro-electronic systems at two temperatures $T_1 > T_2$, we obtain:

$$\lambda_1 = F \times e^{\frac{-E_a}{kT_1}}$$

and

$$\lambda_2 = F \times e^{\frac{-E_a}{kT_2}}.$$

Hence the ratio λ_2/λ_1 represents the acceleration rate due to the temperature difference; thus :

$$\frac{\lambda_2}{\lambda_1} = e^{\left(\frac{-E_a}{kT_1} - \frac{E_a}{kT_2}\right)} = e^{-\frac{E_a}{k} \times \left(\frac{1}{T_1} - \frac{1}{T_2}\right)}.$$

Therefore,

$$\lambda_1 = \lambda_2 \times e^{-\frac{E_a}{k} \times \left(\frac{1}{T_1} - \frac{1}{T_2}\right)}. \tag{26.1.13}$$

Considering that failure time has a function of the exponential distribution we have:

$$MTTF_1 = \frac{1}{\lambda_1}$$

and

$$MTTF_2 = \frac{1}{\lambda_2}.$$

Hence,

$$MTTF_1 = MTTF_2 \times e^{\frac{E_a}{k} \times \left(\frac{1}{T_1} - \frac{1}{T_2}\right)}. \tag{26.1.14}$$

The relationship of the Arrhenius model and probability distributions such as Weibull and lognormal, consult [124, 448]. Finally, it is worth remarking that the activation energy, E_a, is empirically estimated by varying the environment temperature, verifying the respective time to failure, and estimate the activation energy by

$$E_a = \frac{k \ln\left(\frac{\lambda_2}{\lambda_1}\right)}{\frac{1}{T_1} - \frac{1}{T_2}}. \tag{26.1.15}$$

Example 26.1.5. Assume a network switch has a time to failure distributed according to an exponential distribution with failure rate equal to $\lambda_2 = 2.5 \times 10^{-5}\,h^{-1}$ at temperature $20^0\,C$ [160, 407]. Assuming the activation energy is $E_a = 0.6\,eV$ [253, 450, 451], the mean time to failure of the network switch at $32^0\,C$ may be estimated using the Arrhenius formula by first converting the temperatures from Celsius scale to Kelvin. Hence

$$T_2 = 20^0\,C = 293.15\,K,$$

and

$$T_1 = 32^0\,C = 305.15\,K.$$

As $k = 8.62 \times 10^{-5}\,eV/K$, we have

$$\lambda_1 = \lambda_2 \times e^{-\frac{E_a}{k} \times \left(\frac{1}{T_1} - \frac{1}{T_2}\right)}$$

$$\lambda_1 = 2.5\,10^{-5} \times e^{-\frac{0.6}{8.62 \times 10^{-5}} \times \left(\frac{1}{305.15} - \frac{1}{293.15}\right)}$$

$$\lambda_1 = 6.36\,10^{-5}\,h^{-1}.$$

Thus,

$$MTTF_1 = \frac{1}{\lambda_1} = \frac{1}{6.36\,10^{-5}\,h^{-1}} = 15{,}723.37\,h.$$

$\square$

Eyring Model

The Eyring[2] model extends the Arrhenius model by including other stress variables as required. These variables may represent stress parameters such as humidity and voltage, for instance. The Eyring model represents the reaction rates (λ) by

$$\lambda = F\,T^\alpha\,e^{\left(-\frac{E_a}{kT} - \sum_{i=1}^{n} S_i\left(B_i + \frac{C_i}{T}\right)\right)}, \tag{26.1.16}$$

---

[2]Henry Eyring was a chemist best known for his theory of absolute reaction rates and the theory of the activated elaborate chemical transition state reactions [213].

where α, B_i, C_i, D_i, and E_i are constants determining stress interaction and S_i are stress parameters. It is worth noting that if α, B_i, C_i, D_i, and E_i are all zero for all i, the Eyring model is reduced to the Arrhenius model.

As an example consider a case that $B_i = 0$, $\forall i$, $i > 2$, $i \in \mathbb{N}$, $\alpha = C_i =$, $D_i = E_i = 0$ $\forall i$, $i \in \mathbb{N}$, and $S_1 = \ln(1/V)$, where V is the electrical tension. Therefore, we have

$$\lambda = F T^0 e^{\left(-\frac{E_a}{kT} - B \ln(\frac{1}{V})\right)},$$

$$\lambda = F e^{\left(-\frac{E_a}{kT}\right)} \times e^{-B \ln(\frac{1}{V})},$$

$$\lambda = F e^{\left(-\frac{E_a}{kT}\right)} \times e^{-B \ln(\frac{1}{V})},$$

$$\lambda = F V^{-B} e^{\frac{-E_a}{kT}} \tag{26.1.17}$$

Assuming that the time to failure is exponentially distributed, we have:

$$MTTF = \frac{V^B e^{\frac{E_a}{kT}}}{F}. \tag{26.1.18}$$

This expression is a two-stress Eyring model with temperature and electrical tension as stress parameters, such that the temperature follows the Arrhenius model and the electrical tension obeys the inverse power relationship.

Example 26.1.6. Now consider an electro-electronic system operating at temperature T_2 and with its power source providing electrical tension equal to $V_2 \in VR$, where VR is the voltage range supported by the electro-electronic system. If the system's failure rate is well represented by Equation 26.1.17, then we have

$$\lambda_2 = F V_2^{-B} e^{\frac{-E_a}{kT_2}}.$$

Likewise,

$$MTTF_2 = \frac{V_2^B e^{\frac{E_a}{kT_2}}}{F}.$$

Now assume the temperature changes to T_1 ($T_1 > T_2$) and the power sources bounce the voltage and stabilize at V_1 ($V_1 > V_2$). Hence,

$$\lambda_1 = F V_1^{-B} e^{\frac{-E_a}{kT_1}}$$

and

$$MTTF_1 = \frac{V_1^B e^{\frac{E_a}{kT_1}}}{F}.$$

Therefore,

$$\lambda_1 = \lambda_2 V_1^{-B} V_2^B e^{\frac{E_a(T_1 - T_2)}{kT_1 T_2}} \tag{26.1.19}$$

and

$$MTTF_1 = MTTF_2 \times V_1^B V_2^{-B} e^{\frac{E_a(T_2 - T_1)}{kT_1 T_2}} \tag{26.1.20}$$

Assume the activation energy is $E_a = 0.6\,eV$, and $B = 1.5^3$. Consider $MTTF_2 = 20000\,h$ for $T_2 = 295.15\,K$ and $V_2 = 3\,V$. $MTTF_1$ is estimated adopting Equation 26.1.20 for $T_1 \in (295.15\,K, 304.15\,K)$ and $V_1 \in (3V, 5V)$ and is shown in Figure 26.4.

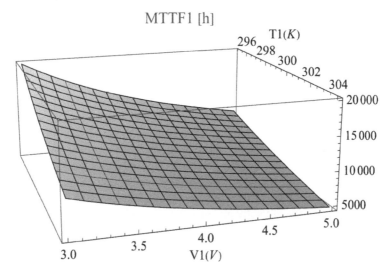

Figure 26.4 Eyring Model - Two-Stress Parameters - Temperature and Electrical Tension.

The number of accelerated life testing models is extensive; discussing additional models and methods is beyond the scope of this text. However, the attentive reader may refer to the bibliography cited in this section for material discussing them.

26.2 SOME NOTABLE FAULT INJECTION TOOLS

This section provides a glimpse of a set of key fault injection tools. Among them, some traditional fault injection platforms from the 80s and 90s are briefly discussed.

---

[3]B may be estimated through experiments and regression analysis as E_a.

These leading platforms provide the grounds for more recent tools. Besides, the section also highlights a few more recent appliances. Nevertheless, it does not intend to offer a comprehensive overview of present-day tools at hand; instead, it only offers some relevant initiatives in the field.

- **Czeck, Segall, and Siewibrek**

Czeck, Segall, and Siewibrek proposed a software fault insertion tool for emulating transient faults in the processor data path, control path, memory system, and transmission bus. The motivation for implementing such a tool was to reduce the complexity of hardware fault insertion and the respective automation processes. Besides, software inserted faults are repeatable within a system and across architectural and implementation boundaries. This tool supports defining the location, timing, and duration of the inserted faults [89].

- **FIAT**

The Fault-Injection-based Automated Testing environment (FIAT) is an automated real-time distributed accelerated fault injection environment implemented to emulate hardware and software faults to support validation and uncover deficiencies in systems' error detection mechanisms, recovery procedures to guide tradeoffs between alternative designs. Faults are introduced by a fault injection library linked with the target process for corrupting memory on requests from an external program. A library code is also employed to watch the process behavior and for data gathering. Such a solution intends to subdue the operating system's security mechanisms that prevent external processes from altering the state of a target process. FIAT also provides a user interface and a hardware/software structure for aiding the definition of workloads, faults, for managing remote experiments, and for data analysis. FIAT provides the analyst with means for defining fault classes, choosing where, when, and how long errors will strike, and how they will communicate with executing object code or data. One of the significant flaws of FIAT was linking the fault injection library at compilation time using the object or the source code of the target. This procedure is unsuitable for third-party software [374, 375].

- **FOCUS**

FOCUS is a design automation platform for analyzing jet-engine controllers that employ a simulation environment based on SPLICE for tracking the impact of transient faults. The simulation environment feeds the analysis software with faults to discover critical design features that may lead to system failures and enable the identification of fault propagation paths and the most sensitive modules to fault propagation [75].

- **MESSALINE**

MESSALINE is a pin-level fault injection platform composed of four modules: the injection module, the activation module, the collection module, and the management module. The activation module assures the correct initialization of the target system.

The collection module is used to observe the target system. Finally, the management module is accountable for the automated and parameterizable generation of the test sequences, controlling the execution runtime, and storing the result for post-test analysis. The first three modules are hardware modules, whereas the management module is implemented as a software component [19, 20].

- **RIFLE**

RIFLE is a hardware fault injection mechanism that injects faults at the pin-level of hardware modules such as the processor, the memory, the bus, controllers, or other devices. The injection of faults is deterministic and can be reproduced if required. RIFLE can also detect particular states in which the injected faults do not harm the target system. The preeminent idea of RIFLE is to couple trigger and tracing methods adopted in digital logic analyzers with the logic demanded by the pin-level fault insertion. The tracing data is adopted for describing faults and their influence on the target system and for error propagation process analysis [250].

- **DEFINE**

DEFINE is a distributed fault injection and monitoring environment to evaluate system dependability, analyze fault propagation, and validate fault-tolerant mechanisms. DEFINE can inject hardware faults (emulation) and software faults into a distributed system and observe their impact and propagation among machines. It applies two fault injection methods: the first employs the hardware clock that interrupts to control fault injection and activation; the second adopts software traps to inject and monitor fault activation. DEFINE consists of four parts: a controller, a software monitor, a fault injector, and a workload generator. A target system is a group of connected machines. Therefore, DEFINE should be installed on a machine that is not part of the target system for not being affected by the faults [458].

- **MEFISTO-C**

MEFISTO-C [144] is an upgraded version of MEFISTO (Multi-level Error/Fault Injection Simulation Tool) [192]. MEFISTO-C uses a VHDL simulator for injecting faults via simulator commands that alter variables and signals defined in VHDL models. It grants users a set of predefined fault models, features to set up and conduct fault injection attacks. MEFISTO-C supports estimating fault-tolerance mechanisms' coverage, investigating distinct VHDL abstraction-levels mappings, and validating fault-tolerant mechanisms.

- **FERRARI**

The Fault and ERRor Automatic Real-time Injector (FERRARI) is a software fault injection tool that emulates transient errors and permanent hardware faults by corrupting the executing target program's state. This is accomplished by using traps and system calls to enable software to emulate the effects of faults and errors. One of FERRARI's key features is to support the control to define the type, location, and time of fault and error injection. The fault injection mechanism is carried out by the concurrent execution of the target program and the fault injection mechanism process, which modifies the execution state of the target program. FERRARI comprises four modules: the initializer and activator, the user information, the fault and error injector, and the collector and analyzer. The manager module controls these modules by coordinating the information flow and commands among the four modules [202].

- **XCEPTION**

Xception is a fault injection platform for dependability analysis that generates faults by software and monitors faults' activation to observe their impacts on the system behavior. XCEPTION uses a set of debugging and performance monitoring features, such as performance counters and breakpoint registers - existing in processors - to inject faults by software and observe the faults' activations and their influence on the target system. It supports a comprehensive collection of fault triggers such as spatial, temporal, and e data memory fault triggers. The target application is not modified, no software traps are inserted, and it is not required to execute the target application in special trace mode. The injected faults can be adopted to emulate physical faults, even affecting the internal target processor units. Xception consists of a kernel module, a fault setup module, and the Experiment Manager module (EMM). The kernel module consists of the exception handlers and the code for performing fault injection. The fault setup module is a library of functions whose only task is to receive the fault parameters from the host and pass them to the kernel. Fault setup is accomplished by invoking the library function, StartXception(), from any processor in the target system. The target application or a dedicated process can be invoked if the application source code is not available. The EMM uses a distinct kernel for conducting fault injection experiments. The EMM runs on a host system and provides the user interface for fault definition, automatic fault injection experiment control, and collection of results. The target system is regarded as composed of the processor, system buses, and memory, where the processor is further divided into its functional units [69].

- **FTape**

FTape (Fault Tolerance and Performance Evaluator) generates software-implemented fault injection under stressful workload generation to increase the likelihood of errors spread to produce failures. FTAPE emulates physical faults by software and monitors workload activity. For instance, a memory location can be flipped to emulate the impact of an alpha particle on a memory bit. The fault injector emulates faults on CPU registers, memory locations, and disks and combines stressful workload generation to evaluate error propagation by monitoring workload activities. FTape also supports defining the fault injection spot, instant, and workload threshold to enable fault generation. Probability distributions may also be employed to specify the fault generation instant and location randomly. The tool comprises three main parts: the fault injector, the monitoring module, and a synthetic workload generator. The primary goal of the workload generator is to sustain a controllable workload that may disseminate erroneous states due to injected faults [440].

- **MAFALDA**

MAFALDA (Microkernel Assessment by Fault Injection and Design Aid) is an experimental platform for backing the characterization of the failure modes in the presence of injected faults and modules wrapping focused on microkernels for enhancing dependability. Its fault injector offers two types of fault injections. The first type consists of randomly altering a chosen byte among the byte string that composes the set of parameters provided to the microkernel during the invocation of one of its primitives. Hence, when workload demands the execution of one of these primitives, it fails since the corresponding functional component tested is corrupted, while the other primitives continue stable. The second type of fault injection emulates a physical fault or a software fault into the microkernel. The injection process consists of corrupting a randomly picked byte within the address space of the targeted functional module, that is, its text segment and its data segment. Such microkernel fault injection uses debugging hardware features existing in most processors to inject faults by software and monitor the activation of the faults in the same manner as Xception [69]. The measures offered by MAFALDA are a summary of the events witnessed during the fault injection attack, including a) errors distribution, b) errors propagation, c) notifications distribution, such as exceptions, errors status, and d) the corresponding latencies when appropriate such as generated by exceptions [362].

- **VFIT**

VFIT (VHDL-based Fault Injection Tool) is a fault-injection tool equipped to inject faults into VHDL models at the gate, register, and chip levels. It is possible to define the injection time and duration through various probability distribution functions. A fault injection intervention consists of injecting faults into the model according to the parameters' values. When a fault is injected, the model's behavior is assessed, and at the end of the attack, the values of some specified parameters are obtained. The tool is composed of a configuration module, a parser, a VHDL injector library, a GUI, a macro-injection library, and the injection manager [156].

- **G-SWFIT**

G-SWFIT (Generic Software Fault Injection Technique) is a tool that aids in emulating software faults through a library of fault operators. The faults are directly injected into the target executable code. Each fault emulation operator in the library consists of a machine-code level pattern matching code changes depicting the most common software faults (bugs) seen for that code pattern. The fault emulation method changes the binary code of software modules by injecting specific changes that reflect the code generated by the compiler if the expected fault were in the high-level source code. A library of fault emulation operators previously specified for a target platform guides the injection of code modifications. The fault emulation involves scanning the target code for particular low-level instruction patterns and changing the code in the places identified to emulate the expected high-level faults. The code changing tool contains a disassembler to translate the executable file into assembly code where the machine-code patterns are browsed and the mutations are inserted. The G-SWFIT fault emulation operators are defined around two concepts: (1) Searching defined patterns to identify locations where to emulate a given fault; and (2) Low-level mutation, which consists of code replacing applied to locations where the intended fault emulation is meant to occur [114].

- **PreFail**

PreFail is a programmable failure-injection tool for automating multiple-fault injection and analysis. It enables checkers to formulate policies to denote sets of multiple-fault combinations expected to traverse. PREFAIL is divided into two parts: (1) the fault-injection engine, which allows setting execution points of the system under test, besides being accountable for injecting faults; and (2) the fault-injection driver that assists testers expressing pruning policies. PREFAIL provides faults' abstraction levels and enables specifying the execution points where sequences of faults are injected. Moreover, it also profiles such fault sequence executions. Testers can adopt the abstraction levels to specify pruning policies [199].

- **AFEX**

The AFEX (Automated Fault Explorer) is a cluster-based testing system applied to traverse for high-impact faults. It relates the impact of earlier injected faults to dynamically explore the space's structure and choose new faults for subsequent inspections. The inspection method proceeds until a particular objective is reached, such as a specified level of code coverage, a threshold on the faults' influence level, finding some disk faults that suspend the DBMS, or a time limit. AFEX investigates the injected faults for analyzing redundancy strategies, then groups, classifies and sorts them by severity to support developers' decision processes [35].

- **FIM-SIM**

FIM-SIM is a fault injector module for CloudSim (a cloud-based simulation framework) [162] for supporting the cloud engineers to test and verify their infrastructures. FIM-SIM follows the event-driven model and inserts faults in CloudSim based on statistical distributions. The fault injector module extends the CloudSim core functions with FaultGenerator, FaultEvent, and FaultHandlerDatacenter. The entity FaultGenerator is accountable for starting the simulation, supervising other entities from the system, inserting faults at specific instants based on time probability distributions. The entity FaultEvent defines the fault sources, destinations, instants of injection, and types. Finally, FaultHandlerDatacenter processes fault events sent by the FaultGenerator, updates the cloudlet execution/status according to the fault event type, and manages virtual machine migration [309].

- **ProFIPy**

ProFIPy is a tool intended for supporting fault injection on high-level domain-specific language (DSL) similar to Python. ProFIPy is provided as a software-as-a-service to aid users in building programs blended with fault injection features. The tool compiles the DSL program plus the fault (bug) specification and automatically generates fault-injected versions of the original program. These versions may then be executed to support the program analysis under the influence of faults. In addition, the fault specification outlines how the program's source code should be converted to inject software bugs (faults) [82].

- **EucaBomber**

EucaBomber supports fault injection on Eucalyptus cloud computing platform (software and hardware) and estimates system and components' availability. The tool emulates faults at virtual machines, Eucalyptus components, operating systems, and physical infrastructure. EucaBomber 2.0 [60] introduced new features to the original implementation of EucaBomber [408, 409] to support virtual machine managing functions. For example, the tool may take the system or some of its components to unavailable states by emulating components' faults. Moreover, it can also execute automatic repair events in components that do not require human intervention. The fault and repair time events are implemented using a random variate supported by the FlexLoadGenerator package [148].

The EucaBomber kernel was implemented using Java language with the support of the FlexLoadGenerator package. Multiple threads implement the code that drives the faults to the system and its components. Each thread may specify complex scenarios with multiple failure modes and repair actions that denote different fault sequences.

The **Infrastructure Failures and Repairs Module** generates events that emulated hardware failures. An implementation of such a feature adopts the hibernation commands of the operational system, which stop the machine's activity for a period adjusted according to a user-defined parameter values of a time random variate. When the hibernation period is over, the previous system state is resumed by calling a repair function whose delay also obeys a user-defined time random variate. Other strategies are also applied to emulate hardware failures such as total machine shutdown and repair events by using the network to send a "magic package" as Wake-On-Lan technology (*WOL*), for instance.

The **Eucalyptus Components Failures and Repairs Module** focuses on interacting with high-level Eucalyptus components. The failure events of this type operate at Eucalyptus components processes using the service commands for handling Linux processes. These commands stop, suspend, resume, and start processes of the selected component, dependent on other system modules and components. Hence, the dependency chain must be carefully supervised to avoid erroneous behavior. For accomplishing this, it is highly recommended to parallel processing to close the gap between the emulation platform and the actual occurrence of faults in existing systems.

The **Virtual Machines Failures and Repairs Module** emulates faults at the client services running on virtual machine processes. The status of such processes is provided to the cloud manager. Failures events injected are emulated using a terminate routine of the cloud environment, and the repair events are emulated by creating new virtual machines.

26.3 SOFTWARE-BASED FAULT INJECTION

It is worth mentioning again that software-based fault injection tools may be applied to inject software faults in a system, emulate hardware faults on existing hardware systems or hardware functional prototypes, and simulate hardware and software faults in models. This section presents an overview of general software-based fault injection architecture and its components.

An architecture of a generic fault injection tool may be depicted by the diagram shown in Figure 26.5. This environment is composed of a system under test (SUT), and a Fault Injector Computer (FIC) commanded by an operator. The FIC is represented here only by its fundamental subsystems: the computer hardware, the computer operating system (OS), and the Fault Injector (FI). Many other software subsystems may be required to make the system operational, such as language interpreters, databases, and libraries, for instance.

The Fault Injector is composed of a Fault Injector Kernel (FIK) and a set of libraries. For example, the diagram depicted in Figure 26.5 depicts the following libraries: Statistics Library, Probability Distributions Library, Models' Library, Fault Mechanisms' Library, User Interface Library, and Context-Specific Library. The Fault Injector Kernel controls the whole set of activities such as choosing a time distribution that represents a given time to failure or time to repair, calling the respective distribution function, waiting until the respective time elapses, monitoring the system under test, choosing the fault injection method to be applied to a specific fault injection, and injecting the fault. It also provides the means for accessing functions to support operators interacting with each specific system under test. Besides, composing a fault injection approach may reuse the previous model stored in the Models' library.

When defining a fault injection process, the components of the system under test should be represented (model) so the FIK may recognize the dependencies between the system's components and respective infrastructure to avoid generating impossible events. For instance, assume the system under test is a computer with hardware infrastructure, operating system, and several software subsystems upon the operating system. Then, if the operating system has suffered a fatal failure, it does not make sense to insert failure in any software system that depends on the operating system since OS failure has already caused the failure of dependent subsystems. Likewise, the repairing action related to those dependent subsystems should only be carried out after repairing the operating system, which can only be repaired if the hardware infrastructure is operational. The system's model representation may be coded as part of FIK (see Example 24.3.6 - Appendix E) or may be a data structure which is handled by an interpreter such as the strategy adopted in Section 14.2.

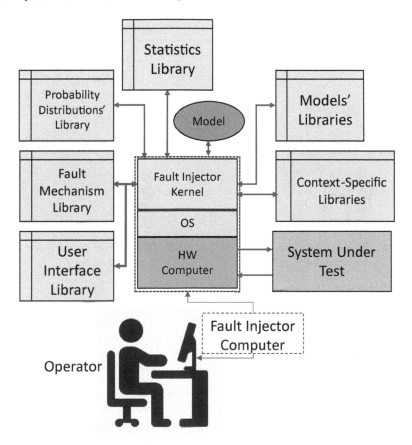

Figure 26.5   An Architecture of Generic Fault Injection Tool.

The Statistics Library provides a set of statistical methods for parameter estimation. The Probability Distributions Library supports random variate generation, probability calculation, and moments estimation. The Models' Library stores a set of models that can be reused when building a new fault injection plan. The Fault Mechanisms' Library provides a set of methods for injecting or emulating fault in a system or even for simulating faults if the system under test is still a simulative model. The User Interface Library provides a function for supporting the interaction between the Fault Injector and the operator. Finally, the Context-Specific Library provides a set of functions customized for each particular system under test.

The system under test may be a system that does not share the same hardware infrastructure as Figure 26.5 suggests or might be a software system that shares the same hardware infrastructure of the computer that injects faults in SUT. For example, Figure 26.6 shows a software system under test (SUT) that shares the same hardware

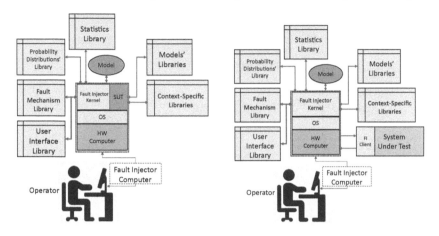

Figure 26.6 *SUT* Sharing the Hardware Infrastructure of *FIC*.

Figure 26.7 *SUT* has a Software Client Component of the *FI*.

and host operating system of Fault Injector Computer. On the other hand, Figure 26.7 depicts a *SUT* that is entirely independent of the *FIC*. Therefore for supporting the fault injection on *SUT* by the *FI* and monitoring it, a Fault Injection Client component is inserted in *SUT* to handle the commands sent by *FI* and to send back data from the *SUT* that may not be directly accessible from the *SUT* external interface.

Figure 26.8 depicts a system under test, *SUT*, and a Fault Injector Computer, *FIC*. *SUT* is composed of one hardware server, the respective host operating system, and two virtual machines (VM_1 and VM_2), besides an external storage system (*ST*). Let us assume the system is operational if either or both virtual machines are operational, and the storage system is also functional, that is, $((VM_1 = UP \lor VM_1 = UP) \land ST = UP) = TRUE$.

The Fault Injector (*FI*) injects faults (emulation) on the *SUT*'s components and monitors the system availability. The system is assumed to be available if at least one virtual machine is operational and the storage system is properly functioning. The monitoring subsystem (part of the *FI*) is configured to periodically check the status of each virtual machine i through a function $checkVM(i)$. This function replies *TRUE* if the VM_i is operational and *FALSE* otherwise. Likewise, the monitoring subsystem also periodically checks the status of the storage system i through a function $stdCheck(i)$. The function $checkST(i)$ replies *TRUE* if the storage system i is operational; otherwise, it replies *FALSE*. The time between samples is called *tbs*. Hence, after observing the *SUT* for a period T, we obtain a sample of size $n = T/tbs$. If m out of n samples are *TRUE* observations, the steady-state availability may be estimated by

$$A = \frac{UT}{T} = \frac{m \times tbs}{n \times tbs} = \frac{m}{n},$$

which is the ratio between the uptime (*UT*) and the observational period T.

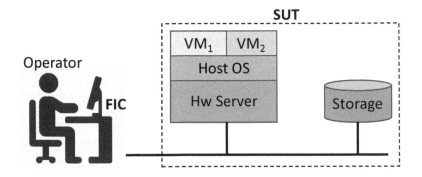

Figure 26.8 High-Level Architecture of the *SUT*.

As already mentioned, the system's model may be coded as part of *FIK* or may be a data structure handled by a model's interpreter. In this specific case, the system model is represented by the SPN shown in Figure 26.9 and Table 26.3. Therefore, *FIK* has an *SPN* interpreter that evaluates which events (faults and repairs) can occur depending on the structural and data dependencies and the stochastic-time structure.

The *SUT*'s initial state depicts two virtual machines and external storage systems as functionally operational. This state is depicted in SPN by the following marking:

$$M_0^T = (m_{vm1u}, m_{vm1d}, m_{vm2u}, m_{vm2d}, m_{osu}, m_{osd}, m_{hwu}, m_{hwd}, m_{stu}, m_{std}).$$

$$M_0^T = (1, 0, 1, 0, 1, 0, 1, 0, 1, 0).$$

The *FI* evaluates which events can possibly occur at this state. The possible events are $F1, F2, OSF, HWF$, and STF. None of these transitions are immediate; then the stochastic delay related to each enabled timed transition is generated. The transition with the smallest generated delay is chosen to be fired. Let us assume $F2$ is the transition with the smallest generated delay. This transition represents the failure event of the $VM2$. The *FI* waits until the delay elapses. After that, $F2$ is fired. Such a firing removes one token from place $VM1U$ and stores one token in place $VM1D$. Besides, $F2$ firing also calls a function to emulate the virtual machine failure. Here, we denote such a function by $killVM(i)$, which kills the virtual machine process i. The new marking is

$$M_1^T = (1, 0, 0, 1, 1, 0, 1, 0, 1, 0).$$

It is worth mentioning that the monitoring process is concurrently running with fault injection processes. The monitoring process counts the number of events that do not denote the *SUT* in the available state. At marking M_1, the transitions enabled are

$R1$, $F2$, OSF, HWF, and STF. As in the previous marking, none of these transitions are immediate; then the delay of each enabled timed transition is generated. Let us assume $R2$ is the transition with the smallest generated delay. The FI waits until the delay elapses. After that, $R2$ is fired. This transition represents the $VM2$ repair. Firing $R2$ removes one token from place $VM1D$ and stores one token in place $VM1U$. When $R2$ is fired, the virtual machine is repaired. The repair is conducted by restarting the respective virtual machine by calling the function $startVM$. This process goes on by firing enabled transitions and calling the respective functions that emulate faults and repair actions until a stop condition is reached. In such a state, the point estimation and confidence intervals of system availability, mean time to failure, mean time to restore, and other related measures are provided.

For supporting the hardware server and the storage subsystem failures, those should support emulating failure. These events may be implemented, for instance, by switching off the respective subsystems. For automatically emulating the repair of this system, strategies such as the Wake-On-Lan technology should be supported; otherwise, an external interaction is required.

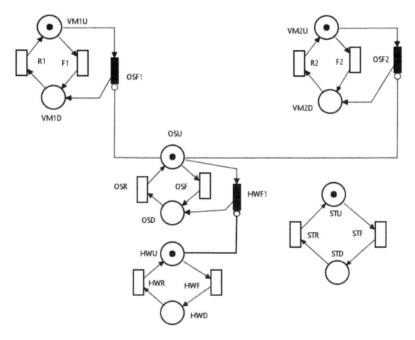

Figure 26.9 Model's Architecture of the SUT

Table 26.3

Transitions' Attributes

Transition	Guard	π (Priority)	ω (Weight)	λ (Rate)
F1		1		λ_{F1}
R1	#$OSD = 0$	1		μ_{R1}
F2		1		λ_{F2}
R2	#$OSD = 0$	1		μ_{R2}
OSF1		1	1	
OSF2		1	1	
OSF		1		λ_{OS}
OSR	#$HWD = 0$	1		μ_{OS}
OSF1		1	1	
HWF		1		λ_{HW}
HWR		1		μ_{HW}
STF		1		λ_{ST}
STR		1		μ_{ST}

EXERCISES

Exercise 1. What are the aims for using fault injection?

Exercise 2. Explain what are **a**) hardware-based, **b**) software-based, and **c**) hardware-software-based fault injectors?

Exercise 3. Software-based fault injectors may be employed **a**) to inject actual software faults in a system, **b**) to emulate hardware faults, and **c**) to simulate hardware and software faults in the models. Explain each of these mechanisms.

Exercise 4. What do you understand by an invasive or a non-invasive fault injection mechanism? Give examples.

Exercise 5. Explain the purpose of the fault acceleration mechanisms and where these mechanisms are usually applied.

Exercise 6. What are failure scaling factors? Explain.

Exercise 7. Consider a stress experiment was carried out, and a sample of two hundred $TTFs$ was collected. The $MTTF$ calculated from the sample was $MTTF_s = 246.3\,h$. (a) If the compression factor is constant and equal to $CF = 1/8$, what is the mean time to failure at normal operation conditions? (b) If the probability distribution function of the TTF is exponentially distributed, present the CDF and the cumulative hazard function at normal conditions.

Exercise 8. Consider a system whose time to failure is dependent on the voltage, V, provided by the power supplier and obeys the *IPL*

$$TTF = 8.5 \times 10^7 V^{-2},$$

If $MTTF_2$, for $V_2 = 110V$, is $9000h$, what is the mean time to failure, $MTTF_1$ for the voltage $V_1 = 130V$?

Exercise 9. Six sets of twenty similar gadgets were tested under six different temperatures (in Celsius degrees) until all gadgets of each set failed (complete data). Then, the average failure rate of each set was recorded. The temperatures and the average failure rates (in failures per hour - fph) are depicted in Table 26.4.

Table 26.4

Failure Rate ($\lambda(s)$) × Temperature (in Celsius degree)

s (°C)	$\lambda(s)$ (fph)
20	8.00×10^{-5}
22	8.70×10^{-5}
24	9.30×10^{-5}
26	1.16×10^{-4}
28	1.57×10^{-4}
30	2.33×10^{-4}

Assume the device's failure rate follows a function such as

$$\lambda(s) = C \, e^{A \times s} \, fph,$$

where s is the temperature in Celsius degree. (a) Use regression to find out the parameters A and C. (b) Plot the $\lambda(s) \times s$, and (c) Plot the $1/\lambda(s) \times s$.

Exercise 10. Consider a storage system has a constant failure rate equal to $\lambda_2 = 4 \times 10^{-5} h^{-1}$ at temperature $T_2 = 22°C$. Assume the activation energy is $E_a = 0.75eV$. Using the Arrhenius formula, (a) estimate the failure rate of the storage system at $T_1 = 35°C$ and (b) the respective mean time to failure.

Exercise 11. Two sets of twenty electronic components were tested in two different temperatures, $T_1 = 20°C$ and $T_2 = 40°C$. We assume the failure rates are constant in each temperature. The average failure rate at T_1 was $\lambda_1 = 8.1067\,10^{-5}\ fph$ and the average failure rate at T_2 was $\lambda_2 = 1.268\,10^{-3}\ fph$. If the failure rate grows with the temperature according the Arrhenius law, (a) estimate the activation energy of the substance used to build the electronic devices. (b) Estimate the failure rate and the $MTTF$ of a electronic component at $T_3 = 30°C$.

Exercise 12. Assume an electro-electronic system operating at temperature $T_2 = 293.15\,K$ and its power source operates at $V_2 = 3.8\,V$. Now consider the temperature changes to T_1 ($T_1 > T_2$) and the power sources bounce the voltage and stabilize at V_1 ($V_1 > V_2$). If the system's failure rate is well represented by the Eyring model, the activation energy is $E_a = 0.49\,eV$, $B = 1.5$, $MTTF_2 = 25000\,h$ for T_2 and V_2, estimate the $MTTF_1$ for $T_1 \in (293.15\,K, 302.15\,K)$ and $V_1 \in (3.8V, 5.2V)$ and draw the respective plot.

Bibliography

1. 3DMark - Technical Guide. Updated September 18, 2020.

2. J. A. Abraham, "An Improved Algorithm for Network Reliability," in IEEE Transactions on Reliability, vol. R-28, no. 1, pp. 58-61, April 1979. doi: 10.1109/TR.1979.5220476

3. Anderson, T. W., and D. A. Darling. "Asymptotic Theory of Certain 'Goodness of Fit' Criteria Based on Stochastic Processes." The Annals of Mathematical Statistics, vol. 23, no. 2, pp. 193–212, 1952.

4. Anderson, T. W., and D. A. Darling. "A Test of Goodness of Fit." Journal of the American Statistical Association, vol. 49, no. 268, pp. 765–769, 1954.

5. Automotive Engineering Council. http://aecouncil.com/ Retrieved at 5/10/2021.

6. Francisco Airton Silva, Sokol Kosta, Matheus Rodrigues, Danilo Oliveira, Teresa Maciel, Alessandro Mei, and Paulo Maciel. Mobile Cloud Performance Evaluation Using Stochastic Models. IEEE Transactions on Mobile Computing. 2018. ISSN: 1536-1233.

7. A. Jensen. Markov chains as an aid in the study of Markov processes. Skand. Aktuarietidskrift, 3:87–91, 1953.

8. Ajmone Marsan, Marco and Conte, Gianni and Balbo, Gianfranco. A Class of Generalized Stochastic Petri Nets for the Performance Evaluation of Multiprocessor Systems. ACM Trans. Comput. Syst. 1984. Vol: 2. n:2. pages: 93–122. issn:0734-2071. ACM.

9. Ajmone Marsan, M. and Bobbio, A. and Donatelli, S. Petri nets in performance analysis: An introduction. Lectures on Petri Nets I: Basic Models: Advances in Petri Nets. Springer Berlin Heidelberg. isbn: 978-3-540-49442-3. pages:211–256. 1998

10. Akhmedjanov, F. M.. Reliability databases: State-of-the-art and perspectives. Denmark. Forskningscenter Risoe. Risoe-R No. 1235(EN) 2001.

11. Algirdas Avizienis. 1967. Design of fault-tolerant computers. Causes and symptoms of logic faults in digital systems. In Proceedings of the November 14-16, 1967, fall joint computer conference (AFIPS '67 (Fall)). Association for Computing Machinery, New York, NY, USA, 733–743. DOI:https://doi.org/10.1145/1465611.1465708

12. Mukhtar M. Ali. Stochastic Ordering and Kurtosis Measure. Journal of the American Statistical Association. Vol.:69. Number: 346. Pages:543-545, Taylor & Francis. 1974.

13. Virgilio A. F. Almeida and Jussara M. Almeida. 2011. Internet Workloads: Measurement, Characterization, and Modeling. IEEE Internet Computing 15, 2 (March 2011), 15–18. DOI:https://doi.org/10.1109/MIC.2011.43

14. H. H. Amer and E. J. McCluskey, "Calculation of Coverage Parameter," in IEEE Transactions on Reliability, vol. R-36, no. 2, pp. 194-198, June 1987. doi: 10.1109/TR.1987.5222338

15. P. Ameri, N. Schlitter, J. Meyer and A. Streit, "NoWog: A Workload Generator for Database Performance Benchmarking," 2016 IEEE 14th Intl Conf on Dependable, Autonomic and Secure Computing, 14th Intl Conf on Pervasive Intelligence and Computing, 2nd Intl Conf on Big Data Intelligence and Computing and Cyber Science and Technology Congress(DASC/PiCom/DataCom/CyberSciTech), Auckland, 2016, pp. 666-673, doi: 10.1109/DASC-PICom-DataCom-CyberSciTec.2016.120.

16. Anselone, P. M. Persistence of an Effect of a Success in a Bernoulli Sequence. Journal of the Society for Industrial and Applied Mathematics. 1960, Vol. Vol. 8, No. 2.

17. Araujo, Camila and Silva, F and Costa, Igor and Vaz, Fabiano and Kosta, Sokol and Maciel, Paulo. Supporting availability evaluation in MCC-based mHealth planning. Electronics Letters. Vol: 52. Number:20. pp:1663–1665. IET. 2016.

18. Eltton Araujo, Paulo Pereira, Jamilson Dantas, and Paulo Maciel. Dependability Impact in the Smart Solar Power Systems: An Analysis of Smart Buildings. ENERGIES (BASEL). 2020. ISSN: 1996-1073

19. J. Arlat, Y. Crouzet and J. -. Laprie, "Fault injection for dependability validation of fault-tolerant computing systems," [1989] The Nineteenth International Symposium on Fault-Tolerant Computing. Digest of Papers, Chicago, IL, USA, 1989, pp. 348-355, doi: 10.1109/FTCS.1989.105591.

20. J. Arlat et al., "Fault injection for dependability validation: a methodology and some applications," in IEEE Transactions on Software Engineering, vol. 16, no. 2, pp. 166-182, Feb. 1990, doi: 10.1109/32.44380.

21. M. F. Arlitt and C. L. Williamson, "Internet web servers: Workload characterization and performance implications," IEEE/ACM Transactions on Networking (ToN), vol. 5, no. 5, pp. 631–645, 1997.

22. T. F. Arnold, "The Concept of Coverage and Its Effect on the Reliability Model of a Repairable System," in IEEE Transactions on Computers, vol. C-22, no. 3, pp. 251-254, March 1973. doi: 10.1109/T-C.1973.223703

23. Arrhenius, Svante. "Über die Reaktionsgeschwindigkeit bei der Inversion von Rohrzucker durch Säuren" Zeitschrift für Physikalische Chemie, vol. 4U, no. 1, 1889, pp. 226-248. https://doi.org/10.1515/zpch-1889-0416

24. R. B. Ash, Basic Probability Theory, Wiley, New York, 1970.

25. Bruno Silva, Paulo Maciel, Eduardo Tavares, Carlos Araujo, Gustavo Callou, Erica Souza, Nelson Rosa, Manish Marwah, Ratnesh Sharma, Tom Christian and J. Paulo Pires. ASTRO: A Tool for Dependability Evaluation of Data Center Infrastructures. In: IEEE International Conference on Systems, Man, and Cybernetics, 2010, Istanbul. IEEE Proceeding of SMC, 2010.

26. Bruno Silva, Paulo Maciel, Gustavo Callou, Eduardo Tavares, Jair Figueiredo, Erica Sousa, Carlos Araujo, Fábio Magnani and Francisco Neves. ASTRO: An Integrated Environment for Dependability and Sustainability Evaluation. Sustainable Computing, Informatics and Systems. Elsevier. 2012. ISSN: 2210-5379.

27. AUERBACH STANDARD EDP REPORTS 1 - An Analytic Reference Service for the Electronic Data Processing Field. Prepared, Edited and Published by AUERBACH Corporation. Philadelphia, Penna. Vol. 1. 1962.

28. A. Avizienis, Fault-tolerance: The survival attribute of digital systems, in Proceedings of the IEEE, vol. 66, no. 10, pp. 1109-1125, Oct. 1978, doi: 10.1109/PROC.1978.11107.

29. Avizienis, A. Toward Systematic Design of Fault-Tolerant Systems. IEEE Computer. 1997 , Vol. Vol. 30, no. 4.

30. Avizienis A., Laprie J. C., Randell B.. Fundamental Concepts of Computer System Dependability. IARP/IEEE-RAS Workshop on Robot Robots in Human Environments – Seoul, Korea, May 21-22, 2001

31. Avizienis A., Laprie J. C., Randell B.. UCLA CSD Report no. 010028 LAAS Report no. 01-145 Newcastle University Report no. CS-TR-739. 2001

32. D. Avresky, J. Arlat, J. -. Laprie and Y. Crouzet, "Fault injection for formal testing of fault tolerance," in IEEE Transactions on Reliability, vol. 45, no. 3, pp. 443-455, Sept. 1996, doi: 10.1109/24.537015.

33. Backblaze Hard Drive Data and Stats. https://www.backblaze.com/b2/hard-drive-test-data.html. Retrieved on 5/11/2021.

34. Bahga, A. and Madisetti, V.K. Synthetic workload generation for cloud computing applications. Journal of Software Engineering and Applications, 4(07), p.396. 2011.

35. Radu Banabic and George Candea. 2012. Fast black-box testing of system recovery code. In Proceedings of the 7th ACM european conference on Computer Systems (EuroSys '12). Association for Computing Machinery, New York, NY, USA, 281–294. DOI:https://doi.org/10.1145/2168836.2168865

36. Barabady, J., & Kumar, U. (2007). Availability allocation through importance measures. International Journal of Quality and Reliability Management, 24(6), 643–657.

37. Barlow, Richard E. s.l., Mathematical reliability theory: from the beginning to the present time. Proceedings of the Third International Conference on Mathematical Methods In Reliability, Methodology And Practice, 2002.

38. Gely P. Basharin, Amy N. Langville, Valeriy A. Naumov. The life and work of A.A. Markov. Linear Algebra and its Applications. Volume 386. 2004. Pages 3-26. ISSN 0024-3795. https://doi.org/10.1016/j.laa.2003.12.041.

39. Board of Directors of the American Institute of Electrical Engineers. Answers to Questions Relative to High Tension Transmission. s.l. : IEEE, September 26, 1902.

40. Benard, A. and Bos-Levenbach, E. C. (1953): Het uitzetten van waarnemingen op waarschijnlijkheids-papier. Statistica Neerlandica, Vol. 7 pp. 163-173. English translation by Schop, R. (2001): The Plotting of Observations on Probability Paper. Report SP 30 of the Statistical Department of the Mathematics Centrum, Amsterdam. http://www.barringer1.com/wa.htm

41. Benso, Alfredo and Prinetto, Paolo. Fault Injection Techniques and Tools for Embedded Systems Reliability Evaluation. isbn: 1441953914. Springer Publishing Company, Incorporated. 2010.

42. Bernard, A. and Bos-Levenbach, E.J. The plotting of observations on probability-paper. Stichting Mathematisch Centrum. Statistische Afdeling. Stichting Mathematisch Centrum. 1955.

43. Bernstein, S.. "Sur l'extension du théorème limite du calcul des probabilités aux sommes de quantités dépendantes." Mathematische Annalen 97 (1927): 1-59. ¡http://eudml.org/doc/182666¿.

44. G.Berthelot. Checking Properties of Nets Using Transformations. Advances in Petri Nets, vol 222, Lecture Notes in Computer Science, Springer Verlag, Edited by G. Rozenberg, pp 19-40, 1986.

45. E. Best, Structure Theory of Petri Nets: the Free Choice Hiatus, LNCS vol. 254, Springer Verlag, 1987

46. Birnbaum, Z. W., J. D. Esary and S. C. Saunders. Multi-component systems and structures and their reliability. Technometrics. 1961, Vol. 3 (1).

47. Birnbaum, Z. W.: On the importance of different components in a multi-component system. Technical Report Number 54, May 20th, 1968, University of Washington. Contract N-onr-477(38).

48. Birnbaum, Z. W.: On the importance of different components in a multi-component system. In: Krishnaiah, P. R. (ed.) Multivariate Analysis–II, pp. 581–592. Academic Press (1969)

49. Wallace R. Blischke, D. N. Prabhakar Murthy, [ed.]. Case Studies in Reliability and Maintenance. Hoboken: John Wiley & Sons, 2003. p. 661.

50. Joseph K. Blitzstein, Jessica Hwang. Introduction to Probability, Chapman & Hall/CRC Texts in Statistical Science. 596 Pages. Published 2014 by Chapman And Hall/CRC. ISBN-13: 978-1-4665-7557-8. ISBN: 1-4665-7557-3

51. Richard Blum. Professional Assembly Language. Wiley Publishing, Inc. ISBN: 0-7645-7901-0. 2005

52. Bolch, G., Greiner, S., Meer, H., Trivedi, K. S. Queueing Networks and Markov Chains - Modeling and Performance Evaluation with Computer Science Applications. John Wiley & Sons. 2006.

53. Jan Lodewijk Bonebakker Findin.g representative workloads for computer system design. PhD Thesis. Sun Microsystems, Inc., USA. 2007

54. George Boole. An Investigation of the Laws of Thought. 1854. Project Gutenberg's. Release Date: July 19, 2017.

55. J.-Y. Le Boudec, Performance Evaluation of Computer and Communication Systems. EPFL Press, Lausanne, Switzerland. 2010.

56. W. G. Bouricius, W. C. Carter, D. C. Jessep, P. R. Schneider and A. B. Wadia, "Reliability Modeling for Fault-Tolerant Computers," in IEEE Transactions on Computers, vol. C-20, no. 11, pp. 1306-1311, Nov. 1971. doi: 10.1109/T-C.1971.223132

57. Box, G. E. P., and D. R. Cox. "An Analysis of Transformations." Journal of the Royal Statistical Society. Series B (Methodological), vol. 26, no. 2, 1964, pp. 211–252. JSTOR, www.jstor.org/stable/2984418.

58. Box, G. E. P.; Muller, Mervin E. A Note on the Generation of Random Normal Deviates. Ann. Math. Statist. 29 (1958), no. 2, 610–611.

59. Wilfried Brauer and Wolfgang Reisig. Carl Adam Petri and "Petri Nets". Fundamental Concepts in Computer Science. 3:129–139. 2007

60. J. Brilhante, B. Silva, P. Maciel and A. Zimmermann, "EucaBomber 2.0: A tool for dependability tests in eucalyptus cloud infrastructures considering VM lifecycle," 2014 IEEE International Conference on Systems, Man, and Cybernetics (SMC), 2014, pp. 2669-2674, doi: 10.1109/SMC.2014.6974330.

61. W. Buchholz, "A synthetic job for measuring system performance," in IBM Systems Journal, vol. 8, no. 4, pp. 309-318, 1969, doi: 10.1147/sj.84.0309.

62. Bucklew, James. Introduction to Rare Event Simulation. isbn.: 1441918930. Springer. 2010.

63. Buzacott, J. A. Markov approach to finding failure times of repairable systems. IEEE Transactions on Reliability, Volume 19, issue 4, pages: 128-134. 1970

64. G. Callou, E. Sousa, Maciel, and F. Magnani, "A formal approach to the quantification of sustainability and dependability metrics on data center infrastructures," in *Proceedings of DEVS*.   San Diego, CA, USA: SCS, 2011, pp. 274–281

65. G. Callou, P. Maciel, F. Magnani, J. Figueiredo, E. Sousa, E. Tavares, B. Silva, F. Neves, and C. Araujo, "Estimating sustainability impact, total cost of ownership and dependability metrics on data center infrastructures," in *Sustainable Systems and Technology (ISSST), 2011 IEEE International Symposium on*, May 2011, pp. 1 –6

66. Calzarossa, Maria Carla; Della Vedova Marco L.; Massari, Luisa; Petcu, Dana; Tabash, Momin I. M.; Workloads in the Clouds. Book chapter in Principles of Performance and Reliability Modeling and Evaluation: Essays in Honor of Kishor Trivedi on his 70th Birthday. Pages:525-550. ISBN: 978-3-319-30599-8. Springer International Publishing. 2016.

67. Campos, Eliomar and Matos, Rubens and Maciel, Paulo and Costa, Igor and Silva, Francisco Airton and Souza, Francisco. Performance evaluation of virtual machines instantiation in a private cloud. 2015 IEEE World Congress on Services. pp: 319–326. IEEE. 2015

68. HP Capacity Advisor 7.4 User Guide. HP Part Number: T8670-90054. Published in September 2014.

69. J. Carreira, H. Madeira and J. G. Silva, "Xception: a technique for the experimental evaluation of dependability in modern computers," in IEEE Transactions on Software Engineering, vol. 24, no. 2, pp. 125-136, Feb. 1998, doi: 10.1109/32.666826.

70. J. V. Carreira, D. Costa and J. G. Silva, "Fault injection spot-checks computer system dependability," in IEEE Spectrum, vol. 36, no. 8, pp. 50-55, Aug. 1999, doi: 10.1109/6.780999.

71. Cassady, C. R., Pohl, E. A., & Jin, S. (2004). Managing availability improvement efforts with importance measures and optimization. IMA Journal of Management Math, 15(2), 161–174.

72. Cassandras, Christos G., Lafortune, Stéphane. Introduction to Discrete Event Systems. SBN 978-0-387-68612-7. Springer-Verlag. 2008.

73. Giovanni Chiola and Marco Ajmone Marsan, Gianfranco Balbo and Gianni Conte. Generalized stochastic Petri nets: A definition at the net level and its implications. IEEE Transactions on Software Engineering. Vol.: 19. pages: 89-107. 1993.

74. Choi, Byoung Kyu and Kang, Donghun. Modeling and Simulation of Discrete Event Systems. isbn.: 111838699X. Wiley Publishing. 2013.

75. G. Choi, R. Iyer and V. Carreno, "FOCUS: an experimental environment for validation of fault-tolerant systems-case study of a jet-engine controller," Proceedings 1989 IEEE International Conference on Computer Design: VLSI in Computers and Processors, Cambridge, MA, USA, 1989, pp. 561-564, doi: 10.1109/ICCD.1989.63428.

76. Chung, Christopher A., Simulation Modeling Handbook: A Practical Approach. isbn.:0849312418. CRC Press, Inc. 2003.

77. Church, R. M. (1979). How to look at data: A review of John W. Tukey's Exploratory Data Analysis. Journal of the Experimental Analysis of Behavior, 31(3), 433–440.

78. Ciardo, Gianfranco and Muppala, Jogesh and Trivedi, Kishor S., On the Solution of GSPN Reward Models. Performance Evaluation. Vol:12. number:4. issn:0166-531. Elsevier. 1991.

79. Clark, Christopher and Fraser, Keir and Hand, Steven and Hansen, Jacob Gorm and Jul, Eric and Limpach, Christian and Pratt, Ian and Warfield, Andrew. Live migration of virtual machines. Proceedings of the 2nd conference on Symposium on Networked Systems Design & Implementation - Volume 2. NSDI'05. pp.: 273–286. USENIX Association. 2005

80. W. G. Cochran, "The Chi-Square Test of Goodness of Fit," Annals of Mathematical Statistics, Vol. 23, No. 3, 1952, pp. 315-345. doi:10.1214/aoms/1177729380

81. Costa, Igor and Araujo, Jean and Dantas, Jamilson and Campos, Eliomar and Silva, Francisco Airton and Maciel, Paulo. Availability Evaluation and Sensitivity Analysis of a Mobile Backend-as-a-service Platform. Journal on Quality and Reliability Engineering International. Vol: 32. Number:7, pp: 2191–2205

82. Cotroneo, Domenico, L. Simone, Pietro Liguori and R. Natella. "ProFIPy: Programmable Software Fault Injection as-a-Service." 50th Annual IEEE/IFIP International Conference on Dependable Systems and Networks (DSN). 364-372. 2020.

83. Cox, D. . A use of complex probabilities in the theory of stochastic processes. Mathematical Proceedings of the Cambridge Philosophical Society, 51(2), 313-319. 1955. doi:10.1017/S0305004100030231

84. Cramèr, H. "On the Composition of Elementary Errors". Scandinavian Actuarial Journal. (1): 13–74. 1928

85. Yves Crouzet, Karama Kanoun. System Dependability: Characterization and Benchmarking. A.Hurson, S.Sedigh. Advances in Computers. Special issue: Dependable and Secure Systems Engineering, Elsevier, pp.93-139, 2012, 978-0-12-396525-7.

86. M. Curiel and A. Pont, "Workload Generators for Web-Based Systems: Characteristics, Current Status, and Challenges," in IEEE Communications Surveys & Tutorials, vol. 20, no. 2, pp. 1526-1546, Second quarter 2018, doi: 10.1109/COMST.2018.2798641.

87. H. J. Curnow, B. A. Wichmann, A synthetic benchmark, The Computer Journal, Volume 19, Issue 1, 1976, Pages 43–49, https://doi.org/10.1093/comjnl/19.1.43

88. Sidney J. Cutler,Fred Ederer. Maximum utilization of the life table method in analyzing survival. Journal of Chronic Diseases. Volume 8, Issue 6, Pages 699-712 Elsevier. December 1958.

89. Edward W. Czeck and Zary Z. Segall and Daniel P. Siewiorek. Software implemented fault Insertion: An (FTMP) Example. Technical Report CMU-CS-87-101. Carnegie Mellon University. January 1987.

90. Dâmaso, A., Rosa, N., & Maciel, P. (2017). Integrated Evaluation of Reliability and Power Consumption of Wireless Sensor Networks. Sensors (Basel, Switzerland), 17(11), 2547. doi:10.3390/s17112547

91. Julien Danjou. Serious Python.Publisher: William Pollock. ISBN-13: 978-1-59327-878-6. 2020

92. Dantas, Jamilson and Matos, Rubens and Araujo, Jean and Maciel, Paulo. An availability model for eucalyptus platform: An analysis of warm-standby replication mechanism. Systems, Man, and Cybernetics (SMC), 2012 IEEE International Conference on. pp.: 1664–1669. IEEE. 2012.

93. Dantas, Jamilson and Matos, Rubens and Araujo, Jean and Maciel, Paulo. Eucalyptus-based private clouds: availability modeling and comparison to the cost of a public cloud. Computing. Vol.: 97. number: 11. pp.:1121–1140. Springer. 2015

94. Jamilson Dantas, Rubens Matos, Carlos Melo and Paulo Maciel. Cloud Infrastructure Planning: Models Considering an Optimization Method, Cost and Performance Requirements. International Journal of Grid and Utility Computing. 2020. ISSN: 1741-8488 (Online). ISSN: 1741-847X (Print).

95. Jamilson Dantas, Rubens Matos, Jean Teixeira, Eltton Tullyo and Paulo Maciel. Estimating Capacity-Oriented Availability in Cloud Systems. International Journal of Computational Science and Engineering. 2020. ISSN: 1742-7193 (Online). ISSN: 1742-7185 (Print).

96. Davison, A. C. and Hinkley, D. V., Bootstrap Methods and Their Application, Cambridge University Press, New York, NY, USA, 2013.

97. B. Silva and Paulo Romero Martins Maciel and Eduardo Tavares and Armin Zimmermann.Dependability Models for Designing Disaster Tolerant Cloud Computing Systems. The Third International Workshop on Dependability of Clouds, Data Centers and Virtual Machine Technology (DCDV). 2013

98. Denning, P. J., Buzen, J. P. The Operational Analysis of Queueing Network Models. Acm Computing Surveys, 10, 3, 225-261, September 01, 1978.

99. Desel, Jörg and Esparza, Javier, Free Choice Petri Nets, 1995, isbn: 0-521-46519-2, Cambridge University Press.

100. Desel, Jörg. Basic linear algebraic techniques for place/transition nets. Lectures on Petri Nets I: Basic Models: Advances in Petri Nets. Springer Berlin Heidelberg. pages:257–308. isbn:978-3-540-49442-3. 1998.

101. Desel, Jörg, W. Reisig. Place/Transition nets. Lectures on Petri Nets I: Basic Models: Advances in Petri Nets. Springer Berlin Heidelberg. pages:122–173. isbn:978-3-540-49442-3. 1998.

102. Desrochers, A.A. and Al-Jaar, R.Y., Applications of Petri Nets in Manufacturing Systems: Modeling, Control, and Performance Analysis, IEEE Press. 1995.

103. Dhillon, B. S. (Balbir S.),. Applied Reliability and Quality: fundamentals, methods and applications. London : Springer-Verlag, 2007.

104. DiCiccio, Thomas J.; Efron, Bradley. Bootstrap confidence intervals. Statist. Sci. 11 (1996), no. 3, 189–228. doi:10.1214/ss/1032280214. https://projecteuclid.org/euclid.ss/1032280214

105. J. Dickinson, G. S. Chakraborti, Nonparametric Statistical Inference, Marcel Dekker, Inc., Fourth Edition, 2003.

106. Dienes, P. The Taylor series: an introduction to the theory of functions of a complex variable. Dover, 1957. "An unabridged and unaltered republication of the 1st edition [1931] with errata incorporated into the text."

107. J. J. Dongarra, C. B. Moler, J. R. Bunch, and G. W. Stewart. LINPACK Users' Guide.1979. Pages: 364

108. Dongarra, J.J., Luszczek, P. and Petitet, A. (2003), The LINPACK Benchmark: past, present and future. Concurrency Computat.: Pract. Exper., 15: 803-820. doi:10.1002/cpe.728

109. Development and Evaluation of a Fault-Tolerant Multiprocessor Computer, Vol III, FTMP Test and Evaluation Charles Stark Draper Laboratories, 1983. NASA Contract Report 166073.

110. https://linux.die.net/man/1/dstat. Retrieved at 8/6/2020.

111. http://linuxadministrative.blogspot.com/2014/06/dstat-command-examples.html. Retrieved at 8/7/2020.

112. Dubrova, Elena. Fault-Tolerant Design. ISBN:1461421128. Springer Publishing Company. 2013.

113. Jeff Duntemann. Assembly Language Step-by-Step - Programming with Linux. Third Edition. ISBN: 978-0-470-49702-9. Wiley Publishing. 2009.

114. J. A. Duraes and H. S. Madeira, "Emulation of Software Faults: A Field Data Study and a Practical Approach," in IEEE Transactions on Software Engineering, vol. 32, no. 11, pp. 849-867, Nov. 2006, doi: 10.1109/TSE.2006.113.

115. Ebeling, C.E., An Introduction to Reliability and Maintainability Engineering, ISBN: 9781577666257, second edition, 2010. Waveland

116. L. Eeckhout, H. Vandierendonck and K. De Bosschere, "Designing computer architecture research workloads," in Computer, vol. 36, no. 2, pp. 65-71, Feb. 2003, doi: 10.1109/MC.2003.1178050.

117. L. Eeckhout and K. Hoste, "Microarchitecture-Independent Workload Characterization" in IEEE Micro, vol. 27, no. 03, pp. 63-72, 2007. doi: 10.1109/MM.2007.56.

118. Efron, Bradley and Hastie, Trevor. Computer Age Statistical Inference: Algorithms, Evidence, and Data Science. isbn: 1107149894. Cambridge University Press. 2016.

119. Efron, B. Bootstrap Methods: Another Look at the Jackknife. Ann. Statist. 7 (1979), no. 1, 1–26. doi:10.1214/aos/1176344552. https://projecteuclid.org/euclid.aos/1176344552

120. Efron, Bradley. "Nonparametric Estimates of Standard Error: The Jackknife, the Bootstrap and Other Methods." Biometrika 68, no. 3 (1981): 589-99. doi:10.2307/2335441.

121. Efron, Bradley, and Robert J. Tibshirani. An introduction to the bootstrap. CRC press, 1994.

122. Paul Ellgen. Thermodynamics and Chemical Equilibrium. 2021. Retrieved July 14, 2021, from https://chem.libretexts.org/@go/page/151654

123. Elsayed, E. A. (1996). Reliability engineering. Reading, Mass: Addison Wesley Longman.

124. Elsayed A. Elsayed. Accelerated Life Testing. Book chapter. Pages: 415-428. In Handbook of Reliability Engineering. ISBN: 978-1-85233-453-6. DOI: 10.1007/b97414. Springer-Verlag. 2003.

125. Edited by G. Somasundaram and A. Shrivastava. Information Storage and Management. John Wiley & Sons. ISBN: 978-0-470-61833-2, 2010.

126. Enderton, Herbert B. Elements of Set Theory. ISBN:978-0-12-238440-0. Copyright 1977 Elsevier Inc. All rights reserved 1977.

127. Electronic Parts - Reliability Data 2014. Prepared by Quanterion Solutions Incorporated for Reliability Information Analysis Center. ISBN-13: 978-1-933904-66-5. 2014.

128. Epstein, Benjamin and Sobel, Milton. Life Testing. Journal of the American Statistical Association. Sep. 1953, Vol. Vol. 48, No. 263.

129. Ericson, Clifton. Fault Tree Analysis - A History. Proceedings of the 17th International Systems Safety Conference. 17th International Systems Safety Conference, 1999.

130. A. K. Erlang. Principal Works of A. K. Erlang - The Theory of Probabilities and Telephone Conversations. First published in Nyt Tidsskrift for Matematik B. 1909, Vol. Vol 2

131. Principal Works of A. K. Erlang - The Theory of Probabilities and Telephone Conversations. First published in Nyt Tidsskrift for Matematik B. 1909, Vol. Vol 20.

132. Eva Ishay. Fitting Phase-Type Distributions to Data from a Telephone Call Center. Research Thesis. HAIFA, October 2002

133. Brian S. Everitt, Sabine Landau, and Morven Leese. Cluster Analysis (5th. ed.). Wiley Publishing. 2011.

134. Fanban - Open Source Performance and Load Testing Tool. http://faban.org/. Retrieved at 9/23/2020.

135. L. Feinbube, L. Pirl, P. Tröger and A. Polze, "Software Fault Injection Campaign Generation for Cloud Infrastructures," 2017 IEEE International Conference on Software Quality, Reliability and Security Companion (QRS-C), Prague, Czech Republic, 2017, pp. 622-623, doi: 10.1109/QRS-C.2017.119.

136. Feitelson, Dror G. Workload Modeling for Computer Systems Performance Evaluation. isbn:1107078237. Cambridge University Press. 2015

137. Feitelson D.G. (2002) Workload Modeling for Performance Evaluation. In: Calzarossa M.C., Tucci S. (eds) Performance Evaluation of Complex Systems: Techniques and Tools. Performance 2002. Lecture Notes in Computer Science, vol 2459. Springer, Berlin, Heidelberg. https://doi.org/10.1007/3-540-45798-4˙6

138. W. Feller, An Introduction to Probability Theory and Its Applications, Vols. I, II, Wiley, New York, 1968.

139. Domenico Ferrari. 1984. On the foundations of artificial workload design. SIGMETRICS Perform. Eval. Rev. 12, 3 (August 1984), 8–14. DOI:https://doi.org/10.1145/1031382.809309

140. J. Jair Figueiredo, Paulo Maciel, Gustavo Callou, Eduardo Tavares, Erica Sousa and Bruno Silva. Estimating Reliability Importance and Total Cost of Acquisition for Data Center Power Infrastructures. In: Proceedings of the 2011 IEEE International Conference on Systems, Man, and Cybernetics (IEEE SMC 2011). Anchorage, Alaska, USA, 2011.

141. Jason Fink, Matt Sherer, Kurt Wall. Linux Performance Tuning and Capacity Planning. Sams, Indianapolis, Indiana, 46290 USA. ISBN: 0-672-32081-9. 2002

142. Ronald Aylmer Sir Fisher. On a Distribution Yielding the Error Functions of Several Well Known Statistics. Proceedings International Mathematical Congress, Toronto. 2, pp. 805-813. 1924.

143. K. Florek, J. Łukaszewicz, J. Perkal, Hugo Steinhaus, S. Zubrzycki Colloquium Mathematicum 2, 282-285 DOI: 10.4064/cm-2-3-4-282-285. 1951

144. P. Folkesson, S. Svensson and J. Karlsson, "A comparison of simulation-based and scan chain implemented fault injection," Digest of Papers. Twenty-Eighth Annual International Symposium on Fault-Tolerant Computing (Cat. No.98CB36224), Munich, Germany, 1998, pp. 284-293, doi: 10.1109/FTCS.1998.689479.

145. Catherine Forbes, Merran Evans, Nicholas Hastings, Brian Peacock. Statistical Distributions. John Wiley & Sons, Inc. ISBN: 978-0-470-39063-4. 2011.

146. L. Fratta and U. Montanari, "A Boolean algebra method for computing the terminal reliability in a communication network," in IEEE Transactions on Circuit Theory, vol. 20, no. 3, pp. 203-211, May 1973. doi: 10.1109/TCT.1973.1083657

147. H. E. S. Galindo, W. M. Santos, P. R. M. Maciel, B. Silva, S. M. L. Galdino and J. P. Pires, "Synthetic workload generation for capacity planning of virtual server environments," 2009 IEEE International Conference on Systems, Man and Cybernetics, San Antonio, TX, 2009, pp. 2837-2842, doi: 10.1109/ICSMC.2009.5346600.

148. Hugo Galindo, Erico Guedes, Paulo Maciel, Bruno Silva and Sérgio Galdino. WGCap: a synthetic trace generation tool for capacity planning of virtual server environments. In: IEEE International Conference on Systems, Man, and Cybernetics, 2010, Istanbul. IEEE Proceeding of SMC, 2010.

149. Gan, F. F., and K. J. Koehler. "Goodness-of-Fit Tests Based on P-P Probability Plots." Technometrics 32, no. 3 (1990): 289-303. doi:10.2307/1269106.

150. Gareth James, Daniela Witten, Trevor Hastie, and Robert Tibshirani. An Introduction to Statistical Learning: with Applications in R. Springer Publishing Company, Incorporated. 2014.

151. Jean-Claude Geffroy,Gilles Motet. Design of dependable computing systems. ISBN:1-4020-0437-0. 2002. Kluwer Academic Publishers

152. Silva, B. and Maciel, P. and Brilhante, J. and Zimmermann, A. GeoClouds Modcs: A performability evaluation tool for disaster tolerant IaaS clouds. Systems Conference (SysCon), 2014 8th Annual IEEE. pp.: 116-122. doi: 10.1109/SysCon.2014.6819245. 2014

153. German, Reinhard. Performance Analysis of Communication Systems with Non-Markovian Stochastic Petri Nets. 2000. isbn:0471492582. John Wiley & Sons, Inc. New York, NY, USA.

154. Reinhard German and Christoph Lindemann. Analysis of stochastic Petri nets by the method of supplementary variables. Performance Evaluation. Volume: 20, number: 1, pages: 317-335. issn: 0166-5316. 1994

155. Garth A. Gibson. Redundant Disk Arrays: Reliable, Parallel Secondary Storage. Thesis Ph.D. Thesis in Computer Science. University of California, Berkeley, April. 1991.

156. Gil, Daniel, Juan Carlos Baraza, Joaquin Gracia, and Pedro Joaquin Gil. "VHDL simulation-based fault injection techniques." In Fault injection techniques and tools for embedded systems reliability evaluation, pp. 159-176. Springer, Boston, MA, 2003.

157. Gilbreath, J., "A High-Level Language Benchmark," Byte, vol. 6, no. 9, September 1981, pp. 180–198.

158. Girault, Claude and Valk, Rudiger, Petri Nets for Systems Engineering: A Guide to Modeling, Verification, and Applications, isbn:3642074472, Springer Publishing Company, Incorporated, 2010.

159. Gnedenko, Igor A. Ushakov. Probabilistic Reliability Engineering. s.l. : Wiley-Interscience, 1995.

160. Demis Gomes, Guto Leoni, Djamel Sadok, Glauco Gonçalves, Patricia Endo, and Paulo Maciel. 2020. Temperature variation impact on estimating costs and most critical components in a cloud data centre. Int. J. Comput. Appl. Technol. 62, 4 (2020), 361–374. DOI:https://doi.org/10.1504/ijcat.2020.107426.

161. Anatoliy Gorbenko, Vyacheslav Kharchenko, Alexander Romanovsky. On composing Dependable Web Services using undependable web components. Int. J. Simulation and Process Modelling. Nos. 1/2, 2007, Vol. Vol. 3.

162. Tarun Goyal, Ajit Singh, Aakanksha Agrawal. Cloudsim: a simulator for cloud computing infrastructure and modeling, Procedia Engineering, Volume 38, 2012, Pages 3566-3572, ISSN 1877-7058, https://doi.org/10.1016/j.proeng.2012.06.412.

163. Gravette, M. A., & Barker, K. (2014). Achieved availability importance measures for enhancing reliability centered maintenance decisions. Journal of Risk and Reliability, 229(1), 62–72.

164. Gray, G. (1985). Why Do Computers Stop and What Can Be Done About It?. Tandem TR 85.7.

165. Franklin A. Graybill (Author), Hariharan K. Iyer. Regression Analysis: Concepts and Applications. ISBN-13: 978-0534198695. ISBN-10: 0534198694. Duxbury. 1994.

166. Chiola, G. and Franceschinis, G. and Gaeta, R. and Ribaudo, M. GreatSPN 1.7: Graphical Editor and Analyzer for Timed and Stochastic Petri Nets. Perform. Evaluation. Vol: 25. number:1-2. pages:47-68. isssn:0166-5316. Elsevier. 1995

167. Grinstead, Charles Miller, and James Laurie Snell. Introduction to probability. American Mathematical Soc., 2012.

168. Grottke, M., Matias, R., Trivedi, K. (2008). The fundamentals of software aging. In IEEE International Conference on Software Reliability Engineering Workshops.

169. Almir Guimarães, Paulo Maciel, Rivalino Matias, Bruno Silva, and Bruno Nogueira. An analytic approach for optimization of computer network design considering the integration of the communication and power infrastructures. International Journal of Network Management. 2021. ISSN: 1099-1190

170. Haas, Peter J. Stochastic Petri Nets: Modelling, Stability, Simulation. Springer, New York. pages:85–445, year: 2002. isbn: 978-0-387-21552-5, doi:10.1007/0-387-21552-2˙9.

171. (Godfrey Harold. A Course of Pure Mathematics. Third Edition. Cambridge at the University Press. 1921. ps.: The Project Gutenberg EBook. Release Date: February 5, 2012.

172. Boudewijn R. Haverkort. Markovian Models for Performance and Dependability Evaluation. Lectures on Formal Methods and Performance Analysis, Springer, 2001

173. Boudewijn R. Haverkort. Performance of Computer Communication Systems: A Model-Based Approach. John Wiley & Sons, Inc. New York, NY, USA, 1998.

174. Harchol-Balter, M. Performance Modeling and Design of Computer Systems: Queueing Theory in Action. Cambridge: Cambridge University Press. 2013 doi:10.1017/CBO9781139226424

175. Heath, Thomas, History of Ancient Greek Mathematics. Vol I. Oxford Press. 1921.

176. B. Herington, D. & Jacquot. The HP Virtual Server Environment: Making the Adaptive Enterprise Vision a Reality in your Data Center. Prentice-Hall, 2006.

177. Herzog, Ulrich. Formal Methods for Performance Evaluation. Book chapter. pp: 1-37. Formal Methods for Performance Evaluation. Lectures on Formal Methods and Performance Analysis. Springer Berlin Heidelberg. Editors:Brinksma, Ed, Hermanns, Holger, Katoen, Joost-Pieter, ISBN: 978-3-540-44667-5. 2001.

178. Hogg, R. V., Tanis, E. A., Probability and statistical inference, New York, Macmillan, 1977.

179. András Horváth, Marco Paolieri, Lorenzo Ridi, Enrico Vicario. Transient analysis of non-Markovian models using stochastic state classes. Performance Evaluation. North-Holland. Volume: 69. Issue: 7-8. Pages: 315-335. 2012.

180. Horváth, Gábor". Moment Matching-Based Distribution Fitting with Generalized Hyper-Erlang Distributions, Springer Berlin Heidelberg, Analytic and Stochastic Modeling Techniques and Applications: 20th International Conference, ASMTA 2013, Ghent, Belgium, July 8-10, 2013. Proceedings

181. Mei-Chen Hsueh, T. K. Tsai and R. K. Iyer, "Fault injection techniques and tools," in Computer, vol. 30, no. 4, pp. 75-82, April 1997, doi: 10.1109/2.585157.

182. https://linux.die.net/man/1/httperf. Retrieved at 10/3/2020.

183. Hu, Tao and Guo, Minyi and Guo, Song and Ozaki, Hirokazu and Zheng, Long and Ota, Kaoru and Dong, Mianxiong. MTTF of composite web services. Parallel and Distributed Processing with Applications (ISPA), 2010 International Symposium on. pp.: 130–137. IEEE. 2010.

184. P. H. Starke and S. Roch. INA - Integrated Net Analyzer - Version 2.2. Humbolt Universität zu Berlin - Institut für Informatik. 1999.

185. Intel Distribution for LINPACK Benchmark. https://software.intel.com/content/www/us/en /develop/documentation/mkl-linux-developer-guide/top/intel-math-kernel-library-benchmarks//intel-distribution-for-linpack-benchmark/ /overview-of-the-intel-distribution-for-linpack-benchmark.html. Retrieved at 9/8/2020.

186. ITIC 2020 Global Server Hardware, Server OS Reliability Report. Information Technology Intelligence Consulting Corp. February/March2020

187. B. Silva and Paulo Romero Martins Maciel and Armin Zimmermann. Performability Models for Designing Disaster Tolerant Infrastructure-as-a-Service Cloud. The 8th International Conference for Internet Technology and Secured Transactions (ICITST). 2013.

188. Jain, R., The art of computer systems performance analysis: Techniques for experimental design, measurement, simulation, and modeling. New York: Wiley. 1991.

189. Jean Araujo, Rubens Matos, Verônica Conceição, Gabriel Alves and Paulo Maciel. Impact of Capacity and Discharging Rate on Battery Lifetime: A Stochastic Model to Support Mobile Device Autonomy Planning Pervasive and Mobile Computing. Journal Pervasive and Mobile Computing. 2017. Online ISSN 1574-1192. Print ISSN 1574-1192.

190. Banks, Jerry, John S. Carson, and Barry L. Nelson. 1996. Discrete-event system simulation. Prentice-Hall. 4th Edition. isbn.: 10: 0131446797. 2004.

191. Edited by Jerry Banks. Handbook of Simulation: principles, methodology, advances, applications, and practice; John Wiley and Sons, Inc. isbn: 0471134031. 1998.

192. E. Jenn, J. Arlat, M. Rimen, J. Ohlsson and J. Karlsson, "Fault injection into VHDL models: the MEFISTO tool," Proceedings of IEEE 24th International Symposium on Fault-Tolerant Computing, Austin, TX, USA, 1994, pp. 66-75, doi: 10.1109/FTCS.1994.315656.

193. Arnulf Jentzen and Peter Kloeden. Taylor Approximations for Stochastic Partial Differential Equations. Series: CBMS-NSF Regional Conference Series in Applied Mathematics 83. Publisher: SIAM. ISBN: 9781611972009. 2011

194. Hao Jiang and Constantinos Dovrolis. 2005. Why is the internet traffic bursty in short time scales? SIGMETRICS Perform. Eval. Rev. 33, 1 (June 2005), 241–252. DOI:https://doi.org/10.1145/1071690.1064240

195. Joanes, D. N., and C. A. Gill. "Comparing Measures of Sample Skewness and Kurtosis." Journal of the Royal Statistical Society. Series D (The Statistician), vol. 47, no. 1, 1998, pp. 183–189.

196. Johnson SC. Hierarchical clustering schemes. Psychometrika. 1967 Sep;32(3):241-54. doi: 10.1007/BF02289588. PMID: 5234703.

197. Johnson, Mark E., Gary L. Tietjen, and Richard J. Beckman. "A New Family of Probability Distributions With Applications to Monte Carlo Studies." Journal of the American Statistical Association 75, no. 370 (1980): 276-79. doi:10.2307/2287446.

198. Johnson, Barry W. Design &Amp; Analysis of Fault-Tolerant Digital Systems. ISBN: 0-201-07570-9. Addison-Wesley Longman Publishing Co., Inc. 1988

199. Pallavi Joshi, Haryadi S. Gunawi, and Koushik Sen. 2011. PREFAIL: a programmable tool for multiple-failure injection. In Proceedings of the 2011 ACM international conference on Object-oriented programming systems languages and applications (OOPSLA '11). ACM, New York, NY, USA, 171–188. DOI:https://doi.org/10.1145/2048066.2048082

200. Juhás, Gabriel and Lehocki, Fedor and Lorenz, Robert. Semantics of Petri Nets: A Comparison. Proceedings of the 39th Conference on Winter Simulation: 40 Years! The Best is Yet to Come. Washington D.C. 2007. isbn: 1-4244-1306-0. page: 617–628. IEEE Press.

201. Joseph Juran, A. Blanton Godfrey. Juran's Quality Handbook. Fifth Edition. ISBN 0-07-034003-X. McGraw-Hill. 1998

202. G. A. Kanawati, N. A. Kanawati and J. A. Abraham, "FERRARI: a flexible software-based fault and error injection system," in IEEE Transactions on Computers, vol. 44, no. 2, pp. 248-260, Feb. 1995, doi: 10.1109/12.364536

203. E. L. Kaplan and Paul Meier. Nonparametric Estimation from Incomplete Observations. Journal of the American Statistical Association, Vol. 53, No. 282 (Jun. 1958), pp. 457-481

204. Kailash C. Kapur and Michael Pecht. 2014. Reliability Engineering (1st. ed.). Wiley Publishing.

205. Richard M. Karp and Raymond E. Miller, Parallel program schemat, Journal of Computer and System Sciences, vol.: 3, number: 2, year:1969, issn:0022-0000.

206. Kaufman, L. and P. Rousseeuw. Finding Groups in Data: An Introduction to Cluster Analysis. John Wiley. isbn: 978-0-47187876-6. doi: 10.1002/9780470316801. 1990.

207. W R Keesee. A METHOD OF DETERMINING A CONFIDENCE INTERVAL FOR AVAILABILITY. NAVAL MISSILE CENTER POINT MUGU CA. DEFENSE TECHNICAL INFORMATION CENTER. Accession Number: AD0617716. 09 July 1965.

208. Law, A. M. and W. D. Kelton (1991). Simulation Modeling and Analysis, second edition. McGraw-Hill, New York.

209. M. Khatiwada, R. K. Budhathoki and A. Mahanti, "Characterizing Mobile Web Traffic: A Case Study of an Academic Web Server," 2019 Twelfth International Conference on Mobile Computing and Ubiquitous Network (ICMU), Kathmandu, Nepal, 2019, pp. 1-6, doi: 10.23919/ICMU48249.2019.9006650.

210. https://www.iec.ch/si/binary.htm. Retrieved at 5/2/2020.

211. Kim, Dong Seong and Machida, Fumio and Trivedi, Kishor S. Availability Modeling and Analysis of a Virtualized System. Proceedings of the 2009 15th IEEE Pacific Rim International Symposium on Dependable Computing. PRDC '09. isbn:978-0-7695-3849-5. doi: 10.1109/PRDC.2009.64. IEEE Computer Society. 2009.

212. Kim, Dong Seong and Machida, Fumio and Trivedi, Kishor S. Availability modeling and analysis of a virtualized system. Dependable Computing, 2009. PRDC'09. 15th IEEE Pacific Rim International Symposium on. pp.: 365–371. IEEE, 2009.

213. Kimball, E. Harvey Fletcher and Henry Eyring: Men of Faith and Science. Dialogue: A Journal of Mormon Thought, 15(3), 74-86. 1982.

214. Ronald S. King. Cluster Analysis and Data Mining: An Introduction. Mercury Learning & Information, Dulles, VA, USA. 2014.

215. Anil K. Jain and Richard C. Dubes. Algorithms for clustering data. Prentice-Hall, Inc., USA. 1988.

216. Andrey Nikolaevich Kolmogorov. Kolmogoroff, A. Über die analytischen Methoden in der Wahrscheinlichkeitsrechnung (in German) Mathematische Annalen. Springer-Verlag, 1931.

217. Maha Kooli, Alberto Bosio, Pascal Benoit, Lionel Torres. Software testing and software fault injection. DTIS: Design and Technology of Integrated Systems in Nanoscale Era, Apr 2015, Naples, Italy.

218. Israel Koren, C. Mani Krishna. Fault-Tolerant Systems. Morgan Kaufmann Publishers Inc. 2007. ISBN: 10: 0-12-088568-9

219. G. Kotsis, K. Krithivasan and S. V. Raghavan, "Generative workload models of Internet traffic," Proceedings of ICICS, 1997 International Conference on Information, Communications and Signal Processing. Theme: Trends in Information Systems Engineering and Wireless Multimedia Communications (Cat., Singapore, 1997, pp. 152-156 vol.1, doi: 10.1109/ICICS.1997.647077.

220. Kotz, Samuel, and Saralees Nadarajah. Extreme value distributions: theory and applications. World Scientific, 2000.

221. K. Krishnamoorthy. Handbook of Statistical Distributions with Applications. Chapman & Hall/CRC. ISBN 1-58488-635-8. 206.

222. A. N. Kolmogorov, Sulla determinazione empirica di una legge di distribuzione, Giornale dell'Istituto Italiano degli Attuari, 4:83–91, 1933.

223. V. G. Kulkarni. Introduction to Modeling and Analysis of Stochastic Systems. Springer. 2011. ISBN:978-1-4419-1771-3.

224. Zuo, Way Kuo and Ming J. Optimal Reliability Modeling - Principles and Applications. s.l. : Wiley, 2003. p. 544.

225. Kuo, Way and Zhu, Xiaoyan. Importance Measures in Reliability, Risk, and Optimization: Principles and Applications. 2012. ISBN: 111999344X, 9781119993445. Wiley Publishing

226. Lance, G., & Williams, W.T. A General Theory of Classificatory Sorting Strategies: Hierarchical Systems. Comput. J., 9, 373-380. 1967.

227. Laprie, J.C. Dependable Computing and Fault Tolerance: Concepts and terminology. Proc. 15th IEEE Int. Symp. on Fault-Tolerant Computing. 1985.

228. J.C. Laprie. Dependability: Basic Concepts and Terminology. s.l. : Springer-Verlag., 1992.

229. Jerald F. Lawless. Statistical Models and Methods for Lifetime Data, Second Edition. First published:13 November 2002 Print ISBN:9780471372158 —Online ISBN:9781118033005 —DOI:10.1002/9781118033005. 2003 John Wiley & Sons

230. Lawless, J. F. Statistical models and methods for lifetime data. Hoboken, N.J: Wiley-Interscience. 2003.

231. M. Le and Y. Tamir, "Fault Injection in Virtualized Systems—Challenges and Applications," in IEEE Transactions on Dependable and Secure Computing, vol. 12, no. 3, pp. 284-297, 1 May-June 2015, doi: 10.1109/TDSC.2014.2334300.

232. Lee, Elisa T. and Wang, John Wenyu. Statistical Methods for Survival Data Analysis. isbn: 1118095022. 4th edition. Wiley Publishing. 2013.

233. Leemis Lawrence M. Reliability - Probabilistic Models and Statistical Methods. Second Edition. isbn: 978-0-692-00027-4

234. Lehmer, D. H., Proceedings 2nd Symposium on Largescale. Digital Calculating Machinery, Cambridge, Harvard University Press, pp. 141-146, 1951.

235. Lehn, M., Triebel, T., Rehner, R. et al. On synthetic workloads for multiplayer online games: a methodology for generating representative shooter game workloads. Multimedia Systems 20, 609–620 (2014). https://doi.org/10.1007/s00530-014-0359-z

236. Leithold, Louis, and Louis Leithold. The calculus 7th Edition. New York: HarperCollins College Pub. 1996.

237. Lewis, Byron C., and Albert E. Crews. "The Evolution of Benchmarking as a Computer Performance Evaluation Technique." MIS Quarterly, vol. 9, no. 1, 1985, pp. 7–16. JSTOR

238. Lilja, D. (2000). Measuring Computer Performance: A Practitioner's Guide. Cambridge: Cambridge University Press. doi:10.1017/CBO9780511612398

239. C. Lindemann. Performance Modelling with Deterministic and Stochastic Petri Nets. John Wiley and Sons. 1998.

240. https://people.sc.fsu.edu/~jburkardt/c_src/linpack_bench/linpack_bench.c. Retrieved at 10/10/2020.

241. John D. C. Little. Little's Law as Viewed on Its 50th Anniversary. Oper. Res. 59, 3. May 2011. 536–549. DOI:https://doi.org/10.1287/opre.1110.0940

242. https://www.netlib.org/benchmark/livermorec. Retrieved at 10/18/2020.

243. Roy Longbottom. Roy Longbottom's PC Benchmark Collection. http://www.roylongbottom.org.uk/. Retrieved at 9/8/2020.

244. Lyu, Michael R. Software Fault Tolerance. John Wiley & Sons, Inc. ISBN: 0471950688. New York, NY, USA. 1995.

245. Machida, F. and Andrade, E. and Kim, D.S. and Trivedi, K.S. Candy: Component-based Availability Modeling Framework for Cloud Service Management Using SysML. Reliable Distributed Systems (SRDS), 2011 30th IEEE Symposium on. pp.: 209–218. IEEE. 2011.

246. Paulo Maciel, Kishor Trivedi, Rivalino Matias and Dong Kim. Dependability Modeling. In: Performance and Dependability in Service Computing: Concepts, Techniques and Research Directions ed. Hershey, Pennsylvania: IGI Global, 2011.

247. P. Maciel, K. S. Trivedi, R. Matias, and D. S. Kim, "Dependability modeling," in Performance and Dependability in Service Computing: Concepts, Techniques and Research Directions. Hershey: IGI Global, 2011.

248. Maciel, Paulo; Dantas, Jamilson; Melo, Carlos; Pereira, Paulo; Oliveira, Felipe; Araujo, Jean; Matos, Rubens; A survey on reliability and availability modeling of edge, fog, and cloud computing, Journal of Reliable Intelligent Environments pages:2199-4676, Springer. 09/18/2021 , 10.1007/s40860-021-00154-1

249. MacQueen, James. Some methods for classification and analysis of multivariate observations. Proceedings of the fifth Berkeley symposium on mathematical statistics and probability. Vol. 1. No. 14. 1967.

250. Madeira H., Rela M., Moreira F., Silva J.G. (1994) RIFLE: A general purpose pin-level fault injector. In: Echtle K., Hammer D., Powell D. (eds) Dependable Computing — EDCC-1. EDCC 1994. Lecture Notes in Computer Science, vol 852. Springer, Berlin, Heidelberg. https://doi.org/10.1007/3-540-58426-9˙132

251. H. Madeira, D. Costa and M. Vieira, "On the emulation of software faults by software fault injection," Proceeding International Conference on Dependable Systems and Networks. DSN 2000, New York, NY, USA, 2000, pp. 417-426, doi: 10.1109/ICDSN.2000.857571.

252. Magee, Jeff and Kramer, Jeff, Concurrency: State Models &Amp; Java Programs, 1999, isbn:0-471-98710-7, John Wiley & Sons, Inc., New York, NY, USA.

253. J. A. Manion, R. E. Huie, R. D. Levin, D. R. Burgess Jr., V. L. Orkin, W. Tsang, W. S. McGivern, J. W. Hudgens, V. D. Knyazev, D. B. Atkinson, E. Chai, A. M. Tereza, C.-Y. Lin, T. C. Allison, W. G. Mallard, F. Westley, J. T. Herron, R. F. Hampson, and D. H. Frizzell, NIST Chemical Kinetics Database, NIST Standard Reference Database 17, Version 7.0 (Web Version), Release 1.6.8, Data version 2015.09, National Institute of Standards and Technology, Gaithersburg, Maryland, 20899-8320. Web address: https://kinetics.nist.gov/

254. Mann, Nancy R., and Frank E. Grubbs. "Chi-Square Approximations for Exponential Parameters, Prediction Intervals and Beta Percentiles." Journal of the American Statistical Association 69, no. 347 (1974): 654-61. doi:10.2307/2285996.

255. Marsaglia, G., & Marsaglia, J. Evaluating the Anderson-Darling Distribution. Journal of Statistical Software. 2004.

256. Marsan, Marco Ajmone and Balbo, G. and Conte, Gianni and Donatelli, S. and Franceschinis, G. Modelling with generalized stochastic Petri nets. isbn:9780471930594, Wiley. 1995

257. M. Ajmone Marsan and G. Chiola. On Petri Nets with deterministic and exponentially distributed firing times. In G. Rozenberg, editor, Adv. in Petri Nets 1987, Lecture Notes in Computer Science 266, pages 132–145. Springer-Verlag, 1987.

258. M. Ajmone Marsan, G. Balbo, A. Bobbio, G. Chiola, G. Conte, and A. Cumani. The effect of execution policies on the semantics and analysis of stochastic Petri nets. IEEE Transactions on Software Engineering, pages:832-846. SE-15:832-846, 1989

259. Mathis, Matthew and Semke, Jeffrey and Mahdavi, Jamshid and Ott, Teunis. The macroscopic behavior of the TCP congestion avoidance algorithm. SIG-COMM Comput. Commun. Rev. pp.: 67–82. Vol: 27. no: 3. issn:0146-4833. doi:10.1145/263932.264023. ACM. 1997.

260. Rubens Matos, Paulo Maciel, Fumio Machida, Dong Seong Kim, Kishor Trivedi. Sensitivity Analysis of Server Virtualized System Availability. IEEE Transaction on Reliability. Volume 61, Number 4, Pages 994-1006. Published on December 2012. ISSN: 0018-9529.

261. MATOS, R. S.; MACIEL, P. R.; SILVA, R. M. Qos-driven optimization of composite web services: an approach based on grasp and analytic models. International Journal of Web and Grid Services, v. 9, n. 3, p. 304–321, 2013.

262. R. Matos, E. C. Andrade and P. Maciel, "Evaluation of a disaster recovery solution through fault injection experiments," 2014 IEEE International Conference on Systems, Man, and Cybernetics (SMC), San Diego, CA, USA, 2014, pp. 2675-2680, doi: 10.1109/SMC.2014.6974331.

263. Rubens Matos, Jean Araujo, Danilo Oliveira, Paulo Maciel and Kishor Trivedi. Sensitivity Analysis of a Hierarchical Model of Mobile Cloud Computing. Elsevier Journal Simulation Modelling Practice and Theory. Volume 50, January 2015, Pages 151–164. ISSN: 1569-190X.

264. Rubens Matos, Jamilson Dantas, Jean Araujo, Kishor S. Trivedi, and Paulo Maciel. Redundant Eucalyptus Private Clouds: Availability Modeling and Sensitivity Analysis. Journal of Grid Computing. 2016. Online ISSN 1572-9184. Print ISSN 1570-7873.

265. Rubens Matos, Jamilson Dantas, Eltton Araujo, and Paulo Maciel. Bottleneck detection in cloud computing performance and dependability: Sensitivity rankings for hierarchical models. Journal of Network and Systems Management (JONS). 2020. ISSN: 1064-7570.

266. Philippe Maurine, Karim Tobich, Thomas Ordas, Pierre Yvan Liardet. Yet Another Fault Injection Technique: by Forward Body Biasing Injection. YACC'2012: Yet Another Conference on Cryptography, Sep 2012, Porquerolles Island, France.

267. Michael P. McLaughlin. Compendium of Common Probability Distributions. Compendium of Common Probability Distributions Second Edition, v2.7. Copyright 2014 by Michael P. McLaughlin. All rights reserved. Second printing, with corrections.

268. McMahon, F H. The Livermore Fortran Kernels: A computer test of the numerical performance range. United States: N. p., 1986.

269. Meeker, W. Q., & Escobar, L. A. Statistical methods for reliability data. New York: Wiley. 1998.

270. Rosangela Melo, Maria Clara Bezerra, Jamilson Dantas, Rubens Matos, Ivanildo José de Melo Filho, Aline Santana Oliveira, Fábio Feliciano and Paulo Maciel. Sensitivity Analysis Techniques Applied in Video Streaming Service on Eucalyptus Cloud Environments. Journal of Information Systems Engineering & Management. 2018. ISSN: 2468-4376 (Online).

271. Melo, Carlos; Araujo, Jean; Dantas, Jamilson; Pereira, Paulo; Maciel, Paulo. A model-based approach for planning blockchain service provisioning. Computing. Springer. A10.1007/s00607-021-00956-4. 05/23/2021.

272. Carlos Melo, Paulo Pereira, Jamilson Dantas, and Paulo Maciel. Distributed Application Provisioning over Ethereum based private and permissioned Blockchain: Availability modeling, capacity, and costs planning. The Journal of Supercomputing. 2021. ISSN: 1573-0484.

273. Paulo Maciel, Rubens Matos, Bruno Silva, Jair Figueiredo, Danilo Oliveira, Iure Fé, Ronierison Maciel, and Jamilson Dantas. Mercury: Performance and Dependability Evaluation of Systems with Exponential, Expolynomial and General Distributions. , In: The 22nd IEEE Pacific Rim International Symposium on Dependable Computing (PRDC 2017). January 22-25, 2017. Christchurch, New Zealand.

274. Bruno Silva, Rubens Matos, Gustavo Callou, Jair Figueiredo, Danilo Oliveira, João Ferreira, Jamilson Dantas, Aleciano Lobo Junior, Vandi Alves and Paulo Maciel. Mercury: An Integrated Environment for Performance and Dependability Evaluation of General Systems. In: Proceedings of Industrial Track at 45th Dependable Systems and Networks Conference (DSN-2015). June 22 – 25, 2015. Rio de Janeiro, RJ, Brazil.

275. Philip M. Merlin. A Study of the Recoverability of Computing Systems. Ph.D. thesis, University of California, Irvine. January 1974.

276. Philip M. Merlin and David J. Farber. Recoverability of Communication Protocols–Implications of a Theoretical Study. IEEE Transactions on Communications, vol. 24, no. 9:1036 – 1043, September 1976

277. Mike Julian. Practical Monitoring: Effective Strategies for the Real World. ISBN-10: 1491957352. O'Reilly Media. 2017

278. Milner, Robin. Elements of Interaction: Turing Award Lecture. Commun. ACM. Volume: 36. Number:1. Pages: 78–89 Jan. 1993. ISSN:0001-0782. New York, NY, USA

279. Silvio Misera, Heinrich Theodor Vierhaus, and Andre Sieber. 2007. Fault Injection Techniques and their Accelerated Simulation in SystemC. Proceedings of the 10th Euromicro Conference on Digital System Design Architectures, Methods and Tools (DSD '07). IEEE Computer Society, USA, 587–595.

280. von Mises, R. E. Wahrscheinlichkeit, Statistik und Wahrheit. Julius Springer.1928.

281. Mark L. Mitchell, Alex Samuel, Jeffrey Oldham. Advanced Linux Programming. ISBN-10: 0735710430. New Riders Publishing. 2001

282. Mobley, R. Keith, Lindley R. Higgins, and Darrin J. Wikoff. Maintenance Engineering Handbook. New York: McGraw-Hill, 2008.

283. Cleve Moler and Charles Van Loan, Nineteen Dubious Ways to Compute the Exponential of a Matrix, SIAM REVIEW, Vols. 20, Issue 4, 1978.

284. Cleve Moler and Charles Van Loan, Nineteen Dubious Ways to Compute the Exponential of a Matrix, Twenty-Five Years Later, SIAM REVIEW, Vols. 45,Issue 1, 2003.

285. On the Integration of Delay and Throughput Measures in Distributed Processing Models. Ph.D. thesis. UCLA. Los Angeles. USA.

286. Molloy, M. K. Performance Analysis Using Stochastic Petri Nets. IEEE Trans. Comput. Vol. 31. n:9. 1982. ISSN: 0018-9340. IEEE Computer Society.

287. Montgomery, D. C., Runger, G. C., Applied statistics and probability, for engineers, Hoboken, NJ: Wiley., Addison-Wesley, Reading, Massachusetts, 2007.

288. Douglas C Montgomery; Elizabeth A Peck; G Geoffrey Vining. Introduction to linear regression analysis. Fifth Edition. John Wiley & Sons, Inc. ISBN 978-0-470-54281-1. 2012.

289. Moore, Edward F. Gedanken-Experiments on Sequential Machines. The Journal of Symbolic Logic. Mar. 1958, Vols. Vol. 23, No. 1, Association for Symbolic Logic.

290. E.F. Moore, C.E. Shannon. Reliable circuits using less reliable relays. Journal of the Franklin Institute.Volume 262. Issue 3. 1956. Pages 191-208. ISSN 0016-0032.

291. Les Cottrell, Warren Matthews and Connie Logg. Tutorial on Internet Monitoring and PingER at SLAC. http://www.slac.stanford.edu/comp/net/wanmon/tutorial.html. 1996.

292. David Mosberger and Tai Jin. Httperf—a tool for measuring web server performance. SIGMETRICS Perform. Eval. Rev. 26, 3 (Dec. 1998), 31–37. DOI:https://doi.org/10.1145/306225.306235

293. Silva, Manuel. 50 years after the Ph.D. thesis of Carl Adam Petri: A perspective. IFAC Proceedings Volumes 45, no. 29 (2012): 13-20.

294. Jogesh K. Muppala and Gianfranco Ciardo and Kishor S. Trivedi. Stochastic Reward Nets for Reliability Prediction. Communications in Reliability, Maintainability and Serviceability. Pages: 9-20. 1994.

295. T. Murata. Petri Nets: Properties, Analysis and Applications. Proc. IEEE. April. no. 4. year:1989. pages:541-580

296. https://www.nagios.com/. Retrieved at 5/19/2020.

297. NASCIMENTO, Rilson Oscar Do; Mark Wong; MACIEL, P. R. M. DBT-5: A Fair Usage Open-Source TPC-E Implementation for Performance Evaluation of Computer Systems. DOI.: 10.6084/m9.figshare.13123280. In: WPerformance – 2007, 2007, Rio de Janeiro. DO XXVII CONGRESSO DA SBC, 2007.

298. Nascimento, R., Maciel, P. DBT-5: An Open-Source TPC-E Implementation for Global Performance Measurement of Computer Systems. Computing and Informatics, 29 (5), 719-740. 1335-9150. DOI.: 10.6084/m9.figshare.13123319. 2010

299. Pablo Pessoa do Nascimento, Paulo Pereira, Jr Marco Mialaret, Isac Ferreira, Paulo Maciel, A methodology for selecting hardware performance counters for supporting non-intrusive diagnostic of flood DDoS attacks on web servers, Computers & Security,Volume 110,ISSN 0167-4048, https://doi.org/10.1016/j.cose.2021.102434. 2021.

300. Roberto Natella, Domenico Cotroneo, and Henrique S. Madeira. 2016. Assessing Dependability with Software Fault Injection: A Survey. ACM Comput. Surv. 48, 3, Article 44 (February 2016), 55 pages. DOI:https://doi.org/10.1145/2841425

301. Natkin, G.F.S. Matrix Product Form Solution For Closed Synchronized Queuing Networks. Petri Nets and Performance Models. 1990. IEEE Computer Society.

302. Les Reseaux de Petri Stochastiques et leur Application a l'Evaluation des Systém Informatiques. PhD thesis. CNAM. Paris

303. http://www.netresec.com/?page=NetworkMiner. Retrieved at 5/19/2020.

304. Neumann, J. V. Probabilistic logics and the synthesis of reliable organisms from unreliable components. Annals of Mathematics Studies. CE Shannon and McCarthy, 1956, Vol. 34, AutomataStudies.

305. M. F. Neuts, Matrix-Geometric Solutions in Stochastic Models: An Algorithmic Approach. Dover, 1981.

306. Bob Neveln. Linux Assembly Language Programming. Publisher(s): Prentice-Hall. ISBN: 0130879401. 2000

307. https://linux.die.net/man/8/ngrep. Retrieved at 5/19/2020.

308. Ningfang Mi, Qi Zhang, Alma Riska, Evgenia Smirni, Erik Riedel, Performance impacts of autocorrelated flows in multi-tiered systems, Performance Evaluation, Volume 64, Issues 9–12, 2007, Pages 1082-1101, ISSN 0166-5316, https://doi.org/10.1016/j.peva.2007.06.016.

309. Nita, Mihaela-Catalina, Florin Pop, M. Mocanu and V. Cristea. "FIM-SIM: Fault Injection Module for CloudSim Based on Statistical Distributions." Journal of telecommunications and information technology 4. 2014.

310. http://nmon.sourceforge.net/pmwiki.php. Retrieved at 5/19/2020.

311. NOGUEIRA, Meuse; MACIEL, P. R. M. . A Retargetable Environment for Power-Aware Code Evaluation: An Approach Based on Coloured Petri Net.In: Power and Timing Modeling, Optimization and Simulation (PATMOS), 2005, Leuven. Lecture Notes in Computer Science, 2005.

312. NOGUEIRA, Meuse; VASCONCELOS NETO, Silvino; MACIEL, P. R. M.; LIMA, Ricardo Massa Ferreira; BARRETO, Raimundo. Embedded Systems' Software Performance and Energy Consumption by Probabilistic Modeling: An Approach Based on Coloured Petri Nets.In: Application and Theory of Petri Nets and Other Models of Concurrency, 2006, Turku. Lectures Notes in Computer Science – Proceedings of the Application and Theory of Petri Nets and Other Concurrency Models. Heidelberg, Germany: Springer Verlag, 2006.

313. J. R. Norris, Markov Chains, Vols. Cambridge University Press, 1997.

314. Nonelectronic Parts Reliability Data (NPRD-2016). Quanterion Solutions Incorporated . ISBN-13: 978-1-933904-76-4. 2016.

315. https://linux.die.net/man/5/ntp.conf. Retrieved at 5/14/2020.

316. William H. and Teukolsky, Saul A. and Vetterling, William T. and Flannery, Brian P. Numerical Recipes 3rd Edition: The Art of Scientific Computing. isbn:0521880688. Cambridge University Press. 2007

317. Mohammed S. Obaidat and Noureddine A. Boudriga. 2010. Fundamentals of Performance Evaluation of Computer and Telecommunications Systems. Wiley-Interscience, USA.

318. Danilo Oliveira, Nelson Rosa, André Brinkmann and Paulo Maciel. Performability Evaluation and Optimization of Workflow Applications in Cloud Environments. Journal of Grid Computing. 2019. ISSN: 1572-9184 (Online).

319. O'NEILL, M. The Genuine Sieve of Eratosthenes. Journal of Functional Programming, 19(1), 95-106. 2009. doi:10.1017/S0956796808007004

320. OREDA Offshore Reliability Data Handbook. 4th Edition. Publisher: Høvik. Norway. 2002.

321. OREDA. Offshore & Onshore Reliability Data. https://www.oreda.com/. Retrieved at 5/5/2021.

322. Diego Perez-Palacin, José Merseguer, and Raffaela Mirandola. 2012. Analysis of bursty workload-aware self-adaptive systems. In Proceedings of the 3rd ACM/SPEC International Conference on Performance Engineering (ICPE '12). Association for Computing Machinery, New York, NY, USA, 75–84. DOI:https://doi.org/10.1145/2188286.2188300

323. Diego Perez-Palacin, Raffaela Mirandola, José Merseguer, Accurate modeling and efficient QoS analysis of scalable, adaptive systems under bursty workload, Journal of Systems and Software, Volume 130, 2017, Pages 24-41, ISSN 0164-1212, https://doi.org/10.1016/j.jss.2017.05.022.

324. Papazoglou, M. P.. Service-oriented computing: Concepts, characteristics and directions. Proceedings of the Fourth International Conference on Web Information Systems Engineering. WISE '03, pages 3–12, Washington, DC, USA. IEEE Computer Society. 2003.

325. Emanuel Parzen. Stochastic Processes. Dover Publications Inc. 1962.

326. PCMark - Technical Guide. Updated September 10, 2020.

327. Karl Pearson F.R.S., X. On the criterion that a given system of deviations from the probable in the case of a correlated system of variables is such that it can be reasonably supposed to have arisen from random sampling, Philosophical Magazine Series 5, Vol. 50 , Iss. 302,1900

328. Witold Pedrycz. Knowledge-Based Clustering: From Data to Information Granules. Wiley-Interscience, USA. 2005.

329. Pelluri, Sudha and Keerti Bangari. "Synthetic Workload Generation in Cloud". International Journal of Research in Engineering and Technology 04. 2015. 56-66.

330. Paulo Pereira, Jean Araujo, Jamilson Dantas, Matheus Torquato, Carlos Melo and Paulo Maciel. Stochastic Performance Model for Web-Server Capacity Planning in Fog Computing. The Journal of Supercomputing. 2020. ISSN: 1573-0484 (Online). ISSN: 0920-8542 (Print).

331. Pereira, Paulo; Melo, Carlos; Araujo, Jean; Dantas, Jamilson; Santos, Vinícius; Maciel, Paulo; Availability model for edge-fog-cloud continuum: an evaluation of an end-to-end infrastructure of intelligent traffic management service; The Journal of Supercomputing; 1573-0484; 10.1007/s11227-021-04033-7. 09/03/2021.

332. Paulo Pereira, Carlos Melo, Jean Araujo, and Paulo Maciel. Analytic Models for Availability Evaluation of Edge and Fog Computing Nodes. The Journal of Supercomputing. 2021. ISSN: 1573-0484.

333. https://docs.microsoft.com/en-us/windows-server/administration/windows-commands/perfmon. Retrieved at 5/19/2020.

334. Peterson, James Lyle. Petri Net Theory and the Modeling of Systems. isbn:0136619835. 1981. Prentice-Hall PTR. Upper Saddle River, NJ, USA

335. Carl Adam Petri. Kommunikation mit Automaten. Schriften des Rheinisch-Westfälischen Institutes für Instrumentelle Mathematik an der Universität Bonn Nr. 2, 1962

336. Communication with Automata. New York: Griffiss Air Force Base, Technical Report, RADC TR-65-377-vol-1-suppl-1 Applied Data Research, Princeton, NJ, Contract AF 30(602)-3324, 1966

337. Editor: Hoang Pham. Handbook of Reliability Engineering. ISBN: 978-1-85233-453-6. DOI: 10.1007/b97414. Springer-Verlag. 2003.

338. Phone Arena - Phone News, Reviews and Specs. `http://www.phonearena.com/`. 2019. Online. Accessed 20-May-2019.

339. Pierce, W. H. Failure-tolerant computer design. New York: Academic Press, 1965. ISBN:978-1-4832-3179-2.

340. Pietrantuono, R.; Russo, S. Software Qual J (2019). https://doi.org/10.1007/s11219-019-09448-3, Springer US Print ISSN 0963-9314, Online ISSN 1573-1367. 2019

341. T. F. da Silva Pinheiro, F. A. Silva, I. Fe, S. Kosta, and P. Maciel. Performance prediction for supporting mobile applications' offloading. The Journal of Supercomputing, 74(8):4060–4103, Aug 2018.

342. Plackett, R. L. "Karl Pearson and the Chi-Squared Test." International Statistical Review / Revue Internationale De Statistique 51, no. 1 (1983): 59-72. doi:10.2307/1402731.

343. Pólya, G., Über den zentralen Grenzwertsatz der Wahrscheinlichkeitsrechnung und das Momentenproblem, Mathematische Zeitschrif, vol.: 8, 171-181, 1920

344. R. E. Barlow and F. Proschan. Mathematical Theory of Reliability. New York: John Wiley, 1967. SIAM series in applied mathematics.

345. J. D. Esary and F. Proschan. A Reliability Bound for Systems of Maintained, Interdependent Components. Journal of the American Statistical Association. 1970, Vol. Vol. 65, No. 329.

346. R. E. Barlow and F. Proschan. Proschan, R. E. Barlow and F. Statistical Theory of Reliability and Life Testing: Probability Models. New York. : Holt, Rinehart and Winston, 1975. Holt, Rinehart and Winston, New York, 1975.

347. Semyon G. Rabinovich. Evaluating Measurement Accuracy. Springer. ISBN 978-1-4419-1455-2. DOI 10.1007/978-1-4419-1456-9. 2010

348. Bharat Rajaram. Technical White Paper: Understanding Functional Safety FIT Base Failure Rate Estimates per IEC 62380 and SN 29500. Texas Instruments. June 2020

349. Kandethody M. Ramachandran and Ramachandran Tsokos and Chris P. Tsokos, Mathematical Statistics with Applications, Elsevier Academic Press, ISBN 13: 978-0-12-374848-5. 2009

350. C. Ramchandani. Analysis of Asynchronous Concurrent Systems by Timed Petri Nets. Technical Report: TR-120, Massachusetts Institute of Technology, Cambridge, MA, USA, February 1974.

351. Dunn-Rankin, Peter, Gerald A. Knezek, Susan R. Wallace, and Shuqiang Zhang. Scaling methods. Mahwah, N.J. USA. Lawrence Erlbaum Associates, 2004.

352. Rausand, M., System Reliability Theory: Models, Statistical Methods, and Applications. ISBN: 9780471471332. Wiley Series in Probability. Wiley. 2004.

353. Philipp Reinecke, Levente Bodrog, and Alexandra Danilkina. Phase-Type Distributions. Resilience Assessment and Evaluation of Computing Systems, Springer Berlin Heidelberg, 2012

354. W. Reisig. On the Semantics of Petri Nets. pp.:347-372. In Formal Models in Programming. Edited by E.J. Neuhold and G. Chroust. Proceedings of the IFIP TC2 Working Conference on The Role of Abstract Models in Information Process. Vienna. Austria. January-February. 1985. isbn: 0444878882.

355. Renata Pedrosa, Jamilson Dantas, Gabriel Alves, and Paulo Maciel. Analysis of a Performability Model for the BRT System. International Journal of Data Mining, Modelling and Management. 2018. ISSN Online 1759-1171 and ISSN print: 1759-1163

356. Alvin C. Rencher and G. Bruce Schaalje. Linear models in statistics. Second Edition. Wiley. ISBN 978-0-471-75498-5. 2008.

357. Richard L. Burden and J. Douglas Faires. Numerical Analysis, Ninth Edition. ISBN-13: 978-0-538-73351-9. Brooks/Cole, Cengage Learning. 2011.

358. *Lecture Notes on Petri Nets I: Basic Models.*Lecture Notes in Computer Science - Advances in Petri Nets, Springer-Verlag, Edited by W. Reisig and G. Rozenberg. 1998.

359. *Lecture Notes on Petri Nets II: Applications.* Lecture Notes in Computer Science - Advances in Petri Nets, Springer-Verlag, Edited by W. Reisig and G. Rozenberg. 1998.

360. Ripley, Brian D. Stochastic Simulation. isbn.: 0-471-81884-4. John Wiley & Sons, Inc. 1987

361. Robinson, Stewart.Simulation: The Practice of Model Development and Use.isbn:0470847727. John Wiley & Sons, Inc. 2004. USA.

362. Manuel Rodríguez, Frédéric Salles, Jean-Charles Fabre, and Jean Arlat. 1999. "MAFALDA: Microkernel Assessment by Fault Injection and Design Aid". In Proceedings of the Third European Dependable Computing Conference on Dependable Computing (EDCC-3). Springer-Verlag, Berlin, Heidelberg, 143–160.

363. Fabrizio Romano, Dusty Phillips, Rick van Hattem. Python: Journey from Novice to Expert. Packt Publishing. ISBN: 9781787122567. 2016.

364. Ross, Sheldon M.Simulation, Fourth Edition. isbn.: 0125980639.Academic Press, Inc. 2006.

365. Sheldon M. Ross. Introduction to Probability and Statistics for Engineers and Scientists. Elsevier Academic Press. ISBN 13: 978-0-12-370483-2. 2009.

366. Cisco Catalyst 3750 Data Sheet. http://tinyurl.com/38krjm. October. 2013.

367. G. Rozenberg, P. S. Thiagarajan, Petri Nets: Basic Notions, Structure, Behaviour, LNCS vol. 424, Springer Verlag, 1986

368. E. M. Salgueiro, P. R. F. Cunha, P. R. M. Maciel, J. A. S. Monteiro and R. J. P. B. Salgueiro, "Defining bandwidth constraints with cooperative games," 2009 International Conference on Ultra Modern Telecommunications & Workshops, St. Petersburg, Russia, 2009, pp. 1-8, doi: 10.1109/ICUMT.2009.5345534.

369. https://www.sisoftware.co.uk/2019/07/18/sisoftware-sandra-20-20-2020-released/ Retrieved at 9/19/2020.

370. Sato, N. and Trivedi, K. S.Stochastic modeling of composite web services for closed-form analysis of their performance and reliability bottlenecks. Proceedings of the 5th international conference on Service-Oriented Computing. ICSOC '07, pages 107–118, Berlin, Heidelberg. Springer-Verlag.. 2007.

371. Schaffer, Simon. Babbage's Intelligence: Calculating Engines and the Factory System. Critical Inquiry. The University of Chicago Press, 1994, Vol. 21, No. 1.

372. Schmidt Klaus. High Availability and Disaster Recovery: Concepts, Design, Implementation. isbn: 3642063799, 9783642063794. Springer Publishing Company, Incorporated. 2010.

373. Schrijver, Alexander, Theory of Linear and Integer Programming, John Wiley & Sons, Inc., isbn:0-471-90854-1, New York, NY, USA, 1986.

374. Z. Segall et al., "FIAT-fault injection-based automated testing environment," [1988] The Eighteenth International Symposium on Fault-Tolerant Computing. Digest of Papers, Tokyo, Japan, 1988, pp. 102-107, doi: 10.1109/FTCS.1988.5306.

375. Z. Segall et al., "FIAT - Fault injection-based automated testing environment," Twenty-Fifth International Symposium on Fault-Tolerant Computing, 1995, ' Highlights from Twenty-Five Years'., Pasadena, CA, USA, 1995, pp. 394-, doi: 10.1109/FTCSH.1995.532663.

376. Eugene Seneta. Markov and the Creation of the Markov Chains. School of Mathematics and Statistics, University of Sydney, NSW 2006, Australia

377. Seongwoo Woo. Reliability Design of Mechanical Systems. Second Edition. ISBN 978-981-13-7235-3. Springer Nature Singapore Pte Ltd. 2017.

378. Woo, Seongwoo. Reliability Design of Mechanical Systems: a Guide for Mechanical and Civil Engineers (Second edition.). Springer. 2020

379. Shannon, C. E. A Mathematical Theory of Communication. The Bell System Technical Journal. July, October, 1948, Vols. pp. 379–423, 623–656, Vol. 27.

380. Shetti, N. M. (2003). Heisenbugs and Bohrbugs: Why are they different?DCS/LCSR Technical Reports, Department of Computer Science, Rutgers, The State University of New Jersey.

381. Martin L. Shooman. Reliability of Computer Systems and Networks: Fault Tolerance, Analysis, and Design. 2002 John Wiley & Sons, Inc. ISBN: 0-471-29342-3

382. Ellen Siever, Stephen Figgins, Robert Love, and Arnold Robbins. Linux in a Nutshell, Sixth Edition. O'Reilly Media, Inc. ISBN: 978-0-596-15448-6. 2009

383. J. Sifakis. Use of Petri nets for Performance Evaluation. 3rd Intl. Symposium on Modeling and Evaluation, IFIP, North-Holland, pages 75–93, 1977.

384. Sifakis, Joseph, Structural properties of Petri nets, Mathematical Foundations of Computer Science, Springer Berlin Heidelberg, pp 474–483, 1978.

385. Silva, Manuel; Terue, Enrique; and Colom, José Manuel.Linear algebraic and linear programming techniques for the analysis of place/transition net systems. Lectures on Petri Nets I: Basic Models: Advances in Petri Nets. Springer Berlin Heidelberg. isbn:978-3-540-49442-3. pages: 309–373. 1998.

386. Manuel Silva.50 years after the Ph.D. thesis of Carl Adam Petri: A perspective. WODES. 2012.

387. F. A. Silva and M. Rodrigues and P. Maciel and S. Kosta and A. Mei. Planning Mobile Cloud Infrastructures Using Stochastic Petri Nets and Graphic Processing Units. 2015 IEEE 7th International Conference on Cloud Computing Technology and Science (CloudCom). DOI: 10.1109/CloudCom.2015.46. 2015

388. Silva, Francisco Airton and Zaicaner, Germano and Quesado, Eder and Dornelas, Matheus and Silva, Bruno and Maciel, Paulo. Benchmark applications used in mobile cloud computing research: a systematic mapping study. The Journal of Supercomputing. Vol.:72, number: 4. pp:1431–1452. Springer. 2016

389. Silva, Francisco Airton and Kosta, Sokol and Rodrigues, Matheus and Oliveira, Danilo and Maciel, Teresa and Mei, Alessandro and Maciel, Paulo. Mobile cloud performance evaluation using stochastic models. IEEE Transactions on Mobile Computing. Vol: 17. Number: 5. pp:1134–1147. IEEE. 2017

390. Bruno Silva, Rubens Matos, Eduardo Tavares, Armin Zimmerman and Paulo Maciel. Sensitivity Analysis of an Availability Model for Disaster Tolerant Cloud Computing System. International Journal of Network Management. 2018. ISSN: 1099-1190 (Online).

391. D. Leu, M. Silva, J. Colom, T. Murata. *Interrelationships among Various Concepts of Fairness for Petri Nets*. Proceedings of the 31st Midwest Symposium on Circuits and Systems. IEEE Computer Society Press,1988.

392. J.M.Colom, M.Silva. Convex Geometry and Semiflows in P/T Nets. A Comparative Study of Algorithms for Computation of Minimal P-Semiflows. Lecture Notes in Computer Science, vol-483, p. 79-112, Springer-Verlag, Edited by G. Rozenberg 1990.

393. J.M.Colom,M.Silva. Improving the Linearly Based Characterization of P/T Nets. Lecture Notes in Computer Science, vol-483, p. 113-145, Springer-Verlag, Edited by G. Rozenberg, 1990.

394. F.Dicesare, G. Harhalakis, J.M. Proth, M. Silva, F.B. Vernadat. Practice of Petri Nets in Manufacturing. Chapman and Hall, 1993.

395. Y. Choi, J. Silvester and H. Kim, "Analyzing and Modeling Workload Characteristics in a Multiservice IP Network," in IEEE Internet Computing, vol. 15, no. 2, pp. 35-42, March-April 2011, doi: 10.1109/MIC.2010.153.

396. Richard Simard and Pierre L'Ecuyer. Computing the Two-Sided Kolmogorov-Smirnov Distribution. Journal of Statistical Software.Vol. 39, number: 11. 2011. ISSN:1548-7660. Pages:1–18. DOI:10.18637/jss.v039.i11

397. Dandamudi, Sivarama P. Guide to Assembly Language Programming in Linux. ISBN 978-0-387-26171-3. Springer. 2005.

398. Service Level Agreement - MegaPath Business Access and Value-Added Services. http://tinyurl.com/cwdeebt. October. 2012.

399. J. G. Smith and H. E. Oldham, "Laser testing of integrated circuits," in IEEE Journal of Solid-State Circuits, vol. 12, no. 3, pp. 247-252, June 1977, doi: 10.1109/JSSC.1977.1050886.

400. Alan Jay Smith. 2007. Workloads (creation and use). Commun. ACM 50, 11 (November 2007), 45–50. DOI:https://doi.org/10.1145/1297797.1297821

401. Smith David J., Reliability, Maintainability and Risk - Practical methods for engineers. Eighth edition 2011. ISBN:978-0-08-096902-2

402. Smith David J., Reliability, Maintainability and Risk - Practical methods for engineers. Ninth edition 2017. ISBN:978-0-08-102010-4

403. Sneath, Peter HA. "The application of computers to taxonomy." Microbiology 17.1 (1957): 201-226.

404. https://www.iana.org/assignments/service-names-port-numbers/service-names-port-numbers.xhtml. Retrieved at 5/18/2020.

405. https://www.solarwinds.com/network-performance-monitor. Retrieved at 5/19/2020.

406. Hbrekke, Solfrid; Hauge, Stein; Xie, Lin; Lundteigen, Mary Ann. Failure rates of safety-critical equipment based on inventory attributes. Safety and Reliability – Safe Societies in a Changing World. Proceedings of ESREL 2018, June 17-21, 2018, Trondheim, Norway, 2419-2426

407. R. Souza, G. Callou, K. Camboin, J. Ferreira and P. Maciel, "The Effects of Temperature Variation on Data Center IT Systems," 2013 IEEE International Conference on Systems, Man, and Cybernetics, 2013, pp. 2354-2359, doi: 10.1109/SMC.2013.402.

408. D. Souza, R. Matos, J. Araujo, V. Alves and P. Maciel, "EucaBomber: Experimental Evaluation of Availability in Eucalyptus Private Clouds," 2013 IEEE International Conference on Systems, Man, and Cybernetics, Manchester, UK, 2013, pp. 4080-4085, doi: 10.1109/SMC.2013.696.

409. Souza, D., Rúbens de Souza Matos Júnior, J. Araujo, Vandi Alves and P. Maciel. "A Tool for Automatic Dependability Test in Eucalyptus Cloud Computing Infrastructures." Comput. Inf. Sci. 6 (2013): 57-67.

410. https://www.spec.org/30th/timeline.html. Retrieved at 9/19/2020.

411. SR-332 Issue 4. https://telecom-info.njdepot.ericsson.net/site-cgi/ido/docs.cgi?ID=SEARCH&DOCUMENT=SR-332. Retrieved at 5/7/2021.

412. Peter H. Starke. Remarks on Timed Nets. Petri Net Newsletter, 27:37–47, August 1987.

413. Stewart, William J., Probability, Markov chains, queues and simulation. Published by Princeton University Press. 2009.

414. Stewart, William J., Introduction to the Numerical Solution of Markov Chains. Published by Princeton University Press. 1994.

415. Stewart, James. Essential calculus: early transcendentals. Belmont, CA: Thomson Higher Education. 2007.

416. Stott, H. G. Time-Limit Relays and Duplication of Electrical Apparatus to Secure Reliability of Services at New York. s.l. : IEEE, 1905.

417. Gilbert Strang. Calculus. MIT. Publisher: Wellesley-Cambridge Press. ISBN 13: 9780961408824. 1991.

418. Stuart, H. R. Time-Limit Relays and Duplication of Electrical Apparatus to Secure Reliability of Services at Pittsburg. s.l. : IEEE, June 1905.

419. Rai, Suresh, Malathi Veeraraghavan, and Kishor S. Trivedi. "A survey of efficient reliability computation using disjoint products approach." Networks 25, no. 3 (1995): 147-163.

420. Cisco Systems: Switch dependability parameters. http://tinyurl.com/cr9nssu. October. 2012.

421. Symons F. J. W., Modelling and Analysis of Communication Protocols using Numerical Petri Nets, Ph.D Thesis, University of Essex, also Dept of Elec. Eng. Science Telecommunications Systems Group Report No. 152, May 1978.

422. http://man7.org/linux/man-pages/man2/syscalls.2.html. Retrieved at 5/1/2020.

423. https://github.com/sysstat/sysstat. Retrieved at 5/4/2020.

424. Tausworthe, Robert C. Random numbers generated by linear recurrence modulo two. Math. Comp. 19, 201–209, 1965.

425. Telcordia-Bellcore SR-332. http://www.t-cubed.com/faq˙telc.htm. Retrieved at 5/7/2021.

426. https://www.tcpdump.org/. Retrieved at 5/19/2020.

427. S. J. Einhorn and F. B. Thiess. "Intermittence as a stochastic process". S. J. Einhorn and F. B. Thiess, "Intermittence as a stNYU-RCA Working Conference on Theory of Reliability. Ardsley-on-Hudson, N. Y., 1957.

428. German, Reinhard and Kelling, Christian and Zimmermann, Armin and Hommel, Günter. TimeNET: A Toolkit for Evaluating non-Markovian Stochastic Petri Nets. Perform. Evaluation. Vol: 25. number:1-2. pages:69-87. isssn:0166-5316. Elsevier. 1995

429. Tobias, P. A., & Trindade, D. C. (2012). Applied reliability. Boca Raton, FL: CRC/Taylor & Francis.

430. Matheus D'Eça Torquato, Marco Vieira and Paulo Maciel. A Model for Availability and Security Risk Evaluation for Systems with VMM Rejuvenation enabled by VM Migration Scheduling. IEEE Access. 2019. ISSN: 2169-3536 (Online).

431. Matheus D'Eça Torquato and Paulo Maciel. Availability and Reliability Modeling of VM Migration as Rejuvenation on a System under Varying Workload. Software Quality Journal. 2019. ISSN: 1573-1367 (Online).

432. Torquato, Matheus; Maciel, Paulo; Vieira, Marco; Model-Based Performability and Dependability Evaluation of a System with VM Migration as Rejuvenation in the Presence of Bursty Workloads. Journal of Network and Systems Management. 1573-7705. 10.1007/s10922-021-09619-3. 09/14/2021

433. Transaction Processing Performance Council. http://www.tpc.org/. Retrieved at 9/20/2020.

434. http://www.tpc.org/tpcc/detail5.asp. Retrieved at 8/7/2020.

435. T. Triebel, M. Lehn, R. Rehner, B. Guthier, S. Kopf and W. Effelsberg, "Generation of synthetic workloads for multiplayer online gaming benchmarks," 2012 11th Annual Workshop on Network and Systems Support for Games (NetGames), Venice, 2012, pp. 1-6, doi: 10.1109/NetGames.2012.6404028.

436. Triola, E. F., Elementary statistics (second edition), Pearson Education, 2013.

437. Kishor S. Trivedi. Probability and Statistics with Reliability, Queuing, and Computer Science Applications, 2nd Edition. John Wiley & Sons. 2001.

438. Robin A. Sahner, Kishor S. Trivedi, Antonio Puliafito. Performance and Reliability Analysis of Computer Systems - An Example-Based Approach Using the SHARPE Software Package. s.l. : Kluwer Academic Publishers. p. 404. 1996

439. Trivedi, K. S., Grottke, M. (2007). Fighting Bugs: Remove, Retry, Replicate, and Rejuvenate. IEEE Transactions on Computers, 4(20), 107–109.

440. T. K. Tsai, Mei-Chen Hsueh, Hong Zhao, Z. Kalbarczyk and R. K. Iyer, "Stress-based and path-based fault injection," in IEEE Transactions on Computers, vol. 48, no. 11, pp. 1183-1201, Nov. 1999, doi: 10.1109/12.811108.

441. Dimitri P. Bertsekas, John N. Tsitsiklis. Introduction to Probability,2nd Edition. Hardcover. 544 Pages. Published by Athena Scientific ISBN-13: 978-1-886529-23-6. ISBN: 1-886529-23-X. 2008

442. Tukey, John W., Exploratory data analysis,1977, Reading, Mass.

443. https://www.ubuntupit.com/most-comprehensive-list-of-linux-monitoring-tools-for-sysadmin/ Retrieved at 4/29/2020.

444. James Rumbaugh, Ivar Jacobson, and Grady Booch. 2004. Unified Modeling Language Reference Manual, The (2nd Edition). Pearson Higher Education.

445. Ushakov, Igor. IS RELIABILITY THEORY STILL ALIVE?, e-journal Reliability: Theory & Applications. March 2007, Vol. 2, No 1.

446. Ushakov, Igor. IS RELIABILITY THEORY STILL ALIVE? e-journal Reliability: Theory & Applications. March 2007, Vol. Vol. 2, No 1.

447. Valmari, Antti, The state explosion problem, Lectures on Petri Nets I: Basic Models: Advances in Petri Nets, pages:429–528,isbn:978-3-540-49442-3, Springer Berlin Heidelberg, 1998.

448. Vassiliou P., Mettas A., El-Azzouzi T. Quantitative Accelerated Life-testing and Data Analysis. In: Misra K.B. (eds) Handbook of Performability Engineering. Springer. London. 2008. https://doi.org/10.1007/978-1-84800-131-2˙35

449. W. E. Vesely, F. F. Goldberg, N. H. Roberts, D. F. Haasl. Fault Tree Handbook. Systems and Reliability Research Office of Nuclear Regulatory Research U.S. Nuclear Regulatory Commission Washington, D.C. 20555. Date Published: January 1981

450. Vishay Semiconductors. Reliability. VISHAY INTERTECHNOLOGY. Document Number: 80116. Rev. 1.3, Feb-2002.

451. Vishay Semiconductors. Quality and Reliability. VISHAY INTERTECHNOLOGY. INC. ENVIRONMENTAL, HEALTH AND SAFETY POLICY. Document Number: 82501. Rev. 1.3, 26-Aug-2005.

452. HP Insight Dynamics - VSE and HP VSE Management Software 4.1 Getting Started Guide, January 2009.

453. Implementing a Virtual Server Environment: Getting Started, January 2009.

454. Introduction to the HP Virtual Server Environment, January 2009

455. Christian Walck. Hand-Book on Statistical Distributions for Experimentalists. Internal Report SUF–PFY/96–01 Stockholm, 11 December 1996, first revision, 31 October 1998, last modification 10 September 2007

456. Josephine L. Walkowicz. Benchmarking and Workload Definition. A Selected Bibliography with Abstracts Systems and Software Division. Institute for Computer Sciences and Technology. National Bureau of Standards. U.S. DEPARTMENT OF COMMERCE. Washington, D.C. 20234. 1974.

457. David Watts. Lenovo x86 Servers Top ITIC 2020 Global Reliability Survey. Information Technology Intelligence Consulting Corp. March 2, 2020.

458. Wei-Lun Kao and R. K. Iyer, "DEFINE: a distributed fault injection and monitoring environment," Proceedings of IEEE Workshop on Fault-Tolerant Parallel and Distributed Systems, College Station, TX, USA, 1994, pp. 252-259, doi: 10.1109/FTPDS.1994.494497.

459. Weicker, Reinhold P. "Dhrystone: a synthetic systems programming benchmark." Communications of the ACM 27, no. 10 (1984): 1013-1030.

460. Weicker, Reinhold P. 1990. An Overview of Common Benchmarks. Computer 23, no.12. 65-75 (December 1990), 65–75. DOI:https://doi.org/10.1109/2.62094

461. Wendai Wang and D. B. Kececioglu, "Confidence limits on the inherent availability of equipment," Annual Reliability and Maintainability Symposium. 2000 Proceedings. International Symposium on Product Quality and Integrity (Cat. No.00CH37055), Los Angeles, CA, USA, 2000, pp. 162-168. doi: 10.1109/RAMS.2000.816301

462. Peter H. Westfall. Kurtosis as Peakedness, 1905–2014. R.I.P. The American Statistician. Vol:68. Number:3. Pages:191-195. Taylor & Francis. 2014

463. https://www.netlib.org/benchmark/whetstone.c. Retrieved at 10/7/2020.

464. Mark Wilding and Dan Behman. Self-Service Linux. Prentice-Hall. ISBN 0-13-147751-X. 2005

465. Wilmink F.W., Uytterschaut H.T. Cluster Analysis, History, Theory and Applications. In: Van Vark G.N., Howells W.W. (eds) Multivariate Statistical Methods in Physical Anthropology. Springer, Dordrecht. https://doi.org/10.1007/978-94-009-6357-3˙11. 1984.

466. https://www.winpcap.org/windump/. Retrieved at 5/19/2020.

467. https://www.wireshark.org/. Retrieved at 5/19/2020.

468. Cluster Analysis, Wolfram Language Documentation Center. 2020. https://reference.wolfram.com/language/guide/ClusterAnalysis.html. Retrieved at 12/22/2020.

469. Wayne B. Nelson. Accelerated Testing: Statistical Models, Test Plans, and Data Analysis. Wiley Series in Probability and Statistics. Book. ISBN: 9780470317471. 2009. Wiley.

470. https://docs.microsoft.com/en-us/windows/win32/perfctrs/performance-counters-portal. Retrieved at 4/29/2020.

471. K. Lai, D. Wren. Fast and Effective Endpoint Security for Business – Comparative Analysis. Edition 1, PassMark Software. 15 June 2010.

472. J. Han, D. Wren. Consumer Security Products Performance Benchmarks. Edition 2. PassMark Software. 13 January 2020.

473. Device Reliability Report Second Half 2020 UG116 (v10.14). https://www.xilinx.com/support/documentation/user˙guides/ug116.pdf. April 23, 2021. Retrieved at 5/10/2021.

474. Yeo, In-Kwon, and Richard A. Johnson. "A New Family of Power Transformations to Improve Normality or Symmetry." Biometrika, vol. 87, no. 4, 2000, pp. 954–959. JSTOR, www.jstor.org/stable/2673623.

475. Yim, O, & Ramdeen, K. T. Hierarchical Cluster Analysis: Comparison of Three Linkage Measures and Application to Psychological Data, The Quantitative Methods for Psychology, 11(1), 8-21. doi: 10.20982/tqmp.11.1.p008. 2015.

476. J. Yin, X. Lu, X. Zhao, H. Chen and X. Liu, "BURSE: A Bursty and Self-Similar Workload Generator for Cloud Computing," in IEEE Transactions on Parallel and Distributed Systems, vol. 26, no. 3, pp. 668-680, 1 March 2015, doi: 10.1109/TPDS.2014.2315204.

477. Young, Derek Scott. Handbook of regression methods. CRC Press, 2018.

478. Zenie, Alexandre. Colored Stochastic Petri Nets. International Workshop on Timed Petri Nets. IEEE Computer Society. pages: 262–271, 1985. isbn: 0-8186-0674-6

479. Zimmermann, Armin. Stochastic Discrete Event Systems: Modeling, Evaluation, Applications. isbn.: 3540741720. Springer-Verlag. 2007.

480. Zuberek, W. M. Timed Petri Nets and Preliminary Performance Evaluation. Proceedings of the 7th Annual Symposium on Computer Architecture. Pages: 88–96. ACM. 1980. La Baule, USA.

Appendices

A MTTF 2oo5

$$MTTF = A + B + C + D.$$

$$MTTF = \int_0^\infty 10e^{-2\lambda t}(1-e^{-\lambda t})^3 \, dt + \int_0^\infty 10e^{-3\lambda t}(1-e^{-\lambda t})^2 \, dt +$$

$$\int_0^\infty 5e^{-4\lambda t}(1-e^{-\lambda t}) \, dt + \int_0^\infty e^{-5\lambda t} \, dt.$$

First consider A:

$$A = \int_0^\infty 10e^{-2\lambda t}(1-e^{-\lambda t})^3 \, dt.$$

Let $u = 1 - e^{-\lambda t}$, then $e^{-\lambda t} = 1 - u$, and $du = \lambda e^{-\lambda t} \, dt$. Hence

$$A = \frac{10}{\lambda} \int_0^\infty e^{-\lambda t}(1-e^{-\lambda t})^3 \lambda e^{-\lambda t} \, dt.$$

As when $t = 0$, $u = 0$, and $t \to \infty$, $u = 1$, then

$$A = \frac{10}{\lambda} \int_0^1 (1-u)u^3 \, du.$$

$$A = \frac{10}{\lambda} \left(\int_0^1 u^3 \, du + \int_0^1 u^4 \, du \right)$$

$$A = \frac{10}{\lambda} \left(\left. \frac{u^4}{4} \right|_0^1 + \left. \frac{u^5}{5} \right|_0^1 \right)$$

$$A = \frac{1}{2\lambda}.$$

Now consider B:

$$B = \int_0^\infty 10e^{-3\lambda t}(1-e^{-\lambda t})^2 \, dt.$$

Let $u = 1 - e^{-\lambda t}$, then $e^{-\lambda t} = 1 - u$, $e^{-2\lambda t} = (1 - u)^2$, and $du = \lambda e^{-\lambda t} dt$. Thus

$$B = \frac{10}{\lambda} \int_0^\infty e^{-2\lambda t} (1 - e^{-\lambda t})^2 \lambda e^{-\lambda t} dt.$$

As when $t = 0$, $u = 0$, and $t \to \infty$, $u = 1$, then

$$B = \frac{10}{\lambda} \int_0^1 (1 - u)^2 u^2 du = \frac{1}{3\lambda}.$$

Now take C:

$$C = \int_0^\infty 5 e^{-4\lambda t} (1 - e^{-\lambda t}) dt.$$

Let $u = 1 - e^{-\lambda t}$, then $e^{-\lambda t} = 1 - u$, $e^{-3\lambda t} = (1 - u)^3$, and $du = \lambda e^{-\lambda t} dt$. Hence

$$C = \frac{5}{\lambda} \int_0^\infty e^{-3\lambda t} (1 - e^{-\lambda t}) \lambda e^{-\lambda t} dt.$$

As when $t = 0$, $u = 0$, and $t \to \infty$, $u = 1$, then

$$C = \frac{5}{\lambda} \int_0^1 (1 - u)^3 u \, du = \frac{1}{4\lambda}.$$

Now take D:

$$D = \int_0^\infty e^{-5\lambda t} dt = \frac{1}{5\lambda}.$$

Therefore

$$MTTF = \frac{1}{2\lambda} + \frac{1}{3\lambda} + \frac{1}{4\lambda} + \frac{1}{5\lambda} = \frac{77}{60\lambda} =$$

$$\frac{1}{\lambda} \sum_{i=2}^5 \frac{1}{i}.$$

B Whetsone

```
/*
 * C Converted Whetstone Double Precision Benchmark
 * Version 1.2 22 March 1998
 *
 * (c) Copyright 1998 Painter Engineering, Inc.
 * All Rights Reserved.
 *
 * Permission is granted to use, duplicate, and
 * publish this text and program as long as it
 * includes this entire comment block and limited
 * rights reference.
 *
 * Converted by Rich Painter, Painter Engineering, Inc.
 * based on the www.netlib.org benchmark/whetstoned
 * version obtained 16 March 1998. A novel approach was
 * used here to keep the look and feel of the FORTRAN version.
 * Altering the FORTRAN-based array indices,
 * starting at element 1, to start at element 0 for C, would
 * require numerous changes, including decrementing the variable
 * indices by 1. Instead, the array E1[] was declared 1 element
 * larger in C.  This allows the FORTRAN index range to function
 *  without any literal or variable indices changes.  The array
 * element E1[0] is simply never used and does not alter the
 * benchmark results.
 *
 * The major FORTRAN comment blocks were retained to minimize
 * differences between versions.  Modules N5 and N12, like in
 * the FORTRAN version, have been eliminated here.
 *
 * An optional command-line argument has been provided [-c] to
 * offer continuous repetition of the entire benchmark.
 * An optional argument for setting an alternate LOOP count is
 * also provided.  Define PRINTOUT to cause the POUT() function
 * to print outputs at various stages.  Final timing
 * measurements should be made with the PRINTOUT undefined.
 *
 * Questions and comments may be directed to the author at
 * r.painter@ieee.org
 */
/*
C*************************************************************
C     Benchmark #2 -- Double  Precision Whetstone (A001)
C
C     o This is a REAL*8 version of
C the Whetstone benchmark program.
C
```

```
C      o DO-loop semantics are ANSI-66 compatible.
C
C      o Final measurements are to be made with all
C WRITE statements and FORMAT sttements removed.
C
C***********************************************************
*/

/* standard C library headers required */
#include <stdlib.h>
#include <stdio.h>
#include <string.h>
#include <math.h>

/* the following is optional depending on the timing function
                                                      used */
#include <time.h>

/* map the FORTRAN math functions, etc. to the C versions */
#define DSIN sin
#define DCOS cos
#define DATAN atan
#define DLOG log
#define DEXP exp
#define DSQRT sqrt
#define IF if

/* function prototypes */
void POUT(long N, long J, long K, double X1, double X2,
          double X3, double X4);
void PA(double E[]);
void P0(void);
void P3(double X, double Y, double *Z);
#define USAGE "usage: whetdc [-c] [loops]\n"

/*
COMMON T,T1,T2,E1(4),J,K,L
*/
double T,T1,T2,E1[5];
int J,K,L;

int
main(int argc, char *argv[])
{
/* used in the FORTRAN version */
long I;
long N1, N2, N3, N4, N6, N7, N8, N9, N10, N11;
double X1,X2,X3,X4,X,Y,Z;
long LOOP;
int II, JJ;
```

```
/* added for this version */
long loopstart;
long startsec, finisec;
float KIPS;
int continuous;

loopstart = 1000; /* see the note about LOOP below */
continuous = 0;

II = 1; /* start at the first arg (temp use of II here) */
while (II < argc) {
if (strncmp(argv[II], "-c", 2) == 0 || argv[II][0] == 'c') {
continuous = 1;
} else if (atol(argv[II]) > 0) {
loopstart = atol(argv[II]);
} else {
fprintf(stderr, USAGE);
return(1);
}
II++;
}

LCONT:
/*
C
C Start benchmark timing at this point.
C
*/
startsec = time(0);

/*
C
C The actual benchmark starts here.
C
*/
T  = .499975;
T1 = 0.50025;
T2 = 2.0;
/*
C
C With loopcount LOOP=10, one million Whetstone instructions
C will be executed in EACH MAJOR LOOP..A MAJOR LOOP IS EXECUTED
C 'II' TIMES TO INCREASE WALL-CLOCK TIMING ACCURACY.
C
LOOP = 1000;
*/
LOOP = loopstart;
II   = 1;

JJ = 1;
```

```
IILOOP:
N1  = 0;
N2  = 12 * LOOP;
N3  = 14 * LOOP;
N4  = 345 * LOOP;
N6  = 210 * LOOP;
N7  = 32 * LOOP;
N8  = 899 * LOOP;
N9  = 616 * LOOP;
N10 = 0;
N11 = 93 * LOOP;
/*
C
C Module 1: Simple identifiers
C
*/
X1  =  1.0;
X2  = -1.0;
X3  = -1.0;
X4  = -1.0;

for (I = 1; I <= N1; I++) {
    X1 = (X1 + X2 + X3 - X4) * T;
    X2 = (X1 + X2 - X3 + X4) * T;
    X3 = (X1 - X2 + X3 + X4) * T;
    X4 = (-X1+ X2 + X3 + X4) * T;
}
#ifdef PRINTOUT
IF (JJ==II)POUT(N1,N1,N1,X1,X2,X3,X4);
#endif

/*
C
C Module 2: Array elements
C
*/
E1[1] =  1.0;
E1[2] = -1.0;
E1[3] = -1.0;
E1[4] = -1.0;

for (I = 1; I <= N2; I++) {
    E1[1] = ( E1[1] + E1[2] + E1[3] - E1[4]) * T;
    E1[2] = ( E1[1] + E1[2] - E1[3] + E1[4]) * T;
    E1[3] = ( E1[1] - E1[2] + E1[3] + E1[4]) * T;
    E1[4] = (-E1[1] + E1[2] + E1[3] + E1[4]) * T;
}

#ifdef PRINTOUT
IF (JJ==II)POUT(N2,N3,N2,E1[1],E1[2],E1[3],E1[4]);
#endif
```

```
/*
C
C Module 3: Array as parameter
C
*/
for (I = 1; I <= N3; I++)
PA(E1);

#ifdef PRINTOUT
IF (JJ==II)POUT(N3,N2,N2,E1[1],E1[2],E1[3],E1[4]);
#endif

/*
C
C Module 4: Conditional jumps
C
*/
J = 1;
for (I = 1; I <= N4; I++) {
if (J == 1)
J = 2;
else
J = 3;

if (J > 2)
J = 0;
else
J = 1;

if (J < 1)
J = 1;
else
J = 0;
}

#ifdef PRINTOUT
IF (JJ==II)POUT(N4,J,J,X1,X2,X3,X4);
#endif

/*
C
C Module 5: Omitted
C   Module 6: Integer arithmetic
C
*/

J = 1;
K = 2;
L = 3;
```

```
for (I = 1; I <= N6; I++) {
    J = J * (K-J) * (L-K);
    K = L * K - (L-J) * K;
    L = (L-K) * (K+J);
    E1[L-1] = J + K + L;
    E1[K-1] = J * K * L;
}

#ifdef PRINTOUT
IF (JJ==II)POUT(N6,J,K,E1[1],E1[2],E1[3],E1[4]);
#endif

/*
C
C Module 7: Trigonometric functions
C
*/
X = 0.5;
Y = 0.5;

for (I = 1; I <= N7; I++) {
X = T * DATAN(T2*DSIN(X)*DCOS(X)/(DCOS(X+Y)+DCOS(X-Y)-1.0));
Y = T * DATAN(T2*DSIN(Y)*DCOS(Y)/(DCOS(X+Y)+DCOS(X-Y)-1.0));
}

#ifdef PRINTOUT
IF (JJ==II)POUT(N7,J,K,X,X,Y,Y);
#endif

/*
C
C Module 8: Procedure calls
C
*/
X = 1.0;
Y = 1.0;
Z = 1.0;

for (I = 1; I <= N8; I++)
P3(X,Y,&Z);

#ifdef PRINTOUT
IF (JJ==II)POUT(N8,J,K,X,Y,Z,Z);
#endif

/*
C
C Module 9: Array references
C
*/
J = 1;
```

```
K = 2;
L = 3;
E1[1] = 1.0;
E1[2] = 2.0;
E1[3] = 3.0;

for (I = 1; I <= N9; I++)
P0();

#ifdef PRINTOUT
IF (JJ==II)POUT(N9,J,K,E1[1],E1[2],E1[3],E1[4]);
#endif

/*
C
C Module 10: Integer arithmetic
C
*/
J = 2;
K = 3;

for (I = 1; I <= N10; I++) {
    J = J + K;
    K = J + K;
    J = K - J;
    K = K - J - J;
}

#ifdef PRINTOUT
IF (JJ==II)POUT(N10,J,K,X1,X2,X3,X4);
#endif

/*
C
C Module 11: Standard functions
C
*/
X = 0.75;

for (I = 1; I <= N11; I++)
X = DSQRT(DEXP(DLOG(X)/T1));

#ifdef PRINTOUT
IF (JJ==II)POUT(N11,J,K,X,X,X,X);
#endif

/*
C
C       THIS IS THE END OF THE MAJOR LOOP.
C
*/
```

```
if (++JJ <= II)
goto IILOOP;

/*
C
C       Stop benchmark timing at this point.
C
*/
finisec = time(0);

/*
C--------------------------------------------------------------
C       Performance in Whetstone KIP's per second is given by
C
C (100*LOOP*II)/TIME
C
C       where TIME is in seconds.
C--------------------------------------------------------------
*/
printf("\n");
if (finisec-startsec <= 0) {
printf("Insufficient duration- Increase the LOOP count\n");
return(1);
}

printf("Loops: %ld, Iterations: %d, Duration: %ld sec.\n",
LOOP, II, finisec-startsec);

KIPS = (100.0*LOOP*II)/(float)(finisec-startsec);
if (KIPS >= 1000.0)
printf("C Converted Double Precision Whetstones: %.1f MIPS\n",
        KIPS/1000.0);
else
printf("C Converted Double Precision Whetstones: %.1f KIPS\n",
        KIPS);

if (continuous)
goto LCONT;

return(0);
}

void
PA(double E[])
{
J = 0;

L10:
E[1] = ( E[1] + E[2] + E[3] - E[4]) * T;
E[2] = ( E[1] + E[2] - E[3] + E[4]) * T;
E[3] = ( E[1] - E[2] + E[3] + E[4]) * T;
```

```
E[4] = (-E[1] + E[2] + E[3] + E[4]) / T2;
J += 1;

if (J < 6)
goto L10;
}

void
P0(void)
{
E1[J] = E1[K];
E1[K] = E1[L];
E1[L] = E1[J];
}

void
P3(double X, double Y, double *Z)
{
double X1, Y1;

X1 = X;
Y1 = Y;
X1 = T * (X1 + Y1);
Y1 = T * (X1 + Y1);
*Z  = (X1 + Y1) / T2;
}

#ifdef PRINTOUT
void
POUT(long N, long J, long K, double X1, double X2, double X3,
                                               double X4)
{
printf("%7ld %7ld %7ld %12.4e %12.4e %12.4e %12.4e\n",
N, J, K, X1, X2, X3, X4);
}
#endif
```

C Linpack_Bench

```c
# include <stdlib.h>
# include <stdio.h>
# include <math.h>
# include <time.h>

int main ( );
double cpu_time ( );
void daxpy ( int n, double da, double dx[], int incx, double dy[],
                                                      int incy );
double ddot ( int n, double dx[], int incx, double dy[],
                                            int incy );
int dgefa ( double a[], int lda, int n, int ipvt[] );
void dgesl ( double a[], int lda, int n, int ipvt[], double b[],
                                                    int job );
void dscal ( int n, double sa, double x[], int incx );
int idamax ( int n, double dx[], int incx );
double r8_epsilon ( );
double r8_max ( double x, double y );
double r8_random ( int iseed[4] );
double *r8mat_gen ( int lda, int n );
void timestamp ( );

/**************************************************************/

int main ( )

/**************************************************************/
/*
  Purpose:

    MAIN is the main program for LINPACK_BENCH.

  Discussion:

    LINPACK_BENCH drives the double precision LINPACK benchmark
                                                      program.

  Modified:

    25 July 2008

  Parameters:

    N is the problem size.
*/
{
```

```
# define N 1000
# define LDA ( N + 1 )

  double *a;
  double a_max;
  double *b;
  double b_max;
  double cray = 0.056;
  double eps;
  int i;
  int info;
  int *ipvt;
  int j;
  int job;
  double ops;
  double *resid;
  double resid_max;
  double residn;
  double *rhs;
  double t1;
  double t2;
  double time[6];
  double total;
  double *x;

  timestamp ( );
  printf ( "\n" );
  printf ( "LINPACK_BENCH\n" );
  printf ( "  C version\n" );
  printf ( "\n" );
  printf ( "  The LINPACK benchmark.\n" );
  printf ( "  Language: C\n" );
  printf ( "  Datatype: Double precision real\n" );
  printf ( "  Matrix order N               = %d\n", N );
  printf ( "  Leading matrix dimension LDA = %d\n", LDA );

  ops = ( double ) ( 2 * N * N * N ) / 3.0 + 2.0 *
                                ( double ) ( N * N );
/*
  Allocate space for arrays.
*/
  a = r8mat_gen ( LDA, N );
  b = ( double * ) malloc ( N * sizeof ( double ) );
  ipvt = ( int * ) malloc ( N * sizeof ( int ) );
  resid = ( double * ) malloc ( N * sizeof ( double ) );
  rhs = ( double * ) malloc ( N * sizeof ( double ) );
  x = ( double * ) malloc ( N * sizeof ( double ) );

  a_max = 0.0;
  for ( j = 0; j < N; j++ )
  {
```

```
    for ( i = 0; i < N; i++ )
    {
      a_max = r8_max ( a_max, a[i+j*LDA] );
    }
  }

  for ( i = 0; i < N; i++ )
  {
    x[i] = 1.0;
  }

  for ( i = 0; i < N; i++ )
  {
    b[i] = 0.0;
    for ( j = 0; j < N; j++ )
    {
      b[i] = b[i] + a[i+j*LDA] * x[j];
    }
  }
  t1 = cpu_time ( );

  info = dgefa ( a, LDA, N, ipvt );

  if ( info != 0 )
  {
    printf ( "\n" );
    printf ( "LINPACK_BENCH - Fatal error!\n" );
    printf ( "  The matrix A is apparently singular.\n" );
    printf ( "  Abnormal end of execution.\n" );
    return 1;
  }

  t2 = cpu_time ( );
  time[0] = t2 - t1;

  t1 = cpu_time ( );

  job = 0;
  dgesl ( a, LDA, N, ipvt, b, job );

  t2 = cpu_time ( );
  time[1] = t2 - t1;

  total = time[0] + time[1];

  free ( a );
/*
  Compute a residual to verify results.
*/
  a = r8mat_gen ( LDA, N );
```

```
for ( i = 0; i < N; i++ )
{
  x[i] = 1.0;
}

for ( i = 0; i < N; i++ )
{
  rhs[i] = 0.0;
  for ( j = 0; j < N; j++ )
  {
    rhs[i] = rhs[i] + a[i+j*LDA] * x[j];
  }
}

for ( i = 0; i < N; i++ )
{
  resid[i] = -rhs[i];
  for ( j = 0; j < N; j++ )
  {
    resid[i] = resid[i] + a[i+j*LDA] * b[j];
  }
}

resid_max = 0.0;
for ( i = 0; i < N; i++ )
{
  resid_max = r8_max ( resid_max, fabs ( resid[i] ) );
}

b_max = 0.0;
for ( i = 0; i < N; i++ )
{
  b_max = r8_max ( b_max, fabs ( b[i] ) );
}

eps = r8_epsilon ( );

residn = resid_max / ( double ) N / a_max / b_max / eps;

time[2] = total;
if ( 0.0 < total )
{
  time[3] = ops / ( 1.0E+06 * total );
}
else
{
  time[3] = -1.0;
}
time[4] = 2.0 / time[3];
time[5] = total / cray;
```

```
  printf ( "\n" );
  printf ( "Norm. Resid Resid MACHEP X[1] X[N]\n" );
  printf ( "\n" );
  printf ( "  %14f %14f %14e %14f %14f\n", residn,
           resid_max, eps, b[0], b[N-1] );
  printf ( "\n" );
  printf ( "Factor Solve Total MFLOPS Unit Cray-Ratio\n" );
  printf ( "\n" );
  printf ( "%9f %9f %9f %9f %9f %9f\n",
           time[0], time[1], time[2], time[3], time[4],
           time[5] );

  free ( a );
  free ( b );
  free ( ipvt );
  free ( resid );
  free ( rhs );
  free ( x );
/*
  Terminate.
*/
  printf ( "\n" );
  printf ( "LINPACK_BENCH\n" );
  printf ( "  Normal end of execution.\n" );

  printf ( "\n" );
  timestamp ( );

  return 0;
# undef LDA
# undef N
}
/*************************************************************/

double cpu_time ( void )

/*************************************************************/
/*
  Purpose:

    CPU_TIME returns the current reading on the CPU clock.

  Discussion:

    The CPU time measurements available through this routine
    are often not very accurate.  In some cases, the accuracy
    is no better than a hundredth of a second.

  Licensing:

    This code is distributed under the GNU LGPL license.
```

```
  Modified:

    06 June 2005

  Author:

    John Burkardt

  Parameters:

    Output, double CPU_TIME, the current reading of
                        the CPU clock, in seconds.
*/
{
  double value;

  value = ( double ) clock ( )
        / ( double ) CLOCKS_PER_SEC;

  return value;
}
/******************************************************/

void daxpy ( int n, double da, double dx[], int incx,
                             double dy[], int incy )

/******************************************************/
/*
  Purpose:

    DAXPY computes constant times a vector plus a vector.

  Discussion:

    This routine uses unrolled loops for increments equal
                                               to one.

  Modified:

    30 March 2007

  Author:

    FORTRAN77 original by Jack Dongarra, Cleve Moler,
    Jim Bunch, Pete Stewart.
    C version by John Burkardt

  Reference:

    Jack Dongarra, Cleve Moler, Jim Bunch, Pete Stewart,
```

```
        LINPACK User's Guide,
        SIAM, 1979.

        Charles Lawson, Richard Hanson, David Kincaid, Fred Krogh,
        Basic Linear Algebra Subprograms for Fortran Usage,
        Algorithm 539,
        ACM Transactions on Mathematical Software,
        Volume 5, Number 3, September 1979, pages 308-323.

      Parameters:

        Input, int N, the number of elements in DX and DY.

        Input, double DA, the multiplier of DX.

        Input, double DX[*], the first vector.

        Input, int INCX, the increment between successive entries
                                                    of DX.

        Input/output, double DY[*], the second vector.
        On output, DY[*] has been replaced by DY[*] + DA * DX[*].

        Input, int INCY, the increment between successive entries
                                                    of DY.
*/
{
  int i;
  int ix;
  int iy;
  int m;

  if ( n <= 0 )
  {
    return;
  }

  if ( da == 0.0 )
  {
    return;
  }
/*
  Code for unequal increments or equal increments
  not equal to 1.
*/
  if ( incx != 1 || incy != 1 )
  {
    if ( 0 <= incx )
    {
      ix = 0;
    }
```

```
    else
    {
      ix = ( - n + 1 ) * incx;
    }

    if ( 0 <= incy )
    {
      iy = 0;
    }
    else
    {
      iy = ( - n + 1 ) * incy;
    }

    for ( i = 0; i < n; i++ )
    {
      dy[iy] = dy[iy] + da * dx[ix];
      ix = ix + incx;
      iy = iy + incy;
    }
  }
/*
  Code for both increments equal to 1.
*/
  else
  {
    m = n % 4;

    for ( i = 0; i < m; i++ )
    {
      dy[i] = dy[i] + da * dx[i];
    }

    for ( i = m; i < n; i = i + 4 )
    {
      dy[i  ] = dy[i  ] + da * dx[i  ];
      dy[i+1] = dy[i+1] + da * dx[i+1];
      dy[i+2] = dy[i+2] + da * dx[i+2];
      dy[i+3] = dy[i+3] + da * dx[i+3];
    }
  }
  return;
}
/****************************************************************/

double ddot ( int n, double dx[], int incx, double dy[],
                                             int incy )

/****************************************************************/
/*
  Purpose:
```

```
    DDOT forms the dot product of two vectors.

  Discussion:

    This routine uses unrolled loops for increments equal
                                            to one.

  Modified:

    30 March 2007

  Author:

    FORTRAN77 original by Jack Dongarra, Cleve Moler, Jim Bunch,
    Pete Stewart.
    C version by John Burkardt

  Reference:

    Jack Dongarra, Cleve Moler, Jim Bunch, Pete Stewart,
    LINPACK User's Guide,
    SIAM, 1979.

    Charles Lawson, Richard Hanson, David Kincaid, Fred Krogh,
    Basic Linear Algebra Subprograms for Fortran Usage,
    Algorithm 539,
    ACM Transactions on Mathematical Software,
    Volume 5, Number 3, September 1979, pages 308-323.

  Parameters:

    Input, int N, the number of entries in the vectors.

    Input, double DX[*], the first vector.

    Input, int INCX, the increment between successive entries in DX.

    Input, double DY[*], the second vector.

    Input, int INCY, the increment between successive entries in DY.

    Output, double DDOT, the sum of the product of the corresponding
    entries of DX and DY.
*/
{
  double dtemp;
  int i;
  int ix;
  int iy;
  int m;
```

```
  dtemp = 0.0;

  if ( n <= 0 )
  {
    return dtemp;
  }
/*
  Code for unequal increments or equal increments
  not equal to 1.
*/
  if ( incx != 1 || incy != 1 )
  {
    if ( 0 <= incx )
    {
      ix = 0;
    }
    else
    {
      ix = ( - n + 1 ) * incx;
    }

    if ( 0 <= incy )
    {
      iy = 0;
    }
    else
    {
      iy = ( - n + 1 ) * incy;
    }

    for ( i = 0; i < n; i++ )
    {
      dtemp = dtemp + dx[ix] * dy[iy];
      ix = ix + incx;
      iy = iy + incy;
    }
  }
/*
  Code for both increments equal to 1.
*/
  else
  {
    m = n % 5;

    for ( i = 0; i < m; i++ )
    {
      dtemp = dtemp + dx[i] * dy[i];
    }

    for ( i = m; i < n; i = i + 5 )
```

```
    {
      dtemp = dtemp + dx[i  ] * dy[i  ]
                    + dx[i+1] * dy[i+1]
                    + dx[i+2] * dy[i+2]
                    + dx[i+3] * dy[i+3]
                    + dx[i+4] * dy[i+4];
    }
  }
  return dtemp;
}
/*********************************************************/

int dgefa ( double a[], int lda, int n, int ipvt[] )

/*********************************************************/
/*
  Purpose:

    DGEFA factors a real general matrix.

  Modified:

    16 May 2005

  Author:

    C version by John Burkardt.

  Reference:

    Jack Dongarra, Cleve Moler, Jim Bunch and Pete Stewart,
    LINPACK User's Guide,
    SIAM, (Society for Industrial and Applied Mathematics),
    3600 University City Science Center,
    Philadelphia, PA, 19104-2688.
    ISBN 0-89871-172-X

  Parameters:

    Input/output, double A[LDA*N].
    On intput, the matrix to be factored.
    On output, an upper triangular matrix and the multipliers
    used to obtain it.  The factorization can be written
    A=L*U, where L is a product of permutation and unit lower
    triangular matrices, and U is upper triangular.

    Input, int LDA, the leading dimension of A.

    Input, int N, the order of the matrix A.

    Output, int IPVT[N], the pivot indices.
```

```
    Output, int DGEFA, singularity indicator.
    0, normal value.
    K, if U(K,K) == 0.  This is not an error condition for
    this subroutine, but it does indicate that DGESL or
    DGEDI will divide by zero if called.
    Use RCOND in DGECO for a reliable indication of
    singularity.
*/
{
  int info;
  int j;
  int k;
  int l;
  double t;
/*
  Gaussian elimination with partial pivoting.
*/
  info = 0;

  for ( k = 1; k <= n-1; k++ )
  {
/*
  Find L = pivot index.
*/
    l = idamax ( n-k+1, a+(k-1)+(k-1)*lda, 1 ) + k - 1;
    ipvt[k-1] = l;
/*
  Zero pivot implies this column already triangularized.
*/
    if ( a[l-1+(k-1)*lda] == 0.0 )
    {
      info = k;
      continue;
    }
/*
  Interchange if necessary.
*/
    if ( l != k )
    {
      t = a[l-1+(k-1)*lda];
      a[l-1+(k-1)*lda] = a[k-1+(k-1)*lda];
      a[k-1+(k-1)*lda] = t;
    }
/*
  Compute multipliers.
*/
    t = -1.0 / a[k-1+(k-1)*lda];

    dscal ( n-k, t, a+k+(k-1)*lda, 1 );
/*
```

```
  Row elimination with column indexing.
*/
    for ( j = k+1; j <= n; j++ )
    {
      t = a[l-1+(j-1)*lda];
      if ( l != k )
      {
        a[l-1+(j-1)*lda] = a[k-1+(j-1)*lda];
        a[k-1+(j-1)*lda] = t;
      }
      daxpy ( n-k, t, a+k+(k-1)*lda, 1, a+k+(j-1)*lda, 1 );
    }

  }

  ipvt[n-1] = n;

  if ( a[n-1+(n-1)*lda] == 0.0 )
  {
    info = n;
  }

  return info;
}
/************************************************************/

void dgesl ( double a[], int lda, int n, int ipvt[],
                              double b[], int job )

/************************************************************/
/*
  Purpose:

    DGESL solves a real general linear system A * X = B.

  Discussion:

    DGESL can solve either of the systems A * X = B or
                                          A' * X = B.

    The system matrix must have been factored by DGECO
                                              or DGEFA.

    A division by zero will occur if the input factor
    contains a zero on the diagonal.  Technically this
    indicates singularity but it is often caused by improper
    arguments or improper setting of LDA.  It will not occur
    if the subroutines are called correctly and if DGECO has
      set 0.0 < RCOND or DGEFA has set INFO == 0.

  Modified:
```

```
      16 May 2005

  Author:

    C version by John Burkardt.

  Reference:

    Jack Dongarra, Cleve Moler, Jim Bunch and Pete Stewart,
    LINPACK User's Guide,
    SIAM, (Society for Industrial and Applied Mathematics),
    3600 University City Science Center,
    Philadelphia, PA, 19104-2688.
    ISBN 0-89871-172-X

  Parameters:

    Input, double A[LDA*N], the output from DGECO or DGEFA.

    Input, int LDA, the leading dimension of A.

    Input, int N, the order of the matrix A.

    Input, int IPVT[N], the pivot vector from DGECO or DGEFA.

    Input/output, double B[N].
    On input, the right hand side vector.
    On output, the solution vector.

    Input, int JOB.
    0, solve A * X = B;
    nonzero, solve A' * X = B.
*/
{
  int k;
  int l;
  double t;
/*
  Solve A * X = B.
*/
  if ( job == 0 )
  {
    for ( k = 1; k <= n-1; k++ )
    {
      l = ipvt[k-1];
      t = b[l-1];

      if ( l != k )
      {
        b[l-1] = b[k-1];
```

```
      b[k-1] = t;
    }

    daxpy ( n-k, t, a+k+(k-1)*lda, 1, b+k, 1 );

  }

  for ( k = n; 1 <= k; k-- )
  {
    b[k-1] = b[k-1] / a[k-1+(k-1)*lda];
    t = -b[k-1];
    daxpy ( k-1, t, a+0+(k-1)*lda, 1, b, 1 );
  }
}
/*
  Solve A' * X = B.
*/
else
{
  for ( k = 1; k <= n; k++ )
  {
    t = ddot ( k-1, a+0+(k-1)*lda, 1, b, 1 );
    b[k-1] = ( b[k-1] - t ) / a[k-1+(k-1)*lda];
  }

  for ( k = n-1; 1 <= k; k-- )
  {
    b[k-1] = b[k-1] + ddot ( n-k, a+k+(k-1)*lda, 1, b+k, 1 );
    l = ipvt[k-1];

    if ( l != k )
    {
      t = b[l-1];
      b[l-1] = b[k-1];
      b[k-1] = t;
    }
  }
}
  return;
}
/********************************************************/

void dscal ( int n, double sa, double x[], int incx )

/********************************************************/
/*
  Purpose:

    DSCAL scales a vector by a constant.

  Modified:
```

```
  30 March 2007

Author:

  FORTRAN77 original by Jack Dongarra, Cleve Moler,
  Jim Bunch, Pete Stewart.
  C version by John Burkardt

Reference:

  Jack Dongarra, Cleve Moler, Jim Bunch, Pete Stewart,
  LINPACK User's Guide,
  SIAM, 1979.

  Charles Lawson, Richard Hanson, David Kincaid, Fred Krogh,
  Basic Linear Algebra Subprograms for Fortran Usage,
  Algorithm 539,
  ACM Transactions on Mathematical Software,
  Volume 5, Number 3, September 1979, pages 308-323.

Parameters:

  Input, int N, the number of entries in the vector.

  Input, double SA, the multiplier.

  Input/output, double X[*], the vector to be scaled.

  Input, int INCX, the increment between successive
  entries of X.
*/
{
  int i;
  int ix;
  int m;

  if ( n <= 0 )
  {
  }
  else if ( incx == 1 )
  {
    m = n % 5;

    for ( i = 0; i < m; i++ )
    {
      x[i] = sa * x[i];
    }

    for ( i = m; i < n; i = i + 5 )
    {
```

```
      x[i]   = sa * x[i];
      x[i+1] = sa * x[i+1];
      x[i+2] = sa * x[i+2];
      x[i+3] = sa * x[i+3];
      x[i+4] = sa * x[i+4];
    }
  }
  else
  {
    if ( 0 <= incx )
    {
      ix = 0;
    }
    else
    {
      ix = ( - n + 1 ) * incx;
    }

    for ( i = 0; i < n; i++ )
    {
      x[ix] = sa * x[ix];
      ix = ix + incx;
    }
  }
  return;
}
/************************************************************/

int idamax ( int n, double dx[], int incx )

/************************************************************/
/*
  Purpose:

    IDAMAX finds the index of the vector element of maximum
                                            absolute value.

  Discussion:

    WARNING: This index is a 1-based index, not a 0-based
                                            index!

  Modified:

    30 March 2007

  Author:

    FORTRAN77 original by Jack Dongarra, Cleve Moler,
    Jim Bunch, Pete Stewart.
    C version by John Burkardt
```

```
  Reference:

    Jack Dongarra, Cleve Moler, Jim Bunch, Pete Stewart,
    LINPACK User's Guide,
    SIAM, 1979.

    Charles Lawson, Richard Hanson, David Kincaid,
    Fred Krogh,
    Basic Linear Algebra Subprograms for Fortran Usage,
    Algorithm 539,
    ACM Transactions on Mathematical Software,
    Volume 5, Number 3, September 1979, pages 308-323.

  Parameters:

    Input, int N, the number of entries in the vector.

    Input, double X[*], the vector to be examined.

    Input, int INCX, the increment between successive
    entries of SX.

    Output, int IDAMAX, the index of the element of
    maximum absolute value.
*/
{
  double dmax;
  int i;
  int ix;
  int value;

  value = 0;

  if ( n < 1 || incx <= 0 )
  {
    return value;
  }

  value = 1;

  if ( n == 1 )
  {
    return value;
  }

  if ( incx == 1 )
  {
    dmax = fabs ( dx[0] );

    for ( i = 1; i < n; i++ )
```

```
    {
      if ( dmax < fabs ( dx[i] ) )
      {
        value = i + 1;
        dmax = fabs ( dx[i] );
      }
    }
  }
  else
  {
    ix = 0;
    dmax = fabs ( dx[0] );
    ix = ix + incx;

    for ( i = 1; i < n; i++ )
    {
      if ( dmax < fabs ( dx[ix] ) )
      {
        value = i + 1;
        dmax = fabs ( dx[ix] );
      }
      ix = ix + incx;
    }
  }

  return value;
}
/************************************************************/

double r8_epsilon ( )

/************************************************************/
/*
  Purpose:

    R8_EPSILON returns the R8 round off unit.

  Discussion:

    R8_EPSILON is a number R which is a power of 2 with the
    property that, to the precision of the computer's
    arithmetic,
      1 < 1 + R
    but
      1 = ( 1 + R / 2 )

  Licensing:

    This code is distributed under the GNU LGPL license.

  Modified:
```

```
      01 September 2012

   Author:

      John Burkardt

   Parameters:

      Output, double R8_EPSILON, the R8 round-off unit.
*/
{
   const double value = 2.220446049250313E-016;

   return value;
}
/**********************************************************/

double r8_max ( double x, double y )

/**********************************************************/
/*
   Purpose:

      R8_MAX returns the maximum of two R8's.

   Modified:

      18 August 2004

   Author:

      John Burkardt

   Parameters:

      Input, double X, Y, the quantities to compare.

      Output, double R8_MAX, the maximum of X and Y.
*/
{
   double value;

   if ( y < x )
   {
      value = x;
   }
   else
   {
      value = y;
   }
```

```
    return value;
}
/************************************************************/

double r8_random ( int iseed[4] )

/************************************************************/
/*
  Purpose:

    R8_RANDOM returns a uniformly distributed random number
    between 0 and 1.

  Discussion:

    This routine uses a multiplicative congruential method
    with modulus 2**48 and multiplier 33952834046453 (see
    G.S.Fishman,'Multiplicative congruential random number
     generators with modulus 2**b: an exhaustive analysis
     for b = 32 and a partial analysis for b = 48', Math.
    Comp. 189, pp 331-344, 1990).

    48-bit integers are stored in 4 integer array elements
    with 12 bits per element. Hence the routine is portable
    across machines with integers of 32 bits or more.

  Parameters:

    Input/output, integer ISEED(4).
    On entry, the seed of the random number generator; the
    array elements must be between 0 and 4095, and ISEED(4)
    must be odd. On exit, the seed is updated.

    Output, double R8_RANDOM, the next pseudorandom number.
*/
{
  int ipw2 = 4096;
  int it1;
  int it2;
  int it3;
  int it4;
  int m1 = 494;
  int m2 = 322;
  int m3 = 2508;
  int m4 = 2549;
  double r = 1.0 / 4096.0;
  double value;
/*
  Multiply the seed by the multiplier modulo 2**48.
*/
  it4 = iseed[3] * m4;
```

```
  it3 = it4 / ipw2;
  it4 = it4 - ipw2 * it3;
  it3 = it3 + iseed[2] * m4 + iseed[3] * m3;
  it2 = it3 / ipw2;
  it3 = it3 - ipw2 * it2;
  it2 = it2 + iseed[1] * m4 + iseed[2] * m3 + iseed[3] * m2;
  it1 = it2 / ipw2;
  it2 = it2 - ipw2 * it1;
  it1 = it1 + iseed[0] * m4 + iseed[1] * m3 + iseed[2] * m2 +
                                              iseed[3] * m1;
  it1 = ( it1 % ipw2 );
/*
  Return updated seed
*/
  iseed[0] = it1;
  iseed[1] = it2;
  iseed[2] = it3;
  iseed[3] = it4;
/*
  Convert 48-bit integer to a real number in the interval (0,1)
*/
  value =
      r * ( ( double ) ( it1 )
    + r * ( ( double ) ( it2 )
    + r * ( ( double ) ( it3 )
    + r * ( ( double ) ( it4 ) ) ) ) );

  return value;
}
/****************************************************************/

double *r8mat_gen ( int lda, int n )

/****************************************************************/
/*
  Purpose:

    R8MAT_GEN generates a random R8MAT.

  Modified:

    06 June 2005

  Parameters:

    Input, integer LDA, the leading dimension of the matrix.

    Input, integer N, the order of the matrix.

    Output, double R8MAT_GEN[LDA*N], the N by N matrix.
*/
```

```
{
  double *a;
  int i;
  int init[4] = { 1, 2, 3, 1325 };
  int j;

  a = ( double * ) malloc ( lda * n * sizeof ( double ) );

  for ( j = 1; j <= n; j++ )
  {
    for ( i = 1; i <= n; i++ )
    {
      a[i-1+(j-1)*lda] = r8_random ( init ) - 0.5;
    }
  }

  return a;
}
/************************************************************/

void timestamp ( )

/************************************************************/
/*
  Purpose:

    TIMESTAMP prints the current YMDHMS date as a time stamp.

  Example:

    31 May 2001 09:45:54 AM

  Licensing:

    This code is distributed under the GNU LGPL license.

  Modified:

    24 September 2003

  Author:

    John Burkardt

  Parameters:

    None
*/
{
# define TIME_SIZE 40
```

```
static char time_buffer[TIME_SIZE];
const struct tm *tm;
time_t now;

now = time ( NULL );
tm = localtime ( &now );

strftime ( time_buffer, TIME_SIZE, "%d %B %Y %I:%M:%S %p",
                                                  tm );

printf ( "%s\n", time_buffer );

return;
# undef TIME_SIZE
}
```

D Livermore Loops

```
# include <stdlib.h>          double s;
# include <stdio.h>           double temp;
# include <math.h>            double xnm;
# include <time.h>            double scale;
#include <sys/time.h>         double e6;
                              double e3;
int l;                        double xnc;
int lw;                       double xnei;
int k;                        double xnm;
int kx;                       double a11;
int ky;                       double a12;
int loop=100;                 double a13;
int n=100;                    double a21;
int nl1;                      double a22;
int nl2;                      double a23;
int ii;                       double a31;
int i;                        double a32;
int j;                        double a33;
int ipntp;                    double sig;
int ipnt;                     double ar;
                              double br;
long m, ink, ip, kn, kb5i;    double cr;
long nz, ng;                  double qa;
long jnn;                     double dm22;
long k2;                      double dm23;
long k3;                      double dm24;
long j4;                      double dm25;
long j5;                      double dm26;
                              double dm27;
long k2;                      double dm28;
long k3;                      double c0;
long j4;                      double ar;
long j5;                      double br;
long i1;                      double j11;
long j2;                      double i22;
long lb;                      double tmp;
long zone[300];               double tmp;
long e[96];                   double flx;
long f[96];                   double dk;
long ix[1001];                double dn;
long ir[1001];                double di;
                              double expmax;
double q;                     double stb5;
double r;                     double vstp[101];
double t;                     double vxne[101];
```

```
double vxnd[101];               double xx[1001];
double ve3[101];                double rx[1001];
double vlr[101];                double rh[2048];
double vlin[101];               double ex[1001];
double za[7][101];              double plan[300];
double zp[7][101];              double d[300];
double zq[7][101];              double plan[300];
double zr[7][101];              double d[300];
double zm[7][101];              double b5[101];
double zb[7][101];              double g[1001];
double zu[7][101];              double xx[1001];
double zv[7][101];              double sa[101];
double zz[7][101];              double sb[101];
double px[101][25];             double b[64][64];
double p[512][4];               double c[64][64];
double cx[101][25];             double u1[2][101][5];
double h[64][64];               double u2[2][101][5];
double vy[25][101];             double u3[2][101][5];
double vf[7][101];              double du1[101];
double vh[7][101];              double du2[101];
double vg[7][101];              double du3[101];
double vs[7][101];              double x[1001];
double vx[1001];                double y[1001];
double xx[1001];                double z[1001];
double grd[1001];               double u[1001];
double ex1[1001];               double v[1001];
double xi[1001];                double w[1001];
double dex1[1001];              double vsp[101];
double dex[1001];

struct timeval begin, end;

int main ( )
{
// Start measuring time
gettimeofday(&begin, 0);

//    Kernel 1 -- hydro fragment

for ( l=1 ; l<=loop ; l++ ) {
for ( k=0 ; k<n ; k++ ) {
x[k] = q + y[k]*( r*z[k+10] + t*z[k+11] );
}
}

//    Kernel 2 -- ICCG excerpt (Incomplete Cholesky Conjugate
                                                   Gradient)

for ( l=1 ; l<=loop ; l++ ) {
        ii = n;
      ipntp = 0;
```

```
        do {
            ipnt = ipntp;
          ipntp += ii;
            ii /= 2;
            i = ipntp - 1;
              for ( k=ipnt+1 ; k<ipntp ; k=k+2 ) {
                  i++;
                  x[i] = x[k] - v[k  ]*x[k-1] - v[k+1]*x[k+1];
              }
        } while ( ii>0 );
    }

//   Kernel 3 -- inner product

    for ( l=1 ; l<=loop ; l++ ) {
        q = 0.0;
        for ( k=0 ; k<n ; k++ ) {
            q += z[k]*x[k];
        }
    }


//  Kernel 4 -- banded linear equations

    m = ( 1001-7 )/2;
    for ( l=1 ; l<=loop ; l++ ) {
        for ( k=6 ; k<1001 ; k=k+m ) {
            lw = k - 6;
            temp = x[k-1];

            for ( j=4 ; j<n ; j=j+5 ) {
                temp -= x[lw]*y[j];
                lw++;
            }
            x[k-1] = y[4]*temp;
        }
    }



//      Kernel 5 -- tri-diagonal elimination, below diagonal


    for ( l=1 ; l<=loop ; l++ ) {
        for ( i=1 ; i<n ; i++ ) {
            x[i] = z[i]*( y[i] - x[i-1] );
        }
    }

// Kernel 6 -- general linear recurrence equations

    for ( l=1 ; l<=loop ; l++ ) {
```

```
        for ( i=1 ; i<n ; i++ ) {
            for ( k=0 ; k<i ; k++ ) {
                w[i] += b[k][i] * w[(i-k)-1];
            }
        }
    }


//  Kernel 7 -- equation of state fragment

    for ( l=1 ; l<=loop ; l++ ) {
        for ( k=0 ; k<n ; k++ ) {
            x[k] = u[k] + r*( z[k] + r*y[k] ) +
                   t*( u[k+3] + r*( u[k+2] + r*u[k+1] ) +
                     t*( u[k+6] + r*( u[k+5] + r*u[k+4] ) ) );
        }
    }


//   Kernel 8 -- ADI integration

    for ( l=1 ; l<=loop ; l++ ) {
        nl1 = 0;
        nl2 = 1;
        for ( kx=1 ; kx<3 ; kx++ ){
            for ( ky=1 ; ky<n ; ky++ ) {
                du1[ky] = u1[nl1][ky+1][kx] - u1[nl1][ky-1][kx];
                du2[ky] = u2[nl1][ky+1][kx] - u2[nl1][ky-1][kx];
                du3[ky] = u3[nl1][ky+1][kx] - u3[nl1][ky-1][kx];
                u1[nl2][ky][kx]=
                    u1[nl1][ky][kx]+a11*du1[ky]+a12*du2[ky]+
                    a13*du3[ky] + sig*(u1[nl1][ky][kx+1]-
                    2.0*u1[nl1][ky][kx]+u1[nl1][ky][kx-1]);
                u2[nl2][ky][kx]=
                    u2[nl1][ky][kx]+a21*du1[ky]+a22*du2[ky]+
                    a23*du3[ky] + sig*(u2[nl1][ky][kx+1]-
                    2.0*u2[nl1][ky][kx]+u2[nl1][ky][kx-1]);
                u3[nl2][ky][kx]=
                    u3[nl1][ky][kx]+a31*du1[ky]+a32*du2[ky]+
                    a33*du3[ky] + sig*(u3[nl1][ky][kx+1]-
                    2.0*u3[nl1][ky][kx]+u3[nl1][ky][kx-1]);
            }
        }
    }


//   Kernel 9 -- integrate predictors

    for ( l=1 ; l<=loop ; l++ ) {
        for ( i=0 ; i<n ; i++ ) {
            px[i][0] = dm28*px[i][12] + dm27*px[i][11] +
```

```
                dm26*px[i][10] + dm25*px[i][ 9] +
                dm24*px[i][ 8] + dm23*px[i][ 7] +
                dm22*px[i][ 6] + c0*( px[i][ 4] +
                px[i][ 5]) + px[i][ 2];
        }
    }

//    Kernel 10 -- difference predictors

    for ( l=1 ; l<=loop ; l++ ) {
        for ( i=0 ; i<n ; i++ ) {
            ar          =          cx[i][ 4];
            br          = ar - px[i][ 4];
            px[i][ 4] = ar;
            cr          = br - px[i][ 5];
            px[i][ 5] = br;
            ar          = cr - px[i][ 6];
            px[i][ 6] = cr;
            br          = ar - px[i][ 7];
            px[i][ 7] = ar;
            cr          = br - px[i][ 8];
            px[i][ 8] = br;
            ar          = cr - px[i][ 9];
            px[i][ 9] = cr;
            br          = ar - px[i][10];
            px[i][10] = ar;
            cr          = br - px[i][11];
            px[i][11] = br;
            px[i][13] = cr - px[i][12];
            px[i][12] = cr;
        }
    }


// Kernel 11 -- first sum

    for ( l=1 ; l<=loop ; l++ ) {
        x[0] = y[0];
        for ( k=1 ; k<n ; k++ ) {
            x[k] = x[k-1] + y[k];
        }
    }

// Kernel 12 -- first difference

    for ( l=1 ; l<=loop ; l++ ) {
        for ( k=0 ; k<n ; k++ ) {
            x[k] = y[k+1] - y[k];
        }
    }
```

```
//    Kernel 14 -- 1-D PIC (Particle In Cell)

   for ( l=1 ; l<=loop ; l++ ) {
      for ( k=0 ; k<n ; k++ ) {
         vx[k] = 0.0;
         xx[k] = 0.0;
         ix[k] = (long) grd[k];
         xi[k] = (double) ix[k];
         ex1[k] = ex[ ix[k] - 1 ];
         dex1[k] = dex[ ix[k] - 1 ];
      }
      for ( k=0 ; k<n ; k++ ) {
         vx[k] = vx[k] + ex1[k] + ( xx[k] -
         xi[k] )*dex1[k];
         xx[k] = xx[k] + vx[k]  + flx;
         ir[k] = xx[k];
         rx[k] = xx[k] - ir[k];
         ir[k] = ( ir[k] & 2048-1 ) + 1;
         xx[k] = rx[k] + ir[k];
      }
      for ( k=0 ; k<n ; k++ ) {
         rh[ ir[k]-1 ] += 1.0 - rx[k];
         rh[ ir[k]   ] += rx[k];
      }
   }


// Kernel 15 -- Casual Fortran. Development version

   for ( l=1 ; l<=loop ; l++ ) {
      ng = 7;
      nz = n;
      ar = 0.053;
      br = 0.073;
      for ( j=1 ; j<ng ; j++ ) {
         for ( k=1 ; k<nz ; k++ ) {
            if ( (j+1) >= ng ) {
               vy[j][k] = 0.0;
               continue;
            }
            if ( vh[j+1][k] > vh[j][k] ) {
               t = ar;
            }
            else {
               t = br;
            }
            if ( vf[j][k] < vf[j][k-1] ) {
               if ( vh[j][k-1] > vh[j+1][k-1] )
                  r = vh[j][k-1];
               else
```

```
                                r = vh[j+1][k-1];
                        s = vf[j][k-1];
                }
                else {
                    if ( vh[j][k] > vh[j+1][k] )
                            r = vh[j][k];
                    else
                            r = vh[j+1][k];
                        s = vf[j][k];
                }
                vy[j][k] = sqrt( vg[j][k]*vg[j][k] +
                                        r*r )* t/s;
                if ( (k+1) >= nz ) {
                    vs[j][k] = 0.0;
                    continue;
                }
                if ( vf[j][k] < vf[j-1][k] ) {
                    if ( vg[j-1][k] > vg[j-1][k+1] )
                            r = vg[j-1][k];
                    else
                            r = vg[j-1][k+1];
                        s = vf[j-1][k];
                        t = br;
                }
                else {
                    if ( vg[j][k] > vg[j][k+1] )
                            r = vg[j][k];
                    else
                            r = vg[j][k+1];
                        s = vf[j][k];
                        t = ar;
                }
                vs[j][k] = sqrt( vh[j][k]*vh[j][k] +
                                        r*r )* t / s;
            }
        }
    }

//    Kernel 16 -- Monte Carlo search loop


    ii = n / 3;
    lb = ii + ii;
    k3 = k2 = 0;
    for ( l=1 ; l<=loop ; l++ ) {
        i1 = m = 1;
        label410:
        j2 = ( n + n )*( m - 1 ) + 1;
        for ( k=1 ; k<=n ; k++ ) {
            k2++;
            j4 = j2 + k + k;
```

```
            j5 = zone[j4-1];
            if ( j5 < n ) {
                if ( j5+lb < n ) {                      /* 420 */
                    tmp = plan[j5-1] - t;               /* 435 */
                } else {
                    if ( j5+ii < n ) {                  /* 415 */
                        tmp = plan[j5-1] - s;           /* 430 */
                    } else {
                        tmp = plan[j5-1] - r;           /* 425 */
                    }
                }
            } else if( j5 == n ) {
                break;                                  /* 475 */
            } else {
                k3++;                                   /* 450 */
                tmp=(d[j5-1]-(d[j5-2]*(t-d[j5-3])*
                (t-d[j5-3])+(s-d[j5-4])*(s-d[j5-4])+
                (r-d[j5-5])*(r-d[j5-5]))));
            }
            if ( tmp < 0.0 ) {
                if ( zone[j4-2] < 0 )                   /* 445 */
                    continue;                           /* 470 */
                else if ( !zone[j4-2] )
                    break;                              /* 480 */
            } else if ( tmp ) {
                if ( zone[j4-2] > 0 )                   /* 440 */
                    continue;                           /* 470 */
                else if ( !zone[j4-2] )
                    break;                              /* 480 */
            } else break;                               /* 485 */
            m++;                                        /* 455 */
            if ( m > zone[0] )
                m = 1;                                  /* 460 */
            if ( i1-m )                                 /* 465 */
                goto label410;
            else
                break;
        }
    }


//   Kernel 17 -- implicit, conditional computation

    for ( l=1 ; l<=loop ; l++ ) {
        i = n-1;
        j = 0;
        ink = -1;
        scale = 5.0 / 3.0;
        xnm = 1.0 / 3.0;
        e6 = 1.03 / 3.07;
        goto 161;
160:    e6 = xnm*vsp[i] + vstp[i];
```

```
            vxne[i] = e6;
            xnm = e6;
            ve3[i] = e6;
            i += ink;
            if ( i==j ) goto 162;
161:        e3 = xnm*vlr[i] + vlin[i];
            xnei = vxne[i];
            vxnd[i] = e6;
            xnc = scale*e3;
            if ( xnm > xnc ) goto 160;
            if ( xnei > xnc ) goto 160;
            ve3[i] = e3;
            e6 = e3 + e3 - xnm;
            vxne[i] = e3 + e3 - xnei;
            xnm = e6;
            i += ink;
            if ( i != j ) goto 161;
162:;
        }


//   Kernel 18 - 2-D explicit hydrodynamics fragment


    for ( l=1 ; l<=loop ; l++ ) {
        t = 0.0037;
        s = 0.0041;
        kn = 6;
        jnn = n;
        for ( k=1 ; k<kn ; k++ ) {

          for ( j=1 ; j<jnn ; j++ ) {
             za[k][j] = ( zp[k+1][j-1] +zq[k+1][j-1] -
                         zp[k][j-1] -zq[k][j-1] )*
                         ( zr[k][j] +zr[k][j-1] ) /
                         ( zm[k][j-1] +zm[k+1][j-1]);
             zb[k][j] = ( zp[k][j-1] +zq[k][j-1] -
                         zp[k][j] -zq[k][j] ) *
                         ( zr[k][j] +zr[k-1][j] ) /
                         ( zm[k][j] +zm[k][j-1]);
          }
        }
        for ( k=1 ; k<kn ; k++ ) {

           for ( j=1 ; j<jnn ; j++ ) {
              zu[k][j] += s*( za[k][j]   *( zz[k][j]
                                        - zz[k][j+1] ) -
                             za[k][j-1] *( zz[k][j]
                                        - zz[k][j-1] ) -
                             zb[k][j]   *( zz[k][j]
                                        - zz[k-1][j] ) +
                             zb[k+1][j] *( zz[k][j]
```

```
                                        - zz[k+1][j] ) );
                    zv[k][j] += s*( za[k][j]    *( zr[k][j]
                                          - zr[k][j+1] ) -
                                  za[k][j-1] *( zr[k][j]
                                          - zr[k][j-1] ) -
                                  zb[k][j]    *( zr[k][j]
                                          - zr[k-1][j] ) +
                                  zb[k+1][j] *( zr[k][j]
                                          - zr[k+1][j] ) );
             }
        }
        for ( k=1 ; k<kn ; k++ ) {

            for ( j=1 ; j<jnn ; j++ ) {
                zr[k][j] = zr[k][j] + t*zu[k][j];
                zz[k][j] = zz[k][j] + t*zv[k][j];
            }
        }
    }


//   Kernel 19 -- general linear recurrence equations


    kb5i = 0;
    for ( l=1 ; l<=loop ; l++ ) {
        for ( k=0 ; k<n ; k++ ) {
            b5[k+kb5i] = sa[k] + stb5*sb[k];
            stb5 = b5[k+kb5i] - stb5;
        }
        for ( i=1 ; i<=n ; i++ ) {
            k = n - i ;
            b5[k+kb5i] = sa[k] + stb5*sb[k];
            stb5 = b5[k+kb5i] - stb5;
        }
    }


//   Kernel 20 -- Discrete ordinates transport,
                   conditional recurrence

    for ( l=1 ; l<=loop ; l++ ) {
        for ( k=0 ; k<n ; k++ ) {
            di = y[k] - g[k] / ( xx[k] + dk );
            dn = 0.2;
            if ( di ) {
                dn = z[k]/di ;
                if ( t < dn ) dn = t;
                if ( s > dn ) dn = s;
            }
            x[k] = ( ( w[k] + v[k]*dn )* xx[k] +
```

```
                          u[k] ) / ( vx[k] + v[k]*dn );
              xx[k+1] = ( x[k] - xx[k] )* dn + xx[k];
          }
      }

//    Kernel 21 -- matrix*matrix product

      for ( l=1 ; l<=loop ; l++ ) {
          for ( k=0 ; k<25 ; k++ ) {
              for ( i=0 ; i<25 ; i++ ) {
                  for ( j=0 ; j<n ; j++ ) {
                      px[j][i] += vy[k][i] * cx[j][k];
                  }
              }
          }
      }


//    Kernel 22 -- Planckian distribution


      expmax = 20.0;
      u[n-1] = 0.99*expmax*v[n-1];
      for ( l=1 ; l<=loop ; l++ ) {
          for ( k=0 ; k<n ; k++ ) {
              y[k] = u[k] / v[k];
              w[k] = x[k] / ( exp( y[k] ) -1.0 );
          }
      }

//    Kernel 23 -- 2-D implicit hydrodynamics fragment

      for ( l=1 ; l<=loop ; l++ ) {
          for ( j=1 ; j<6 ; j++ ) {
              for ( k=1 ; k<n ; k++ ) {
                  qa = za[j+1][k]*zr[j][k] + za[j-1][k]*
                       zb[j][k] + za[j][k+1]*zu[j][k] +
                       za[j][k-1]*zv[j][k] + zz[j][k];
                  za[j][k] += 0.175*( qa - za[j][k] );
              }
          }
      }

//    Kernel 24 -- find location of first minimum in array

      x[n/2] = -1.0e+10;
      for ( l=1 ; l<=loop ; l++ ) {
          m = 0;
          for ( k=1 ; k<n ; k++ ) {
              if ( x[k] < x[m] ) m = k;
          }
```

```
    }


// Stop measuring time and calculate the elapsed time

    gettimeofday(&end, 0);
    long seconds = end.tv_sec - begin.tv_sec;
    long microseconds = end.tv_usec - begin.tv_usec;
    double elapsed = seconds + microseconds*1e-6;

    printf("Duration: %.6f sec.\n \n",elapsed);
  return 0;

}
```

E MMP - CTMC Trace Generator

```
Clear[st]; Clear[tb]; Clear[tm]; Clear[ta]; Clear[gt]; Clear[nt];
Clear[tl];Clear[tr]; Clear[tbt]; Clear[alpha]; Clear[beta]; Clear[n];
Clear[lambda]; Clear[mu]; Clear[omega1]; Clear[omega2];
ClearAll;
datag = {}; datatbt = {}; st0d = {}; st1d = {}; st2d = {}; st3d = {};
datag = Append[datag, {"Transaction Instance", "Transaction Type",
       "Event Occurrence Instant", "Bytes Transfered"}];
datatbt = Append[datatbt, {"Time Between Transactions"}];
tr = 0; tbt = 0; ta = 0; tl = 0; tb = 0; tm = 0; tbt = 0; bg = 0;
gt = 0; nt = 1000; st = 0; n = 1;
alpha = 5; beta = 10; lambda = 350; mu = 700;
omega1 = 1/2500; omega2 = 1/5000;
While[True,
  Label[st0];
  st = 0;
  tb = Extract[RandomVariate[ExponentialDistribution[beta], 1], 1];
  tm = Extract[RandomVariate[ExponentialDistribution[mu], 1], 1];
  If[tb < tm,
   st0d = Append[st0d, tb];
   gt = gt + tb;
   Goto[st2];
   ];
  st0d = Append[st0d, tm];
  tbt = tm;
  bg = Extract[RandomVariate[ExponentialDistribution[omega1], 1],
    1];
  gt = gt + tm;
  tr = 1;
  datatbt = Append[datatbt, tbt];
  datag = Append[datag, {n, tr, gt, bg}];
  n++;
  If[n > nt,
   Break[];
   Goto[st1];
   ];
  Label[st1];
  st = 1;
  tb = Extract[RandomVariate[ExponentialDistribution[beta], 1], 1];
  tm = Extract[RandomVariate[ExponentialDistribution[mu], 1], 1];
  If[tb < tm,
   st1d = Append[st1d, tb];
   gt = gt + tb;
   Goto[st2];
   ];
  st1d = Append[st1d, tm];
```

```
tbt = tm;
bg = Extract[RandomVariate[ExponentialDistribution[omega1], 1],
  1];
gt = gt + tm;
tr = 1;
datatbt = Append[datatbt, tbt];
datag = Append[datag, {n, tr, gt, bg}];
n++;
If[n > nt,
 Break[];
 ];
Goto[st0];
Label[st2];
st = 2;
ta = Extract[RandomVariate[ExponentialDistribution[alpha], 1], 1];
tl = Extract[RandomVariate[ExponentialDistribution[lambda], 1],
  1];
If[ta < tl,
 st2d = Append[st2d, ta];
 gt = gt + ta;
 Goto[st0];
 ];
st2d = Append[st2d, tl];
tbt = tl;
bg = Extract[RandomVariate[ExponentialDistribution[omega2], 1],
  1];
gt = gt + tl;
tr = 2;
datatbt = Append[datatbt, tbt];
datag = Append[datag, {n, tr, gt, bg}];
n++;
If[n > nt,
 Break[];
 ];
Goto[st3];
Label[st3];
st = 3; [
ta = Extract[RandomVariate[ExponentialDistribution[alpha], 1], 1];
tl = Extract[RandomVariate[ExponentialDistribution[lambda], 1],
  1];
If[ta < tl,
 st3d = Append[st3d, ta];
 gt = gt + ta;
 Goto [st0];
 ];
tbt = tl;
bg = Extract[RandomVariate[ExponentialDistribution[omega2], 1],
  1];
st3d = Append[st3d, tl];
gt = gt + tl;
tr = 2;
datatbt = Append[datatbt, tbt];
datag = Append[datag, {n, tr, gt, bg}];
n++;
```

```
  If[n > nt,
   Break[];
   ];
  Goto[st2];
  ];
Print["Global Time (s) = ", gt];
Print["sts0= ", N[Total[st0d]]];
Print["sts1 = ", N[Total[st1d]]];
Print["sts2 = ", N[Total[st2d]]];
Print["sts3 = ", N[Total[st3d]]];
Print["ps0= ", N[Total[st0d/gt]]];
Print["ps1 = ", N[Total[st1d/gt]]];
Print["ps2 = ", N[Total[st2d/gt]]];
Print["ps3 = ", N[Total[st3d/gt]]];
Print["ps0+ps1+ps2+ps3 = ",
  N[(Total[st3d] + Total[st2d] + Total[st1d] + Total[st0d])/gt]];
Export["dattrafmmp4.csv", datag];
Export["datatbtmmp4.csv", datatbt];
Print["End"];
```

Milton Keynes UK
Ingram Content Group UK Ltd.
UKHW050306161024
449569UK00037B/24

9 781032 306407